HENRY CLAY FRICK

AN INTIMATE PORTRAIT

HENRY CLAY FRICK

AN INTIMATE PORTRAIT

BY

MARTHA FRICK SYMINGTON SANGER

ABBEVILLE PRESS   PUBLISHERS

NEW YORK LONDON PARIS

Project Management and Development: Joseph Publishing Services
Editors: Susan Costello, Catherine Marshall, Susan Leon, Elsa van Bergen
Art Director: Alex Castro
Production Editor: Owen Dugan
Production Manager: Lou Bilka

First edition
10 9 8 7 6 5 4 3 2

Library of Congress Cataloging-in-Publication Data
Sanger, Martha Frick Symington.
Henry Clay Frick : an intimate portrait / Martha Frick Symington Sanger.
    p.   cm.
Includes bibliographical references and index.
ISBN 0-7892-0500-9
1. Frick, Henry Clay, 1849-1919. 2. Businessmen—United States—Biography.
3. Capitalists and financiers—United States—Biography. I. Title.
HC102.5.F75S32   1998
338.092—dc21
[B]   98-18031

Pages 2-3: The West Gallery at 1 East Seventieth Street, 1927, author's collection.

Page 4: Sir Gerald Kelly (1879-1972), *Henry Clay Frick in the West Gallery of The
    Frick Collection*, 1925, Oil on canvas, 48 x 40 in. (120 x 100 cm), collection of
    Henry Clay Frick, III.

Page 9: John Christen Johansen, *Henry Clay Frick*, The Frick Collection.

Pages 11-12: All photographs are from the author's collection except:
    Henry Clay Frick, Frick Archives; author's photograph, The Maryland Horse
    Breeders Association, Inc.

Printed and bound in Italy.

Because of my mother
MARTHA FRICK SYMINGTON
(1917-1996)

❖

For the descendants
of
HENRY CLAY FRICK

❖

In memory of my great aunt
HELEN CLAY FRICK
(1888-1984)

Death ends a life, but does not end a relationship,
which struggles on in the survivor's mind
toward some resolution . . . it never finds.

—Robert Anderson, *I Never Sang for My Father*

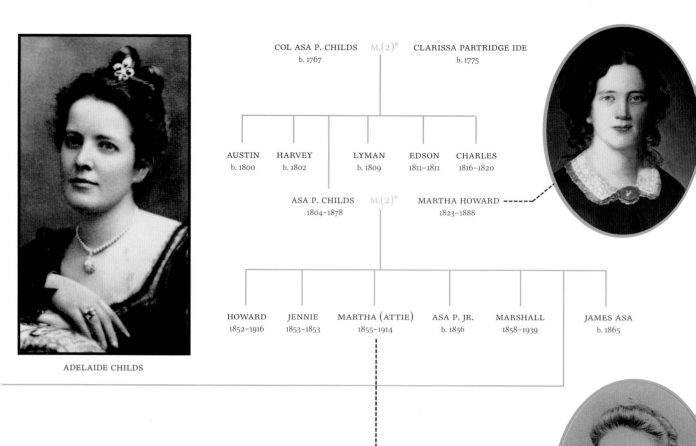

ADELAIDE CHILDS

COL ASA P. CHILDS
b. 1767
M.(2)*
CLARISSA PARTRIDGE IDE
b. 1775

AUSTIN
b. 1800

HARVEY
b. 1802

LYMAN
b. 1809

EDSON
1811–1811

CHARLES
1816–1820

ASA P. CHILDS
1804–1878
M.(2)*
MARTHA HOWARD
1823–1888

HOWARD
1852–1916

JENNIE
1853–1853

MARTHA (ATTIE)
1855–1914

ASA P. JR.
b. 1856

MARSHALL
1858–1939

JAMES ASA
b. 1865

A Genealogy of
Henry Clay Frick
and
Adelaide Childs

(2)* designates second marriage

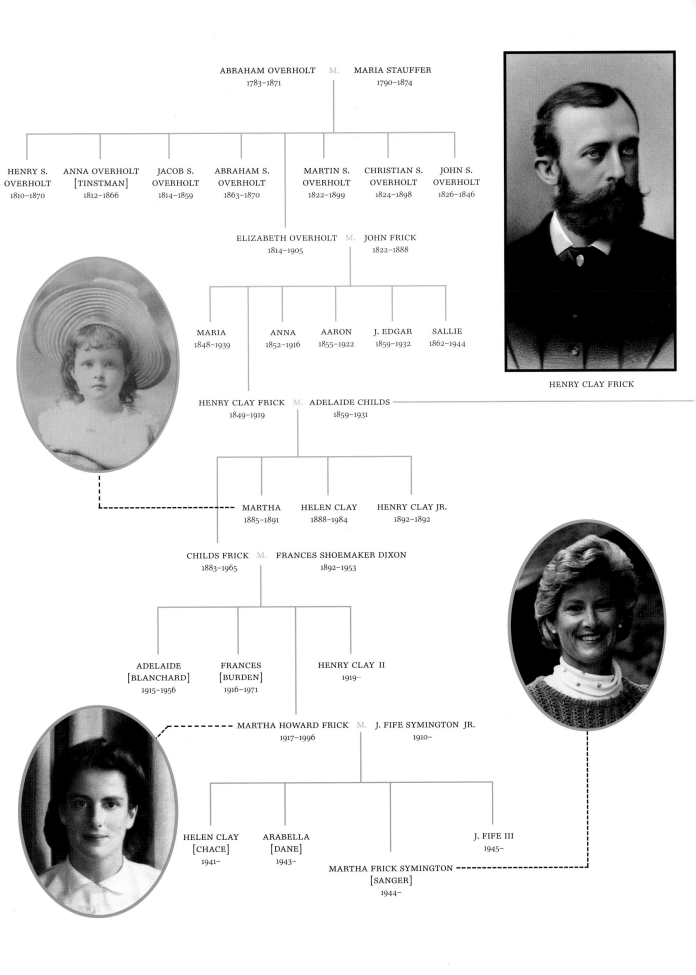

ABRAHAM OVERHOLT   M.   MARIA STAUFFER
1783–1871   1790–1874

HENRY S. OVERHOLT	ANNA OVERHOLT [TINSTMAN]	JACOB S. OVERHOLT	ABRAHAM S. OVERHOLT	MARTIN S. OVERHOLT	CHRISTIAN S. OVERHOLT	JOHN S. OVERHOLT
1810–1870	1812–1866	1814–1859	1863–1870	1822–1899	1824–1898	1826–1846

ELIZABETH OVERHOLT   M.   JOHN FRICK
1814–1905   1822–1888

MARIA	ANNA	AARON	J. EDGAR	SALLIE
1848–1939	1852–1916	1855–1922	1859–1932	1862–1944

HENRY CLAY FRICK

HENRY CLAY FRICK   M.   ADELAIDE CHILDS
1849–1919   1859–1931

MARTHA	HELEN CLAY	HENRY CLAY JR.
1885–1891	1888–1984	1892–1892

CHILDS FRICK   M.   FRANCES SHOEMAKER DIXON
1883–1965   1892–1953

ADELAIDE [BLANCHARD]	FRANCES [BURDEN]	HENRY CLAY II
1915–1956	1916–1971	1919–

MARTHA HOWARD FRICK   M.   J. FIFE SYMINGTON JR.
1917–1996   1910–

HELEN CLAY [CHACE]	ARABELLA [DANE]		J. FIFE III
1941–	1943–		1945–

MARTHA FRICK SYMINGTON [SANGER]
1944–

Introduction

Although my great-grandfather, Henry Clay Frick, died in 1919, he has remained a living presence within our family. Because he was renowned as an art collector, respected as an industrial genius, and despised as an oppressor of labor, the combination of his memory and reputation makes him a difficult ancestor to understand and embrace.

The recent death of my mother has made me realize how complex this accommodation is for me, in particular. I am the fifth Martha in the Childs and Frick families (see foldout opposite). Martha is a lovely, traditional name for a daughter, but, because of one predecessor named Martha, it resonates hauntingly across generations of our family.

The first two Marthas were my great-grandfather's mother-in-law, Martha Howard Childs, and her unmarried daughter of the same name. The third Martha was a Frick, Martha Howard, and it was for her that both my mother and I were named. This short-lived child has had more influence on the family than anyone except her father. Born in 1885 and the first daughter of Henry Clay Frick and Adelaide Howard Childs Frick, she was nicknamed "Rosebud" because of her creamy complexion and soft red curls. By all accounts, she was a beautiful and endearing daughter. The circumstances of her death in 1891, one week prior to her sixth birthday and after suffering a four-year, harrowing illness, haunted Frick for the remainder of his life as intensely as the Frick family is beset by his memory, reputation, and near-living presence.

Martha's legacy is one of grief and disappointment. My maternal grandmother, Frances Dixon Frick, was married to Childs Frick, the only surviving son of Henry Clay Frick and older brother of the ill-fated Martha. The pressure on Frances to produce a son who would bear Henry Clay Frick's name was enormous. But she gave birth to two daughters and then in 1917 to a third, my mother. Longing to please her father-in-law, my grandmother named her third daughter for the only individual she would have known to be more important to Henry Clay Frick than life itself—Martha Howard Frick, his deceased child.

Frances Frick produced a son two years later, named him Henry Clay Frick II, and soon focused all her attention on this long-awaited grandchild. Henry Clay Frick's death months after this boy was born did nothing to dilute Frances's affection.

With the inevitability of genetics, my mother also gave birth to three daughters—and then a son. But my brother's birth in 1945, twenty-six years after my great-grandfather's death, came at a time when she would have felt less pressure to perpetuate the name of Henry Clay Frick. She named her son, therefore, after her husband. But my mother, like my grandmother, had been disappointed by the birth of a third daughter. She well knew the family significance of the ill-fated Martha Howard Frick. Reminding me that I was the dead child's namesake, she warned that I was a spare child and that I was cursed, like all the Frick Marthas.

As a child and young woman, I did not think much about the curse and whether or not it existed. Nor did I think much about my great-grandfather, his art collection, his role as an industrialist, or his reputation as an oppressor of the working class. But in my mid-forties the past asserted itself, and I came to suspect that Henry Clay Frick's posthumous influence on me was more profound than I had realized. After my sixteen-year marriage to a grandson of Planned Parenthood's founder, Margaret Sanger, ended in divorce, I discovered that Alexander Berkman, Frick's would-be assassin during the 1892 Homestead steel strike—a strike that drew national and international attention as a near-civil war between labor and management—had become one of Sanger's lovers. I also learned that when Berkman attacked Frick, Martha, who had died the previous year, appeared to Frick in a visitation as clearly as if she were alive.

❖

To DISCERN THE INNER MOTIVATIONS of a subject as unrevealing as Frick would be difficult for any biographer, and it poses particular problems for a descendant. Although separated from him by three generations, and thus distant from him, I am nevertheless closer than someone who was not exposed to the Martha legacy and the Frick ethos since childhood. As a child, I visited my great-aunt Helen Clay Frick, the only surviving daughter of Henry Clay Frick, at the Frick Art Reference Library in New York; her farm in Bedford Village, New York; her father's summer home, Eagle Rock, in Prides Crossing, Massachusetts; as well as at Clayton, the family home in Pittsburgh, now a museum. Together we visited her father's birthplace in West Overton, Pennsylvania (also a museum), and often she accompanied me as I wandered through the galleries of the Frick Collection in New York. Although she rarely mentioned Martha, she spoke often of her father, but always in hallowed terms. My latter-day quest, therefore, was a difficult one. Martha was a mystery to me. Moreover, Henry Clay Frick had constructed the fortress of his privacy well: he was taciturn, brusque in his personal relationships, committed virtually nothing of a personal nature to paper, and guarded most of his feelings—although his anger was famous and never forgotten by those who experienced it. Helen jealously guarded this fortress.

My greatest insights about Martha, my great-grandfather, his art, and what I came to realize was their remarkably interwoven relationship came from a combination of factors. To help me, my uncle, Henry Clay Frick II, M.D., granted me free and singular access to Frick family papers. Located in the Frick Archives at Clayton and owned by the Helen Clay Frick Foundation, this extensive repository of family letters, diaries, news articles, business records, and memorabilia dating from 1800 was stored haphazardly in hundreds of unopened boxes. They told much of Frick's story, and records in other public and private repositories, such as the Henry Clay Frick Birthplace in West Overton, Pennsylvania; the David C. Duniway archives in Portland, Oregon; the Andrew W. Mellon papers in the office of Paul Mellon; the Frick Art Reference Library in New York; the Rockefeller Archive Center in Pocantico Hills; the Knoedler Gallery archives in New York; the Wallace Collection archives; as well as the archives of U. S. Steel supplemented the family papers. I visited places that revealed more—Frick's birthplace; the Edgar Thomson steel mill; the now defunct H. C. Frick Coke Company's coke works in Pennsylvania's Fayette County; the broken dam at South Fork, Pennsylvania, that caused the 1889 Johnstown Flood; the site of the 1892 Pinkerton battle at Homestead; and the place where Frick's near assassination and Martha's "visitation" occurred. Places I discovered, like the house in Cresson Springs, Pennsylvania, where Martha died in 1891, as well as courthouse and cemetery records in Pittsburgh and Wooster, Ohio, where Frick's siblings had lived, lent still more detail and depth.

Many insights came from spending hours of contemplation in Clayton, as well as in the Frick Collection, on Mondays, when the houses are closed to visitors. I was allowed to roam freely from basement to third floor, so that I could be still with my research and feel the houses as homes. This experience was greatly enhanced by my years in psychoanalysis; the writings on death and dying by modern-day theorists and clinicians such as Barbara Sourkes, Elisabeth Kübler-Ross, Theresa Rando, Albert Cain, Vamik Volkan, and Beverly Raphael, to name a few; and the sharing of family stories. Certainly as I roamed Henry Clay Frick's museums, I felt his sorrow, and I often felt he was not far away. Soon I realized this reaction expressed a truth about both houses and the art they displayed—there was a far more profound psychological relationship between the man and his paintings than has been understood.

❖

Many times when alone in the Frick Collection, I stood before Johannes Vermeer's *Officer and Laughing Girl* (fig. i-1), thinking about Henry Clay Frick and his daughter, Helen, my great-aunt. While wondering if the portrait, a life-long favorite of his, could be a metaphor for their relationship, I came to realize that its vanishing point may be seen as more than a technique of perspective in art.

The vanishing point in art refers to a technique of composition based on the combined sciences of optics and geometry. It dictates that all parallel lines, like railroad tracks and telegraph wires along a straight corridor, converge at a specific point on the horizon. This both creates a sense of space and directs the viewer's eye.

Just as these lines draw the eye through the foreground of a painting and into a point in the distance, so too, emotional trauma can lead the biographer to the core of her subject's humanity. This psychological vanishing point, therefore, may be used as a lens to identify the wound in the psyche where unconscious forces merge, that deep inner space where the greatest pain becomes the driving force of the subject's life.

The vanishing point for Henry Clay Frick, the event that fractured his inner life and polarized other forces around it, or rendered them invisible, was the death of Martha, his beloved Rosebud.

Childhood mortality was an everyday reality in the Victorian era. In the nineteenth century, nearly one-half of all deaths were of children, and one out of every five children under the age of five died. Yet if a child's death was more expected, its reality was, as it is now, the most devastating experience a parent can suffer. Some parents never recovered and were dominated for the remainder of their lives by unresolved grief. In 1848, as noted by Ann K. Finkbeiner in *After the Death of a Child,* a Fanny Longfellow poignantly confided in her diary after the death of her eighteen-month-old baby: "As I controlled her life before birth, so does she [control] me now." And Thomas Mellon, Henry Clay Frick's banker and mentor, wrote in old age about the death of his young son Selwyn in words reflecting both his imagined fault and real guilt, what psychologists today call survivor's guilt: "Time has brought me consolation in all other deaths but this: for Selwyn I cannot be comforted. The recollection of every little unkindness I subjected him to affects me with remorse. . . . His earnest and beseeching look of entreaty rejecting the medicine I was trying to force on him from time to time in vain hope of saving his life, still accuses me of cruelty."

Fig. i-1. Johannes Vermeer (1632–1695), *Officer and Laughing Girl*, 1655–60.
Acquired in 1911, Oil on canvas, 19⅞ x 18⅛ in. (50.5 x 46 cm).
The Frick Collection

In our culture, women have always had permission to grieve. Those of Frick's time observed rigid mourning customs, which were an integral part of their culture. The best known, most deeply affected, and certainly the most powerful of these women was Queen Victoria. An only child whose father died when she was one year old, Victoria assumed the throne of England at eighteen. When her beloved husband, Prince Albert, died in his prime in 1861, he was mourned by "the widow of Windsor," as she became known, through a series of rituals, such as having his chamber pot scalded daily and returned to its place beneath his bed, bringing hot water to his dressing room each evening, and changing his towels and bed sheets each day.

Frick's wife, Adelaide, could outwardly express the family's bereavement following Martha's death through illness, depression, and by wearing mourning jewelry and black mourning clothes for the first two years and then mauve for the third. But for Frick, as for all men of that time, illness was not acceptable and there were no prescribed rituals. As is typical of those who suffer from what we now call chronic grief syndrome, Frick seems to have been as controlled by Martha's death as was Longfellow and as guilt-ridden as Thomas Mellon. He also seems to have suffered an initial absence of expressed emotion, followed by a delay in the onset of the mourning process. His papers reveal a highly disciplined, private man who rarely, if at all, permitted himself confidences. Though silent about his despair, his archives, nevertheless, provide other footprints to follow: his choice of paintings and his obsessive attachment to them.

Commenting upon the aestheticism of Frick's highly selective purchases, Charles Ryskamp, former director of the Frick Collection, quotes a comment made about the great Russian collector S. I. Shchukin: "He put [his collection] together masterpiece by masterpiece, as if he were stringing a necklace." In fact, Henry Clay Frick's selective purchases were highly psychological, both on the literal and the symbolic level. Indeed, I have determined that certain of the paintings served as reminders of specific, Martha-related anniversaries or of gifts Frick gave her, such as her dog and the doll she held at the moment of her death. In fact, Frick's great longing to remain connected to Martha may have been the reason he became almost obsessed with other elements of his past, transferring his Martha-longing onto paintings linking him to deceased friends and to events and places of his past.

❖

Fig. i-2. Fifteenth Century Book of Hours.
The Walters Art Gallery, Baltimore

J UST AS HENRY CLAY FRICK'S COLLECTING EYE was uniquely shaped by grief, grief
was also part of the motivation behind several major nineteenth-century art collections in the United States. Perhaps the spirit of a century that emphasized formal
mourning and paid tribute to both its living and its dead through architecturally elaborate structures, whether capitols or mausoleums, encouraged a form of explicit, visible
remembrance. Whatever encouragement was provided by society, however, highly
personal reactions to death and loss were the shaping factors for the collections
founded by contemporaries of Henry Clay Frick.

William Thompson Walters lost his pious wife, Ellen, in 1862 to pneumonia. At the
time, he and his family were living in Paris to avoid the Civil War. After his wife's death,
William Walters began to create a commemorative collection of drawings and paintings on the theme of prayer, and he dedicated it to the deceased Ellen. His son, Henry
Walters, who was fourteen years old when his mother died and later founded the Walters Art Gallery in Baltimore, Maryland, with a rare book collection second only to J. P.
Morgan's, was, according to Lilian Randall, manuscript curator at the gallery, undoubtedly influenced by his father's collection. She notes that Henry's first-ever rare book
purchase was a late fifteenth-century French book of hours (fig. i-2), thought to have

Fig. i-3. Studio of Francisco de Zurbarán (b. 1598-1664?),
Virgin of Mercy, 1630-65.
Oil on canvas, 54¾ x 42 in. (142 x 108.8 cm).
The Isabella Stewart Gardner Museum

Fig. i-4. Isabella Stewart Gardner with her son, Jackie.
The Isabella Stewart Gardner Museum

been owned by a woman because of the image of Death striking down a young woman. The flyleaf bears a penciled notation by Walters: "My first manuscript purchase."

J. P. Morgan's first known purchase was a portrait of a young woman. Acquired in 1861, it is said to resemble his young wife, Mimi, who had just died from tuberculosis. More interesting, according to Morgan's biographer, Ron Chernow, Morgan had only a modest collection until his father's death in 1890. Then the international banker developed such an obsessive need to collect, he began buying entire collections en bloc, to preserve cultural history. As Chernow notes, "a savior complex" best described the near-compulsive hoarding that characterized Morgan's collecting pattern.

Two collections founded by women, both prominent individuals and famous collectors of Henry Clay Frick's day, were shaped by death as well, those of his friend Isabella Stewart Gardner, wife of the wealthy Bostonian businessman John Lowell Gardner, and Jane Stanford, wife of Leland Stanford, Sr., president and builder of the Central Pacific Railroad and the Southern Pacific Railroad, California governor, and U.S. senator from California.

Gardner, a woman of delicate health who spent her mornings in bed, had had difficulty bearing her only child, a son, only to lose him in 1865 at the age of eighteen months. Warned not to become pregnant again, Gardner later suffered a miscarriage and almost died. In 1888, she acquired a seventeenth-century painting by the studio of Zurbarán entitled *Virgin of Mercy* (fig. i-3) in which, according to Hilliard T. Goldfarb, director of the Isabella Stewart Gardner Museum in Boston, the Christ Child bears some resemblance to her infant son (fig. i-4). She placed the painting in her bedroom above her bed, and in 1903, five years after her husband's death, when the Florentine palazzo housing her art collection was completed, she placed the painting in its Spanish Chapel. As Goldfarb says of the Spanish Chapel, it is "clearly dedicated . . . to her infant son Jackie, who died nearly fifty years earlier."

Jane Stanford's grief reaction was more pronounced. She had been childless for eighteen years when she finally gave birth to Leland Stanford, Jr., in 1869. He died of typhoid fever in 1884, at age fifteen, when in Florence with his parents. His distraught parents had a plaster cast made of his bust and head. When transporting his body home to California via Paris and New York, they daily visited his remains, first in a Paris mortuary and later in a Sunday-school room in New York's Grace Church. They then placed the body in a one-room mausoleum in California, located one hundred yards from their house in Menlo Park. A mosaic of two life-size angels lifting the limp form of their son toward heaven and a posthumous portrait by E. Norjot rested behind the marble sarcophagus containing Leland's bronze casket and purple pall. Jane, who had the only key to the mausoleum, continued to visit her son every day. She brought fresh flowers and sat for hours on one of the two Venetian chairs placed in front of the sarcophagus.

But Jane's mourning soon took on larger, art-related proportions. While her husband began to plan Stanford University in memory of their son, Jane began to construct a museum and collect antiquities. Because young Leland had started his own collection of antiquities and had fashioned two museum rooms on the third floor of his parents' home in San Francisco to display his treasures, Jane dismantled these rooms and had them installed in the heart of the museum. For a time, she kept these rooms locked so she could visit in privacy. Later she expanded the museum collection in the way she felt her son would have done, had he lived. By 1900, the Leland Stanford, Jr., Art Museum was the largest privately owned museum in America.

More significant, however, Jane Stanford commissioned several posthumous portraits of her son. Some show the boy at his desk or contemplating Greek ruins. Others are disturbing. One, painted by Charles Landelle just after Leland's death, shows Jane and her husband with Leland hovering behind them in a mist. Another, by Emile Munier (fig. i-5), shows the boy as an angel comforting his weeping mother, who is

Fig. i-5. Emile Munier (1810–1895), *Leland Stanford, Jr.*
as an Angel Comforting his Grieving Mother, 1884.
Oil on canvas, 37 x 30½ in. (94 x 77.5 cm).
Stanford University Art Museum

dressed in a Madonna-blue robe. Still another, by Salviati of Venice, shows Leland at Christ's feet as he blesses the children. And yet one more, a painting entitled *Spring-time, Palo Alto,* by Thomas Hill, depicts three generations of the Stanford family; it includes Leland, Jr., and his two grandmothers, all of whom were dead at the time the painting was commissioned. After her husband's death in 1893, Jane Stanford built and dedicated the Stanford Memorial Church to *his* memory. A stained-glass window in the west arcade contains the figure of a dead boy, who resembles their son, being taken to heaven by an angel.

HENRY CLAY FRICK'S LIFE AND ART have never before been viewed through the psychological lens of mourning for several reasons. The first was his daughter Helen, who suffered the loss of two siblings before the age of four and who from age three, when her sister Martha died, became her father's consoler and companion. The apparent "laughing girl" in Frick's life, she had from childhood forward carried her own sorrows while also playing a major role both in mitigating her father's anguish and in the formation of his art collection. She knew well her father's personal associations with his art and feared that people might see him as a sentimental collector after his death. Equally determined to rise above her own distress and to erase the dark side of Frick's legacy as a major industrialist, she furiously guarded his privacy and the sanctity of his art collection, initiating numerous lawsuits against those who threatened the private nature of his collection. To say the very least, she did not encourage an analysis of his paintings or the motivations behind his choices.

Second, the Frick family papers have been unavailable for study by scholars. Access to even Frick's business papers has been limited to the business historians John Ingham and Kenneth Warren and to Andrew Carnegie's biographer, the late Joseph Wall.

Third, only in recent decades has the traditional approach to art history and biography expanded to include psychological interpretation. In the past, art collections have been presented solely in aesthetic and historical terms. Increasingly, however, there is greater understanding of the unconscious. Many are now aware that its language is based not on spoken words, but on the symbolic—what a person collects, creates, or even wears.

Fourth, the artworks at Clayton (only recently open to the public) and in New York have never been studied together as one entity, with each work viewed as equal to another *in its meaning to Henry Clay Frick,* rather than in its ranking in the hierarchy of art. The book has, therefore, dictated a unique format. For aesthetic reasons, I have chosen to place all citations in endnotes listed by page number and an identifying phrase. More important, the paintings Frick collected, and the archival photographs from his day, appear throughout the book to illustrate the story of his life. Those artworks now in the Frick Collection, or at Clayton, and those once owned by Henry Clay Frick but now in private collections or other museums, are not grouped by collection, nor are they presented by century, school, nationality, or even their date of acquisition. Rather, the paintings appear as I believe they did to Henry Clay Frick— as haunting, luminous links to his past. Often a painting is juxtaposed with an archival photograph to heighten the reader's understanding of the autobiographical nature of the acquisition. For easy reference, the date of acquisition is included in the caption for each painting reproduced in the book and after those only mentioned in the text. A figure number accompanies every illustration. There is also a chronological list of these paintings in the Appendix.

Now the book belongs to you. If nothing else, I hope that it fully honors the privilege given me and faithfully satisfies the demands of such an intimate portrait.

M. F. S. S., April, 1998

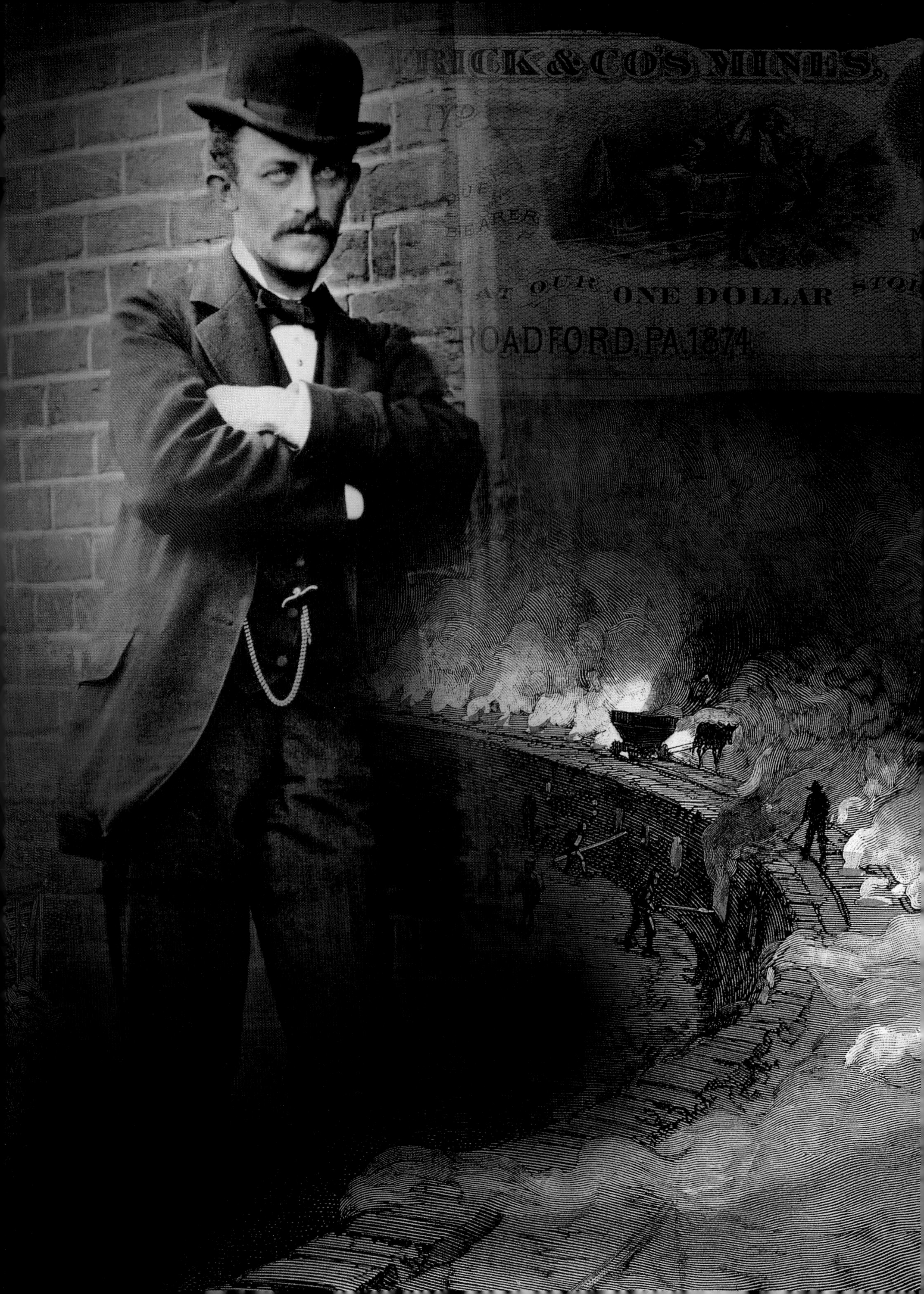
RICK & CO'S MINES,
BEARER
AT OUR
ONE DOLLAR
ROADFORD PA 1874

Birth of a Millionaire

They say Clay is in critical condition.
They don't think he can get well.

—Abraham Tinstman, 1875

Fig. 1-1. The springhouse where Henry Clay Frick was born on
December 19, 1849.
West Overton Museums Archives

H ENRY CLAY FRICK, named for the then-retired Whig statesman Henry Clay, former speaker of the U.S. House of Representatives and known as the Great Compromiser, was born on December 19, 1849, in a two-room springhouse in West Overton, Pennsylvania, just north of Connellsville (fig. 1-1). His maternal grandparents, Abraham and Maria Stauffer Overholt, were German Mennonites and, by agrarian standards, wealthy. Abraham Overholt, described by his grandson A.O. Tinstman as "a pretty tight sort of fellow," owned the one-street village of West Overton, founded in 1800 by Abraham's father, the weaver Henry Overholt, who had moved there from Bucks County, Pennsylvania, in 1800. More important, Abraham also owned much of the surrounding farm land, land that produced the grain for his six-story rye whiskey distillery and flour mill.

Fig. 1-2. The Overholt Homestead in West Overton where Henry Clay Frick spent the first thirty years of his life.
West Overton Museums Archives

Frick's parents, however, were poor. When his mother, Elizabeth Overholt Frick, announced her engagement to John W. Frick, a locally born, red-haired rowdy whose father was a Mennonite and paternal grandmother was a red-haired Irishwoman, Abraham was furious. John Frick was four years Elizabeth's junior and earned a hundred dollars a year in the West Overton distillery. But Elizabeth was three months pregnant, and so Abraham consented to the marriage. The Fricks, however, were not in great favor with Abraham.

Today, the casual eye marks West Overton village as a romantic place. The Overholts' charming, double-porched, brick Homestead (fig. 1-2) still looks out over the picturesque springhouse where Clay, as his family called their second child, was born. Only a few hundred yards to the north stands a large brick barn for cattle, pigs, and farm horses, while to the east looms the distillery building (fig. 1-3). To the south, a smokehouse, a dressy brick barn where the Overholts' horses and carriages were stabled, and a small kitchen garden once planted with herbs and flowers, border a front yard once filled with apple trees. The quaint setting, nestled in country that rolls in ever larger waves eastward to the Allegheny Mountains, or flattens as it extends westward to Pittsburgh and Ohio, reminds the visitor of a quieter life, long since passed.

Although there was peace and beauty in the village of Henry Clay Frick's birth, there was little romance. In this distillery town, as was true elsewhere, alcohol—a staple of the day—was freely available. Diseases such as cholera, dysentery, and typhoid were everpresent dangers. Many children did not attain the age of five. Nevertheless, Elizabeth Frick had been lucky in childbearing. A daughter named Maria was born in 1847, two years before Clay, and now, in Clay, they had a son. By naming him after a great American statesman, perhaps his parents hoped Clay Frick would emulate Henry Clay and become a strong individual, run the family business, and perhaps become a man of national importance.

At Clay's birth, their hopes seemed oddly placed. The mantle seemed far greater than the child could support. As Clay grew from infancy to boyhood, his delicate frame and fragile health increasingly warned of weakness, not strength. A sickly boy, he suffered from chronic indigestion and a weak heart. Unable to work in the fields like other Mennonite children, he was housebound and primarily occupied with helping his mother. In return, Clay was doted on by his mother and maternal grandmother. With his soft eyes and curly hair, he was their favorite, but he was also their constant concern.

Fig. 1-3. The Overholt Distillery in West Overton.
West Overton Museums Archives

Though Clay was the second child, he grew up as the eldest. In August 1852, when Maria was four and Clay three, Elizabeth Frick gave birth to her third child, Anna. Abraham, on hearing the news from a villager, hurried over to see this new granddaughter. As he was admiring her, however, Maria, who was outside playing, dropped a wagon handle on Clay's hand, severely cutting it. Abraham, who must have been anxious for his daughter Elizabeth and upset by the injury to his grandson, immediately gathered Maria in his arms and took her back to the Homestead, where she had been born, to raise as his own. Thus in one tumultuous moment, a badly injured Clay, age three, had his older sister taken away, and perhaps in his child's mind, felt that he had been the cause. As he settled back into family life as the eldest, adjusting to the loss of his older sister, the arrival of the new baby, and his parents' preoccupation with the baby, he could easily have felt guilty, perhaps even abandoned and punished. Whatever the emotional and psychological impact, however, as the oldest he began to help his mother raise his sister Anna, just as he would assist her with his three other siblings (one of them retarded) who would come in rapid succession.

In the spring of 1855, Henry Clay Frick's life was further disrupted. Almost six years old, he was taken by his father to Van Buren, Ohio. The trip was designed for Clay to meet his paternal grandfather, Daniel Frick, who was on his deathbed. It was the first time Clay had been separated from his mother and grandmother and the first time he had been deprived of their watchful eyes and tender care. Upon arrival in Van Buren, Clay contracted scarlet fever—then a highly contagious, life-threatening disease that caused kidney and heart damage.

The disease, marked by a rash, peeling skin, high fever, rapid pulse, nausea, headache, and muscle pain, exacerbated Clay's congenital conditions and perhaps, in following the disease pattern, caused a collapse into rheumatic fever, followed by an attack of inflammatory rheumatism. The latter disease—now known to be a disorder of the autoimmune system causing the body to attack itself—would plague Clay his entire life. It inflicts intense muscle pain, swollen joints and, since it takes months, even years to subside, can so damage the heart muscle and valves that blood is unable to flow normally through the heart chambers. Known today as rheumatoid arthritis, or "the great crippler" because it is progressive and has no known cure, when this disease attacks, it ultimately renders the person bedridden and helpless as a baby.

Henry Clay Frick remained in Van Buren for two months until he was strong enough to travel home to West Overton, where his mother had just given birth to her fourth child, a retarded son named Aaron. A full year passed before Clay fully recovered. He remained so frail that over the next seven years he would have only a sporadic education, unable much of the time to walk the mile to school (fig. 1-4). In times of heavy snow, the miller's son carried him to school on his back. When riding in a

Fig. 1-4. The West Overton schoolhouse where Henry Clay Frick received his early, sporadic education.
West Overton Museums Archives

carriage, because he was susceptible to motion sickness, his mother placed foolscap paper on his stomach.

Nevertheless, the slender, fair-skinned, gray-eyed boy, with auburn-tinged curls inherited from his father, soon learned to compensate for both his lack of education and his frailty. Although he played a rigorous game called bullpen with the other boys, and joined his mother and siblings in the harvest field, running barefoot as he gathered the fallen grain from the stubble, he preferred to apply himself in areas where precision of mind, not strength of body, was required. He became expert at pitching horseshoes and, as J. M. Hantz, a contemporary, noted, was known for his hand-eye coordination—his ability to "make more ringers than any boy in town." He said, "if a shoe was placed in a position to make a ringer by one on the opposite side Frick would knock it out of place if it could at all be done."

Too weak to bat and run, he served as the umpire and scorekeeper for roundball games. He excelled at Authors, chess, checkers, and quoits—all of which demanded mental accuracy and skill, not physical strength. And he fixed things around the house, occasionally helped feed the hundreds of cattle, or drove pigs from the barn to the distillery hog pens for fattening. As far as farm work was concerned, his main

Fig. 1-5. Henry Clay Frick at age fourteen.
West Overton Museums Archives

responsibility was lifting the gate that allowed the distillery mash to run into troughs that fed 2,000 pigs.

But Frick had another personal struggle. He was a gentle, aesthetic-looking and shy child (fig. 1-5), so shy and self-conscious that he constantly elicited ridicule. According to a family diary, when first faced with girls, he broke down completely. When reciting "Twinkle, Twinkle, Little Star" as a young boy, he stumbled his way through so badly that his schoolmates laughed derisively.

Nevertheless, Clay was determined in his schoolwork. According to his cousin, Isaac Sherrick, whose brother sat next to Frick in school, Clay started school a year behind because of his health. Within a year, however, he caught up and was seen helping the younger children, especially in math, even then a strong subject for him. As Isaac's sister Ella wrote, he was "one of the most perfect little gentlemen . . . in its most comprehensive sense to cover not only manner, but mind and morals as well." According to her, he never "utter[ed] a coarse word, or was . . . guilty of a rude action." Clay was also so great a thinker, Ella Sherrick felt that "had there been a library available . . . he would have become a great reader."

Always "neat and careful about his appearance," Clay's "quiet dignity" was part of his power, even though he was given to blushing, something Ella remembered him doing when she came into a store where he was clerking. She was wearing a new dress and when she asked, "Why the blushes?" the subject was immediately dropped. But as she recalled, "the result was most peculiar for never again did I see him color like that, even under the most trying circumstances." In wondering how he controlled it, Ella said, "I could never imagine. Will power, I guess."

And yet, Henry Clay Frick was an odd mixture of sensitivity and fury. Of dry humor and quick temper, at school Clay received his share of "hickory oil," as whippings with the hickory cane were called. He was quick to defend young girls against the hickory stick. When, for example, Isaac and Ella's sister Susan was told by the teacher she would be whipped if she did not do her work better, Clay "was angry clear through." He told the teacher that if he beat his cousin Susan, he would whip *him*—a statement that had an immediate effect. As Clay's contemporary and childhood friend, Charles F. Booher, remembered him, Clay was "strong willed—more so than most boys." He was someone who would fight without a great deal of provocation, particularly when he thought his rights were being trampled upon. As Booher noted, "There was not a cowardly bone in his body."

In fact, Henry Clay Frick seemed to hide his frailties and infirmities in a protective shell, choosing to present a tough facade. Never one to use his physical weakness as an excuse, he earned money gathering wheat sheaves in the fields for his father, money he used to buy clothing for the following year. Clay rose to the challenge of hard work—a self-mastery and determination that later in life would serve him well. *The Meadow Mart* (a newsletter from Shreve, Ohio), quoting Frick many years later, best exhibits Frick's public attempt to downplay his childhood frailty:

> We children had to help to the limit of our strength. Before I was eight, I had learned how to drop corn, help in the harvest field, tend cattle, and perform a hundred variety of chores. So badly were my services needed in the earning of family living that I was allowed to go to school only in the winter months.

Within his family the work ethic was so strong that Frick later admitted to his friends the thing that "most annoyed him was the man that had never accomplished anything worthwhile." He repeatedly claimed, "Everyone was put in this world to work . . . some people have an idea that money grows on trees."

While farming is by nature a life of hard work with little financial promise, the harsh quality of Clay's home life was exacerbated by the fact that his land-rich grandfather Abraham, with two whiskey businesses (the one located in West Overton and the other a twenty-to-thirty-acre complex on the banks of the Youghiogheny River in nearby Broad Ford) and a genteel home full of lithographs, prints, and portraits of U.S. presidents did nothing to ease the burden borne by John and Elizabeth. Clay and his family had few amenities and, consequently, few luxuries. Clay also experienced repeated moves, each one occurring at about the time his mother delivered her babies, because his father rented a new place to live every two years when the leases ran out on the farms he worked.

In these boyhood years, as much as John Frick's negative role-modeling may have sparked Frick's desire to succeed, Abraham, with his business acumen, energy, and determination, showed him the way to achieve success. An immaculate dresser and austere figure, he often rode with Clay around the undulating West Overton farm land. As Clay's cousin Ella Sherrick wrote, the two made "a very pretty pair . . . one so fresh and young, the other old and gray and very dignified." In time, Clay became a skilled horseman and drove Abraham and his two horses, a bay and a gray, everywhere. As the two inspected the planting and harvest fields, Abraham Overholt explained the workings of the farm machinery and farming methods to him, often complimenting a deserving farmer on a neatly planted crop.

Although tight-fisted, Abraham was far-sighted and fair. He started the school system in the West Overton area and took such a paternal interest in his neighbors' welfare that he was often addressed as "Grandpap Overholt." He had undoubtedly told Clay of the time he sent two of his sons, who were then young men, to buy up as much wheat as they could in Ohio. Abraham feared his own wheat crop was going to be poor, causing high prices and shortages in the West Overton region. When the shortage did occur, people flocked to him. A few local farmers tried to buy the bulk of Abraham's Ohio grain, saying they would be willing "to pay high for it." But Abraham sold them, and others, only enough for their own needs, and did so at cost. So Clay, while unable to play and attend school like other children, did receive unique and early training in supply and demand—although he would never be known to sell at cost.

Perhaps Clay received another kind of education from Abraham as well. This grandfather was quick to make a decision, and though noble and dignified, he was a man with a temper so fierce that it was said of his rage, "If one got it, all felt it." There was a sign over the mantel in the springhouse where Clay was born that read: "If you want to know who's boss, just start something." In 1844, when the Democrat James K. Polk defeated Henry Clay in the presidential election, two stonemasons working in West Overton hoisted a Polk sign on the distillery building. According to a family diary, Abraham came out of the building "very angry, with his under lip protruding," and stood by as his son Martin shot it down on his order.

His behavior was, in fact, so rash that he risked excommunication from the Mennonite church. Although his wife was a daughter and granddaughter of Mennonite ministers, and he permitted evening prayer meetings in his home, Abraham refused to take part in the traditional Mennonite footwashing ceremony. During the Civil War, in defiance of his pacifist religion, he supplied the Union troops with his Old Farm Rye Whiskey. The pride of Abraham's life, the whiskey was considered "the 'best likker' in the 'hull kentry.'" People said the supply never equaled the demand. Every morning on rising Abraham descended the stairs, entered the sitting room, removed the whiskey decanter from the cabinet, and downed a glass, together with a sugar loaf kept in the sugar box on the mantel, before visiting the outhouse.

Abraham was tough, competitive, and strict. On the road, he refused to allow anyone to pass him and quickly out-galloped any challengers. At meals, his commanding eye imposed silence more forcefully than any words he could have uttered. When he wished something passed to him, he would silently point, instead of asking. He would banish to the kitchen anyone who laughed during meals, and if his hot mush and milk were cooked improperly, he would glower and send the food back to the kitchen.

From his earliest days, however, Clay was competitive with his stern grandfather. Ashamed of his own father, perhaps even his own frailty, Clay looked to Abraham as the person he must surpass. According to a family diary, Clay was described by his peers as a "hustler." He used to say to his sister Maria, "Oh, I'll be worth $200,000 some day." His first cousin and best friend, Abraham Tinstman, who was fifteen years older than Clay and ran Abraham's other distillery at Broad Ford, founded in 1855, as well as the farm and family timber business, remembered Clay claiming a greater dream: "There is nothing to hinder me from being worth one million dollars, and I propose to be worth that."

In 1863, a year after his mother produced her sixth and last child, and as the Civil War raged, Clay, age fourteen, began his quest. He clerked at his Uncle Christian Overholt's store in West Overton (fig. 1-6), conveniently located across the street from the house John Frick was then renting. The following year, he discarded all his dark, shoddy, ill-fitting farming clothes and declared he would now clothe himself. He appeared one morning in a pair of black boots with yellow stitching, which cost sixteen dollars, and according to family lore, "smiled contentedly that everyone noted his extravagance." But at the end of six months, he also showed them how frugal he was. The boots still shone like new, as did the yellow stitching. Many years later, when Clay told his son Childs this story, he confided that going barefoot in the summer was not such an inconvenience.

At sixteen, Clay moved to Mt. Pleasant where he helped put a roof on the family barn and for the next three years clerked for his Uncle Martin Overholt. He began frequenting the Baptist church and attended Westmoreland College, where he took courses in math and history and donated *The Life of Napoleon Bonaparte* (which fascinated him) and works by Sir Walter Scott to their library. He also attended Otterbein College in Westerville, Ohio, for six weeks, but the majority of his time was spent

Fig. 1-6. Christian Overholt's West Overton store.
Frick Archives

weighing sugar, measuring cloth, handling dairy products, sweeping the floor in the evenings after his elders went to bed. At night he slept on a mattress which he spread on the counter.

In 1868, however, Henry Clay Frick got fired for some still unknown reason. John Frick saw him walking back to West Overton and, upon learning that his son had been discharged, said, "[You] better go down and tell [your grandmother] right away." Clay replied that such was his exact intent and after his confession, Abraham swung Clay up on his elegant bay horse, rode him to the distillery at Broad Ford (fig. 1-7), located a few miles south of West Overton, and asked Abraham Tinstman to give his grandson a job as an office boy with a salary of $25 a month.

Clay must have considered how he might now achieve his dream of making $1 million with an annual salary of $300, and at the age of sixteen, realized that he would need capital. One day, when Abraham Overholt visited the distillery, with a directness that always characterized Clay, the boy turned to him and asked, "Grandfather, won't you tell me as near as you can what my share in your estate would be. If I had it [now] I could make so much more out of it than you are."

Abraham warned his grandson, "It will be time enough to know that after I am gone."

As Abraham did not seem anywhere near death, an industrious Henry Clay Frick set out to pursue his million dollar dream. For the next few months, the bookkeeper at Broad Ford taught him accounting, but at nineteen, Clay left West Overton to work in Pittsburgh. He became a Baptist, as did his parents and many other Mennonites who were shedding their German heritage, and rented a room in Allegheny City, now the North Side of Pittsburgh. With the large, dark shape of Coal Hill looming over the confluence of the Allegheny, Monongahela, and Ohio rivers, Clay daily walked the bridge across the Allegheny to Macrum and Carlisle, a wholesale and retail dealer in trimmings, embroideries, skirts, corsets, hosiery, gloves, fancy goods, and notions. He was placed in charge of the linen and lace department and received $6 a week for his efforts. The position, secured for him by his Uncle Christian, also kept Clay connected to the feminine world on which he had been dependent from an early age, a world that had given him the reputation of being both very polite and considerate of young girls, a world that knew him as the handsome young man often seen helping women with their baskets and babies when on the train from Mt. Pleasant to Broad Ford.

Moreover, the position satisfied Clay's innate love of finery. He had always appreciated textiles, perhaps because weaving, as well as distilling, was an Overholt family

Fig. 1-7. The Overholt distillery in Broad Ford.
Carnegie Library, Connellsville

tradition. And to further satisfy this passion for clothing, while still wearing the traditional drab black and white of the Mennonite sect, he borrowed $50 from a relative, bought himself a church suit, and attended services at the first Presbyterian Church, recently built by Asa P. Childs, who would later become Clay's father-in-law, and William K. Thaw, Pittsburgh's noted businessman and art collector.

The position at Macrum satisfied other interests as well—his love of math and his appreciation for art. In the evenings, he studied accounting at Iron City Commercial College. On Sundays, he saw, and perhaps met, William K. Thaw, who collected works by local artists and had just opened the Pittsburgh School of Design for Women. During the week, perhaps inspired by Thaw, and certainly by the lithographs, prints, and portraits of the U.S. presidents in his grandfather's home, Clay ventured to Schuchmann's Lithography, conveniently located above Macrum's. Sellers of maps, landscapes, architectural and machine drawings, prints and engravings, Schuchmann's might well have had a collection of engravings reproduced by the naturalized Frenchman Michel Knoedler, who had managed the New York branch of the well-known French engraving firm Goupil et Cie. And if Clay had seen them, perhaps there at Schuchmann's, the seed was sown for his eventual relationship with the art dealer's grandson, Roland Knoedler, the man who would one day play a prominent role in the formation of Henry Clay Frick's art collection.

According to one story, Henry Clay Frick was an aspiring artist. In the late 1860s, Andrew Mellon, who became a lifelong friend of Clay's and whose father, Judge Thomas Mellon, was a contemporary and friend of Abraham Overholt's, was working in the same Pittsburgh company as Frick. Apparently, Andrew Mellon had decided to take a walk in the yard during lunch hour and came upon Frick hiding behind a shed, painting. Frick was so embarrassed by having been discovered, he pleaded, "Andy, please don't tell any of the fellows that you saw me here painting. They would think me a sissy."

In a month or two, Clay left Macrum's and took up a position at Copper's, a fashionable dealer in mourning clothes and black dress goods. But this position, too, was short-lived. In that spring of 1868, Clay contracted typhoid fever and was forced to return to West Overton. Nursed by his mother, grandmother, and older sister, Maria, who administered homeopathic remedies, brought him fresh spring water, and read him the Sermon on the Mount to satisfy his constant request, he began to recover.

Rather than returning to Pittsburgh after his illness, he worked at the West Overton distillery until he was strong enough to make the daily trip to his grandfather's flour mill and distillery at Broad Ford. In addition to the routine tasks of weighing grain and flour and selling lumber, he helped the bookkeeper with the accounts. Even at this age, Clay was recognized in the community as having extraordinary bookkeeping skills, as well as good judgment. His ability in conducting business and managing employees was often noted, and his account books, filled with his beautiful handwriting, were as accurate as they were artistic and neat. After three months of work without pay, Frick was rewarded with the news he would receive a $1,000-a-year salary.

There was no mistaking that Henry Clay Frick was a determined young man. Alfred Emerson, a local laborer, noted this quality when, many years before, Clay had stepped on what Emerson called "the first rung of the ladder" of his career. At that time, Clay had apparently asked a Mr. Longsdorf in West Overton if he knew where he could get a job. When Longsdorf advised him that a man at the Broad Ford mill was about to quit, Clay and Emerson walked that evening from West Overton to Broad Ford. In the morning, when Clay asked his Tinstman cousin for the job, Tinstman hired him to take care of the office. In an aside to Emerson, Tinstman said he had never seen a colder day and suggested they might have some fun with the lad. Tinstman told Clay the first thing they would do would be to take inventory at the saw mill, and he instructed Clay to get a tablet and pencil and mark down all that was measured, fully expecting that within minutes, because of the cold, Clay would run to the fire to get warm. But the two men measured and measured until noon, and as Emerson recalled, Clay "dident [sic] squeal." After lunch, when Tinstman announced that they would start another project, to his surprise Clay said, "No, we will finish the sawmill first." Although it did not take long to finish the job, Tinstman, knowing Clay "had the laugh on them," said to Emerson, "What in the name of common sense is in him that we couldn't Freeze him?"

Soon even Clay's determination would be tested by the death of his grandfather and the disappointment of his hopes for an inheritance. Around 6 A.M. on January 15, 1870, eighty-six-year-old Abraham (fig. 1-8) awoke with a severe pain in his head. As was his habit, he went downstairs, drank a glass of his favorite whiskey, and ate a sugar loaf. With lantern in hand, he visited the outhouse. Concerned when he did not return, the family went to the outhouse and found him prostrate on the floor. He had died of apoplexy.

Abraham, however, was not as successful a businessman as had been assumed. At the end of his life in 1870, his West Overton distillery and farm were surviving on a hand-to-mouth basis and the distillery at Broad Ford was bankrupt. As both distilleries were owned in partnership, and Abraham's two surviving sons, Christian and Martin, were heavily in debt to him and bankrupt, the distillery partnerships had to be dissolved and many of Abraham's assets sold.

After the dissolution, Abraham's estate totaled about $395,000 (approximately $4.5 million today). The legacy was divided into six shares, one to each of his deceased sons' widows; one to each of his two surviving, but bankrupt sons; one to Clay's mother,

Fig. 1-8. Abraham Overholt.
Frick Archives

Elizabeth; and one to his widow. As Abraham's favorite grandchild, Clay had always assumed he would be given a legacy, but nothing was set aside for him or his siblings except a small stipend for Maria, Clay's older sister, whom Abraham had raised.

Clay was twenty years old (fig. 1-9), had a limited income, and no formal education. His health was poor, but he enjoyed the physical and emotional support of his Overholt mother and grandmother. Above all, he burned with determination and ambition. As a child he had fed cattle and driven pigs. But he had long since repudiated farm life. He was now convinced that his fortune lay beneath, not above, the ground.

Clay decided, therefore, to go into coal mining and the then fledgling coking business. Abraham Tinstman, who became the sole owner of the Broad Ford distillery on Abraham's death to resolve the debt, owned the nearby Morgan Mines in partnership with Col. A. S. M. Morgan from Pittsburgh. Morgan and Company had 111 coke ovens and held almost entire control of the Connellsville coke business with earnings close to $110,000 a year.

Even though financial insecurity and the threat of death would continue to stalk Clay through early manhood, he would soon show more than his grandfather's ghost who was boss.

❖

THE FIELDS OF WESTMORELAND COUNTY ARE PEACEFUL, undulating pasture and crop lands, not unlike Constant Troyon's *A Pasture in Normandy* (fig. 1-10). They stretch gracefully eastward to the Allegheny Mountains, while to the west, many fast-moving streams join the broad, smooth Youghiogheny River, whose waters flow as gently as the river in Aelbert Cuyp's *Cows and Herdsman by a River* (fig. 1-11), and make their way into the Monongahela River east of Pittsburgh. This swift-moving highway winds past the now deserted sites of steel mills and into the city itself. Then, at the apex of the triangle that defines downtown Pittsburgh, the Monongahela joins the Allegheny River to form the Ohio River, one of the great arteries of commerce to the heart of the American continent in the eighteenth and nineteenth centuries.

At the time of Henry Clay Frick's birth in 1849, the Youghiogheny, Monongahela, and Allegheny rivers supplied transportation for goods going to market in Pittsburgh, then thriving as an iron and glass-making center and a river port for shipping freight and coal, as well as pioneers who were settling the West and dreaming of California gold. Yet beneath the placid surface of West Overton and the surrounding hills of Westmoreland and Fayette counties there rested an underground treasure that was of immensely greater value than California gold. It would give birth to Henry Clay Frick's fortune and become a major force in America's transition from an agrarian to an industrial society.

In an underground trough three miles wide and forty-miles long lay a rich bituminous coal deposit. It was located within fifty miles of the city's mills and was part of the Pittsburgh seam which covered large areas of southwestern Pennsylvania, Ohio, and parts of West Virginia. Plentiful and pure, it became famous because it made superb coke. Like ore and limestone, coke was an essential ingredient to the making of iron and iron's later refinement—steel.

Fig. 1-9. Henry Clay Frick
at age twenty-one.
West Overton Museums Archives

Coke—the name derives from the contraction of the words coal and cake—is a pure form of carbon that produces an intense, smokeless heat. In Clay's time, coke was made by the beehive process, named for the brick ovens, roughly shaped like beehives, which burned the coal of the Pittsburgh seam into coke. In the process, bituminous coal was dropped into the ovens from larries that ran along a track on top of the banks of ovens. The coal was fired through an opening in the front of each oven which was then sealed with bricks. The coal cooked for forty-eight or seventy-two hours, depending on the quality of coke desired. Once the impurities—sulfur and phosphorous—

Fig. 1-10. Constant Troyon (1810–1865), *A Pasture in Normandy,* c. 1850.
Acquired in 1899, Oil on panel, 17 x 25⅝ in. (43.2 x 65.1 cm).
The Frick Collection

Fig. 1-11. Aelbert Cuyp (1620–1691), *Cows and Herdsman by a River,* c. 1650.
Acquired in 1902, Oil on oak panel, 19¾ x 29¼ in. (50.2 x 74.3 cm).
The Frick Collection

were burned off, the final form of coke was pure carbon. When "drawn" from the oven and watered down, the coke broke into gray lumps and was then loaded into railroad cars and shipped to the mills.

Ultimately, 44,000 coke ovens, connected in rows or banks, would line the hills and pastures of the Connellsville Coke Region, as Westmoreland and Fayette counties became known. And the coal mines that fed these ovens would form vast underground labyrinths beneath the Allegheny foothills. No one realized, however, the implications of this sleeping fortune, a fortune that would soon be carried to the market place by the vast river network and burgeoning railroad system.

In 1870, when Henry Clay Frick entered the coal and coke business, no one guessed that within ten years thousands of immigrant workers would silently mine coal beneath the quiet pastures, moving like ants along their carefully measured and constructed tunnels. Neither did anyone suspect that in twenty years the peaceful hills and hamlets along the streams and rivers would become the sites of these two major industries, a place where strife between labor and management would turn the Coke Region into a bloody battlefield.

❖

ALTHOUGH FEW IN SOUTHWESTERN PENNSYLVANIA before the Civil War could have grasped the potential of the coal that underlay their land, they knew it existed. As early as 1830, some farmers were mining the coal beneath their fields and turning it into coke. Abraham Overholt had mined coal from the hill behind his house and used it to heat his home and fuel his distilleries. He, too, had experimented with the making of coke in beehive ovens located in a pasture next to his West Overton home. The war had spurred the growth of both industry and railroads in the North, and Overholt was a man of business as well as a farmer. In 1868, he loaned his grandson Abraham Tinstman $20,000 to invest in the lucrative Morgan Mines which were located in the Broad Ford Run Valley close to his distillery.

To the uninitiated, one sees nothing unusual when driving around the area. But to Clay and those familiar with the black riders of coal that stretched horizontally across the bluff outcroppings, the easy calculation of acreage multiplied by the thickness of the seam, made the volume of coal readily apparent.

Clay knew that the Morgan Mines were earning Tinstman about $110,000 a year in profits. Disappointed in his expectations of an inheritance from his grandfather, not wishing to farm, and sensing something of the future importance of coal and coke, he decided to go into partnership with Tinstman, his cousin J. S. R. Overholt, and Joseph Rist.

With his father co-signing the note, he took out a $5,000 life insurance policy and confidently borrowed $75,000 against his mother's and grandmother's inheritance—agreeing to pay the trustees $12,514.16 with interest—in order to develop the mines on 125 acres of coal land adjoining the Broad Ford distillery.

Clay mentally attacked this enterprise with a brute force equal to the muscle power of the local miners he hired. He also demanded much of himself physically. He often walked from West Overton, through Scottdale, across Jacob's Creek, through the valley where Tinstman had his Morgan Mines, to the Broad Ford distillery—and back again at night.

Originally called the Broad Ford Mines, the partnership was soon referred to as Frick and Company, perhaps because Clay became the manager. He decided to continue working at the floundering Broad Ford distillery, using his bookkeeper's salary for living expenses. He took no salary from his new company, hoping that he could simultaneously build the company's earnings and reduce its debt.

With the lands acquired and the partnership formed, in March 1871, Frick then sought funding for building fifty coke ovens. His family background gave him access to Judge Thomas Mellon (fig. 1-12), one of the most powerful entrepreneurs in western Pennsylvania. A farm boy who had graduated from college, studied law, and become a jurist, Mellon had retired from the bench to manage his many business interests, and in 1870, founded the Mellon Bank in Pittsburgh. Judge Mellon's father, Andrew, had been a close friend of Abraham Overholt's and often brought his son Thomas to play with Frick's mother, the young Elizabeth Overholt.

Despite the advantage of the family connection, Frick was only twenty-one years old, with refined boyish looks, and untried in business. At the age of fifty-seven, Mellon was a formidable and almost legendary figure—and he had lost money in the notoriously unstable coke industry. Somehow the meeting turned out well for Frick, perhaps because Mellon recognized in his young visitor something of himself and certainly because he recognized something of the future importance of coke. Mellon was famously stern and candid, with no use for circumlocutions. And Frick, even as a young man, was well organized, spoke in a low warm voice, his eyes intent and steady. Interested in the immaculately dressed man before him, and appreciative of the steadfast determination of the Overholt family, Mellon agreed to lend Frick $10,000 at 6 percent interest, payable in six months, for building his ovens.

As construction began on the Frick Works (but called the Novelty Works by Clay), Clay noted that on April 27 he had six ovens burning and would have fifteen finished by April 29. Perhaps sensing that it would be more economical to build another fifty

ovens while the crew was already on the site, he returned to Judge Mellon in July and asked for a second loan of $10,000. The loan officer reviewing the application recommended the loan be denied. But Judge Mellon, impressed by Frick's vision, as well as his frugal life-style—Frick was living in a clapboard shack and his combination office and living room was filled with mining maps as well as prints and sketches, some done by himself—was of another mind. He told his son Andrew that "the loans being made to Mr. Frick were larger than Mr. Frick's material resources justified but that he was of a character to succeed." He was "pleased with the type of statement which Mr. Frick furnished of his affairs in which everything was frankly set forth, the favorable with the unfavorable."

Judge Mellon then sent his own mining partner, James B. Corey, to make an independent examination of Frick's coke works. When Corey arrived at Frick's shack, he found Frick was not home. Corey settled in and mentally appraised Frick's living space. Apparently, the two-room cabin serving as home and office was so well organized that Corey thought "he would like to see more of the young man with the cast-iron nerve." After spending a day and a night with Frick, Corey was conquered. His report to the Judge was brief: "Give him the money." His reasons: "Lands good, ovens well built; manager on job all day, keeps books evenings, may be a little too enthusiastic about pictures but not enough to hurt; knows his business down to the ground."

Having secured the loan, Frick built the extra ovens at his Novelty Works, fired them, and opened still another coke works, the Henry Clay, a 100-oven complex adjacent to his Henry Clay mine. This mine was strategically located across from the Frick Works, at the juncture of the Pittsburgh and Connellsville Railroad and the private railroad Tinstman had built through the valley to his Morgan Mines.

From the start, the coke business was good. Clay shipped his product to Chicago, Milwaukee, Salt Lake City, and other western cities. As he had every reason to anticipate a profitable future, he began compiling a three-page description for the executors of Abraham Overholt's estate concerning deeds for lands that Frick and Company might purchase with loans from the beneficiaries of Abraham's estate. As business grew and Clay systematically began to repay his outstanding loans from company earnings, he began to reinvest profits in more coking coal lands and more ovens along Tinstman's railroad.

Then suddenly, after his ovens had been in operation only two years, on September 16, 1873, a financial panic—in the making since the beginning of the Civil War— hit Wall Street. The financial collapse was soon followed by an industrial depression. By the end of the year, more than five thousand commercial enterprises had failed. The iron mills shut down, the demand for coke fell catastrophically, and coal mines were left idle. Many people who operated coke works were forced to abandon them, and the demand for coke in the Connellsville region was all but extinguished. Frick and Company seemed doomed, along with Clay's hopes for making his fortune.

His partners were unable to put any of their resources into the company, as they were overextended and needed all their cash to safeguard their other investments. Nevertheless, with Pittsburgh as a major railroad center, inland port, and manufacturing center, Clay remained convinced the economy would recover, and with its rebound, industry would have an insatiable demand for his coke. He decided, therefore, to keep his ovens in operation, further anticipating that were he to leave his new works idle, the operations would deteriorate, causing a greater financial liability than running his company at a loss.

He mortgaged a farm he and his father had purchased with assets from his mother's and grandmother's shares of Abraham's estate and used the money to buy more lands at depressed prices. He hustled to pay off debts, maintained the condition of his ovens, and kept himself in touch with his few remaining customers, ever gambling the market would recover.

Figs. 1-13, 14. Davidson Coke Works, railroad tracks, and Henry Clay Frick's coke cars.
Private collection

At two o'clock one morning, shortly after the panic of 1873 hit, Clay called at the home of Joseph Myers, a farmer and neighbor of John Frick's, from whom Clay had borrowed $10,000. The note had his father's name on it for security, as well as Abraham Tinstman's, and another cousin's. Clay told Myers that one cousin backing the note had failed and Tinstman was about to fail. When Frick pleaded with Myers, "I don't want you to close me out," Myers replied, "John W. Frick is still on the note and I won't close you out."

Determined never to default on a note bearing his signature, Clay then set up an arduous work schedule. He began his day at two or three in the morning, hitching up the mine mules he traditionally drove to Sunday dinner at the Overholt Homestead and driving them around the hillsides to canvass the potential coal lands selling at panic prices. He studied the bare rock outcroppings, known as "coal fronts"—lines of bluff hills that revealed the black seams of coal compressed between the rocks—which not only charted the outer boundaries of the coal seam, but pointed to the rich vein of Connellsville coking coal sixty feet below the ground.

After mentally appraising these coal fronts and following their path along the bluff hills, he would return to Broad Ford, monitor his coke works, and then, acting as both his own sales agent and manager, board the train to Pittsburgh at seven o'clock in the morning. Reaching his small office by ten o'clock, he "legged it" from factory to factory to get orders for his coke, left town at three, was home by six, at which time he picked up his mail, went over the details of his mining operation, and, after responding to every communication, he finally went to bed.

During this time, Abraham Tinstman had nearly rebankrupted the Overholt distillery and farm operation. Like many other people in the area, he was also so personally overextended that he had to sell several of his properties at greatly reduced prices. Faced with the prospect of losing his home to foreclosure, he began to sell his Frick and Company shares back to Clay. Additionally, because the demand for iron and steel goods had dropped, as had the demand for coke, traffic on his private railroad (figs. 1-13, 14) was slack. As a result, Tinstman further anticipated suspending shipments on his railroad, an action that would have forced the closure of the remaining active coal mines and coke works in the area.

Knowing the closure of the railroad would be a certain death blow for Frick and Company, and motivated by a real desire to rescue his cousin and partner, Clay searched for a solution. One evening, as Frick rode the Pittsburgh and Connellsville Railroad home to Broad Ford, it occurred to him that if a railroad was the problem, a railroad might be the solution. Although the time was not right to ask a railroad company to invest capital, he decided to offer Tinstman's private line to the B&O Railroad. Tinstman's feeder line connected the region's best and most productive coal mines and coke works to the Pittsburgh and Connellsville Railroad and was a line on which the B&O depended for freight. The B&O was the oldest commercial railroad in the country, but it had been thwarted by politics and public opinion to such an extent that not until 1871 had it been able to break the Southwestern Pennsylvania Railroad's monopoly on the lucrative freight market in the Pittsburgh-Connellsville area. In that year, the B&O had finally connected its 150-mile track from Baltimore, the chief railroad center in America, through Cumberland, Maryland, to the Pittsburgh and Connellsville line running through Connellsville, the chief mining center, past the Broad Ford distillery and on into Pittsburgh, the chief manufacturing center.

When Clay got off the train that evening, instead of hitching up his mine mules as usual, he borrowed Billy, his friend Gen. Cyrus Painter Markle's gray, high-stepping pacer and spent the evening riding around the country, visiting Tinstman's stockholders and arguing that they should sell. He was successful. The stockholders only wanted to get the railroad running, not turn a profit, and they feared, like Tinstman, the loss of their homes to foreclosure. With options to sell properly signed and executed, Frick presented his proposal to the B&O executives at the general offices in Connellsville. The B&O, anxious to expand its business in what it called an area "without a peer anywhere in this world for freight tonnage," and knowing the "Vanderbilt Roads" were planning to build a railway in the area as well, decided to buy the strategic ten-mile railroad. When the market for coke recovered, the B&O would own not only the feeder line already supplying much needed freight, but a branch railroad through a valley lined on either side by the purest bituminous coking-coal mines in the country—and the largest concentration of producing coke ovens in the area.

As negotiator and intermediary, Clay requested a $50,000 commission and gave them forty-eight hours to accept his proposition. The B&O agreed to buy the owners out at cost. They paid $200,000 for the railroad and gave Clay his commission. Clay then used the money to pay off debt, reinvest in his operations, and acquire more coking-coal lands at depression prices, as he continued to absorb Tinstman's interests and those of his failing partners.

This commission, combined with the assurance the railroad would stay in operation, placed Clay in a far more secure financial position. But to further strengthen his financial base, because money was in short supply, he decided to pay his employees' wages in Frick dollar bills (fig. 1-15)—nearly exact copies in size, shape, color, and typography of the currency in use during the Civil War. They soon became the common currency of the area. He also built his first company store, the Union Supply Company, at Broad Ford. The men, who usually came to his clapboard shack to receive their pay, were now paid at the company store.

Fig. 1-15. Frick Dollar Bill.
Frick Archives

In the midst of this struggle to keep his business in operation, Frick suffered a deep loss. In December 1874, a few months after the completion of the railroad deal, his eighty-three-year-old grandmother, Maria Overholt—his spiritual mainstay and most ardent supporter—died. She had been ill for a number of years, but she had remained a woman quaint and neat, tender and loving. Saving of everything, when her youngest son died at age twenty of typhoid, she had forever kept his personal effects beneath her bed. A true matriarch, whose greatest tragedy was that only three of her eight children survived her, she nevertheless had forty-eight grandchildren, including Henry Clay Frick, and twenty-five great-grandchildren. She was known as a "monument to Christian learning," she had what was described as a "sweet face, loving heart, and . . . winning voice," and so important was she to Clay that he visited her regularly throughout her illness.

The passing of Maria Overholt in 1874 left the twenty-five-year-old Clay Frick disconsolate. Tinstman noted Clay "wasn't the brooding kind and never showed much of what he felt but he couldn't seem to smile and his eyes were very sad." Depleted by his rigorous schedule of hustling coke, exhausted from raising cash to pay off loans on time, and anxious about his financial situation, he had already become dangerously thin and very pale. By February 1875, just two months after his grandmother's death, Clay became critically ill. He had gone to a dance in Connellsville wearing light shoes, and after boarding a train to Akron, Ohio, he suffered an attack of inflammatory rheumatism so severe that the conductor on the return train had to carry him from the train to his room. The night watchman from the Broad Ford distillery sat with him at night, helping to care for him, while three doctors, two from Connellsville and one

Fig. 1-16. Henry Clay Frick after his 1875 illness.
Frick Archives

from Pittsburgh, treated him. They wrapped him in seven pounds of wool and gave little hope for his recovery. With his loving and supportive grandmother dead, there seemed a great chance that Clay would follow her to the grave.

Clay was soon moved from his shack at Broad Ford and given a sunny third floor room in the Homestead. Abraham Tinstman, upon coming to bathe and feed Clay, noted the gravity of the situation in his diary on February 2, 1875: "They say Clay is in critical condition . . . they don't think he can get well." Many years later, however, Clay's daughter Helen recalled her father saying that when he heard the doctors' grim prognosis, he "made up his mind he would get well and from that day he began to recover."

A full year passed before he returned to health, and for months he had to be washed and dressed daily, like an infant. For a long time he was too depleted to sit up in bed, but by that spring of 1875, though weak and still house-bound, he amused himself by watching people outside his window on the busy distillery street. Slowly he began to stabilize (fig. 1-16), and although he had to walk with crutches for a few months, by summer he began to venture out into the coal lands again. He had purchased Billy, General Markle's gray pacer, after closing the railroad deal, and now the horse provided him a second piece of good fortune. He resumed his survey of the surrounding hills, following the outline of the coal bluffs. He analyzed the length and width of these riders, as he simultaneously calculated the potential value of the coal beneath the land. He watched as the value of the coal lands declined, buying out his overextended partners and rivals who continued to falter under the ongoing financial pressures of the day.

Of all the properties, his cousin Tinstman's lucrative Morgan Mines were the ones Clay most coveted. The profitability of these mines had been the catalyst for his own mining venture, and they had continued both to dominate the area and be Frick and Company's largest competitor. Once, in 1874, Morgan and Tinstman had tried to consolidate their mines with Frick and Company, but as Clay offered $550,000 against their $650,000 asking price, the deal did not go through.

By October 1875, however, Tinstman and Morgan were forced to sell their operation, and Clay stepped in as buyer. Tinstman's poor money management had driven him into bankruptcy and had harmed the Overholt businesses. Although Frick and Abraham Tinstman remained friends throughout their lives, and Tinstman would make a slight comeback in the coke business, certain of Tinstman's relatives remained bitter that Clay, not Abraham, had become the wealthier man. On May 13, 1891, Henry Clay Frick wrote to Mrs. Joseph Rice in Danville, Iowa, saying: "I regret very much you are under the impression that Mr. Tinsman [*sic*] assigned his wealth over to me when he went into bankruptcy. Such was not the case. Mr. Tinsman had no wealth to assign, and I lost as much by his failure as anyone, and I think probably more than anyone." In fact, in an agreement dated October 11, 1875, Frick had taken the unusual step of having the deed to the Morgan Mines executed and delivered "upon the understanding that if . . . Tinstman within two years . . . should pay said notes amt'g in all to $60,000 together with any interest on the $10,000 note, . . . [the] deed of conveyance should become null and void."

Assured a first option on the Morgan Mines, and loaning them $8,000 to stay in operation, Clay improved his position through other investments as well. Although the contemplative time spent riding around the countryside, thinking, recuperating, and planning had won him Tinstman's coveted mines, over the previous four years Clay had also become the sole owner of Frick and Company.

Now, for the first time, Frick felt he had attained enough financial security to leave his agrarian roots behind. He rented rooms in Pittsburgh's fashionable Monongahela House (fig. 1-17), located on the section of the Monongahela riverbank known as the Mon Wharf. Grand and sumptuous, it satisfied Frick's love of finery. The hotel was five stories high with a lobby trimmed in gold. It featured an impressive walnut staircase, richly decorated bedrooms, and riverside balconies overlooking both the Mon Wharf—the heart of Frick's and Pittsburgh's commerce—and the Point where the Monongahela, Allegheny, and Ohio rivers combine.

Additionally, Clay paid off the last of Joseph Myers's $10,000 note, saying to his father's farmer-neighbor-friend, "This is the best investment I ever made." He became the sole trustee of his mother's share of Abraham Overholt's estate, now perhaps enhanced by his grandmother's death, by replacing his uncles, one of whom had not only commingled his mother's inheritance with his personal moneys, but had also gone bankrupt.

On one of the many weekends he spent in Abraham Tinstman's home, however, Frick found time to bring him *The Complete Works of Shakespeare* and, for his wife, a Dolly Varden dress, designed after the one worn by the gaily dressed coquette in Charles Dickens's historical novel *Barnaby Rudge* that is set against the London riots

Fig. 1-17. The Monongahela House was as much the hub of society as the Mon Wharf was the hub of commerce.
Carnegie Library, Pittsburgh

of 1780. The latter was a telling gift, for strikes and riots were beginning to be a part of community life. A coal strike in the anthracite region of Pennsylvania put a premium on Connellsville coke because the anthracite furnaces were unable to obtain suitable coal, and turned to Connellsville coke, spreading its reputation wider.

Ever more confident that coke was the fuel of the future, Clay acquired still more coal lands. So convinced was he of the potential of a stretch of farm land a mile or so from the Overholt Homestead (now referred to as Morewood), he traded, acre for acre, the surface rights of four farms (one of which belonged to his father and lacked coal) for all the coal on the Morewood farm. According to a family diary, when the Frick and Company store at Morewood opened in 1877, certain of the investors and suppliers were present: Howard Childs of the prominent Pittsburgh shoe manufacturing family; Carter C. Beggs, a Pittsburgh oil broker; and Col. James Schoonmaker, who had large coke operations contiguous to Frick's and was both chairman and one-fourth partner of the Morewood Coke Company. Frick and Overholt relatives were in attendance as well. As this diary reveals, "John Frick was a very proud father." Father, son, suppliers, and partners had reason to be proud. Within five years the store profits were eighty to one hundred thousand dollars.

The Morewood dedication ceremony was perhaps the last time Henry Clay Frick could take full pleasure in one of his achievements in the Coke Region. As industrialism spread rapidly through the United States, the tensions it created mounted and then exploded locally and nationally over the next decades. Just a few months after the dedication, thousands of railroad workers struck over a wage cut. Massive rioting in Pittsburgh and throughout the nation suggested a social revolution. Angry mobs looted, burned, and destroyed railroad property. The Pennsylvania state militia was brought in to restore order.

The 1877 railroad strike (fig. 1-18) was felt in the Coke Region by both labor and management. And Henry Clay Frick's response to it suggested that he was changing, along with the country. In the Connellsville area, many local citizens were sworn in as deputies to help keep the peace. Strikers living in company houses or railroad housing were threatened with eviction. As a foretaste of the strikebreaker he would become, Clay warned the strikers occupying shacks on Tinstman's old railroad to vacate. When one striker, James King, refused to leave, Clay went to King's house with a deputy and asked King, "Were you not told to get out?" When King replied yes, Clay demanded, "Then why do you not go?" King, knowing that the B&O now owned the railway, replied, "This is not your property." Clay and the deputy decided to follow the common practice with strikers and evict King, so, while Clay went to mail some

Fig. 1-18. Rioting at the rail depot during the 1877 Pennsylvania railroad strike.
Antique Prints

Fig. 1-19. The Henry Clay coke works stood in the shadow of an Overholt distillery warehouse at Broad Ford.
Frick Archives.

letters, the deputy carried King's bed outside. He put it on the coke pile and then added King's personal effects, right down to his razor. When Clay, who only weighed 130 pounds and had recently knocked an insolent villager off his feet, returned and found King still refusing to leave, he and the deputy picked the man up and threw him into the creek.

In 1877, Clay won another victory. Abraham Tinstman had not been able to buy back his interest in the Morgan Mines, and so the mines officially became Henry Clay Frick's property. But in victory, Clay decided that rather than take on more debt, he would sell shares in Frick and Company and form a partnership with two friends, the brothers of a prominent New York banking family, Edmund M. and Walton Ferguson. In 1871, Edmund had moved from Connecticut to Fayette County where he manufactured coke. Although in the fall of 1874 Edmund had moved to the fashionable Shadyside district in Pittsburgh, he maintained his own coke interests and in 1878 became Clay's partner. The following year his brother, Walton, moved from New York to Shadyside and became Clay's partner as well.

But as Clay entered this pivotal moment of his company's development and his financial career, he was again struck by inflammatory rheumatism. This time, however, he stayed at Edmund M. Ferguson's house in Pittsburgh while recovering, and in March 1878 the partnership, called H. C. Frick and Company, was consummated. As before, he spent a year recuperating, but in 1879, when his health was almost fully restored, the economy finally recovered. Although 50,000 commercial enterprises, including a majority of the railroads, had gone bankrupt, Clay's business exploded proportionately when the demand for coke skyrocketed. He had expanded his 1870 original coal acreage from a nucleus of 125 acres to a block of almost 3,000 contiguous acres. His first fifty ovens at the juncture of his cousin Abraham Tinstman's private railroad and the Pittsburgh and Connellsville Railroad—the railroad Clay sold to the B&O when Tinstman was going bankrupt—translated into well over one thousand working ovens with an 8,750-ton daily capacity. The ovens now stretched nearly the full length of his cousin's former railroad and lined both sides of the small Broad Ford Run Valley, the valley a few miles south of West Overton where, fittingly, his grandfather's distillery was also located (fig. 1-19).

The H. C. Frick Coke Company now employed a thousand people and shipped a hundred cars of coke a day. The company was responsible for eight out of every ten

Fig. 1-20. *Harper's Weekly,* Jan. 30, 1886, "Among the Coke Furnaces of Pennsylvania."
Charles Graham wood engraving
Historical Society of Western Pennsylvania

tons of Connellsville's coking coal, the highest grade coking coal mined in America. As Clay watched his ovens belch fire, flame, and smoke twenty-four hours a day, the price of coke climbed from the 1873 depressed price of $0.90 a ton to $2, $3, $4, and $5 a ton. And he had the satisfaction of knowing that the product once known as Connellsville Coke was now called Frick Coke. Clay was selling $30,000 worth of coke a day and pocketing a $20,000-a-day profit. No wonder that the previously unknown Mennonite farm boy from Westmoreland County was now hailed as "The Coke King."

An accident of birth, grit, attention to detail, and prudent business skills had enabled Frick to triumph during the depression where others had failed. In ten years, as he acquired the most valuable coal properties yet known, not one loan had been defaulted. And more important, Henry Clay Frick had satisfied his childhood longing—the making of a million dollars.

But his success brought darkness to the hills and fields of Fayette and Westmoreland counties (fig. 1-20). In 1879, when the depression ended and the agrarian culture was fading, trees were already dying from the smoke of coke furnaces that settled as clouds over the valley. The first large sink holes were appearing in local pastures as mine tunnels collapsed. And day and night those working the ovens and mining the coal either died in accidents or hacked and coughed from breathing the polluted air above and below ground. The fresh streams and rivers were becoming polluted, and soon typhoid would become a leading cause of death.

ON DECEMBER 19, 1879, Frick quietly celebrated his thirtieth birthday and his hard-earned million dollar fortune. At the end of the day, he walked to the store near his room in George Washabaugh's house near Broad Ford, bought a Havana cigar on credit, strolled placidly back to the Washabaughs' house, and went to bed.

But more than the making of Henry Clay Frick's first million had occurred. The man had hardened. At age twenty-one, when he first ventured into the coke business, a photograph (see fig. 1-9) reveals that his blue eyes were soft, skin luminous, and mouth gentle. With his curly hair, doelike eyes, and sensitive lips, he resembled the young Shelley. Although the aesthetic sense suggested by these youthful features remained a part of Clay Frick, his appearance, as well as his demeanor, changed dramatically by the end of his second decade.

Now, as a thirty-year-old millionaire, the combination of his ten-year battle to survive the 1873 panic, his physical exhaustion from hard work, and the debilitating effects of inflammatory rheumatism, as well as his grief over the death of his grandmother, had caused Clay's warm eyes to become cold. A photograph taken at age thirty (see fig. 1-40) shows that his mouth was set, his jaw clenched, and his neck muscles tight. Gone was the lush crop of curls. The frail child whose health was nurtured by mother and grandmother, the delicate boy whose disciplined mind had been shaped by both the weakness of his body and the harsh work ethic of his grandfather and Mennonite faith, the determined teenager who once clerked in linens, lace, mourning clothes, and black dress goods, the young man who was afraid of being called a sissy, but always dressed immaculately, would in three years become the largest supplier of coke in what would then be the nation's greatest coke-producing center.

Seemingly hardened and impervious to pain, a ruthless Henry Clay Frick was born. Fifteen years passed before the slightest echo of his childhood in the once virgin countryside, the grandparents who mentored him, or the midnight ride through the coke country would surface. In 1895, a delayed reaction to the 1891 death of his daughter Martha, combined with the extraordinary experience of her sudden, after-death visitation unlocked these memories. Images long stored in his psyche flashed in his mind's eye and became the shaping factor of his art collection.

His acquisition in 1895 of Jules Breton's *The Last Gleanings* (fig. 1-21) and others by Jean-François Millet, whose paintings evoke the noble yet punishing quality of farming life, mirrored the harsh aspects of Frick's farming-family childhood, softened by his mother's care. In the former painting, the sun sets as a jubilant, barefoot boy runs toward an old woman, his mother, and a teenage girl who carry large bundles of gleanings. He is waving a prize—a sheaf of wheat with grain intact. When added to the growing pile on the women's shoulders, the stalk promised flour for the winter and fresh bedding for the year.

Of the Millets, *La Fermière* (fig. 1-22), recalled nearly exactly the landscape of Clay's parents' small farm and evoked a daily scene—his tiny mother on her way to milk cows in the harsh winter weather. *The Knitting Lesson* (fig. 1-23) described the everyday chore of mending and making clothes. *La Sortie* (fig. 1-24) and *Woman Sewing by Lamplight* (fig. 1-25), acquired just after Frick's mother's death, rekindled his experience of the warmth and security of mothering. *The Sower* (fig. 1-26) acquired in 1899—ten years after his father's death and on Frick's fiftieth birthday—recalled Frick's dirt-farming father, while *End of Day* (fig. 1-27) sanctified the exhaustive, yet sacred nature of the agrarian work ethic.

Neither did Frick forget his grandparents when forming his collection. In 1906, the same year he acquired *Woman Sewing by Lamplight*, he acquired *Self-Portrait* (fig. 1-28) by Rembrandt—a painting of this Mennonite-sympathizing artist who was raised in a farming and brewing family and had created this portrait in his own bankrupt years.

Fig. 1-21. Jules-Adolphe Breton (1827–1906), *The Last Gleanings*, 1895.
Acquired in 1895, Oil on canvas, 36½ x 55 in. (92.7 x 139.7 cm).
The Henry E. Huntington Library, Art Galleries, and Botanical Gardens,
San Marino, California

Fig. 1-22. Jean-François Millet (1814–1875), *La Fermière*, c. 1868–70.
Acquired in 1897, Pastel on blue gray wove paper, 15½ x 20¾ in. (39.4 x 52.7 cm).
Frick Art and Historical Center

Fig. 1-23. Jean-François Millet (1814–1875), *The Knitting Lesson,*
c. 1858–60.
Acquired in 1898, Black chalk on dark cream laid paper,
14 x 11 in. (35.6 x 27.9 cm).
Frick Art and Historical Center

Fig. 1-24. Jean-François Millet (1814-1875), *La Sortie.*
Acquired in 1908, Black and white chalk on cream laid paper,
15¼ x 12⅜ in. (38.7 x 31.3 cm).
Frick Art and Historical Center

Fig. 1-25. Jean-François Millet (1814–1875), *Woman Sewing by Lamplight*, 1870–72.
Acquired in 1906, Oil on canvas, 39⅝ x 32¼ in. (100.7 x 81.9 cm).
The Frick Collection

Fig. 1-26. Jean-François Millet (1814–1875), *The Sower*.
Acquired in 1899, Pastel on tan wove paper, 12⅛ x 9⅝ in. (30.8 x 24.5 cm).
Frick Art and Historical Center

Fig. 1-27. Jean-François Millet (1814–1875), *End of Day*.
Acquired in 1904, Pastel on cream laid paper, 9¼ x 12⅞ in. (23.3 x 32.7 cm).
Frick Art and Historical Center

Fig. 1-28. Rembrandt Harmensz. van Rijn (1606–1669), *Self-Portrait*, 1658.
Acquired in 1906, Oil on canvas, 52⅝ x 40⅞ in. (133.7 x 103.8 cm).
The Frick Collection

According to his only surviving daughter, Helen Clay Frick, late in Frick's life he said "that if he could be given the choice of different kinds of ability, he would prefer being a painter like Rembrandt than anything else." Although this comment can be understood as Henry Clay Frick's basic appreciation of the artist, perhaps he was also reacting to Rembrandt's ability—in depicting his own deep-set eyes, ponderous brow, and protruding lower lip—to kindle Frick's memory of the paradox of his own land-rich but cash-poor forebear, Abraham Overholt (see fig. 1-8).

Old Woman with a Book (fig. 1-29), then considered Rembrandt's portrait of his mother, when juxtaposed to a photograph of Frick's Mennonite grandmother, Maria Stauffer Overholt (fig. 1-30), seems to visually recall this determined little woman. Apart from the fact that the photograph was taken in 1855, when six-year-old Frick was critically ill with inflammatory rheumatism and his grandmother daily read him the Bible, on close inspection, the photograph shows her holding reading glasses similar to those held by the old woman in the painting. More important, the photograph shows Frick's grandmother resting these glasses in a position remarkably similar to the unusual way the subject in *Old Woman with a Book* holds hers.

The portrait cost Frick $200,000 and he seemed to attach much emotion to the painting. He bought it almost fifty years after his grandmother's death, when his wife became a grandmother. Later, however, he was advised that the painting was by Carel van der Pluym, not Rembrandt, and Frick—who rarely lost his temper, but when he did, like his grandfather, "all felt it"—took the reattribution as a personal insult and exploded. Now considered a "problem painting" by the Frick Collection, in an odd coincidence, it hangs on the wall in the Trustees Room—the wall against which the headboard of Henry Clay Frick's deathbed rested in 1919.

Echoes of the once virgin West Overton countryside also resounded in the collection. As we have seen, Constant Troyon's *A Pasture in Normandy* bears a remarkable similarity to the hills and fields of Frick's childhood, the pasture land that held his fortune. Similarly, Aelbert Cuyp's *Cows and Herdsman by a River* evokes the broad, smooth-flowing Youghiogheny River that runs alongside the Broad Ford distillery and the sawmill where Clay got the laugh on his elders. Together the paintings recall the environment that supported Abraham Overholt's farming and rye whiskey business, the fields that after Abraham's estate had been dispersed had left a $395,000 fortune. And together the paintings bespeak the calm preceding the human, social, and environmental chaos born of Henry Clay Frick's million-dollar dream.

Many of the landscape paintings Frick eventually acquired may also have reminded him of specific places he knew. Jacobus Hendrikus Maris's painting of *The Bridge* (fig. 1-31), depicting a small canal bridge with roads on both banks, bears striking resemblance to a bridge Clay often crossed—the Brownsville Bridge across Dunlap's

Above: Fig. 1-29. Carel van der Pluym (1625–1672), *Old Woman with a Book.*
Acquired in 1916, Oil on canvas, 38⅝ x 30¾ in. (98.1 x 78.1 cm).
The Frick Collection

Right: Fig. 1-30. Maria Stauffer Overholt.
West Overton Museums Archives

Above: Fig. 1-31. Jacobus Hendrikus Maris (1837–1899),
The Bridge, 1885.
Acquired in 1914, Oil on canvas,
44⅜ x 54⅜ in. (112.7 x 138.1 cm).
The Frick Collection

Left: Fig. 1-32. The Brownsville Bridge.
National Museum of American History,
Smithsonian Institution

Fig. 1-33. Fritz Thaulow (1847–1906), *Village Night Scene*, 1895.
Acquired in 1895, Oil on canvas, 25¼ x 36 in. (64.1 x 91.4 cm).
Frick Art and Historical Center

Fig. 1-34. Jean-Charles Cazin (1841–1901), *Sunday Evening in a Miner's Village*, c. 1892.
Acquired in 1895, Oil on canvas, 32 x 46 in. (64.77 x 81.28 cm).
Frick Art and Historical Center

Above: Fig. 1-35. Pierre-Etienne-Théodore Rousseau
(1812–1867), *The Village of Becquigny,* c. 1857.
Acquired in 1902, Oil on mahogany panel,
25 x 39⅜ in. (63.5 x 100 cm).
The Frick Collection

Right: Fig. 1-36. Map of West Overton, 1864.
West Overton Museums Archives

Fig. 1-37. Meyndert Hobbema (1638–1709), *Village with Water Mill Among Trees.*
Acquired in 1911, Oil on oak panel, 30 x 43½ in. (94.3 x 129.8 cm).
The Frick Collection

Fig. 1-38. Rembrandt Harmensz. van Rijn (1606-1669), *The Polish Rider*, c. 1655.
Acquired in 1910, Oil on canvas, 46 x 53⅛ in. (116.8 x 134.9 cm).
The Frick Collection

Creek on U.S. 40 (fig. 1-32). The first cast-iron bridge in America, the once wooden structure is like a canal bridge in that the road makes a right-angle turn onto the bridge. It was once crossed by the statesman Henry Clay, when he was on his way to the nation's capital. His stagecoach was upset while making the sharp turn onto the rain-soaked bridge, and Clay fell into a mud hole, causing him to remark, "This was probably the first time Clay from Kentucky was used to fill a mud hole in Pennsylvania."

Although evening village scenes of the Mennonite West Overton community would perhaps also be evoked by Fritz Thaulow's *Village Night Scene* (fig. 1-33) and Jean-Charles Cazin's *Sunday Evening in a Miner's Village* (fig. 1-34), neither are as compelling as Pierre-Etienne-Théodore Rousseau's *Village of Becquigny* (fig. 1-35). The latter bears similarity to an 1864 view of West Overton's single, long, straight, tree-lined avenue, dotted with family houses, as seen from the springhouse where Frick was born (fig. 1-36). A poignant acquisition, the Rousseau paid tribute to the West Overton family village that had been Frick's home for thirty years, a place central to the vast seam of coking coal that had made his fortune. Another village scene, at the Jacob's Creek Crossing, could have been later remembered by Frick in the Dutch Mennonite Meyndert Hobbema's *Village Among Trees* (1902) and the same artist's *Village with Water Mill Among Trees* (fig. 1-37).

Most significant, however, is Rembrandt's *The Polish Rider* (fig. 1-38)—a painting that may have reminded Frick of the pivotal moment of his career, his inspired night-ride around the countryside on the gray horse Billy when securing permission to sell Tinstman's private railroad to the B&O. The painting, acquired in 1910 on the thirtieth anniversary of Frick's making his first million, interested Frick because, as he said, it was "unique as being one of the few equestrian portraits ever done by the artist." In another respect, however, close examination of the countryside of Frick's fortune also gives weight to the thought that the painting evoked his important midnight ride. The Polish Rider carries a war hammer strongly resembling a miner's pick, and the cliff in the background recalls the bluff outcroppings characteristic of the landscape Frick canvassed that night on Billy. Additionally, apart from the fact that Coal Hill (Mt. Washington) was a familiar landmark to Clay when he was in Pittsburgh selling his coke (fig. 1-39), he had seen it daily when, as a teenage boy, he worked in Pittsburgh as a clerk. Moreover, Coal Hill was the first place to use the Connellsville coke and give it its early reputation.

Just as the Polish Rider is considered a Christian Knight, so also was Clay. In 1872, he had the Degree of Master Mason conferred on him, and he later became secretary and treasurer of King Solomon's Lodge No. 346 of Free and Accepted Masons in Connellsville. In 1874 he had drawn his Mark—three beehive ovens—in the "Mark" book of the Urania Chapter No. 192 at Greensburg, and on May 3, 1880, just before he left on a

Fig. 1-39. Coal Hill (Mt. Washington) businesses were the first to use Connellsville coke. Frick saw the large cliff as a teenager when crossing the bridge from Allegheny City to his workplace in Pittsburgh.
Historical Society of Western Pennsylvania

tour of Europe, Clay had had the three highest Orders of the Masonic York Rite—the Orders of the Knights of the Rose Croix, the Knights of Malta, and Knights Templar—as well as the highest Orders of the Scottish Rite, conferred on him. Thus, the young Clay Frick had become a Christian Knight, something that may also have drawn him to Rembrandt's portrait of *The Polish Rider*.

S IR OSBERT SITWELL SAYS of the Polish Rider's horse: it "attains spiritually to the grandeur and terror of one of the horses in the Apocalypse." And of the Polish Rider he says that he proceeds on a "solitary journey from birth to death."

In 1870, Henry Clay Frick was imbued with such energy, and had embarked on just such a solitary journey. By 1880, he had become cold, ruthless, and inured to sentiment and pain. Only power, control, and money seemed his gods. With aestheticism and compassion largely divorced from consciousness, the thirty-year-old millionaire, Henry Clay Frick, would soon know the full meaning of "grandeur" and "terror."

Fig. 1-40. Henry Clay Frick at age thirty.
West Overton Museums Archives

CHAPTER II

Honeymoons and Horrors

*Rosie has taken cold which has settled in her hip so that she can scarcely bear
to put her right foot down. The doctor does not think it will prove very serious,
but has not made up his mind fully.*

—Henry Clay Frick, 1894

ALTHOUGH HENRY CLAY FRICK REFERRED to the ten years spent making his first
million in the coke industry as "an awful time," these years of accumulation had
been worth the hard work and suffering. Apart from successfully building his coke
business, Frick had established himself as a person of economic prominence. And
now he began to enjoy his wealth, aligning, preparing, and acquiring for himself all the
things that would identify him as a person of social standing as well.

In November 1878, Frick, together with Benjamin Ruff, a tunnel contractor and
coke dealer who often stayed at the Monongahela House, acquired from the Pennsylvania Railroad an abandoned canal reservoir in the Allegheny Mountains located
forty miles northeast of Pittsburgh. The small body of water was in an enclave about
two miles from the Pennsylvania Railroad's South Fork station, on the main line from
Pittsburgh to Cresson Springs and Altoona. This enclave was situated between the
steel town of Johnstown to the south and the fashionable Queen Anne style gothic
Mountain House resort built by the Pennsylvania Railroad at Cresson Springs to the
north. Frick and Ruff were developing an exclusive, lakeside club to accommodate the
increasingly popular sports of boating and fishing—a private club that could offer an
alternative to the five-story, land-locked, public resort at Cresson. They solicited fourteen other investors and Frick, as the largest stockholder, became a member of the

Fig. 2-1. Henry Clay Frick (standing, far left) leaves for his first trip abroad with
Andrew W. Mellon (seated), A. A. Hutchinson, and Frank Cowen, 1880.
Carnegie Library, Pittsburgh

executive committee of what was soon to be known as the South Fork Fishing and
Hunting Club.

Although Frick had rented rooms in the Monongahela House in 1875, and kept a
room in the Washabaughs' house near Broad Ford, returning often to survey his coke
works and bring fresh oranges to his friends' children, he now decided to live in the
famous hotel permanently. On taking up residence, his collection of prints, lithographs, and oil paintings—only some of which remain in his collection today—was so
vast, two men took two days to hang them. With sumptuous hotel furnishings and a
view of the Mon Wharf, where he had peddled his coke those long ten years and conducted business with men in the wrought iron and shoe business, men who were also
art collectors, Frick could only have experienced a great sense of satisfaction.

But Henry Clay Frick was never content for long. In May 1880, on yet another quest,
he reentered the Mellon Bank to pay a visit that was different than those of the past.
He had come to invite Andrew Mellon, who at age twenty-five had just assumed the
presidency of the Mellon Bank, to spend the weekend with him in the West Overton
area. Mellon accepted and upon arrival, he was disappointed to find his host sitting at
a table stacked with books. Afraid he was in for a long weekend, Mellon, whose own

eyes were tired from hours of reading to his father, Judge Mellon, nevertheless greeted Frick and joined him at the table. To his surprise, Frick then invited him on a trip to Europe that Frick had planned with two other men (fig. 2-1). One, Frank Cowan, was a congenial young man who wrote poetry, sang beautifully, and told delightful stories—something that appealed to Mellon because he, like Frick, was quiet, introverted, and not much of a conversationalist. The other companion was an older man, A. A. Hutchinson, who had the reputation of being very dull—which did not appeal to Mellon. He nevertheless accepted the invitation because something Frick had said gave him a vague indication that there was a "special reason" for including Hutchinson.

On June 21, 1880, Frick and Andrew Mellon arrived in New York to begin their trip. As they traveled up Fifth Avenue, the Coke King, excited by the prospect of his first trip abroad, found his eyes appraising the building at 640 Fifth Avenue, the home of the "Railroad King," William Henry Vanderbilt, head of the House of Vanderbilt, art collector, and the richest man in America. His mansion, actually twin houses connected by a single-story vestibule, took up the entire block between Fifty-first and Fifty-second Streets. The most opulent home of its day, it had been built in eighteen months with seven hundred men working night and day. Separated from the busy street by a wide strip of grass and a sandstone wall, the house on the north end of the block was built for William Henry's two married daughters, the southern one for William Henry and his wife, Maria Kissam Vanderbilt. A colossus, the mansion had an extensive art gallery—something that appealed to Frick, who continued to collect art.

As blossoming social ambition combined with his incisive mind, Frick said meditatively to Andrew Mellon: "I suppose those are really the best residences in the city."

A man of few words, Mr. Mellon replied, "I think they are probably so."

Frick, pointing to William Henry's house on the southern corner, questioned Mellon, "I wonder how much the upkeep of the one on that corner would be, say $300,000 a year? I should think that would cover it."

"It might," Mellon replied, as their carriage wound its way through nearby Central Park.

Then, as Mellon smoked a stogie and Frick smoked his customary five-cent cigar, Frick calculated out loud, "that would be 6 per cent on five millions or 5 per cent on six, say a thousand a day."

Turning to Mellon, in his simple, direct way of speaking, Frick said of the house and the required millions, "That is all I shall ever want."

So Frick and his companions sailed to Queenstown, Ireland, and upon their arrival in a Cork market, an old Irish woman caught the spirit of the men before her. As Frick and Mellon paid her for strawberries and cabbage, she remarked, "Your ancestors went away walking sticks of poverty and you've come back monuments of pride."

Their tour took them to Dublin, Blarney—where they kissed the stone while holding the American flag high above their heads, and then to Belfast, the Scottish Highlands, the Lake District, and London. Upon apparently visiting Sir Richard Wallace's five-generation family art collection, Frick claimed that one day, if he were successful, he would like to develop such a collection and give it to his countrymen.

While in London, they also visited "the fair Emma," a lady of the night. And then they were off to Paris where they toured the Louvre, took French lessons, and saw the sights. Next came Belgium, where they visited the World's Fair, and Holland, where they saw King Leopold. They returned to Paris before going on to Venice, and then came back to Paris.

Not until the end of the trip, however, did Frick's "special reason" for inviting the older, dull man finally surface. Frick had planned to give Hutchinson a very good time, guessing that he would want to stay in Europe and sell his coke holdings. When the gentleman announced that he planned to extend his trip around the world, Frick, who had long coveted his coal lands in Connellsville, offered to buy them. As Frick's biographer, George Harvey, notes, Frick "graciously facilitate[d] the execution of [Hutchinson's] bold project," and by 1883 Frick owned Hutchinson's coke interests.

In October, after visiting his mother and siblings, all of whom except Anna had moved to Wooster, Ohio, where John Frick's successful brother Jacob lived, Henry Clay Frick returned to his room at the Monongahela House. He purchased a Tiffany clock and candelabra as well as a painting of Paint Creek in the Allegheny Mountains near Johnstown and the South Fork Fishing and Hunting Club: *Landscape with a River* (fig. 2-2) by Pittsburgh's then most famous artist, George Hetzel, who worked *en plein air* like the Barbizons and founded the artist colony Scalp Level on the outskirts of Pittsburgh.

Still under the spell of William Vanderbilt's house and the European trip, Frick also bought the first four volumes of Edward Strahan's autographed ten-volume edition of *Art Treasures of America,* describing many of the Vanderbilt paintings. Additionally, he acquired two revealing engravings of works by George Henry Boughton that were reproduced by M. Knoedler in New York—Evangeline, the heroine of Henry Wadsworth Longfellow's poem who searches for her bridegroom only to find him dying in Philadelphia, and Priscilla, the heroine who commands her beloved: "Ask me yourself" if you want to marry me.

Although these engravings no longer remain in Frick's collection, they and one other painting—a humorous, but salacious work by Luis Jiménez y Aranda entitled *A Revelation in the Louvre* (fig. 2-3) depicting an elder chaperone pulling a young woman away from a sculpture of a nude male torso—reveal Frick's frame of mind. More a reflection of his burgeoning sexuality than his aestheticism, *In the Louvre* confirmed

Fig. 2-2. George Hetzel (1826-1899), *Landscape with a River,* 1880.
Acquired in 1881, Oil on canvas, 44½ x 29½ in. (113 x 74.9 cm).
Frick Art and Historical Center

Fig. 2-3. Luis Jiménez y Aranda (1845–1903), *A Revelation in the Louvre*, 1881.
Acquired in 1881, Oil on canvas, 22¾ x 16¾ in. (57.5 x 41.3 cm).
Frick Art and Historical Center

the direction his collector's eye had taken. In June 1881 Frick attended a Pittsburgh reception with Andrew Mellon, dressed as was Mellon in his finest clothes. Standing apart from the guests, the two men surveyed the crowd. Mellon noticed that Mr. Frick's "penetrating eyes" were fixed on a tall, slender woman with mahogany brown hair, deep blue eyes, a soft smile, and quiet demeanor.

After a few moments, Frick whispered to Mellon, "There is the handsomest girl in the room. Do you know who she is?"

Mellon, who had once courted the girl, explained that she was Miss Adelaide Howard Childs.

"Daughter of Asa P.?" Frick queried, wondering if the young lady was the daughter of the recently deceased co-owner of Pittsburgh's reputable shoemaking family, and the sister of Howard Childs, who since 1877 had been supplying the company store at Morewood with shoes.

"Yes, the youngest," replied Mellon.

"I want you to introduce me," was Frick's response.

As a young man, Frick's experience with women had been little and inconclusive. According to a childhood friend, Mrs. Adam Whitehead, he was "a hard worker [and] did not 'run around' much, except where business took him." Often he was seen coming out of the Broad Ford office late on Sunday evenings, and although young girls called, and his Broad Ford landlady organized parties, Clay would "go in but not stay, excusing himself on account of business duties." He fancied his cousin, Ella Sherrick, but was so shy that rather than visit her at home, he had his cousin James Overholt deliver his notes. Occasionally, however, the two met outside and took walks. When Ella married in January 1875, just after Maria Overholt's death, Clay gave the newlyweds a silver tureen with ladle and tray. As a groomsman, he also held a party for them in Pittsburgh's Pennsylvania Station before they left for the West.

In 1879, when Frick had his character read by the famous phrenologist O. W. Fowler, who analyzed the shape and size of his cranial bones, Frick gained valuable insight about his reticence with young women. Fowler disclosed that Frick was more "adapted in marriage to a woman much more negative than positive, who does not find any fault; [and] one who never talks back." He advised Frick to take a bride who was "clinging, doting, dependent."

By 1880, Frick seemed to have overcome his apparent shyness, but to no avail. On his European trip, he had fallen in love with the daughter of an American banker in Paris; in fact, he may well have proposed to her, for when he returned home, as George Harvey notes, "[the] understanding . . . proved . . . to have been only tentative and was soon tacitly ignored by mutual assent." Because Frick was now thirty, however, "the inclination persisted [as] the question of future domesticity called for grave attention."

In response to Frick's request for an introduction, Mellon, intent on following the etiquette of the day, searched for an older guest to perform this function. He took such a long time that Frick became impatient, abandoned social etiquette, and approached Adelaide himself. The two fell into conversation, and permission was soon granted for Frick to call the following Sunday. After three months of courtship chaperoned by Andrew Mellon and Adelaide's older sister, Martha Howard Childs, the two became engaged. Frick gave Adelaide enamel opera glasses, a diamond pin with a pearl at each end and a Limoges head in the center, and a pair of gold bracelets made for a Paris exposition.

Later he acquired the then-contemporary American artist Charles Courtney Curran's painting *Woman with a Horse* (fig. 2-4), a painting reminiscent of Adelaide— the

Above: Fig. 2-4. Charles Courtney Curran
(1861–1942), *Woman with a Horse,* 1890.
Acquired in 1890, Oil on canvas,
11½ x 8½ in. (29.2 x 21.6 cm).
Frick Art and Historical Center

Right: Fig. 2-5. Adelaide Howard Frick
driving a carriage, c. 1898.
Frick Archives

Fig. 2-6. Adelaide Howard Childs Frick
in her wedding gown.
Frick Archives

paternal great-granddaughter of a fine New England banking family, and the maternal granddaughter of a highly respected Presbyterian minister. She was, as a later photograph of her driving a carriage shows (fig. 2-5), also an accomplished horsewoman. She often rode her fiancé's horse, Modock, through the deep woods in back of the Pittsburgh suburb of Oakland.

In October, Adelaide went with Frick on a shopping spree to Philadelphia as lavish wedding gifts began to arrive for the newly betrothed couple. Among these, Frick's well-born fiancée received a fine silver tea service from her future in-laws (and paid for by her husband) and diamond earrings from her intended. The wedding, which took place on December 15, 1881, was described as "one of the most notable weddings of the season" (fig. 2-6).

Their six-week honeymoon began in New York, where the new couple visited the Stock Exchange, crossed the Brooklyn Bridge, attended the Metropolitan Opera, toured the Metropolitan Museum of Art, and admired William H. Vanderbilt's twin mansions at 640 Fifth Avenue (fig. 2-7). The groom showered the bride with more beautiful jewelry, and on Christmas day, he took her to lunch at the Windsor Hotel

Fig. 2-7. Henry Clay Frick and Adelaide
on their wedding trip in 1882.
Frick Archives

with fifty-year-old Andrew Carnegie (who had moved from Pittsburgh to New York in 1865) and his mother, neither of whom the Fricks had ever met.

Carnegie, who was fifteen years older than Frick, had emigrated with his parents from Scotland to Pittsburgh in 1848. Then an impoverished thirteen-year-old whose Scottish grandfather Thomas Morrison, uncle, and father were radical labor leaders who advocated abolition of the monarchy and all inherited privilege, Carnegie had seen his father lose his hand-weaving business with the introduction of steam looms. Ashamed of his father's poverty, Carnegie had grown up in a poor district of Pittsburgh where he stoked furnaces in a textile mill. He became a telegraph messenger boy, advanced through the ranks of the Pennsylvania Railroad, invested in the Woodruff Sleeping Car Company—later known as the Pullman Company—and in 1864 entered the iron business.

By 1881, Carnegie was a wealthy man on the verge of becoming America's most famous industrialist. Having been initially preoccupied with resolving his father's shame and his own poverty, Carnegie had long since removed from consciousness his early heritage—his grandfather's, father's, and uncle's advocacy of rights for labor. Interested only in advancing his business concerns, Carnegie, who in 1872 had introduced

America to the Bessemer process of oxygenating molten iron to make steel, had built the Edgar Thomson steel mill in Braddock, near Pittsburgh, in 1873. He now wanted to expand his steel interests. Although he had coke interests of his own, he also wanted to secure a guaranteed supply of high-grade Connellsville coke for his mill and furnaces. Carnegie had researched many options, but one 1881 October day, when visiting his Allegheny cottage at Cresson Springs, he decided that rather than further develop his own coke resources, he would approach Frick with a partnership deal—a deal to which Frick responded, "Will let you know the best we can do," on his wedding day.

Carnegie feared Frick's coke monopoly, had never met Frick, but had used Frick coke for his Lucy Furnaces and his Edgar Thomson rail mill. When the Fricks came to their honeymoon luncheon with Carnegie and his mother, unknown to anyone but Carnegie and Frick, one-half of Frick's coke works were already placed in the partnership. When five foot two Carnegie rose to his feet to toast the Fricks, he surprised both Adelaide and his own mother by telling them that he and Mr. Frick (who was also five foot two) had entered into partnership. Although the partnership did not become final until April 1882, H. C. Frick and Company—renamed the H. C. Frick Coke Company—would be the exclusive supplier of coke for Carnegie's steel mills. Frick would receive shares in Carnegie Brothers and Company (a consolidation of Edgar Thomson and the Lucy Furnaces), and in exchange, by 1883 Carnegie would become the majority shareholder of the H. C. Frick Coke Company—something that appealed to Frick because he would be able to settle the last of his debts from both his earlier coking enterprise and his investment in the South Fork Fishing and Hunting Club.

Andrew Carnegie beamed, "It will be a great thing for Mr. Frick," whereupon Carnegie's domineering mother replied in her heavy Scottish accent, "Surely, Andrew, that will be a fine thing for Mr. Frick, but what will be the gain to oos [us]?"

Over the next eighteen years, the deal would do much for both Carnegie and Frick, but at that time, the partnership announcement heightened the already soaring spirits of the honeymooners. Flowers arrived for Adelaide from Carnegie, and Frick urged Adelaide to write him a thank-you note. Adelaide did as she was asked, but Frick never mailed the letter. The flowers had actually been ordered by him.

High with happiness, the two climbed Bunker Hill in Boston; visited Independence Hall in Philadelphia; toured the Smithsonian Institute, the House of Representatives, and the Senate in Washington, D.C.; and also attended the trial of Charles J. Guiteau, President James A. Garfield's assassin. Adelaide poked Guiteau with her husband's cane as he passed and later, when the couple called on President Chester A. Arthur in the White House, she was given flowers from the White House greenhouses.

Back at the Monongahela House by February 1882, Frick and Adelaide began looking for a house in which to raise a family. But as they searched, Frick was again stricken with inflammatory rheumatism—as was often true during major transitions in his life. Fever, pain in the joints, muscular atrophy, diarrhea, and other gastrointestinal disorders all returned to plague Frick, who once again became bedridden. This time, he was nursed through the ordeal by his bride. Adelaide tried to alleviate his physical suffering by making fleece-lined gloves to keep his hands warm. Though she was very attentive, when Adelaide left with her mother to attend social engagements, Frick would tease his bride about "leaving him alone."

By spring he was better, and, acting on a tip from Andrew Carnegie's brother Thomas, Frick bought a small, two-story Italianate house in the fashionable East End of Pittsburgh, where the business elite lived (fig. 2-8). Naming the house Clayton, after himself, he hired the important Pittsburgh architect Andrew Peebles to make renovations. Although Frick kept title of the land, he gave the house to Adelaide, two months pregnant at the time, as a belated wedding present.

By all accounts, this was a good time for Frick and his twenty-six-year-old bride. They reveled in wealth's pleasures—beautiful clothes for her, splendid carriages and horses for them both, as well as art objects to adorn their new home. Together the happy couple studied Edward Strahan's *Art Treasures of America* and read books on interior decorating and the art of creating a home that was a combined personal and social statement, as well as an environment for children. They traveled to New York and bought furniture from D. S. Hess and china from Davis and Collomore. Visits to art galleries resulted in their collection of paintings becoming enriched by the addition of an engraved portrait of Longfellow and several works by local artists. Two months before their move on January 29, 1883, Frick acquired another painting by George Hetzel, this one entitled *Fruit,* and then, two days before the move, he bought a second painting of fruit, this one by his friend A. Bryan Wall. This artist was a member of Hetzel's Scalp Level School, and his father, Alfred S. Wall, had lived in Mt. Pleasant when Frick was a boy growing up in nearby West Overton.

On January 20, 1883, however, just nine days before he and Adelaide moved into a now eleven-room, fully renovated Clayton, Frick's anxiety surfaced over having his home correctly reflect his new status. He complained to D. S. Hess and Company, "I would like your Mr. Hess to make a run out. I am very much disappointed in some of the furniture and mantels. [It is] really embarrassing to me to show [them] to my friends and say that [they were] purchased in New York."

Mr. Hess soon came out to hang draperies and place the furniture, and on January 29, 1883, with new telephones installed and Adelaide seven months pregnant, Henry Clay Frick took two days off from work to help unpack boxes. In anticipation of his first-born child, Frick gave his wife a baby's high chair marked "Childs," and then, at 2:00 A.M. on March 12, during a thunderstorm, Adelaide gave birth to their

Fig. 2-8. Clayton in 1882 when it was purchased by Henry Clay Frick as a wedding present for his wife, Adelaide.
Frick Archives

son, Childs Frick. Her sister reflected in her diary, "I don't think his Papa ever wrote any words that made him feel so rich and happy as those written in the Bible that day announcing the birth of Childs Frick." Proud of the baby, Frick carried him around the house, burped him regularly, and, for a man who fussed about the details of interior decoration and neatness of dress, never seemed to mind having Childs soil his clothes. As oldest son to four younger siblings, Frick was used to the ways of babies. And as the second child in a large family, he was accustomed to and familiar with the fatigue, discomfort, and frailty of many women after childbirth. As a result, he loved doting on Adelaide and carried her up and down stairs until the doctors said she could walk.

Two weeks after her wedding Adelaide had received a letter from her mother, Martha Howard Childs, saying she was happy that "providence has placed my darling in a position to do good." She also advised, "Strive to be a good, kind, affectionate and loving wife, giving up your own will for that of your Husbands [sic]." And indeed, Adelaide was doing as her mother suggested. In fact, Frick, sensitive to his wife's kindness and her dependencies, was particularly protective of the close relationship Adelaide had with her unmarried sister, Martha. Unlike the placid Adelaide, Martha was daringly independent and headstrong for a woman of her social standing at that time. She refused to marry, sneered at the Bible, eventually drove her own car, and had a

Fig. 2-9. A. Bryan Wall (1861–1935), *Wife and Sister.*
Acquired in 1882, Oil on canvas, 27 x 22 in. (68.6 x 55.9 cm).
Frick Art and Historical Center

house of her own. She claimed that Adelaide would never have become engaged if she, Martha, had been in Pittsburgh that summer. She was so cross that Adelaide had "left home" that she wrote Adelaide the morning after the wedding that she had been crying all day, that she felt her "mate had flown away." She insisted "what a lovely pair we would have made," but confessed that "nothing in the world could make us cease to see and love each other." Perhaps as a way to reassure her that his marriage to Adelaide would not sever the two sisters' bond, in December 1883 Frick commissioned A. Bryan Wall to do a portrait of the sisters entitled *Wife and Sister* (fig. 2-9).

Apart from his sister-in-law's initial disapproval, and the advent of another financial and industrial depression, 1883 remained a satisfying year in Frick's life. In August, he added the Trotter and Standard coke works to the H. C. Frick Coke Company over the protests of Andrew Carnegie. Foreshadowing the complicated relationship that would engulf these men, as Frick incorporated the works, he challenged his senior and largest stockholder:

> I am free to say, I do not like the tone of your letter. Outside of my desire to follow and accept your views as largest stockholder in our Company—I have great admiration for your acknowledged abilities and your general good judgment, and would much prefer to defer to your views—in the matter of the values the properties in question and the propriety of increasing our stock I shall have to differ from you and I think the future will bear me out.

In the fall of that year, Frick again flexed his muscle and defied his superior. When Carnegie refused to purchase Frick's Morewood coke works, citing as his reason that because the coal was largely beneath water level the price of the resulting coke would be too costly, Frick placed the works in a partnership with the owners of some Chicago steel mills. He had long been supplying these mills with Frick coke, and over the years these clients would follow Frick's advice and develop the important South West Coal and Coke Company.

But as 1883 closed, and 1884 unfolded amidst the routine of business management, Frick was greeted with the happy news that Adelaide was again pregnant. After paying $400 over the next thirteen months to the Pittsburgh publishing, bookbinding, and importing firm Glynn and Barrett for an extraordinary four-volume set of Edward Strahan's *Mr. Vanderbilt's House and Collection,* he paid an extra $100 for a twenty-print satin portfolio of Vanderbilt's collection, all of which he hung in Clayton, five of them boasting exquisite gold frames. Beautiful as they were, they paled with the birth of his first daughter, Martha Howard Frick, on August 5, 1885. That Martha's birth would mark the end of the last happy period in Frick's life could never have been foretold.

MARTHA WAS INDEED A REMARKABLE BEAUTY, with her fragile skin and soft red curls. She seemed both a symbol of all the happiness and good fortune the Fricks had thus far enjoyed and a pledge of all the good fortune and happiness that was to come.

When Annie Blumenschine, the teenager hired as companion for the Fricks' children, first saw Martha in early August 1885, she lost her heart to her. Martha was in a brand-new baby carriage lined with gold satin. As Annie later wrote in a 1945 memoir, all she could see of Martha was the "sweetest little face peeping from a little frilly bonnet and two dear little pink hands on the coverlet." Overcome with the child's beauty, Annie said she had to hold her breath. When she asked the nurse the baby's name, the nurse had whispered, "Rosebud." So, in the first years, Martha was called not by her Christian name, but by "Rosebud." With her tiny red curls framing her face like immature petals, she promised a radiant bloom.

As Martha grew from infancy to toddlerhood, the new partnership between the H. C. Frick Coke Company and Andrew Carnegie entered its third year, Frick's partnership with his Chicago clients remained on solid ground, and the South Fork Fishing and Hunting Club, only sixty miles from Pittsburgh, was a going concern. It now boasted prominent Pittsburghers as members. These included Frick's partner Andrew Carnegie, who was also in partnership with the Cambria Iron Company in Johnstown, the largest iron and steel producer in the country and the largest manufacturer of steel rails and iron wheels for the Pennsylvania Railroad, as well as other affiliated railroads; Frick's banker and longtime family friend, Andrew Mellon; his attorney the poker-playing enthusiast Philander Knox, who was secretary of the club and Carnegie's legal advisor; and the head of the Pittsburgh Division of the Pennsylvania Railroad, Robert Pitcairn. Members of Adelaide's family vacationed there regularly, and Frick's new Pittsburgh social friends and neighbors, the Benjamin Thaws and Charles Clarkes, built cottages on the lake. Moreover, Joseph R. Woodwell—a successful hardware manufacturer and famous Pittsburgh artist who lived next door to Clayton, introduced Frick to many artists in Europe, and told him tales of his adventures with members of the Barbizon school and other European artists who were his friends—often came to South Fork. Always the first to see Frick's most recent acquisitions, Woodwell, like his Barbizon friends on the outskirts of Paris, spent time sketching *en plein air* at the Scalp Level artist colony. A man of passion, Woodwell expressed all the emotion the more taciturn Frick repressed. Woodwell often challenged, "Did you ever study the sky ? Shall I paint it as I see it? That is impossible, but I can try to paint it as I feel it."

Though Frick never appeared to notice the sky or voice deep emotion, in the summer of 1887, his skies were about to darken. Seeming carefree, he sold a one-third interest in the Broad Ford distillery to Andrew Mellon and then took Childs, two-year-old Rosebud, and his wife on a European tour. On July 29, apparently at peace with the world, Frick wrote his friend "Andy" Mellon from Bremen, Germany: "Have not given business a thought." He particularly relished the mineral baths, and during their August stay in Germany, Frick, who rarely socialized, but silently observed people and his environment with a detective's eye, shared his impressions of two of his celebrated covacationers with Mellon: Robert Garrett of the B&O Railroad "does not impress me as being a man of much force," and the prince of Wales "seems to enjoy life very much, & mingles freely with the crowd." If worried about anything, however, he seemed only concerned with his wife's constant shopping expeditions. He expressed concern to his good friend that his wife, "though very well . . . however goes to Frankfurt every day or two . . . as they have fine stores there."

At times, however, Frick was restless. He complained from Dresden: "This everlasting sightseeing is a bore, and I don't see how I could put in the time if it were not for the fact that a Boston couple are traveling with us, and the gentleman a Mr. Hussey is a good fellow and our tastes are similar." In a reflective moment, he advised Mellon, "I don't think it pays to stop over here unless you have a taste for pictures, and after you have made such a trip as we did in '80 all you want is the ocean voyage, and a rest in England and probably a run over to Paris." Then he confessed, "About the first thing I did on arrival here was to look up the fair Emma, [but found] she [had] married an officer."

From his traveling companion John Wanamaker, he acquired J. G. Meyer von Bremen's painting of a mother with two children entitled *The Darlings* (fig. 2-10) and Tito Lessi's *Reading the Newspaper* (fig. 2-11), depicting a jovial, bespectacled man reading the daily news. But once in Paris at the end of August, Frick seemed further disenchanted by his grand tour. He wrote Mellon: "Paris is not so gay and attractive as in '80 and you would notice it at once, the buildings do not look so clean and bright." As he again recalled the spontaneity of their bachelor trip, Frick wrote Mellon, "No more trips for me to Europe which involves sight seeing.'"

The family stayed in Paris from August 24 to September 10 and then departed for a month's stay in London. As was his custom, he dashed through the art galleries, his quick retentive mind grasping every detail so that later, when discussing the paintings with others, his family were astonished by his photographic recall.

"Glad to get where [he] could understand the language," a still frustrated Frick wrote Mellon that his wife "Ada and the rest have gone to Windsor Castle. I did not think I would care to see it and having an excellent courier they do not need me." His tone cheered when he later divulged what he had discovered through a friend: "it is a mistake about that young lady [the fair Emma] being married . . . she is on the stage in Berlin."

Fig. 2-10. J. G. Meyer von Bremen
(b. 1813), *The Darlings.*
Acquired in 1887, Oil on canvas.
Private collection

Fig. 2-11. Tito Lessi (1858-1917),
Reading the Newspaper.
Acquired in 1887/1889, Oil on panel,
7 x 8½ in. (17.8 x 21.6 cm).
Frick Art and Historical Center

Records do not reveal if Frick returned to Emma, but they do show why he was edgy and cross. The real reason he had written Mellon saying he had "not given business a thought" (and yet was perhaps drawn to *Reading the Newspaper*) was that months before his European trip, Frick had resigned as chairman of his H. C. Frick Coke Company over a disagreement with Carnegie about the price of coke and the handling of wildcat strikers that threatened civil authority in the Coke Region.

This breach with Carnegie had been a year in the making. Indeed, the two men seemed to be on the verge of a power struggle. In 1886, Frick had asked Carnegie to make him a shareholder in Carnegie Brothers and Company, but Carnegie had replied that such a move "would be the mistake of your life." Although Carnegie told Frick that his ambition, drive, and genius for financial and business management could make him the largest shareholder of the Carnegie steel concern, he insisted that that concern would still be his, Carnegie's, and not "your work and you could not be proud of it." Carnegie, insisting Frick's idea was "suicidal," further chastised:

> I cannot imagine how your pride permitted you to think for one moment of sinking to an insignificant holder of 4 percent in your own Creation. To think that you could ever be influenced in its councils with such a petty interest is absurd. . . . The idea is suicidal. . . . Every dollar I had, all I could get credit for, I should put into *My Company*, and be the Frick of the Frick Coke Company. . . . I believe you will make more millions by *Concentrating* than by Scattering. . . . I never could advise you to divide your thoughts and time between concerns when your own field was fully open before you. Go in and possess it or sink into merited insignificance!

So adamant was Carnegie that Frick not invest in his steel concerns, he added a postscript: "File this for future reference."

Then, that same year, the hairline cracks that were beginning to splinter the relationship deepened when the deaths of Carnegie's mother and his brother Thomas provided a catalyst for an astonishing philosophical reversal on Carnegie's part. Although as early as 1867 Carnegie had imported foreigners to replace strikers in his iron works, and had continued this practice, he published in 1886 an essay "An Employer's View of the Labor Question," and a book, *Triumphant Democracy*, espousing both the right of workers to organize into unions and the policy that during a strike no man should have his job taken by another. These statements, made during a nationwide strike, when Frick was standing firm against labor and Chicago police opened fire on rioting strikers, suggest not only a sudden collapse by the bereaved Carnegie into the early value system of his male ancestors, but also an obvious ploy on his part to endear himself to the laboring class. More important, Carnegie's calculated reversal might also be seen as an expression of a deeply rooted fear of Frick's ambition and greater managerial genius.

Since Carnegie was now traveling and writing full time, he had good reason to believe that Frick could out-manage him and might, therefore, supplant him.

Carnegie began, therefore, to see Frick as both partner and threat. Frick, on the other hand, still saw himself as Carnegie's partner; he had entered into their partnership thinking that Carnegie favored, as did he, importing other ethnic groups to replace striking workers. Unaware that he now represented Carnegie's alterego and implied nemesis, Frick was shocked by Carnegie's about-face and felt undercut. He saw labor matters as his purview and thought Carnegie's new views weakened his authority and compromised his ability to handle labor uprisings in the Coke Region.

To protect against strikes, wildcat or otherwise, in 1885, when state law prohibited women from working in the mines and coke works, and the coke operators reduced their husbands' wages to reflect their absence, Frick had formed a syndicate with the independent coke operators to control the supply and price of coke, as well as wages. But Andrew Carnegie, who in 1886 had insisted that Frick be seen as commander of the H. C. Frick Coke Company, now in 1887, when wildcatters struck in the Coke Region, used his position as majority stockholder to force Frick to sell him coke at below syndicate prices and to capitulate to the strikers, even though Frick and the coke owners were united in their decision to stand firm against the wildcatters and to import strikebreakers. He forced Frick to betray both his own union policy and the very syndicate of independent coke operators he had formed. The blow to Frick was further exacerbated by the fact that in retribution, the syndicate withheld $90,000 of funds from the H. C. Frick Coke Company for having violated the agreement.

On May 13, 1887, Frick, after having first "clean[ed] the business up and put it in proper shape," had offered to sell his shares in the H. C. Frick Coke Company back to the directors at "low and easy terms." In writing the directors, he warned that by capitulating, they had strengthened the hand of labor and stated: "The loss to the Coke Company may be far more than made up, so far as you are concerned, by gains in your steel interests, but I object to so manifest a prostitution of the Coke Company's interests in order to promote your steel interests."

Headlines in the June 11, 1887, *Pennsylvania Press* read:

CARNEGIE THUNDERS FROM HIS CASTLE IN THE SCOTTISH HIGHLANDS
HIS BOLT WRECKS THE SYNDICATE
FRICK OVERPOWERED RESIGNS
HUNGARIANS DANCE WITH GLEE

Humiliated and betrayed, Frick had suffered a major blow to his authority and his ego. He advised Carnegie, "Whilst a majority of the stock entitles you to control, I deny that it confers the right to manage." At once beaten by Carnegie and the wildcat strikers, Frick was financially and publicly disgraced by his syndicate peers, who condemned him as being a worse sort than the wildcatters. As Henry Phipps, chairman of Carnegie Brothers, warned Andrew Carnegie: "Frick and Company is almost his all, his ewe lamb, put yourself in his place."

Although Frick's offer to sell his company interests was denied, he had nevertheless washed his hands of the whole business, and it was under this cloud that he had departed for Europe. But as Frick toured the Continent, Carnegie, regretting the action he had forced upon his manager-partner, started to make conciliatory gestures. Henry Phipps, who managed other Carnegie interests, had become the new chairman of the coke company, but within months, just as Frick predicted, though Carnegie was receiving guaranteed supplies of coke, he was having to pay 12.5 percent higher wages than his competitors. Thus, when Frick arrived in London on August 2 for the start of his European tour, waiting for him was an invitation from Carnegie to visit him in Scotland, where he was honeymooning with his bride, Louise. Still cross with Carnegie, Frick did not reply and set off with his family for Germany and Paris. But in September, on his return to London, Frick was greeted by what he described in a letter to Andrew Mellon as "a very pressing invitation from Mr. C to visit him at Kilgraston [Scotland]."

As a result, Frick, Adelaide, and her sister Attie (Martha Howard Childs) left Childs and Martha behind in London with a governess and set off for Scotland. During the four-day visit, he and Carnegie "took a long walk and during the stroll [Carnegie] brought up the coke matter which we discussed pleasantly and then dropped it without going into the future." When Frick and his party began their return to London via Glasgow, Loch Katrine, and Loch Lomond, the breach still had not healed. So, perhaps as a way to unwind after the strains and tensions of this visit, Frick and the ladies decided to spend a few days in Edinburgh before joining the children in London at the Hotel Victoria.

When Frick arrived in Glasgow on Wednesday, September 21, however, he found a disturbing telegram informing him that "Rosie" was not well. Unknown to anyone, little Martha had swallowed a pin while the party had been staying in Paris. Without the benefit of modern medical technology and without witnesses to the incident, no one could have suspected the gravity of her situation. Yet Frick immediately took the train to London with his wife and sister-in-law and wrote Mellon, "Rosie has taken cold which has settled in her hip so that she can scarcely bear to put her right foot down." He went on to say, "The doctor does not think it will prove very serious, but has not made up his mind fully. She will not permit him to examine her as he should." Worried about the child (fig. 2-12), he explained, "I should like very much to be at home" and wrote that he had booked passage for an early return, on October 9.

Fig. 2-12. Martha Howard Frick in 1887, a few weeks after ingesting the pin.
Private collection

Although he remained concerned about his young daughter's condition, within months he and Adelaide were distracted by other matters. On November 10, 1887, the *Pennsylvania Press* announced:

FRICK IS BOSS AGAIN

Frick had agreed to reassume chairmanship of the H. C. Frick Coke Company, but only on the condition that the $90,000 withheld by the syndicate be returned. As for Carnegie, he soon began writing Frick adoring notes: "You can't justly estimate what a tremendously big man you are. Perhaps some day you will realize that you are bigger than Prest [*sic*] of P. R. R. Take supreme care of that head of yours. It is wanted again. Expressing my thankfulness that I have found THE MAN."

So with the exception of Martha's ongoing distress, the clouds that had gathered in Henry Clay Frick's life seemed to be dissipating. And as they did, Adelaide announced she was pregnant with their third child. On September 3, 1888, she produced a daughter named Helen Clay. Childs, then six, announced proudly to Annie Blumenschine that he and three-year-old Rosebud had a new baby sister. Annie, anxious to see the new baby for herself, asked to be taken to Mrs. Frick's bedroom. She recalled in her memoir that her mistress was in bed "looking like a princess from a fairy tale" and that beside her was a crib lined in pink satin ribbon and bows. Inside, was what Annie described as another "pink rosebud." From that point on, however, Adelaide insisted everyone was now to address her first daughter as Martha, not Rosebud.

For the next year and a half, as Martha suffered, she began to lose her hair (fig. 2-13). Then, approximately six months after Helen's birth, in the winter of 1889, the nurse who had been changing Martha noticed a small spot on the child's right side that had split open and was oozing pus. Startled, the nurse wiped the pus away and was horrified to find a black pin exiting the wound. In thinking back over the onset of Martha's illness two years before, and her constant suffering since that time, all realized Martha must have somehow swallowed the pin in Paris during the summer of 1887—and that for almost two years, as the pressure from the abscess grew, the pin had been pushing through her body.

Dr. James McClelland, a famous homeopathic doctor in Pittsburgh who studied bacteriology and surgery annually in Vienna, was called immediately. Homeopaths, then at the height of their popularity because they had the lowest mortality rate in patients suffering from typhoid fever and other devastating diseases, believe "likes cure likes," that radical doses of invasive, harmful drugs only alleviate symptoms and work against the natural healing powers of the body. Homeopaths instead administer small doses of remedies prepared from the plant, mineral, and animal world that are said to stimulate a person's own immune system.

Frick was a longtime proponent of homeopathy and a life member of Pittsburgh's Homeopathic Dispensary; moreover McClelland and his brother, who was also a homeopath, was a friend, a true intellectual, a skilled surgeon, and commissioner of health for Pennsylvania. Dr. McClelland said they would have to operate on Martha—even though it was dangerous. Pediatric abdominal surgery was rarely practiced. Such procedures had a high mortality rate because, although the surgical technique was in place, neither asepsis (the prevention of infection in a wound by keeping everything related to the surgical process sterile) nor antibiotics had been discovered. Carbolic acid was poured into a wound to prevent infection.

Limited to the science of his day, Dr. McClelland made a half-inch incision, cleaned the wound, and considered the operation a success. But Martha cried day and night after the operation. The doctors could not tell what the trouble was, for the pin was out and the incision healed over. Unknown to them, however, a peritoneal abscess had formed in the trail left by the pin, and infection was filling Martha's abdominal cavity.

Fig. 2-13. Martha wore a wig to cover her thinning hair.
Author's collection

Unwittingly, the doctors exacerbated the situation because their knowledge of bacteriology was so limited and the practice of aseptic surgery unknown. Instruments were not sterilized; nor had the surgeons scrubbed, or worn sterile protective clothing.

After the operation, as Martha continued to complain, the doctor—perhaps to keep Annie from worrying—said Martha was only teething. But for a long time, Martha was lame. Unable to walk or enjoy the outdoors, she rode in a carriage or a go-cart. And when the artist Roseti composed a family portrait, sensing perhaps that Martha was dying, he portrayed the balding Martha (fig. 2-14) against a backdrop of angels and with lush, auburn-red hair (fig. 2-15).

Although the breach with Carnegie was healed and Martha's scar was forming, the peace in Henry Clay Frick's life had ended. And wounds of several kinds were opening. Like Martha's illness, one of them was physical, silent, and sinister. Seeping lake water was silently eroding the dam at the now fashionable South Fork Fishing and Hunting Club. The worst natural disaster in America's history was about to take place and Frick, among others, would soon be blamed for the death of over two thousand working-class people, many of whom were women and children.

Fig. 2-14. In this 1889 family photograph, Martha shows signs of hair loss.
Frick Archives

Fig. 2-15. Fr. Roseti, *Portrait of Mrs. Henry Clay Frick and Children*, 1889.
Watercolor on opaque white glass,
7½ x 9¾ in. (19 x 24.7 cm)
Property of Henry Clay Frick II, on loan to the Frick Art and Historical Center

Fig. 2-16. South Fork Fishing and Hunting Club lakeside cottages.
Johnstown Area Heritage Association, Johnstown, Pa.

THE SOUTH FORK FISHING AND HUNTING CLUB (fig. 2-16) was a true thorn in the side of the people working in the mills and factories of Johnstown. The club typified the elitism of the upper class—its membership was limited to eighty people, and it was the only Pittsburgh club to own its own grounds at that time. It was completely hidden from coal miners, steel workers, and other local people, people whom the elite perceived as violent and dangerous. To insure privacy, the entire property was posted and fenced. Poachers were thrown off, and in an attempt to hide the club from public scrutiny, the owners illegally incorporated it in Allegheny County, the seat of their own personal affairs, instead of in Cambria County, where the club was actually situated. Thus, in the tranquil setting of the Allegheny Mountains, carefully selected members of the Pittsburgh business, social, and cultural elite could sail, paint, fish, swim, and hunt in complete freedom and security.

The lake created for this mountain retreat out of the small canal reservoir stood fourteen miles north of Johnstown, a city then second only to Chicago as a manufacturing center, and 450 feet above it. The dam that contained this lake was located at the top of the Conemaugh Gorge. Originally the dam was so small and inconsequential that up until 1857 it had contained only a small reservoir for the Johnstown Canal Basin and the Western Division of the Main Line Canal. This dam had been left in ill repair until the Pennsylvania Railroad sold it to Benjamin Ruff who, like Frick, had then lived in the Monongahela House. Besides the dam and abandoned reservoir, they and the fourteen other incorporators bought seventy acres of surrounding woodland with the finest trout streams in the state. It was a site that appealed to Frick enormously. As a boy, he had been fascinated with water power. Once, during a violent rainstorm, he had constructed a dam across a road in West Overton; when it burst the water so damaged the road he was severely punished by his father, who was commissioner of the roads at that time. Later, as chairman of the vast coke company in that same region, Frick had dammed streams and run underground pipes from the Youghiogheny River to feed the reservoirs that held the water needed for his coking operations.

Initial repairs to the club's dam proved unsuccessful, and on Christmas Day 1879, the new construction was washed away in a storm. Work was delayed until the summer of 1880, when Frick was on his trip to Europe with Andrew Mellon. Then again, in February 1881, hard rains damaged the dam, this time forcing the club to assess its members and change its charter to provide for increased membership and solicitation of stockholders.

When the dam was finally completed that summer, it measured 931 feet in length, 270 feet in width at the base, and 72 feet in height (fig. 2-17). Referred to by residents of Johnstown as the Sword of Damocles, the $17,000 structure was an enormous mound of earth dumped between two hills. It was then the largest earthen dam in the world and held at bay the largest artificial lake in the world, a lake measuring seven miles in circumference, a mile wide in places, and three-and-a-half miles long. The lake encompassed more than seven hundred acres, held 20 million tons of water, and was seventy feet deep at some points. Lake Conemaugh, as it was called, was an impressive rival to the small natural lakes in England's Lake District seen by Frick in 1880 on his first trip to Europe.

The waters of long, placid Lake Conemaugh would, however, soon cause havoc. The dam restricted the flow of water into the Little Conemaugh riverbed and kept the water from entering the fourteen-mile-long, rock-walled Conemaugh Gorge, with its 450-foot drop in elevation between South Fork and Johnstown. Within this steep gorge lay the heavily traveled Pennsylvania Railroad roadbed and the tiny mining and manufacturing towns of Mineral Point, East Conemaugh, Franklin, and Woodvale. The safety of the thirty thousand people who had packed their homes within the narrow confines of the gorge, or lived in the town of Johnstown below, was dependent on the dam.

John Fulton, a deeply religious man who was a geologist and the chief engineer for the Cambria Iron Company in Johnstown, had insisted in 1881 that the dam was being

Fig. 2-17. The dam at Lake Conemaugh.
Johnstown Area Heritage Association, Johnstown, Pa.

poorly repaired, that water coming out of the base of the dam was lake water escaping through faulty construction and not a natural spring. Others not only disliked having a lake of 20 million tons of water suspended four hundred feet above their heads, but also resented the flotilla of fifty canoes and rowboats, countless sailboats, an electric catamaran, and two steam-powered yachts that lazed the day away in the sunshine, while they labored in the oppressive heat and frenzy of the mills in the gorge below. A minister from Johnstown, who echoed the town's concerns about the concentration of water that was being held above their heads, prayed, "God have mercy on those people below" in the event that the dam were to break.

And mercy they would need. Although the South Fork Fishing and Hunting Club had transported a thousand black bass from Lake Erie in a special Pullman car fitted with oxygen tanks, similar consideration had not been given to the method of the dam's repair. The old dam had required a complete overhaul and new discharge system, but these former weaknesses had not been addressed sensibly. Over 260,000 tons of material, in the form of mud, straw, manure, rocks, and trees had been tossed from wagons into existing trouble spots in the old dam. The abandoned sluice gates, which had previously controlled the water level of the lake, were missing their cast-iron discharge pipes, and rather than install new pipes, the pipe holes had simply been filled with rubble and sealed.

To accommodate the carriages passing each other on top of the dam as they wound their way back and forth on the two-and-a-half mile trip from the railroad station at South Fork to the cottages, Ruff and Cyrus Unger leveled the top of the dam, lowering it by four feet. Although this procedure made two-way traffic possible, it left the dam lower in the middle than on its sides. The dam's center, therefore, became its weakest point.

There were other engineering faults as well. The spillway (fig. 2-18) on the east end of the dam, the single escape hatch for excess water, was only four-and-a-half feet deep. Because the spillway had a solid rock bottom, it could not be deepened, and could, therefore, only accommodate a limited overflow in an emergency. Furthermore, the flow of water from the lake was restricted by heavy, elevated wire screens that had been spread between the supports of the spillway bridge to keep the bass from jumping out. In addition, wedge-shaped, nail-studded traps, arranged in a zigzag pattern stood out from the spillway screens into the lake itself; they were a further deterrent to fish escaping downstream and a further restriction to the flow of water into the spillway.

Fig. 2-18. The rock-walled, narrow spillway at Lake Conemaugh.
Johnstown Area Heritage Association, Johnstown, Pa.

In 1889, a few months after the pin exited Martha's side—ten years after the incorporation of the club and seven years after the dam's completion—an unusually violent spring hit the region. A historic 52.6 inches of rainfall nationwide established a new national record. In the Pittsburgh area, a February tornado killed seventeen people. On April 6, snow reached an accumulation of up to fourteen feet in the mountains, but it melted immediately and was followed by eight days of rain throughout the remainder of the month. During the last week of May, Pittsburgh, already saturated by eleven days of rain that month, received five additional days of relentless downpour.

Nevertheless, on Memorial Day, May 30, 1889, the town of Johnstown was in a holiday mood. Bands played, flags flew, and its 245 drinking establishments enjoyed a good business. But that night a torrential rainstorm blew in from the Midwest. By morning landslides had occurred, most cellars were flooded, rats could be seen running along fence-tops, and the congested rivers, rising at eighteen inches an hour and traveling at six miles per hour, not only roared their warning, but ripped out their bridges.

Gauges at the lake showed that during breakfast Lake Conemaugh had risen a full five inches. New streams were racing down the tree-stripped mountains and the once peaceful trout streams, which had been lined with moss-covered rock, delicate ferns, and majestic trees, were turning into churning, boiling torrents. The streams were draining into the lake so fast that it was now rising ten to twelve inches an hour.

At the dam site, the battle of man against nature took on horrific proportions. As dense fog clouded the lake and filled the gorge below, frantic attempts were made to bolster the dam, plug leaks, dig a second spillway, enlarge the existing rock-walled spillway, and tear out the screen fish guards that were so filled with debris they impeded the flow of water into the spillway and thus placed extra pressure on the crumbling dam.

In the meantime, however, the spillway water was running seven feet deep through its rock bed, while lake water was spilling over the dam in a sheet and squirting from crevices in the heart of the dam wall. The water from both rain and runoff was now accumulating in Lake Conemaugh at four thousand gallons a second. At the peak of the storm, with few trees left to hold the excess water, ten thousand cubic feet of water drained into the lake every second. The lake rose one inch every ten minutes as six thousand feet of water per second roared into the rock-bound spillway; the heavy screens and wooden traps placed in front of it were clogged with debris, logs, and whole trees uprooted from the hillsides. The Signal Service—the Army Signal Corps' public weather service—called the rainstorm the worst ever recorded for that particular area. Six to eight inches of rain fell in twenty-four hours. Ten inches fell in the tree-stripped mountains.

Fig. 2-19. The broken dam at South Fork.
Johnstown Area Heritage Association, Johnstown, Pa.

At 3:10 P.M. the time bomb at South Fork exploded. With the pent-up fury of the boiling streams and mountain runoff, the pressure of the rapidly accumulating waters broke the faulty dam with a roar (fig. 2-19). Its entire face burst forward as the waters of Lake Conemaugh leapt to freedom in a 450-foot, fourteen-mile free-fall through the Conemaugh Gorge below. The force of the water, carrying a 300-foot section of the dam in front of it, was horrific. The wave hit the gorge like a battering ram, making the hills quake. The water made a low, thunderous rumble and was preceded by a violent wind that blew down small buildings as offerings to the advancing water. The wave from Lake Conemaugh cleared the 100-foot breach in the dam and emptied Lake Conemaugh in forty-five minutes (fig. 2-20).

Jacob Kohler, a resident of South Fork, said, "I saw it coming with the water reaching a height of at least twenty five feet, tearing trees up by the roots and dashing big rocks about as a boy would marbles."

In less than an hour, many of the people who the day before had honored the lives of family members killed in action would themselves be dead. The forty-foot wall of

Fig. 2-20. The empty lake bed at South Fork.
Johnstown Area Heritage Association, Johnstown, Pa.

water, traveling at ten to fifteen miles an hour, missed the town of South Fork, because it was on the side of a hill, and entered a narrow section of the rock-walled gorge containing the Little Conemaugh River. The wave, now seventy-five feet high and traveling at treetop level, crashed into the seventy-five-foot stone viaduct used by the Pennsylvania Railroad to traverse the river's two-mile-long oxbow. Carrying the remains of the destroyed viaduct, the wave obliterated East Conemaugh and its railroad yard and added to its debris numerous eighty-ton locomotives, freight cars, and passenger cars.

When the killer wave fell into Woodvale—the Cambria Iron Company's model town—within five minutes this town of a thousand people, employing mainly women and children in the textile mills, was destroyed. After adding Woodvale to its growing mass, the wave hit the blast furnaces of the Gautier wire works, causing massive explosions and scalding steam. Suddenly 150,000 to 200,000 pounds of Gautier barbed wire joined the massive wall of water, binding together hot metal, almost fifty miles of railroad track, hundreds of houses, a tannery, eighty-nine horses, and thirty tons of hay. The wave killed, on average, one out of every three people in its path.

When the wave hit Johnstown, it was almost solid in form. The city was destroyed in less than ten minutes, only to be compressed into one mass against the Pennsylvania Railroad's stone bridge, located at the triangle where the Little Conemaugh and

Stonycreek meet to form the Conemaugh River. Built by the Pennsylvania Railroad Company just two years before the flood, the stone bridge, though structurally sound, had not been designed to accommodate the flow of water in a large flood. Its stone archways too narrow and its pilings too wide, the railroad bridge became still another South Fork Dam (fig. 2-21). With water and debris unable to flow downriver, the flood wreckage, which now covered sixty acres, pressed against the bridge and extended fifteen feet above it. The dam turned Johnstown into an artificial lake, uglier, smaller, and shallower than Lake Conemaugh.

Although the killer wave's momentum had been arrested, the continuing destruction and havoc were far from over. In the evening, oil tanks in the debris at the stone bridge ruptured and suddenly caught fire. Five hundred women, children, and animals were trapped in the inferno, an inferno that burned for more than two days in full view of the stranded survivors on the hills above. Powerless to reach the victims, the dislocated, dissociated survivors, knowing that family members and friends might be in the fire, listened to the victims' screams long into the night (figs. 2-22, 23).

Fig. 2-21. The Pennsylvania Railroad bridge became another dam.
Johnstown Area Heritage Association, Johnstown, Pa.

Figs. 2-22, 23. Johnstown, Pennsylvania, before and after the flood of 1889. The wave moved from left to right across the area pictured. Note the fire at the Pennsylania Railroad bridge, left side, lower image.

Johnstown Area Heritage Association, Johnstown, Pa.

George Swank, editor for the *Johnstown Tribune,* wrote from his office that the fire "burned with all the fury of the Hell you read about—cremation alive in your own home, perhaps a mile from its foundation; dear ones slowly consumed before your eyes, and the same fate yours a moment later."

William Tice, who was actually pulled from the water at the bridge, said: "I saw hundreds of them as the flames approached throw up their hands and fall backward into the fire, and those who had escaped drowning were reserved for the more horrible fate of being burned to death."

But was being burned to death a more horrible fate than drowning? When the immense wave hit the bridge, it crashed into the cliff wall across Stonycreek, the back-wash creating a whirlpool with men, women and children helplessly caught in the vortex, screaming as they met death by drowning. One witness to the scene, Frank McDonald, said, "They reminded me of a lot of flies on flypaper, struggling to get away with no hope and no chance to save them."

So great had been the destructive force of the wave, almost everyone who survived the flood was left homeless. Property damage was listed at $17 million, an average mill worker's salary at the time being $10 a week. More compelling, of the over two thousand dead:

> Nine hundred and sixty bodies were never found.
> One in three of the bodies found was unidentifiable.
> Ninety-nine entire families were wiped out.
> Ninety-eight children lost both parents.
> Three hundred and ninety-six children under ten years of age
>   had been killed.

Understandably, Conemaugh Valley was christened the Valley of Death.

Some of the South Fork Fishing and Hunting Club's Pittsburgh members refused to believe the tragedy had happened. Louis Clarke told a reporter he did not believe it was the South Fork Dam that had broken. James McGregor told a reporter, "I am going up there to fish the latter part of this month. . . . We have been putting in from fifteen thousand to twenty thousand dollars a year at South Fork, and we should not be likely to drop that much money in a place that we thought unsafe. No sir, the dam is just as safe as it ever was, and any other reports are just wild notions."

And James Reed, partner of Frick's lawyer Philander Knox in the law firm of Knox and Reed, claimed that within days of the disaster he had studied the dam, climbed all over it, and inspected it, and opined that "in the absence of any positive statement to the contrary [he would] continue to doubt, as do many others familiar with the place, that it really let go."

Others, however, knew the truth. The night the dam broke, prominent members of the club met in the East End home of Charles Clarke, whose family had used the club more than almost any other. Perhaps anticipating future lawsuits, they adopted a policy of complete silence: no members were to speak publicly about the club, the dam, or the tragedy. The following day, Saturday, June 1, Robert Pitcairn, head of the Western Division of the Pennsylvania Railroad, called a meeting and formed the Pittsburgh Relief Committee. Henry Phipps, treasurer of Carnegie Brothers and Company, and Frick were appointed to a five-man executive committee, and Dr. James H. McClelland, the physician who was treating Martha, would soon be, as president of the Pennsylvania State Board of Health, in charge of disease control in Johnstown.

Also on June 1, and within hours of the telegraph lines reopening, Frick wrote E. Y. Townsend, the president of Cambria Iron Company, "Words are inadequate to express the deep sympathy we all feel for you, and if we can be of any service, please command us." That same day, dynamite charges were set off at the stone bridge in Johnstown, to break the debris loose. Among the bodies found was that of a woman who had drowned giving birth. The child had not been fully delivered at the time of its mother's death.

On Sunday, the Pittsburgh Relief Committee was in session all day. Twenty-four subcommittees were formed to cover the many aspects of the relief effort. The committee asked the Pennsylvania Railroad and the B&O to restrict ticket sales to only those people with a pass from its headquarters. By late afternoon, a fourteen-car train with thirty physicians, four boxcars of provisions, and Battery B of the 18th Pennsylvania Regiment left for Johnstown. Three other trains, one with nine hundred tents and some boats, another with coffins and undertakers, the third with lumber and fifteen hundred pounds of dynamite, were also dispatched. Typical of the response in the Pittsburgh community, all business activity in the city ceased for two weeks while the Relief Committee assumed primary managerial control of organized relief for Johnstown. The committee alone was responsible for food, money, medicine, burial of the dead, and the abatement of public health problems (fig. 2-24).

When the water began to recede, people working on the wreckage found a halter with a portion of a horse's head still in it. Hundreds of human bodies, some decapitated or otherwise mutilated, were found buried in the mud waiting, like the drowned fish on the bottom of South Fork's emptied lake bed, to be gathered up and carried off in baskets.

Frick certainly had much to do with the swift, efficient response of the Pittsburgh Relief Committee, but he remained publicly silent about the tragedy. He was silent in his correspondence as well. On June 5, he wrote J. C. Morse, president of the Illinois Steel Company in Chicago about a business matter, saying only: "This dreadful catastrophe

Fig. 2-24. The Pittsburgh Relief Committee handled the first rescues and the initial emergency care in Johnstown.
Johnstown Area Heritage Association, Johnstown, Pa.

at Johnstown has demoralized almost everybody, so that nothing can be done, and it is not well to take up the subject any further at the present."

On June 7, he then forwarded donations of $5,000 each from Carnegie Brothers and Company Ltd., Carnegie Phipps and Company, and the H. C. Frick Coke Company to William J. Robinson, treasurer of the Cambria Iron Company. On that same day, the coroners of Westmoreland and Cambria counties, who had been conducting an inquest, rendered their verdict of "death by violence" and held the owners of the club responsible.

On June 8, Frick expressed his desire to bow out of the situation. He wrote Reuben Miller, treasurer of the club, that "Taking a view of the whole situation, we think that the Philadelphia meeting should appoint a committee for Johnstown, and also a finance committee to relieve us, and allow us to get back to our business, which is of pressing importance. Much trouble is before us if we stay with the work, and we can gracefully step out."

Four days later, the situation at Johnstown came under state control. Clara Barton and the Red Cross arrived to care for the flood survivors, and Pitcairn's railroad workers rebuilt the critical viaduct, opening the town to the influx of charitable relief organizations. Relief money began to accumulate as well. Among the thousands of donations, Benjamin Thaw sent $3,000, the Pennsylvania Railroad $5,000, Mellon $2,000, and the South Fork Fishing and Hunting Club gave $3,000 and twelve hundred blankets. Prisoners at the Western Penitentiary baked a thousand loaves of bread, while monetary donations from Buffalo Bill Cody's benefit Wild West Show in Paris, Queen Victoria, the sultan of Turkey, and President Benjamin Harrison pushed the eventual dollar relief fund total to $3.73 million.

By June 13, Frick seemed impatient, particularly with Andrew Carnegie, who had been vacationing in Europe at the time of the disaster. Carnegie had written him about changing coke rates, and Frick had replied that he had made "a fair start towards getting [a] change . . . when this terrible disaster occurred, and since then it has been impossible and out of the question to do anything with the railroad men, as you can readily understand. Everything had been in confusion with the railroads, but things are beginning to shape themselves."

Andrew Carnegie replied to his partners, "Dear Boys, that South Fork calamity has driven all else out of our thoughts for past few days. Glad all is getting back to calm days." He finished his letter saying, "Paris was too hot and too full, we decided to take a run to Rhine regions and enjoyed every day of our excursions. . . . [We] do Norway and Russia, etc. return to Paris about 1st September and sail 18th."

But one wonders more about the effect of this tragedy on Frick. Hard, cold, and silent, Frick neither spoke nor wrote about his reaction. Later on, however, his experience with the Johnstown Flood may have been stirred through certain paintings—Joseph Mallord William Turner's stormy seascapes, *Antwerp: Van Goyen Looking Out for a Subject* (fig. 2-25) and *Fishing Boats Entering Calais Harbor* (fig. 2-26), as well as two Jacob van Ruisdaels: *A Waterfall with Rocky Hills and Trees* (fig. 2-27) and *A Waterfall with a Castle and Cottage* (fig. 2-28). The two Turners, although depicting boats entering harbors then familiar to Frick, also contain raging waves that may have evoked for him the horror and strength of Lake Conemaugh's infamous Wave of Death. The Ruisdaels show storm-filled mountain torrents with water rushing through narrow, rock-walled ravines similar to the insufficient spillway at South Fork.

By contrast, it is not hard to read the intent that drew him to Jean-Baptiste-Camille Corot's four paintings of long, placid lakes surrounded by high hills, scenes painted by Corot only twenty years before the Johnstown tragedy. Frick's praise in 1898 of his first Corot, *Ville d'Avray,* as "the gem of [his] collection," combined with the fact that later, when acquiring three other lakeside Corots, he sold Corot's *Couronne de Fleurs* and *La Seine à Nantes,* suggests that his predilection for lake scenes was related to the unfulfilled dream of owning a lakeside paradise. *The Boatman of Mortefontaine* (fig. 2-29) bespeaks tragedy, as the scene resembles the contours of Lake

Fig. 2-25. Joseph Mallord William Turner (1775-1851), *Antwerp: Van Goyen Looking Out for a Subject*, 1833
Acquired in 1901, Oil on canvas, 36⅛ x 48⅜ in. (91.8 x 122.9 cm).
The Frick Collection

Fig. 2-26. Joseph Mallord William Turner (1775-1851), *Fishing Boats Entering Calais Harbor*, c. 1803.
Acquired in 1904, Oil on canvas, 29 x 38¾ in. (73.7 x 98.4 cm).
The Frick Collection

Fig. 2-27. Jacob van Ruisdael (1628/29-1682), *A Waterfall with Rocky Hills and Trees.*
Acquired in 1901, Oil on canvas.
Private collection

Fig. 2-28. Jacob van Ruisdael (1628/29–1682), *A Waterfall with a Castle and Cottage.*
Acquired in 1918, Oil on canvas, 39¼ x 34 in. (99.7 x 86.3 cm).
Courtesy The Fogg Art Museum, Harvard University Art Museums, gift of Helen Clay Frick, 1953

Fig. 2-29. Jean-Baptiste-Camille Corot (1796–1875), *The Boatman of Mortefontaine*, 1865–70.
Acquired in 1903, Oil on canvas, 24 x 35⅜ in. (60.9 x 89.8 cm).
The Frick Collection

Fig. 2-30. A boat on Lake Conemaugh as seen from the lakeside cottages.
Johnstown Area Heritage Association, Johnstown, Pa.

Conemaugh and its boathouse as seen from the South Fork clubhouse and the house Frick was reputed to have owned (fig. 2-30).

As horrific as it was, the Johnstown Flood of 1889 was only a foreshadowing of the disastrous flood of events awaiting Frick. Although he had been like a fast-moving weather system himself, he had not heard the last from his wilderness retreat, his first real-estate investment gone wrong.

❖

I N THE TEN YEARS SINCE THE INCORPORATION of the South Fork Fishing and Hunting Club in 1879, Henry Clay Frick's H. C. Frick Coke Company had gained control of 22,850 acres of coal lands along the Connellsville seam. He owned two-thirds of the 15,000 ovens in the Connellsville area, three pumping plants with a 5-million-gallon daily capacity, several short railroads, and 1200 coke cars. He employed 11,000 men, and was shipping 1100 carloads of coke a day. When Carnegie entered the business in 1882, the company had been capitalized at $2.1 million. Now it was capitalized at $5 million.

Clayton had been adapted to electricity, and in January 1889, just before the pin exited Martha's side, Frick was elected chairman of Carnegie Brothers and was again asserting himself with Carnegie. Shortly after his appointment, when he fired a negligent accountant, Frick informed Carnegie that he would only be chief executive of a "well managed concern." He insisted: "I must feel that I have the entire confidence of the power that put me where I am, in a place I did not seek. With all that, I know that I can manage both Carnegie Brothers and Company and Frick Coke Co. successfully." For his part, Carnegie said, "I only want to know how your hands can be strengthened."

Although Frick now owned the long-coveted shares in Carnegie's steel concern, headed a division of one of the largest steel operations in the world, and was one of the most powerful men in Pittsburgh, a growing shadow in business and family life stalked his every new gain.

On the business front, all the Connellsville men went out on strike in August 1889. As terrorism, rioting, arson, and murder became rampant, Frick, chairman of the H. C. Frick Coke Company, broke the strike after three months. According to the strikers, Frick enacted a "shoot to kill" policy against rioters using his company's Coal and Iron Police—authorized under Pennsylvania state law in 1866 as protection against violent strikers in the coal and coke regions.

Then, on September 28, Captain Bill Jones, one of the many heroes of the Johnstown rescue effort and an expert in the Bessemer process whom Carnegie had hired away from the Cambria Iron Company, suffered a fatal accident. A blast furnace at the Edgar Thomson works in Braddock had exploded with such force that the roar was heard twelve miles away in Pittsburgh. Six men were burned to cinders where they stood. Captain Bill, the mill's superintendent, was one of three men who took the full blast of forty tons of liquid iron. He was blown backward by the explosion and fell into the casting pit. He died from burns and a fractured skull a few days after Frick visited him in the hospital.

A letter from Andrew Carnegie dated July 23, 1889, from Cluny Castle in Scotland, however, anticipated the personal disaster awaiting Frick. Concerned that his partner was not coming abroad, Carnegie wrote: "We have been alarmed about little Martha, hope your decision not to leave home is not owing to her."

Martha, pale and wan at the Mountain House in Cresson Springs to celebrate her August 5 birthday, had lost her appetite. Fatigue and pain continued to plague her into the next year, with some days better than others, but none particularly bright. One day in September 1890, however, Frick wanted very much to take Martha to lunch with Thomas Lynch, the newly appointed general manager of the H. C. Frick Coke Company, who lived with his family in nearby Greensburg. Particularly pleased to see that Martha was wearing her pretty gingham dress and matching sunbonnet, he left with his daughter feeling very happy. But a few days after their return, the happiness vanished. One of the Lynch's children had died the previous year of diphtheria and Martha, who used this child's chair (brought down that day from the attic especially for the luncheon) caught the disease. Martha, who may have benefited from weekly

Fig. 2-31. The library at Clayton.
Frick Art and Historical Center

injections of the recently discovered diphtheria antitoxin, recovered after several weeks, but suffered bouts of dysentery so severe that the pressure caused a reopening of her wound.

Frick, though concerned about Martha, went forward in his characteristically deliberate and methodical way. In October 1890, he orchestrated the acquisition of the Duquesne steel works located on the Monongahela River just north of Carnegie's Braddock and Homestead mills. Carnegie had sabotaged this rival to his monopoly in the Pittsburgh rail market by sending notices to the railroad purchasing agents that the Duquesne rails, made by an innovative one-step process known as direct rolling, were defective. The mill, already suffering from labor troubles and lack of capital, soon fell to Carnegie. Frick, who later adopted Duquesne's direct rolling process, offered to buy the mill for $1 million in bonds, plus additional cash for inventory—a deal that saw no outlay of money on Carnegie's part, as well as paying Carnegie Brothers and Company $1 million dollars within a year because Frick had planned ahead and established a market for the Duquesne rails.

Then, in January 1891, Frick suppressed rioting workers at the Edgar Thomson mill. He advised Carnegie that the riot was "not anything more than a drunken Hungarian spree," and when Charles Schwab, manager of the Edgar Thomson works, suggested Frick bring in Pinkertons (employees of the Pinkerton National Detective Agency often hired by management to break labor strikes), Frick refused, saying he preferred to have the sheriff and his deputies protect the mill as he did not want to alienate the men and the public.

Against this backdrop of labor violence, but with his personal fortune increasing handsomely, Frick now decided to remodel Clayton, his home for the past eight years. He hired the important architect Frederick J. Osterling for the renovations and moved the family to a rented home on Lilac Street in Shadyside. Clayton, which in a year's time would resemble a small Loire Valley chateau, would boast twenty-four rooms, extra baths, and special details, like a new children's entrance with a miniature sink and oak hat rack that would serve the needs of the three busy children. A new and remodeled library (fig. 2-31), with furniture that included a child-sized leather arm chair to match the adults' set, as well as a children's playroom on the third floor, were also in the offing. As a social statement, however, the renovation would be so extensive and elaborate there could be no doubt as to Frick's importance in Pittsburgh's business and social communities (fig . 2-32). And yet, as the renovations commenced, Frick, perhaps reacting to the constant violence in his life and expressing a rare feeling of insecurity, wrote Osterling: "Please do not make any mistake, but make all your calculations to insure a good, substantial, safe job at my house, so that we will never be in any danger of having the roof blown off, or the house blown down, or be under the necessity of having to strengthen it after it is supposed to be completed."

But storms happen in many different ways, and roofs blow off for many different reasons. As the family was moving out of Clayton for its renovation, the troubles brewing in Frick's business and family life would merge, like parallel lines converging at the vanishing point in a painting, into a singular tragedy.

Fig. 2-32. Clayton, c. 1900.
Frick Art and Historical Center

CHAPTER III

As Martha Dies

Oh, Annie, what shall I do? What shall I do?

—Henry Clay Frick, 1891

EXCEPT FOR THE FACT THAT THE FAMILY MOVED into a rented home in Shadyside while work began on Clayton, 1891 did not have a fortuitous beginning. Apart from the rioting workers at the Edgar Thomson steel mill, the worst disaster in Connellsville mining history occurred at the H. C. Frick Coke Company's Mammoth Mines on January 27, 1891. The Frick mines were known for their high safety standards, particularly ventilation for protection against firedamp—an explosive mixture of methane gas, oxygen, and coal dust. The ventilation system exceeded the state's safety regulations, but that day at Mammoth, after the mine was inspected and vacated, unbeknownst to anyone, a fall of coal occurred, releasing the firedamp. Unaware of the gas, the miners entered with open-flame lights on their helmets; in the subsequent explosion, most of the 134 miners were smothered by the resulting afterdamp, toxic air devoid of oxygen (figs. 3-1, 2).

Immediately the H. C. Frick Coke Company formed a relief committee consisting of their officials, two Roman Catholic priests, a Methodist pastor, and the head of the union, Knights of Labor. A $25,000 long-term care fund was established, widows and orphans received emergency care, safety lamps replaced "naked lamps," and new safety rules were enacted which gave rise to the slogan used in heavy industry today, "Safety Is the First Consideration."

In February, rioting "Hungarians" at Carnegie's Edgar Thomson steel mill were brought under control by Pinkertons. Then a wage agreement with the coke workers expired, just as an industrial depression so severely slowed business that a shutdown of the steelworks had ensued. The shutdown became a lockout, however, with the

Figs. 3-1, 2. Mine cave-in, probably at Mammoth.
Private collection

strikers demanding an eight-hour day and a wage increase just as company officials were demanding a pay reduction. Although the coke operators broke the strike in early February with a pay raise, labor leaders who wanted more were anxious to have the agreement undone.

On February 9, ten thousand men walked out, and on February 27, a reign of terror struck the Coke Region. Immigrant workers rioted at Vanderbilt, near Frick's Adelaide coke works, located near his brother-in-law's farm, across the Youghiogheny River from the distillery at Broad Ford. One of the independent coke operators in the region, W. J. Rainey, hired Pinkertons to defend his Paull and Fort Hill plants, but Frick merely shut his plants down. He had stockpiled a three months' supply of coke in the Carnegie furnaces, and in waiting the strike out, he anticipated that civil authorities would handle the situation—particularly because he sensed that labor leaders were trying to extend the strike to other parts of the Coke Region.

By March 27, the strike momentum seemed to be dwindling, and a thousand men were back on the job. They signed an agreement with the H. C. Frick Coke Company accepting a new wage scale and recognizing the company's right to employ any person or persons it desired and no others, whether they were union or nonunion.

As March 1891 drew to a close with Easter Sunday, home life seemed peaceful by comparison. According to Annie's memoir, Annie had been coaxing Martha to eat and humoring her while teaching the children the story of Christ's crucifixion and resurrection. On March 29, after the children untied the satin bows of their Easter baskets, Frick asked Annie to dress Martha in her best dress for church. Childs put on his best suit, and when it was time to go, Frick gave Martha and Childs each a quarter. Noticing Annie's look, he asked if a quarter was enough. She said it was not because there was to be a special collection that day for the Children's Hospital, and she had more than that to give herself. Frick's eyes flashed a quick understanding. With a subtle smile on his lips, he took from his pocket a ten dollar bill which he placed in Martha's hand. Martha kissed her father good-bye and settled into the waiting carriage.

Annie thought Martha and Childs looked radiant as they walked up the aisle to the altar and gave the minister their donations for the needy children. Indeed Martha was radiant. When she returned from the altar, her face burst out in a smile and as Annie said later, "many heads were turned because she did look so beautiful." Martha turned to Annie, hugged her, and said, "Annie dear, this has been the nicest Sunday I ever had."

For Henry Clay Frick, however, the day would not radiate such joy. Indeed, it would go down as perhaps the worst Sunday he had ever experienced. Not because of Martha's health, but because the dividing line between civil authority and lawlessness in the West Overton Coke Region was again to be tested. Carnegie, using the lighthearted

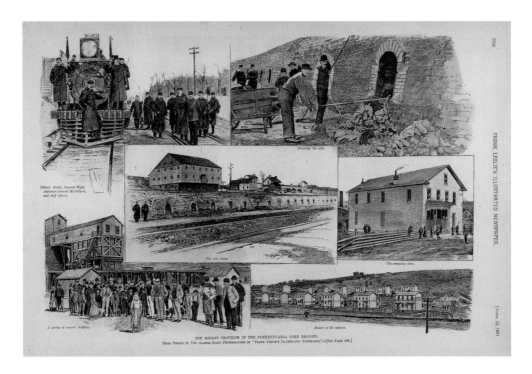

Fig. 3-3. Morewood Coke Works, H. C. Frick Coke Company.
Frank Leslie's Illustrated Weekly, April 25, 1891.
Historical Society of Western Pennsylvania

style he employed when granting press interviews, said from New York, "The iron
trade is as you know the jumping jack of business, the king or the pauper." But the situation was not so simplistic. Since February, in what the *Greensburg Record* called
"the storm center of the great conflict between capital and labor," neither the labor
leaders nor the independent coke operators were satisfied.

In a letter written in March 1891, Frick had complained to J. C. Morse, president
of Union Steel in Chicago: "I don't know when business seemed so utterly lifeless as at
present. No demand whatever for rails; no demand for billets. . . . it looks as if the time
had about arrived when we should post at the coke works the scale of wages we are
willing to pay, and make an effort at some of these works to start."

Nevertheless, Frick hoped that by the second week of April he would have all his
coke works operating. Apart from the fact that the Trotter coke plant, the stronghold
of the labor leaders, was up and running, the antiunion sentiment in the press and
public opinion seemed with him.

On Easter Sunday, March 29, 1891, however, as the Frick family celebrated Christ's
resurrection and the children were tucked in bed, the sun set, only to rise the next day
on the worst insurrection in the history of the H. C. Frick Coke Company. Easter Sunday had been quiet in the Coke Region, but on Monday the coke that had been left to

charge—to bake for the prescribed three days—would be ready to be drawn from the Morewood ovens. Morewood (fig. 3-3) was the largest and most sophisticated of the company's plants, the coal field acquired by Frick in 1877 when trading, acre for acre, the surface of his father's and three other farmers' pastureland for Morewood's coal rights. Because Frick feared the strikers would attack the Morewood men coming back on the job and keep them from pulling the coke, he asked the newly elected governor, Robert E. Pattison—a prolabor Democrat who had just recaptured his seat from the Republicans—to send the National Guard Police of Company E, Regiment 10, stationed in nearby Greensburg, to protect the works and assist his own Morewood deputies.

His request was denied. Frick, knowing the newly formed United Mine Workers of America, a coalition of two existing rival mine unions, had chosen the Connellsville area as the place to test its authority, therefore decided to protect his plant his own way. He organized the local police, together with sixty-five guards at the Morewood plant, and instructed the Morewood guards to shoot to kill only if their verbal order to halt failed to stop the strikers' advance. On Monday morning, March 30, a group of a thousand well-organized, angry, immigrant workers—who refused the new wage scale and who refused to allow others to work in their stead—rioted at Morewood. The

Fig. 3-4. Morewood Riots.
Harper's Illustrated Weekly, April 18, 1891.
Historical Society of Western Pennsylvania

rioters, who had crowded out the more peaceful Irish, Welsh, and German miners, were not naturalized American citizens, understood no English, and had to be instructed by impromptu sign language. At 2 A.M., fifteen hundred of these men attacked the Jimtown plant and bombed the West Leisenring works. Another thousand then marched on the Standard plant where they tore down telephone and telegraph wires to Morewood. They then divided themselves into four groups and in a well-planned, carefully thought out attack, the mostly intoxicated immigrants marched on Morewood. Armed with revolvers, stones, iron bars, and every other conceivable weapon, each division was headed by a brass band, playing sacred music. Each started its march from a different direction, down four different hills surrounding the coke works. As they met in the valley and turned on Morewood, they played the *Marseillaise,* burned their coking tools, demolished windows in the Morewood company store, tore up the railroad tracks in and around the plant, and wrecked the plant's high wooden fence. They jeered at the guards' halt order, fired three shots at the guards, and advanced to the sound of beating drums. The Morewood guards then opened fire, killing, according to the *Greensburg Daily Tribune,* seven men and wounding twenty-one others. Each of the dead was shot through the head or chest. Not one had a bullet hole in the back. At 9 A.M. the angry mob attacked again. Four more strikers were killed, and twenty-five more were wounded.

Overnight, Morewood, a plant with the most expensive mining system in the region, became the focal point of a 25,000-man strike in the bituminous coke fields (fig. 3-4). The plant was forced to close for a day, and on Tuesday, March 31, 1891, the *New York Times* reported a statement by Frick: "Heretofore he had not antagonized labor, but in the future he did not propose to sit idly by and see his property destroyed. He says the men are satisfied with the scale of wages he offered, but that labor leaders will not permit them to return to work as their positions depend upon the success of the strike." Determined to exhaust the resources of civil authority in both Westmoreland and Fayette counties, Frick warned the public, "The fight from this time will be bitter."

When work commenced at Morewood a day later, the conviction behind this statement was borne out. The fence around the works had been repaired and the guards armed with Winchester rifles. Thomas Lynch, general manager of the H. C. Frick Coke Company, described by the *Greensburg Daily Tribune* as "a stubby little Irishman [who] is as mild as a zephyr and as deliberate as death," said to the press: "The Frick Coke Company is not going out with guns and clubs to drive the strikers to work, and the Frick Coke Company will not permit the strikers to go out with guns and clubs and drive men who want to work away from our plants." He warned: "If these powers are not sufficient, the H. C. Frick Coke Company . . . will bring into the region uniformed men, armed and prepared for battle, and they will be ordered to shoot, and shoot to kill anyone who interferes with our men or our arrangements."

Fearing yet another attack on Morewood, Frick, whose deputies were deserting, wrote Governor Pattison: "It seems to me to be of the utmost importance that you should order the 18th Regiment forward immediately to Morewood," and warned that if he refused a second time "much damage will be done." The following day, Frick sent Carnegie his statement for release in Pittsburgh's morning papers:

> These ignorant people are simply the tools working out the plans and designs of others. . . . The public should not allow itself to be blinded to the real authors of the present trouble. The controversy is now not one between our company and its employees but is between the lawful authority of our Commonwealth and a mob of irresponsible men in the hands of cunning demagogues. This breach of the peace and violation of the law of our land is not the result of a sudden gush of uncontrollable passion, but is the result of a deep laid scheme, and well planned attempt, to over-ride the civil authority of our state.

He also noted that of the reported eleven killed and forty-six wounded "not a single employee of the Morewood coke works . . . is found among [them]."

Ten thousand strikers poured into the Mt. Pleasant–West Overton area the following day. As mob violence ruled the area, and as the residents in Frick's hometown became increasingly alarmed about their lives and property, Governor Pattison finally relented and sent in the militia. But Frick vowed he would never again sit idly by and see his property destroyed. In a front-page article in the *New York Times* on Friday, April 3, he stated:

> We placed our men and property in the hands of the lawful authorities for protection. . . . This is no quarrel about wages, but only whether our men working are to be shot down at midnight and our property destroyed by rioters. The authorities must settle this, and we will know whether mobs or law is the rule.

In the meantime, on April 4, as the 8th and 10th Regiments of the Pennsylvania National Guard settled in at Mt. Pleasant, the strikers began to bury their dead. A miserable rain that had turned the streets to mud now changed to snow. A five-car trainload of mourners arrived at the depot, and a cortege of six thousand subdued mourners marched past the H. C. Frick Coke Company offices on their way to the cemetery.

In anticipation of the evictions from company housing that traditionally followed strikes and riots, Frick asked Capt. R. J. Linden, of a cavalry unit known as the First City Troop of Philadelphia, to send four of his best men, who would operate under his personal instructions, to the Coke Region. Four days later, as saboteurs dynamited water tanks at the H. C. Frick Coke Company, Frick began planning the wholesale eviction of strikers from their homes in the company towns. Worried about increased violence, he again wrote Capt. Linden and this time requested he send fifty men to the nearby Leisenring No. 2 plant, where they would be sworn in as Coal and Iron Police.

He also warned Carnegie, who still opposed Frick's importing of other immigrant groups to replace the strikers, "We must keep at this persistently and patiently, and I am satisfied we will, before many days, get in pretty good shape." But still the strike wore on. Father M. A. Lambing of Scottdale, who was both a priest and a friend of Frick's, urged the men to return to work, while carloads of Blacks from Virginia arrived to replace those who would not do so. Frick advised Carnegie, "It will be some time before they will amount to much as miners and coke drawers, but they will learn, and their introduction will have a good effect on the old men, who certainly will not like to see their jobs taken by others." On April 20, Frick tightened the noose. He ordered one hundred Pinkertons to Leisenring No. 2 to safeguard, as Frick wrote Carnegie, "a large number of men willing to work if properly protected."

With his men in place, Frick's evictions from company housing began (fig. 3-5). On April 21 the *New York Times* noted the strikers' wives were "driven wild." They took axes to the police and shot deputies through the head; at Adelaide a pitched battle broke out when a "Hungarian" striker tried to shoot the sheriff, but accidentally killed his sweetheart who was, as the *Times* recounted on April 23, "fighting [the sheriff] with the ferocity of a young lioness."

By April 25, threats on Frick's life also became reality. The Pittsburgh police were informed that a carpenter named Timmons, from the nearby town of Braddock, saw twelve "Hungarians" working in a gully in Homewood, loading dynamite sticks. Each man had taken twenty dynamite sticks and departed for Braddock where they had made known their intention, as *The Dispatch* reported, to "blow up the bad man Frick." Frick did not take the threat seriously; in fact, the *Pittsburgh Leader* claimed that he looked upon it "as a huge joke," saying, "I am not afraid of being blown up . . . I laughed quite heartily . . . and shall not lose any sleep on account of what Mr. Timmons says."

Nevertheless, Frick was losing sleep—for a different reason. Once forced, as he had said in 1887, "to prostitute" the coke company, Frick was now accused of divided loyalties, managing the strike for the benefit of the coke company, not the steel mills. Although the output of coke from the H. C. Frick Coke Company had been severely compromised by the strike and rioting, J. C. Morse, among others, was demanding more coke for his steel mills. In an attempt to placate Morse and elicit his patience and understanding, Frick wrote that he was "putting the matter fully and fairly" before him, "in justice" to him. Recognizing he was "suffering for coke," he explained there

Fig. 3-5. Eviction of strikers and their families from company housing during the
Morewood riots drove women to violence and caused much distress.
The New York Society Library

had been "no disposition on my part to take care of [H. C. Frick Coke Company] interests" first. He explained: "We are not sparing any effort or expense to win this strike,
and win it soon. Of course we must look for some black eyes before we finally succeed,
but after we do win it . . . we will not have much trouble for a long time to come."

By the end of May, Frick won the fifteen-week strike and immediately withdrew
seventy-five of the one hundred Pinkertons from the Coke Region. But as he continued evicting strikers from company housing, more than "some black eyes" awaited
him. Frick, perhaps for the first time in his life, would not have the last laugh.

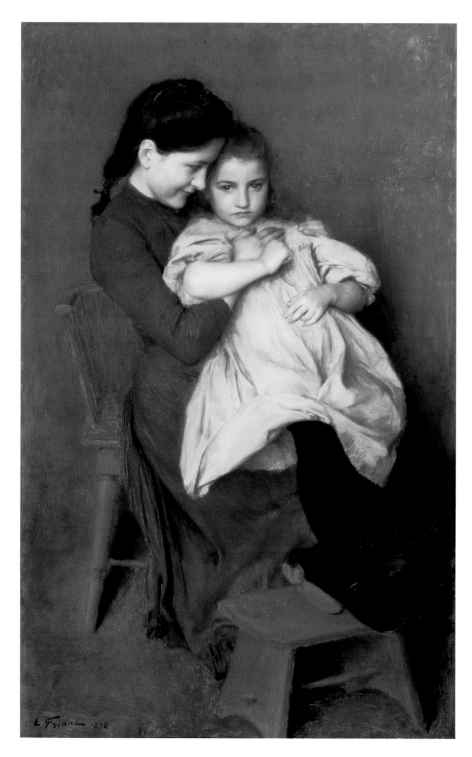

Fig. 3-6. Emile Friant (1863–1932), *Chagrin d'Enfant*, 1897.
Acquired in 1899, Oil on panel, 17¼ x 27¼ in. (43.8 x 69.2 cm).
Frick Art and Historical Society

MARTHA'S HEALTH was now noticeably worse. When in New York prior to the Morewood riots, Frick had taken her and Childs on a rare shopping spree. He had purchased a bicycle for Childs, a tricycle for Martha, and a doll for Helen. When the presents arrived at their rented Shadyside home, Childs started to ride his bike but Martha asked to walk. When Annie spoke to Adelaide about Martha's reluctance to ride the tricycle, Adelaide said Martha just needed to get used to it and would probably enjoy riding it more as time went on. But by late June 1891, Martha asked Annie not to bring the tricycle out from the cellar anymore.

The Doctors McClelland called every day to see the children, but generally did no more than examine Martha and give the women something to rub on Helen's gums, as she was teething. Annie noticed, however, that Martha had begun to cling to her and seemed fearful of letting her out of her sight. Most of the time Martha preferred to have Annie play with her by tossing a large rubber ball or, since Martha had outgrown her afternoon nap, Annie would sit with her on the front porch in the shade and play a game of jacks. Often Martha would say, "Annie, dear, tell me a story." She would sit on a little chair beside Annie, but soon would ask to sit in Annie's lap saying, "Put your arms around me. Please hold me Annie dear."

Frick, who like the entire family was devoted to Annie, undoubtedly was deeply touched by these scenes. Indeed, he may not have recognized their import at the time, but certainly they were remembered in 1899 when he acquired *Chagrin d'Enfant* (fig. 3-6), a painting by the contemporary French realist Emile Friant depicting a teenager holding a young, deeply troubled girl in her lap. As can be seen in the juxtaposition of *Chagrin d'Enfant* with a photograph of Annie holding her own child (fig. 3-7), the young girl in the Friant painting closely resembles Annie Blumenschine, and the child, though slightly older and larger than Martha at this time, resembles Martha with her distended abdomen and long auburn hair.

At that time in 1891, however, as Annie held Martha, Frick obviously had no idea how grave his daughter's situation was. One day, the mind-over-matter Frick asked Annie to dress Martha in her very best dress because he wanted to walk with her to his lawyer Philander Knox's house. Frick beamed when he saw Martha, with her red curls neatly in place. Annie agreed that Martha "looked just like a beautiful doll." No sooner had he begun his walk, however, than he returned to

Fig. 3-7. Annie Blumenschine Stephany holding her son Clayton.
Author's collection

Clayton and asked for Annie. Disturbed by the loose stocking on Martha's right leg, he asked Annie to smooth the stocking and tighten her garter. Although Annie explained that Martha had asked her to loosen the supporter more and more each day because it was too tight, she did as Frick asked. But as Martha walked away down the sidewalk, Annie noticed she was limping slightly.

When father and daughter returned, Frick seemed worried. He had noticed the limp and asked Adelaide to be sure to have the doctor look at Martha in the morning. That night, as Annie put the child to bed, she looked at the side where the scar was. When Martha quickly put her hand over it, Annie asked her if it hurt. Martha replied it did not, but refused to let Annie touch her side.

When the Doctors McClelland came the next morning, they proclaimed that Martha had "a little gas on her stomach" and gave her small doses of their homeopathic remedies. But Annie knew that the medicine was ineffective. Martha pleaded to have the supporter on the right side loosened and constantly put her hand over the scar as if to protect it. Although Annie asked Martha again to please tell her if her side was hurting, Martha continued to reply it did not. Annie noticed, however, that Martha's limp was getting worse and she seemed to tire more easily than ever.

As June warmth began to turn into July heat, the final stages of Martha's long, slow death from peritonitis and septicemia began. Bacteria had claimed Martha's abdominal cavity and bloodstream. Her vital organs, starved for nutrients and oxygen, were now on the verge of collapsing, one after the other, like dominos.

One evening in early July, Annie, Childs, and Martha went to the rear lawn to play ball after supper, whereupon Martha began to cry and complained to her father that Annie would not play ball with her and did not love her anymore. Frick asked Childs and Annie if they had played fair and when they said they had, Frick carried Martha to the living room couch. With Martha still crying and insisting Annie did not love her anymore, Frick teased, "Annie, do you think it would help if I had her red curls cut off?"

Aghast, Annie replied, "Oh, please don't cut off her beautiful red curls. I know my darling will stop crying for me if you will just please leave us alone."

Frick returned to the dinner table and Annie put her arms around Martha, telling her over and over how much she loved her. She kissed Martha and hugged her. When her crying stopped and the tears were dried, certain Martha was all right, Frick and Adelaide came in and kissed her.

But Martha was not all right. Annie took her upstairs, put her into a bed which had been placed next to her parents' because she had been so sick, tucked her in for the night, told her a bedtime story, heard her prayers, and promised to love her always. But at about midnight, Martha called out to her mother saying she was sick to her stomach and had a pain in her right side. From then on until morning Adelaide and

Frick took turns attending their daughter. In the morning they called for Annie because Martha was crying for her. Annie dressed as quickly as possible and found Martha "very ill indeed." She also found that Adelaide, who was worn out from lack of sleep, had retired to the front room to rest. Frick, although dressed for work, delayed his usual 7 or 8 A.M. appearance at the office, called the Doctors McClelland, and waited for one of them to arrive.

The one who came was not alarmed and put everyone's fears to rest. He said the pain was caused by vomiting because Martha had eaten something at lunch that did not agree with her. Although others in the family had eaten the same food as Martha and no one else in the house had been sick, the doctor insisted bad food was the problem. He left some pills for the child and promised to return in the afternoon to see how she was doing.

Fig. 3-8. Martha with eyebrows and hair pencilled in.
Frick Archives

When the doctor returned, Martha was worse and had developed a fever. She was still complaining about "the dear pain" in her side. By evening, on the third visit that day, both Doctors McClelland came and the two seemed more puzzled than ever. They continued to claim Martha just had an upset stomach which they called acute indigestion.

Within days Martha became too ill to be left alone at any time, day or night (fig. 3-8). Adelaide, weakened from two and a half months in bed because, at the moment of the Morewood riot, she began suffering with neuralgia of the head, pain along the nerves that now involved her ears, nevertheless stayed with Martha while Childs and Annie took their meals. When Frick arrived home in the evening, he would relieve her.

Martha's situation was now out of control. Her kidneys had obviously begun to fail, for she was unable to retain any food or liquids, not even pills or water. As a result, the bedding had to be changed constantly, and to keep the nurse from hurting her, Annie would have to put her arms around the child. Worse, the day nurse, who had been taught "the art" of making a bed, first rolled Martha to one side, then rolled the old sheets up against her back, placed the new sheets on the bed, rolled the loose portion next to the old, rolled Martha back over the pile of linen sheets, rubber sheets, and draw sheets, and then snapped the fresh sheets taut and smooth beneath her. Thankfully, that evening, as the day nurse collected her pay, she announced she would not return. Relieved to have this nurse gone, Annie soon realized the new nurse was more heartless than the last.

Another doctor, Frick's personal physician and neighbor, Lawrence Litchfield, examined Martha. He advised Frick to get a hospital nurse, as Martha was in very serious condition and required special care. When this woman arrived, Adelaide briefed her about Martha's illness and gave her instructions as to what the doctors had ordered. But when Martha saw the nurse, she screamed and refused to allow the woman to touch her. To Annie's horror, the nurse then demanded that Adelaide and Annie leave the room so she could manage the child in her own way. In a short time, they heard Martha screaming, "Go away! Go away!" and then, more desperately, "I want my Mamma dear. I want my Annie dear."

The new nurse had warned that if Annie entered the room, she would leave. To keep the peace, Adelaide asked Annie to return home. Because they planned to take Martha to the Mountain House at Cresson Springs, hoping to restore her health with the medicinal spring water and cool, clean air of the Allegheny Mountains, Adelaide dispatched Annie with the request she obtain permission to come with them. As soon as Annie's mother saw her, she asked her daughter if she had been ill. Thin and pale, Annie confessed she had not been able to eat or sleep because of Martha's illness. She begged her mother to allow her to go to Cresson and permission was granted. Adelaide was greatly relieved because Martha had cried for her the whole time she was gone. But the nurse was not so happy to see Annie. When her shift was over, she announced that she would not come back because, in her opinion, Martha was just spoiled. She took her pay and, as Annie said, "left in a huff."

So Adelaide, Annie, and Frick became Martha's nurses. A routine was established. Adelaide took charge of Martha the first part of the night. Frick stayed in the room until about two or three in the morning when Annie would be sent in because Martha would invariably be calling for her.

Martha was thinner than ever, the last of her beautiful red curls were falling out from her high fever, and she was too weak to raise her head. Whenever she was lifted, no matter how gently, Martha, no longer stoic, would cry constantly of the "dear pain" in her side. Additionally, because the summer heat was terrific, they had to fan her continuously. The filthy air, heavy with the smoke of the steel mills, draped over them like a pall. Some days the fog hung so fiercely over the river valleys that the smoke from the steel mills could not rise farther than the tops of the houses, its thickness permeating everything. The dirt and grime settled indiscriminately on hair, skin, and furniture alike.

When Frick slept on a couch in the den, Annie stayed close beside Martha, holding her hand because she was so restless. Annie bathed her hot forehead and whispered some comforting words to ease her pain. But every time Annie let go of Martha's hand, she would whisper, "Don't leave me, Annie dear. Don't leave me." One evening, however, Annie felt faint and made her way to the couch to lie down. There was a dim light in the room and she could see Martha's "little white face" as she rested there. Annie later said she must have had a dream because Adelaide's maid, whose room was right across from Martha's, heard Annie crying. When she awakened, Annie explained she had seen "[her] little darling in a white casket and . . . the angels carrying her to Heaven." Annie insisted that what she had seen was true, that Martha had died; no one could convince her otherwise. Attie brought her a glass of Adelaide's wine and asked her not to mention anything about her vision to Adelaide or Frick as "they would feel very bad."

In the meantime, one of the Drs. McClelland encouraged Frick to take Martha to Cresson Springs as soon as possible. On Tuesday, June 30, at ten minutes past four in the afternoon, he telegraphed the Mountain House: "Can you give me four good rooms for the month of July, to arrive tomorrow night?" That same day, he also wired Andrew Carnegie in London: "Mrs. Frick does not improve very rapidly, and we have had a very sick little girl for two weeks past." Hoping against hope, he said, "We think she is better, however, now and hope to be able to move her to Cresson some day this week."

Hopes were high. The Mountain House, fifty miles from Pittsburgh and a few miles north of the still devastated town of Johnstown and the abandoned South Fork Fishing and Hunting Club, was high enough in the Allegheny Mountains to offer relief from Pittsburgh's heat (fig. 3-9). The fashionable resort, advertised as being "the place of restoration for all forms of human suffering," also was close enough to be a safe journey for Martha. Instructions were sent to the Mountain House to make the Carnegie Cottage ready for the Frick family. They were coming with a sick child, her pet dog Brownie, Helen, Childs, Attie, a maid, a new nurse, Annie, a butler, Dr. James McClelland, and George Megrew, Frick's personal manservant, needed at Cresson

Fig. 3-9. The Mountain House at Cresson Springs.
The Library Company of Philadelphia, Pa.

because long-distance phone calls and telegrams inquiring about Martha's health had to be received and answered.

Frick then ordered a private car to be attached to the rear of the next train headed from Pittsburgh to Cresson. Not trusting anyone but himself to handle Martha, he carried her to the carriage and onto the waiting train.

And so Frick, then the most powerful man in Pittsburgh, certainly at the peak of his financial career, was faced with having to take his still incapacitated wife and his dying child from their rented home in Shadyside eastward to Johnstown. As though having to reenter an old wound, Frick would have to take his entire family up through the Conemaugh Gorge where the formal search for bodies from the 1889 flood still continued. He would have to take Martha across the stone bridge into Johnstown, the town only two years into its reconstruction, the city still described by Cyrus Elder, chief counsel for the Cambria Iron Company and the only Johnstown member of the South Fork Fishing and Hunting Club, as a place "of unspeakable griefs and dreadful memories."

Though Frick's reaction to this ride through the Valley of Death is not known, Annie did record in her memoir that the trip from Pittsburgh to Cresson proved a great strain on Martha. When she arrived at the Carnegie Cottage she was very much fatigued and still would not allow a nurse to touch her. Frick placed her on her bed, but she was so weak she scarcely moved and seemed unconscious most of the time. Dr. James McClelland tried to reassure everyone by saying she would be all right after resting, but later, when she awoke, she called for her "Papa dear" and asked him not to leave her. When Frick went to the Mountain House to register, Martha called for "Mama dear," and when the nurse returned with pills, the child screamed so loudly that Adelaide asked Annie to give them to her.

From then on, Annie herself tended Martha. Although the nurse and Annie were assigned a room with a double bed, Annie rarely slept there. Most of the time, she napped in a chair or lay down on the couch in Martha's room without so much as undressing. Meals were haphazard as well.

Weekdays were hardest on Annie. Frick had to be in Pittsburgh for business reasons and he would hardly be gone before Martha would ask, "Is this the day my Papa dear is coming?"

The strain was hard on Frick too. On Monday, July 20, 1891, Frick wrote Martha:

My sweetest little Daughter,

    How sorry I was to leave you yesterday evening and how happy I would be if I had the time to stay with you and take you out driving everyday.

    You must be patient little girl and eat what your Mamma says is good for you, and you will soon get well and strong. And how happy we will all be when you can run and play as you did a few weeks ago. I was so pleased to hear from George that you slept well last night.

    Many kisses and much love

Papa

Torn between the pressure of his business life and caring for his family, Frick brought Martha a present, a book or a toy, each time he returned to Cresson. Although Martha was now too sick to be interested in gifts, she did respond to a question her father asked her as he was leaving for Pittsburgh. He had asked her to tell him what she wanted most so he could buy it for her. She replied that what she wanted most of all was "a doll for her Annie dear." Annie tried to change her mind, but Martha insisted her "Papa dear" buy the doll.

Indeed, Frick did as Martha asked and bought her a doll. Knowing it was for Annie, he bought one with Annie's same blue eyes and brown hair. When the package arrived the next day, it was addressed to Martha. Annie opened it on Martha's bed and, with Martha insisting the doll was for her, she "accepted it with her love," and named the doll "Rosebud."

Fig. 3-10. Pierre-Auguste Renoir (1841–1919), *Mother and Children*, 1874–76.
Acquired in 1914, Oil on canvas, 67 x 42⅝ in. (170.2 x 108.3 cm).
The Frick Collection

Fig. 3-11. Martha and the girl holding a doll in Renoir's
Mother and Children clasp their hands similarly.
Author's collection

One must wonder whether Frick was recalling his last gift to Martha when twenty-three years later he acquired Pierre-Auguste Renoir's *Mother and Children* (fig. 3-10)—a painting that was originally entitled *Governess and Children*. The painting depicts a young woman walking in a park with two strawberry-haired girls, the oldest of whom is the same age as Martha was in 1891, a child whose hands clasp a doll in the same way Martha once held her favorite ball (fig. 3-11), a child whose doll resembles the mother-governess in the painting.

Martha had been begging to be taken outside. Although the next door cottage was empty and the lawn outside would be quiet, the doctor felt she was too sick to be moved. But when Frick returned to Cresson, he asked the doctor to please let him take her out, "to satisfy her longing." The doctor relented, saying if she were put in a baby carriage very carefully, Martha could go out for about half an hour.

So Frick brought the baby carriage to her bedroom, lifted Martha from her bed, and placed her in the carriage. Then, with Childs and Annie at the front of the carriage and Frick at the rear, they carried it onto the lawn. Martha's dog, Brownie, was so delighted to see his playmate coming out the door, he began barking, and, as Annie wrote, Martha was "so pleased."

After placing the carriage under a shady tree on the vacant lot next door, Frick heard an organ-grinder playing in the distance. He asked Childs to bring the man over so Martha could request a tune. At the time, Frick was sitting on the porch of the vacant house, Annie was beside the carriage, holding Martha's hand, and Childs was restraining Brownie, hoping to keep him from biting the organ-grinder. As the man started to play, to every one's surprise, the tune was Martha's favorite, "Little Annie Rooney Is My Sweetheart." Childs and Martha believed the tune had been written just for their Annie because she was so petite. They liked to call her "Little Annie Rooney."

As Martha smiled at her, with what Annie described as "an angelic look that was heartbreaking," the scene was too much for Frick. According to Annie, he went to the side of the cottage so no one, most particularly Martha, would see him cry.

As the organ-grinder continued to play, he started to switch tunes. Martha called, "Stop, not that," for she wanted him to play her favorite song over again. After a while Frick returned and gave Childs a ten dollar bill to give the organ man, a gift Annie said he accepted "with surprise and bows of thanks." He seemed so pleased that on leaving he played "Little Annie Rooney" until he was out of sight and hearing.

Martha, tired now, asked Childs to kiss her and then told Childs she wanted to kiss her "Annie dear." Frick heard all of this and was deeply touched when Martha, in a weak voice, then asked, "I want my Papa dear to kiss me and take me home." They had taken Martha on her final outing.

Later in the week, Otis Childs, Adelaide's cousin and like Frick a partner in the Carnegie Steel Company, came to visit. He arrived from Pittsburgh with Frick and because he was a favorite of Martha's, all hoped his presence would cheer her up. But Otis was ill prepared for what he saw. Martha, whose emaciated body told him she was dying of starvation and dehydration, was only a shadow of her former self. The beautiful child he had known so well had vanished. Her lovely curls were gone; her face and hands were thin and pale. It was all he could do to control his emotions. Tentatively he asked her, "Do you know who this is, Dear?"

Martha looked at him and answered, "My Cousin Otith." Although this seemed to please him, he went to the hall crying, overcome with grief.

Everyone knew the worst was happening, but no one could face the truth. Although Helen's room was across the hall from Martha and Adelaide, her nurse, Nanna, had been instructed to keep the three-year-old child away from the house so that Martha could have quiet. But at dinner time, Annie brought Helen in to see her "dear Tissie," as she called Martha, because she could not pronounce "sister."

When Annie took Helen to Martha, Helen would pat Martha's hand and kiss it saying, "My Tissie sick, my dear Tissie sick." Martha, pleased to see Helen, kept saying to her, "My baby dear, my baby dear," as she smiled weakly until exhausted, and fell asleep.

Annie felt that Martha seemed to know she was about to die. She would ask for one member of the family after the other to come in and see her. She kept asking for her "Baby dear," and begged for Childs, who was, as Annie described, "so pleased." But Martha, suffering constant pain, was too feeble to talk. When Adelaide, her sister, and Frick came to her, they, too, left the room brokenhearted.

On July 20, at 12:10 P.M., Frick, who was back in Pittsburgh, responded to a concerned telegram from his wife. She must have been pressing him to send Carnegie's doctor, Jasper Garmany, chief assistant to Dr. Fred S. Dennis, a prominent surgeon and director of the new Carnegie Laboratory at Bellevue Hospital in New York, to examine Martha. Bellevue had the distinction of being the first institution of its kind in the United States for teaching and researching bacteriology and pathology as they related to surgical wounds. Although abdominal surgery had always been an option, its high mortality rate had led Frick to believe that homeopathy was the best treatment for his daughter. Homeopathy, however, was a subject of varying medical opinion. Referred to by Arpad G. Gerster, M.D., in the first American textbook on asepsis, *The Rules of Aseptic and Antiseptic Surgery* (1890), it was noted as "a subject of hot controversy to this day."

Frick, at a loss and now believing the surgeons should visit Martha, wired his wife saying he had also received Dr. McClelland's telegram, that "no doubt everything possible is being done for Martha, but it will do no harm to have Dr. Garmany from New York out. Just have telegram from him. Will reach New York in morning. Will arrange to have him out. Will not be up until I can reach him there."

The next day, July 21, at 12:03 P.M., Adelaide wired Frick back: "Had a restless night. She is very weak this morning and refuses to eat." Adelaide was obviously upset and continued to press for both her husband's return and the New York doctor's visit. Two hours later, he told her that he and one of the Drs. McClelland would be on the four-thirty train and that Dr. Garmany was taking the eight o'clock train that night for Cresson. Then, after a quick trip to Cresson, Frick returned to Pittsburgh. He wrote from the Duquesne Club what turned out to be his last letter to Martha. Addressed to Miss Martha H. Frick, Cresson, Pa., c/o the Carnegie Cottage, it read:

> *My Dear Sweet Little Daughter,*
> *I just have a telegram from Mama saying you will not eat anything.*
> *Won't you try hard to eat something to please me, or to drink milk.*
> *If you do so you will soon get strong. Try to do so to please*
> *Papa*

As Annie notes in her 1945 memoir, when Frick returned to Cresson on July 28, he felt hopeful. Dr. Garmany had arrived with another surgeon, both of whom had not only performed abdominal surgery, but had also studied the principles and techniques of antisepsis with Dr. Dennis. Five years before, Garmany and Dennis had seen Carnegie through a near life-threatening bout of typhoid fever at Cresson. As Annie described Garmany, he was "one of the highest priced specialists in New York," and she wrote that he was going to charge Frick "five or ten thousand dollars to come and perform an operation on Martha in the morning" which he believed would save the child's life.

When the surgeons arrived, Martha took one look at the strange men and began to scream. The doctors and Frick left the room and went into the nurse's room next door to look at her charts. When they left, Martha cried, "Annie dear, hold my hand."

Shortly, the surgeons came back in. They examined Martha's side which was by now very much distended and more painful than ever. The doctors were careful throughout their examination, but Martha howled from pain the whole time and was completely exhausted when they were finished.

Annie stayed with Martha and comforted her while the doctors and Frick went into the sitting room for a consultation. When it was over, Frick beckoned to Annie to come into the hall where the doctors and the nurse had gathered. They explained that an abdominal inflammation was causing Martha's intense pain and that it was evident a pus pocket had formed. Because of Martha's critical condition, and her now very weak heart, it was doubtful she would be able to survive an operation. The doctors could offer very little hope, but if Annie could persuade Martha to swallow their pills, they would operate early in the morning in the hope of saving her life.

They gave Annie two pills, one for Martha and the other for her to take as a way to coax Martha into swallowing hers. They promised Annie the pill would do her no harm, placed them in her hand, and then asked her to repeat everything they had said.

Annie took the pills in to Martha and showed them to her, saying as she put one in Martha's mouth and one in her own mouth, "One pill is for you, Darling, and I am taking one too."

In a minute or two, Annie exclaimed, "My that tasted good; I wish I had another one. The doctor has promised to give us another one later."

But Martha, her strength spent, would not be coaxed. She put her hand to her mouth and took the remainder of her pill in her fingers and said, "Here Annie, dear, you can have mine."

The surgeons and Frick were on the other side of the hall door which was ajar. On hearing that Martha would not take the pill from Annie, Frick gave a grief-stricken cry. Annie went to the hall to tell them how sorry she was, but they knew she had done her best. Frick then walked the doctors over to the Mountain House. He returned to find Adelaide in what Annie described as a "highly nervous state." Attie was doing her best to console Adelaide, but she was as disconsolate as her sister.

Annie picked up Helen, who had been left alone in the bedroom with the crying women and brought her in to see her "Tissie." Helen kept complaining, "My Tissie sick, my Tissie sick" and frightened by the sight, pleaded with Annie, "Wannie, please make my Tissie's pain go away."

That night, July 28, Frick remained with Martha while Annie went to the hotel for dinner. When dinner was over, Adelaide, Attie, Frick, and Annie took turns staying with Martha. By ten o'clock Annie said she was about ready to faint as she had been up since five o'clock in the morning, so Frick made everyone go to bed. He explained his intention to stay up all night with his sick child and give everyone else a rest.

Annie climbed the carved oak stairs to the assigned bedroom in which she had yet to sleep. Childs greeted Annie in the upstairs hall and asked if she thought Martha was going to die. Annie took him by the hand and together they knelt and prayed for God to save the child they both loved.

At three o'clock in the morning, the maid came to Annie's room and woke her from a much-needed sleep to tell her Martha was calling for her. Annie went down the steps so fast, she later wondered why she didn't fall. Frick was in the downstairs hall waiting for her, and after apologizing, he said Martha was calling for her so continually he feared she was getting worse.

Just then Annie heard Martha's weakened voice calling, "I want my Annie dear." Annie went to the left side of her bed, but Martha kept begging, "Come close, I want you in my bed beside me."

Annie lay on the bed beside her, trying not to touch her body. But Martha whispered again, "Hold my hand, Annie dear."

Annie said, "I am holding your hand, Dearie," but Martha answered, "I want you to hold my other hand too, and come closer."

So Annie took both Martha's hands and soon Martha became quiet. Frick, who had been in the doorway watching, was thankful Martha was now resting, and so went to his room to get some sleep.

By seven the next morning, everyone in the house was awake and knew for certain that Martha did not have much longer to live. Childs and Annie went to the Mountain House for breakfast at about eight o'clock, and when they returned, although Martha was calling for Annie, her voice sounded different.

Annie knew immediately that something was very wrong, a suspicion that was verified when the nurse, who was meant to stay with Martha, rushed out of her own room and left for breakfast at the Mountain House the moment Annie appeared. Later Annie realized the nurse must have known what had happened to Martha while she and Childs were at breakfast and had deliberately stayed in her room. Stepping into Martha's room, Annie noticed a peculiar odor. She went to the right side of

Martha's bed, and as she unfolded the sheets, she saw Martha's old scar had ruptured, and foul-smelling pus that measured a half-a-cup was draining from Martha's side. Trembling, hardly able to breathe, Annie ran across the hall and called for Frick to come quickly.

Frick came at once and shook all over when he saw what had happened. He looked at Annie, saying over and over again, "Annie, what shall I do? What shall I do?"

Annie ran to the Mountain House for the doctors who were sitting together in the dining room. They saw immediately from the expression on her face that something had happened.

When they saw Martha, they said that it was too late now to operate, that Martha would not be able to stand the shock. After the doctors and nurse were finished attending her wound, Martha cried again for Annie to hold her. Embracing the child, Annie prayed, bargaining with God to take her life, not the child's, as Martha had everything in the world to live for.

Patting and comforting Martha, Annie put her arms around her as tenderly as she could. Martha, sweet and patient, kept pleading, begging Annie over and over again, "Don't leave me Annie, dear. Don't leave me Annie, dear." She also asked for her "Mama, dear" and then for her "Papa dear."

About three hours later, at noon, with her mouth puckered as if for a kiss, Martha said, "Kiss me, Annie dear." Martha's breathing was so labored, Annie did not want to take her breath away and so kissed her on the forehead. Martha, surprised, said, "Annie, dear, don't you love me anymore?" Annie replied, "Oh, my darling, of course I love you and I will always love you as long as I live." Martha gave her an angelic smile and looked pleased.

Annie went to the hall door and called Frick. He was with Adelaide, who had become hysterical with grief. When he entered the room, Martha recognized him but was too weak to speak. Annie said to Frick, "I think she wants you to kiss her." As he did, Martha gave him a smile, turned her eyes to Annie and said, with pauses between her words, "Annie dear, take—that—away."

Annie had tucked a linen napkin under Martha's chin because so much water or saliva was coming from her mouth.

Frick gave his dying daughter his hand to bite as a way to alleviate her pain, but her last words had been spoken. In just one more breath, Martha passed away.

❖

THAT SUMMER OF 1891, as Henry Clay Frick alternated between the Mountain House and Pittsburgh, he had succeeded in quelling the riots at Morewood and ruthlessly evicting the striking families from his company houses. His chilling treatment of working-class families would never seem to bother him, but at forty-two years of age, he had nonetheless been scarred as he helplessly watched his daughter die. The scar would be invisible to the outer world, but the nightmare, like Martha's teeth marks on his hand, would be carried to his own deathbed in 1919.

In the meantime, the saddened Mountain House community came to the cottage to pay their respects and, as far as a summer resort could be, the Mountain House became a place of mourning. Tennis players stopped their games, the usual afternoon baseball match was canceled, and a perceptible hush fell over everything.

The next morning, Robert Pitcairn's private Pullman car was attached to a special locomotive. Adelaide, Attie, Annie, and Frick, leaving Childs and Helen behind in Cresson, took Martha's body back to Shadyside for burial. Following the exact path the Wave of Death had taken the day of the Johnstown Flood, and traveling at about the same speed, the special engine pulled the car down through the towns of Mineral Point, East Conemaugh, and Franklin. It pulled them over the bare rock which had once been and would never be again Woodvale, the town filled with the women and children who worked in the textile mills. Following the tracks as they curved through Johnstown, beneath the high ridge overlooking the site where most of the almost seven hundred unidentified flood victims were buried in the New Grandview Cemetery, the train continued out of the valley, across the infamous stone bridge.

That same day, Frick, who was a trustee of the Homewood Cemetery, paid $10,185 for a 240-square-foot burial lot on top of a barren hill in the cemetery's section 14. The newly opened section, designed primarily for private mausoleums and large monuments, has the highest vantage point in the cemetery and is located only a block from Clayton. At the time, the new section had only seven graves, most of which were children's. After Frick trimmed the trees between the lot and Clayton, a tenth of a mile away in the valley below, there was an unobstructed view of Martha's grave when the family eventually returned to their home.

Saturday, August 1, 1891, the day of Martha's funeral, Annie recalled everyone was up at daybreak, doing their best to ease the heartache felt by the dead child's parents. Adelaide was being as brave as she could be. Frick was trying to be calm, making every effort to comfort and console his wife.

Telegrams and messages were sent and delivered. Flower arrangements bearing messages of sympathy and condolence arrived. By four in the afternoon, the time of the service, the small rented home on Shadyside was packed with friends and relatives.

Martha's body was dressed in white and placed in a white, embossed velvet coffin, advertised as a Jewel Box because it helped beautify the death scene, and like a lady's "jewel casket," it held all that was precious. The coffin was trimmed in solid silver and bore a silver nameplate.

When the funeral service began, Annie stayed in the bedroom with Martha's coffin. George Megrew ushered in the close relatives and friends and seated them throughout the house while Adelaide, her sister, and Frick, who apparently wanted complete privacy, stayed in an upstairs bedroom.

After the funeral, the sad task of reorganizing their lives without this much loved daughter began. As if wanting nothing further to do with Paris, or with any reminder of where Martha had swallowed the pin, Adelaide asked her husband to place the two gold bracelets made for the Paris Exposition and given to her as an engagement present in his safe deposit box, where they remained until after Frick's death in 1919. Martha's toys were placed in a newly purchased trunk and packed away until the family returned to Clayton and the toys could be put in what became known as "Martha's Closet" at the top of Clayton's attic stairs.

At the same time, Frick received an invitation from E. M. Ferguson, his close Pittsburgh friend and first business partner in the H. C. Frick Coke Company, to bring his wife and children to Fishers Island, an island resort off the Connecticut coast. E. M. Ferguson and his brother Walton, both of whom had frequented the South Fork Club, bought the island in 1889, just after the Johnstown Flood, largely with the profits from their investment in Frick's coke company.

Frick, unable to move back into Clayton because the renovations were not complete, and sensing that Pittsburgh's heat, combined with the sad memories of Shadyside, were more than he and his family could bear, decided to accept Ferguson's invitation. He had a private railroad car attached to the rear of the Pullman train headed for New York and arranged an unscheduled stop at the Cresson Springs station to collect Childs, Helen, Brownie, the trunks, and the remaining staff from the Carnegie Cottage.

As the train approached the station at Cresson, Adelaide and Attie, anxious to see Helen and Childs, pressed their heads against the train window. When the train stopped, Frick, the brakeman, and the conductor were off the train quickly. In responses that almost seem to presage the course each child's life would take, Frick rushed straight to Helen, picked her up in his arms, held her close, and kissed her over and over again as he carried her to the train. While Childs and Helen's nurse followed behind, and Brownie was put in a dog box in the baggage car, Frick placed Helen in her mother's lap. Adelaide's arms wrapped around Helen, and as she kissed her only remaining daughter again and again, Frick looked on with tears in his eyes.

When Childs came on the train, however, he was greeted with what bordered on coldness and indifference. As Annie recalled, he kissed and greeted his parents in a formal manner, but it was to Helen that all eyes had turned. As Childs sat down next to Annie, Helen suddenly twisted around. She looked at everyone with a puzzled expression. No one dared breathe as they knew what was coming. Then Helen called out, "Where is my Tissie?" Receiving no response, with her voice firmer than before, Helen insisted, "I want my Tissie." She then turned to Annie, on whom all eyes were fixed, and demanded, "Wannie where is my Tissie? I want my Tissie."

Annie had braced herself for the inevitable question and replied calmly, "Darling, I can't get your dear sister as she has gone to heaven."

Helen, having no conception of what death and heaven meant, looked at Annie and ordered her in an imperious voice, "Wannie, you go to Heaven and get my Tissie for me. I want my Tissie right away."

This was too much, and the entire family broke down in tears. Helen, sensing she had done some inexplicable harm, began saying over and over, "Don't cry, Mama, don't cry, Papa."

Although Helen's questions were painful to Adelaide and Frick, Childs's reaction was equally upsetting. His eight-year-old mind *could* understand the finality of death. He asked Annie all about Martha, how she looked and what her casket was like. Annie, quite sensibly, answered the questions honestly, telling Childs that his father had taken her into Martha's room after the undertaker had placed Martha in her coffin, and that his sister had looked like "a little angel asleep in a white satin-lined casket."

After listening to the details of Annie's and his parents' sad return to Shadyside, Childs sat at the window and watched the scenery go by, and Helen fell asleep. Later, after Helen had awakened, the family was served dinner in their private coach by the Pullman chefs. The waiter came in, pulled down the table, and placed a wine glass at every place except the children's. Frick poured the wine and said to Annie, who drank wine only for medicinal purposes, "Annie, I want you to drink that wine and also eat your dinner, as you are in need of it and I have paid for it." When Annie refused the wine, Frick explained it was champagne, and Adelaide, who often drank to console herself, nodded to Annie to do as her husband asked.

As it turned out, neither wine nor the trip to Fishers Island offered much solace. True, the outside world had hardly heard of Fishers Island, so the grieving family continued to have privacy. But their first day there was Wednesday, August 5, 1891, which would have been Martha's sixth birthday. Although they were all trying their best to console each other, as Annie later wrote, "the heartache still remained." Adelaide and Attie locked themselves away in their darkened bedrooms and cried compulsively; Annie brought them tea and cocoa and held them as they cried. She revealed in her

Fig. 3-12. The Haystock Cottage, Fishers Island, where the Frick family stayed.
The Henry L. Ferguson Museum, Fishers Island, New York

memoir that "her own heart ached so [she] could hardly contain [herself]. [She] knew what a heartbreaking day this was" (fig. 3-12).

As the women grieved openly, Frick, still preoccupied with running the Carnegie empire, showed no emotion and returned to work. He left within a few days for Pittsburgh, returning to the island for weekends.

In September, the island interlude drew to a close, and the family returned to Shadyside to begin adjusting anew to Martha's absence. Childs was enrolled in the nearby Sterrett School, and after Gus, the coachman, drove Annie and Childs to school, Annie would return to shop with Adelaide and Attie, or drive with Adelaide to the cemetery. They seemed to establish a new routine, but in their grief, Martha, though dead, remained a living presence.

❖

No one could have guessed what the nature of the mourning process would be for this grieving family—whether their mourning would be completed by eventually letting go of the emotion attached to Martha, or whether this emotion would intensify over time. But Frick, who probably had no conscious memory of the removal of his older sister Maria from their home when he was only three, undoubtedly harbored an unconscious guilt over that event, a guilt leaving him too vulnerable for the memory of Martha's death to fade. Having already "lost" one little girl that age in his sister Maria, in Martha's death Frick experienced a reenactment—greatly magnified—of the same scenario. The acquisitions Frick made some twenty-four and twenty-eight years after Martha's death testify to the intensity and longevity of his mourning. In 1915, Frick bought a painting by Francis Cotes of five-year-old Francis Vernon (fig. 3-13), who died at age eight. Apart from the fact that the portrait subject strongly resembles an 1887 photograph of the four-year-old Childs (fig. 3-14), taken the week before Martha ingested the pin, Childs was eight years old when he watched five-year-old Martha die. More

Right: Fig. 3-13. Francis Cotes (1726–1770),
Francis Vernon, 1757.
Acquired in 1915, Pastel on paper affixed to canvas,
49 x 55⅞ in. (124.4 x 141.9 cm).
The Frick Collection

Above: Fig. 3-14. Childs Frick at age four.
Author's collection

Fig. 3-15. Johannes Vermeer (1632-1675), *Mistress and Maid*, 1665-70.
Acquired in 1919, Oil on canvas, 35½ x 31 in. (90.2 x 78.7 cm).
The Frick Collection

significant, Frick acquired the painting in what would have been Martha's thirtieth birthday year, had she lived.

In 1919, he bought Johannes Vermeer's *Mistress and Maid* (fig. 3-15). The last painting he ever acquired before his own death, *Mistress and Maid* depicts a woman whose concentration is interrupted by the delivery of a letter from her maid, a letter that has caused the woman obvious concern. This could have evoked the frantic correspondence between Henry Clay Frick and his wife, and Frick's own desperate letters to Martha. Additionally, the small, silver-trimmed jewel casket in the painting, though made of wood, could easily have activated in Frick's mind his memory of the silver-trimmed casket, reserved for children, in which Martha was buried (fig. 3-16). The jewel casket in *Mistress and Maid,* used by Vermeer to connote purity and innocence, or perhaps vanity, had a greater meaning in Frick's day: by 1891 casket had replaced the word coffin and was a term whose original meaning described a container for precious objects. Moreover, after the horrific loss of life and mutilation of bodies in the carnage of the Civil War, the deceased body was suddenly perceived not as an "unimportant shell" but as something precious. The Victorians expanded this idea by designing burial caskets that were lined, cushioned, and designed to open from the side like a lady's jewel casket, rather than by removing a lid. The widely read essays in very popular children's periodicals of the time also were spoken of as short literary "gems." One such magazine was entitled *The Young People's Casket.* In fact, Frick, who often referred to his wife and children as "My Jewels," in 1885, just after Martha's birth, had written those very words across a photograph of Adelaide, Childs, and Martha (fig. 3-17).

Other facts also point to Frick's association of this painting to Martha's death. In an odd coincidence, *Mistress and Maid* entered Frick's collection in the summer of 1919, close to the July anniversary of Martha's death and the August anniversary of her birth. Evidently the painting held a special fascination for Frick. He changed his position at the dining room table in his summer home at Eagle Rock, Massachusetts, so he could better see it. And more compelling, a few days before his own death in 1919, as Frick stood in the West Gallery of his New York mansion in front of *Mistress and Maid,* he said to a friend that he wanted the Frick Collection to be his monument—and that he hoped the public would get as much pleasure from his art collection as he had.

But in 1891, the first Christmas after Martha's death indicated what would be this family's mourning pattern, a pattern where birthdays and anniversaries would increasingly show themselves as their hardest moments. On Adelaide's birthday, December 16, Childs gave his mother a book of poems entitled *Comfort.* It was dedicated to "the toilers and sufferers on the way to the 'better country'" and had a special, rosebud pink cover embroidered with pansies. It also contained a poem, "Papa's Little Girl," written in memory of a seven-year-old child whose "sweet, pathetic voice still said,

Fig. 3-16. The white jewel casket used for Martha's remains was similar to that used
for the body of Johnny Frederick Schultz (shown above), 1893.
The Burns Archives

'I'm Papa's little girl.'" Adelaide so loved the poem that she marked its location and pressed numerous pansies, Martha's favorite flower, between the pages. She placed it by her bedside, where it remains to this day in the Clayton house-museum. Predictably, as the first family Christmas without Martha approached, everyone's emotions intensified. Since the family was still in deep mourning, there would be no Christmas tree, no holly wreaths, nor decorations of any kind.

There was, nevertheless, a certain amount of excitement. As often happens after the death of a child, the grieving parents immediately tried to replace the lost child with a newborn. Adelaide was pregnant, and a special pregnancy it would be. A true replacement child, the new baby would be due on or about the first anniversary of Martha's death, or what would have been her seventh birthday on August 5. The doctors, concerned for everyone's health—including Adelaide's—visited the family daily. They prescribed medicines and advised all of them to keep busy so they would not worry too much and make themselves sick for the holidays.

According to Annie's memoir, a few close friends and relatives sent presents which were saved for Christmas Day. And the family did minimal shopping. Adelaide wrapped a picture of the children for Annie and bought a silver frame for Attie in which she placed a picture of Martha inscribed "Attie's Heart's Ease," for that had been Attie's pet name for her namesake, Martha.

On Christmas Eve, Annie, who had been sent by Adelaide to pick up the frame for Attie's picture, did some shopping of her own. She bought Childs a harmonica because, as she said, he "wanted a mouth organ more than anything else." Although Helen had many dolls, Annie decided to buy her a rubber one that squeaked when it was squeezed. Annie thought it would be a perfect gift for Helen because she could play with it in the bathtub. But she missed Martha intensely, and so she stopped at a florist and bought flowers for Martha's grave—Adelaide and Frick wanted Annie to go with them to the cemetery after breakfast Christmas morning.

All the way home, Annie wished she could immediately take the flowers "to the little grave [she] loved so much," but she knew she couldn't. It was already getting dark and Adelaide would not allow her out after dark, particularly since no streetcars went to the cemetery and it was a five-mile walk round trip from their rented home. Annie knew she would have to wait for the morning, but for her, the waiting felt like an eternity.

Fig. 3-17. Henry Clay Frick inscribed this photograph
of Adelaide, Childs, and Martha: "My Jewels."
Frick Art and Historical Center

In the meantime, the Borntraegers, who lived next door to Clayton on Home-wood Avenue, sent over a Christmas gift for Childs and one for Helen as well. According to Annie, Adelaide allowed them to open their presents early. When Childs opened his, he found, to his delight, a set of building blocks.

Helen's present came in a large box, so Adelaide asked the butler to carry it to her in the nursery and there, as she helped Helen undo the wrapping, the angel appeared, in the form of an imported wax doll. It was about the size of an infant and had blue eyes and golden curls. It was dressed in fine netting and had wings of spangled silver and gold that sparkled and gleamed in the night. The angel doll had a hook from which it could be fastened to a Christmas tree or a chandelier. It also had a music box inside with a key to wind it.

Adelaide wound it and then had the butler hang it from the nursery room chandelier. It played two Christmas carols which sounded so beautiful that everyone stood looking up at it, listening to the music in silence. Adelaide and Annie were mute with emotion for they had the same thought—that in this angel doll, Martha's spirit had returned.

That night, Adelaide let Helen's nurse go and asked Annie to stay in Helen's room. Helen, thrilled to have Annie to herself, said, "Go home quick, Nanna, so Wannie can read me a story." As Annie sat by her bed, she held Helen's little hands through the crib bars and told her the story of the babe in the manger. Before Annie had a chance to finish, however, Helen was fast asleep.

In the meantime, Childs had been in the living room hanging Helen's, Annie's, and his own stocking on the mantel. After Helen had fallen asleep, he gave Annie his whistling sound, which meant he was ready for his bedtime story. Annie told him a story, heard his prayers, and then, after tucking her presents for Childs and Helen in their stockings, she checked to see that her flowers had enough water. By then it was nine o'clock, her regular bedtime, so she arranged her clothes on a chair, complete with her coat and hat, in anticipation of the early morning visit to Martha's grave.

Annie went over to see if Helen was all right; finding her "sleeping like a little angel," she turned the oil lamp low and knelt beside the window to say her prayers. As she looked into the night sky, she saw what she called "Martha's Star." Promising Martha she would bring flowers to her grave in the morning, Annie finished her prayers and turned from the window. Looking up at the chandelier, she noticed the angel doll had cast "a life size shadow on the ceiling, which made it look like [their] dear angel, Martha."

Adelaide came in at midnight to check on Helen, something she always did before retiring. Finding Helen comfortably asleep, she looked at Annie, who was asleep in the bed next to Helen's, and as she looked at Annie's face, she noticed it was turned toward the ceiling and smiling. Following the direction of her smile upward through the warm glow of the bedroom, Adelaide's eyes met the shadow of the angel doll.

But in the morning, the angel's spell was broken. Helen stood up in her bed demanding, "Wannie, where is Santa Claus?"

A short time later, Helen was brought downstairs into the living room to search through the stockings for the gifts from Santa. Frick and Adelaide did not come into the room, but just stood in the doorway, as Annie wrote, "looking so very sad because . . . Martha was not with [them]." Then the carriage arrived to take them to the cemetery. Adelaide asked Annie to get her flowers as it was time to leave. Startled, Annie answered, "My flowers are gone and I have been to the cemetery already."

Adelaide looked at Annie in bewilderment and said it was not possible, that she had checked on Annie during the night and found her asleep in her bed. Annie, also puzzled, said perhaps she had just dreamed she had been to the cemetery with her flowers, but the flowers were not in the vase.

Since Childs and Helen did not want Annie to go to the cemetery, and Annie's flowers were gone, she stayed behind with the children. When Frick and Adelaide returned from the cemetery, they were badly shaken. Adelaide immediately asked Annie to come to her room, and Frick called Dr. Litchfield. They both looked so worried that Annie noted in her memoir, she was "grief stricken."

When Annie asked if her flowers were on the grave, Adelaide replied that they were and that she and Frick had seen the impression of Annie's pleated skirt and knees beside what Adelaide described as "the little frosted grave." Annie's hand marks were visible where she had arranged the flowers, and Adelaide said her footprints were "imbedded in the hoar frost all the way to the cemetery."

But Adelaide was less concerned about the flowers than about the danger to which Annie had subjected herself. She explained that they had told the coachman, Gus, to drive slowly so they could trace her footsteps. Thus they had determined that Annie had walked the entire five miles to the cemetery, passing such dangerous places as Bruce's Ice Pond. Adelaide started to cry and said, "If a man had thrown you in that ice pond we would never have found you and your Mama would never have forgiven me!" Worse, at the intersection of Fifth and Shadylane, Adelaide and Frick had seen Annie's footprints intermixed with wagon wheels, horses' hoofs, and the footprints of a man or two.

On hearing this, Annie began to cry for she knew she had upset Adelaide. She apologized for causing so much anxiety and worry, but said she could not account for what happened. Adelaide, grateful that Annie was not hurt and appreciating how much she "held their dear child in [her] thoughts," then insisted Annie tell her all she could remember.

Annie could recall only very little—that she was beside Martha's grave, that she placed her flowers on it, said some prayers, and sang some Christmas carols. She said she had her prayer book and hymnal, but it was too dark to see; she knew the hymns by heart anyway. She could see lights in the distance, "had no fear whatever," and although she must have stayed by the grave for nearly an hour, she had not felt the cold.

After questioning one of the cooks, the Fricks learned that Annie had rattled the door knob at five in the morning. On hearing the noise, the bewildered cooks had opened the door for her. They noticed she had a prayer book in her hands, and when they asked where she had been, knowing it was far too early for any church services, Annie "just stared at [them] and went up the stairs to the nursery."

The conclusion was that Annie had either walked in her sleep or had been in a trance. The doctor prescribed a tonic and warned her not to go out alone at night and to get more outdoor exercise and sunshine. The doctors also advised Frick that as soon as Christmas was over, Adelaide and the children should leave Shadyside. Since Adelaide was already having trouble with her pregnancy, the lease on the Shadyside house was almost up, and the renovations at Clayton were not due to be completed until the spring, Frick took the doctor's advice and made train reservations for New York.

In New York after this first Christmas without Martha, the family grieved and remained alert to any sign that she was still with them. And in their longing for Martha they found her everywhere. Annie's memoir reveals that a carriage was kept at their disposal, and Adelaide and the children often went to Central Park where they had once sat with Martha, watching people walking and children playing. Childs and Helen bought nuts and crackers so they could feed the squirrels and the birds, but the park reminded them all of Martha. Moreover, although Adelaide was holding the promise of a new child and New York represented a welcome change of scene, when back in their hotel at night, all remembered Martha's distinctive laughter and waited for it to ripple through the living room where she had once played Parlor Car and turned somersaults.

At night, Annie and Childs said their prayers together. Although they tried to console each other, there seemed no relief for either of them. Annie mourned the little bed next to her own, the bed in which Martha had slept, the bed which had not yet been removed. And at the end of the day, Annie would go to the window, whisper a prayer, and then cry herself to sleep.

Many years later, Frick's grief was manifested in George Romney's *Lady Hamilton as 'Nature'* (fig. 3-18). This painting was purchased at a time when Martha, had she lived, would have been the same age as the teenage Lady Hamilton when she sat for Romney. Thus, like the Cotes portrait, it has an age association with Martha's death. Furthermore, Lady Hamilton's position is exactly that of Childs holding Martha's dog,

Fig. 3-18. George Romney (1734–1802), *Lady Hamilton as 'Nature'*, 1782.
Acquired in 1904, Oil on canvas, 29⅞ x 24¾ in (75.8 x 62.9 cm).
The Frick Collection

Brownie, in a Christmas photograph taken at Clayton in 1892, when Brownie became Martha's surrogate in the family photographs (fig. 3-19). The dog had recently suffered a blow, leaving him unable to use his hind legs.

In 1891, Andrew Carnegie, sensing the family's grief at this first, particularly painful juncture, had advised Frick to take a European holiday for a few weeks, saying, "There never is a time when it seems wise to leave, and there scarcely ever comes a time when it is not wise to do so. In your own case, it is the highest wisdom, indeed, I consider it a duty to yourself & others."

But Frick did not take Carnegie's advice, and as 1892 dawned, except for daily bedecking the photograph of Martha over his bedroom mantel with fresh flowers, he showed no outward sign of emotion over her death. With his facade fixed in place, though grieving in silence, a deliberate, methodical, cold man faced the outer world and conducted Carnegie's business.

And by then, Henry Clay Frick needed to maintain a tough facade. Apart from the fact that men of his day were cultured to show no emotion, the renowned strikebreaker was now forcing a confrontation with the labor unions at the famous Homestead steel plant. The coming battle—to be known as the Homestead Steel Strike of 1892—would quickly assume the character of a religious war. Although Frick's victory over labor would be complete and longlasting, it would also deliver him longlasting defeat at a personal and spiritual level. Predictably, both victory and defeat would further intensify his protracted longing for Martha.

Fig. 3-19. Childs Frick holding Brownie, Christmas, 1892.
David C. Duniway Archives

CHAPTER IV

Triumph Over Labor

Even [if it takes] my life itself. I will fight this thing to the bitter end.
I will never recognize the union, never, never.

—Henry Clay Frick, 1892

Life for Henry Clay Frick seemed to test his strength endlessly. Frick endured childhood illness, defeated the 1873 financial panic and nationwide depression, and survived two near fatal attacks of inflammatory rheumatism. He successfully challenged Andrew Carnegie over labor policy, remained publicly silent about the Johnstown Flood and stoic over his daughter's death. If this was any indication of his unrelenting determination, Frick's stand at Homestead would be final proof of his unshakable resolve.

When the family moved to New York in the winter of 1891-1892, after their first Christmas without Martha, Frick, who needed to be in Pittsburgh to oversee the H. C. Frick Coke Company and the Carnegie enterprises, was unable to stay and provide emotional support to his wife and children. He could not afford to collapse into his own grief even if he wanted to, as he was without a doubt entering the most important phase of his business career. His immediate concern was the forthcoming termination, on July 1, 1892, of the union contract with the Homestead mill—a contract he did not want to renew because he wanted to operate nonunion. He was also about to be elected chairman of the two divisions of the Carnegie empire, Carnegie Brothers and Company and Carnegie Phipps and Company. As head of the united Carnegie empire, he was about to centralize a $25,000,000 corporation whose steel production was equal to over one-half Great Britain's total production.

But Henry Clay Frick was also entering this period carrying his resentment of the 1891 Morewood riots. Apart from the fact that the riots had prevented him from tending more completely to Martha during her fatal decline, they had cost the state

Fig. 4-1. The Homestead mill in 1886 at the time of its first labor strike.
Engraving, company advertisement.
Carnegie Library, Pittsburgh, Randolph Harris Collection

$40,000, the coke-carrying railroads $1,250,000, and the coke manufacturers $1 million. Indeed, the riots had intensified both Frick's disgust of labor union leaders and his bitterness over Martha's death.

Since the time Carnegie forced him to capitulate to wildcatters in 1887, Frick had broken every coal strike in both the H. C. Frick Coke Company's region and the Carnegie steel mills. Starting at Morewood, he consistently brought in other ethnic groups willing to work and employed Pinkertons as deputies to either protect his men or evict striking employees from company-owned houses. Although in 1891 the state of Ohio had voted to outlaw the use of Pinkertons as armed guards, Pennsylvania had no such law. As far as protecting and reclaiming the Homestead mill was concerned, Frick's handling of the situation would remain unchanged. He would use his traditional lash and hire Pinkertons to help him throw the unions out of the heart of Carnegie's empire.

Homestead was sacred ground for Frick and Carnegie (fig. 4-1). A highly specialized mill and the most modern plant of its day, it was considered the finest of the Carnegie works. The $6 million mill, with its relentless furnaces and advanced machinery, now manufactured structural iron and steel for bridges and fireproof buildings. Additionally, Homestead was an important producer of armor plate used in the construction of warships for the U. S. Navy, like the *Monterey* and the *Maine*.

Homestead had, however, a long and troubled labor history. Carnegie had purchased the Homestead plant in 1883 at cost from the Pittsburgh Bessemer Steel Company because the former owner was unable to settle with the unions. In 1882 and later, in 1889, before Frick had any managerial responsibilities there, Homestead had been the focal point of two strikes. As labor historians note, both times the workers had used violence and terrorism to win a place for the unions within the mill; they had seized control of the town and fought with local civil law enforcement agents to win their demands, capitulating only when Pinkertons were sent in to break the strike. And both times the workers used Homestead's geographic situation to their advantage. The mill is bordered on the south by the Monongahela River and on the north by a steep hill. With the railroad running east to west through the town, the configuration permitted the strikers to isolate both town and plant from management, the outside world, and the state law enforcement agencies.

In 1889, although the union, the Amalgamated Association of Iron and Steel Workers, accepted a 25 percent wage reduction, it gained a near stranglehold on the mill, winning the right to determine which skilled workers were hired and promoted, job allocation, and how work was to be paced. Additionally, the union could make decisions about the production process, including the quality of the pig iron that should be used and the quantity of scrap. As Henry Clay Frick said many years later, "We had reached the point where the men had become dictators of how our business be run." In the eyes of management, the union was running the plant.

Even though in the spring of 1892 Frick had entered into negotiations with labor, he made no secret of his determination to reject compromise. As the July 1 contract deadline approached, the majority of the workers in the plant—the day and unskilled laborers who were nonunion men and belonged to no lodges—had already signed a new three-year contract with management. Frick preferred to deal with each man on an individual basis and found intolerable what others described as the Amalgamated Association's "unbearable panache." In his view, its demands for higher wages, better hours, and longer contracts for skilled workers threatened to hamper effective, profitable running of the mills. It was his conviction—and Carnegie's as well, even though Carnegie remained opposed to using strikebreakers—that management had the right to hire and fire whomever it wanted, whenever it wanted, and had the right to establish its own rules with its work force.

Frick also felt the union's attempt to obtain higher wages at Homestead was tantamount to extortion. The skilled workers, whose wages were tied to the tonnage produced, had been encouraged by the dramatic increase in production over the previous decade and were demanding a proportionate rise in their wages. But Frick believed the increased production was due to mechanization and production efficiencies, not human labor, however skilled. And he thought the demands themselves were unreasonably high, well beyond the wages of their competitors. Then, too, Frick belittled the workers' fears that "the introduction of more machinery would cause wholesale unemployment" as "unfounded." While admitting that he had "put in one contrivance that saved over four hundred men," Frick noted that the reduction of costs enabled him to employ more men than before and allowed the machinery to do "some of the most trying work formerly performed by hand."

Therefore, as he explained to Carnegie in April 1892, the better strategy would be to confront labor now, rather than have labor later confront them. He then warned Carnegie: "No better time can be selected or expected. We will get ready for a fight immediately. If it be unnecessary, all the better. It may be a stubborn one, but if once gone into, without regard to cost or time, it will be fought to a finish."

In May, Andrew Carnegie, who traditionally went to Scotland in the summer because he was susceptible to sun poisoning, departed for an extended fishing trip. Though Frick was left to face the unions alone, he had encouraged his senior partner to stay out of the country. Indeed, Henry Phipps, who like Frick feared repercussions of his boss's inevitable press interviews advocating softer labor policies, later said he had "rejoiced when we were permitted to manage the affair in our own way." When the fight came, Frick wrote Carnegie, "it would be better that you should postpone your return until spring."

The stand at Homestead, however, was a fight in which Carnegie did not want to be involved. Toward the end of the strike, he would, however, express concern for Henry Clay Frick. Referring to himself as "a very wise man . . . and a true friend," Carnegie would counsel his partner: "This fight is too much against our *Chairman* — partakes of personal issue. It is very bad indeed for you—very and also bad for the interest of the firm." He would also say, "There's another point which troubles me on your account—the danger that the public and hence all our men get the impression that it is *all Frick*—your influence *for good* would be permanently impaired—You don't deserve a bad name, but then one is sometimes wrongfully got."

From the beginning, however, Frick welcomed the strike and showed no interest in protecting his name. With Carnegie out of the country and the July deadline looming, Frick, as the future chairman of the consolidated Carnegie interests, presented the union with a contract it could never accept. Having convinced his senior partner that they might as well have the fight now as later, particularly since they would not be perceived as starving the men into submission since the confrontation was to happen in July, Frick demanded of the union a reduction of the minimum-wage scale based on the price of the products the skilled workers were making. Covering his bases, he then insisted on a change in the date of any future contract with the union—

from July 1 to December 31—knowing that the workmen would fear eviction from company housing in the harsh winter months, and, therefore, be less likely to strike over a new contract.

On the other hand, the union officials believed they were strong enough to defeat Frick. They knew that Homestead had a large contract with the U.S. Navy for armor plate, a contract management needed to complete on time. And because 1892 was an election year, they also believed the prolabor press would capitalize on the plight of the steelworkers and turn sentiment against the capitalist-oriented Republican party. As common practice, laborers worked every day of the year except Christmas and the Fourth of July; they worked from six to six on twelve-hour days. Every two weeks, when the shift "turned," they worked a full twenty-four hours, and then got a day off to catch up on their sleep. The men lived in overcrowded, filthy homes and usually died before the age of forty from either industrial accident or disease.

Thus, both sides were preparing for a confrontation.

⁌

FROM CHRISTMAS 1891 UNTIL MARCH 1892, Adelaide and the children remained in New York. Frick did, however, try to reassure them by calling every night. As Annie noted in her memoir, his phone calls seemed to sustain Adelaide, who was unable to shake her depression and the general lethargy she had been feeling since Martha's death. While her mood improved noticeably on weekends when Frick rejoined his family, as soon as he left for Pittsburgh, she would fall apart, retire to her room, and cry herself to sleep. Her stamina was low, and she was unable to cope with the many decisions she needed to make. Dr. Garmany, the New York surgeon Frick had summoned to Cresson Springs, was treating her for a combination of ailments: an ongoing neuralgia, fragile emotional health, and complications from the first tri-mester of her pregnancy.

Adelaide consoled herself by shopping for the newly renovated Clayton and enlisted the services of A. J. Kimbal, Jr., an important New York decorator. But Frick, who was, in spite of his great wealth, always concerned about his wife's spending habits, seems to have issued a warning when in 1895 he purchased *Manon* (fig. 4-2), a portrait of a self-indulgent beauty described as a woman "too anxious for a life of plea-sure, too young to know the ways of the world and how to avoid its pitfalls." Manon, the antithesis of the Victorian wife who was meant to embody purity and high moral values, is a young woman who renounces convent life, runs away with her lover, seeks

Fig. 4-2. Gustave-Jean Jacquet (1846-1909), *Manon*.
Acquired in 1895,
Oil on canvas, 12¾ x 9 in. (32.4 x 22.9 cm).
Frick Art and Historical Center

a life of luxury to the destruction of all around her, repents too late, and dies. The portrait, by Gustave-Jean Jacquet, was eventually placed above Adelaide's writing desk at Clayton, and although Adelaide continued to spend lavishly on the house—buying bedding, linens, curtains, draperies, books, china, and silver—perhaps she joined her husband, who always wanted the best, in this dark-humored Manon joke. Perhaps, however, Adelaide was also being controlled by her husband's humor, the kind of humor known to be a veiled threat.

But by March, after a sorrow-filled winter in New York, the family was able to move back into Clayton. Yet Adelaide's pregnancy, depression, and general poor health made the return problematic. She had, as her mother had urged, given over her will entirely to her husband, and now her dependency on him seemed accentuated. As Frick's acquisition of Madeleine-Jeanne Lemaire's painting entitled *Expectation* (fig. 4-3), of a woman looking longingly out a window hoping for her husband's return, suggests, Adelaide had apparently taken her mother's advice. Typical of most women of her day, she undoubtedly lived as her mother's letter and family diaries indicate—largely for her husband's return in the evening. Whereas *Manon* was placed above Adelaide's writing desk, Frick hung *Expectation* above his bedroom washstand, positioning it so that the woman in the painting seems to look through the bedroom window to the entrance gates on Penn Avenue below.

Adelaide, though a retiring and undemanding woman, was nonetheless aggravated by the slowness of the workmen at Clayton, fretting as she waited for them to put the finishing touches on $2,700 worth of hardware and to sand and polish $5,300 worth of parquet floors. Woodwork, over which the workmen had splashed and scattered paint, still had to be thoroughly cleaned; shades, curtains, and draperies had to be hung; and dishes and other bric-a-brac, mostly imported, had to be carefully unpacked and put in their proper places.

As she pushed for the house to be completed, Adelaide also asserted her taste. Afraid the stencil wall paintings in the hall were not going to be done to her taste, she had George Megrew, Frick's valet, write that "the halls to suit Mr. and Mrs. Frick must be of a heavy warm character."

Fig. 4-3. Madeleine-Jeanne Lemaire (1845–1928), *Expectation.*
Acquired in 1895, Watercolor, 21½ x 13½ in. (54.6 x 34.3 cm).
Frick Art and Historical Center

Fig. 4-4. Adelaide Frick's dressing table.
Frick Art and Historical Center

Nevertheless, before long the small, two-story Italianate home costing $25,000 that Frick had given Adelaide in 1882 as a wedding present and first enlarged to eleven rooms was successfully transformed by the architect Frederick J. Osterling and A. J. Kimbal, Jr., the decorator, into a showplace that was the equal of any of Pittsburgh's grandest residences. The $131,300 renovations had created a four-story mansion of about twenty-four rooms, outfitted with machine-made custom rugs and a dual system of electricity and gas. The children's entrance, complete with the sink, coatrack, and third-floor playroom envisioned in 1891, were now in place. The new floor plan provided improved plumbing costing $4,000, a pantry, scullery, an enlarged dining room, a solarium, verandah, and portico. Windows had fourteen-karat gold handles. An oak front hall, walnut parlor, mahogany reception room, and Honduran mahogany dining room glistened beneath fashionable aluminum leaf ceilings.

In later life, Helen recalled the meticulous attention her mother had lavished on their new home. "It required the greatest care in order to have a really clean house," Helen said, and in fact, her mother was kept so busy cleaning and arranging things, George Megrew wrote Frick that he thought "she does too much for she gets so very tired."

Annie also recalled Adelaide's behavior from this period. In her memoir, she remembers that one day in early June, Adelaide began cleaning and polishing the jewelry Frick had given her. Because she was still in mourning, most of her jewelry was kept in a secret drawer (fig. 4-4). As was proper for the day, she wore only her wedding ring and one of three black and gold brooches, sedate bereavement jewelry that Frick had given her in December for their tenth wedding anniversary. One was a daisy with a large pearl in the center; another was a flower with a small diamond center. As was typical of mourning jewelry—part of the social custom of the time—both pins were reminders of the inevitability of death. The third was a pansy, often considered the flower of remembrance and reflection, one of Frick's favorites, and the flower Martha had most loved. It thus fulfilled the greater purpose of bereavement jewelry: not only was it suitable for a woman in mourning, it was also a souvenir of the deceased.

Clayton, of course, now bore little resemblance to the house where Martha had been born. Nevertheless, she remained as a living presence. Frederick Wilhelm Stephany, who had been hired to paint murals and decorative details on the interior walls, as if to escape the dreariness of Pittsburgh's yellow clouds and the haze of the thick black smoke from the steel mills which obscured the sun, turned Helen's bedroom into a garden paradise as seen on a radiant spring day. On the ceiling he painted cheerful scenes of hummingbirds, bluebirds, and butterflies rejoicing among playful clouds. Swallows soared, gentle breezes blew, and, where the walls met the ceiling, a cascading trim of white roses, chrysanthemums, and wisteria encircled the room. More important, on the east wall, between the two windows looking out over the garden, he painted one single rosebud, clearly a gesture to Martha. Unlike all the other roses, which were white and in full bloom, this bud was reddish pink and separated from all the other roses on the wall. Detached, falling with its head down, as if someone had dropped it, the rosebud seemed to hang suspended in time and space, isolated and alone.

Another powerful reminder of the long shadow Martha's absence cast on the lives of everyone at Clayton occurred in June, after Adelaide had finished her breakfast. She asked Annie to come into her bedroom, saying she needed her help. When Annie reached her door, Adelaide was holding a wide bolt of pale blue satin ribbon, a pair of scissors, and a door key. She guided Annie across the hall to the blue room where Attie often stayed, unlocked the door, and entered the empty, darkened bedroom. She turned on the lights and there, placed in the center of the room, was something covered with a white sheet, standing on top of another white sheet to protect it from any dirt that might have previously settled on the rug.

Adelaide gave Annie the ribbon and scissors to hold as she uncovered what was to be her new baby's bassinet. It was obvious that she had been hard at work sewing ribbons and bows on the white wicker basket. Annie stood there holding her breath, for she had not known the baby was expected so soon. Seeing Annie's surprise and delight, Adelaide gave her a sweet, knowing look and asked her to hold the bolt of ribbon as she started to measure the width and length of the bed. After Adelaide had cut the ribbon to the right length, Annie wove the ribbon through the open spaces. And Adelaide, perhaps hopeful the new baby would make up for her loss of Martha, perhaps praying for good luck and blessing the bed in which the replacement child would soon lie, kissed her fingers every time she touched the ribbon or the bassinet.

By lunch time the trimming was complete. Adelaide and Annie took a moment to silently admire their work. Then Adelaide kissed the bassinet lovingly, draped the sheet back over it, turned off the lights, and locked the door. She was worried that Childs, with his nine-year-old inquisitive mind, would see the bassinet and ask awkward questions.

But Childs raised other concerns. He had developed a chronic throat disorder and had recently lost a great deal of weight. Since the doctors thought his poor health was due to his confinement in the mornings to the third-floor schoolroom with his tutor, they prescribed a tonic and instructed Childs to take a lot of outdoor exercise.

Thus, after classes in the upstairs schoolroom were over and the tutor had left, Annie and Childs would spend the rest of the day walking and playing games in the garden. If it were raining, the coachman would take them on sightseeing trips and Helen would come along.

At a deeper level, however, Childs's health problems may have been a somatic manifestation of his mourning for Martha. Just as that first Christmas at Shadyside and in New York without her had brought fresh waves of grief and mourning, so would the first anniversary of Martha's death, and that day was fast approaching. Now it was June 1892, exactly a year from the moment Martha's health had gone into its rapid decline; exactly a year since they had taken Martha to Cresson Springs and watched her die.

Although these months leading up to the anniversary were painful, Annie and Childs comforted and consoled each other. They became close friends in their grief, and Helen, now almost four, sensing their despair, tried to comfort them both. As Annie wrote in her memoir, "no one could withstand a child's happy laughter or bright childish sayings for long." Thus, little Helen became Annie's and Childs's tonic, their "greatest blessing and comfort through their sorrowing times."

As much as Helen gave them relief, however, the fear that someone else might die never lifted. That fear was not as much about contracting a disease or suffering a fatal accident as it was about a larger threat: the ever present worry that someone in the family would be killed by an anarchist or some other opponent of capitalism. Frick had become a symbol of capitalist oppression at a time when the national mood of the working class had grown sullen and dangerous. From the end of the Civil War to 1892, 11 million immigrants had entered America. Strikes occurred on an average of twelve hundred times a year. Labor unrest seemed to be approaching a form of class warfare. And threats on Frick's life by anarchists and the labor union were rumored in the newspapers. As cranks and fanatics constantly called Clayton, the safety of his wife and children was endangered as well. Even the daily mail was viewed with suspicion, and anyone found to be loitering outside Clayton's iron fence was immediately questioned.

Simultaneously, labor problems within the steel industry, and most particularly within the Homestead plant, were reaching an exploding point. The interests of management and labor were so diametrically opposed, their champions were like adversaries in a religious war. The Amalgamated Association of Iron and Steel Workers —representing the craft unions or the skilled workers of the steel industry—had locked horns with plant owners. Neither the Amalgamated nor the steel magnates were about to convert to the other's faith. Both parties meant to fight to the death so that their own ideology might prevail.

Frick tried to keep his worries to himself, hoping not to cause Adelaide what he called "undue anxiety." He told the staff to keep newspapers out of her sight and instructed them to protect her if something should happen to him. The staff thus became Adelaide's shadow. Should any danger arise, they were to raise the alarm immediately and do everything possible to spare her emotions or to protect her life. Under no circumstances was Adelaide to be allowed outside alone. To Annie he instructed: "After Tie's [Childs's] tutor arrives, I wish you would stay with Mrs. Frick and keep her company as she is not feeling well."

Taking no precautions for himself and using no bodyguards, the forty-three-year-old ironmaster would leave for his office, where he monitored in methodical, meticulous detail the operations of each Carnegie plant and the strategy for the coming fight. As Frick now watched to see that each plant within the Carnegie empire worked with the precision of a clock's interdependent gears, and that company profits and products were being produced with maximum speed, so too he began to implement his plan to cripple the Amalgamated Association and drive the labor unions from Carnegie's mills.

In 1889, when Carnegie wrote his "Dear Boys" letter about the "calamity" at South Fork, he said of that year's impending Homestead strike, "Don't be alarmed at the bluster at Homestead [,] *in their hearts* they know that the game is up. . . . This knowledge prevents any earnest fight. They only will make a show of it to scare other manfrs [*sic*]."

By January 1891, however, Carnegie's tone had changed. He wrote Frick, "I shall look forward with great interest to the result of a thorough investigation of Homestead labor forces. There is certainly $300,000 a year unaccounted for, as between [18]89 and [1890]." A few months later, Carnegie had written Frick, "My hope is you will . . . *concentrate* upon this business and make it the greatest ever seen—even Chicago should rank second."

Frick would accomplish all that Carnegie asked, but in making the business "the greatest ever seen," the confrontation with labor at Homestead would prove to be far more than the 1889 "bluster." As chairman of the consolidated Carnegie empire, Frick would drive the unions from the Carnegie works, set the labor union movement back forty years, and make them second to none in steel production.

❖

On June 12, 1892, Frick began to set his trap. He began building a bullpen around the plant—a three-mile-long, twelve-foot-high fence of stout stockade planks (fig. 4-5). An impressive edifice, the *Pittsburgh Post* described it as a massive board wall, stronger than any ordinary fence. Semicircular in shape, it stretched from the east riverbank through the town, where it divided mill from town, to the river's west bank. The subject of endless newspaper cartoons and editorials, the fence was pierced with two hundred holes, three inches in diameter, just the size and height to accommodate rifle barrels (fig. 4-6). It was further fortified by a jagged, three-strand barbed wire fence on top. The whitewashed edifice stood in defiant contrast to the grayness of mill and town where, except after a heavy rain, the stunted trees were blackened with dust.

The workers' densely packed homes, a calamity of filth and squalor, had been located so close to the mill that before the construction of the fence, it was hard to tell where the mill ended and the town began. Every able-bodied man and youth in the town of approximately seven thousand people worked in the mill and had always been free to drift between home and plant. Now the workers were completely severed from that six-hundred-acre site because even on the river side, the Monongahela's deep, swift-running waters—the water itself contaminated with human sewage, mill waste, and chemicals—served as a barrier. Only the piers below the gray stone, arched pumping station on the river, and certain designated, well-guarded gates facing the town, provided access to the plant.

Although the mill was an intolerable workplace, the men were nevertheless emotionally and physically attached to it. Upset as they might have been by their new

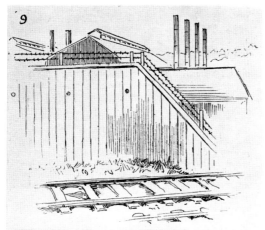

Above: Fig. 4-5. The fence at Homestead
built to separate mill and town.
Carnegie Library, Pittsburgh

Left: Fig. 4-6. Rifle holes in the fence at Homestead.
Frank Leslie's Illustrated Weekly, July 14, 1892.
New York Society Library

isolation, even more galling was the fact that they were required to build platforms inside the mill yards for company guards and searchlights. Moreover, they saw pipes for high pressure hoses being laid behind the guard stations, while boxes of explosives and guns were being quietly carried into the Homestead plant.

Understandably, overnight, the press labeled the Homestead plant "Fort Frick." Although some workers jokingly peered through the holes and said confidently it was "only the bottom of the ninth inning and the ball game wasn't over yet," the headline in *The Dispatch* on June 12 was less cavalier:

PREPARING FOR WAR

But neither the press, nor anyone else, knew Frick had done more than build a fence to fortify Homestead. With the lesson of Morewood from April 1891, he activated what would prove to be the boldest plan allowable under law to further insure the safety of the Homestead plant. He contacted the Pinkerton Agency and requested that three hundred guards be reserved for his use in the first week of July.

On June 25, Frick posted a formal notice on his bullring fence, declaring that henceforth the managers of the company would deal with their employees only on an individual basis. He also furnished Robert Pinkerton with the details of his plan. Anticipating that Homestead might again become a Morewood situation—or, worse, a workers' republic in revolt for a third time—he requested the guards "as a measure of precaution against interference with our plan to start operation of the works, July 6th, 1892." Frick, still operating against Carnegie's wish that he not replace the strikers with men willing to work, expected "some demonstration of violence upon the part of those whose places have been filled," but hoped that his guards would not need to use their guns. He further warned Pinkerton that the situation required "absolute secrecy" regarding the movement of these men onto the premises. He continued: "[We] will notify the Sheriff and ask that they be deputized either at once or immediately upon an outbreak of such character as to render such a step desirable." Then, on June 30, Frick closed the giant plant and locked almost four thousand men out of their jobs.

The ominous headline read:

THE DIE IS CAST

On July 1, Frick, working closely with his lawyer and Carnegie Steel's general counsel, Philander Knox, announced that all the company's plants previously operating individually had been merged into one self-governing unit with himself as chairman of the new company, Carnegie Steel, and that its partner, the H. C. Frick Coke Company, would remain its sole supplier of coke. As head of the largest steel company in the world, the largest coke company in the world, and as employer of more than thirty thousand men, Frick thus became one of the leading employers in the world, or, as a great many of the men had come to think of him, a leading oppressor of the working class.

The quiet within the mill yards, locked and emptied, was likened to "the stillness in a cemetery at midnight." *The New York Times* noted on July 2, "It is evident that there is no 'bluffing' at Homestead. The fight there is to be to the death between the Carnegie Steel Co. Ltd. with its $25,000,000 capital and the workmen."

On Sunday, July 3, "a genuine old fashioned drizzle . . . transformed the dust [and] carpeted streets into rivers of sticky, yellow mud. . . . the weather forced the populace to remain indoors, and it proved to be a damp, dull, and unprofitable day." In anticipation of the Fourth of July, the Advisory Committee of the Amalgamated Association, fifty men who also managed the town, closed down all but two bars in Homestead.

They knew that the men, who traditionally drank for stimulation, relaxation, or simply to wash the dust and minuscule grains of steel down their throats, could easily get out of control.

In reality, Independence Day was taking on a fierce, new meaning. The workers, their livelihood locked away from them by management, decided to fight back and locked management out of the mill as well. They constructed bulwarks outside Frick's fence and positioned themselves so that neither management nor strikebreakers could enter—thereby turning Frick's lockout into a strike.

The Advisory Committee, a mixture of labor leaders, strikers, and townspeople, then proceeded to put together what was later called "as perfect a system of military tactics as ever defended a fort from the outside." They divided the entire work force of four thousand men into three divisions, alternating in eight-hour shifts. Divided into subgroups, their duty was to guard the key entrances to the plant at the riverfront, the water gate, the gray-stone pump house, the railroad station, and the four gates into the works. Eight hundred non-English-speaking Slavs and Poles were organized by interpreters and stood ready to do whatever they were told. A picket line was formed along the waterfront. One thousand men patrolled the river on both sides, five miles upstream and five miles down (fig. 4-7). A patrol fleet was put in service on the water, and at night fires were lit at intervals along the shore.

Fig. 4-7. Searchlights installed by the strikers scanned the Monongahela River to prevent infiltration of the mill.
Frank Leslie's Illustrated Weekly, July 14, 1892.
New York Society Library

Telegraph wires were run into the Amalgamated headquarters and an observatory was erected on top, which commanded a sweeping view of "Fort Frick." To facilitate communication, a steam whistle was placed on top of the electric light works in the town; the men were thus able to determine from the number of whistle blasts where the strikebreakers had penetrated their line and where they were to go. As had happened in 1882 and 1889, every road in the borough was blockaded, the railroad depot was surrounded by armed guards, and Homestead was isolated. On Independence Day, the town was again a workers' republic in revolt.

❖

At Clayton, Frick was about to have his own Fourth of July celebration. Childs had persuaded his father to buy some firecrackers and balloons, even though Adelaide felt that since the family was still in mourning, they should not be involved in any celebrations. Moreover, the lawn by Penn Avenue—where Frick wanted to set up the platform—had just been sodded. He insisted that the spot he had chosen was the best place because everyone on the street and in the neighboring houses could see the display. He said to Adelaide, "Ada, I do not intend to damage the lawn, but if I should do so, I certainly will have it repaired."

Frick proceeded with his plans and soon large boxes marked "Explosives—Handle With Care," arrived at Clayton for storage in the carriage house. Frick assured Adelaide he ordered only a hundred dollars worth, not enough to make a lot of noise. He also said he intended to set off most of the firecrackers himself and would personally help Childs with the smaller ones.

When the Fourth arrived, Frick and his son carried the explosives from carriage house to lawn. Suddenly, Frick reappeared with a hatchet, lumber, and nails. He started building a rough platform and nailed some boards upward so the rockets, floral bombs, meteors, vertical wheels, parachutes, and tricolor candles could have a proper launching pad. But when dinner came, and the family ate on the porch overlooking the launch pad, Adelaide grew tearful. She, like everyone else, had started to think about last year's holiday and Martha's precipitous decline. As the darkness descended and sadness began to permeate the group, Frick suddenly rose and said, "I think we had better get the fireworks started."

Frick went with Childs to set off the balloons, causing a burst of color. The "tense spell," as Annie described the moment, was broken. But the deep heartache of Martha's absence had not been eased. And although the skies over Homestead had been as alive with rockets and candles as at Clayton, the great works on the river, usually alive with its own flame and fire, had been dark and silent. The union guards made their rounds and kept their watch. The quiet was not to last long. Believing that he was "only letting . . . [his] property lie idle awaiting one of the worst bodies of men that ever worked in a mill," Frick concluded, "it was better to have trouble, if . . . [he] were to have it, at once."

Frick, therefore, advised Robert Pinkerton that he was ready to begin transporting the security company's men from Ashtabula, Ohio, to Homestead the following night, July 5, 1892, with their arrival at Homestead planned for 3 A.M. on July 6. Frick cabled an anxious Carnegie that he would, "of course, keep within the law, and do nothing that is not entirely legal." The trains carrying the three hundred Pinkertons arrived at Bellevue, five miles downriver from Pittsburgh, on schedule and with their coaches darkened. Not a single man was armed, but unlabeled crates contained two hundred and fifty Winchester rifles, three hundred pistols, and ammunition had been stored on their train. At midnight, July 5, the Pinkertons boarded two barges. Recently purchased by the Carnegie Steel Company, each had a hatch on top; tug boats would accompany them upriver so the guards could land on the piers inside the Homestead plant just beneath the pump house, the heart of the mill.

The general superintendent of the Homestead plant, who was to travel on the barges with the Pinkertons, was cautioned by Philander Knox to break no laws. No matter what indignities he might be subjected to in protecting Homestead, he and the Pinkertons were to "do no act of aggression, but should confine themselves to protecting themselves and the company's property."

Fog was thick on the river, at 2:45 A.M. on July 6, but one of the barges was nevertheless sighted two miles downriver from Homestead. A horseman rode at full speed to inform the strikers' headquarters, and the war began. The Amalgamated whistles sounded the alarm. Women, men, and boys ran to the river's edge carrying clubs, revolvers, rifles, hoes, and the staves of picket fences. Hundreds of mill men and their sympathizers joined them, and by 3:30 A.M. one thousand men were posted at the various landing places and entrances to the mill.

When the barges were about one mile from Homestead, the strikers opened fire, continuing the barrage until the tugboat reached the pier. Balls fired by small arms and rifles struck the pilothouse and smokestacks of the tug. But because no one was hurt, the Pinkertons were not given guns and did not return the fire. The captain of the first barge tried to land at a spot on the banks inside the plant. Seeing this, a mob of strikers

Fig. 4-8. The battle at the Pinkerton landing site.
Frank Leslie's Illustrated Weekly, July 14, 1892.
New York Society Library

charged over the riverbank. They ran to the fence, tore it down, got inside the mill, and seized control of the plant, screaming, "Don't let the blacksheep land!" (fig. 4-8).

The first wave attacked and tried to stop the Pinkertons from putting out a gangplank. The head of the striking workers yelled to the commander of the tug, "In the name of God and humanity, don't attempt to land! Don't attempt to enter these works by force!"

The reply from the tugboat came back: "We were sent here to take possession of this property and to guard it for this company. . . . If you men don't withdraw, we will mow every one of you down and enter in spite of you. You had better disperse, for land we will!"

In a volley of shots—shots the Pinkertons later disclaimed because they only fired a general volley in retaliation when they saw their men hit—thirty strikers went down. Others retreated behind iron-plate barricades or inside the pump house where they could fire on the Pinkertons through the arched windows. One worker, twenty-eight-year-old John E. Morris, who was positioned in the pump house overlooking the barges, popped his head out during a lull in the firing to get a look at the battle. A bullet ripped through his forehead, knocking him off the building. Screaming, he fell sixty feet into the ditch below.

In the meantime, other strikers were trying to sink the barges with cannon fire from two antique Civil War cannons. One shot blew a hole in the roof of a barge. Another inadvertently decapitated one of their own men, a twenty-three-year-old striker.

The strikers also opened a natural gas main next to the pumping station, ignited it, and threw Fourth of July rockets into the flames, hoping the rockets or dynamite would blast the barges out of the water. Not meeting with success, they pumped oil into the Monongahela and set fire to both a raft and a railroad car of burning oil, hoping they would crash into the barges, ignite the oil slick, and incinerate the Pinkertons. These efforts also failed.

The battle raged from barge to pump house for the next fourteen hours. According to Leon Wolff's account in *Lockout,* at 7 P.M. the Pinkertons raised a white flag of surrender. The man who waved it was shot down and as another Pinkerton was killed, one hundred armed strikers swarmed aboard the second barge. Each Pinkerton had his pistol taken and his uniform jacket removed and tossed into the river. The rifle crates were seized, food was distributed to the women and children, and the barges were torched.

Because the Homestead jail was too small to hold all the Pinkertons, the strikers marched them through the town, up the hill, to the skating rink. The women, the power behind the striking men, chanted, "Kill the murderers," and bludgeoned the unarmed Pinkertons with clubs as they were marched through the Homestead grounds (fig. 4-9). Children pelted them with rocks. A woman poked a man's eye out with an umbrella. People kicked a guard who was on his knees, begging for mercy, and clubbed him until he was unconscious. Others threw sand in the Pinkertons' eyes and punched their faces with bare fists. Someone else slugged each passing Pinkerton with a large stone wrapped in leather, tied to a rope that was short enough to make the blows land accurately behind each man's ear.

Although only three Pinkertons and seven workers were killed, and sixty people wounded—fewer than in the Morewood riots the year before—the Homestead battle became overnight a national news event. The ten Pittsburgh papers and an extensive national press corps highlighted the intense ideological differences between labor and management, and their fine illustrators drew pictures of the battle and more cartoons of the fence.

Initially, the Homestead men who had fought for their job security, the safety of their homes, and their very survival believed themselves victorious. Ecstatic in their defiance of management, they now controlled the town of Homestead, the Homestead plant, and the waterfront as well.

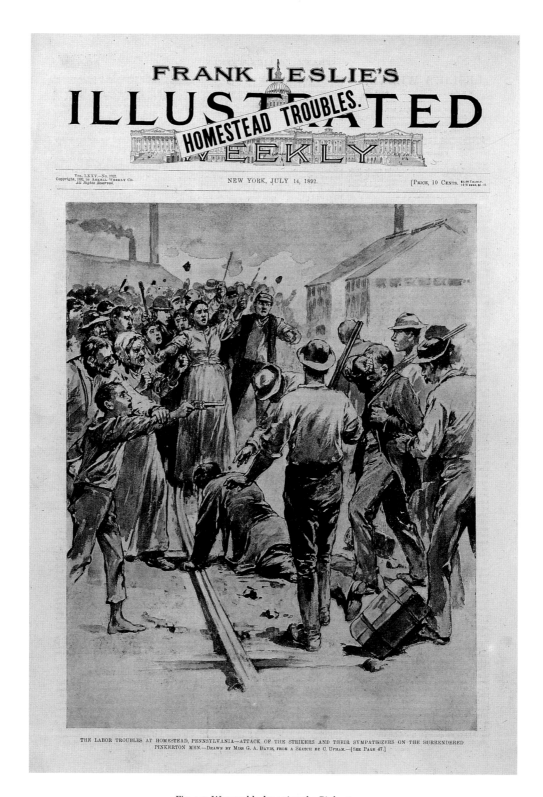

FRANK LESLIE'S
ILLUSTRATED
HOMESTEAD TROUBLES.
WEEKLY

Vol. LXXV.—No. 1922.
Copyright, 1892, by ARKELL WEEKLY CO.
All Rights Reserved.

NEW YORK, JULY 14, 1892.

[PRICE, 10 CENTS. $4.00 YEARLY.
IN ADVANCE, $1.15

THE LABOR TROUBLES AT HOMESTEAD, PENNSYLVANIA—ATTACK OF THE STRIKERS AND THEIR SYMPATHIZERS ON THE SURRENDERED PINKERTON MEN.—DRAWN BY MISS G. A. DAVIS, FROM A SKETCH BY C. UPHAM.—[SEE PAGE 47.]

Fig. 4-9. Women bludgeoning the Pinkertons.
Frank Leslie's Illustrated Weekly, July 14, 1892.
New York Society Library

But Frick had not given up. And the following day, July 7, Andrew Carnegie cabled from Pitlochry, Scotland: "All anxiety gone since know you stand firm[.] Never employ one of these rioters[.] Let grass grow over works."

Frick said to the press:

> While nobody could regret the occurrences of the last few days more than myself, yet it is my duty, as the executive head of the Carnegie Company, to protect the interest of the association. . . . The matter is out of our hands now. We look to the sheriff to protect our property. The men upon our properties are not strikers, they are lawbreakers. . . . I will hold conferences with nobody. . . . the supremacy of the law is the only question involved.

As far as the law was concerned, Frick was soon to discover that a far greater "law" than that of the land was dictating the course of his life.

❖

ON JULY 7, THE STRIKERS BURIED the unfortunate John Morris, killed at the pump house, and two other of their dead. Morris's widow said of Frick, "There is no more sensibility in that man than in a toad."

But Frick had not come out of the battle unscathed. In a moment of bitter irony, the day after the Morris burial, Adelaide went into labor and nearly died giving premature birth to Martha's replacement child—a sick baby boy. Adelaide placed her newborn son in the blue satin bassinet she had blessed with good luck kisses. To lessen the confusion in the household, Childs was immediately sent to Fishers Island with George Megrew. Helen, however, remained behind at Clayton (fig. 4-10).

But the crisis in Henry Clay Frick's home was of little consequence to the public as news of the Homestead tragedy spread and was debated. Were the strikers guilty of murder? Had Frick conspired to commit murder? On July 9, the local headline read:

FRICK MAY BE INDICTED

One newspaper claimed, "If he was not in the right [to hire the Pinkertons], then the case against him becomes strong. The protection of human life is the first consideration of the law. The protection of property is a secondary consideration."

Frank Leslie's Illustrated Weekly took the alternate view—management had the right to hire and fire whomever it pleased, and to establish its employees' salaries. Additionally, because the authorities failed to give management the necessary protection,

Fig. 4-10. Clayton at the time of the Homestead strike.
Frank Leslie's Illustrated Weekly, July 14, 1892.
New York Society Library

it had no other recourse than to hire an outside security force: "It is the sheerest nonsense to say that employers in this country may not protect themselves against anticipated or actual assault, within the limitations of the law, by such agencies as they may elect."

On July 12, after local police were unable to establish order in Homestead, Governor Robert Pattison finally ordered mobilization of 8,500 members of the Pennsylvania State Militia—cavalry and troops. Locomotives pulling ninety-five coaches arrived at the Munhall station in Homestead at 9:20 A.M. Four thousand heavily armed men were stationed near the front gate of the mill. By 10:00 A.M., the Carnegie officials were back in the mill office. The rest of the militia set up camp on Munhall Hill, a hill so high it had an uninterrupted view of the Homestead plant, the town, and the river below.

Relieved, Carnegie cabled Frick: "Governors action settles matters[.] all right now[.] No compromise." Two days later, in referring to the startup prognosis of the mill, he wrote, "Starting a few months sooner or later is nothing compared with the right class of men," adding the postscript, "Homestead had the refuse from old works."

Although he had communicated with his cousin George Lauder that "Matters at home *bad*—such a fiasco. . . . still we must keep quiet and so do all we can to support Frick and those at the seat of war," he reassured Frick by cable that he had "not spoken written or cabled one word to anybody" and intended to "continue silent." He again cabled Frick the same day: "Am with you to the end whether works run this year next or ever[.] No longer question of wages or dollars."

The question, in fact, had silently turned from wages, dollars, or "the right class of men," to murder. Unknown to Carnegie, Frick, or the militia, a twenty-one-year-old, black-haired, black-eyed Russian Jew from Lithuania named Alexander Berkman had now arrived in Pittsburgh, determined to take the law into his own hands (fig. 4-11). A member of the most radical fringe of the anarchist movement in New York, he was an outspoken,

Fig. 4-11. Alexander Berkman.
Harper's Weekly, August 6, 1892.
New York Society Library

brooding man with a fiery temper. Sallow-skinned and described by his contemporaries as a "cigarette fiend," he believed in taking direct action; if opportunity offered, he would not hesitate to murder a wealthy businessman abusing the poor. Those who knew Berkman said he was an intelligent man, but very rash; morose, yet violent when angered, he was considered so unstable that most anarchists would have nothing to do with him. He lived with Emma Goldman in New York, and together they preached the combined virtues of free love and "dynamite and death to all capital."

As Goldman later wrote in *Living My Life,* the Homestead battle "sounded the awakening of the American worker, the long-awaited day of his resurrection. The native toiler had risen, he was beginning to feel his mighty strength, he was determined to break the chains that held him in bondage." An equally inspired Berkman stated:

> The spirit of the heroic past [Russia] was reincarnated in the steel workers of Homestead, Pennsylvania. What a supreme joy to aid in this work! That is my natural mission. . . . The people, the toilers of the world, the producers—Comprise, to me, the universe. . . . They alone count. The rest are parasites, who have no right to exist. . . . The removal of a tyrant, of an enemy of the people, is in no way taking of a life. . . . If the latter demand his [own] life, so much the better.

Berkman and Goldman felt that "A blow aimed at Frick would . . . strike terror in the enemy's ranks and make them realize that the proletariat of America had its

Fig. 4-12. The Carnegie Steel offices,
site of the assassination attempt.
Carnegie Library, Pittsburgh

avengers." For Berkman the assassination of Frick—a symbolic act, not a personal assault—was justified because Frick "incarnated the spirit of the furnace [and was] the living symbol of his trade."

Upon arriving in Pittsburgh, Berkman first went to Homestead and then to Clayton. He strolled down Shadyside's broad, tree-lined avenues. He noted the "joyous and care-free" ladies in fine clothes and carriages. Though irritated by their smiles and laughter, for an instant the bucolic setting made him nostalgic: "Ah, life could be made livable, beautiful! Why should it not be? Why so much misery and strife? Sunshine, flowers, beautiful things all around me. This is life! Joy and peace." Suddenly, violent thinking pierced the mood: "Probably they are laughing at me. Laugh! Laugh! You despise me. I am of the People, but you belong to the Fricks. Well, it may soon be our turn to laugh."

Unwittingly, Frick gave Berkman his chance. On July 16, four days after the gates of Homestead were opened, Frick, with his mill now under protection of the state government, posted a notice on his Homestead fence stating that beginning July 21, any former employee who had not taken part in the strike and had not reapplied for his job would have his position given to a nonunion, imported strikebreaker.

Berkman viewed Frick's ultimatum as "the last word of Caesar." He decided to kill Frick on Saturday, July 23, because Frick was rumored to be leaving Pittsburgh for a few days in New York. Moreover, as Clayton was heavily guarded, he had decided to kill Frick in his office where, unbelievably, with no sign of a guard, Frick could be seen at his desk from the public hall, a hall anybody could reach simply by going up the elevator (fig. 4-12).

From Berkman's memoir and newspaper accounts of the day, the details of the assassination attempt can be constructed. The whole incident began at 1:55 P.M. that Saturday afternoon. Berkman brushed by an astounded attendant, stepped into the office on the left, and faced Frick (fig. 4-13). He later recalled that "for an instant, the sunlight, streaming through the window, dazzled [him]." "Fr——," he began, as the look of terror on Frick's face struck him speechless, knowing the look was "the dread," as Berkman recalled, "of the conscious presence of death." Then, with a quick motion, he drew the revolver. Frick clutched the arms of his chair with both hands, attempting to rise. Berkman took aim at Frick's head. Frick averted his face. Berkman pulled the trigger and "there [was] a flash, and the high-ceilinged room reverberate[d] with the booming of a cannon." Berkman remembered "a sharp piercing cry" and saw Frick on his knees, his head against the armchair, a stream of blood gushing from his neck. The bullet had pierced the lobe of Frick's left ear, entered his neck at the base of his skull, and penetrated to the middle of his back.

Berkman felt "calm and possessed, intent upon every movement" of Frick, who lay "head and shoulders under the large armchair, without sound or motion."

"Dead?" Berkman wondered. He decided to make sure. About twenty-five feet separated them. Berkman took a few steps toward Frick, when suddenly John G. A. Leishman, the vice president of Carnegie Steel, who had been sitting at the desk talking to Frick and was stunned by the swift attack, leaped to his feet. Instinctively, with his eyes bulging out, Leishman grabbed Berkman.

Frick screamed, "Murder! Help!"

Astonished, Berkman realized his assassination attempt had failed.

Fig. 4-13. Alexander Berkman's attempted assassination of Henry Clay Frick.
Harper's Weekly, August 6, 1892.
New York Society Library

"Alive?" he gasped, as he threw Leishman aside, and fired for a second time at the "crawling figure of Frick."

Again Frick started back, but after a minute, he began to swoon. Berkman's second shot, deflected by Leishman's hand, had lodged in the right side of Frick's neck, causing another stream of blood to run down over his clothing.

"I have missed!" Berkman despaired as he and Leishman struggled across the room.

Berkman tried to throw Leishman off, but the man held on. Then, noticing an opening between his victim's arm and body, Berkman thrust the revolver into Frick's side, intending to pull the trigger for a third time. But Leishman anticipated his move. He caught Berkman's wrist, and swung his arm up and back. The third bullet crashed into the wall as Leishman held the arm with the pistol with one hand and seized Berkman by the throat with the other.

"Not dead?" Berkman realized with amazement as he began to crawl, in Frick's direction, thinking he "must get the dagger from his pocket" (fig. 4-14).

Frick, recovered from the shock of his two wounds by the sound of the third shot hitting the wall, got to his feet and threw himself on the struggling men. Round and round the trio wrestled, getting nearer to the front windows all the time. Though slight in build, Berkman seemed possessed of Herculean strength.

Twice Berkman nearly wrenched himself loose, trying hard to free the hand in which he held the pistol. Once he succeeded and pulled the trigger, but the pistol misfired. Leishman seized the hand again and held it. Frick grasped the man about the waist, pinioning the other hand. All three appeared about to fall. As they swayed back and forth, not a word was uttered. Frick was becoming weak, his blood staining his assailant's clothing.

A carpenter named Andy rushed in on the scene with his hammer in hand and began to strike uncontrollably at Berkman's head.

"Where is the hammer? Hit him, carpenter!" yelled those who had rushed into the office. A blow hit Berkman in the head, stunning him enough to cause him to drop the gun. The carpenter, intent on striking again, missed his mark and Frick, although weak from the loss of blood, commanded:

"Don't kill him, I tell you; let the law take its course."

Berkman, though dazed, was able to wrench his left hand free and plunge it into his back pocket.

"I have it!" Berkman exclaimed to himself, as he unleashed his crude, stilettolike knife. The knife

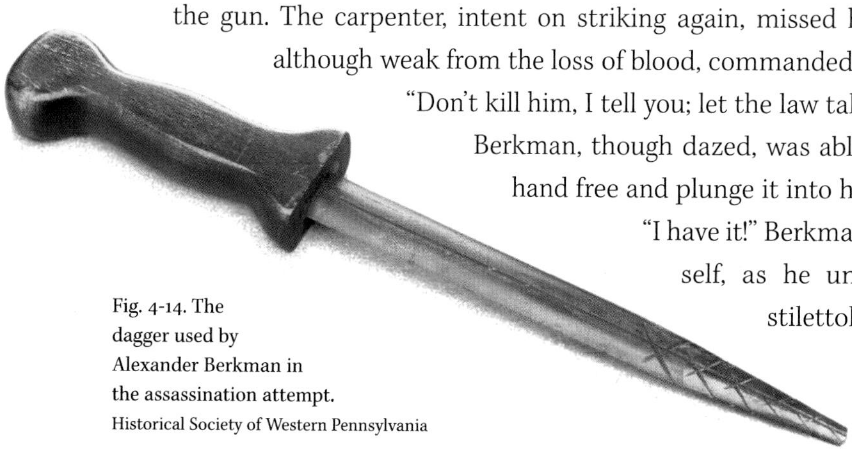

Fig. 4-14. The dagger used by Alexander Berkman in the assassination attempt.
Historical Society of Western Pennsylvania

flashed through the air and was driven with force into Frick's back. With hardly an instant's pause it was withdrawn and again driven forward into Frick's hip, right side, and left leg below the knee. Berkman heard Frick cry out in pain. There was much shouting and stamping until Leishman finally succeeded in tripping the assailant. Berkman went down on the floor as Frick and Leishman bent over him.

The assault and subsequent struggle, though seeming suspended in time, was over in a flash.

When the authorities arrived, they found all three men on the floor. The deputy sheriff drew his gun and was going to shoot the assassin on the spot, but Frick insisted once again, "Don't shoot! Leave him to the law; but raise his head and let me see his face."

Policemen, clerks, workmen in overalls, surrounded Berkman. Frick, supported by several men, stood in front of his would-be-assassin. Frick looked like death. His face was ash gray; his beard was streaked with red blood oozing from his neck wound. For a moment, as Berkman looked at Frick, he felt "a feeling as of shame" coming over him. But the next moment he was "filled with anger at the sentiment, so unworthy of a revolutionist."

The police asked, "Mr. Frick, do you identify this man as your assailant?" as an officer pulled Berkman's head back by the hair. Berkman's eyes met Frick's, and as he looked at Frick full in the face, with defiant hatred, Frick nodded weakly.

But the struggle was not yet finished. When someone noticed that Berkman was chewing something, they pried his mouth open. They found a capsule containing enough fulminate of mercury to blow the whole building apart. At that point, Leishman fainted.

Frick stood up and leaned on his desk for a full minute. Then he said with a forced smile, "Well, I believe I feel like fainting."

Hands reached out to support him and lift him gently onto the lounge chair. Dr. Lawrence Litchfield, who was summoned to the scene, immediately called Dr. J. J. Buchanan, a surgeon who had just started his practice at Mercy Hospital the year before. Buchanan lived near the Carnegie Steel Company's office and, as one of the first surgeons in Pittsburgh to practice aseptic surgery, was the only Pittsburgh doctor who kept a black bag of sterile instruments with him for emergencies.

The two doctors quickly began to tear off Frick's clothing. Ready to probe for the bullets, Dr. Buchanan started to give Frick anesthesia, but Frick refused to take it, saying this way he could better help Buchanan feel his way to the bullets. Frick then added with a smile, "Don't make it too bad, Doctor, for you know I must be at the office on Monday."

Fig. 4-15. Henry Clay Frick goes home in an ambulance.
Frank Leslie's Illustrated Weekly, August 6, 1892.
New York Society Library

Frick directed Dr. Buchanan as the surgeon probed his neck and back. It took two individual searches, one for each bullet. The first bullet was found with "unerring precision." The second bullet, however, took Dr. Buchanan another two hours to locate. Frick suddenly felt metal hit metal and said simply, "There, that feels like it."

After the bullet was removed, Frick began to complain of numbing in one of his legs, saying he could not control it with ease. Dr. Buchanan felt certain that one of the bullets had caused partial paralysis, but on further examination, he discovered two gashes from the assassin's knife, each located on the underside of Frick's leg and so deep that the tendons had almost been severed.

Saturated in blood, Frick, with bullets removed and wounds dressed, suddenly announced he wanted to walk downstairs and go home in his carriage. The doctors said that his "was the most magnificent exhibition of courage they had ever seen," but instead they ordered Frick an ambulance from Mercy Hospital, believing there was little if any hope for his recovery.

To their astonishment, Frick, who on their arrival had seemed to be unconscious and dying, now suddenly moved from the chair where the doctors had operated on him, to his desk. As if motivated by some mysterious, life-giving force, he picked up the train of thought interrupted by Berkman's attack and took up his affairs exactly where he had left off. Frick completed the day's paperwork, signed letters, and concluded an important loan deal.

He sent a telegram to his mother: "Was shot twice but not dangerously." And then sent a telegram to Andrew Carnegie, assuring him that there was no need for him to come home, saying that he was still in shape to "fight the battle out."

At 6 P.M., four hours after Berkman's attack, Frick prepared a statement for the press from his office: "This incident will not change the attitude of the Carnegie Steel Company toward the Amalgamated Association. I do not think I shall die, but whether I do or not, the Company will pursue the same policy and it will win."

He also sent a message to Clayton by special messenger. Adelaide was not to be told about the attack because it was feared the shock might kill her. The message was delivered, rather, to Attie, who then came rushing down to the office to see her brother-in-law. Although the operation to extract the bullets was not yet over when she arrived, Frick greeted her quite cheerfully saying, "Hello, I am glad to see you. What do you think? I am not hurt much." She returned to Clayton promising not to tell Adelaide anything about what had happened.

The doctors kept Frick at the office until long past seven and watched him constantly. A crowd of two thousand people had gathered, screaming at Berkman as he was dragged out of Frick's office, "Lynch him. Shoot him. Kill him." They now kept vigil, certain the Carnegie officials would soon announce Frick's death.

The doctors placed Frick on an iron cot and carried him downstairs to the iron-wheeled Mercy Hospital ambulance that would transport him over the cobblestone streets back to Clayton (fig. 4-15). Before leaving the building, wanting no future reminders of his assassin, Frick ordered all his office furniture removed. Then, covered in blankets, his head and face swathed in bandages, two crystal blue eyes peeped out with what seemed to be a half-amused expression. As Frick passed, he glimpsed an Inspector Sylvus, who was at the front of the building commanding a squad of officers, and said, "I'll be back Monday."

WHILE FRICK WAS DEFYING both medical reason and medical wisdom, Attie returned to Clayton, where Annie described her as "shaking like a leaf." When she recounted the events of the day to Annie, they agreed at once that Adelaide, still fragile after childbirth and only out of bed that day for the first time, must be shielded from the news. As Attie said to Annie, "Just tell my sister anything you can think of just so she will not hear the confusion when they bring him home."

While the baby slept in his bassinet and the afternoon wore on, Adelaide still did not suspect that anything was wrong. But the blistering heat wave had made Clayton so unbearable that upstairs, two windows had been opened in Adelaide's room, one window looking out over the garden, the other toward Penn Avenue. Annie had been trying to keep Adelaide's thoughts occupied by telling her about Martha's pet dickey bird who had died that day. And as she was telling Adelaide how they had buried the bird with a proper service, she suddenly heard a newsboy on Penn Avenue calling,

ALL ABOUT HENRY CLAY FRICK BEING SHOT

Although Annie ran to the window and closed it before Adelaide could register what had been said, Adelaide asked why she had closed the window. Annie simply told her she felt hot air blowing through the window and feared Adelaide would be in a draft. But when Frick finally arrived at Clayton, at eight o'clock that night, Adelaide became hysterical. Ten minutes before his arrival, Attie had told Adelaide that her husband had been shot. Hoping to minimize her sister's anxiety, Attie explained there had only been one wound, it was superficial, and Frick was in no danger.

Upon Frick's arrival, however, Adelaide's worst fears were realized. She could hear the confusion of labored footsteps, as the four men carrying him up the stairs in the cot struggled under their patient's one hundred and sixty pounds. And when the men stopped in front of her door, Frick, trying not to let on he was badly hurt, politely asked Adelaide how the baby was. Then he said in as casual a tone as he could muster, "Ada . . . , I will be in to see you as soon as I get washed and cleaned up."

At that, Adelaide gasped, "Oh, something has happened!" Annie threw her arms around her and tried to comfort her saying, "There, there, dear, everything will be all right." But Adelaide was sobbing and struggling with Annie, pleading, "Annie, I must get up, I must get up."

The doctors came in to calm Adelaide and gave her, Annie, and Attie some pills to quiet them all before redressing Frick's wounds, which had bled through his bandages and clothing. Then the nurse lifted Adelaide from her bed into her rocking chair. Together the nurses and Adelaide's brother, Marshall Childs, who lived nearby, pulled Adelaide and the chair through Frick's dressing room, into his bedroom. Then they put her in bed beside Frick. Adelaide's voice was so weak, it trembled when she spoke to him.

The nurse entered the room and then closed the doors so Adelaide and Frick, who wanted to be alone, could have their privacy. It was the exact same week during which Martha had died one year before; the first anniversary was only six days away.

Both Adelaide and Frick had been sedated, and the nurse, who had remained in the room, put a chair at Adelaide's side of the bed. Soon she asked Annie to sit there while she had her dinner and boiled her instruments, for Frick had previously ordered that only Annie should stay in his room while the nurse was gone. The nurse told Annie to ring for her if Adelaide or Frick wakened.

As Annie remembered, they lay in bed, their eyes closed, neither speaking a word. Afraid to even breathe, Annie was sure Adelaide and Frick had died, for they never moved once while the nurse was gone.

At nine o'clock, although Adelaide had nursed the baby before she was taken into her husband's room, the nurses brought her back into her room, put her in her own bed, and got her settled in time for the baby's next feeding. Frick fell in and out of consciousness. His body began to battle the summer heat, which reached over a hundred in the shade. He fought off a high fever, infection, the fear of blood poisoning, and almost certain death.

Some morning headlines sneered:

TOO BAD—SERVES HIM RIGHT
FRICK IS A DIRTY DOG AND DESERVES TO DIE

The Amalgamated Association, however, wanting to clear its name, immediately condemned "the unlawful act of . . . wounding." *The New York World* had the most balanced view: "Those who hate him most admire the nerve and stamina of this man of steel whom nothing seems to be able to move."

Carnegie cabled: "Too glad at your escape to think of anything[.] Never fear my brave dear friend my appearing on the scene as long as you are able to direct matters from house and unless partners call. Be careful of yourself[.] Be careful of yourself is all we ask." Judge Thomas Mellon wrote his protégé urging "the necessity of quiet and mental repose . . . duty to yourself, your family, and the public demands it."

Frick, however, eschewed the well-meaning advice of his family and business associates, who urged him to take it easy during his convalescence. He read the papers, continued to run Carnegie Steel, and monitored the ongoing negotiations concerning the Homestead strike from his sickbed. The doctors insisted that he not read about the attempt on his life, as it might "cause [his] fever to rise," but Frick said he would worry more if details were kept from him, if he was not constantly informed. He said with a laugh: "It will not hurt me; this is very interesting reading."

Frick had been lucky. Had Berkman been more professional and less of an idealist, Frick, most assuredly, would have been dead. Apart from the fact that Berkman's gun had been old and rusty, and Berkman was known to be a poor shot, his eight-inch stiletto—a common file set in a common pine handle—was dull and defective. Moreover, one wound revealed that Berkman's knife had struck Frick's ninth rib, thus preventing the blade from penetrating his right lung. In another wound the blade had broken off two inches inside Frick's body, narrowly missing his spinal cord and vital organs. In taking inventory of his wounds, the doctors were amazed how many of them were near misses.

On July 30, Tom Carter, President Harrison's personal friend and chosen political advisor, as well as head of the Republican National Committee, asked a mediator, John Elmer Milholland, to try to negotiate between Frick and the labor union. He was worried about the negative effect the Homestead strike would have on the November presidential election. Milholland approached the striker who had been in charge on the morning the Pinkertons had landed. Between them they drew up the strikers' final terms and sent them to Carnegie, who was on a coaching trip through the Scottish Highlands. Carnegie's reply was "See Frick."

Milholland did and later wrote:

> He was able to see me and discuss the subject with clearness and decision, not withstanding his weakened condition. The settlement as proposed he declared to be "utterly impossible". . . . he would not, so long as he remained in charge of the plants "deviate one iota from the lines he had laid out to follow" and was following them to their logical lengths. . . . His powerful jaws came together like a steel trap when he referred to the "murderous" exhibitions of the strikers, but while he spoke with great intensity of feeling there was no undue excitement throughout the interview. . . . as he lay there as white almost as the sheet itself, I realized that I was talking to a man of absolute nerve, with a will of iron; one who knew his own mind and indulged in no illusions as to the difficulties in the way of carrying out his purpose.

Frick said he would "fight the strike out on the lines that he [Frick] had laid down. . . . if it takes all summer and all winter, and all next summer and all next winter. Yes, even my life itself. I will fight this thing to the bitter end. I will never recognize the Union, never, never!"

On September 17, 1892, one month before the end of the Homestead strike, Frick expressed this determination through an art acquisition. He acquired from J. J. Gillespie's a small painting of a donkey, the steady, stubborn little beast of burden, entitled *Mine Mule* (fig. 4-16) by James Bonar. In a wry gesture, he placed it at the top of Clayton's back stairs, the stairs he had been carried up when returning from the assassination attempt. George Harvey, Frick's biographer, commented that Frick's "notably quick mind did not respond readily to wit; he hardly ever laughed; his real delight lay in humor, the subtler the better, which never failed to elicit that 'slow, understanding smile.'" In purchasing *Mine Mule,* Frick had laughed, albeit in a dark-humored way, about his workers, his mulish stance at Homestead, and his near loss of life. Though donkeys carry burdens and mules are determined, Frick knew that mine mules were the most carefully and respectfully tended and the most valuable possessions of all mining equipment. Often stabled underground, they hauled coal to the surface, and if a miner were ever lost in the dark, tunneled caverns of the mine, the mule, "given its head," would lead him to safety. One mule at the Union Coke Works near Morewood was a legend. Held up as an archangel of antiunionism, the old mule had never missed a day's work, except when the works were temporarily shut down.

Frick's *Mine Mule* was just as special. While the painting suggests the well-known story of the loyal mule and the determination noted by Milholland, it suggests more strongly Frick's view of labor. In an obvious dig at laborers, perceived by him and

Fig. 4-16. James Bonar (1864–1942), *Mine Mule*.
Acquired in 1892, Oil on canvas, 7¾ x 9¾ in. (19.7 x 24.8 cm).
Frick Art and Historical Center

others of the wealthy class as beasts of burden, the donkey carrying high explosives wears a sign: "Non-Union Helper."

When visiting Frick, although Milholland sensed the depth of Frick's determination, he was struck by something far more intense. He felt that Frick's "normal cool resolution [showed] something of a fanatical quality." Neither he nor any one else, however, knew that Frick's determination to break the Amalgamated Association had gone beyond contempt for labor union leaders; his personal conviction had turned into religious ideology. Indeed, according to George Harvey, twenty years passed before Henry Clay Frick would acknowledge that when Berkman aimed the gun at his head and fired the first shot, Martha had appeared at his side. As Frick himself revealed to an Ohio news reporter, he saw her "as clearly and as real as if she had been physically present—indeed for an instant her presence was so real and corporal that he [had] felt like stretching out his arms to her." In 1912, when Frick was building his New York home, he was asked by a friend if it were true that Martha had appeared to him during Berkman's attack. Frick nodded in quiet assent. Berkman had been more vocal. He

Fig. 4-17. Pascal-Adolphe-Jean Dagnan-Bouveret (1852–1929), *Christ and the Disciples at Emmaus,* 1896-97.
Acquired in 1897, Oil on canvas, 78 x 110½ in. (198.1 x 280.7 cm).
Carnegie Museum of Art, Pittsburgh, gift of Henry Clay Frick, 1898

claimed he had missed Frick's head because he, Berkman, had been "dazzled" by sunlight streaming through the window. But as Frick privately believed, Berkman missed because he had been "dazzled" by the spiritual light surrounding Martha's apparition, not by the sun. Frick's office window faced due north.

❖

FRICK HARBORED HIS SECRET and fervently held his belief in Martha's divine intervention until his death. As a result, the grief over his lost daughter and the experience of her apparition profoundly affected his relationship with the union, Carnegie, his wife, his surviving children, and the ultimate shape of his art collection. Martha, the child who swallowed the pin in the summer of 1887 just after Frick had resigned as chairman of his H. C. Frick Coke Company; the child who had a pin exit her side just months before the dam broke at South Fork; the child Frick neglected during the 1891 Morewood riots as she went into her fatal decline; the child who could not be saved by Carnegie's doctors or all the money in the world; this child, who died in the Carnegie Cottage, had reappeared from the dead in a supernatural flash of light to save the father who could not save her. This child had become the silent cross beneath which Frick would now purge Homestead.

Although Frick felt Martha's visitation was too poignant and private to share, within the family there was an understanding that because his longing for Martha remained profound, his thoughts could not help but return to her. Louise Dilworth Childs wrote her mother, Mrs. George W. Dilworth: "This week is the anniversary of Martha's death which will be hard for him to think of as Martha C. [Attie] told me . . . that Mr. F. had never gotten over Martha's death, and now being confined to his bed will give him so much time to think and recall this time last year."

Although Frick did not acknowledge Martha's apparition until 1912, his secret was revealed in certain works of art acquired in 1895, when he seems to have suffered a delayed reaction to Martha's death. Additionally, in 1897, when Frick saw P. A. J. Dagnan-Bouveret's *Christ and the Disciples at Emmaus* (fig. 4-17) his silence indicated the direction his art collecting was taking. In that painting, describing the disciples' experience of Christ appearing to them in a postdeath visitation three days after his crucifixion, a burst of brilliant light emanates from Christ's head as he reveals himself. Still later, the vision of Martha would echo in Sir Thomas Lawrence's portrait *Miss Louisa Murray* (fig. 4-18). The subject is a love-child who floats like an apparition through the air with haunting eyes, curly hair, and forehead like Martha's. Her skirt is full of pansies, Martha's favorite flower.

Fig. 4-18. Sir Thomas Lawrence (1769–1830), *Miss Louisa Murray*, 1827.
Acquired in 1916, Oil on canvas, 36½ x 28⅞ in. (92.7 x 73.3 cm).
The Frick Collection

Henry Clay Frick's convalescence was going smoothly, but his three-week-old infant son, ill since birth, was failing. Nurse Grandison, daughter of a minister and a greatly respected African-American woman who was caring for the baby, believed the problem lay in the fact that he was not taking enough nourishment, a situation that seemed odd, particularly since Adelaide had plenty of milk. A newspaper article claimed that poison was involved:

> A sensational chapter is added to the Frick tragedy by the receipt of a startling letter [in Wooster, Ohio] this evening. Robert Alexander, a Pittsburgh fresco artist working here, tonight received a letter from his sweetheart, who is employed as a domestic in the Frick household. Within the past four days an attempt had been made to poison the entire Frick household. Mrs. Frick and her infant son were made dangerously ill, and the wife of Mr. Frick's coachman is in dying condition. Strenuous efforts . . . had been made to suppress the facts, while detectives were employed to ferret out the perpetrators of the outrage.

Although the story is impossible to authenticate, what is documented is the fact that the child's doctors had examined the baby every day, and could not decide what to do, for they could not make a diagnosis.

Then one morning, Frick, although ever preoccupied with the Homestead situation, called out happily from his room. Pleased by an article supporting him against the Amalgamated Association, he said jokingly, "Ada dear, I am going to call our son 'Charles Dana,' after the editor of the *New York Sun*."

Adelaide replied, "Yes, dear," and then whispering, she turned to Annie and confided, "I have named my baby 'Henry Clay Frick, Jr.'"

In fact, the baby had yet to be christened, and Annie was becoming increasingly alarmed about his health. On the morning of August 3, she was in the room alone with Adelaide and the baby while Nurse Grandison was downstairs preparing breakfast. Glancing down at the baby, Annie noticed how very pale he was. She did not want to call Adelaide to the bassinet because, except to be placed in Frick's bed the night her husband had been wounded, Adelaide had not been allowed out of her own bed.

Annie felt the baby was dying. Knowing he, like Martha and the other children, had not been baptized because Frick, a Mennonite who had turned Baptist and Freemason in the late 1870s, did not practice infant baptism, she took a glass, filled it with water and returned to the bassinet. When no one was looking, she baptized the baby "Henry Clay Frick, Jr."

When she returned with the papers, she found the Doctors McClelland and Frick's two surgeons in Adelaide's bedroom. The baby was having convulsions and because Adelaide was unable to withstand the realization that her new baby was dying, she had been moved to Frick's bedroom.

The doctors had decided there was nothing to be done to save the child. About 8 A.M., as the doctors, Nurse Grandison, Attie, and Annie watched helplessly, Henry Clay Frick, Jr., suffered another convulsion and died of unexplained internal hemorrhage.

Attie broke the news to Adelaide and Frick who, as Annie explained, were not in any shape either physically or emotionally to "stand such sorrow." The baby had died on Wednesday, August 3, the same week Martha had died the prior year, and two days short of Martha's seventh birthday, had she lived.

To further complicate the tragedy, the Carnegie Company called Frick to advise him of the results of the inquest into the Homestead case. The headline in the morning paper delivered by Annie was confirmed:

MR. FRICK TO BE ARRESTED

Warrants were issued for the arrest of all Carnegie officials. The Pinkertons were charged with murder. Some Carnegie officials were arrested, and some surrendered. Their bail was set at $10,000 each. Frick's arrest was to be delayed until he had recovered from his wounds.

When Frick heard the charges against him, the *Commercial Gazette* said "he was not ruffled in the least." In fact, they reported that he said nothing. But for the first time since the shooting, he did not read his morning mail. His legal fate, the fiasco of a corporation on trial—these must have seemed bitterly irrelevant to him at this moment. He had his infant son's funeral to arrange.

Frick invited very few of his business friends to attend, deciding that this child's funeral would be attended primarily by family. The undertaker and minister were called. Then, as was common practice of the day, Adelaide requested a photographer be summoned to take pictures of the dead baby (fig. 4-19). Dressed in a long, white lace day dress, he was placed in the blue and white bassinet Adelaide had so lovingly prepared only weeks before. He was then moved from Adelaide's room into Helen's room, in front of the fireplace, where his posthumous photograph was taken both in his bassinet and posed in his nurse's lap.

The funeral was set for the following day, Thursday, August 4, for it was important to have the baby buried before Martha's birthday the next day. Adelaide and Frick refused to receive any visitors and Frick, anxious about his wife's health, sat up most of the night of August 3 beside her bed, sleeping for only an hour or two at a time.

On the morning of August 4, just before the minister arrived at Clayton to perform the funeral service, Frick asked Annie to come to his bedroom. Perhaps needing privacy because he was so weak and Adelaide so frail, Frick had positioned some chairs inside his bedroom so he and his wife could hear the service below without being seen. He was sitting on his thirty-three-year-old wife's right, holding onto her.

She was trembling so badly, Frick beckoned Annie to sit on his wife's left side. As Annie did so, she took hold of Adelaide's left hand, and although Frick held her right one, Annie feared Adelaide might still fall off her chair.

The choir was in the downstairs hall. The minister stood on the stair landing with the stained-glass window entitled *Love in the Tower* behind him. As the choir sang past the minister up to Frick and Adelaide, it was clear to Annie the only thing that could have given the couple the strength to endure the service was "God himself." Then just past noon, August 4, 1892, the mortal remains of Henry Clay Frick, Jr., who had been placed in a fine, plush casket with a solid silver nameplate, were accompanied by the mourners to the Homewood Cemetery and lowered into a small grave beside his sister Martha.

Fig. 4-19. Posthumous photograph of Henry Clay Frick, Jr.,
in the bassinet trimmed by his mother, Adelaide Frick.
Frick Archives

James Howard Bridge, Herbert Spencer's former secretary and Andrew Carnegie's literary assistant, later noted the baby's tragedy: "Born in the midst of the excitement and dead because of it." And yet, Frick, who had now lost two children in a year and had almost lost his wife in childbirth, went on as if nothing had happened.

Presenting his ever determined face to his family, the forty-three-year-old industrialist remarked at breakfast the day after the baby's funeral—as he was to do every August 5 thereafter—that it was Martha's birthday. This day he commented that had Martha lived, she would have been seven years old. This was a sacred number, symbolic of the completion of time, a number revered in antiquity and in the Freemasonry ethos, to which Frick subscribed.

Then Henry Clay Frick turned to face the world. At 9:45 A.M., he left Clayton for his office. Only two weeks from the day he was almost fatally wounded, with scars on his neck and ears, and stiffness in his shoulders, he rode a Duquesne trolleycar from outside his home and walked into his office as if absolutely nothing had happened. Saying he "had too much to do to stay away from the office any longer," and "hop[ing] his friends and the public [would] drop [the subject of the assassination attempt] as he has done," as the press noted, he "engaged with all his energies in his business as quietly as if yesterday he had been at his desk, instead of attending the funeral of his child."

Writing from Scotland the following day, Carnegie cheered: "Hearty congratulation from all here upon your return to the post of duty[.] Every thing is right when you and Mrs. Frick are right[.] Every other consideration insignificant."

Despite Frick's profound personal losses, his physical strength had largely returned, his resolve to see the strike out was still firm, and his experience of Martha's visitation was still a secret. He had shown no concern for the tragedy of working-class families, most particularly those who had struck his plants in the Coke Region or the Homestead mill, and no outward emotion on the death of two children. But future art acquisitions would reveal that his emotional breaking point was moving to the surface, even as he returned to work and displayed a courteous, armor-plated facade. He celebrated Martha's birthday by going into his private room, lighting a cigar, asking the heads of the departments to report to him as usual, and burying himself in his morning mail.

Frick announced he would continue to ride in carriages and open streetcars at fixed hours. He dismissed all police protection, saying it was for Adelaide's peace of mind, and refused to have any personal bodyguards. He said to a *New York Times* reporter, "If an honest American cannot live in his own home without being surrounded by a body guard, it is time to quit." On August 13, however, armed guards were brought back to Clayton. Frick did not want them, but his friends insisted he be protected because a friend of Alexander Berkman's, whose name was Aaronstamm, had apparently been sent to complete the job Berkman had bungled. Officials of the Carnegie Company were receiving threatening letters, and their secretary, Francis Lovejoy, had been warned he only had two days to live. This second assassination attempt had originated in Vienna and had been revealed to the New York police by the Austrian vice-consul.

Frick went out of town for a few days on a fishing trip. Adelaide, who had been described in the newspapers just four years before as "young, fair and charming . . . the fortunate owner of carriages, horses, diamonds and all the beautiful things that money can buy," began to accumulate a wardrobe of black as she retreated further into the world of depression and chronic ill health. She had lost Martha, Martha's replacement child, and would soon lose herself as well.

Within months Annie eloped with Lewis Stephany, the son of the interior decorator at Clayton. She remained a close friend of the family and kept Martha's "Rosebud doll" as a poignant reminder of the Frick family. They, and ironically, the doll would eventually play a role in the lives of her own five children. Annie named her first child, a boy, Clayton; and her second, a girl, was called Helen Frick Stephany. Annie gave her Martha's "Rosebud doll." But Martha's tragedy seemed to continue through the doll. In 1902, when little Helen was eight years old, she came down with typhoid fever and died. Although Annie packed Martha's doll away in a trunk in the attic, its apparent curse lasted into the next generation, when Annie gave it to her granddaughter, also named Martha. One day Martha, who was returning home from college, found her mother, Elizabeth, who had been picking mint in the garden, running into the house covered with yellowjackets. She screamed for Martha to spray her with water, but Martha was unable to spray the bees off in time. Elizabeth fell dead to the floor.

⁘

FRICK WAS SUFFERING DEEPLY, but none was the wiser. Following his infant namesake's funeral, he continued to go about his business as usual. And as the strike wore on, Frick brought strikebreakers into the mill by way of the riverbank and housed them within the mill yards, still enclosed by his fence. The scabs worked and slept inside the mill in the record heat which, in some departments, reached one hundred and fifty degrees. According to the *New York Times*, some died in the mill from poisoning by arsenic and croton oil with powders of antimony slipped into their food by undercover agents of the union.

On August 17, a cheerful Frick wrote Andrew Carnegie: "We will be amply repaid for all of our trouble [in this world] and in the near future. We shall be able to get closer to our men, and when they once become acquainted with us they will find that we are probably about the best friends they have."

Carnegie congratulated him: "The whole public is at your feet, and I am obliged to paint your history every day; and, of course, you may suspect, I never fail to add 'that is the kind of fellows our firm is made up of—the ablest and best set of men in the world; all not only partners but friends.'"

Carnegie, weary of the anticapitalist press and concerned for the Homestead men, wanted to make a conciliatory gesture to Homestead by building a library overlooking the mill. Hoping to ingratiate himself with the workers by taking this interest in their cultural development, on August 29 he wrote Frick: "I am glad you see the need for this institution, and of other things of similar character calculated to produce feelings of harmony and friendship between us and all our men." Wishing "the break would come" and anxious about the hiring policy to follow once the strike was over, he cautioned Frick that every one of the twenty-three partners in the company would "sink [the] works rather than dismiss one man," particularly since they had lost the fight.

Frick, however, having made such a concession to Carnegie in 1887, determined never to do so again. Unlike Carnegie, he had no sympathy for the men who challenged his authority and seized the mill. He was now only interested in "the firmness with which these strikers hold on." On August 31, with the protection of a detective, he inspected the mill for the first time since the strike. Pleased with what he saw, he said, "The strike is a thing of the past." The strength of his conviction was about to be borne out, he wrote Andrew Carnegie on September 10, and urged him to remain calm:

> I with you, most heartily wish the break would come, but we will have to exercise a little more patience, and it will come eventually, and when once we demonstrate to our workmen that they can have only one master, and that it is better for them that it should be so, we will be able to accomplish wonderful results at all our works. We cannot expect that the public should understand just how kindly we do feel towards those who are in our service; that we are just as anxious for their welfare as we are for our own. We must expect to be misrepresented, but time will cure this all, if we are right, and there is no question but what we are right in this matter. . . . There is nothing personal in this matter, so far as I am concerned. . . . if we want to get the full benefit of all that we have gone through, there must be no deviation from the policy we have been pursuing all along. After it is all over, if it is thought someone else can do better, the position is open for him. I have never sought responsibility, nor, to my knowledge have I ever shirked it.

On September 24, Carnegie wrote his friend the eighty-three-year-old English prime minister, William E. Gladstone: "The pain I suffer increases daily." And that same day, concerned about the strain Frick was under, he warned Frick from Scotland:

I think many times a day how slender the thread is upon which we depend—
your good health—any ordinary man would have broken down ere this—you
may not until all is quiet but then you will feel it. I never felt "nerves" until
Louise was out of danger & then I couldn't walk a few squares—keep before you
a grand tour round the world—Mrs. Frick Miss Childs [Attie] you, children
under charge of some relative. . . . there is nothing so full of intense interest as a
visit to Japan China India.

Within a week he wrote Frick, again offering advice:

We have had our trials in all this business—hard enough in some respects
harder to hear standing apart in inaction, than in the midst of the excitement
but these melt into nothingness compared to your *Home agonies*. I don't see
how you can stand them. If you are like me you will stand until all is quiet and
you are out of it and then give way. I have not been so well the past two weeks
principally because there is less excitement and besides, fishing is over. . . .
I hope to get my mind somewhat off [Homestead] by rushing through Italy
etc.—fresh sights do much. . . . Business be hanged.

But Frick showed no signs of a man about to break down. He only longed to break the strike, a wish granted on November 18, 1892. The strikers, forced to give up from lack of money, fell to Frick. He had used the best and most astute lawyers available, had been unwavering in his stand, and as would later be decided by a congressional investigation, he had fought the Amalgamated Association within the confines of existing laws, breaking none of them.

The strikers, on the other hand, were charged with breaking the law. They had shown themselves to be an armed mob which had torn down company fences; occupied the plant; armed themselves with rifles, pistols, and cannon; and taken illegal possession of private property. The strikers had forcibly and unlawfully barred the Carnegie Steel Company from its own property and prevented it from operating.

By seizing Homestead, the strikers forced the government to consider the issue of workers' rights versus the rights of management and private property. In the end, the law protecting the sanctity of private property prevailed. Hours after the strike fell apart, Frick sent Carnegie a concise telegram, "Victory—Early."

From the Scottish highlands, Carnegie cabled Frick: "Through the war at last. What a relief." And a week after the victory, as a still euphoric Carnegie left for Rome, he wrote Frick: "Life is again worth living . . . . Havent [*sic*] we had a blundering time of it ever since we owned Homestead." He almost sighed, "now for long years of peace and prosperity." And he confessed, "I am now interested in art matters. Until your cable my mind was always running away with me to Pittsburgh."

Frick cabled back: "Our victory is now complete and most gratifying. Do not think we will ever have any serious labor trouble again. . . . Let the Amalgamated still exist, and hold full sway at other people's mills. That is no concern of ours." Saying, "We had to teach our employees a lesson, and we have taught them one they will never forget," Frick predicted: "It is hard to estimate what blessings will flow from our recent complete victory, both to the owners and the employees of the Carnegie Steel Ltd."

One of the blessings for Frick was that the Homestead victory broke the back of the unions in more places than just Carnegie's empire. Within a year, the Amalgamated lost 12,000 of its 24,000 dues-paying members. And then on June 4, 1893, the *Post* confirmed the decision of those investigating murder charges against Henry Clay Frick: "We are fully satisfied that no just cause existed for the finding of an indictment for murder or any other criminal offense against the laws of the Commonwealth of Pennsylvania."

Nevertheless, to some, Henry Clay Frick's name went down in infamy. The radical fringe of the labor movement became obsessive in its hatred of him. The U.S. House of Representatives, which investigated the Homestead strike, had a milder reaction; they were of the opinion that "Mr. Frick, who is a businessman of great energy and intelligence, seems to have been too stern, brusque and somewhat autocratic." Indeed, as time went on, the predominant perception of Henry Clay Frick was that of a villain, a malevolent persecutor of the working class.

But Frick did not care. While his boss remained abroad until January 1893, Henry Clay Frick, legally exonerated, his victory over labor and his antiunion policy vindicated, continued on with his work. Yet Frick, his once dark brown beard now whitened, still found no inner peace. The cost of victory and the trauma of Martha's death, now compounded by the death of his infant namesake, could be seen in the symbolic names of six parallel streets outside the Homestead mill. Starting at his semicircular wooden fence, later to become a brick wall, the streets stretched up the steep hill overlooking the plant. Three on the north end honor the Carnegie family: Margaret, for Andrew Carnegie's mother and daughter; Louise, for Carnegie's wife; and Andrew, for Andrew himself.

Two streets on the south end also run up the hill. One honors Ulysses S. Grant, commander of the victorious Union armies in 1865 and eighteenth president of the United States, whose initials were said to stand for "Unconditional Surrender." The other is named Harrison Street. Only five foot six, Benjamin Harrison, also a Civil War hero and twenty-third president of the United States at the time of the Home-

Fig. 4-20. Philips Wouwerman (1619-1668), *Cavalry Camp.*
Acquired in 1901, Oil on oak panel, 16¾ x 20¾ in. (42.5 x 52.7 cm).
The Frick Collection

stead strike, lost his Republican reelection bid that year largely because of Homestead. Tragically, Harrison's wife died on October 25, 1892, just a few weeks before the election and the strike settlement.

But most interesting, at the center of these streets, sandwiched between the group named after the Carnegie family to the north and those honoring the two presidents to the south, there is a street named Martha. It is closest to the main gate of the Homestead plant and ends at the top of the hill where the state militia camped when the government opened Homestead's gates to its owners. It is an outlook not unlike the one depicted in Philips Wouwerman's *Cavalry Camp* (fig. 4-20), acquired by Frick in 1901 when Homestead became the property of U.S. Steel. The apex of the street has the most panoramic view of the Homestead plant, the gray-arched pumping station, and the Pinkerton landing site. Martha Street, along with Grant Street, borders the Carnegie Company's General Office at Homestead.

SOME HAVE SAID the closest Henry Clay Frick ever got to a blast furnace was the day he died. Frick, however, lived in a blast furnace of rage. Two paintings he later acquired would seem to validate this statement: El Greco's violent *Purification of the Temple*, originally called *The Cleansing of the Temple* (fig. 4-21) and Edouard Manet's *The Bullfight* (fig. 4-22). Frick, who once consoled a friend on a death in the family by referring to his belief in a higher power, had from childhood read and studied the Bible. He rarely acquired religious works of art, making this purchase of *Purification of the Temple* a significant statement. Certainly, the painting's cold, brilliant coloring describes Christ's rage at the moneychangers, but it also describes the quality of Frick's own deep-seated anger at the labor unions in his mills. Indeed, his intent was, like Christ's, to "cast out all them that sold and bought in the temple," to cleanse Homestead of the craft unions who, like the moneychangers, had turned it into a "den of thieves."

Frick undoubtedly saw parallels between himself and the rageful Christ. Just as Christ intended his Father's temple to become a house of devotion, Frick contemplated Homestead as a smooth-running plant entirely subservient to him. Like both the artist El Greco and Christ, Frick wanted a reformation in his church. Much as Christ's first act on entering his Father's temple was to cleanse it of the moneychangers (who were in consort with the Romans), Frick's first act as chairman of the newly unified Carnegie Steel Company was the ouster of the craft unions (who were in consort with the Amalgamated Association) from his own temple, Homestead.

Additionally, just as Christ was determined to be master in his Father's house and sacrificed himself for all humanity on behalf of his Father, Frick had willingly sacrificed himself for the antiunionists in the name of his father-figure and boss, Andrew Carnegie. In fact, Carnegie often referred to Frick's duty as chairman as being sacred and would later refer to the purged Homestead as the "church of true faith."

The angry Christ who wields his lash upon the cringing, fleeing moneychangers—a Christ described by the art historian Richard B. Woodward as exhibiting "muscular Christianity"—could only have evoked for Frick his own "muscle" as he executed his Homestead purge. Indeed, the expulsion in the painting takes place beneath bas-reliefs of Adam and Eve's expulsion from the garden and Abraham's sacrifice of Isaac, events that echo the ruthlessness of Christ's and Frick's purges. Significantly, Christ's disciples, much like Frick's partners, are seen sitting quietly in a corner watching Christ's fury.

As for the Homestead purification, Frick was no less ruthless than Christ in his moment of blind rage. Ever loyal to his beliefs, determined to fulfill his mission at the expense of mockery, degradation, and physical attack, Frick stayed his course.

Although *Purification of the Temple* pays tribute to the ruthless quality of Frick's antiunion ideology and his bottled-up emotions, and recalls the site of the Homestead

Fig. 4-21. El Greco (1541-1614), *Purification of the Temple*, c. 1600.
Acquired in 1909, Oil on canvas, 16½ x 20⅝ in. (41.9 x 52.4 cm).
The Frick Collection

Fig. 4-22. Edouard Manet (1832–1883), *The Bullfight*, 1864.
Acquired in 1914, Oil on canvas, 18⅞ x 42⅞ in. (47.9 x 108.9 cm).
The Frick Collection

battle, with its gray, stone-arched pump house, *The Bullfight* (once called *An Incident in the Bullring* and exhibited in his second-floor sitting room, in a specially designed panel above the mantelpiece facing *Purification of the Temple*) illustrates the intensity of the attack Frick felt he had endured. What he may have recalled in 1914, when he saw the fence in Manet's painting, was the semicircular Homestead fence and an inner fence, resembling a bullring, that encircled the Homestead Works' General Office because railroad tracks separated the office from the main plant (fig. 4-23). When illustrations of Fort Frick are juxtaposed with Manet's bullring, the similarity is apparent, particularly if one considers that Manet's focus on bulls killing matadors, rather than matadors killing bulls, was one of the artist's many political statements. According to Homer Saint-Gaudens, director of Fine Arts at the Carnegie Institute in the 1930s, Manet was an artist who "battled contemporary opinion, glorying in the banner of reform." For Manet, bullfighting spoke to the struggle between life and death, victim versus oppressor, a dance of death, the triumph of the persecuted. For Frick, the bull is the scapegoat, Christ figure, or sacrificial animal, much as he regarded himself as a sacrificial victim of the labor leaders and the anarchist's attack. Frick understood well the irony of scapegoating. An avid reader, he was so impressed with William George Jordan's philosophy in *Self Control: Its Kingship and Majesty,* he passed the book around to his friends. Jordan wrote:

When the gray heron is pursued by its enemy, the eagle, it does not run to escape; it remains calm, takes a dignified stand, and waits quietly, facing the enemy unmoved. With the terrific force with which the eagle makes its attack, the boasted King of the Birds is often impaled and run through on the quiet, lance-like bill of the heron. The means that man takes to kill another's character becomes suicide of his own.

And so Frick had baited the strikers into storming his mill and breaking the law. But when "the bull" cleared the ring and "Christ" cleansed the temple, more than matadors and moneychangers had been expelled. Indeed, Carnegie was ever haunted by the Homestead tragedy: "Nothing I have ever had to meet in all my life, before or since, wounded me so deeply. No pangs remain of any wound received in my business career save that of Homestead. It was so unnecessary." In a solemn moment after his Homestead victory, Frick, in a rare expression of vulnerability, referred to it as a "lamentable matter" and said to Carnegie, "[I] am sure I never want to go through another such fight."

On November 17, 1892, the day before the strike was broken, Carnegie wrote Frick from Venice. In expressing his sympathy for the defeated strikers, Carnegie may also have planted a seed that eventually drew Frick to *Purification of the Temple*. He wrote

Fig. 4-23. Fort Frick.
Historical Society of Western Pennsylvania, courtesy William J. Gaughan

jubilantly: "I got one big 'religious' picture (fine copy) might do for Schwab at Homestead—I think there is a church of the true faith there. We must show our men there who have gone into the best of all Unions—a union with their Employers—that they are no longer considered as outcasts . . . important give Homestead evidence of our tender regard now."

But Frick, having driven out the union, was interested in another church of the true faith. Not about to be forgiving, exhibiting neither charity nor tender regard for the strikers, he and others within the Carnegie works drew up a blacklist. No strikers were rehired.

In his *Prison Memoirs of an Anarchist,* Berkman voiced his bitterness, writing that Frick survived because the greatest surgeons in America had been called to his bedside, that his wealth had enabled him to recover. He also fumed, "It was mainly his cowardice that saved him—he hid under the chair! Played dead! And now he lives, the vampire."

Vampire or not, victorious Frick was nevertheless a casualty of Homestead. In 1893 an orchestrion (fig. 4-24), a large musical instrument containing miniature drums, cymbals, and other orchestral instruments, arrived at Clayton. Chosen by Carnegie for Frick, it played many songs, including one of Frick's favorites, the overture from Friedrich von Flotow's opera *Martha,* with the theme of "The Last Rose of Summer" occurring throughout.

Fig. 4-24. The orchestrion at Clayton.
Frick Art and Historical Center

I live in a dream.
A dream that never dies.
I hear her gentle voice.
I see her lovely eyes.
She frowns, and all my world
Is filled with pain.
But when I see her smile,
My heart revives again.

*

In my dream, she is all my own. . . .
Ah, how fair she appears
Like an angel from the skies!
Ah, how dear is the sight
To my lonely, longing eyes!
Then how soon she is gone
And the dream dies away!

Adelaide placed an enormous collage of Martha's life and an equally large collage of posthumous photographs of the infant Henry Clay Frick, Jr., in her bedroom; Frick wore Martha's favorite flower, a pansy—the flower of lover's longing—in his lapel. And he commissioned a Roman sculptor, Orazio Andreoni, to create a life-size marble bust of Martha with arms folded, resting on a cloud. A cut rose, symbolizing both Martha's nickname and her short life, and a pansy rest beneath her arms. In an unusual practice for his day, Frick placed the bust in the Clayton reception room. Later he surrounded it with the Millets that recalled his childhood (fig. 4-27). Even today, the bust remains a living presence in the Clayton house-museum.

Frick also had Martha's likeness engraved onto his checks, and in 1895, he commissioned Théobald Chartran to do her posthumous portrait wreathed in spring flowers (see fig. 5-13). A radiant composition, it is an almost calculated effort to erase the memory of the emaciated, suffering child whose slow death the family had shared and witnessed. In particular, Chartran gave Martha abundant, long auburn hair, hair which throughout her four-year illness had constantly fallen out. As if promising the hope for Martha's transcendence, three narcissus—symbols of triumph over sin and selfishness—were placed at her heart. The rest of the garland is replete with buttercups, forget-me-nots, and poppies, the latter symbolizing sorrow and death.

Martha the child became, for Frick, Martha the vision, both devil and angel of Frick's soul. And so to this extent, the portrait *Miss Louisa Murray*, of the love-child so resembling Martha who floats through Sir Thomas Lawrence's canvas like an apparition, also affirms a father's torment. As if the painting itself describes the fluid time boundaries of a paranormal experience where past, present, and future seem to exist in the same moment, in actuality Miss Murray would have been twenty-five months and ten days old when Lawrence did her portrait, not the six-year-old Lawrence presented in the painting. The portrait, therefore, becomes a still more intriguing link to Martha. Martha was twenty-five months old when she swallowed the pin, and she died just days before her sixth birthday. And although Miss Murray had lived to adulthood, she died in 1891, the same year as Martha.

Henry Clay Frick still had not divulged that Martha had appeared at his side during Berkman's attack. Two decades later, however, when he moved into his new home in New York, certain paintings hanging in his bedroom seemed to confirm his experience (figs. 4-25, 26). *Lady Hamilton*, recalling the 1892 Christmas photograph of Childs holding Martha's dog and suggesting what Martha would have looked like had she lived to be Lady Hamilton's age in the portrait, was placed on the wall at the foot of his bed. *Miss Louisa Murray*, the apparition, hung on the wall to the right of his bed. *Lady Hamilton* suggests Frick's longing for the beauty of life, life as it would have been had Martha lived, while *Miss Murray* suggests the nightmare of Frick's incessant

Fig. 4-25. Henry Clay Frick's bedroom (north wall) at 1 East Seventieth Street, New York, 1927.
Author's collection

Fig. 4-26. Henry Clay Frick's bedroom (east wall) at 1 East Seventieth Street, New York, 1927.
Author's collection

Fig. 4-27. The reception room at Clayton with Martha as a living presence
among the family-associated Millet paintings.

Frick Archives

search for his dead daughter. As Charles Anderson, author of the first quasi-empirical study of complicated mourning notes, reminders of the deceased also create "internal persecutors," and the mourner's dreams can "assume a nightmarish character." This can be particularly understood in the disturbing portrait of Miss Murray.

And in time we shall see that Frick's inner disquiet would be much like a recurring nightmare. With Martha's likeness on his checks (fig. 4-28), every transaction Frick ever made, every bill he ever paid, every debt he ever settled, every painting he ever bought was settled in memory of Martha. The imprint of Martha's likeness was a signature as binding as the letters in his own name.

Fig. 4-28. Henry Clay Frick's check bearing Martha's likeness.
Frick Archives

CHAPTER V

Emotions, Apparitions, and Art

[I] feel now that I need such a rest as is only obtained by almost entire freedom from business cares.

—Henry Clay Frick, 1894

A temporary respite will restore you. . . . trips to Europe, recreation, hasnt [sic] that been my text. You can take a long holiday, go to Egypt.

—Andrew Carnegie, 1894

IN 1893, THE YEAR AFTER THE HOMESTEAD STRIKE, severe industrial depression once again overwhelmed the country. While six hundred banks and a third of the railroads went bankrupt, many steel concerns experienced temporary shutdowns, some falling into receivership. Carnegie's company was not without its troubles. The U.S. government filed suit against Carnegie Steel for delivering faulty armor plate. Although the government won its case, the combination of fine, damage to the company's reputation, and depression did not prevent the company from doing a lucrative business. In fact, Carnegie Steel was able to seize any business at any price, largely because costs had fallen dramatically after the labor unions were driven from the Carnegie mills. Additionally, the work force had been reduced by 25 percent, wages had been reduced because of the depression, the mill was "running full" (seven days a week), and the men were working a day and night shift (called a turn) twice a month. More important, Frick, who had long used connecting railroad spurs in his coke operations, now initiated the additional cost-saving enterprise of unifying the Carnegie empire by building a switching railroad—a system of railroad spurs connecting the many company plants to the major transportation systems in the Pittsburgh area. Called the Union Railway, the one-hundred-mile interplant railway consolidated the mills into one working unit. It streamlined the transport of raw materials and semifinished products, carried as much freight as any of the major national rail systems,

Fig. 5-1. On vacation in Scotland, c. 1895. At center, Andrew Carnegie, surrounded by family and friends. Seated to Carnegie's left are (clockwise) Childs Frick, unidentified man, Helen Clay Frick with Adelaide Frick, tutor Clyde Duniway (seated behind Carnegie), Henry Clay Frick (standing), and to the right of Carnegie, Martha Howard Childs. Four others are unidentified.

David C. Duniway Collection

provided complete control of the company's yards, and eliminated the company's costly switching charges. In fact, so streamlined were the company operations that in 1893 the company attained its largest share of national steel production; and although profits were down 25 percent, the company boasted a net gain of $4.2 million.

Inside this fast-paced, smooth-running machine, however, stress fractures had developed between Frick and Carnegie that threatened its ultimate stability. With Frick's power within the company heightened by his position as sole executive head, and with his unprecedented, unilateral victory over labor, Andrew Carnegie, awed by Frick's management genius, now began to fear that the public would see Frick, not him, as the King of Carnegie Steel. To preserve his crown, Carnegie began making some of the company's decisions without consulting Frick—a tactic that would soon embitter Frick, destroy their relationship, pit partners against partners, and strain Frick to the point of emotional collapse.

Over the previous twelve years, the personal and business relationship of these strong-willed men, with their mutual passion for moneymaking and their ability to succeed, seemed, by and large, to have been friendly. Both men traveled in Europe, were avid readers, and enjoyed art and music. Their wives were friends, and the two families always visited each other when abroad (fig. 5-1). In fact, Carnegie took a genuine interest in Frick's children. In 1898, when Carnegie's daughter Margaret was one year old, he wrote Frick that when the public saw Helen and Margaret together, "the public will vote them a pair." And whenever the Fricks came to stay in Scotland, Carnegie enjoyed taking Childs hunting and fishing, often commenting on the boy's sensitive and gentlemanly nature.

Even in business the two industrial titans showed compatibility. Both had photographic memories and a tremendous capacity for assimilating detail. They were men of great vision, with a ruthless penchant for keeping costs low at the expense of their employees. Moreover, they were successful at "picking the bottom"—buying when prices were low and waiting out depressions.

Fig. 5-2. Andrew Carnegie in the Scottish Highlands.
Carnegie Mellon University Archives

But in reality, the men were as opposite as two human beings could possibly be. Carnegie, fourteen years Frick's senior, was spontaneous, affable, and fun-loving. A smooth talker (particularly to the press), he made decisions rapidly, acted on impulse, flourished when around people who flattered him, and, as an intuitive genius, overflowed with ideas. Energized by activities at home, and by his travels abroad, he was ever the schemer who loved to play people against each other and more than once forced a partner into retirement by buying him out at a ruthlessly low price. When his brother Tom died in 1886, had Frick not intervened, Carnegie would have seized Tom's shares in the company, thereby preventing his brother's widow from realizing her rightful inheritance.

And yet, as the largest shareholder of Carnegie Steel, he was an absent partner. He hired others to mind the shop, held no title or position within his own company, rarely stayed for any length of time in Pittsburgh, and almost never attended board meetings. Yet Carnegie was, despite his casual posture, aware of every aspect of the company's operations. He reviewed the board's lengthy minutes and was in intimate contact with the firm managers, firing off frequent and lengthy memorandums, comments, and suggestions. Not unlike what we call today "a Monday-morning quarterback," Carnegie watched from afar as the organizational capabilities of his carefully selected young protégés turned his dreams to gold (fig. 5-2).

More than anything, Carnegie relished publicity, and he so longed to be loved and admired by the public, although his philanthropy was genuine, he made certain it was well-publicized and bore his name. And, as we have seen, he gave softhearted, pro-labor press interviews calculated to endear himself to the working man—something that justly earned him the reputation of hypocrite.

Carnegie, however, saw himself as a social philosopher and aspired to be publicly recognized as the equal to Henry Ward Beecher, Matthew Arnold, Herbert Spencer, and other great thinkers and social Darwinists of the day. He not only sought their society, but in 1886, as described above, published a political manifesto, *Triumphant Democracy*. He fooled no one, however. As John Ingham notes in his introduction to the reprint edition of *The History of the Carnegie Steel Company* by James Howard Bridge, Carnegie was "little liked or even respected." In an ironic convergence of attitude, both his Pittsburgh peers and its working class—though not the press—saw through his facade.

Nonetheless, people seemed to forgive Carnegie his faults. Of the two men, Frick was the one who constellated bitterness and hatred. And yet, despised as Frick was, no one ever perceived him as pandering, glib, or hypocritical. As the younger Homestead workers said, "It is better to confront a Frick with a hard heart than a Carnegie with a false tongue." At least Frick's enemies always knew where he stood, and his few

Fig. 5-3. Henry Clay Frick, c. 1890.
Frick Archives

intimate friends enjoyed his rock-solid loyalty. An abrupt, straightforward man, he was without pretense and played within the rules of the day. Having worked in a farming family that tested him to the limit of his own strength, and having won his fortune in a grueling ten-year period plagued by ill health, he had neither sympathy for humanitarian concerns nor interest in social policy. Within Carnegie Steel, maintaining harmony among partners was of prime importance to Frick; but as company peacemaker, he was perceived as dour and taciturn. Ice cold, with a mysterious underlying passion that was visible in his art collection and in his occasional bouts of rage, he was usually courteous to the point of deference. When amused, however, his humor was often cynical and dark. In fact, his expletives were known for their near surgical sarcasm. His smile, according to one associate, served "as an answer to, or acknowledgment of, Carnegie's jest and habitual enthusiasms."

Unlike globe-trotting Carnegie, Frick was happiest when alone, either at home or in his office monitoring the company's accounts and concentrating on its business. In contrast to Carnegie's gregariousness, Frick's conversation was largely about money and business (fig. 5-3). As the grandson of William H. Vanderbilt, Cornelius Vanderbilt,

Jr., would remember in his 1935 memoir, *Farewell to Fifth Avenue,* "no other guest in our house mentioned the word 'dollar' so often."

Withdrawn and highly introverted, Henry Clay Frick was a facts-and-figures man—rational, diligent, analytic, methodical. Though in his own words he was "absolutely opposed to newspaper interviews of any kind," when forced to speak to the press, his statements were deliberate, concise, and unemotional. Once, during a financial panic, this quality was noted, together with his wry wit. When a reporter asked him for a comment on the financial situation, Frick's response was simply, "The U.S.A. is a great and growing company. P.S. This information is confidential and not for publication."

Unlike Carnegie, public opinion was of no importance to Henry Clay Frick. Nor was being liked or admired. Only logic born of practicality and his own sense of justice shaped his judgment. To that end, in an effort to avoid the press and safeguard the privacy of both his business and private life, he neither wrote nor published anything. Unlike Carnegie, when Frick gave to charity, his gifts were anonymous.

Except for their 1887 clash—when Frick resigned as chairman of the coke company because Carnegie had forced him to capitulate to wildcatters—the two men's personality differences had not materially threatened their relationship or the Carnegie Steel Company. As opposite halves of a whole, with varying insights, they brought an undeniable depth to management and a clear vision for the company's growth. When Carnegie presented his endless flow of ideas, Frick sorted through them, advised Carnegie of their worth, and, when necessary, as in Homestead, served as his hatchet man. Moreover, with Frick on the job in Pittsburgh, Carnegie could travel and pursue his literary interests, trusting Frick to do what he most enjoyed—organize and manage two of the nation's most powerful manufacturing concerns.

But now, with empire built, unified, and running smoothly under Frick's sole executive control, Carnegie's jealousy began to disrupt the firm and irritate Frick. Historians have traditionally noted that in the early years of their partnership Frick may have resented being subordinate to Carnegie in his own H. C. Frick Coke Company. But with the singular exception of Frick's 1887 capitulation to the wildcatters, Carnegie traditionally submitted to Frick.

Over the years, friction over labor policy had remained a constant between Frick and Carnegie, but Frick had had his way, apart from the 1887 debacle. During the 1891 Morewood riots, Frick brought in Pinkertons and strikebreakers against Carnegie's advice. Then, in 1892, Frick orchestrated the events at Homestead while Carnegie—who at first supported Frick's Homestead stand, but turned on him when the press reacted unfavorably—was safely silenced in Scotland. Later, Frick tolerated Carnegie's public expression of loyalty and such hypocrisy as Carnegie's post-Homestead praise of him before the Homestead workmen, even when Carnegie suggested he rehire the very strikers who had bludgeoned and murdered the unarmed Pinkertons. Frick, however, had refused to comply with what must have seemed a ludicrous suggestion, particularly in light of the financial shortfall these strikers had caused the company, his own near death from an assassin's attack, the death of his infant son, and the near death of his wife during the strike.

But then, the ever glib and impetuous Carnegie was often blind to Frick's emotions and, therefore, tactless. In August 1892, one year after Martha's death, a month after Frick's recovery from the attempted assassination, and days after the death of Frick's infant son, Carnegie rejected the drawings Frick had submitted for the World's Columbian Exposition in Chicago. In so doing, he said, "[It is] too Frenchy for my taste. It is most pretentious. The hanging chains upon it would do for a lot in a cemetery. . . . rather than have such a spread-eagled thing, I should vote to have no exhibition at all."

But now, in 1894, as the post-Homestead era commenced with Frick as chairman of both the H. C. Frick Coke Company and the consolidated Carnegie steel empire, as well as the national and international opponent of unionism, issues of long-range planning compounded the strain between the two industrialists. As chairman and chief executive officer, Frick realized the strategic advantage of Carnegie Steel having its own ore supply. He wanted to invest with Henry Oliver, a plow and steel manufacturer from Pittsburgh who hoped to sell Carnegie an interest in the valuable Minnesota iron ore lands in the Mesabi range located off Lake Superior. The seam had a high ore content and was so close to the surface that it could be scooped up off the surface, rather than deep-mined, and shipped with a minimum of labor or machinery. Carnegie quipped, however, "Oliver's ore bargain is just like him—nothing in it. . . . [Ore] never has been very profitable, and the Massaba is not the last great deposit that Lake Superior is to reveal." Adding injury to insult, Carnegie advised Frick to go fishing: "With fly-fishing and whist as passions, you will not be badly off for old age when it comes."

Frick did not turn to fly-fishing or whist. In spite of Carnegie's protests, Frick struck a deal with Oliver that spring. Knowing the obvious, that iron ore together with limestone and coke were necessary ingredients for the making of steel, Frick was determined to have a guaranteed supply of ore for his mills, just as he had a guaranteed supply of coke. Cost-saving measures being ever on his mind, he saw the value in shipping the ore down the thousand-mile waterway of the Great Lakes by company steamer, rather than rail, knowing that the ships would save the company half a million dollars a year in freight charges.

Then, to add to this tension, labor unrest again surfaced in the Coke Region. Andrew Carnegie wrote Frick from Sorrento, Italy: "When any of you overworked slaves need a change take a boat for Naples, hence to Capri and Amalfi—if that don't cure, take to prayer, steadily. Its [*sic*] your only chance."

One can only imagine Frick's reaction to Carnegie's quip when on April 3, the biggest riot yet witnessed in the Coke Region broke out. Marked by violence, bloodshed, and angry parades of over one thousand marchers tramping through the towns of Connellsville, Mt. Pleasant, and Scottdale, the riot had two aims: to make the H. C. Frick Coke Company their target because it refused to shut down during the strike, and to prevent those who wanted to work in the Coke Region from doing so.

On April 6, the rioting reached tragic proportions for Frick. J. H. Paddock, the popular chief engineer of the H. C. Frick Coke Company, was brutally murdered at the company's Davidson plant. Paddock, a thirty-year-old father of four, had tried to calm three hundred strikers who had marched upriver from Vanderbilt, ransacking workers' homes at Adelaide. They crossed the Youghiogheny River at the Broad Ford Distillery and encountered Paddock, who suggested in a mild and pacific manner that they were on the company's grounds. As the engineer started back toward the coal screening plant, or tipple, the crowd began to stone him. Paddock ran up the tipple, but as he jumped down onto the ovens to make his escape, he fell. The strikers then beat him to death with clubs and stones, which they left by his body. The murderers were apprehended as they ran through Broad Ford and attempted to cross the bridge

Fig. 5-4. The home of Morris Ramsay at the time of the Morewood riots in 1891.
His pregnant wife, soon to be widowed, is leaning out of the parlor window.
Courtesy Marjorie R. Laing

to Adelaide. In what would turn out to be his last visit to the Coke Region, Frick said at the funeral of this man, who had been in his employ for twelve years, "If the sheriff of Westmoreland County had done his duty . . . Paddock would still be alive."

For Frick, Paddock's loss was particularly bitter. The prior year the H. C. Frick Coke Company's Morewood superintendent, Morris Ramsay, who had named his infant daughter after Frick's wife, Adelaide, was fatally injured in a carriage accident (figs. 5-4, 5). Although Ramsay was sent by Frick to a Pittsburgh hospital, he died in surgery. Frick served as a pallbearer at Ramsay's funeral and offered financial aid to his devastated widow.

Now, one year later, he had lost another superintendent and young family man to tragedy. Forced to spend his days coping with the strike's fallout, including the demands of some to outlaw foreign labor in the area, Frick, ever the businessman, and cognizant of the tremendous manpower needed to sustain the coke company, told the *Commercial Gazette:* "It is not the intention of our company to shut out the foreign workmen now employed, and they will not be discriminated against in the future. They are not so bad as represented. Of course they are credulous and easily misled but if they are given fair treatment, it will be found that they will conduct themselves properly. . . . We shall not discriminate against them or in their favor. They are good workmen and will not be discharged."

Fig. 5-5. Morris Ramsay, the forty-four-year-old Morewood superintendent, was fatally injured in an 1892 carriage accident.
Courtesy Marjorie R. Laing

Carnegie, who was in Sussex, England, when the riot occurred, continued to be blissfully detached from Frick's problems. Concerned only about his own health, and cheering the long-range advantages of the industrial depression, he wrote Frick on April 21: "I am sorry you are having a coke strike around you, but this will not trouble us. . . . nothing is so beneficial as a serious [industrial] depression. It puts things on the right footing. . . . I am now entirely well. I eat and sleep well. . . . [but] have many qualms of conscience while all you fellows are working hard, but so far I have compounded my conscience by knowing that I have really had a serious attack of the grippe."

Perhaps the depression and strike did not trouble Carnegie. And perhaps suffering from the grippe eased Carnegie's conscience. But not so for Frick. Anxious and worried, as late as July 14, Frick, who canceled his own planned vacation to Europe with his family, wrote Andrew Mellon: "Regret very much I could not accompany [the family] but knew I would not enjoy it with the coke strike still unsettled. The stubborn Hungarian is making a stiff fight this time, and when the end is to come I would not care to prophesy."

Not until March of the following year did the end come. And then it came because of a preemptive move against the labor leaders—a caveat that ended labor strikes in the Coke Region until 1922. The independent coke operators (led by the H. C. Frick Coke Company) announced a voluntary increase in wages of 15 percent for mining and other laborers. Additionally, they promised to reduce wages only if they found their business under dire economic stress.

But another end was at hand as well. Although Frick had traditionally been a team player, had held his temper, and had remained publicly respectful toward his glib "friend," partner, and boss, he had now had his fill of Carnegie. In October 1894, Frick, with Carnegie's approval, had been in secret negotiations with Russia for an armor plate contract. Carnegie, however, without consulting Frick, gave a press interview and revealed the company's bid, thereby enabling the Bethlehem Steel Company, which had not yet placed its bid, to win the contract. A livid Frick could not suppress his indignation and advised an associate, Lt. C. A. Stone, in Washington, D.C., that the impetuous, indiscreet Carnegie was "not able to contain himself at any time or under any conditions. . . . If it was an employee of this company, we would have no further use for his services. It is unfortunate . . . that our leading stockholder is a little injudicious at times." As Frick voiced his outrage, he warned Carnegie that these "little things" (the fact that Carnegie had enabled Bethlehem Steel to undercut Carnegie Steel) should be borne "in mind when comparison is being made between one management and another."

Carnegie, smarting from this put-down, became more determined than ever to deal behind Frick's back. Knowing full well Frick's sensitivity to his meddling in H. C. Frick Coke Company matters, he nonetheless decided to merge the coke works of an independent coke operator in the Connellsville area, W. J. Rainey, into the H. C. Frick Coke Company. Although Frick had long considered Rainey both a "rascal" and "thief," and had often expressed his reluctance to do business with him, Carnegie began negotiations without Frick's knowledge. Upon learning of Carnegie's actions, Frick told John Walker, a stockholder in and director of the H. C. Frick Coke Company who had once been chairman of Carnegie, Phipps, and Company, that "leaving my feelings out of the question, he [Carnegie] has already done the Frick Coke Co. great harm."

By December 17, 1894, two days before his forty-fifth birthday, Frick had been pushed too far. He informed Carnegie of his intent to resign in January. Both interesting to note and in keeping with his character, in so doing, Frick did not mention Carnegie's many tactless comments, his frustration with him over Oliver's ore deal, or the faux-pas with the Russian contract. He did not comment on Carnegie's blithe response to Paddock's murder and the coke riot at Adelaide or the Rainey situation. Nor did he admit to other strains—the recent tragedies in his personal life. Frick instead merely explained that the years since 1889, the time of the Johnstown Flood and his promotion to chairmanship of Carnegie Brothers and Company, "had been trying ones." For six years he had not taken a day's rest. He had spent long hours at the office when he had completely restructured Carnegie's steel interests and had beaten labor while augmenting his, Carnegie's, and their partners' fortunes. "My mind from necessity has been so absorbed in bookkeeping after the interests of this great concern, I have had no time for anything else and feel now that I need such a rest as is only obtained by almost entire freedom from business cares."

Frick, who was exhausted, assured Carnegie his decision to resign was made "after the most serious consideration." He had told Carnegie the affairs of the association were in "splendid shape . . . in every way better than at any time in the past and the outlook for the future very bright."

And bright the financial future was.

Since 1889, when Frick became chairman of Carnegie Brothers and Company, through 1892 when he became chairman of Carnegie Steel, and by the end of 1894, he had increased the net profits of the Carnegie Steel Company from approximately $3.5 million to over $4 million. Annual production of steel had gone from a little over five hundred thousand tons to slightly more than one million tons. The company had agencies in all principle cities in the nation and was exporting steel to Mexico, Cuba, and South America. As far as coke was concerned, it produced 50 percent of America's output and was the largest coke producer in the world. A foundation, therefore, had been laid for tremendous future profit.

Perhaps for all these reasons, Carnegie, who should have otherwise been pleased that his back-parlor dealing had brought Frick to submission, was suddenly alarmed at the prospect of losing his best manager and chief executive. He therefore refused to accept Frick's resignation, insisting instead that Frick fulfill the "sacred obligations . . . due your partners." Confessing that "no brain, no not even yours and your temperament (the latter as rare as the former) could stand [the pressure]," Carnegie advised: "A temporary respite will restore you. . . . Trips to Europe, recreation, hasnt [sic] that been my text—not purely because we should thereby have the resources of your rare ability longer, but I can say because I like you and yours as friends." Recognizing Frick's "unequaled financial ability," Carnegie also advised Frick that his "partners had a claim upon" him. "You can take a long holiday, go to Egypt," for Egypt was a country full of mystery and discovery, and certainly the most exciting of all places to visit in the winter as jewels and relics surfaced daily from new archaeological sites.

In this December 18 letter, Carnegie explained to Frick just how much he was in need of a vacation. Apparently the two men had recently dined together, and Carnegie had noticed Frick's haggard state. Thus, a seemingly sympathetic Carnegie went on to describe Frick's condition:

> your face appears to me as it was the other night when you came to us after dinner. It was worn, you were tired, over strained, long meetings, vital questions, discussions had worn you out. I am not alone in seeing recently that just as I was this time last year, so now you require just what I did and if you can only be restored as I have been, to pristine health you will return and smile at matters which now (in your tired state) seem gigantic and annoying. . . . All your partners ask (at least I ask) is that you will be patient, try the cure—not one of them would endanger your health.

But in extending his hand in compassion, Carnegie nevertheless referred to Frick's resignation as an "improper act," couching this remark with the real reason he wanted Frick to take the cure and return to the company smiling at matters that he well knew annoyed him. Banking on Frick's pattern of promoting harmony and loyalty within the company, the fifty-nine-year-old Carnegie, always looking for a chance to manipulate a partner, offered to let Frick buy him out. As Carnegie criticized Frick's recent behavior, he explained:

> I cannot consider your note for one moment because you will decide upon reflection that it would not be worthy of you to retire without proper notice to your partners and friends. . . . I have told you of my desire to sell to you and my partners and that I only waited until our affairs were in order when such a proposition could be made without adding to your cares. It is I who should be relieved my Dear Friend not you—altho I do feel for you as one who has been compelled to do far more than any one else could have stood. You are yet young and should be my successor as chief ironer—a post I have told you I aimed at your being and left it to you to say when you felt the Company was ready to take my interest.

But Carnegie, who in 1892 began construction of a library at Homestead (fig. 5-6) that was, as he said to Frick, "calculated to produce feelings of harmony and friendship between us and our men," badly misplayed his hand. On December 18, Frick discovered that the solicitous Mr. Carnegie was selling 32,000 shares of H. C. Frick Coke Company stock through a broker at below par. When Frick challenged, "What will Rainey think?" Carnegie claimed he was doing nothing underhanded and knew nothing of the transaction. He said to Frick, "Be just my friend."

Fig. 5-6. The Homestead Library.
Carnegie Library, Pittsburgh

Moreover, on December 23, Carnegie wrote Frick that a celebration over the opening of the Homestead Library would grant him a close to his career in an appropriately fitting and grand manner. "My wish is to close my business career fittingly—a splendid close. The opening of the Library, or rather handing it over to good old Pittsburgh would furnish this. Suppose I announce then—this day I have handed over all my business interests to my dear friends and trusted partners. . . . The main point with Mrs. Carnegie and me is the fitting close of my business life. Both set much store on this [October 1895] ending. . . . Assist me then to realize my aim. All of you take the wealth and give me dignified retirement. You will have my blessing."

Frick was not duped. He knew Carnegie's methods, had no interest in a trip to Egypt, did not want Carnegie's share of the business, and did not care to organize a fitting and dignified close to Carnegie's career. Nor, for that matter, did he want Carnegie's blessing. Frick simply wanted out. So, on Christmas Eve, an angry Frick replied, "I do not wish to purchase your interest or any part of it." He did, however, make one concession. In one of his more cynical remarks, Frick said he would "defer further action regarding his resignation until early January to give [Carnegie] ample time to arrange his plans to purchase my interest and relieve me."

On December 30, the situation then became further inflamed. Frick learned Carnegie had called a special meeting of the coke company to which he, as chairman and founder, had not been invited. Frick wrote Carnegie, "And so Mr. Rainey is delighted

Fig. 5-7. Henry Phipps, c. 1890.
Carnegie Library, Pittsburgh

to have anyone 'you desire' present at next meeting. How kind of him, how considerate of you, and what a Solomon he has proved himself to be in not mentioning my name."

By New Year's Day, 1895, the stress fractures finally and irrevocably had given way. Frick discovered that over Christmas, Carnegie had written their mutual friend and company treasurer, Henry Phipps (fig. 5-7), who was then at Knebworth House in England, that Frick was an unwell, "disordered man." Infuriated that Carnegie had capitalized on his confession of fatigue, Frick confronted Carnegie about this slanderous assault on his character, warning him by letter: "It is high time you should stop this nonsensical talk about my being unwell and overstrained and treat this matter between us in a rational business like way. If you don't, I will take such measures as will convince you that I am fully competent to care for myself in every way."

Frick, threatening Carnegie for trying to discredit him and sabotage his good relationship with Phipps, further insisted what Carnegie wrote about his health was "start to finish untrue & you know it. " He claimed that if "a man penned a sillier lot of nonsense" then he would like "as a curiosity" to see it. He ended this New Year's letter by condemning Carnegie on all fronts—for his financial irresponsibility, for the damage he had caused the coke company, for his undercutting press interviews, his interference in the management of Carnegie Steel, and for his tactlessness. Frick seethed:

> Who has been taking care of the credit of both concerns for the last several years—endorsing individually their paper, even putting up his own securities? While you have been drawing millions from one of them.
>
> Why do you force me to call your attention to these things and which can be verified by the books. . . . I desired to quietly withdraw, doing as little harm as possible to the interests of others, because I had become tired of your business methods, your absurd newspaper interviews and personal remarks and unwarranted interference in matters you know nothing about.

And as Frick raged at Carnegie, he reminded his senior partner that he knew Carnegie's game: "It has become your custom for years when any of your partners disagreed with you to say they were unwell." Thus, he issued Carnegie this New Year's ultimatum: "I warn you to carry this no further with me, but come forward like a man and purchase my interest, and let us part before it becomes impossible to continue to be friends."

No longer able to play both ends against the middle, Carnegie replied on January 3, "I wish to be friends as much as you do." Claiming he was now writing in "the most sacred manner . . . as your best friend & you know it," he agreed to accept Frick's resignation, but did so with a stinging rebuke: "It is simply ridiculous, my dear Mr. Frick, that any full-grown man is not to make the acquaintance of Mr. Rainey, or anyone else, without your august permission—really laughable." And as Carnegie went on to deny having made comments to Phipps about Frick's health, he wrote:

> Never to a soul have I ever *intimated* you were not yourself. You have yourself to blame that another knows it—who has not seen it for himself—so there. . . . No use corresponding any more; you are determined to resign. All right. I am forced to agree the work of the C.C.Co. & F. C. Co. is too much for any man. You shall withdraw quietly, and if you wish it, I shall co-operate with you. . . . No one values you more highly as a *partner,* but for being Czar and expecting a man shall not differ with you and criticize you, No. Find a slave elsewhere, I can only be a man and a friend. You are not well my Friend—You are not well.

In good health or not, Frick was out, but not for long. As had happened in 1887 when Frick resigned as chairman of the H. C. Frick Coke Company, the partners became alarmed at losing him. Henry Phipps lamented to his son, Jay, that "this Christmas to me has been marked by a series of serious cables from A. C." In fact, he told Carnegie that "unless something was done . . . [he] wished to retire." Phipps felt that in this case, Frick was "the wronged one & had [his] sympathies & best support." Phipps wrote Carnegie of his admiration and loyalty to Frick, as well as about his misgivings if the company were forced to go forward without him. He advised Carnegie:

> In my opinion, there is not in our Country the equal of our chairman, he fills more fields, and does the duties better than any man I know in active business. . . . Mr. Frick is first, and there is no second, nor fit successor, with him gone, a perfect Pandora's box of cares and troubles would be upon our shoulders. . . . troubles unnumbered—unending, life too short, the game not worth the candle, the closing of a career that could only be disappointing, the community, too eager to speak, would say too truly, "what an ending was that!"

Phipps further cautioned Carnegie: "You may be sure, if we are on earth, it won't be a Heaven under such circumstances. When fair times come again, an arrangement can be made where by we can have a haven of enjoyment and rest, instead of what may beset us any day, a sea of trouble, cares and anxieties."

Most of the partners were as concerned about a Frick-Carnegie split as Phipps. They too urged Carnegie to keep Frick, and warned of damage to the company if the argument became protracted and made public. The partners devised a way to reinstate Frick, while satisfying Carnegie and minimizing what Frick described as the "confining and exhaustive details which . . . constantly require the attention of the Chairman." They voted to retain Frick as chairman of the board of managers and created the new position of president for John G. A. Leishman, the Carnegie Steel executive who had been present at the time of Berkman's assassination attempt.

While initially Carnegie did not favor having two executive heads of the company, he relented, calling Frick's position largely honorary. A now magnanimous Carnegie, who never mentioned the pressure Phipps and others put on him, stated that Frick had come to him begging for a nominal office to "spare him[self] humiliation." Carnegie noted, at the time, Frick's "dejected, haggard, penitent, and distressed state," and said he, Carnegie, "against my business judgment and actuated solely by pity, and anxious to do everything I could to spare him humiliation," promised Frick he would consider the subject. Then, after the fact, a seemingly pleased Carnegie ticked off the advantages of Frick's new position: Frick would be isolated from people needing to see the president; he would not have to be called from home for special meetings; he was better held as the "reserve."

In Leishman, however, the managers had chosen a president both weak and ineffective. The man who had fainted during Frick's struggle with Berkman was largely regarded as a pawn in Frick's hand and as one of Frick's more loyal colleagues. Thus, although 5 percent of Frick's 11 percent share in the company was transferred to Leishman, Frick remained the dominant influence within the company, but with less of the daily burden.

In losing almost 50 percent of his shares, however, Frick had lost the 1894 power struggle. Nevertheless, he met with Rainey and maintained a superficial friendship with Carnegie; Frick seemed to have "recovered his equilibrium." But Frick was far from stable. The long-delayed grief reaction over Martha's death, though pushed closer to the surface, was still simmering silently within. Over the next five years, while Carnegie and Frick's troubled relationship moved toward a final rupture, so too Frick's hold on his emotions would come nearer to collapse.

❖

Fig. 5-8. The 1895 Loan Exhibition in the Carnegie Art Gallery.
Carnegie Library, Pittsburgh

Beginning in 1895, the intense pace of Frick's business life was decreased, and since he was no longer the company lightening rod, he had fewer crises commanding his attention. Increasingly, therefore, he had more time to satisfy his mounting passion for collecting art, a passion that had largely been overshadowed by business since the mid-1880s.

Returning to art, however, would satisfy more than Frick's aesthetic needs. In the aftermath of the 1894 power struggle, Frick knew he had no friend in Carnegie. And in this realization, Frick may have begun considering the direction his life would take in retirement; art collecting would furnish him a new "career." Perhaps he also hoped that through art he could stay at the forefront of Pittsburgh society and remain competitive among his business peers, most particularly Andrew Carnegie. In 1895 Carnegie was preparing to open the Carnegie Art Gallery in Pittsburgh (fig. 5-8), combined with a library and a natural history museum. In fact, the gallery was to open with a loan exhibition composed of the finest modern paintings donated by artists, private collectors, and dealers of importance in America and Europe. The following year, the Carnegie International—an annual exhibition modeled after the Paris Salon with medals, prizes, and jury system—would begin, as would a chronological collection of American art, developed by purchasing the best American paintings exhibited

Fig. 5-9. Roland Knoedler with Andrew Mellon and Henry Clay Frick.
Frick Archives

in the Internationals. More important, the exhibition was to "strike as high a key as possible" in order to catch the attention of America and the art world. The hope was that all eyes would turn from New York, where Carnegie had resided since 1865, but was one among many notables in America's celebrated art capital, to Pittsburgh, also an art center, where Carnegie, though absent, nonetheless remained an icon. And, in this attempt to bolster the culture of his "hometown," already boasting seventy-five serious private art collections, Carnegie believed he would bring "sweetness and light" to Pittsburgh's working class, and, one could imagine, to himself.

After announcing his plans, Carnegie, who knew little about art, retreated to the background and, as was his custom, sat back as his appointees brought his vision from dream to reality. Henry Clay Frick, already treasurer of the Carnegie Library, was asked to be treasurer of the Carnegie Art Acquisition Fund, as well as to join the many trustees of the Carnegie Art Institute. Although at the time Frick had a small collection of his own and hosted many meetings at Clayton when developing the jury system for the International exhibitions, he was not asked to be on the Fine Arts Committee, the committee controlling the gallery.

Whether Frick took this as a slight is not known, but one can imagine that had he been included, he would have enjoyed the honor. Enthusiastic about the 1895 loan exhibition in particular, and perhaps even remembering both his teenage delight in art when working in Pittsburgh and his own desire to found a collection for the benefit of his countrymen, Frick advised Carnegie that he intended to ask the railroad men to help promote the exhibition by lowering train fares into the city. "Stopped at the Library on my way this morning. They are making fine progress in hanging pictures. They will create a sensation. I think the Railroad Companies should make special rates to enable people from country towns to visit Pittsburgh during the time the gallery remains open. It will be a long time before the people of this district will have such an opportunity to view so fine a collection."

However interested he was in helping the country townspeople come to the exhibition, Frick was eager to have the employees of the Carnegie Steel Company attend the opening exercises on November 5. Frick even told Carnegie the seventy-five tickets he was given as a trustee would be allocated to employees before personal friends.

The forthcoming loan exhibition also opened the floodgates of his own art collecting passion. With time now to search out worthy paintings, Frick had made the acquaintance through Charles Carstairs, a sophisticated Philadelphia art dealer from a brewing family, of Roland Knoedler (fig. 5-9), an expert in French painting. Knoedler ran a family art gallery in New York, had just opened galleries in London and Paris, and was already selling art to Pittsburgh collectors. More significant, Knoedler was a family man, as well as a popular figure with artists, musicians, and actors. He could, as his colleagues noted, "shake the hand of his richest friend, [and] . . . with the other shake the hand of the poorest artist." "Warm" and "endearing," Knoedler was known for his "sympathetic understanding of a person's need."

Although Frick had collected art nearly all his life, great wealth, feelings of loss, and time on his hands had unmistakably pushed him to a new threshold. Whether or not Carstairs and Knoedler fully understood, or played up to, Frick's grief is a question that can never really be answered. But certainly, since the gift of a good salesman is the ability to read a client, Knoedler and Carstairs—like other of Frick's eventual dealers, including Thomas Agnew and Sons in London, Arthur Tooth and Son, the Durand-Ruel gallery, and Joseph Duveen—must have had some sense of Frick's melancholy and were influenced by it when presenting pictures to him. Psychologists now recognize that pathological grief is characterized by an intense, long-lived melancholy, a type of all-consuming longing for the deceased, dominating the bereaved's inner life. One would suspect the dealers knew Frick's was a rich emotional field to mine.

Through these dealer friends, therefore, and with the encouragement of his next-door neighbor and exuberant artist friend Joseph Woodwell, who was on the Fine Arts Committee, Frick was introduced to many contemporary French artists. With Knoedler serving as conduit, Frick began collecting at a feverish pace, buying according to the fashion of the day: anecdotal genre scenes, history paintings, and landscapes by contemporary French artists and the Barbizon School. Additionally, Frick, who in 1887 wrote his friend Andrew Mellon that sightseeing was a bore, now toured Europe with enthusiasm. He sought out historical sights, great cathedrals, the Paris Salon, mosaic factories, and artists' studios. He knocked on the doors of private homes reputed to have valuable paintings and introduced himself with the sole purpose of persuading the owner to sell. In 1895, so furious was his collecting pace, he purchased eighteen paintings, establishing an aggressive style that for the next five years saw him, on average, acquire one painting a month. "More hurry. . . . More hurry. Great Hurry! Only half seen," complained a traveling companion as Frick dashed through galleries and museums. Since the Carnegie loan exhibition was to open with paintings from the most important private collections in Pittsburgh and the rest of the country, Frick wanted to insure that both he and his collection would be properly represented.

So Henry Clay Frick, who previously had collected art to decorate his home and display his wealth to guests, now seemed to collect to maintain, and perhaps improve, his position among his peers, as well as to express his all-consuming grief. In a move that could be seen only as calculated, Frick commissioned Knoedler's French artist friend, Théobald Chartran (fig. 5-10), to do a portrait of himself (fig. 5-11), as well as individual gift-portraits of Andrew Carnegie (fig. 5-12), Henry Phipps, Judge Thomas Mellon, and the 1896 president-elect William McKinley. After the 1894 power struggle with Carnegie, Frick, though demoted, is portrayed as a man in charge. Unlike the dejected, haggard, penitent man Carnegie had described, Frick looks fit, prosperous, energized, and in complete control as he sits at a paper-laden desk.

As Chartran worked on the portraits of Frick and others of his circle, he also spent time with the Frick family. His youth and sense of fun brought moments of laughter back into a very saddened household. An aristocratic, heavily mustached man who

Above: Fig. 5-11. Théobald Chartran (1849–1907), *Portrait of Henry Clay Frick,* commissioned in 1896.
Private collection

Opposite: Fig. 5-10. Théobald Chartran, 1898.
Frick Archives

Fig. 5-12. Théobald Chartran (1849-1907), *Portrait of Andrew Carnegie*, commissioned in 1895.
Oil on canvas, 46½ x 35 in. (118.1 x 88.9 cm).
Carnegie Museum of Art, Pittsburgh, gift of Henry Clay Frick, 1896

radiated what his friends called "strength and the spirit of conquest," he delighted the Frick family with his antics. Dressed in a long gown with a high collar and large, dramatic, black, swashbuckling hat which sat crooked on his head, he looked like a "musketeer." He thrilled Helen by painting whimsical watercolors of her canaries and apple blossoms on Clayton's glass porch doors, as he also toyed with Frick's art collection by adding brush strokes to the glass protecting his paintings from the harmful Pittsburgh air. A clever cartoonist as well as a serious portraitist and painter of religious art, Chartran converted cows to buffaloes and people to ghostly figures. So amused was the family by these touch-ups to Clayton and Frick's paintings, they were allowed to remain there for a long time.

The fun-loving Chartran also endeared himself in other ways. He, like Knoedler and Carstairs, became a close personal friend of Frick's. According to his contemporaries, he had "a sympathy which sometimes overwhelms us, attracts us, and delivers us to a newcomer with all the trust and abandon that one would not often grant people of one's own family. . . . There was nothing sickly or tortured or worried in him. . . He gave the impression of a human being happy to live."

Thus it was that Frick asked Chartran to do a posthumous portrait of Martha (fig. 5-13). Chartran portrayed her in the blossom of health and happiness. And in 1896 he painted eight-year-old Helen, showing this child wearing around her neck a locket containing a miniature copy of his Martha portrait of the previous year (fig. 5-14).

In Frick's collecting pattern, however, one can glean from the paintings retained from this period a subtle indication of a rationale more deeply rooted than his attempt to maintain a place in the close-knit Carnegie circle, his commitment to Carnegie Steel's employees and county towns, or even his desire to be part of the national and international art scene—his longing to have Martha return as a living presence in his life. July 1895 would have been the tenth anniversary of Martha's birth, and it was at this time when Knoedler brought Frick, who now traveled to Europe regularly, to the studio of the prestigious French artist Adolphe-William Bouguereau. As DeCourcy McIntosh notes in *Collecting in the Gilded Age,* Pittsburgh collectors had been having "a love affair with this artist." So "phenomenal" was Pittsburgh's Bouguereau "epidemic," owning one of his paintings was then considered "one of the defining elements of taste in Pittsburgh."

Frick's extraordinary reaction to a particular painting in Bouguereau's studio, however, went beyond the Pittsburgh-artist romance, beyond the need for status. The unendurable emotions, long withheld, quietly emerged when he saw a life-size portrait, entitled *L'Espieglèrie (Mischievous Girl)* (fig. 5-15), of a child with long wavy hair. A typical Bouguereau figure, she is "alarmingly present" and flashes eyes that simultaneously challenge and seduce. The girl so resembled Martha, a stunned Frick purchased it immediately.

Fig. 5-13. Théobald Chartran (1849-1907), *Portrait of Martha Howard Frick*, 1895.
Oil on panel, 22½ x 19 in. (57.1 x 48.3 cm).
Frick Art and Historical Center

Fig. 5-14. Théobald Chartran (1849–1907), *Portrait of Helen Clay Frick*, 1896.
Oil on panel, 22½ x 19 in. (57.1 x 48.3 cm).
Private collection

In the presence of a brilliant art dealer and soft-spoken, sympathetic artist, who within the last decade had himself suffered the loss of a child in infancy, a sixteen-year-old son, a wife, and an eight-month-old baby two months after his wife's death, Frick's emotional control had broken, and grief for his dead daughter finally surfaced, albeit silently. As if using the painting to fill the void Martha had left in Clayton, he placed the portrait in his daughter Helen's bedroom. He also placed an artist-inscribed print of the painting, given to Helen by Bouguereau, above the governess's desk in Helen's third-floor playroom.

And then, at home in Pittsburgh, still under the spell of the Bouguereau and his fallen Rosebud, perhaps even influenced by Carnegie's desire to create for his gallery a "chronological collection," Frick's collecting eye sharpened. He and John A. Brashear, the famous Pittsburgh astronomer, had become friends. Many were the times Brashear came to Clayton and kept Frick spellbound as he showed him the colors of the spectrum and talked of the stars. As if stimulated by these evenings, Frick, who was always prone to collecting the anecdotal, continued his own form of "chronology," acquiring and retaining those paintings evoking for him the same real-life image, stored in his memory, until brought to life in the painting with the same intensity as Martha's apparition. Further remembering Martha, Frick acquired Jean-Baptiste Robie's *Flower Piece—Roses* and two paintings by the great French contemporary master Jean-Léon Gérôme: *Prayer in the Mosque of Quat Bey* (fig. 5-16) and his 1893 *Painting Breathes Life Into Sculpture* (fig. 5-17). Although he sold the Gérômes four years later, one can understand what may have drawn him to all three, particularly the latter two works. *Prayer in the Mosque* depicts a man and his child in a mosque with, as the art historian Gabriel Weisberg notes, "spectacular light effects streaming through stained glass windows." The work may well have evoked for Frick his experience of the spiritual light surrounding Martha's apparition. *Painting Breathes Life Into Sculpture* describes an artist applying paint to sculpted figurines, a polychrome technique Gérôme often used to bring "a curious life-likeness" to his sculptural works. This painting, Gérôme's response to critics who felt his realism had gone too far, seems both an extension of Martha's apparition and Frick's experience of seeing his dead daughter come alive in works of art.

René Gimpel, a famous art dealer of the day, once remarked that the 1895 Bouguereau purchase marked the true beginning of Frick's art collection, and perhaps he was correct. If longing for Martha underlay his art acquisitions, a mourning that by extension could be transferred onto other paintings evoking deceased friends and places and events from his past, then certain other works from his artist friends entering his collection that year also testified both to Frick's emerging collecting pattern and to the start of his own "chronological collection."

Fig. 5-15. Adolphe-William Bouguereau (1825-1905), *L'Espieglèrie (Mischievous Girl)*.
Acquired in 1895, Oil on canvas.
Private collection, courtesy of Sotheby's, Inc., New York

Fig. 5-16. Jean-Léon Gérôme (1824-1904), *Prayer in the Mosque of Quat Bey*, 1895.
Acquired in 1895, whereabouts unknown, 30¼ x 39½ in. (76.5 x 100 cm).
Frick Art Reference Library

Perhaps remembering his long hours in the harvest fields as a child, he bought Jules Breton's previously mentioned *The Last Gleanings* (see fig. 1-21), depicting a barefoot boy, women, and other children gathering sheaves of grain at sunset. Francisco Domingo y Marques's personally inscribed painting entitled *Landscape with Two Riders* (1895), depicts a sight once familiar to the younger Clay Frick: two well-dressed riders, one astride a bay, the other astride a gray, converse with each other as their horses trot by a shepherd and his flock. More compelling, the two previously mentioned, large, romantic images that Frick chose to elevate over his desk in the library at Clayton, Fritz Thaulow's *Village Night Scene* (see fig. 1-33) and Jean-Charles Cazin's *Sunday Evening in a Miner's Village* (see fig. 1-34) seem to further evoke both the mood of West Overton, his boyhood home, and Broad Ford, the place where he began to build his fortune, the heartland of the H. C. Frick Coke Company. All three paintings, deliberately and unabashedly nostalgic, are interesting for their autobiographic implications and in their stark contrast to the heartless and thereafter so vilified man of the

Fig. 5-17. Jean-Léon Gérôme (1824–1904), *Painting Breathes Life Into Sculpture*, 1893.
Acquired in 1895, Oil on canvas, 19¾ x 27 in. (50.2 x 68.9 cm).
The Art Gallery of Ontario

Fig. 5-18. Jean-Charles Cazin (1841–1901), *The Pool—Grey Night*, 1886.
Acquired in 1895, Oil on canvas, 21¾ x 17¾ in. (45.1 x 55.2 cm).
Frick Art and Historical Center

Homestead steel strike. Yet, these are the paintings, particularly the latter two, with their romantic portrayal of his hometown, chosen by Frick to grace his work area.

The paintings Frick selected to hang above his desk, as well as a third work by Cazin, *The Pool—Grey Night* (fig. 5-18), placed in the connecting upstairs living room, seem to indicate that Frick was at last recognizing and giving expression to the deep shadows in his psyche. Of all the artists collected at this time, Cazin seemed to be Frick's favorite, particularly those works that featured the otherworldly effects of diffuse starlight, moonlight, or lamplight. As Frick instructed Knoedler, "I am relying on you to see that I get the first opportunity at any of Mr. Cazin's pictures which you might consider masterpieces, and also anything else that may come up of any other first class artist which you think particularly fine."

Whether acting consciously or unconsciously, by associating Martha with the girl subject in Bouguereau's painting, and by associating his other paintings with the Coke Region of his birth, Henry Clay Frick, though collecting within the fashionable norms of his day, seemed to have placed an idiosyncratic, personalized signature on his choices: each painting gave voice to loss, each painting brought back to life an image from his past—an image firmly etched but long dormant in his mind's eye. Although in five years he began to collect Old Masters, even then his acquisitions were marked by this same apparent sentimentality. They, too, carried an extraordinary visual recollection of the past, suggesting that Henry Clay Frick's paintings were highly emblematic expressions, a way for him to voice the silence of his longing, the experience of Martha's apparition, and his attempt to link himself to Martha and his past.

True, when the Carnegie Art Institute opened in 1895, art defined prestige and position. And as the artists Frick collected also became his friends, staying with him at Clayton and serving as jurors and members of the foreign advisory committee for the Internationals, art was fun. Clearly, he took lighthearted pleasure in his new endeavor. After purchasing over eighteen paintings from Knoedler and seven from other dealers (spending $76,563.24, or the equivalent of $1.5 million today) in his first major year of collecting, Frick wrote J. C. Morse of Care Parrs Banking Company on September 26, 1895, that the pictures he had purchased abroad had arrived safely. "It seems to me better to have a certain amount of such things than the same value in bonds in the Safe Deposit Company, as you can draw your dividend daily." A month later, he again wrote Morse and expanded his sentiments: "I get more real pleasure out of this than anything that I have ever engaged in, outside of business. Nothing like having a hobby of some kind, I find."

And it was a hobby—at first. But Frick was also enacting a mourning ritual, attempting to make sense of death and loss. Paintings offered him a way to connect himself to Martha and, by extension, to his past. Like visitations from the dead, the

Fig. 5-19. John W. Beatty (1851–1924), *Harvest Scene.*
Acquired in 1895, Oil on canvas, 19½ x 29 in. (49.5 x 73.6 cm).
Frick Art and Historical Center

Fig. 5-20. A. Bryan Wall (1825–1896), *Shepherd and Sheep.*
Acquired in 1895, Oil on canvas, 19½ x 29¼ in. (49.4 x 74.2 cm).
Frick Art and Historical Center

portraits and landscapes acquired and retained in his collection seem to be visions of people, places, and events, as clearly as if they had come back to life in the paintings. Henry Clay Frick was living in two separate worlds: the outer world of daily routine and an encapsulated inner world, a place of mourning where grief and art silently connected him to the spirit world, a world as real to him as Martha's apparition had been.

Remaining in his Clayton collection today are paintings recalling his outer world: William Michael Harnett's *Still Life* (c. 1895) and scenes of places he knew—a Claude Monet entitled *Bords de la Seine* (1901), Martin Rico y Ortega's *Fisherman's House on the Island of Venice* (1895), as well as paintings commissioned from Thaulow. Also remaining are works by his three Scalp Level artist friends on the Carnegie Fine Arts Committee—*Harvest Scene* (fig. 5-19) by the Fine Arts director, John W. Beatty; A. Bryan Wall's *Shepherd and Sheep* (fig. 5-20); and Joseph R. Woodwell's *Landscape*.

Others would serve as warnings. Jacquet's painting of the extravagant *Manon* (see fig. 4-2), as we have seen, and *Tigers Drinking by a Lotus Pool* (fig. 5-21) by the British artist John Macallan Swan, bought from the 1896 Carnegie International, are examples. As mentioned before, Frick said nothing about the portrait of *Manon*, other than placing it above Adelaide's desk. He did, however, say of the sinister painting of stealthy tigers who drink with gleaming eyes alert to approaching danger or prey, "It seems to improve on acquaintance. We have it hung in a very bad place in our house, but hope to improve on that." The painting, however, never found a better place in Clayton. Rather, Frick exhibited it in his office at the Carnegie Company.

So excited was he by his new acquisitions during the summer of 1895, Frick wrote Knoedler, "All the paintings purchased by you are on the wall, except three Cazins, the frames of which are in place." He also made an extensive list for the 1895 Carnegie loan exhibition. When he found certain of his paintings had not been selected for the exhibition, he demanded that John W. Beatty, director of the Fine Arts Committee, explain why they had been omitted. Frick was in fact so angry, he wrote the art dealer from J. J. Gillespie and Company who was charged with the task of removing his paintings: "[They] had better not send for his [paintings] until he heard from Beatty." Cross that, among others, the Bouguereau painting recalling Martha had been turned down, he also wrote Beatty, "I furnished you with a very complete list, carefully made out, so there could be no mistake. . . . If you have intentionally left out the three named, I would like to know why."

Art was important to Frick at many levels and for many reasons. But in 1897, after another year of collecting that included the purchase of Virgile Narcisse Diaz de La Peña's haunting *The Pond of Vipers* (fig. 5-22), as well as other darkly wooded, mysterious landscapes, the force driving his collector's eye would be further revealed in other acquisitions still remaining in the Clayton collection: *Christ at Emmaus* (see fig. 4-17),

Fig. 5-21. John Macallan Swan (1847–1910), *Tigers Drinking by a Lotus Pool.*
Acquired in 1898, Oil on canvas, 44½ x 69½ in. (112.7 x 176.7 cm).
The Art Museum, Princeton University, gift of Helen Clay Frick, 1937

Fig. 5-22. Virgile Narcisse Diaz de La Peña (1807-1876), *The Pond of Vipers*, 1858.
Acquired in 1896, Oil on canvas, 22 x 30 in. (55.9 x 76.2 cm).
Frick Art and Historical Center

which, as we saw, recalls the brilliant light surrounding Martha's postdeath visitation, and *Consolatrix Afflictorum* (fig. 5-23). These paintings illustrate more clearly than any others how fiercely the combination of Frick's snapshot recall, his surfacing melancholia, and Martha's apparition affected his collecting eye.

❖

CHRIST AT EMMAUS AND *CONSOLATRIX AFFLICTORUM,* arguably among the most personally revealing paintings in Frick's collection, are by the French artist Pascal-Adolphe-Jean Dagnan-Bouveret, a photographer and artist once of the realist school and later a symbolist. Frick and Adelaide knew Dagnan, who was a small man, not more than five foot one or two, with dark hair, a dark beard, and deep-set, intense eyes. Regarded by his contemporaries as "a man who comes to feel instinctively the thoughts in the mind of another person with whom he is in intimate relationship, [and] arrives at a sympathetic knowledge of what is inside," Dagnan had an ability to express a person's inner soul and psychology. Perhaps this was the quality that most endeared him to Frick and Adelaide, for his contemporaries noted he "radiated sympathy which overflowed." Moreover, Dagnan-Bouveret, as is widely believed today, had also lost a child. And by the late 1890s, he, like Frick, was preoccupied with the mystical and supernatural. As man and artist, Dagnan-Bouveret was perfect for Frick, his aesthetic an ideal complement to Frick's emotional state and collecting pattern. As Gabriel Weisberg writes, this artist exhibited a "curious blending of the real with the unreal."

Of the first religious painting acquired by Frick, originally called *Supper at Emmaus* or *Christ Blessing the Bread,* but today known as *Christ and the Disciples at Emmaus* (referred to hereafter as *Christ at Emmaus*), the *Chicago Tribune* warned:

IT WILL CAUSE A SHOCK.
EUROPE CONSIDERS IT SCANDALOUS.
FRICK BUYS A FREAK.

Dagnan-Bouveret's agent, Arthur Tooth, however, boasted that the artist "has surpassed himself; that he considers it his masterpiece." Frick, pleased by the importance of his acquisition, on October 21, 1897, introduced Carnegie to Dagnan-Bouveret by writing: "Am quite anxious that he and Mrs. Carnegie should see the picture you are painting for me, as the chances are it will eventually find a resting place in the institution which he has founded."

Fig. 5-23. Pascal-Adolphe-Jean Dagnan-Bouveret (1852–1929), *Consolatrix Afflictorum*, 1899.
Reserved in 1898, Oil on canvas, 88 x 77 in. (223.5 x 195.6 cm).
Frick Art and Historical Center

In the last two years, Frick and Carnegie seemed to have resolved their differences. In 1897, company profits had climbed to $7 million, and as both men pursued their interest in art, Frick seemed content to help bring Carnegie's Art Institute to completion. When Carnegie, who had been abroad since May, saw *Christ at Emmaus,* he wrote Frick of the vast, six-and-a-half-by-nine-foot canvas, "It is the best modern picture of Christ I have seen by far. Color exquisite, and beautiful—very. It is really great."

The press, however, sneered at the painting because Dagnan-Bouveret had, in its opinion, committed sacrilege by including himself and his family in the biblical scene. In addition—in the kind of gratuitous commentary that would always shadow public discourse regarding Henry Clay Frick's collection—the press noted that in the artist's reference to the blessing of the broken body (the body of sacrifice), "Mr. Frick's employees in Homestead have often been in a position to know what a blessing bread must be."

Responding to the outrage prompted by the inclusion of himself and his family in the religious scene, Dagnan remarked that the three figures represented "the modern world face to face with the divine mystery"; the woman and child were still able to kneel before Christ and show faith, while the man was not. Both Dagnan and Frick also explained to the press that precedent for including contemporary personages in religious works was set by "the Catholic painters in the Middle Ages and the Renaissance [who] used to introduce the figure of the donor worshipping the divine person of the Madonna." Although Dagnan-Bouveret's critics were forced to agree that artists like Titian, Rembrandt, and Paolo Veronese had honored their patrons in this way, they warned that Veronese was "cited before the holy office for the crime of heresy" and denounced Dagnan-Bouveret as being no more than a "skeptic theologian."

Dagnan-Bouveret remained steadfast. As if describing Frick's own situation, he responded that modern man, with his reliance on science and rational thought, was concerned more with the expansion of his own powers and control over the external world than with his soul. He wrote of his portrait subject, the nineteenth-century man, "His brow is care worn with the anxiety which has desolated his heart."

But far more than this had inspired Frick's acquisition of the painting and his defense of it. He had visited Dagnan's studio in August 1897, the summer after Dagnan exhibited his prize-winning *Madonna of the Rose* at the first Carnegie International. Frick and Adelaide were in Paris at the time, and the dealer Edmund Simon took Frick to Dagnan's studio specifically to see *Christ at Emmaus.* Although the artist had just started the painstaking process of blocking out the painting's details, using composite photography and tracing-paper overlays to place his figures on the canvas and enhance their realism, Frick was struck by the artist's initial effort. He immediately contracted to buy the painting, the purchase seeming a sudden, almost compulsive move, because up until that time, Frick's acquisitions were typically landscapes, portraits, still lifes, and genre scenes of medium size and mid-market price.

There was, perhaps, a legitimate personal reason why he was so inexplicably drawn to this piece of religious art. Edgar Munhall comments that when Frick saw the painting, he was no doubt as "dazzled" by the sunburst emanating from Christ's head as he had been "dazzled by the apparently living image of his dead daughter" during Berkman's attack. Frick, had, after all, been taken by Edmund Simon to Dagnan's studio in the month of August, a time when Frick's thoughts were, as Munhall conjectures, intensely preoccupied with Martha, her death, and her apparition. In his heightened emotional state, Frick undoubtedly reexperienced the sensation of the child's apparition and correlated the blinding light of her visitation with Dagnan's sunburst depiction of Christ's postdeath appearance to the disciples during supper at Emmaus.

Additionally, the painting's actual subject matter could easily have resonated with Frick. Apart from the fact that he was raised in the strict Mennonite tradition of New Testament Christianity, later becoming a Baptist and a Freemason, he was a man intimate with both scripture and mythology. Just as Christ's sudden appearance brought proof of resurrection and an afterlife to the disciples, so too Frick's vision of Martha had given him a sudden affirmation, strengthening his messianic conviction to fight out the strike and to fight for his own life as well. Certainly, just as the disciples' faith was turned to devotion by the vision of the risen Christ, the strength of Frick's conviction about Homestead was further fortified by his vision of his beloved daughter.

Frick's deeper response to the painting seemed to relate not only to the visual and metaphysical effect of Martha's visitation but also to a darker reaction to her death: a father's grief turned into survivor's guilt. All grief researchers agree: in acute grief, apart from intense preoccupation with images of the deceased, feelings of guilt populate the bereaved's mind, and these include the failure to do right at the time of death, or even negligence. As an editorial in the *Canadian Medical Association Journal* entitled "Death in Childhood" notes: "often the parents' minds will dart restlessly about in search of some failure or error on their part that may have influenced the situation . . . . what may seem almost an eagerness for self-reproach." Ann Finkbeiner says in *After the Death of a Child*, "Guilt is one way to explain the death: I should have prevented it; I am to blame; I am guilty."

Martha's death, seen in this way, provided great potential for guilt: had someone watched her more carefully, she might never have ingested the pin during that 1887 Paris summer. Worse, since no one suspected the nature of her discomfort until the pin exited her side two years later, any momentary lack of compassion on Frick's part could have later been interpreted by him as cruelty. Compounding this self-imposed guilt, Frick had delayed bringing Carnegie's surgeons to Martha until too late, affording

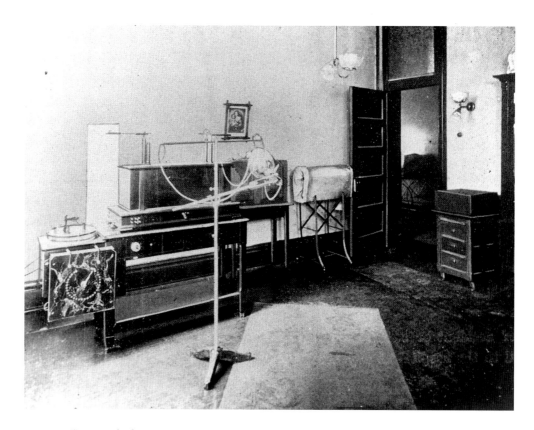

Fig. 5-24. The first X-ray machine at Mercy Hospital was donated by Henry Clay Frick in 1896.
Mercy Hospital Archives, Pittsburgh

him ample reason to feel implicated in her death. When expressing this guilt only in terms of his preoccupation with business, he would eventually confess to an Ohio newspaper reporter that he felt Martha's death "more painfully" because he blamed himself for not being able "to attend her more constantly" during her fatal illness. There was much truth to this statement. In 1891, as Martha slipped into her final decline, he had been so focused on quelling the Morewood riots, he had, by his own admission, hardly spent more than an hour or two with his family.

With this confession of guilt and negligence, he also may have seen Martha's death as a form of punishment—the price exacted for the fortune accumulated. Like most of his contemporaries, Frick had been immersed in the Christian tradition where hell and damnation are ever-present realities. In fact, in the months prior to seeing Dagnan's painting, certain of his actions would suggest that he might have been consumed with easing the crushing burden of guilt he carried. For a few years, he had been preoccupied by the welfare of children, giving donations to the Kindergarten Association and purchasing a new site for the Kingsley Settlement House, dedicated to the education and welfare of underprivileged children, agreeing to underwrite its renovation. Additionally, Frick served on the board of the Pittsburgh Free Dispensary, and in 1896 he donated a newly invented X-ray machine (fig. 5-24) to Mercy Hospital, as well as new instruments and antiseptic equipment to the Homeopathic Hospital. His thinking behind these gestures is inescapable: had this machine and the new antiseptic techniques been available in 1887 when Martha swallowed the pin, or when her wound was lanced in 1889, she, like him, might still be alive.

A fragment of a letter from Dagnan-Bouveret to his wife in April 1898, though containing a reference to a hospital Frick had not built, nevertheless confirms Frick's state of mind. Dagnan says the painting "corresponded so intimately to his [Mr. Frick's] dreams"; all the studies for the painting were reserved for "the main room of a hospital which he [Mr. Frick] had built after the death of his little girl." Dagnan further mentions to his wife that a certain person named Engel-Gros has asked to stay at the chateau de Ripaille "so that he could paint his [Frick's] 'two little girls'"—presumably the one that lived and the one that died.

Significantly, apart from the fact that the paintings Frick had already purchased for himself were expressions of loss and links to the spirit world, and apart from his redemptive social acts through monetary contributions, there is evidence to suggest that he was also displacing his long pent-up guilt as rage against Carnegie. Beverly Raphael, author of *The Anatomy of Bereavement*, makes the point that a person who is locked into pathological mourning will often direct anger, born of the bereaved's self-imposed guilt and sense of personal negligence, onto someone who was also connected to the death. This anger may be transferred to a spouse, or if one defends against that, onto a person outside the family. In Frick's case, Carnegie was an obvious target. When Martha swallowed the fatal pin, Frick was in Europe recovering from his forced capitulation to wildcat strikers' demands and his resignation from his coke company. Furthermore, Martha had gone into her fatal decline when Frick was preoccupied with events in the Coke Region, the time he failed to call Carnegie's surgeons until it was too late. Perhaps as a way to let Carnegie know that he perceived Martha as a sacrificial lamb—that her death had been both the price Frick had paid and the true cost of Carnegie Steel's success, a sacrifice Frick recognized he had been bound to make in fulfillment of his "sacred duties"—he had a plaque attached to the painting when he gave it to the Carnegie Art Institute. It read: "Given in honor of Martha Howard Frick by her Parents."

Apart from using the words "in honor of," not "in memory of," specific elements in the painting point to this guilt-ridden theme of blame, sacrifice, and resurrection. In a break from artistic tradition, *Christ at Emmaus* depicts a woman rather than a man serving Christ, an obvious reference to the serving girl, Martha—the Martha who complained to Christ at a feast the week before the crucifixion that she always labored

Fig. 5-25. Pascal-Adolphe-Jean Dagnan-Bouveret (1852–1929),
Detail, *Christ and the Disciples at Emmaus*, 1896–97.
Oil on canvas, 78 x 110½ in. (198.1 x 280.7 cm).
Carnegie Museum of Art, Pittsburgh, gift of Henry Clay Frick, 1898

and toiled, while her sister Mary sat at Christ's feet in rapture. But she is also the Martha of the resurrection, the Martha who so doubts that Christ can raise her brother Lazarus, dead four days, that Christ first teaches the lesson of resurrection and the afterlife to her by indeed performing that miracle.

Professor W. W. Martin wrote in the *Pittsburgh Post* on Sunday, November 27, 1898, of Dagnan-Bouveret's serving girl, as if he, too, were linking the child Martha to the Martha of scripture: "The face of the Christ is most remarkable, but scarcely less so is the face of the young maid, clothed like the Christ in spotless white robes. . . . She approaches the table bearing the platter upon which is the meat. But she has paused, beautiful in her simple loving modesty like a lily in its charm of form and lovely purity. She looks at Christ with that undisturbed, confident gaze as if in the Master all the noblest hope and thoughts of her life were realized." Martin then noted the plaque attached to the painting and went on to say: "One cannot separate this figure from the inscription upon the magnificent picture frame. . . . Somehow we feel could she [Martha] who is daily kept in memory be given place in a painting, not otherwise could she appear than does this beautiful, sweet, singularly pure and charming face."

Historically the serving girl in the painting may have represented the biblical Martha, but the person described by Martin as "beautiful, sweet, singularly pure and charming," was, in the painting, the antithesis of these qualities. She is gaunt. Her long, reddish hair is held under a tight-fitting hood, her startling blue eyes bulge out of her head in an astonished, somewhat ghoulish fashion. The serving girl seems an apparition—if not a harbinger of death, then a vision of death itself.

Martin was wrong: the girl in the painting (fig. 5-25) is not Frick's Martha. A more compelling argument would be that his Martha was instead represented and symbolized by both Christ's brilliant auburn hair and the tender leg of lamb on the serving girl's platter—the Lamb of God—the sacrificial offering, the broken body that was cleansed with her blood. And now Martha, the sacrificial lamb, had paid the ultimate price for Frick's fortune, a fortune made by being Carnegie's hatchet man in both the

Coke Region and the steel mills. Her visitation during Berkman's assassination attempt provided Frick with his near-religious conviction to see the strike through, even if it killed him. Martha was Frick's own sacrificial meal, the food and strength for his journey. And his self-imposed guilt served another purpose—as an unconscious way to remain connected to the child. Guilt, like paintings, emotional pain, and longing, creates a place where the bereaved can live in spirit together with the deceased.

Adding to this argument, and to the significance Frick must certainly have attached to *Christ at Emmaus,* is the fact that the canvas was completed by August 1898, the seventh anniversary of Martha's death, an anniversary when Victorians believed the soul of the deceased, if not baptized, would reappear. Moreover, seven is a sacred number to Freemasons. A perfect number, it represents the completion of time: the seven days of the week; the seven altars of Mithra; the sabbath on the seventh day; the seven days of notice to Noah before the flood; the seven persons on the ark; the seven days the ark rested on Mt. Ararat on the seventh month; and the seven years it took Solomon to build the temple which was dedicated in the seventh month and celebrated for seven days.

The finished canvas, however, posed a dilemma for Frick. Although in 1897 he had considered giving the painting to the Carnegie Institute, he now vacillated. The relationship with Carnegie was again turning stormy, the price of coke being one of the issues. As a result, Frick wrote Edmund Simon to "Please bear in mind that I explicitly stated to you I had not made up my mind what I would do with it. I did not buy it with the intention of presenting it to anybody, and so stated to you." But on Saturday, July 9, 1898, two weeks short of the seventh anniversary of Martha's death, Frick made the decision to go ahead. He wrote his friend William F. Frew, director of the Carnegie Art Institute, who headed a committee to secure the painting from Frick: "Mrs. Frick and I have the honor to present in memory of our daughter Martha to the Carnegie Institute *Les Disciples d'Emmaus [Christ at Emmaus]* by Dagnan-Bouveret."

Frick referred to Martha as "their little girl . . . who has fallen asleep," and the painting, acknowledged as the most valuable work owned by the largely empty gallery and the most spiritual of any religious painting yet to come to America, became the focus of sermons as well as the centerpiece of the coming 1898 Carnegie International. And it served another purpose. Henry Clay Frick was asked to join the Fine Arts Committee of the Carnegie Institute. As the gracious words of thank-you-note-etiquette of the day flowed, Frick could certainly feel that his position both among his business peers and in the art community was secure.

In the meantime, Frick acquired a small copy of the painting for Clayton. Painted by a student of Dagnan-Bouveret's, and seen by Frick when visiting Dagnan's studio, it was one-third the size of the original. Known as *Pilgrims at Emmaus,* the picture arrived at Clayton in December 1898. Frick placed it above the mantel in the upstairs living room and continued weaving his tapestry by balancing the painting on either side with the 1895 Chartran portrait of Martha and his portrait the following year of Helen wearing around her neck a locket bearing a miniature of the Martha painting.

In addition to acquiring a copy of *Christ at Emmaus* for Clayton, Frick softened the loss of the painting by purchasing a second Dagnan-Bouveret of still deeper symbolism. On Friday, July 8, 1898, the day before he wrote Mr. Frew from Paris of his decision to donate *Christ at Emmaus* in honor of Martha, Henry Clay Frick had purchased Dagnan's life-size work, *Consolatrix Afflictorum*.

One of the largest paintings in Frick's collection (measuring 7'3" x 6'4") as well as one of the most expensive he had yet acquired, *Consolatrix* is a picture that would intrigue him throughout his life. It depicts the Madonna in a green robe, seated in a woods like a Celtic priestess—Queen of Earth, Queen of Nature, the fecund divinity of the lower realm dominated by fertility and decay, not the celestial queen traditional to most Christian art. One of her eyes looks at the Christ Child in her lap, the other at a modern-day man prostrate at her feet. Hummingbirds, whose feathers were often used for mourning jewelry, swarm around the Christ, while a hart or a prepubescent deer is sheltered beneath her cape. Three angels stand behind her. The left angel wears violets, the death flower prized for its perfume yet pitied for the shortness of its life. The central angel wears baby's breath, and the angel to the right, lilacs—another spring flower most often associated with death, and, ironically, the spring flower commemorating the Frick's rented home on Lilac Street where Martha fell into her fatal decline. Additionally, the Madonna's wreath of five daisies, each with its single bright eye, seems to represent the divine, intuitive eye, the eye of Christ and his five wounds.

So fascinated was Frick by the painting that as late as 1903, Knoedler wrote Dagnan on Frick's behalf, seeking the painting's "full particulars." In his reply, the artist said that only a scholar or poet could "interpret what [he] wished to convey." He said, "A picture of this kind cannot be explained, or rather it explains itself—Each person interprets it according to the way in which it appeals to his imagination." He did, however, offer various thematic possibilities for consideration: "the religious idea which consoles, or Nature, who reserves for those who suffer a word of comfort; it matters not. I had no precise idea. Like the timid fawn which has sought a refuge in the folds of the simple cloak, the man in trouble, who has fallen prostrate, is also seeking sanctuary. And this refuge I wished it to express the widest possible idea:—Peace and Love."

In an additional note, Dagnan expanded upon the notion of "Peace and Love." He said the man prostrate at the Madonna's feet was meant to represent "the man of the world who in seeking . . . rest has chosen the loneliness of a wood for . . . solitude and 'The Peace which Passeth all Understanding.'" According to Dagnan, this weary, spiritual man seeking rest "has centered his soul and in a vision [of the Christ Child with his Mother feeding the hummingbirds and sheltering the animals of the forest] he sees revealed the simplicity of Love and Peace." The man, wrote Dagnan, has found "consolation in solitude and the awakening of a new life in him has begun."

Certainly, at the time Frick saw the painting in 1898, he could only have been as struck by the emotionality of the work as he had previously been blinded by the brilliance of the ascending Christ in *Christ at Emmaus*. Dagnan's vision for the green-cloaked Madonna, his translucent Christ Child, and the angels with their Celtic references, coupled with his own experience of Martha's apparition and the known Celtic belief in reincarnation, must certainly have spoken to Frick (whose paternal grandmother was Irish) at the deepest level. Moreover, Frick had reached a time in his life when sorrow and solitude continued to weigh heavily on his heart, a time when "peace which passeth all understanding" was for him glimpsed only through art—a peace realized only after sorrow has become so intense it causes the kind of soul-death which, from its ashes, gives birth to the ultimate peace and love described by Dagnan.

Consolatrix resounds with evocations of death and resurrection. In addition to the keen associations Frick drew from it about Martha, its purchase date coincided with the seventh anniversary of the birth of Henry Clay Frick, Jr. More fascinating, although Dagnan-Bouveret traditionally placed his own family in his paintings, he seems to have used a photograph of the Frick nurse holding the deceased baby as a model for the painting. Additionally, he seems to have used pictures of the Frick family for the Madonna, the Christ Child, and the man despairing at the Virgin's feet. Juxtapositions of Frick family photographs with Dagnan's portrait subjects reveal just this: the resemblances are unmistakable. The posthumous photograph of Henry Clay Frick's infant son (fig. 5-26), when compared to the disturbing Christ Child (fig. 5-27), suggests the baby may have been used as the model for the Christ. The painting depicts an infant Christ who seems translucent, almost fetal in character. Like a premature baby's, the infant's eyes sink in their sockets and do not appear fully developed. Even the shape of the infant's head seems awkward, as if compressed by a difficult journey through the birth canal. His peculiarly high forehead appears distorted; the oddly cupped, shell-like ears and the bridge of the nose are set in unusually low positions. The likeness of the Christ Child to the posthumous picture of little Henry Clay Frick, Jr., is nothing less than astonishing.

Dr. Joseph Greenberg, a neonatalist at Mercy Hospital in Pittsburgh, has studied the photograph of the deceased baby. Although he could not determine the cause of death, Dr. Greenberg did comment on the peculiarly low forehead, low ears, and low bridge of the nose, suggesting that these characteristics were perhaps genetic traits, not symptoms of disease. He was correct about the genetics. Henry Clay Frick and his

Fig. 5-26. Posthumous photograph of Henry Clay Frick, Jr., being held by Nurse Grandison, 1892.
Frick Art and Historical Center

son Childs (fig. 5-28) had the low "Overholt" fore-heads, low ears, and a low bridge to the nose. More-over, they had the "Frick" oddly shaped, shell-like ears, just like the deceased baby, and just like the Christ Child in *Consolatrix*.

What is more compelling, the Christ Child may well have represented another tragic loss in Frick's life. On April 23, 1897, two years before the acquisi-tion of this painting, thirty-seven-year-old Ade-laide, had apparently suffered a miscarriage. In his 1897 condolence letter, Carnegie wrote, "Its [*sic*] too bad Dr. Garmany treated Helen so badly when he had promised her a dear sister. . . . Love to the dear mother. She has to be careful too not to break down."

Although Adelaide refused to have her portrait done by Dagnan-Bouveret, and the French actress Julia Bartet is believed to have been the model for the Madonna, close inspection of the Madonna's face (fig. 5-27) reveals its similarity to Adelaide's (see fig. 5-28) at that period. Dagnan, who knew the Fricks personally and had photographs of the fam-ily members, may well have used her face as model for the Madonna's to lure Frick into the purchase. And it is also quite plausible that Dagnan used the green cape and sacrificial grapes to imply that Ade-laide embodied the Madonna's allusion to nature's inevitable cycle of death and rebirth, the death of the Frick's two children and the recent miscarriage. Perhaps the artist felt about women and Adelaide as Charles Swinburne describes the winter and spring aspects of nature in *The Devouring Mother:* "You are crueler, you that we love, than hatred, hunger, or death; You have eyes and breasts like a dove, and you kill men's hearts with a breath."

If so, then perhaps Frick's 1895 acquisition of *Manon* (see fig. 4-2), the pleasure-seeking young girl who repents too late and dies in degradation, was a dark-humored joke. Perhaps even in that purchase

Fig. 5-27. Pascal-Adolphe-Jean Dagnan-Bouveret
(1852–1929),
Detail, *Consolatrix Afflictorum*, 1899.
Reserved in 1898, Oil on canvas, 88 x 77 in. (223.5 x 195.6 cm).
Frick Art and Historical Center

Above, Fig. 5-28. Adelaide
Howard Childs Frick.
Frick Art and Historical Center

Right, Fig. 5-29. Henry Clay
Frick and son Childs.
Frick Art and Historical Center

Frick saw in Adelaide the dark side of femininity. And therefore, perhaps *Consolatrix*
pulled exquisitely both upon Frick's mysticism and his sublimated anger at his wife.
As he became preoccupied with the afterlife, he may have seen Adelaide as a negligent
mother who should have prevented the death of their children. Certainly, in his pain,
Frick could have transferred his own guilt and blamed his wife as much as he blamed
Andrew Carnegie for Martha's death.

Whatever Frick's feelings, the hart beneath the Madonna's cape marks the painting as funereal. The hart points the way to full spirituality. In biblical writings, the hart
typically voices the despair of the soulless, of a man such as the one in the painting, a
man such as Frick. The forty-second psalm, often recited at funerals, begins:

> As the hart panteth after the fountains of water, so my soul panteth
>   after thee, O God . . .
> My tears have been my meat day and night . . .
> Whilst my bones are broken, my enemies who trouble me have
>   reproached me :
> Whilst they say to me day by day: Where is thy God?

Fig. 5-30. The Clayton dining room with *Consolatrix Afflictorum.*
Frick Art and Historical Center

Certainly the man's shell-shaped ears strongly resemble those of Henry Clay Frick in a picture with his son Childs (fig. 5-29). And certainly in 1899 Frick was having a spiritual awakening. Though Dagnan claimed that the man in his painting "returns to his fellow men with purer thoughts and comforted," Frick continued to grieve, but only through the silence of art. In fact, his mourning remained so intense, he placed *Consolatrix* in front of the Clayton dining room fireplace (a facsimile of a beehive coke oven) where it made a free-standing, false wall. When eating dinner, as the orchestri-on played the "Ave Maria" and excerpts from Flotlow's opera *Martha,* Frick could look down the table at his wife, and into the face of the Madonna (fig. 5-30).

CHAPTER VI

Pittsburgh Exodus

The Senior . . . for sometime has stumbled badly.

—Henry Clay Frick, 1899

Frick goes out. . . . He is too old, too infirm in health and mind . . .
I have nothing but pity for Frick. . . .
His recent exhibition [behavior] is childish.

—Andrew Carnegie, 1899

BEYOND UNDERLINING FRICK'S DELAYED AND DISTURBED REACTION to Martha's death, the arrival of *Consolatrix Afflictorum* announced a coming death: Frick's relationship with Andrew Carnegie. In 1889, when Frick took over as chairman of Carnegie Brothers and Company, Carnegie had cheered his partner, "The Man": "F is a marvel. Lets all get F's [Fricks]." He had warned Frick, "Take supreme care of that head of yours. It is wanted." Then, in 1892, when Frick was attacked by Berkman, Carnegie announced, "If his health be spared, I predict that no man who ever lived in Pittsburgh and managed business here will be better liked or more admired than my friend and partner Henry Clay Frick." By 1899, however, Carnegie was no longer infatuated with Frick. He was ready to wield Frick a death blow.

Two portraits might be considered emblematic of the continuing difficulties between the two millionaires and of the darker nature of Frick's collecting pattern. He acquired the long-coveted collector's prize, Hans Holbein the Younger's *Sir Thomas More* (fig. 6-1) in 1912 and the same artist's *Thomas Cromwell* (fig. 6-2) in 1915. Both were men who fell to the scaffold in the sixteenth-century: Sir Thomas More, a man who lived by the letter of the law, and who was so just and uncompromising he accepted the death penalty rather than accept Henry VIII as supreme head of the church, was beheaded by Henry's trusted advisor, Thomas Cromwell, who later suffered the same fate.

Frick family legend claims that the martyr More, who placed his own conscience before secular authority, depicts Henry Clay Frick: the man who insisted that rioting

Fig. 6-1. Hans Holbein the Younger (1497/98–1543), *Sir Thomas More*, 1528.
Acquired in 1912, Oil on oak panel, 29½ x 23¾ in. (74.9 x 60.3 cm).
The Frick Collection

Fig. 6-2. Hans Holbein the Younger (1497/98–1543), *Thomas Cromwell*.
Acquired in 1915, Oil on oak panel, 30⅞ x 25⅜ in. (78.4 x 64.4 cm).
The Frick Collection

Fig. 6-3. Andrew Carnegie seated at his desk containing
the drawer labeled "Gratitude and Sweet Words."
The New-York Historical Society

immigrants had liberty but not license; the man who during the Homestead strike insisted on the Carnegie Steel Company's right to manage and enter its own property; the man who insisted Berkman be left to the law; the man who would soon tell Carnegie, "We will see what the Judge and jury of Allegheny County have to say about the matter."

Family legend also says that Thomas Cromwell depicts Andrew Carnegie. In her adult years, when Helen Frick took her father's great-grandchildren through his collection, she often commented on the brilliant way Holbein painted Cromwell's "greedy little hands." Certainly the visible likeness between Carnegie's hands (fig. 6-3) and Thomas Cromwell's in the previous image is noticeable. In the photograph, Andrew Carnegie sits at his desk that, according to Carnegie's biographer, Joseph Wall, had a drawer labeled "Gratitude and Sweet Words," into which Carnegie's secretary placed favorable press reports about her boss.

But in 1898, three years into Frick's honorary position as chairman of the board of managers of Carnegie Steel and at the time when Frick acquired *Consolatrix* and gave *Christ at Emmaus* to the Carnegie International, past betrayals and present disagreements between Frick and Carnegie again brought the men into conflict. Frick, as chairman of the H. C. Frick Coke Company, had entered into a verbal agreement, effective January 1899, to sell coke to Carnegie Steel at a permanent price of $1.35 a ton, fifteen cents below the market rate. Although the price of coke had gone up, and Carnegie had the benefit of buying coke at a greatly reduced price, he feared that if the price were to fall below $1.35, he would be locked into an inflated rate. Frick, on the other hand, was dissatisfied because the price of coke had actually increased and, because he had already given Carnegie a discount, he felt he was taking a double hit and missing out on the rise in the coke market. Frick, therefore, began to bill Carnegie Steel at ever increasing rates ranging from $1.45 to an eventual $1.75 per ton.

In the summer of 1898, Frick declined an invitation to stay with Carnegie in his newly purchased Skibo Castle in Scotland (fig. 6-4), saying that it was "too damp and although Adelaide wanted a trip abroad, he and Helen did not." Frick realized,

Fig. 6-4. Skibo Castle, c. 1899.
Frick Archives

however, that Adelaide needed a complete rest, and so he told Carnegie they were going to Aix-les-Bains. But more was at work than Adelaide's heath. Frick and Henry Phipps, concerned over the consolidation of steel organizations by the richest man in America, J. P. Morgan, into the Federal Steel Company, warned that Chicago, not Pittsburgh, would soon be the nation's steel center. They felt the time had come to sell the Carnegie Steel Company. But Carnegie, who four years before had tried to coax Frick into buying him out, now felt the steel concern only needed reorganization. His rationale surfaced when his wife Louise expressed her desire that he sell. As Carnegie's cousin George Lauder, a partner and stockholder in Carnegie Steel, described the scene, Carnegie turned on her "quite savagely and went into a tirade on men who retired dying . . . that he would be laying down a crown."

Nevertheless, Frick was asked to explore the possibility of selling the company to Morgan or John D. Rockefeller. Various proposals were made, but none were acceptable to either potential buyers or to Carnegie. Then in March 1899, William H. Moore of Chicago, who had just completed other mergers and was famous for manipulating the stock of his new companies, approached Frick and Phipps. Carnegie sailed for Scotland in April; by May, Frick and Judge Moore (he was an excellent "judge" of horseflesh) put together a syndicate to buy out Carnegie. Both Phipps and Frick knew Carnegie generally disliked speculators and disapproved of Judge Moore in particular. Thus, the Moore connection was not disclosed when Frick and Phipps told Carnegie they had an offer of $250 million for Carnegie Steel and $70 million for the H. C. Frick Coke Company. They secured an option from Carnegie for ninety days with a deposit of $1.17 million of which Frick, Phipps, and another Carnegie associate put up $170,000. The time limit on their option ran out, however, because a minor financial panic delayed the funding of their deal. Phipps and Frick visited Carnegie at Skibo in August, certain that Carnegie would renew their option. But when they arrived, they learned Carnegie had pocketed their $1.17 million deposit. He had discovered the principal in the deal was Moore and that Frick and Phipps were to be paid a $5 million commission, something Frick hotly denied. As retribution, Carnegie, who was building a four-story addition to his white sandstone castle that would include a library, study, music room, drawing room, billiard room, and indoor pool with heated sea water, and was also building a permanent New York residence on Ninety-fourth Street and Fifth Avenue, teased that he was redecorating his Scottish castle with "just a nice little present from Mr. Frick."

Frick, though tempting fate by dealing with Judge Moore, was so infuriated by Carnegie's behavior, he intensified his attempt to sell the company and followed suit with his own "interior decorating." That same summer of 1899, he sold the two Gérômes he had purchased in 1895 and acquired more works by Daubigny, Chelminski, Israel,

Inness, Millet, and Troyon. He also purchased his second placid lakeside Corot, *The Pond,* and Friant's previously mentioned *Chagrin d'Enfant* (see fig. 3-6) from the Paris Salon—the painting that may have poignantly evoked for Frick the onset of Martha's fatal decline—the time when Annie held Martha in her lap and read her stories, the time when he was preoccupied with the Morewood riots, the time when he carried his dying child from the Cresson Springs train station to the Carnegie Cottage where she died. In 1897, Emile Friant had sent Knoedler the sketch for the painting, then called *Two Sisters.* The title changed to *Consolation,* and later, in 1898, when the finished work was delivered to Knoedler's Paris address in time for Frick's arrival, it was called *Chagrin d'Enfant*—perhaps, as McIntosh notes, to "shift the focus" to the younger child. As we know, Frick bought the painting. The child model for this genre scene, as Knoedler undoubtedly told Frick, died not long after Friant finished the painting.

But at this moment in Frick's life, art provided no escape. Summer was always a time of special sadness, when Martha's death was of particular torment. As Frick grieved, so too his anger at Carnegie roared. He told the Carnegie managers, "The Senior . . . for sometime has stumbled badly," and as Carnegie took the opportunity to issue a torrent of criticism at them all, Frick grew resentful. In reply to the jabs, Frick told the managers, "If Mr. Carnegie wishes to review past actions, we have as much right to review other things. . . . I think we have blundered about in proportion to our interests in the concern."

Unlike the 1894 breach, when the partners were behind Frick, loyalties within the concern this time had become divided. If they went against Frick and he won, Frick could ruin them. If the managers went against Carnegie, and he won, he could ruin them as well. For his part, Frick was not beyond trying to endear himself to his partners. When he sent Charles Schwab, Carnegie's new favorite and now president of Carnegie Steel, a painting of Homestead entitled *The Smoky City,* by Frick's artist friend Thaulow, the maneuver won Frick a rewarding response from Schwab: "I am yours to command always"—a response that would soon show itself false.

In October 1899, upon Carnegie's return from Scotland, Frick's disenchantment with the titan escalated when his senior partner began to confront him on the price of coke, still climbing well beyond the agreed $1.35 a ton. Carnegie fumed, "No Sir, Frick can't repudiate contracts for any company which myself and friends control. We are not that kind of cats."

But Frick was wearing two hats; he was president of Carnegie Steel's board of managers and chairman of the H. C. Frick Coke Company, the sole supplier of coke to the steel company. And so, regardless of the fact that Carnegie was the major shareholder of the coke company, Frick threatened to stop shipping coke to Carnegie's mills. To make matters worse, in November, after Frick tried to sell a recently purchased piece of land at Peter's Creek to Carnegie Steel for what Carnegie complained was five times its purchase price, Carnegie accused Frick of committing an "improper act" and complained to others that the land had been sold at an inflated price.

Frick claimed the land had been part of an even trade for real estate near his Clayton home. Furious with Carnegie, Frick also felt his coke company was being used by Carnegie at great cost to the non-steel company shareholders. Apart from the fact that the shareholders were not getting a full price for the coke, $6 million of the coke company's credit had been used for the steel concern. As for the Peter's Creek problem, Frick questioned the board of Carnegie Steel: "Why was he not man enough to say to my face what he said behind my back? . . . Harmony is so essential for the success of any organization that I have stood a great many insults from Mr. Carnegie in the past, but I will submit to no further insults in the future." Frick refused to sell the land until Carnegie gave him a full apology.

Carnegie, however, denied having made the statement, saying, "I shall receive your unmeritted invective in silence. . . . When you get your usual calm and if you come to me, I shall tell you all the circumstances. . . . I am not guilty and can satisfy you of this, also of the folly of believing tale bearers, a mean lot."

Concerned about Frick's state of mind, George Lauder wrote Carnegie on November 24, 1899, and noted Frick's "angry craziness, which seems to be promoted altogether by personal feeling." He urged Carnegie "to cut loose from such a disturbing element," saying, "He is scarcely responsible for many of his sayings and doings and, now that the sting of failure last summer [the failed Moore syndicate to buy out Carnegie] is added, the less said about his condition of mind the better, it is probably more a misfortune than a fault to be thus constituted."

Carnegie, infuriated by Frick's insults, and convinced Frick was too unbalanced to manage a big concern, replied, "Frick goes out. . . . He is too old, too infirm in health *and mind* . . . I have nothing but pity for Frick. . . . His recent exhibition [behavior] is childish." Anticipating the removal of Frick and again having what he referred to as "a happy and united family," Carnegie said to Lauder he had decided:

> to tell Mr. Frick in the kindest manner that I mean divorce under "Incompatibility of Temper." I shall tell him never had anything but happy family until he came into it—and I am not going to have anything else—It is divorce between us as far as management of our business is concerned—no feeling—only I believe our best interests demand an end to quarreling. . . . Mr. Frick has no right to ask what passes between partners, all being confidential and sacred, and if any of our boys asked they should at once decline to be made tale bearers.

With Carnegie's decision to divorce Frick, Charles Schwab came to Clayton on the evening of December 4 with a letter requesting Frick's immediate and quiet resignation from Carnegie Steel. Frick apparently grew so enraged, Schwab left the house with Frick's anger "ringing in his ears."

Nevertheless, the next day, Frick resigned as chairman of the board of managers of the Carnegie Steel Company, in order "to prevent the evil which might result from discord." He repurchased a painting by an American artist, Frank D. Millet, entitled *How the Gossip Grew* and gave it to Mrs. Francis Lovejoy, the wife of the Carnegie company's secretary. He also offered to sell his interests to Carnegie, the price to be fixed by disinterested arbitrators, or, if that was not agreeable, he offered to purchase Carnegie's interests on the same terms Carnegie had required of him in 1894. Carnegie, insisting that Frick become the "King" of his own company by owning the majority of the coke company stock, subsequently offered to sell Frick his shares, so Frick would not "be in the ridiculous position of not being Coke King." Shortly thereafter, however, Carnegie decided against Frick having this controlling share.

At the January 8, 1900, board meeting of the H. C. Frick Coke Company, which Carnegie had padded with his supporters, a contract was approved requiring the coke company to sell its product to Carnegie Steel for $1.35 per ton, even though the market price had reached $3.50. The board also decided to require the coke company to refund any charges made over and above that amount to Carnegie Steel. Frick walked out of the meeting, saying to Carnegie, "You will find there are two sides to this matter."

The following morning, Frick was seated at his desk in his private office in the Carnegie building. He had just lighted a fresh cigar and, having finished dictating answers to various business communications, was reading a personal letter from a friend and stockholder in the steel company, A. R. Whitney, who was vacationing in Colorado. As a contemporary described the scene:

> Raising his eyes upon hearing the door open and close, he beheld without appearance of emotion the familiar figure of Mr. Carnegie poised at the entrance. Half rising, [Frick] stood in an attitude of expectancy while the unheralded visitor, with a cheery, "Good morning, Mr. Frick," stepped jauntily forward and, in response to a grave bow, placed himself gingerly upon the edge of a chair obviously assigned to callers. Having simultaneously resumed his own seat, Mr. Frick, without speaking, looked . . . inquiringly into Mr. Carnegie's defiant eyes.

Frick listened quietly to Carnegie as he demanded Frick accept the terms of the new coke contract and agree to bring no lawsuits against the Carnegie Steel Company.

Frick asked, "And if I don't accept this contract and am successful in enjoining the Frick Coke Company from making any deliveries to Carnegie Steel, what then?"

Carnegie replied he intended to invoke the Iron Clad Agreement—an agreement antedating the creation of the present Carnegie Steel Company but never signed by the current partners. Under the terms of the agreement, Carnegie could force Frick to sell his holdings back to the company over a period of time at book, not market value. Assessed at book value, Frick's share would amount to only $4.9 million, instead of $15 million at market value. More than that, as Frick's biographer, George Harvey, notes, the payments to Frick would come in such small, five-year installments that company profits would more than make up the deficit, "with a net gain to Mr. Carnegie, as the holder of a majority interest, of many millions." The insult to Frick was insufferable.

The bad blood between Frick and Carnegie had become like firedamp, that highly explosive mixture of air, coal dust, and methane gas that is just as likely to sponta- neously combust as it is to explode when touched by a miner's candle. In a rare out- burst of temper, a temper so violent that people who had seen it never forgot it, Frick leaped from his chair and flared at Carnegie: "For years I have been convinced that there is not an honest bone in your body. Now I know that you are a god damned thief. We will have a judge and jury of Allegheny County decide what you are to pay me."

Andrew Carnegie ran from Frick's office, pale-faced and trembling. Philander Knox recalled the scene, saying, "the white whiskers of the Scotch iron-master sang like the needles on the barrel of a music box in the breeze made by Carnegie's energy in seeking a place where Frick was not." Frick had run after Carnegie and slammed the door behind him with such force it could be heard all over the building.

With Carnegie gone, Frick returned to his desk, and in the same cool manner he had exhibited seven years before when attacked by Alexander Berkman, went back to work. He looked at his watch and, as was his custom, cleared his desk before lunch. On the way to the Duquesne Club, he stopped by to see his friend and associate, John Walker. "John," he remarked meditatively, "I lost my temper this morning . . . for the first time in years." "Oh, well," replied a smiling Walker, "I knew you had one. . . . Washington lost his once, you know." Though Frick may well have laughed at Walker's quip, there was no going back: the explosion had contaminated his relationship with Carnegie forever.

Within two days of Frick's outburst, Carnegie, more determined than ever to seize Frick's assets, persuaded the board of the Carnegie Steel Company to invoke the Iron Clad Agreement and force Frick to sell his shares back to the company at book value. Thirty-two of the thirty-six board members voted with Carnegie. Only H. M. Curry, who was ill and refused to side with Carnegie because he wanted to die an honest man; Francis Lovejoy, who resigned as secretary and a member of the board; and

Henry Phipps, who had previously warned Carnegie of "the hastiness of one, and the touchiness of another," stood by Frick.

Frick hired John A. Johnson, Pennsylvania's best lawyer, and David T. Watson, who was a friend of Frick's, a fellow art collector, a client of Knoedler's, as well as the country's finest trial lawyer. In February, they filed an equity suit against Carnegie in the Allegheny County Court of Common Pleas charging him with fraud and malice. The news shocked the financial and industrial worlds both nationally and internationally. With the bulk of his fortune at risk, Frick quietly and carefully began preparing his case.

> [Frick] gave his undivided attention to the matter, not only gathering the data required down to the minutest detail but sifting and analyzing it with the painstaking thoroughness of a trained mind; inviting and even suggesting innumerable questions for himself to answer; proposing lines of bold attack supported by facts and arguments; and generally laying a broad foundation for comprehensive presentation of a case punctuated and enlivened by severe and caustic phrasing of his own devising.

Stating Carnegie had "conceived a personal animosity . . . without good reason, and [was] actuated by malevolent motives," Frick insisted Carnegie had taken possession of his interest in the Carnegie Company and was "carrying on said business . . . as if [Frick] had no interest therein." His brief for an equity suit against the Carnegie Steel Company charged Andrew Carnegie with trying to drive him from the firm and "appropriate my interest at less than one quarter of the value he demanded of his own and at less than one sixth of what he declares is the value of it at this time."

In an affidavit, Carnegie, complaining Frick had "filed an abusive Bill against me," charged him with an "ungovernable temper." He stated Frick was "a man of imperious temper, impatient of opposition, and disposed to make a personal matter of every difference of opinion, even on questions of mere business policy. At times moreover, he gives way to violent outbursts of passion, which he is either unwilling or unable to control. He demands absolute power and without it is not satisfied."

As was typical of the Carnegie loyalists, a Mr. Bilderback wrote Carnegie, "[we] will triumphantly defeat this ingrate Frick in his attempt to defame you and make a public exhibition of your business . . . the people of Pittsburgh are on your side."

With the lawsuit filed, however, and with Carnegie Steel Company's documents showing the real, not the published profits, Andrew Carnegie's hypocrisy was publicly exposed. Although Frick had willingly been Carnegie's hatchet man, and had carried for Carnegie the industrial evil he could not live with, he was no longer the only man held blameful. Carnegie showed himself to be as culpable and as two-faced as many often suspected.

Although Carnegie's biographer Joseph Wall maintains that Carnegie was torn between the rights of labor and his own need to be a superindustrialist, being "torn" would connote a constant and conscious pulling between two opposites, something Carnegie did not display. More likely, Carnegie compartmentalized his actions so successfully that he could be both friend and enemy of labor, just as he could both command and blame Frick. Richard T. Crane, a prominent member of the Chicago manufacturing elite, painted the best portrait. He said Carnegie was "the Dr. Jekyll of library building, and the Mr. Hyde of Homestead rioting and destruction." His two sides seemed not to communicate with each other.

Despite his prolabor stance, Carnegie had truly been the workingman's enemy. The great friend of labor had made 200 percent annual returns at a time when most businesses were making only 10 percent on invested capital. The record showed these profits were based on the sale of steel produced at $12 a ton and sold for $23.75, the excessive price demanded even though a high tariff protected the American industry and its workers from cheap foreign steel. Regardless of Carnegie's generous philanthropic program, the profits he was making were a flagrant violation of the working class whose adoration Carnegie continually sought.

Devastated by the personal ramifications of this disclosure—Carnegie's letters to Frick revealing his duplicitous behavior were ready for publication in the press, and his personal wealth of $25 million in 1900, when unskilled labor earned $0.15 an hour, was to be announced—Carnegie agreed to a final settlement March 22, 1900. With Phipps as mediator, and Andrew Carnegie's two sides perhaps communicating for the first time, the H. C. Frick Coke Company and the Carnegie Steel Company were combined into a new company, the Carnegie Company, capitalized at $320 million—$250 million for the steel company and $70 million for the coke concern. Frick's stock was hand delivered by an appointee of Carnegie's, and although Frick was barred from holding any managerial position, he received more than $15 million in securities and more than $15 million in bonds, significantly more than the $4.9 million he would have received if Carnegie had had his way. With the lawsuit dropped, on April 18, 1900, Frick severed his last, formal tie to Andrew Carnegie. In explaining the situation to Whitney, Frick said, "Settlement made. I get what is due me. All well. I, of course, have not met this man Carnegie and never expect nor want to." In June, he chartered a yacht called the *Shemara* and sailed with family and friends along the east coast.

For his part, Carnegie, in obvious response to the shattering experience of being publicly exposed and now searching for redemption, published a book containing "The Gospel of Wealth" and other essays addressing such matters as trusts, labor, and the merits of a "scientific" philanthropy, advocating the distribution of one's entire wealth during one's lifetime for the benefit and advancement of society. The book was rife with such claims as, "I would as soon leave to my son a curse as the almighty dollar," and "The man who dies thus rich, dies disgraced." All supported his conviction that he was now a "mere trustee and agent for his poorer brethren, bringing to their service his superior wisdom, experience, and ability to administer, doing for them better than they would or could do for themselves." Carnegie also wrote, however, "pity the poor millionaire, for the way of the philanthropist is hard."

Carnegie, who now seemed to remember that his own grandfather, uncle, and father had championed the rights of labor in Scotland before a labor movement existed, appeared to be reverting, as he had in 1886, to his early family value system as a way to regain his fallen crown. In presenting this new public face, he designed a mask to hide his public embarrassment, justify both his life and his behavior, and soften his crushing defeat by Frick.

Frick, though vindicated and victorious, had a hollow victory. Although now a supremely wealthy man, he was a man not only emotionally bankrupt, but bankrupt in Pittsburgh business and social circles as well. All but two partners had voted against him, reminding him that, in a sense, he had never belonged. Out of place as a child in the agrarian family to which he was born, he had been a newcomer to the steel industry, and a newcomer to Pittsburgh society on his marriage in 1881. Now, he was once again a misfit. As a result, his bitterness toward Carnegie escalated. Almost immediately, he ceased lending his art collection to the Carnegie Institute's International Exhibition, something he had done since 1895. He wrote to his artist friend John W. Beatty: "I went over the matter very fully with Mrs. Frick after you left, and I think it only proper to say to you now that you cannot count on *any* pictures from our collection for your exhibition this fall. Mrs. Frick has so much feeling about the matter that I would not want to go against her wishes, and notify you this early that you may not be put to any inconvenience."

Frick also resigned as treasurer of both the Carnegie Library and the Carnegie Institute. He was replaced by Charles Schwab, the recently elected president of Carnegie Steel, who had acted as attorney-in-fact for Carnegie when notifying Frick that his shares in the Carnegie Steel Company had been confiscated by the company. Schwab's loyalty to Carnegie was later rewarded by a rumored annual compensation of $1 million.

Nevertheless, Frick kept a sharp eye on the Carnegie Company. Soon, he became aggravated by Schwab's management style. In August 1900, he wrote Carnegie what turned out to be his last letter to his former partner: "You cannot trust many by whom you are surrounded to give you facts. . . . You are being out generalled all along the line, and your management of the company has already become the subject of jest."

And now, with increased time on his hands, the ache for Martha and memories of the past sounded louder than ever in Henry Clay Frick's Clayton art collection. In 1897

Fig. 6-5. Jean-Charles Cazin (1841-1941), *The Dipper*.
Acquired in 1898, Oil on canvas, 23⅝ x 28¾ in. (60 x 73 cm).
Frick Art and Historical Center

he had purchased, along with Dagnan-Bouveret's *Christ at Emmaus,* the first of thirteen works by Jean-François Millet he would acquire: *La Fermière,* a drawing that depicts a tiny woman, not unlike Frick's own mother, battling the harsh winter wind as she approaches an emaciated cow. In 1898 came a Dagnan-Bouveret portrait of Childs Frick, as well as Jean-Charles Cazin's mystical *The Dipper* (fig. 6-5) and John Swan's previously mentioned *Tigers Drinking* (see fig. 5-21). More poignant, Frick acquired two more Millets recalling childhood memories: *Shepherd Minding Sheep* and *The Knitting Lesson* (see fig. 1-23), evoking his mother's devoted care in the face of their harsh agrarian life. In 1899, the artist's study of Christ's head from *Christ at Emmaus* came as a gift to Adelaide. Moreover, on the approximate tenth anniversary of his farmer father's death and on his own fiftieth birthday, Frick's memories of his hometown surfaced in two works already mentioned: Millet's *The Sower* (see fig. 1-26) and Troyon's *A Pasture in Normandy* (see fig. 1-10), a work resembling the countryside of his birth and fortune.

But another note sounded as well. With his fortune enhanced, Frick began to acquire some of the more prestigious Old Masters, elegant portrait subjects dressed, sometimes, in fanciful hats, but always in fine lace and satin: George Romney's *Mary Finch-Hatton* (1898), John Hoppner's *The Honorable Lucy Byng* (1899), and Jean-Marc Nattier's *Elizabeth, Countess of Warwick* (1899). And so too Henry Clay Frick's attraction to portraits recalling close friends such as Théobald Chartran (fig. 6-6), broke through when he acquired a hallmark of sophistication, *Portrait of a Young Artist* (fig. 6-7), then attributed to Rembrandt.

In five years, Frick had formed the nucleus of a great collection. And he had set his "chronological" collection's tone. In the same amount of time, Carnegie's hope to create his own chronological collection of American art had failed, as had his dream of making Pittsburgh an art capital. Although the annual Internationals continued, they did so without the standard of excellence Carnegie had hoped to achieve. In 1896, the difficulty of mounting an exhibition of high quality was clear when Frick loaned certain paintings to "give tone to their exhibition." The poor quality was further affirmed when Frick also suggested that Knoedler come to Clayton for the weekend, rather than attend the opening. As Frick advised, the "exhibition was [not] going to be a particularly fine one, so far as the American artists are concerned." In fact, by 1897 Frick, Carnegie, and the Fine Arts Committee had been forced to secretly buy paintings as a way to convince the artists and public there was demand for the art.

So in a sense, Frick had a unilateral victory over Carnegie. Yet the break, and the animosity it aroused, left him, at age fifty-one, Pittsburgh's odd man out. And so Henry Clay Frick began laying the foundation for a permanent exodus from Pittsburgh, an exodus that would be marked by a few exquisitely well timed gestures, as

Fig. 6-6. The young Théobald Chartran.
Frick Art Reference Library

well as certain ironic coincidences. He had been considering either adding an art gallery to Clayton or building a home on nearby Gunn's Hill overlooking the steel mills to the south and Martha's grave to the north. He now advised his Chicago architect, D. H. Burnham, that he would do neither. Instead, he commissioned Burnham to make a cenotaph (a monument erected in honor of a person whose body is elsewhere) for his graveyard plot at the Homewood Cemetery. Then, a month after ordering the cenotaph, *Consolatrix* arrived at Clayton and joined the Chartran portraits of Martha and Helen, the copy of Dagnan's *Christ at Emmaus,* Emile Friant's *Chagrin d'Enfant,* as well as Frick's first lakeside Corot and the symbolic paintings by Cazin, Troyon, Thaulow, and Millet.

In 1900, he acquired only two paintings: William Henry Hunt's *Bird's Nest* and Antoine Vollon's *Still Life with Apples and Roses.* But he did begin work on perhaps his most cynical gesture, the Frick Building (fig. 6-8), a twenty-story white granite structure with stained-glass windows by John La Farge. It was to be the tallest and finest office building in Pittsburgh. More important, it was positioned to cast a shadow across the Carnegie Building. As E. R. Graham, Burnham's partner in the building's construction, said, "Frick poisoned himself with hatred for Carnegie."

Frick, however, was proud of his coup. Perhaps as a subtle reply to Carnegie's hope that the public would vote their daughters a pair, Frick announced the office building would belong to his daughter Helen, now age twelve.

In November 1900, a team of twenty-two dark brown horses pulled a massive wooden crate up Homewood Avenue, past Clayton, to the Homewood Cemetery (fig. 6-9). The crate, which sat precariously on a flat wagon, contained Frick's forty-seven-ton cenotaph. As the enormous monument, shaped like a sarcophagus and made of priceless, pale pink granite from Westerly, Rhode Island, was hauled up Homewood Avenue, the team parked on the left-hand side of the road, directly in front of Clayton. The horses lined the dirt road as if outlining Clayton's entire western boundary. A single white horse, placed in the middle of the team, was centered opposite Clayton's

Fig. 6-7. Rembrandt Harmensz. van Rijn (1606-1669), follower of, *Portrait of a Young Artist*, 164[7?].
Acquired in 1899, Oil on canvas, 39⅛ x 35 in. (99.4 x 88.9 cm).
The Frick Collection

Fig. 6-8. The Frick Building was positioned to cast a shadow on the Carnegie Building.
Carnegie Library, Pittsburgh

front door and a nurse, dressed in black clothes, and two small children stood on Clayton's lawn, looking at the procession.

Weeks later, as Frick grew impatient with the progress of his monument, he wrote Burnham, "It seems to me there is no reason why the people putting up that monument for me in Homewood Cemetery should not be at work. I believe they have the granite on the ground. Can't they be hurried up?"

But nothing seemed to go along faster. Not the placement of the cenotaph, not the slackening of Frick's bitterness toward Carnegie, and certainly not the lessening of his now active mourning. As is often the case when a person continues to resist acceptance of a loved one's death, Frick, though with his own grave monument in place, still had not provided gravestones for his two dead children. Their graves remained small, unmarked, grass-covered mounds, bearing no formal acknowledgment of the lives prematurely ended.

But with death, loss, and misfortune increasingly compounding within Frick's inner world, so too his outer world fortune continued to grow. In May 1901, despite another major financial depression, Frick's net worth doubled. J. P. Morgan had purchased the Carnegie Company (which in 1900 had made a $40 million profit) and had merged both it and Federal Steel into the U.S. Steel Corporation, a $1.402 billion trust that was larger than Rockefeller's Standard Oil and represented 60 percent of the steel industry in America.

To close the deal, however, Frick's services had been requested. Morgan needed Rockefeller's holdings in the Mesabi Range to guarantee a ready supply of iron ore for the making of steel. Morgan and Rockefeller did not get along with each other, but both men knew and respected Frick. So on Frick's advice, Rockefeller sold to Morgan at $8.5 million for his fleet of ore boats and $80 million for his Mesabi property. Subsequently, Morgan bought the Carnegie Steel Company for $303 million, and the H. C. Frick Coke Company became part of this vast trust.

Frick coke from the east now met the iron ore shipped from the west in U.S. Steel's Pittsburgh mills. U.S. Steel controlled more than half of all the known iron-ore resources in America, as well as almost the entire Connellsville coking-coal seam, thus assuring its supply of the two finest-grade natural resources necessary to making steel. Although Frick had been denied a managerial position on the Carnegie Company board, he became a director of U.S. Steel. Carnegie, on the other hand, was given no position. He had opted for bonds, not stocks, and so had neither business connections with his former partners nor a voice in U.S. Steel management. William Corey, who succeeded Schwab as president of U.S. Steel in 1903, lent further insight. He claimed that one of the many reasons U.S. Steel paid "very liberally" for the Carnegie Company was "for the elimination of Mr. Carnegie." For his part, Carnegie, now the richest man in America, remarked lightheartedly about his fortune stashed in a Hoboken vault. He said to his friend and cousin Lauder, "Pray sleep soundly—all is fixed—your Bonds and mine go as our partners' go—into vaults." But, as Joseph Wall notes, Carnegie's favorite lines from Robert Burns, "Thine own reproach alone do fear," had returned to haunt him. When he sailed for Scotland in March 1901 he wrote despairing memos to himself: "father bereft of his sons," "abandoned & alone," "no more whirl of affairs . . . occupation gone. Advise no man quit business."

Frick had clearly won. In 1901, perhaps to celebrate his defeat of Carnegie, he bought a painting entitled *The Bracelet* and gave it to his art-collector friend and attorney, David T. Watson.

Fig. 6-9. Henry Clay Frick's cenotaph was parked outside the Clayton gates prior to
the team of horses pulling it up the hill to the Homewood Cemetery.
Carnegie Library, Pittsburgh

Fig. 6-10. Théobald Chartran (1849-1907),
Signing of the Peace Protocol Between Spain and the United States, August 12, 1898, 1899.
Acquired in 1902, Oil on canvas, 62½ x 82⁄16 in. (157.8 x 208.4 cm).
The White House, gift of Henry Clay Frick, 1902

In 1902, when Carnegie returned to New York, he moved into his four-story, sixty-four room, $1.5 million new home and continued to sleep in the brass bed he had used as a child growing up in Pittsburgh.

Frick now rented an apartment in New York's Sherry Hotel. As if to herald the end of his own battle with Carnegie, he gave the newly elected president, Theodore Roosevelt, Chartran's *Signing of the Peace Protocol Between Spain and the United States, August 12, 1898* (fig. 6-10), a painting commissioned by Frick to commemorate the end of the Spanish-American War, a painting that symbolically avenged the sinking of the *Maine* (fig. 6-11). When in New York, he daily frequented the Holland House, the principal meeting place of the most powerful men in the steel industry. By 1903, with the ouster of Schwab from chairmanship of U.S. Steel for gambling and other irresponsible behavior, Henry Clay Frick began to regularly attend directors' meetings, as well as finance and long-range planning meetings.

With this peace and new fortune, however, Frick was not lulled into blind loyalty to the new company. When the price of U.S. Steel stock fell from fifty-five to nine, causing the company to withhold dividends, Frick began selling its stock and purchasing railroads. In 1904, he sold Morgan the property at Peter's Creek that had precipitated the final break with Carnegie in 1899. And as his fortune and reputation as mogul and advisor to U.S. Steel grew, Frick was also named a director of the Pennsylvania Railroad, as well as the Reading; the Chicago and Northwestern; the Union Pacific; the Atchison, Topeka and Santa Fe; the Baltimore and Ohio; and the Norfolk and

Fig. 6-11. The *Maine*. Inscribed by Henry Clay Frick: "As it is now."
West Overton Museums Archives

Fig. 6-12. Eagle Rock, the summer home of Henry Clay Frick.
Private collection

Western. By 1906, he had invested $6 million in each concern and was the largest individual private stockholder of railroads. Moreover, in 1906, Frick realized another dream. He had correctly guessed that Chicago would become the nation's steel center, and he now sold U.S. Steel another valuable piece of land—a tract west of Indiana Harbor.

Frick continued to take other new steps as well. Some of his decisions included refusing invitations to turn his prodigious energies and talents to public service, including an offer to become secretary of the U.S. Treasury (and other federal positions that continued until 1907). Similarly, he rejected an invitation from Attorney General Philander Knox, whose appointment to that position had been suggested by Frick in 1896, to become senator from Pennsylvania. Instead, Frick focused on relocating himself and his family. They had summered on Boston's North Shore for a number of years and often visited their artist friend, Joseph Woodwell, at the Magnolia artist colony. Frick played golf with the Republican stalwarts, and he and Adelaide socialized with their many friends from New York and Chicago. Frick bought property from Judge Moore in Prides Crossing, Massachusetts, overlooking the Atlantic Ocean. Construction did not begin on the house to be called Eagle Rock (fig. 6-12), named for the eagles nesting there, until 1904, and Frick would not move in until 1906;

yet the purchase of the land marked the end of a major chapter in Henry Clay Frick's business and private life.

There was little to hold him to Pittsburgh now. In 1880, his parents and all but one sibling had left West Overton (fig. 6-13). Tired of riots and the smoke-filled coking environment, they had joined Frick's sister Maria, her husband, and John Frick's uncle in Wooster, Ohio. Frick managed their finances from his Pittsburgh office, and after his father's death in 1888, he stayed in close touch with his mother and oldest sister (whose son eventually ran Frick's private office), as well as with his siblings and Overholt and Frick cousins. Together the family cared for Aaron, Frick's mentally challenged brother, who by 1900 was committed to the Massillon State Mental Hospital.

His mother, who had been failing for a number of years, died in October 1905. Frick was called to her bedside, but arrived too late to say his final good-byes. Although Adelaide still had family in Pittsburgh, Frick had neither family nor other significant ties to the area, no real work to do, no frontier (other than art) to conquer,

Fig. 6-13. *Center:* Elizabeth Overholt Frick and John Frick. *From top left running clockwise by birth order:* Maria Frick Overholt, Anna Frick Braddock, Aaron Frick, Jay Edgar Frick, Sallie Frick Lott.
West Overton Museums Archives

Fig. 6-14. John White Alexander (1856-1915),
Detail, *The Crowning of Labor,* 1905-08.
Oil on canvas, 48 panels, approximately 3,900 square feet total.
Carnegie Museum of Art, Pittsburgh

and nothing but bitter reminders of Andrew Carnegie on which to feed. When his former partner's art gallery opened to the public as a greatly expanded complex encom-
passing a library, a music hall, and a natural science museum, Frick, with neither coke
nor steel company to manage, left the Pittsburgh manufacturing center, his home of
fifty-one years, for New York, headquarters for U.S. Steel, and the art and financial capital of the nation. In the new Carnegie Institute, John Alexander White's murals, entitled *The Crowning of Labor* (fig. 6-14), romanticize the harsh life of the working class
and show an armor-suited Carnegie being crowned by an angel as the "Knight of
Labor." Frick, in New York, rented William H. Vanderbilt's famous mansion at 640 Fifth
Avenue. This was the house he had coveted since 1880 when, as a new millionaire, it

had inspired him to comment, "It is all I shall ever want." This house once held the original paintings whose reproductions Frick had long owned, the house with a picture gallery and gold-gilt front doors copied after Lorenzo Ghiberti's *Gates of Paradise*, a house indeed as described in the lease: "fully fitted and furnished."

Leaving Carnegie's propaganda art behind, Frick packed up his family and some fifty of Clayton's approximately one hundred paintings, including Breton's *The Last Gleanings* (see fig. 1-21), Dagnan-Bouveret's *Consolatrix* (which he placed at the foot of the grand staircase), and Friant's *Chagrin d'Enfant*. To those who asked why he was leaving Pittsburgh, Henry Clay Frick, using his paintings as metaphor for himself, simply replied in his dark-humored, Carnegie-obsessed way, that Pittsburgh's bad air was damaging his art collection. Most of his paintings were, in fact, protected by glass.

As Frick entered the New York art, social, and financial milieu, both he and Knoedler could take satisfaction that his collection was as important an entrée into New York as it had been a playing card in his final years in Pittsburgh. The majority of his paintings could be attributed to Knoedler, and with this move to New York and the augmentation of Frick's personal wealth, the art dealer could expect to further influence his friend. Catering to Frick, Roland Knoedler booked Frick's passages to Europe, lent the family his Paris apartment, sent them flowers, secured tickets to the opera and ballet, and continued to introduce them to important artists. In fact, Frick so trusted Knoedler's taste, he loaned him money to acquire paintings to sell in his gallery. For his part, Knoedler knew his client friend well. He repaid the debt on time and would eventually be responsible for having sold Frick the majority of the paintings in his collection. The intimate nature of this friendship was revealed on June 29, 1905, just a few days prior to Frick's departure for Europe. Frick celebrated his move east by writing a teasing, but complimentary letter to Knoedler: "I am practicing golf daily. Expect to be in shape to give you a stroke a hole, and beat you about five up and two to play. Everything going well. Your monument in New York looks fine. It will be the best advertisements [*sic*] you ever had."

If 640 Fifth Avenue (fig. 6-15) was to become a monument to Knoedler, the house also seemed tailor-made for Frick. As early as the mid-1880s, Frick had developed a business relationship with William H. Vanderbilt by personally subscribing $250,000 to the building of the privately funded Vanderbilt railroad through Connellsville. By June 1883, the burgeoning business relationship had become a thriving social one as well. Frick and Adelaide stayed with Vanderbilt and his wife, Maria Kissam, in Saratoga, a time when Adelaide became so homesick for her three-month-old baby, Childs, she refused to come down for dinner.

Now, in 1905, Frick had become a Vanderbilt look-alike. Vanderbilt, in the eight years of collecting from his father's to his own death, spent $1.5 million on two hundred paintings. Frick owned about $1.3 million worth of art. His H. C. Frick Coke Company, which had become a division of U.S. Steel in 1901 and was merged into the company in 1903 had taken on Vanderbilt proportions. In 1871, the coke company had owned only 600 acres in a remote area called Broad Ford. It now boasted over 53,837 acres of coal properties on the valuable Connellsville coke seam. Frick's coke company, which started with 50 "Novelty" ovens and a few mules, now owned 10,148 beehive ovens, 700 mules and horses, 21 locomotives, 1,600 railroad cars, and 43 mines which honeycombed the hills with 41 miles of railroad track above ground and 225 miles of subterranean mine track. By 1906, Frick's once pick-and-shovel mining operation yielded a record 19,170,740 tons of coal. His small railroad system of 1880, then confined primarily to the narrow little valley north and east of Broad Ford, now had both the B&O Railroad and the Southwestern Pennsylvania running through it, their lines so close to each other they could almost touch. In addition, Frick's network of mine and yard tracks connected into the major trunk lines of the Coke Region, all of which flowed smoothly into his Union Railroad and his network of railroad spurs. When Henry Clay Frick reinvested in railroads and became the largest private stockholder of railroads in the country, the 640 Fifth Avenue residence, built by William H. Vanderbilt, "Railroad King" of 1880, became, therefore, the perfect home for the burgeoning art collector and "Railroad King" of 1905.

While Frick remained a legal resident of Pennsylvania, he also maintained a Pittsburgh office in his Frick Building and returned often to Clayton. From 1900 to 1905, his days were filled with activity and planning, and we can glean from his acquisition pattern that during these five years Frick continued weaving his tapestry. Wouwerman's *Cavalry Camp* (see fig. 4-20), discussed previously, is a painting that may well have rekindled his memory of the military encampment at Homestead overlooking the mill, now a division of U.S. Steel, on the hill where Martha Street was located. He also bought Johannes Vermeer's *Girl Interrupted at Her Music* (see fig. 10-39), as well as Turner's stormy seascape, *Antwerp* (see fig. 2-25), a painting he may have associated with the raging wave of the Johnstown Flood of 1889, and Jacob van Ruisdael's *A Waterfall with Rocky Hills and Trees* (see fig. 2-27), a painting that evokes the rock-walled spillway at South Fork. This same year, he acquired Monet's *Bords de la Seine à Lavacourt,* depicting a scene familiar to him.

In 1902, when Frick rented the apartment in New York's Sherry Hotel, he collected more telling art, art that reflected the high society into which he was moving, the man he was becoming, and the wife he wanted to present to New York. Two works by Sir Joshua Reynolds were acquired from a distinguished British family: portraits of Sir George Howland Beaumont, the acclaimed "leader of taste in the fashionable world," and his wife, Lady Margaret Beaumont. A member of Parliament, who also painted

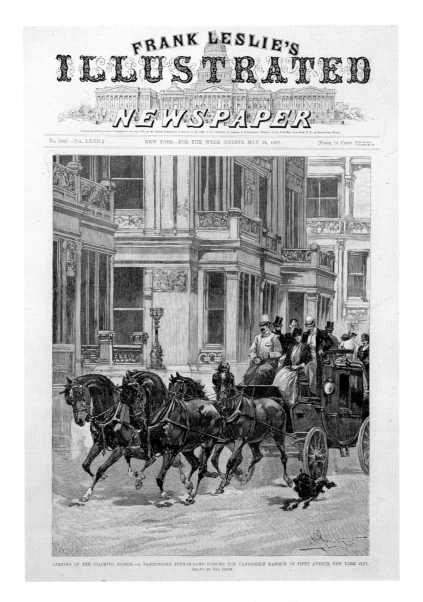

Fig. 6-15. William Henry Vanderbilt's 640 Fifth Avenue.
Frank Leslie's Illustrated Weekly, May 30, 1891.
New York Society Library

landscapes, Beaumont was a friend and patron of such artists as Constable and Gainsborough. As a connoisseur and collector, he made a lasting impression with his bequest to England of sixteen paintings—the nucleus of London's National Gallery. Lady Beaumont was described by a contemporary as an art connoisseur and devoted wife whose "greatest object seems to be the preservation of her husband's affections."

Another painting acquired in 1902 showed, more than any other purchase at that time, how Henry Clay Frick's youthful love of trimmings and lace still flourished. Certainly his appreciation of beautiful material manifested itself in the 1892 interior

Fig. 6-16. Sir Joshua Reynolds (1723–1792), *Selina, Lady Skipwith*, 1787.
Acquired in 1906, Oil on canvas, 50½ x 40¼ in. (128.3 x 102.2 cm).
The Frick Collection

Fig. 6-17. Sir Joshua Reynolds (1723-1792), *Elizabeth, Lady Taylor,* 1780.
Acquired in 1910, Oil on canvas, 50⅛ x 40¼ in. (127.3 x 102.2 cm).
The Frick Collection

Fig. 6-18. Sir Thomas Lawrence (1769–1830), attributed to, *Marquise de Blaizel*.
Acquired in 1902, Oil on canvas, 29¼ x 24¼ in. (74.3 x 61.6 cm).
Frick Art and Historical Center

decoration of Clayton and in the French gowns he bought for Adelaide. But the purchase of Sir Joshua Reynolds's *Selina, Lady Skipwith* (fig. 6-16), *Elizabeth, Lady Taylor* (fig. 6-17), and what was then considered Sir Thomas Lawrence's *Marquise de Blaizel* (fig. 6-18) bespoke another passion: hats. Frick was said by his daughter Helen to be "very particular about hats and always expressed himself frankly," often exclaiming to her, "That's quite a hat you have on—or where's that hat going?" and then adding "You come with me and I will select a hat for you."

But more significant than the paintings seeming to give voice to Frick's passion were the paintings appearing to express where Frick had been. As previously mentioned, Rousseau's *Village of Becquigny* (see fig. 1-35) bears similarity to an 1864 view of West Overton, as seen from the springhouse where Frick was born (see fig. 1-36). As Frick further wove this theme of childhood and birthplace of his fortune through his tapestry, he acquired Cuyp's *Cows and Herdsman by a River* (see fig. 1-11)—the painting suggesting the Youghiogheny River as it meanders past the Overholt Distillery in Broad Ford. He also acquired Hobbema's *Village Among Trees* (see fig. 1-37). It recalls the Mennonite community near Jacob's Creek through which Frick walked nearly every Sunday of his millionaire-making decade.

In 1903, perhaps in further recognition of the high society he and Adelaide were now entering, Frick acquired more beautiful ladies by Gainsborough and Romney, *Mrs. Charles Hatchett* and *Miss Frances Mary Harford*. But a darker note is again heard in the previously mentioned Corot painting of *The Boatman of Mortefontaine* (see fig. 2-29), a scene very like the view of Lake Conemaugh from the South Fork clubhouse. In 1904 came Charles-François Daubigny's *Dieppe*, a harbor Frick knew well, and one other painting alluding to the power of raging water—Turner's giant wave in the storm-tossed painting *Fishing Boats Entering Calais Harbor* (see fig. 2-26). Three Millets arrived—*End of Day* (see fig. 1-27), *Resting in the Shade*, and *The Gleaners*—joining Anton Mauve's *Shepherd* in rekindling hometown memories.

But far more important were the two paintings reminding Frick of his daughters, the one who lived and the one who had died: George Romney's *Lady Hamilton* (see fig. 3-18), a Martha look-alike (had she lived), and Sir Thomas Lawrence's *Julia, Lady Peel* (fig. 6-19), a Helen look-alike, or so said Frick. Obviously struck by the similarity between Lawrence's portrait subject and a behatted Helen (fig. 6-20), he teased her, claiming that in a hundred years, people would point to Julia, Lady Peel, and say, "There's Miss Frick." A year later Helen retaliated by pointing to her father's newly acquired El Greco, *St. Jerome* (fig. 6-21), and saying, "And they will say that you look like Greco's saint!" (fig. 6-22).

During 1905, however, and in this first year living in the Vanderbilt house, Frick gave $100,000 for the creation of the American Academy of Rome and acquired the

Fig. 6-19. Sir Thomas Lawrence (1769-1830), *Julia, Lady Peel*, 1827.
Acquired in 1904, Oil on canvas, 35¾ x 27⅞ in. (90.8 x 70.8 cm).
The Frick Collection

Fig. 6-20. Helen Clay Frick in a feathered hat, c. 1900.
Private collection

prestigious Titian portrait of Pietro Aretino, the satirist whom people paid to insure he not write about them. The painting, of course, expressed Frick's penchant for privacy and his aversion to newspaper interviews. Additionally, he acquired Van Dyck's portrait of Senator Ottaviano Canevari, perhaps a reference to Philander Knox, who had just been elected senator from Pennsylvania, as well as Sir Henry Raeburn's *Mrs. James Cruikshank* and Gabriel Metsu's *Lady at Her Toilet*. More important, he bought two paintings evoking the confluence of the Allegheny, Monongahela, and Ohio rivers at the Point in Pittsburgh: Salomon van Ruysdael's *River Scene: Men Dragging a Net* (fig. 6-23) and Cuyp's *Dordrecht: Sunrise*. Both paintings were, like all the others, fashionable to collect, but they are also reminiscent of scenes from Frick's early life.

Fig. 6-21. El Greco (1541–1614),
Detail, *St. Jerome*, 1590–1600.
Acquired in 1905, Oil on canvas,
43½ x 37½ in. (110.5 x 95.3 cm).
The Frick Collection

Fig. 6-22. Henry Clay Frick, c. 1917.
Frick Archives

His later acquisitions of Cuyp's *River Scene* (1909), as well as what was then considered Jan van de Cappelle's *A View of the River Maas Before Rotterdam* (fig. 6-24), repeat these themes. Together, these Dutch river scenes, as can be seen in their juxtaposition with pictures of Pittsburgh's Point in Frick's day (fig. 6-25), recall the contour of the Ohio riverbank as well as Pittsburgh's unmistakable landmark across the water, the high steeple in the background. Of this, the seventeenth-century Dutch van Ruysdael is particularly evocative. Although it describes a scene like the nineteenth-century Point (known as the Golden Triangle because Pittsburgh had one half the nation's wealth and banks full of gold) as seen from the Ohio River, it was painted in Flanders two hundred years before Frick first worked in Pittsburgh as a teenage boy.

In 1906, Frick expanded his collection of elegantly dressed ladies with Reynolds's *Selina, Lady Skipwith.* He acquired Hals's *Portrait of a Painter,* and as we saw previously, Rembrandt's *Self-Portrait* (see fig. 1-28), a painting evoking the facial characteristics of his Mennonite grandfather, Abraham Overholt. Millet's *Woman Sewing by Lamplight* was also added, a very clear statement of the ongoing dynamic shaping Frick's collecting pattern. His ninety-six-year-old mother, who suffered from dropsy, had died, one week before he moved into the Vanderbilt house. Here, as elsewhere, Frick's mourning seems to express itself in images relating to childhood and primary caretakers.

In 1907, Henry Clay Frick acquired another gracious lady, Van Dyck's beautifully gold-costumed *Marchesa Giovanna Cattaneo*. But, in this second year of his mother's death—an anniversary year considered by most authorities on mourning to be more painful than the first anniversary of a loved one's passing—he also bought a small, very stark, fifteenth-century *Pietà* (fig. 6-26) depicting the Virgin supporting the lacerated body of a grim-faced Christ. This image—of the Madonna cradling her dead son, much as in other paintings she cradles her newborn Christ Child—seems again an expression of Frick's mourning, of his longing to recapture a lost embrace. Other than his two lugubrious Dagnan-Bouverets, this *Pietà* was the only religious work of art he had then acquired.

If Henry Clay Frick's contemporaries missed the deeper significance of his collection of riverscapes, landscapes, lake scenes, or even Lady Hamilton holding the dog resembling Martha's Brownie, one person may have guessed the force fueling his passion. A check dated November 23, 1900, paying for Frick's granite memorial, though signed by Frick in his usual firm hand and engraved with Martha's likeness, is slightly different from others. As if recognizing Martha's death had been the cost of Frick's fortune, some unidentified person defiled the canceled check (fig. 6-27) by drawing extra strands of hair on Martha's balding head and scribbling a dark, sinister beard, the size and shape of Frick's, across her innocent, child's face.

And so the loss of Martha seemed to underlie all Frick's longing. As he searched for harmony in art, new losses simply rekindled the ever resounding heartache of her death, while the paintings, with their symbolic appeal, kept the intensity of his torment alive. Neither new art acquisitions, change of residence, nor the Vanderbilt picture gallery mitigated this sorrow. Superficially Henry Clay Frick's art collection caused public excitement. Privately, however, it heightened a mourning that remained concealed and unchanged.

While art consumed Frick's pain and passion, Andrew Carnegie continued to be the target of Frick's rage. Although each man lived for another nineteen years, the wound between them never healed. In his autobiography, Andrew Carnegie mentioned Henry Clay Frick only once, in a passing reference. And in April 1919, in what would turn out to be the last year of life for both Frick and Carnegie, Frick would make clear what he thought of his old adversary. He had written Judge Elbert H. Gary, the head of U.S. Steel, about the state of Carnegie's 2,811 libraries, libraries on which Carnegie had spent $350 million. Given as new buildings, but without books or endowment, some

Fig. 6-23. Salomon van Ruysdael (1600?-1670), *River Scene: Men Dragging a Net*, 1667.
Acquired in 1905, Oil on canvas, 26¼ x 35⅛ in. (66.7 x 89.2 cm).
The Frick Collection

Fig. 6-24. Jan van de Cappelle (c. 1624-1679), follower of, *A View of the River Maas Before Rotterdam*.
Acquired in 1906, Oil on oak panel, 36½ x 61 in. (92.7 x 154.9 cm).
The Frick Collection

Fig. 6-25. *The Point—Pittsburgh*, 1890.
From a sketch by Mrs. Wilim King.
Historical Society of Western Pennsylvania

Fig. 6-26. *Pietà*. French, probably south of France, fifteenth century.
Acquired in 1907, Tempera or mixed technique on panel, 15⅝ x 22 in. (39.7 x 55.8 cm).
The Frick Collection

of them were in financial trouble. Frick said it was up to the Carnegie Corporation of New York, not U.S. Steel, to "make good [Carnegie's] promises . . . in regard to the libraries." He said Carnegie's record in other matters was "beyond repair" and that should the corporation "fail . . .[in] their apparent duty" and U.S. Steel have to assist, "it should only be with the understanding that the communities . . . should also assist, and that the title of the library should be changed."

Henry Clay Frick had stated his position in 1912—he would never reembrace Andrew Carnegie. Their mutual friend, James Howard Bridge, came to Frick coaxing, "Mr. Carnegie told me to tell you that he is getting along in years, and that he would like to shake hands with you before he dies and let bygones be bygones." But Henry Clay Frick, as the Frick family story goes, refused, angrily declaring that he would "see Carnegie in Hell which is where we both are going."

At the time, however, to the outside world, Frick did not seem to be living anywhere near Hell. He and his family continued to travel abroad and seemed to derive great pleasure from their wealth and art collection. But the combined effect of Frick's money, masterpieces, and mourning severely eroded the emotional, psychological, and spiritual well-being of himself and his family, particularly seventeen-year-old Helen.

Fig. 6-27. The defiled canceled check for the cenotaph.
Frick Archives

CHAPTER VII

Bridging the Hereafter

Henry Clay Frick: *"How interesting it would be if all these
people could come to life and tell us what they know. . . .
If only they could talk."*

James Howard Bridge: *"But they can and do."*

Henry Clay Frick: *"And tell me, what do they say?"*

—James Howard Bridge, *Portraits and Personalities
in the Frick Galleries,* 1930

*That his firstborn girl baby held to the end first place
in the shrine of his heart there can be no question.*

—George Harvey, *Henry Clay Frick: The Man,* 1930

In 1906, the year Henry Clay Frick moved into his summer home at Eagle Rock, and one year after establishing his residency at 640 Fifth Avenue, he took the final meaningful steps sealing his decision to renounce Pittsburgh. He bought a glamorous piece of property on the corner of Fifth Avenue and Seventieth Street, now the site of the Frick Collection. This $2.25 million lot was one of the last remaining prestigious locations along Fifth Avenue, and the only property on a knoll except for Andrew Carnegie's new home on Ninety-first Street and Fifth Avenue. Indeed, people said Frick now intended to make Carnegie's house "look like a miner's shack."

At the time of purchase, the site housed the Lenox Library, an architectural treasure designed by the Vanderbilts' favorite architect, Richard Morris Hunt. The library's book collection was scheduled to be removed to the New York Public Library, then under construction at Forty-second Street, but progress on the new facility was slow. Although Frick contemplated building a permanent New York home on the Lenox Library site, he was forced to wait until 1912, when the New York Public Library was complete and he could take title to his new property.

In those years from 1906 to 1912, Frick patiently bided his time with philanthropic pursuits. When his friend John A. Brashear, a former millwright who made astronomical lenses for use in observatories around the world, expressed his desire to provide better education for the children of foreign-born parents in the Pittsburgh public

Fig. 7-1. Henry Clay Frick with members of the U.S. Steel finance committee.
From left to right: George Baker, Henry Clay Frick, George W. Perkins, Percival Roberts, Jr., Elbert H. Gary.
Carnegie Library, Pittsburgh

school system, Frick gave him an anonymous gift of $250,000. Later to be known as the Henry Clay Frick Educational Commission, it provided the school system with much needed equipment and granted scholarships for teachers so that their teaching skills might be enhanced.

Frick also remained an active director of U.S. Steel (fig. 7-1), the railroads, many banks, and civic organizations, while managing his fortune from a Wall Street office. He continued to travel abroad and, when home, played golf, bridge, and poker either at the Links Club on Long Island or the Myopia Hunt Club in Hamilton, Massachusetts. On the eve of the devastating 1907 stock market crash, he, together with Judge Gary of U.S. Steel, took a midnight train with a special locomotive and Pullman car to Washington, D.C., to seek permission from President Theodore Roosevelt to take over the Tennessee Coal and Iron Company, a move designed to protect the banking house of J. P. Morgan (then akin to the present-day Federal Reserve); they required Roosevelt's promise not to invoke the Sherman Antitrust Act against them. Frick remained a force in the Republican party through his personal friendship with President William Howard Taft and Senator Philander Knox. And, as he continued to collect art, Frick annually transferred his paintings from the rented Vanderbilt house to Eagle Rock so he could enjoy his masterpieces during the summer months. Indeed, Frick's paintings were always around, embracing him. When in Pittsburgh, conducting family business from the Frick Building, he stayed at Clayton, enveloped by the art at once poignantly reminding him of Martha and linking him to her.

When the contents of the Lenox Library were finally moved to the New York Public Library in 1911, Frick began finalizing his plans for his permanent New York residence. Appreciating the architectural beauty of the Lenox Library building, he offered to have it re-erected, at his expense, in Central Park. But his offer caused controversy among various state officials, who opposed increasing the number of buildings in the park, so Frick withdrew his offer and had the building demolished.

By 1912, Frick was still deciding whether or not to house his art collection in his permanent New York home or in an art gallery wing he was considering adding to Eagle Rock. Undoubtedly, Frick remembered seeing the Wallace Collection—the three-generation family collection given to the city of London after Lady Wallace's death in 1897. When he made his first trip abroad in 1880 with Andrew Mellon, he saw this museum, filled with the most important collection of French eighteenth-century paintings outside France; the finest collection of Sèvres porcelain in the world; European armor; and paintings of the English, Dutch, and Spanish schools from the seventeenth, eighteenth, and nineteenth centuries, all of which had inspired his wish to eventually give an art collection to his countrymen. Now the Wallace seemed to have shaped his own collection for, with the exception of European armor, it included, among others, such fashionable works as John Constable's *Salisbury Cathedral* (see fig. 10-4) and Turner's *Mortlake Terrace: Early Summer Morning* (see fig. 10-5), a painting offered to Frick in 1908, but bought by Andrew Mellon, who then sold it to Frick for twice what he had paid. In 1909, Cuyp's *River Scene* entered the collection, along with two long-separated portraits by Sir Anthony Van Dyke: *Frans Snyders* and *Margareta Snyders.* In 1910, apart from two portraits by Frans Hals and one by Reynolds, of *Elizabeth, Lady Taylor,* came Rembrandt's *The Polish Rider* (see fig. 1-38) and *Quay at Amsterdam* by the Mennonite Jacob van Ruisdael. Then, in 1911, he greatly expanded his collection with the addition of Romney's *Charlotte, Lady Milnes,* a painting joining that artist's *Henrietta, Countess of Warwick, and Her Children*; Hobbema's *Village with Water Mill Among Trees* (see fig. 1-37); and Gainsborough's *Frances Duncombe.* Two of Frick's favorites, Vermeer's *Officer and Laughing Girl* (see fig. i-1)—the first Vermeer painted with a vanishing point—and Diego Velázquez's portrait of the great collector and victorious general, *King Philip IV of Spain* (fig. 7-2), arrived this year as well.

One wonders, however, whether these paintings held deeper clues to Frick's collecting pattern than mere appreciation of the artists and the quality of the Wallace Collection. Frick's choices seemed still to be motivated by loss. In expanding his collection of elegantly dressed ladies by Reynolds and Romney, he further allowed himself to give expression to his love of hats, lace, and trimmings. By extension, the Velázquez portrait of Philip IV bears such resemblance to Chartran's 1896 portrait of Henry Clay Frick, one wonders if Frick, with his fondness for finery, had seen himself in the royal portrait. Gabriel Weisberg comments in *Collecting in the Gilded Age:* "Chartran maintained an accurate likeness and often conveyed a sense of fashion with even rather 'reserved' and 'unemotional sitters.'" And, as mentioned before, William Larimer Mellon recalls in *Judge Mellon's Sons,* the young Frick was "a model in manners . . . [and] masculine dress as well. . . . dressed as if the minute in which you saw him was the most important occasion of his life."

Beyond lace, trimmings, shimmering satin, and rich brocade, however, lay another poignant note. Frick also seemed to be trying to fuse the present with the past by reuniting portraits of specific families, perhaps as a statement of his own and his family's emotional distress. Frick had acquired Jean-Marc Nattier's *Elizabeth, Countess of Warwick* in 1899 and enhanced the acquisition in 1904 with the purchase of Romney's portrait of Lady Hamilton, who was both Elizabeth's sister-in-law and mistress to Elizabeth's son Charles Greville prior to her marriage to Sir William Hamilton.

In 1908, he bought yet another Romney, this one a portrait of Elizabeth's grandchildren and daughter-in-law, Henrietta, Countess of Warwick. Apart from the fact that the subjects of these portraits were all related, and Lady Hamilton reminiscent of Martha, the young boy and girl in Romney's *Henrietta, Countess of Warwick, and Her Children* (fig. 7-3) evoke images of what Henry Clay Frick, Jr., and Martha would have looked like had they lived. It is intriguing to note that in this painting the boy is clutching his distended right side, a gesture that could have stimulated Frick's memory of the pain in Martha's right side, or even of his infant namesake, who died of internal bleeding.

Frick also reunited the portraits of married couples long separated. He rejoined Sir Henry Raeburn's portrait of Mrs. James Cruikshank (1905) with his portrait of her husband, the British West Indies sugar magnate James Cruikshank (1911). In his wife's fiftieth birthday year, and his own sixtieth, obviously relishing the idea of reuniting couples through his art collection, he rejoined Van Dyck's portraits of Frans and Margareta Snyders (1909). Apart from alluding to the Fricks, the paintings echo Frick's friendship with Joseph R. Woodwell, his joyful artist friend and Clayton neighbor whom he had visited every Sunday since the early 1880s. The acquisition must have certainly prompted memories of happy times together at Clayton and in Woodwell's

Fig. 7-2. Diego Rodríguez de Silva y Velázquez (1599-1660), *King Philip IV of Spain*, 1644.
Acquired in 1911, Oil on canvas, 51⅛ x 39⅝ in. (129.8 x 99.4 cm).
The Frick Collection

Fig. 7-3. George Romney (1734-1820), *Henrietta, Countess of Warwick, and Her Children*, 1787-89.
Acquired in 1908, Oil on canvas, 79¾ x 61½ in. (202.6 x 156.2 cm).
The Frick Collection

Left: Fig. 7-4. Sir Anthony Van Dyck (1599–1641), *Frans Snyders*, c. 1620. Acquired in 1909, Oil on canvas, 56⅛ x 41½ in. (142.5 x 105.4 cm). The Frick Collection

Above: Fig. 7-5. Théobald Chartran (1849–1907), *Portrait of Joseph R. Woodwell*, 1896. Carnegie Library, Pittsburgh

studio. Frans Snyders (fig. 7-4) bears a similarity to a portrait Chartran did of Joseph Woodwell (fig. 7-5), who often lent Chartran his studio. Just as Snyders often collaborated with Van Dyck in his paintings, Chartran and Woodwell had a close relationship. In fact, a family friend wrote of the Snyders that when Helen's father was in a "holiday mood" he would often comment on the fun they must be having in their reunion.

Frick also continued to collect river and village scenes recalling the West Overton area and to remember deceased friends and events from the past. In 1909, as we know, he purchased the Homestead-related *Purification of the Temple* (see fig. 4-21), a painting he exhibited just inside the *Gates of Paradise,* the gold-gilt bronze doors opening into the Vanderbilt mansion. And in 1910, he acquired a superb character study by Frans Hals entitled *Portrait of an Elderly Man* (fig. 7-6). The subject bears a resemblance to Frick's friend and New York neighbor Henry Osborne Havemeyer (fig. 7-7)—the unsociable, violin-playing art collector who realized a $55 million-a-year profit from his sugar trust, a company that dominated 50 percent of the American market. Havemeyer, a man who had a then famous collection of Rembrandts greatly admired by Frick, died in 1907 at age sixty, during a federal suit against his sugar trust.

Left: Fig. 7-6. Frans Hals (1581/85-1666), *Portrait of an Elderly Man,* c. 1627-30. Acquired in 1910, Oil on canvas, 45½ x 36 in. (115.6 x 91.4 cm). The Frick Collection

Above: Fig. 7-7. Henry O. Havemeyer. Private collection

Though Henry Clay Frick was acquiring the finest examples of European art with Wallace-like perfection, he was also doing so out of deep emotional and psychological needs. In 1912, he decided to house his art collection in New York, not in an art gallery at Eagle Rock. After dismissing the architect D. H. Burnham, whom he had once commissioned for a new Pittsburgh home on Gunn's Hill, as well as for his New York home and the Eagle Rock wing—Frick hired the prestigious firm of Carrère and Hastings (architects for the New York Public Library) to design the house for 1 East Seventieth Street. Although upon his death Frick intended to make the house and art collection a gift to the public, he did not immediately advise his architects of this plan, perhaps to insure the house feel like a home, not a public building. Frick merely said to Thomas Hastings, he wanted "a small house with plenty of light and air."

In April 1912, Charles Carstairs, the Philadelphia art dealer, wrote his brother Roland that Frick was "deeply interested in his new house and loves the plan." By June, however, Hastings was frustrated and exhausted. He complained to James Howard Bridge, who was now Frick's secretary: "I go to see him and talk until I am nervous. When I stop talking he gazes at me in silence in the most disconcerting way. Then I make a few more remarks, which are always received in silence; and when I come away I am exhausted of all nervous energy."

Actually, there was a reason for Frick's silence. That winter, he and his family had traveled to Egypt and visited the great pyramids, the Valley of Kings, and the Temple of Karnak (fig. 7-8). The pharaonic temples, tombs, and mortuaries would have been particularly meaningful to a man who had experienced an apparition, a man preoccupied by death, the afterlife, and the possibility of the immortality of the soul. Lacking a prescribed religious creed, Frick endorsed the concept of a universal religion with its origins in the ancient mystery and initiation religions of Egypt, using myth, allegory, and symbolism as the language to reveal the secrets so occupying Frick's mind—life and death. Architecture and geometry are cornerstones of Masonic philosophy because God is perceived as the grand architect of the universe. Their symbols serve as allegories for man's stages of enlightenment and the development of the self as the world-temple.

The Egyptian mortuaries, while heightening Frick's desire to build a house-museum, could only have furthered his preoccupation with the afterlife and reincarnation, his attempt to remain connected to Martha, and his attraction to paintings recalling his past. Most certainly the Egyptian monuments influenced his vision of his house as

Fig. 7-8. Henry Bacon (1839–1912), *On the Way to Karnak*, watercolor, commissioned in 1912.
Helen Clay Frick and her future sister-in-law, Frances Shoemaker Dixon of Baltimore,
ride donkeys down the Avenue of Sphinxes during the Frick family's 1912 trip to Egypt.
Author's collection

a pyramid or type of grave beyond death, filled with Masonic references and symbolic images of Martha and others now dead, as well as religious iconography of purification and redemption. As a living grave, his new home could provide a meeting place between the living and the dead, between two worlds. It would provide a pathway linking him to the departed, a dwelling place in the hereafter while yet alive, and a place to store his riches and heal his sorrows while paying full honor to Martha.

Frick had continued to seek the opinions of others about the hereafter, and in 1912, about the time he visited Egypt and started construction of his New York mansion, he broke his silence about his 1892 postdeath contact with Martha. Someone had asked Frick if it were true that during Alexander Berkman's assault, Martha's "apparently living image" had "dazzled" him. In the first public acknowledgment of this vision, as George Harvey explained, Frick "bowed his head and nodded in quiet assent." Indeed, Henry Clay Frick's museum-temple-tomb was well on its way to becoming a full expression of this "quiet assent." As Harvey put it, "that [Frick's] firstborn girl baby held to the end first place in the *shrine* of his heart there can be no question."

❖

James Howard Bridge, who was certainly unaware of the Masonic dynamic at work in Frick's mind during this period, *was* aware of his employer's secret desire that the house should become a museum. Bridge wrote Frick, who was then at Eagle Rock, to describe the progress of the house and the guarding of the museum secret:

> As you had chosen to limit his [Hastings's] understanding of what was required, I did not feel at liberty to do more than "suppose" the building were subsequently to be used as a museum; and I found with a few alterations it could be easily adapted to this end. . . .
>
> At the same time, the museum idea does not seem to be of very great importance just now. The thing is to have a worthy & homey residence for yourself. During the next twenty years, you will have lots of time to develop ideas for public work. The home as planned promises to be just that—a home, inside. Exteriorly it will be impressive & beautiful because of its simplicity which by a hairs breath [*sic*] escapes severity.

Frick, however, was quite open about one thing. Although accustomed to living in grand style, within that context he insisted Sir Charles Allom, the decorator of Buckingham Palace, and Hastings use economy and restraint. In June 1913 he instructed

Fig. 7-9. One East Seventieth Street under construction, c. 1913.
UPI/Corbis-Bettmann

Allom, who with Hastings would provide designs for the entire house from organ console to library table desk: "Please see the ceilings are almost plain. From what I see Mr. Hastings is favoring too much carving. Please impress upon him my earnest desire to avoid anything elaborate and show him this." A man of exacting detail, Frick spent hours going over everything from decorative ornamentation to the basement plan (fig. 7-9), again reminding Allom in December: "We desire a comfortable well arranged home, simple, in good taste, and not ostentatious." The following March, he further cautioned Allom, "I do hope we will not make any mistake in having a livable, homelike house and in the best of taste; we depend on you largely that such shall be the result." And, as if confirming this "homelike" desire, in 1913 he acquired another painting perhaps recalling his own family, Van Dyck's *James, Seventh Earl of Derby, His Lady and Child* (fig. 7-10). As the art critic John Russell observes, this was a family that stood "fair and square to the outside world," even though the earl was beheaded for maintaining his loyalty to King Charles I of England. Frick, in standing by his principles at Homestead and suffering the black eyes he knew would come, may well have made a visceral connection between the fate of this family and his own.

As 1914 progressed, however, tension mounted while Frick settled fights between Allom and Elsie de Wolfe, a former actress noted for her fresh, innovative, and pioneering approach to interior decorating whom Frick hired for the second-floor apartments. As the two decorators claimed rooms on each other's floors, Frick advised Miss de Wolfe, "I should think, however, that you might secure better prices. Take your

Fig. 7-10. Sir Anthony Van Dyck (1599-1641), *James, Seventh Earl of Derby, His Lady and Child*, 1632-41.
Acquired in 1913, Oil on canvas, 97 x 84⅛ in. (246.4 x 213.7 cm).
The Frick Collection

time—you know time is money!" He warned her "the shrewd art dealer is always around to take advantage . . . to my mind, the most of them are robbers." He also advised her, "We will go slow in securing furniture for the first floor. I hope to consult you, in whose taste I have the greatest confidence"; then, after she concluded a few more deals on his behalf, he wished her a "happy summer" and wrote "am delighted that you are improving in your bargaining capacity—that is all you need to make you perfect!"

Construction of the house went smoothly, and Adelaide began visiting the site twice a day. Although delighted with the progress, she requested many changes—like ordering wooden doors to go in front of the existing ones of wrought iron and glass at the porte cochere—orders the foreman said "shall be done but some are going to be rather difficult & rather expensive."

In May, Frick went to London to buy light fixtures, candelabras, torchères, and furniture. When he returned home from Europe in June, thrilled with the progress of the house—the West Gallery in particular—he wrote Knoedler: "Went almost immediately to the new house which I found had progressed marvelously. The picture gallery is going to be a dream; I like its proportions immensely."

But something else must have pleased him as well—the iconography and architectural details for his mansion. Indeed, the price Frick paid for his fortune was never far from his consciousness. Bas-reliefs of a boy and girl child encircled the exterior walls of the house (fig. 7-11), something of significance to Frick far beyond their traditional use as architectural ornamentation for a neoclassical, Beaux Arts building. Moreover, two exterior door pediments and two exterior window pediments had been similarly carved. The pediment above the front door (fig. 7-12) shows Mars' helmet resting at the foot of a cherub who holds a mirror for Venus as water runs out of a vessel— the traditional theme of honoring love over war. Each of the other door and window pediments depicts two boys and two girls, the family Frick would have had, had his children all survived. The pediment for the archway on the southwest corner of the building shows the children in an art-related motif (fig. 7-13). More important, behind this pediment, there is a domed loggia leading to an entrance into what is today known as the Enamel Room, a room then designed as Henry Clay Frick's inner sanctum. The dome has carvings on the ceiling showing a boy and girl on a dolphin, the classic reference to the passage of souls across the River to the Island of the Dead (fig. 7-14).

The death and resurrection motifs also continued in the pediment on the northwest corner of the building (fig. 7-15). Perhaps a statement of Frick's ongoing, self-imposed guilt over the death of his children and a recognition of Adelaide's unrelenting depression, it depicts Orpheus, who failed in his attempt to bring his wife from the underworld because he looked over his shoulder too soon. He is seen playing his lyre as a boy and girl sit contentedly to his right, while a boy and girl on his left hide

Fig. 7-11. The pediment over the front door references
the age-old saying "Make love, not War."
The Frick Collection

in fear behind a grotesque mask. Probably carved by Attilio Piccirelli, a sculptor used often by Hastings, the pediments reflect a cruel irony. Attilio, who lost a brother in childhood and whose own marriage was barren, was deeply interested in child psychology. His friend Fiorello La Guardia, who later became mayor of New York, noted of Atillio's hands as he worked, they looked tender as those of "a young mother bathing her new infant."

In July 1914, when floors were being laid on the second floor and Frick's special panel for El Greco's *Purification of the Temple* was being installed above the mantelpiece in his private sitting room, Frick suffered another life-threatening attack of inflammatory rheumatism. Admitting the attack had been "coming on for a long time," Frick had experienced a series of disruptive and disconcerting events. The first occurred that March when fifty-two-year-old George Vanderbilt—Frick's landlord at 640 Fifth Avenue, who was successfully recovering from an appendectomy in Washington, D.C.—dropped dead of heart failure. His body was brought back to New York and rested overnight in his sister's house, the connecting twin to Frick's, to await burial in the Vanderbilt plot on Staten Island.

Thus, Frick's tenancy had come to an abrupt close. As required by the terms of the rental agreement, he had to vacate his home of nine years to make room for its new owner, Grace Vanderbilt. Suddenly in a great hurry, the Frick family moved what they could to 1 East Seventieth Street and Eagle Rock, where they would spend the summer, and Frick began pushing the contractors for an October occupancy.

Then, on June 28, another event occurred that may well have intensified his anxiety. While Frick was attending a U.S. Steel finance committee meeting in New York, Archduke Francis Ferdinand, heir to the throne of Austria, was assassinated in Sarajevo, capital of the Austrian province of Bosnia. Within weeks Europe went to war. The Archduke's assassination most surely rekindled memories of Alexander Berkman's attempt on Frick's life in 1892 and heightened the terrifying reality that an anarchist attack was still an everpresent reality. The *New York Times* described the grim

Fig. 7-12

Fig. 7-13

Fig. 7-14

Fig. 7-15

Figs. 7-12–15. Exterior bas-reliefs and pediments containing putti and children
may be references to Frick's children—the two who lived, the two who died.
The Frick Collection

event with photographic accuracy. Lists of rulers who had fallen to fanatics' hands in the last century appeared, and Berkman himself, who had been released from prison in 1906 after his twenty-two-year sentence had been commuted to eighteen years, boasted that the anarchists and revolutionists had "[struck] down the only man strong enough to continue the iron rule of Emperor Francis Joseph." Moreover, many circumstances of the attack were similar to Berkman's attack on Frick. Just as the twenty-year-old Berkman had stormed into Frick's office and shot him twice in the neck, an angry nineteen-year-old student had jumped on the running board of the Archduke's car and fired two bullets into his neck, piercing his jugular vein and windpipe. The assassin then fired shots into the Duchess's abdomen and throat, killing her as well. *New York Times* articles described how the Duchess clutched her husband's neck with her fingers in a futile effort to stay his wounds as she sank backward into the car, dying as she screamed, "My God! My God!" and expiring as the Archduke, himself a breath away from death, pleaded, "Sophie, remain alive for our children!"

The shots "heard around the world" hit Frick hard, but subsequent "shots" hit him harder. On July 23, 1914, Frick's much-loved sister-in-law, Martha Howard Childs, died unexpectedly. Attie was not only the person to whom Frick looked for fun, frivolity, and humor, but she died the same week as had her little namesake Martha twenty-three years before. In fact, the day of her death was also the twenty-second anniversary of Berkman's attack on Frick, which of course was also the same day Frick experienced the postdeath visitation from Martha, and the day Attie had rushed to his side to comfort her wounded brother-in-law.

These events, abounding in coincidences of birth and death, may have precipitated the recurrence of his illness. As his autoimmune system attacked his own body, he was further plagued by inflamed joints, atrophying muscles, high fever, sweating, diarrhea, and other gastrointestinal disorders. He was again reduced to a helpless state and fully bedridden. Humiliated by his incapacitated state, wincing with pain if someone so much as sat on his bed, Frick dictated a letter to his close friend and lawyer, J. P. Grier. Admitting he was "Helpless as a baby, having to be carried to and from the bathroom," he explained his was "muscular rheumatism of the very worst kind."

Severe anxiety, as is usually the case in the acute stages of this disease, continued, even though Frick appeared arrogant and self-confident. His was a textbook case. Anger and negativism served as a way of disguising vulnerability and fear of breaking down emotionally. This defense mechanism must have been very strong, for Frick's frequent excessive demands so terrorized those around him, they feared the consequences of his ill humor more than his ill health. In fact, Frick's agitation reached such proportions, his doctor, Jasper Garmany, who had failed to save Martha's life in 1891, warned him that his behavior might seriously endanger his health.

But Frick, caught between rage and dependency, was now governed as much by grief as by fear. According to the Vanderbilt biographer, Jerry E. Patterson, William Henry Vanderbilt had a premonition of early death in 1882 when completing his mansion at 640 Fifth Avenue, the "proper setting for his most cherished possessions, his collection of paintings." Perhaps taking the events of the last few months as a bad omen, Frick too may have feared, as had Vanderbilt, that he would die before his collection could be housed in its new home.

Preoccupied with his own battle, and generally unconcerned about the outbreak of war in Europe, Frick wrote in August to his iron-master friend and former Carnegie Steel agent, S. L. Schoonmaker, "Well it is too bad we are to have a war, but it seems it had to come sometime, and it's just as well it should be over." And in thinking about his art collection, and the late July industrial recession igniting Wall Street's fears that gold would be hoarded in London, not New York, a fear that anticipated a collapse in transatlantic trade, Frick advised Charles Carstairs, "Conditions are such at present that I think it wiser to take up some good securities that are selling very low, rather than add to my collection of pictures."

The war in Europe and the battle between Frick's immune system and his body were almost mild in comparison to the attacks Frick made on Sir Charles Allom. Still confined to his bed after eight weeks, in the care of nurses and only able to "move around with difficulty," an incapacitated Frick nevertheless warned the decorator, "I am glad to say that I am well again, and will see that things are pushed from now on." Allom had written him a stern letter on October 30, 1914, explaining:

> locksmiths have been taken off to make rifles, and nothing in the world that we could do could have affected that, any more than we or you could have stopped the war had we desired to do so.
>
> I can tell you that it is just wonderful that this country [England] is proceeding with its work as it is, when it has at least 2 million men under arms, with equipment having to be made for them at forced pressure. It has not only taken men from normal employment, but it has taken material, money, and has even interfered with the shipping of goods. . . . The share which France has taken in your house, has naturally caused delay, for which I am sure you cannot blame me.

Frick, however, was sicker and angrier than ever. He cabled Allom: "Simply outrageous unbusinesslike your dilatory manner completing contracts with me. First contract in many respects notably hardware for doors not even heard of. War excuse absurd."

❖

WHEN MOVING DAY CAME ON NOVEMBER 16, Frick was still suffering from his affliction. Nevertheless, the family moved in and a greatly debilitated Frick oversaw the hanging of his collection. He had always personally directed the unwrapping and placement of every new acquisition, made careful notations of the date of the acquisition and the date of each art work's arrival or departure when transferred from one of his houses to another, and kept a list of where each painting was displayed. This time, he was no less meticulous, particularly as one might suspect that feelings of loss and memories of the deceased were evoked by the accumulation of crated paintings comprising the very essence of his anxiety. Many of his now less fashionable works collected before 1900 remained behind in Pittsburgh, as they had done while Frick lived at 640 Fifth Avenue: the Cazin and Thaulow above his Clayton desk; works by his Pittsburgh artist friends Woodwell, Beatty, and Wall; the smaller copy of *Christ at Emmaus* (see fig. 4-17) given to the Carnegie Art Institute in memory of Martha; and the small Millet drawings. When Frick visited Pittsburgh, perhaps these pictures remained to envelop him in a past he could not leave behind.

But then, since 1895, Frick had continued to buy and sell, as painting after painting either met or did not meet his standard of harmony. Among others, as we have seen, two Rembrandts had been exchanged for Vermeer's *Officer and Laughing Girl* (see fig. i-1), a Monet had been exchanged for a Cuyp, a Velázquez had been credited against a Van Dyck, and a Constable and a Reynolds returned because "the family do[es] not seem to care for [them]." And now, Henry Clay Frick began to reveal, more poignantly than ever, the reasons for his acquisitions, refinements, and choice of exhibition place.

Over the next five years (the last of his life) Frick would change the arrangement of his paintings in 1 East Seventieth Street as new ones arrived and others departed. Certain works, however, remained forever where Frick placed them in 1914. Frick chose Millet's *Woman Sewing by Lamplight* (see fig. 1-25), acquired shortly after his own mother's death in 1905, for the southeast wall of the second-floor breakfast room (fig. 7-16), a placement suggesting comfort and consolation, particularly since Frick would be largely confined to the upstairs in his convalescence and was critically ill with the disease that had plagued him since childhood. To this room, he added Rousseau's *Village of Becquigny* (see fig. 1-35), centering it above the mantel, across from the Millet. Rousseau's West Overton look-alike village, with its angle of view identical to the view from the window in the springhouse of Frick's birth, created an effect that could only have reinforced his much needed feeling of nurturance and protection.

For his own bedroom, he selected his post-Martha devotional, *Lady Hamilton* (see fig. 3-18), the auburn-haired beauty who would have resembled her, holding a dog

Fig. 7-16. The second-floor breakfast room with Millet's *Woman Sewing by Lamplight*, 1927.
Author's collection

resembling Brownie. The painting held a place of honor above the mantelpiece, facing the headboard of Frick's bed.

In the summer of 1914, Frick had said to Knoedler, "I really doubt the wisdom of making a purchase of pictures at this time, and do so rather reluctantly. It is most difficult to tell what the future has in store for us, and at present it seems to me that pictures will decline rather than advance in value." But as 1914 drew to a close, a new home, ample gallery space, the war in Europe, and an almost morbid foreboding and preoccupation with death and the afterlife combined to unleash a flood of collecting, a burst of acquisitions that continued to reincarnate his past.

Of the fifteen paintings Henry Clay Frick acquired at the end of 1914, four were Impressionists. One was the previously mentioned *Mother and Children* by Renoir (see fig. 3-10), the only Renoir in his collection. Frick exhibited *Mother and Children* at the top of the stairs at 1 East Seventieth Street, at the entrance to the family quarters (fig. 7-17). Day and night, everyone in the house passed the life-size painting as they moved up and down stairs, and to and from bedrooms, sitting rooms, and the upstairs

Fig. 7-17. Renoir's *Mother and Children* in the second-floor hall stood
at the entrance to the family's private living quarters.
Author's collection

breakfast room. Whether Frick used the elevator or the stairs, this work, depicting a child holding a doll so like the one he had given Martha days before her death, was the first thing that greeted him. Indeed, the mother in the painting, who wears a hat decorated with clusters of tiny silk rosebuds, and her two daughters must have appeared as if they were walking straight toward him in greeting, just as they would have done if twenty-three years before Martha had been alive and he had come to greet his daughters in Central Park.

El Greco's *Purification of the Temple* was placed in a specially carved panel above the mantel in Frick's second-floor private sitting room (fig. 7-18). The painting's strong associations to Homestead were probably greatly enhanced when Frick hung the newly acquired Manet, *The Bullfight* (see fig. 4-22), across from El Greco's Christ thrashing the moneychangers.

Frick's placement of paintings downstairs was equally poignant. "As requested," Knoedler exhibited Frick's two vast Turners in the main hall (fig. 7-19): *The Harbor of*

Fig. 7-18. Henry Clay Frick's second-floor private sitting room, 1927.
The Frick Collection

Fig. 7-19. The main hall in 1 East Seventieth Street, 1927,
with the Turners placed as Henry Clay Frick requested.
Author's collection

Fig. 7-20. Joseph Mallord William Turner (1775–1851),
Cologne: The Arrival of a Packet-Boat: Evening, 1862.
Acquired in 1914, Oil, and possibly watercolor, on canvas,
66⅜ x 88¼ in. (168.6 x 224.1 cm).
The Frick Collection

Dieppe (1914) and *Cologne: The Arrival of a Packet-Boat: Evening* (fig. 7-20). And no wonder. When the latter painting is juxtaposed with a photograph of the broad, flat sandbank of Pittsburgh's Mon Wharf (fig. 7-21), one senses the painting reminded Frick of his first home and place of business as a new millionaire. Indeed, Turner had lived beneath the Thames Bridge in London, just as Frick lived in the Monongahela House overlooking the Mon Wharf and the packet company. As John Russell wrote, "arrivals and departures by sea were an obsession for Turner," as were the exact maritime details in his harbor scenes. Both paintings, therefore, testify to the fact that Frick, through the Turners, remembered the hustle of life in the hub of wharf life, a life once enjoyed by artist and collector alike.

For the Living Hall, where the family gathered after dinner for coffee before the fireplace, Frick chose his first Italian Renaissance painting, Titian's *Pietro Aretino* (1905). El Greco's stern portrait of St. Jerome (1905)—the Henry Clay Frick look-alike according to his daughter Helen—took its place above the mantel, as did another previously mentioned Frick look-alike, Holbein's *Sir Thomas More* (see fig. 6-1).

Fig. 7-21. The Mon Wharf, as Henry Clay Frick knew it,
with the packet company and the Monongahela House.
Carnegie Library, Pittsburgh

Fig. 7-22. Thomas Gainsborough (1727-1788), *Sarah, Lady Innes,* c. 1757.
Acquired in 1914, Oil on canvas, 40 x 28⅝ in. (101.6 x 72.7 cm).
The Frick Collection

Fig. 7-23. Martha Howard Frick holding a rosebud, 1886.
Frick Art and Historical Center

The library absorbed more family-associated portraits. Thomas Gainsborough's *Sarah, Lady Innes* (fig. 7-22), similar to a portrait of Martha holding a rosebud (fig. 7-23), was placed in the library together with Lawrence's portrait of Julia, Lady Peel (see fig. 6-19), whom Frick had felt bore strong resemblance to Helen. More significant, the library received the Reynolds portraits of the married couple representative of Frick and his wife: the British art patron and collector, Sir George Howland Beaumont and Lady Margaret Beaumont.

But Frick placed another painting in the library as well, the political and social satirist William Hogarth's portrait of Miss Mary Edwards (see fig. 9-35), the richest woman of her day in England. It was given a place of honor above the mantel, and the painting—as we shall see when we turn to examine the effect of Henry Clay Frick's money, masterpieces, and mourning on his family—showed how intense his relationship was with Helen. Indeed, as we shall also see in Edgar Degas's *The Rehearsal* (see fig. 9-33), a painting Frick placed over her writing desk in his upstairs sitting room, the two paintings speak to this relationship. They were powerful messages to Helen as well as symptoms of a grieving father's mourning.

As Frick continued arranging his paintings, Knoedler delivered James Abbott McNeill Whistler's picture of a dead calm ocean, as well as two black-on-black portraits— the artist *Miss Rosa Corder* (fig. 7-24) and the poet *Robert, Comte de Montesquiou-*

Fig. 7-24. James Abbott McNeill Whistler (1834–1903),
Miss Rosa Corder, 1875–78.
Acquired in 1914, Oil on canvas, 75¾ x 36⅜ in.
(192.4 x 92.4 cm).
The Frick Collection

Fig. 7-25. James Abbott McNeill Whistler (1834–1903),
Robert, Comte de Montesquiou-Fezensac, 1891–92.
Acquired in 1914, Oil on canvas, 82⅛ x 36⅛ in.
(208.6 x 91.8 cm).
The Frick Collection

Fezensac (fig. 7-25). Knoedler had purchased the paintings from the casino-owner Richard Canfield the previous day, one week after George Vanderbilt's death. Frick placed the portraits in his business office, together with two of the most astonishing paintings he had yet collected. Ever consumed by morbidity and plagued by longing, Frick still questioned his friends about the hereafter. Preoccupied by Martha's 1892 return from the grave, and repeatedly stunned by portrait subjects resembling his deceased friends, Frick also developed a habit of comparing his age, and the ages of others, to biblical or historical characters. He often said, "It would take only thirty generations of thirty years each to bring us back to the time of Christ." He also enjoyed calculating, "So and so is just the age of Christ when he died, or Lincoln when he was assassinated."

Thus, in 1914, as his inner world became increasingly consumed by these afterlife, age-related associations, he acquired Francisco Goya's portrait *An Officer* (fig. 7-26) and Goya's landlady (fig. 7-27) (now known as *Doña María Martínez de Puga*). Like apparitions themselves, the paintings are near reincarnations of John Singer Sargent's portraits of the Spanish-looking George Vanderbilt (fig. 7-28), who had died only nine months before, and his mother, Maria Kissam Vanderbilt (fig. 7-29), once the landlady of 640 Fifth Avenue. Frick purchased these poignant, afterlife-related portraits from two different dealers on December 5 and 17, 1914, one month after moving into 1 East Seventieth Street, and placed them in his downstairs business office. With a methodology as precise as his own signature, Frick would later juxtapose Goya's officer with Gilbert Stuart's *George Washington* (see fig. 7-71)—George Washington Vanderbilt was his namesake. In this juxtaposition, Frick had taken his predilection for linking objects to deceased friends to still deeper levels. As we know, the beginnings of the Frick-Overholt whiskey fortune and Frick's own coking, railroading, and art-collecting career were all born at Broad Ford—the Delaware Indians' crossing place where in the 1700s the young soldier George Washington recognized the superior quality of the area's coal and became the first white man to traverse the Youghiogheny River.

The balance of the paintings Frick had collected through 1914 were exhibited in the West Gallery. Van Dyck's elegant *Paola Adorno, Marchesa di Brignole Sale* (1914) showed that Frick had not lost his appreciation of ladies' finery. And Maris's *The Bridge* (1914) was again a striking reminder of the countryside of Frick's fortune, in particular the bridge in Brownsville, Pennsylvania. More important, however, the West Gallery received Goya's mighty *The Forge* (fig. 7-30), considered by Charles Ryskamp to have been a "daring acquisition for the time." But for Frick, it was a natural. He was then discussing with Andrew Mellon the merits of the byproduct ovens made by the German firm, Koppers. These ovens captured coke oven smoke and thereby retrieved valuable gas and chemicals. Since both men were anticipating the role these

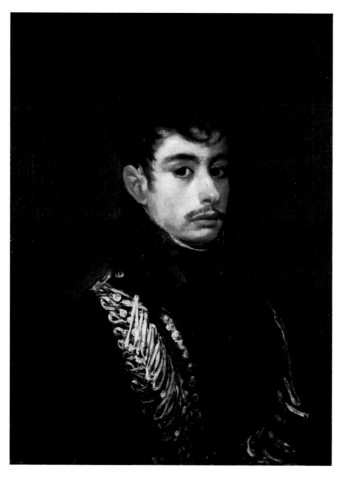

Above: Fig. 7-26. Francisco de Goya y Lucientes (1746–1828),
An Officer.
Acquired in 1914, Oil on canvas, 24⅞ x 19¼ in. (63.2 x 48.9 cm).
The Frick Collection

Right: Fig. 7-27. Francisco de Goya y Lucientes (1746–1828),
Doña María Martínez de Puga, 1824.
Acquired in 1914, Oil on canvas, 31½ x 23 in. (80 x 58.4 cm).
The Frick Collection

Above: Fig. 7-28. John Singer Sargent (1856–1925),
George Vanderbilt.
Oil on canvas, 41 x 45½ in. (104.15 x 115.57 cm).
Biltmore Estates, Asheville

Right: Fig. 7-29. John Singer Sargent (1856–1925),
Maria Kissam Vanderbilt.
Oil on canvas, 50¼ x 68 in. (127.63 x 172. 72 cm).
Biltmore Estates, Asheville

Fig. 7-30. Francisco de Goya y Lucientes (1746-1828), *The Forge*, c. 1815-20.
Acquired in 1914, Oil on canvas, 71½ x 49¼ in. (181.6 x 125.1 cm).
The Frick Collection

Fig. 7-31. Men drawing coke.
Harper's Illustrated Weekly, July 7, 1888.
Historical Society of Western Pennsylvania

U.S. Steel coke ovens might play in the war against Germany, *The Forge* may have spoken to the anticipated fire and frenzy of wartime coke manufacturing. More likely, however, with this purchase Frick was recalling the lurid dance of immigrant workers, in bondage to fire as they toiled day and night in the eerie glow of his coke works. In 1888, twenty-six years before Frick purchased the Goya, *Harper's Weekly* captured the coke workers' rhythm and movements in a drawing of men working a line of beehives like those of the H. C. Frick Coke Company (fig. 7-31). In 1903, this drawing was reproduced by James Howard Bridge, then Andrew Carnegie's secretary, in *The History of Carnegie Steel*—a book Frick helped bring to publication. When he bought *The Forge,* Frick acquired a monumental painting, a masterful comment on his life experience as well as on the frenzy of fire and immigrant labor.

A<small>T THE END OF</small> 1914, Henry Clay Frick was still suffering from inflammatory rheumatism, but his museum-tomb at 1 East Seventieth Street was well on its way toward becoming an elaborate container for his grief, a place giving concrete reality to his meeting place with Martha and bridging the spirit world. Moreover, there was much iconography to suggest this neoclassic museum-grave was also a Masonic shrine, perhaps the "shrine of his heart" alluded to by George Harvey. Possibly a clandestine, private Symbolic Masonic Lodge—a lodge of Master Masons where the First through Third Degrees of Masonry, known as the Symbolic Degrees, are conferred—or even a symbol of this lodge, Frick's new home was splendid as a museum-to-be, evocative when seen as his link to the spirit world, and dramatic as a combined statement of his pathology and his Masonic philosophy.

Throughout his life, Frick had been a generous supporter of his Mother Lodge in Connellsville. He gave them an organ and, in 1904, a silk banner. And certainly in the architectural details of his new home, Frick made many references to the mystery religions, part of the foundation of Freemasonry. Frick chose globes to mark the entrance to the Fifth Avenue garden, an allusion to the two spheres (earthly and celestial) with which Freemasonry is concerned. More important, he had black-and-white, river-pebble mosaic paths laid in the garden itself (fig. 7-32), paths recalling the floor of Solomon's Temple, which was decorated with a mosaic pavement of black-and-white stones representing evil versus good. The pebbles, washed smooth by river water, create a labyrinthine design. The upper path depicts rectangles with fertility symbols, suggesting the paths originally used in Egyptian royal tombs and mortuary temples to protect the deceased. The lower path contains motifs of lyre, bulls' horn, and bucranium (an ox skull adorned with wreathes), recalling the ancient bull-worshipping cult of the Persian hero Mithra, the god of light and wisdom who was worshipped in caves and grottos. This cult is believed to have had a direct relationship to Freemasonry because it had initiation rites centered on death and resurrection, demanded completion of eighty trials of increased difficulty, and conferred seven degrees on initiates. A black-and-white mosaic path surviving from antiquity at Ostia (fig. 7-33) depicts all these elements.

Apart from being symbolic of the search for eternal truth, both upper and lower walkways suggest the black-and-white path on which a candidate stands when the Third Degree of Freemasonry is conferred on him—a ceremony that raises the candidate to Master Mason, member of the Mother Lodge. In the ritual, the candidate undergoes a symbolic death (by murder) and resurrection, setting him on the path to perfection. Indeed, the path embodied such mystical power, Frick's daughter Helen regarded it with suspicion. Careful to walk around it and not step on the cracks, she feared it as some do spilled salt.

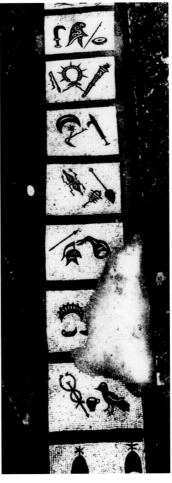

Left: Fig. 7-32. River-pebble mosaic path (after restoration) and the loggia archway.
The Frick Collection

Right: Fig. 7-33. Mithraic path at Ostia.
Archivio Fotografico della Soprintendenza Archeologica di Ostia

At the end of the path, seven "symbolic" steps lead up to an archway defined by two columns—Wisdom, for the wisdom of "The Great Architect" and Master of the Lodge, and Strength, for the stability of the universe and the office of Senior Warden (fig. 7-34). As if Frick were designing the Masonic path to perfection, the archway then leads to the loggia and introduces the third pillar, Beauty, the Temple itself, in this case Frick's inner sanctum, later to be known as the Enamel Room. Thus, in a subtle way, Frick's archway and loggia represent what Masons describe as "the Porchway Entrance to the Holy of Holies in the Temple," known as the Royal Arch Degree (fig. 7-35). An extension of the Third Degree, it anticipates the raising of a candidate to the Fourth Degree and symbolizes the transition stage, his glimpse into the Temple beyond.

Left: Fig. 7-34. The seven steps to the loggia archway may be a reference to
the seven symbolic steps of the Royal Arch Degree.
The Frick Collection

Right: Fig. 7-35. The Royal Arch.
Tracing Board, Museum of the Grand Lodge of Ireland.
Designed J. Harris, 1823.
Courtesy the Grand Lodge of A. F. & A. Masons of Ireland

Frick seems to have repeated this symbolism in the design of the West Gallery
(fig. 7-36). He returned from Egypt in 1912, began construction of the house, and
acquired Paolo Veronese's *Allegory of Vice and Virtue* and *Allegory of Wisdom and
Strength* (figs. 7-37, 38). Each measures approximately 84½ inches by 65¾ inches, and
the vast paintings stood for Frick, as they stand today, like columns between the West
Gallery and his inner sanctum, the Enamel Room. Indeed, they echo the exterior
columns, Wisdom and Strength, leading from the Mithraic path to this room. The cor-
nice above the sculpture in Wisdom and Strength reads in the Masonic tradition:
"Honor and Virtue Flourish after Death." A perfect metaphor for the Masonic Royal
Arch Degree, the paintings, like the columns, may well have symbolized for Frick the

all-important transition from the Third to Fourth Masonic Degree, the passage from death and resurrection to enlightenment, from the porch to the temple.

Although the evidence is not conclusive, because the plans for the house were lost when Hastings's house burned to the ground, and because Freemasonry is a secret society and records, if kept, are not shared, Frick may have been Steward of the Lodge, the officer who collected dues and subscriptions and provided refreshments, something he did when he was treasurer and secretary of his first Lodge in the 1870s. In Frick's Symbolic Lodge, bas-reliefs of cornucopias—a typical Renaissance motif of plenty, as well as the jewel, or insignia, denoting Steward of the Lodge—are carved on the southern and western facades, the two sides of the building enclosing the black-and-white path. Moreover, the black-and-white path (upon which only Master Masons may walk) starts at the dining room and ends at the Enamel Room. There is a suspicion Frick used the inner sanctum as a preparing room for himself and other Master Masons, a suspicion reinforced by the fact that there appears to have been a closet and a way to descend from this room to the basement room, now called the Bowling Alley.

Fig. 7-36. The West Gallery looking toward the Enamel Room.
Author's collection

Fig. 7-37. Paolo Veronese (1528–1588), *Allegory of Vice and Virtue.*
Acquired in 1912, Oil on canvas, 86¼ x 66¾ in. (219 x 169.5 cm).
The Frick Collection

Fig. 7-38. Paolo Veronese (1528–1588), *Allegory of Wisdom and Strength.*
Acquired in 1912, Oil on canvas, 84½ x 65¾ in. (214.6 x 167 cm).
The Frick Collection

Although this subterranean room has always been considered a legitimate bowling alley, evidence suggests otherwise. A former director of the Frick Collection, Everett Fahy, believes it was a meeting room. Walter Cooley, who managed Helen Frick's affairs, said Frick only bowled once in his life: in 1897 when the children's bowling alley was installed at Clayton. "Slapping his hands after throwing a ball, Frick said 'that was the first and last time he would bowl.'" Additionally, this is the only room in the house lacking in Frick's usual harmony of detail. As if the room were converted after Frick's death, it is disjointed and the bowling lanes seem to be both awkward and out of proportion to the space; the hanging shelves are of a different period and style; the lighting in the ceiling is irregularly placed.

Fig. 7-39. The Masonic rug owned by Henry Clay Frick and given to King Solomon's Lodge in Connellsville, Pennsylvania, by Helen Clay Frick. Courtesy of King Solomon's Lodge No. 346, Connellsville

If not a bowling alley, then perhaps this is where the Symbolic Degrees were conferred. Like a Masonic lodge room, the north side, traditionally kept "dark" as a symbolic statement, is windowless. The room runs east to west, has a raised east end, has odd plaques bearing angry medieval faces on the doors (some of which have been removed), and is configured as prescribed by Masonic tradition. A private space, it had an entrance on Seventy-first Street and has the same ceiling motif as Henry Clay Frick's most personal rooms, the Enamel Room and his second-floor sitting room. Additionally, the furniture arriving in 1914 was made of oak, a tree sacred to the Druids. Cushions were covered in blue velvet (perhaps a reference to the Mother Lodge, also known as a Blue Lodge), and a blue and yellow rug with the Masonic symbol for "sacred geometry" may have been there as well. Frick's daughter, Helen, donated such a rug, which is the same size as this room, to Frick's Mother Lodge in Connellsville, Pennsylvania, in 1968 (fig. 7-39).

Apart from the exterior columns and loggia already discussed, Frick seems to have further expressed his Masonic ties through his paintings. *The Polish Rider* (see fig. 1-38) has already been discussed in relationship to his early coking career and his associations with Freemasonry and Christian knighthood. It now becomes important, however, to examine the impact of this knighthood in greater detail. As mentioned in Chapter 1, Frick attained the highest Orders of both the York and Scottish Rites and had many Masonic Degrees and Orders of Knighthood conferred on him.

Above: Fig. 7-40. Sir Peter Paul Rubens (1577–1640), follower of,
A Knight of the Order of the Golden Fleece, seventeenth century.
Acquired in 1915, Oil on canvas, 39¾ x 30½ in. (101 x 77.5 cm).
The Frick Collection

Right: Fig. 7-41. Masonic Funeral Apron, England, c. 1800.
Courtesy of the United Grand Lodge of England

The white lambskin Masonic Apron, an emblem of innocence and purity of soul, as well as the badge of a Mason, is given when a candidate is raised to the First Degree. This all-important apron is alluded to in a painting then considered to be by

Sir Peter Paul Rubens entitled *A Knight of the Order of the Golden Fleece* (fig. 7-40). The knight wears the order's emblem, a golden fleece or lambskin, representing this most illustrious order established in Flanders in 1429 by the duke of Burgundy. The fleece, later symbolized by the Masonic Apron, is so important Masons are required to wear the apron at all lodge functions. During a Masonic funeral service (fig. 7-41) one is usually placed in the casket of the deceased, together with an evergreen branch, as "an emblem of [Masonic] faith in the immortality of the soul." Although Frick felt the painting did not meet his standards, he never sold it as he did others that displeased him.

As we have seen, in the 1870s Frick also became a member of the Knights Templars (fig. 7-42), who at the time of the Crusades were second only to the papacy in wealth and power. They had a naval and merchant fleet and were known as the finest fighting men of their age. As merchant bankers, they handled most of Western Europe's capital. In fact, the origin of modern banking has often been attributed to the Order of the Temple.

Fig. 7-42. The Knights Templar certificate dated and signed by Henry Clay Frick, June 16, 1880.
Frick Archives

The Knights of Malta, another Order conferred on Frick, is the oldest of all semimonastic chivalric orders. These knights sprang into existence with the Crusades, and when they became a military order attending the sick, they were called the Knights of St. John. They warred against enemies of Christianity on land and sea, eventually making their home on Cyprus, then Rhodes, and finally Malta. As a significant naval power, they rivaled the Templars and were as famous for their fleet as they were for their skill in medical care and nursing. When the pope abolished the Knights Templars (because as a body their power was so great the Templars were a law unto themselves), the order was absorbed by the Knights of Malta, who appropriated their riches.

An "appendent" or extra Order in a Commandery of Knights Templar, the Order of the Knights of Malta (conferred after a candidate becomes a member of the Knights Templar) is considered by many Masons to be of questionable honor. Dissolution of the Order has often been argued by Freemasons because of the ancient jealousy between that order and the Templars. Additionally, they claim the Knights of Malta have no history or tradition connecting to Freemasonry as do the Templars, who were also great builders.

Fig. 7-43. The loggia bas-reliefs perhaps alluding to
the Knights Templar and the Knights of Malta.
The Frick Collection

In 1913 Frick had acquired El Greco's portrait of Vincenzo Anastagi, Knight of
Malta and captain of the flagship. With this purchase, he affirmed his own rank as a
Christian Knight and expressed again his fascination with reunion, affirming the union
of the Knights of Malta and Knights Templar. These two Orders are also represented by
four bas-reliefs on the loggia (fig. 7-43); two depict galleys and two depict shields and
armor. The former suggest the Knights Templar, who were wool traders and the only
knights allowed to wear beards; the galleys are replete with motifs of sheep's heads and
a single bearded knight. Among the latter is a shield bearing a caduceus, a symbol of
healing, as a reference to the Knights of Malta. Moreover, there is a helmet with three
white horses on its visor, perhaps representing the three orders of knighthood within

the Order of Knights Templar: the Knights of Malta, the Knights Templar, and the Knight of the Eagle and Pelican (also known as the Knight of the Rose Croix).

The Order of the Knight of the Eagle and Pelican is also the eighteenth degree in the Scottish Rite. One of the many conferred on Frick, symbolized by a pelican piercing its breast, the Order is exclusively dedicated to healing the sick and caring for the wounded. As the pelican commemorates the final triumph of life over death, good over evil, and generally, through the combination of faith and reason, it instructs about triumph over life's sorrows. This is because, according to legend, the father pelican, blinded by the flapping wings of its rebellious young, strikes and kills them; the mother returns to the nest on the third day, lacerates her breast, and feeds her blood to her dead young, thus enabling their rebirth. In the late 1890s when the Clayton house was being renovated as a house museum, the jewel for this Degree (fig. 7-44) was found in Frick's dressing-table drawer, together with a brown soap box lined with paper lace and containing an engraving of Martha's likeness and her hair (fig. 7-45). More telling, a chandelier in the library (fig. 7-46) still hangs before the copy of *Christ at Emmaus,* the painting given to the Carnegie Institute in memory of Martha. The chandelier has the pelican piercing its breast as a repeated motif, as well as small rosebuds (Martha's family nickname) and palms, symbols of a martyr's triumph over death. There is a further, subtle reference to the Knight of the Eagle and Pelican at 1 East Seventieth Street. The black iron fence encircling the building is topped with hundreds of points that resemble long, upright spears placed neatly beside each other in a row. Apart from these spears, the fence has as one of its other prominent motifs a bird, who is a combination of both eagle and pelican, standing on top of a shield (fig. 7-47).

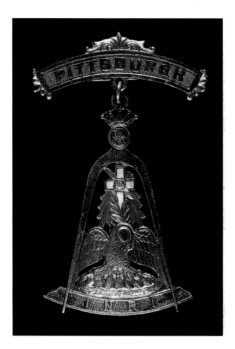

Fig. 7-44. The Masonic jewel belonging to Henry Clay Frick and representing the Knight of the Eagle and Pelican.
Author's collection

References to the Orders of the Scottish Rite occur in bas-reliefs at the base of the grand staircase in the New York house: the Knight of the Brazen Serpent and the Knight of the Royal Axe (fig. 7-48). In ancient rites, the serpent symbolizes the soul's descent into "the infernal regions" and its "resurrection into the grandeur of light, truth, and perfection." The serpent was flung into the breast of an initiate in the ritual of Bacchus Saba-Zeus. Thus the Knight of the Brazen Serpent teaches repentance and reformation. The Knight of the Royal Axe also instructs about repentance and reformation, but through labor and work. In commemorating the building of a Temple, it

Fig. 7-45. Henry Clay Frick kept this box containing Martha's hair, the engraving of her likeness, and the Masonic jewel of the Knight of the Eagle and Pelican, in his Clayton dressing-table drawer.
Frick Archives

Top: Fig. 7-46. The Clayton chandelier bears the dual Christian and Masonic symbol of resurrection, the pelican.
Frick Art and Historical Center

Middle: Fig. 7-47. The fence at 1 East Seventieth Street suggesting the Knight of the Eagle and Pelican.
Author's collection

Bottom: Fig. 7-48. The stair bas-relief in 1 East Seventieth Street alludes to the Knight of
the Brazen Serpent (top left corner) and the Knight of the Royal Axe (middle right.)
The Frick Collection

teaches one to make good products for one's own day and for future generations. This degree, therefore, refers to the four generations of men who cut the cedars of Lebanon to build Noah's Ark, the Ark of the Covenant, Solomon's Temple, and the second Temple. This Order recalls 1 Kings 5: 2, 5, 6, 15: "and behold I propose to build an house unto the name of the Lord my God. . . . Now therefore command thou that they hew me cedar trees out of Lebanon . . . and Solomon had. . . fourscore thousand hewers in the mountains." Frick's bas-relief was thus a daily reminder of his quest, his sorrows, and the healing power of his temple.

Even some of Frick's portraits similarly allude to his Masonic affiliation. Titian's *Portrait of a Man in a Red Cap,* which predates nineteenth-century Freemasonry, was acquired in 1915. But the subject's cap recalls the pillbox red cap worn by Freemasons. Red is also a symbolic or royal color in Freemasonry for it, together with blue and purple, was one of the three colors on the veil of the Temple. Additionally, as the color of fire and therefore of regeneration, red is the color of the Royal Arch Degree, the color of the Knights Templar's cross (meaning martyrdom for the sake of religion), and also the color of zeal, which according to the 1917 edition of the *Encyclopedia of Freemasonry,* "should inspire all who are in search of that which is lost."

The Titian achieves its greatest Masonic import, however, by the fact that Frick exhibited it in the Living Hall beside his recently acquired Giovanni Bellini, *St. Francis in the Desert* (fig. 7-49). Indeed, St. Francis symbolizes the bridge between the nature religions and Christianity. He was a saint long associated with paganism because of his affinity with animals and his Canticle to the Sun, *Brother Sun, Sister Moon.* For Masons, the sun and moon carry much symbolism, as do animals, and together, they are considered part of "the temple of creation."

Frick created many spiritual undercurrents in this Living Hall. He exhibited Bellini's *St. Francis* opposite El Greco's *St. Jerome* (fig. 7-50), a juxtaposition that heightened the direct connection of St. Francis to the nature religions and Freemasonry. St. Francis actually went to the Holy Land, stayed with the Templars, and tried to persuade the sultan to return Jerusalem. He was also an architect and builder. When God called him ("Go now, and rebuild my church which is falling into ruins"), St. Francis took a vow of poverty, carried the stones himself, and built his own order. Thus, the story of St. Francis was a parable for the history of Freemasonry; in the Masonic Lodge, Masons see a symbolic reference to him and the rebuilding of Solomon's temple, upon which the concept of the Masonic Lodge is symbolically constructed. No wonder the painting was one of temple-builder Frick's favorites; no wonder Frick exhibited it in the Living Hall—the most central room in the house and a room whose windows open onto the full length of the black-and-white mosaic path and the Royal Arch.

Fig. 7-49. Giovanni Bellini (c. 1430–1516), *St. Francis in the Desert*, c. 1480.
Acquired in 1915, Tempera and oil on poplar panel, 49 x 55⅞ in. (124.4 x 141.9 cm).
The Frick Collection

Fig. 7-50. El Greco (1541–1614), *St. Jerome,* 1590–1600.
Acquired in 1905, Oil on canvas, 43½ x 37½ in. (110.5 x 95.3 cm).
The Frick Collection

Fig. 7-51. John Hoppner (1758–1810), *The Ladies Sarah and Catherine Bligh*, c. 1790
Acquired in 1915, Oil on canvas, 5⅛ x 40⅜ in. (129.8 x 102.5 cm).
The Frick Collection

THE YEAR 1915 was the thirtieth anniversary of Martha's birth, and so, not surprisingly, it was greeted with a burst of event-related paintings. As previously mentioned, the image of Andrew Carnegie arrived in the form of Holbein's *Thomas Cromwell* (see fig. 6-2) and took its place in the Living Hall as a pair to Frick's Holbein look-alike, *Sir Thomas More* (see fig. 6-1). So too the previously mentioned portrait by Francis Cotes (see fig. 3-13) of eight-year-old Francis Vernon entered the collection, a portrait resembling the young Childs Frick at the time of Martha's death.

Fig. 7-52. Attie— Martha Howard Childs. Author's collection

Frick's preoccupation with death and the afterlife continued throughout 1915 when he acquired John Hoppner's portrait of two dark-haired sisters, *The Ladies Sarah and Catherine Bligh* (fig. 7-51), who resemble Frick's wife Adelaide and his recently deceased sister-in-law, Attie (fig. 7-52). As can be seen by comparing it to the 1883 portrait by A. Bryan Wall entitled *Wife and Sister* (see fig. 2-9), commissioned by Frick to honor the sisters' devotion to each other, Frick seems to have again reunited the women, and restored his sister-in-law as a living presence within a family home in

Fig. 7-53. The dining room at 1 East Seventieth Street with Hoppner's *The Ladies Sarah and Catherine Bligh* over the mantel, 1927. Author's collection

Fig. 7-54. Jean-Honoré Fragonard (1732–1806), *The Progress of Love: Reverie*, 1790–91.
Acquired in 1915, Oil on canvas, 125⅛ x 77⅝ in. (317.8 x 197.1 cm).
The Frick Collection

which she would never dwell. As if in recognition of Attie's place in their lives—her constant presence and devotion to Adelaide, Frick, and their children in times of crisis and tragedy—Frick exhibited *The Ladies Sarah and Catherine Bligh* in a place of honor above the dining room mantel (fig. 7-53).

Although Frick's rheumatism had not abated, as 1915 unfolded, his recurring complaint, "the great trouble . . . is these pictures cost too much money," had stilled. He took comfort in his understanding that "it is difficult to estimate the value of a good picture." But as some worries abated, his longing for Martha, his quest for harmony, accelerated. While the drawing room would have to be remodeled to accommodate them, Frick happily paid Joseph Duveen $1.25 million to acquire from J. P. Morgan's estate sale Jean-Honoré Fragonard's exquisite panels, *The Progress of Love,* originally commissioned by the ill-fated Madame du Barry in 1771 for a new dining pavilion in the garden of her chateau at Louveciennes. But Frick also ordered Duveen: "I think by unremitting attention and your personal attendance . . . [the Fragonard Room will accomplish] perfect success in every detail in pure French style and when finished to be beyond the cirticism [*sic*] of any French expert." Surely it is not so difficult to imagine that these love panels, with their abundance of roses, also spoke to the rose of Henry Clay Frick's heart. The impression must have been all the more palpable whenever "The Last Rose of Summer," the theme from Flotlow's opera *Martha,* often played on the orchestrion at Clayton, was played on the organ at 1 East Seventieth Street. Perhaps an echo of Martha's death can even be seen in the muted rose tones of the wilted, roselike girl in the panel *Reverie*—summer's last rose (fig. 7-54).

Frick's psychic life seemed to turn further and further in on itself. As vanloads of Italian and French Renaissance furniture arrived from Duveen's for consideration, he chastised Hastings: "I think [the house] is a great monument to you, but it is only because I restrained you from excessive ornamentation." Oddly, he then pressed him for the completion of another devotional—a gold-gilt organ screen (fig. 7-55) copied from Luca della Robbia's *Singing Children.* It was to be framed by four wine-colored marble columns carved with grapevines, two columns to be graced with the statue of a boy and two with the statue of a girl. The organ screen would stretch across the east wall of the giant stairwell; the marble columns would raise the four statues above the stairwell like a giant altarpiece. Only the statues of one boy and one girl, however, articulate the child-sacrifice theme. Each has a sacrificial ram carved on its pedestal. Each, thereby, represents Frick's two "sacrificial lambs," his two children who had died at the pinnacle of his Carnegie years (fig. 7-56).

Sigmund Freud, one of the first to examine the mourning process, described, in *Mourning and Melancholia,* just what may have been happening to Frick. If the bereaved cannot withdraw the energy binding him to the deceased loved one and

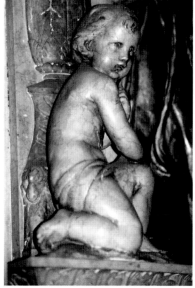

Left: Fig. 7-55. The organ screen with the singing children and four statues possibly representing
Henry Clay Frick's children—the two that lived, the two that died.
Author's collection

Right: Fig. 7-56. The pillar behind the far left statue above the organ screen
has a ram carved beside the girl's lower back.
Author's collection

redirect it to the living, the resistance can be so intense that the bereaved may turn away from reality and cling to the deceased by "a hallucinatory wishful psychosis."

Although Frick's paintings, organ screen, and iconography were symptomatic of this hallucinatory, wishful psychosis, something else was far more telling. In 1915, Frick acquired the Garland Collection of Chinese porcelains, many bronzes, and Limoges enamels from J. P. Morgan's estate, as decorative flourishes. Helen would later explain he bought them so "the rooms would acquire warmth." But the bronzes held a particular fascination for Frick. As if wanting to bring the figures to life, the way his landscapes and portraits so vividly gave birth to images in his mind's eye, he mounted the bronzes on ball bearings so they could easily be studied from every angle. Helen, who as we shall see matured into a highly anxious person, could only have been terrified at seeing the collection revolving at full speed. But Frick, delighted with his invention, played the same joke on the astonished art dealer René Gimpel, whose father in 1904 had sold Frick the daughter look-alikes, *Lady Hamilton* (see fig. 3-18) and *Lady Peel* (see fig. 6-19). Frick sprang from his chair, saying to Gimpel, "Have you seen my new bronzes?" Without waiting for an answer, he added, "Follow me," and took Gimpel into the library, which was lined with low bookcases. As he started one bronze revolving on its ball-bearing mount, he said, "Look at that turning." He then moved around the room making, as Gimpel described, "all the bronzes revolve, and making me go around with him and with them and the room." Gimpel complained, "I would have liked, if not to study them, at least to look at them. But Frick didn't care. The rich child was playing with his toys."

The bronzes, however, were far from toys. When Frick twirled them on their ball bearings, terrifying others as to the object's fate, and starting and stopping them on command, he was controlling both object and person with the same precision he did his own emotions. Stop and start, start and stop. The bronzes allowed Frick to express his longing that fantasy become reality, that he might be able to control the uncontrollable.

On June 24, 1915, however, Frick had brought some measure of control to his life. He signed his will, formalizing his plan to leave his home and his collection to the public. Still suffering from stiff joints and muscle aches, he made his funeral arrangements and ordered a special $5,200 mahogany and bronze coffin lined with blue satin and copper. Sealed at the corners, it was to have a special square end, an engraved inscription, solid copper extension bar handles, and an outside case also of solid copper, braced inside, with all seams sealed. The interior was to be hand-tufted with the best quality Liberty silk, with a hand-tufted mattress—also covered in Liberty silk—and with a matching pillow.

As if to acknowledge the moment, he acquired what would be his fourth and last religious work—Gerard David's plaintive *The Deposition* (fig. 7-57), depicting the Virgin and Mary Magdalen, among others, as they support the dead Christ's body being lifted from the cross. But there is, as the art historian John Russell notes, something unusual about the painting, a singular absence of cruelty: "no real suffering and no real outrage." As he says, Frick chose a version of the Descent from the Cross "where nobody got hurt. Jesus' body is unharmed save for a neat slit on the right side of his chest and two holes on the feet that seem to barely have drawn blood. Even the bystanders are marked . . . by self-control."

When Frick moved into 1 East Seventieth Street, which he described in his will as his "long cherished" and "very dear" dream, he was, in a sense, already dead. Indeed, within the fantasy world he had created, and with the constant covert expectation that the dead can return, a vicious cycle had developed. With the hoped-for reunion never occurring, the loss was constantly reexperienced, the wound constantly reopened.

Fig. 7-57. Gerard David (active 1484–1523), *The Deposition*, 1510-15.
Acquired in 1915, Oil on canvas, 56⅛ x 44¼ in. (142.5 x 112.4 cm).
The Frick Collection

Appropriately, then, in this thirtieth anniversary of Martha's life, when Frick's poignant associations among art, Martha, and deceased family and friends were heightened, Frick extended his hand to the children of others. Though Frick did this consistently and anonymously throughout his life, this time his gesture was discovered. On Christmas Eve, 1915, just two months before his first grandchild was born, Pittsburgh's Bank for Savings failed. Frick held no position in the bank, but he did support the Pittsburgh Board of Education in encouraging children to make regular deposits. He, therefore, made good the $170,000 lost by thousands of children who had entrusted their money to the bank.

❖

HENRY CLAY FRICK HAD ENTERED what would be his last four years of collecting. Although he remained an active golfer (fig. 7-58) and as practical as ever when handling business matters, he dropped so deeply into the spirit world, he would seem fully absorbed by the portrait faces and landscapes before him. George Harvey has noted: "[Frick] loved [his paintings] with a passion as tender as he felt for little children. They rested him, refreshed his mind, soothed his spirit." When alone with his paintings Frick was a different man than the one who dashed through museums and galleries at high speed. As Harvey writes, "Often late at night, at the end of a trying day, when perfect stillness reigned, [Frick] would slip noiselessly, almost furtively, into the darkened gallery, turn on the lights and sit for an hour or more, first on one divan then on another, absorbing solace and happiness through the mirrors of his heart before seeking the mental and physical relaxation of dreamless sleep."

Frick's secretary, James Howard Bridge, noticed a similar effect. Bridge would return to the deserted gallery in the morning and "find [Frick's] cigar ashes around a chair that had been drawn up in front of some old friend."

Helen noted of her father:

> He took so much joy in his paintings, and loved changing them around. . . . I love to think of him in that beautiful room [the West Gallery]—of his wonderful appreciation and understanding of everything there, and the accuracy of his memory when he recounted little incidents connected with the different pictures and how he came to acquire them. He used to say that if he could be given the choice of different kinds of ability, he would prefer being a painter like Rembrandt than anything else.

Fig. 7-58. Henry Clay Frick playing golf in Palm Beach, c. 1916.
UPI/Corbis-Bettmann

Beyond this, however, Sir Joseph Duveen and Sir Charles Allom had invented such a remarkable system of illuminating Frick's portraits and landscapes, they seemed alive. Each one had its own spotlight concealed in the glass ceiling, directed so the light fell only on the canvas, while the frame and surrounding wall were lost in shadow. This system, in Bridge's words, caused visitors "to protest that they have seen changing expressions on the faces of the men and women on the walls." For him, the method of illumination "gave the portraits a weird semblance of light." He claimed that when "sitting alone in their midst, it was easy for me to imagine them as stepping out of the frame and joining each other in friendly talk."

Frick often walked the galleries (fig. 7-59) with his daughter Helen and sighed as he looked at his portraits, "How interesting it would be if all these people could come to life and tell us what they know." To Bridge he mused, "If only they could talk." Bridge would reply, "But they can and they do." Frick's response was, "Well then, what do they say?" Delighted by Bridge's ensuing stories, Frick invariably exclaimed, "I wish you would write that down." Although Bridge had signed an agreement never to discuss the intimate relationship of Frick to his paintings, many years later he did note that when Frick recounted the details of his portrait subjects' lives, he did so as if he had "spoken of some event in his own life." Bridge claimed that "the portraits had become his friends and acquaintances, something more than mere paint and varnish."

And yet, although Frick was personally and deeply involved with his collection, he often asked Helen or anyone present, "Come into the Gallery and let's look at the pictures." It seemed his greatest pleasure came from others enjoying his possessions, most particularly his paintings. For as much as Helen regularly walked through the collection with him, she could not recall his ever refusing anyone admittance. "Certainly they shall have a[n admission] card," she remembered his saying. "Come any day you wish." So much pleasure was derived from others seeing his paintings, he would often step silently in, observe the observers, and then, just as softly, steal out again, unnoticed.

Helen had long understood the healing powers her father's pictures held for him. As we know, her father relished packing up his collection and taking it to Eagle Rock for the summer, a pattern that continued at 1 East Seventieth Street. But as he moved from house to house with his paintings, Helen came to notice how, after moving into his new home, his spirits would lift when the fall season arrived and the paintings

Fig. 7-59. Walter Gay (1856–1937), *Living Hall, 1 East Seventieth Street*, commissioned by Helen Clay Frick, 1926. Oil on canvas, 20 x 26 in. (50.8 x 66 cm). The Frick Art Museum, Pittsburgh

were once again placed in the West Gallery. Of this phenomenon, she wrote, "It seemed as though he could scarcely wait to get back to the Gallery, and after everything was back in place again, he always said, 'the pictures look most beautiful.'"

And beautiful they were. Whether or not he or others fully understood the way these paintings were anchored to Frick's psyche, all could certainly appreciate their harmony of color and artistic brilliance. Throughout 1916, as Henry Clay Frick played golf, monitored his fortune, and honored his directorships, he collected gem after gem and continued to satisfy his love of finery. Frick acquired Gainsborough's *The Mall in*

Fig. 7-60. Thomas Gainsborough (1727-1788), *The Mall in St. James's Park*, c. 1783.
Acquired in 1916, Oil on canvas, 47½ x 57⅞ in. (120.6 x 147 cm).
The Frick Collection

St. James's Park (fig. 7-60), a reflection of the tough-minded (fig. 7-61) industrialist's continuing appreciation of feminine beauty. Indeed, a notation in a diary from his 1912 trip to Egypt indicates Frick's enduring interest in women's clothes. He bought what his daughter described as "twin gowns" in Europe for herself and her sister-in-law to be, Frances Dixon of Baltimore. But of all these examples, his 1915 letter to his daughter-in-law's artistic sister Polly Dixon (who stayed with Helen at 1 East Seventieth Street and took art classes) is the most poignant. In coaxing her to accept his gift of fine clothes, Frick wrote: "It is so innocent, but it really does please the ladies to have fine clothes." In this same letter, he queried, "I wonder if Adelaide [his granddaughter, born in February 1915 and living with her parents in Baltimore] will have a taste for such things when she reaches your age? I am inclined to think that having been born in Philadelphia, she will be exceedingly quiet in her taste and will dress almost entirely in gray."

Fig. 7-61. Henry Clay Frick in Palm Beach, c. 1915. UPI/Corbis-Bettmann

Perhaps because his own wife had retreated to a mourning wardrobe of black and his daughter Helen later insisted on being a plain dresser, Frick continued to feed his love of fine clothing by surrounding himself with his elegant ladies. Gainsborough's *Mall in St. James's Park* certainly depicts a favorite pastime of the collector, walking in parks and watching the ladies. Said Frick of the painting, "I think [it] in every respect a superb picture." And one can understand why. One day, after sitting by the Enamel Room window watching the ladies walk down Fifth Avenue, he said sadly, "No great beauties out today." In fact, as much as Frick loved collecting anecdotes about his portrait subjects' lives, the way real people looked and moved was of keen interest to him. Fascinated by mannerisms, he often sat either by his private sitting room window on the second floor, or at the library window beside his desk, or in the Enamel Room overlooking Fifth Avenue noting the characteristic way people walked.

Whistler's lovely *Mrs. Leyland* came this year too, but Frick remained possessed by his nightmare. Indeed, during this time he acquired the haunting *Miss Louisa Murray* (see fig. 4-18) and placed it to the right of his bed. *Old Woman with a Book* (see fig. 1-29)

also arrived, works we have suggested reminded Frick of his lost daughter and of his grandmother and spiritual mainstay.

More significant, in 1916 he purchased the contemporary artist Eugène Carrière's *Motherhood* (fig. 7-62) featuring a subject much like Adelaide, who was now a grandmother (fig. 7-63). Carrière was known to the Fricks and painted many scenes of mothers holding their children and babies, often using his own wife and friends as models. *The Sick Child* is believed to be a portrait of his own child who, like Martha, had died an untimely death.

As if in recognition of the similarity between Carrière's subject and Adelaide, Frick placed *Motherhood* in his second-floor sitting room next to *Purification of the Temple*, with its Homestead implications and image of Abraham about to sacrifice his son Isaac as an expression of faith. Perhaps this juxtaposition was yet another example of his recognition of the price he and Adelaide had paid during the Homestead strike and a further expression of Frick's desire for a grandson to replace his namesake.

While Frick continued to be haunted by the death of his children, he also acquired his entire François Boucher collection: *The Four Seasons, Girl with Roses,* and eight exquisite panels, *The Arts and Sciences*—works depicting children enacting all the creative endeavors of the human soul (fig. 7-64). The Boucher panels covered the walls of Adelaide's New York boudoir (fig. 7-65) and re-created something familiar to her—the two enormous collages of Martha and the infant Henry Clay Frick, Jr., that lined her Clayton bedroom (fig. 7-66).

Of these panels, one, *Painting and Sculpture,* is particularly revealing. It shows a young boy sculpting a bust of a young girl. This bust, acquired by Frick in 1914, is a copy of *Bust of a Young Girl* (fig. 7-67) by the famous French sculptor François-Jacques-Joseph Saly. Able now to unite this bust with *Painting and Sculpture,* the Fricks, in placing the Saly bust beneath the panel, created yet another poignant reminder of Martha. The girl's sorrowful mouth and dejected, troubled eyes recall Andreoni's bust of a petulant Martha at Clayton (fig. 7-68)—particularly since Saly's subject was then believed to be Madame de Pompadour's daughter Alexandrine d'Etoiles, who had died at an early age.

Martha had been dead twenty-four years, but with the Saly bust beneath the Boucher panel, longing for Martha and the need to feel her as a living presence could only have been increased. Together, the Boucher panels and Saly bust in 1 East Seventieth Street, and the collages and Andreoni bust of Martha in Clayton, underscore how the tragedy, like waves rolling ashore, left Frick and Adelaide a legacy of grief that could not be stilled.

Henry Clay Frick's reaction to a request from the director of the Cleveland Art Museum evidenced his state of mind. Frick often lent his paintings to museums for

Above: Fig. 7-62. Eugène Carrière (1849–1906), *Motherhood,* c. 1880s.
Acquired in 1916, Oil on canvas, 22 x 18¼ in. (55.8 x 46.3 cm).
The Frick Collection

Right: Fig. 7-63. Adelaide Howard Childs Frick as a grandmother, c. 1917.
Author's collection

Fig. 7-64. François Boucher (1703-1770),
The Arts and Sciences: Painting and Sculpture, 1750-53.
Acquired in 1916, Oil on canvas, 85½ x 30½ in. (217.2 x 77.5 cm).
The Frick Collection

Top: Fig. 7-65. The boudoir of Adelaide Howard Childs Frick
at 1 East Seventieth Street, 1927.
Author's collection

Bottom: Fig. 7-66. Adelaide Howard Childs Frick made
a collage of Martha for her Clayton bedroom, c. 1893.
Frick Art and Historical Center

Left: Fig. 7-67. After François-Jacques-Joseph Saly (1717–76), *Bust of a Young Girl.*
Acquired in 1914, Marble, H. 11¾ in. (30 cm).
The Frick Collection, gift of Helen Clay Frick, 1934

Right: Fig. 7-68. Orazio Andreoni, *Portrait of Martha Howard Frick,* 1893.
Commissioned in 1893, Marble, 22½ x 13½ in (57.2 x 34.3 cm)
Frick Art and Historical Center

exhibition, but when the Cleveland director asked him for all the paintings from the West Gallery to exhibit in their opening, Frick replied with his traditional dark humor: "I have your letter of today with Mr. Whiting's letter of the 20th enclosed. I regret that I cannot comply with his *modest* [author's italics] request and his letter to you is herewith returned." Frick did, however, offer to lend the museum Dagnan-Bouveret's *Consolatrix Afflictorum* (see fig. 5-23) instead, but the director declined, saying the painting was too "high in key" for their exhibition. Of course, for Frick, the lugubrious painting with its portrait-like rendition of family members, combined with themes of soul loss, quest for peace, as well as childhood death and resurrection, *was* the ultimate symbol of his entire collection, the "high key" dynamic that fueled his art-collecting passion and fascinated his collector's eye.

❖

Fig. 7-69. James Abbott McNeill Whistler (1834–1903),
Valerie, Lady Meux, 1881.
Acquired in 1918, Oil on canvas, 76¼ x 36⅝ in. (193.7 x 93 cm).
The Frick Collection

By April 1917, Henry Clay Frick saw his $6 million William Penn Hotel and the Union Trust Building, both located in downtown Pittsburgh within a block of his now famous Frick Building, completed. Also by this time, he had spent approximately $12 million on art. David T. Watson, Henry Clay Frick's art-collector friend and lawyer died that same year, and his will stipulated that his art collection be sold and the proceeds used to build a hospital for crippled children on his property. Frick, when asked if he would like to buy any of the paintings, declined.

Fig. 7-70. Nora McMullen Mellon.
Collection of Paul Mellon

Frick's feverish collecting pace was now on the wane. In 1917 and 1918, he did, however, add two more Van Dycks, a Hals, a Gainsborough, two Paters, and a work then attributed to de Hoogh to his collection. He bought a portrait by Reynolds of Lady Cecil Rice, who wears a red rose in her bodice, and he acquired Whistler's *Valerie, Lady Meux* (fig. 7-69), a portrait continuing Frick's familiar pattern of visualizing people lost to him in real life. Lady Meux, a barmaid who married a famous brewer from Hertfordshire, England, bears a certain similarity to Nora Mary McMullen (fig. 7-70), daughter of a famous Hertfordshire brewing family. Nora McMullen married Frick's closest friend and equal shareholder in the Overholt Distillery at Broad Ford, Andrew Mellon, in 1900. She, like Lady Meux, was eccentric and flamboyant. In 1910, the same year Lady Meux died, after a difficult marriage and an angry separation, Nora McMullen Mellon and Andrew filed for divorce. Their divorce became final in 1918, the year Frick bought *Lady Meux*.

Lady Meux also connected Frick to his Masonic heritage. As one of her many colorful acts, she preserved the Temple Bar, a famous Masonic gateway to London, and had it erected on her estate called Theobolds, outside London. Even more fascinating, she was a collector of Egyptian mummies and relics. One such acquisition was a mummy whose coffin bears an inscription promising that the person daring to remove the mummy from its resting place would die childless and suffer a horrible death. Apparently Lady Meux invoked the curse. The man who sold her the mummy was later gored to death by an elephant in Somaliland; Lady Meux was never able to have children.

Frick's final Masonic gesture, however, rests in his purchase of a Gilbert Stuart portrait of George Washington (fig. 7-71), Father of Our Country and, because Washington had his own rye whiskey distilling operation, known also as the Father of the

Fig. 7-71. Gilbert Stuart (1755-1828), *George Washington,* 1795-96.
Acquired in 1918, Oil on canvas, 29¼ x 24 in. (74.3 x 60.9 cm).
The Frick Collection

Fig. 7-72. Currier and Ives, *Washington as a Mason*, 1868.
Engraving.
Courtesy of the Masonic Library and Museum of Pennsylvania

Rye Whiskey Industry. The portrait, acquired in 1918, is significantly the only painting of an American by an American in Frick's New York collection. Moreover, Washington's associations with the region of Frick's youth and fortune extended beyond the former president's own early manhood. He became the leading landowner in western Pennsylvania and owner of a gristmill in Perryopolis, just downstream from the Overholts' Broad Ford distillery. Washington was also considered "a paragon of Freemasonry, an exemplar of its virtues and its graces." He aspired to all Degrees and attained them. He became a Mason in 1752 and was Master of his Lodge. In 1755, as he led the remaining troops to safety after General Braddock's failed attempt to drive the French from the Point in Pittsburgh, George Washington was the only officer not wounded or killed, even though four bullets penetrated his coat. Such an icon was Washington that one of the requirements for all Masonic Lodges is the conspicuous display of his portrait or bust in the Lodge Room (fig. 7-72). No accident, then, that Frick paid the highest price ever for a work by an American artist to secure it. No accident, either, that he chose to exhibit Washington's portrait in his business office at 1 East Seventieth

Street, a room which, like the Enamel Room, also had access to the room called the Bowling Alley.

In July 1918, four years after Frick executed his will, he succeeded in persuading Philander Knox and the U.S. Senate to alter the inheritance tax law so that his heirs would not have to pay a tax on his gift to the public of his house, paintings, and objects of art. Saying he had no objection to a tax on money going to "one of the family," Frick argued successfully that "it did not seem to be just" that his estate would have to pay $10 to $12 million in taxes when his money had been spent over a great many years for the public's benefit.

On October 16, 1918, Charles Knoedler wrote Carstairs in London, "Frick comes in once or twice a week & he never looked better." But he lamented the fact that "there is no business as you know & for some time to come." Although Knoedler had rightly sensed a slowing of Frick's collecting pace, he may well have known Frick's mourning had not abated. In 1919, Frick's seventieth birthday year, and his wife's sixtieth, Knoedler sold Frick Vermeer's *Mistress and Maid* (see fig. 3-15)—the painting recalling the "jewel casket" coffin in which Martha had been buried twenty-eight years before, the painting evoking the frantic correspondence between Frick and his wife in Martha's final days. The last painting Henry Clay Frick acquired, and the only known acquisition of 1919, it arrived at Eagle Rock on the dual anniversary of Martha's death and birth. So drawn was Frick to the painting, in order to have a constant view, he changed his seat at Eagle Rock's dining room table.

By that time, Henry Clay Frick had lived in his "grave surviving death" for five years. Unbeknownst to him, or anyone else, the arrival of *Mistress and Maid* announced the coming end of his mourning. Henry Clay Frick had only four months to live.

❖

EARLY IN HIS BUSINESS CAREER, Henry Clay Frick was asked by a friend whose identity remains unknown, why he, Frick, tried to continue increasing his fortune. Frick replied, "I want money only for the use I can make of it." A few days before his death on December 2, 1919, however, Frick would be talking to another friend, a prominent businessman of wealth known for his tremendous popularity and happy disposition. Although Frick had obviously made great use of his own fortune, he told this friend earnestly, "I am very much richer than you, but I would gladly exchange my wealth for yours if at the same time I could exchange what I get out of my life for what you get out of it." Apparently Frick not only envied this man's popularity, his ability to make friends, and his capacity to enjoy life, but confessed that "it hurt him to think that his fellowmen regarded him as a cold blooded man of affairs interested only in money-making."

This blistering stigma would forever remain synonymous with Henry Clay Frick's name. Humble when responding to questions about his incredible success, he would simply reply: "The demands of modern life . . . called for such works as ours; and if we had not met the demands others would have done so. Even without us the steel industry of the country would have been just as great as it is, though men would have used other names when speaking of its leaders."

This leader, however, would soon leave five-sixths of his now $150 million fortune (approximately $1.4 billion today) to charity. He would also give the public a building and art collection of incomparable beauty (fig. 7-73). And although undoubtedly satisfied that his estate would not be required to pay a substantial inheritance tax, and that he would leave the public a shrine to honor his beloved lost daughter, he could also take comfort in the fact that he had created a place to commune with spirits past. His fortune and his melancholy, however, had done little more than isolate him from his fellowman.

Fig. 7-73. Entrance, 1 East Seventieth Street.
Author's collection

CHAPTER VIII

Final Days

Oh, that I had wings like a dove.

—Psalm 55

AT THE CLOSE OF THE 1919 SUMMER, when Frick was leaving Eagle Rock for New York, his death knell sounded in an ominous way. Helen had a foreboding about her father. He had fainted a number of times and was looking frail. Although he played golf regularly, walked every day, and swam on Eagle Rock's private beach, Helen became anxious about his health, insisting he wear a coat when he traveled in the car. When her father departed for the long drive to 1 East Seventieth Street, he refused to heed her advice. Helen quietly placed a coat on the back seat; although Frick always claimed, "Health is the greatest blessing in the world—without it life would not be worth living," on discovering the coat, he threw it out the car window.

At sixty-nine years of age, he had grown stouter and, as René Gimpel noted, "a more advanced stage of old age accented his crumbling face." His pink complexion was now patchy, his thick white beard finer, but his cold eyes, traditionally grasping and hard under their genial look, remained the same clear, beautiful blue.

Unknown to Frick or others, his heart, damaged by his 1914 attack of inflammatory rheumatism, was weakening. Nevertheless, he was still as mentally tough as he had ever been. Four million American workers had gone out on strike that year and when U.S. Steel fortified its mills against attack and Judge Elbert H. Gary took a tough stand against the strike leaders, Frick complimented him: "You have done your country a great and lasting service. I was glad to see you said that you would not treat with Gompers or with any other Union leaders who come to you as Union men, and that there would be no compromise—That's the stuff!"

With the help of James A. Reed of Missouri, Philander Knox, and other influential Republican senators, Frick lobbied hard to support Henry Cabot Lodge's effort to defeat the League of Nations. Commenting on the plan to allow two-thirds of the league, debtor nations all, to make decisions, Frick said, "Why it seems to me a crazy thing to do."

Of the railroads, his largest investment and the source of his greatest income, however, Frick harbored great concern. In the fall of 1919, with World War I over, the government was about to return the greatly deteriorated railroads to their original owners. During the war, the government had been unable to obtain either capital, labor, or materials for adequate maintenance. The owners had had no choice but to watch helplessly as the government ran their railroads and physically destroyed their property, understanding that winning the war depended upon centralized operation of the railroads. Trains not only moved troops and war materiel, as well as civilian passengers and freight, but they also consumed nearly one-third of the nation's bituminous mined coal and used 40 percent of its steel and iron products. The 635 individual railroad companies had willingly given the War Board power of attorney over their separate properties. No other American industry had been so completely patriotic, and certainly, no other American industry equaled the railroads in manpower and equipment.

With the transfer of the railroads from government to private hands imminent, the owners petitioned Congress for a raise in the rate scale to help underwrite the necessary restoration and rebuilding of their property. Congress began efforts to legislate these rates, but progress was slow. Walker D. Hines, a close personal friend of Frick's who had traveled to Egypt with him and who became a trustee of the Frick Collection after Frick's death, served as director general of the railroads. On October 17, 1919, Frick sent Hines a letter expressing his deep distress about "the appalling conditions which now confront us as a part of the aftermath of the war." Demanding "something must be done at once to avert overwhelming disaster," and concerned about "the dangers which lurk in delay," he insisted the element of "time" was most essential. He wrote: "What the country needs now above all else is restoration of confidence . . . through prompt and decisive action such as would follow naturally and logically your admirable diagnosis." Using the human circulatory system as metaphor for the railroads, Frick went on to note that the circulation of goods was more important than the circulation of money. He expressed his hope that the railroad properties "be given a chance to live and to obtain readily on a fair basis the vast amount of capital whose outlay alone can prevent the choking of the great arteries of commerce."

Further into the letter, however, his metaphor of the circulatory system attained a deeper significance. Although Frick did not mention Martha's death from septicemia, the analogy to her suffocation was explicit. Frick was a life trustee of the Homeopathic Medical and Surgical Hospital and Dispensary in Pittsburgh, an honor one suspects was accompanied by a certain ambivalence, given his decision to treat

Martha's symptoms homeopathically rather than surgically. In 1910, Abraham Flexner, an authority on higher education, particularly in medicine, issued a report that caused sweeping changes in the curriculum and teaching methods in American colleges. Homeopathy was one discipline that fell to his axe. By 1919 many schools no longer taught it at all, and most homeopathic schools had closed. Thus, in his letter Frick insisted: "Upon one point I do not hesitate to express a very positive opinion. . . . Desperate diseases call for drastic remedies. Homeopathic doses in the present condition would be hardly better than none at all." As Frick pressed Hines for a decision, he warned: "It is upon your shoulders and there is no escape."

But as much as the railroad crisis was a reference to Martha's deterioration and his own wrong decision about her medical care, his analogy of the railroads to an impaired circulatory system was a portent of his own death—a death precipitated by ingestion of a fatal substance, exacerbated by wrong medical decisions and his own stubbornness.

Although Frick's final decline lasted only four weeks, not four years as had Martha's, in that time his circulatory system, like the malfunctioning delivery and pick-up system of the railroad, would be impeded. As his diseased heart became increasingly unable to pump blood forward through his circulatory system, fluid from the backed-up blood in the veins would leach into his lungs and other organs. His ankles and other extremities would swell, and as his heart pumped faster and faster to put out more blood, the diseased organ would continue to weaken under the strain. With his heart working against itself, much as his immune system had attacked its own body during his childhood illnesses, Frick's breath would become short, insufficient oxygen would enter his bloodstream, and as the situation developed into a self-feeding, self-destructive cycle, his diseased heart would fail.

I N November 1919, while a coal strike spread nationwide, Frick organized an important luncheon at 1 East Seventieth Street with Boise Penrose, head of the Republican political machine. Frick's daughter Helen—who, unlike her now married brother Childs, still at age thirty-one lived at home with her elderly parents and remained devoted to them—asked if he wanted her to look over the menu. Frick responded that he had already done so and mentioned he had ordered lobster as an entrée. Helen became alarmed because lobster never agreed with him. She begged him to serve something else, but Frick refused, saying, "It agrees with me perfectly now,"

Fig. 8-1. Living Hall in 1 East Seventieth Street where the Frick family enjoyed after-dinner coffee.
Author's collection

and switched his attention to the maids' recent request for a $5 increase in wages due to the cost of shoes and the dilemma of removing the marks made by their white, high-heeled shoes on the floors.

That night, after having dinner with her parents, Helen felt tired and said she thought she would go to bed. According to the diary written to reconstruct the last month of her father's life, Helen had been sitting with her parents in the Living Hall beneath El Greco's *St. Jerome* (fig. 8-1). Frick had been reading the newspaper in the big chair by the right of the sofa while Adelaide played solitaire on the other side. Frick, who was not ready to retire, asked Helen if she would wait for him, whereupon Adelaide said, "Oh, let her go up, she's so tired." Just as Frick replied, "Let her answer for herself," Helen said to her father, "Of course I'll wait." She went over to him, sat alongside his chair, and a few minutes later, walked arm-in-arm with him to the main stair hall.

When they entered the hall, however, her father suddenly went to the hall bench and sat down. Helen asked if he was feeling faint, and when he admitted he was, she dashed up the marble staircase to get him aromatic spirits of ammonia. After taking some, he said it had helped him "very much," but he nevertheless decided to take the elevator to the second floor, rather than climb the stairs. He then confessed to Helen that the lobster must have indeed disagreed with him, as he felt swollen. Helen begged him to take a purgative. He promised to do so later, at midnight, but Helen, fearful her father would not, entered his room, mixed the medicine for him, and with the help of Frick's valet, Oscar, gave him the tonic.

For the next month his health deteriorated, as did his mood.

In the first week of illness, Helen gave him a compound cathartic pill and went to the drugstore where she bought two doses of castor oil, one of which she gave him in mid-afternoon. Later in the day, her father scolded her, "You're no kind of a doctor— that medicine of yours never acted, so I took the second dose."

When Frick's daughter-in-law Frances came to visit and asked how he was feeling, he said he was "fine." He confessed he had lost over six pounds and joked of his newborn grandson and namesake, "if the baby had lost as many pounds as he had in the last day and a half, he wouldn't be here at all."

Though Frick made light of the situation, for the next few days he seemed to drag himself around. He spent a great deal of time on the couch in the library beneath Hogarth's *Miss Mary Edwards* (fig. 8-2), and as he made his way to his office (fig. 8-3),

Fig. 8-2. The library in 1 East Seventieth Street, 1927, where Henry Clay Frick stretched out on the sofa and rested.
Author's collection

Fig. 8-3. Henry Clay Frick's business office in 1 East Seventieth Street.
Author's collection

decorated with the black-on-black Whistlers, Goya's Vanderbilt look-alikes, and Gilbert Stuart's *George Washington* (see fig. 7-71), he often sat a few minutes in the hall on a bench drawn up to the courtyard window, so he could get a sunbath.

Some days during this first week of illness, he went to the Links Club for lunch and sometimes went for a drive in the car. A trustee of the Grant Monument Association, he asked the chauffeur to take him to Grant's tomb across town on Riverside Drive, built in 1892 during the Homestead steel strike. There, Frick's thoughts returned to his Homestead civil war. Perhaps his mind was occupied by the victorious Union commander and later eighteenth president of the United States, who remained haunted by the memory of his men lying three and four bodies deep. Whatever Frick's thoughts may have been as he circled the tomb, when he returned home he asked Helen to have the "Ave Maria" played on the organ and listened to the pleading strains, "Pray, oh, pray for us wretched sinners / Now and when the hour of our death o'er takes us."

One day, Helen walked with him in the walled garden along the Fifth Avenue side of the house. They sat in the sun, looking at the Masonic, black-and-white mosaic path of fertility symbols. Later that day at lunch, as he sat in the dining room with Romney's *Henrietta, Countess of Warwick, and Her Children,* Hoppner's *The Ladies Sarah and Catherine Bligh,* and Gainsborough's *The Mall in St. James's Park* (see figs. 7-3, 51, 60), Frick confessed to Helen he could not bear the thought of being an invalid. He said he would rather not live if he could not do things.

A friend, Mrs. James B. A. Fosberg, stopped in to see him and they had a spirited time together. The first thing Frick said to her was, "How much did you pay for your

Fig. 8-4. The front hall in 1 East Seventieth Street.
Author's collection

shoes? Every maid in the house has asked for a $5.00 increase in wages, on account of the price of shoes." He then admired her hat and said he approved of her suit, whereupon the two of them proceeded to have a heated argument on the subject of "baby bonds." As they conversed, Frick asked her if she had heard that his newest grandchild had been named after him. Mrs. Fosberg said she did know, but "thought it pretty rough on the baby."

"Oh, no," Frick quipped, as he pulled about twenty gold pieces out of his pocket and showed them to her: "I'm feeding him on gold pieces."

When Mrs. Fosberg told him she "supposed he was pawning off counterfeits on the poor baby," Frick responded, "Yes, I have Oscar make them in the cellar." He then departed for his club, "to make," as he said to her, "more for his grandson." Not to be outdone, Mrs. Fosberg made the suggestion that "the grandson might be better off if he [Frick] left what he had already made, at home." As Helen recalled this scene in the front hall (fig. 8-4), her father, "not deigning to reply . . . went out jingling the gold in his pockets."

Before he left, Adelaide and Helen tried to persuade Frick to wear a coat as protection against the damp November air, but as he had done at Eagle Rock a few months

Fig. 8-5. The West Gallery in 1 East Seventieth Street where
Henry Clay Frick often stretched out on a sofa and slept.
Author's collection

before, he refused. The following morning, concerned because she did not find her father in his room, Helen searched the house and discovered him lying on a couch in the West Gallery (fig. 8-5) facing Goya's *The Forge* and Velázquez's portrait of the great collector, King Philip IV of Spain. He had been sick for eight days and now, in addition to having suffered a bad reaction to the lobster, he had contracted a cold and bad cough. Concerned, Helen, who as we shall see, had been a Red Cross nurse in France during the war (fig. 8-6), seized control of his medical care. She called a Dr. Evans, explaining to her father that Dr. Garmany, who had treated his inflammatory rheumatism in 1914 and of whom she had remained suspicious since Martha's death, was not free at the time. After examining Frick, Dr. Evans said her father had a heart block. He explained, however, that "with great care" her father could get along with it for probably ten years.

Worried about this new development, Helen and Adelaide fussed over Frick a great deal and called a Dr. Lewis who came to treat his throat for laryngitis. Helen ordered her father a night nurse and sent him some pink roses with a card that read, "From your best girl." Frick laughed and said, "You are that."

Bedridden and into the second week of illness, Frick received daily visits from Judge Gary, held board meetings for U.S. Steel and the Atchison, Topeka and Santa Fe Railroad in the house, hosted a number of government notables as he continued to lobby to keep the country out of the League of Nations, and discussed art and business with Andrew Mellon. His delight, however, lay in visits from his grandchildren (fig. 8-7). He asked constantly, "When are the children coming?"

His legs and ankles were badly swollen and to add to the household problems, Adelaide, too, had come down with a cold. Though she visited her husband on occasion, during the remaining days of his illness she stayed in her room most of the time, in bed, afraid her cold might make him worse. One afternoon, Frick suddenly dressed and announced he was going out. Helen, ever alert, was able to dissuade him by insisting it was too late and too dark. She brought him into her own little sitting room, and after a visit from J. P. Grier, Frick admitted "he had decided himself not to go out but didn't let on," because Helen had looked so frightened he didn't want to scare her.

Fig. 8-6. Helen, who served as a Red Cross nurse during the war, seized control of her father's medical care.
Pittsburgh Post-Gazette

As he entered his third week of illness, Frick seemed to be realizing that he was indeed a very sick man. He asked his nurse to "go down and ask Miss Helen to look up the Sermon on the Mount for me," adding curtly, "Do you know what that is?" As the afternoon shadows lengthened, he read it, as well as other passages from the Bible. That night, because he was unable to sleep, he sat on the edge of his bed rereading the words so often read to him by his mother and grandmother as he fought for his life through childhood and early manhood.

Finally allowed downstairs to sit with his pictures, he lay on the library couch with a fire blazing beneath Hogarth's portrait of Miss Mary Edwards. Although Frances and Childs wanted Frick in the care of a famous heart specialist from Roosevelt Hospital, Helen—who had witnessed the devastation to culture and human life at German hands during World War I and had developed an inexplicable phobia about Germans—refused to admit him because he had a German-sounding name. In the meantime, much to the concern of both Helen and Childs, Dr. Evans had prescribed an hour's drive through the park. Knowing their father's independent streak, and doubtful he would permit either child to accompany him, they feared Frick might do

Fig. 8-7. Henry Clay Frick's three granddaughters: Martha, Frances, and Adelaide Frick.
Author's Collection

Fig. 8-8. Clayton, Long Island, the house Henry Clay Frick bought
for his daughter-in-law, Frances Dixon Frick.
Author's collection

something impulsive, like drive to Westbury, Long Island—where Childs and Frances's new home, Clayton (fig. 8-8), was located—to see the house and his new grandson.

In the end, Helen managed to join Frick in the car, but as father and daughter approached the corner of Fifth Avenue, he asked Helen, "Did you tell George [the chauffeur] where to go?"

She replied, "Yes, to the park."

Angered, he said, "No, not the park—to Westbury."

Frightened, Helen implored him not to do something so rash. But she protested in vain. Her father turned to her and told her to "obey his orders or get out of the car."

Helen stayed in the car, but begged him to stop at the house for a minute. He said "very well," and when they returned to 1 East Seventieth Street, Helen ran inside, found the nurse, told her to get in her car with all the necessary medicines and to follow quickly, keeping out of sight, until they reached Clayton.

Helen described the ride with her father as being "full of anxiety to me . . . it seemed such a terrible risk. We talked very little and he dozed frequently. . . . It took 45-50 minutes to reach [Childs's] house in Westbury and we were surprised when we turned in at the gates as we had never been there before."

She was also surprised because the nurse had actually arrived first. Helen could see her car parked under the porte cochere, in full sight; however, greatly to her relief, as she wrote in her diary, "Papa never suspected."

René Gimpel once described Frick as having "a rather hard gaze. His features are so regular, his face so pleasant, that he seems benevolent, but at certain moments you see and comprehend that you were mistaken, that his head is there, placed on that body, for his triumph and your defeat." According to Neil Vanderbilt, Frick was "not a man to be permitted in the same room with children."

As far as his grandchildren were concerned, however, Frick was another man. As described by Helen in a diary entitled "Grandfather":

"Papsie!" what a host of happy tender memories this name calls forth, standing for all that is most dear and precious to me. . . . I see that splendid head of his, with its silvery white hair and beard—his large fine brow and clear blue eyes that look you through and through, but with such kindness and sense of humor. His voice, I hear, in its richness and softness of tone—"Well here come the Babies," and out [would] go both his arms to welcome you with hugs.

As she also explained:

Your welfare and happiness were the two things that lay nearest to his heart; that you should have a beautiful home and a splendid, rounded education, were his chief desires for you. . . . frequently he would remark that he wanted you to grow up with good judgment. He never tired of planning how to make you happy—he looked far into the future, and did all in his power to lay the foundation for what he hoped would be useful, contented lives. . . . And yet, he couldn't bear to have you scolded or deprived of anything; if he caught anyone doing either of these things, he would say, "Don't bother her, you don't know how to handle children!"

As Helen noted, her sixty-nine-year-old father was a man who took comfort from a child's warm look, a man who often said, "That child smiled for me." In writing for her niece Adelaide in her adult years, Helen recalled, "Tiny as you were, you seemed to realize that the sweetest smiles you had belonged to Grandfather, and he usually left you thoroughly proud and satisfied."

Frick's joy in the granddaughters was boundless, and so was his pride (figs. 8-9, 10). Frick often commented on the shape of a person's head, indicating whether or not he felt they "had brains." In fact, when he returned from seeing his first grandchild, Adelaide, born February 7, 1915, in Philadelphia, he offered glowing accounts of her "well shaped head and beautifully formed hands." He was convinced from the start that the shape of his first granddaughter's head promised superior intelligence and "good business ability." When Adelaide was only a few months

Figs. 8-9, 10. Henry Clay Frick with his granddaughters
Adelaide and Frances Frick *(above)* and with Adelaide *(below)*.
Author's collection, Frick Archives

old, he carried her into the West Gallery. After walking the length of the room, he insisted she showed "great powers of observation," because her attention was "held by the paintings that were the most worthwhile." So fascinated was he by heads, when his fourth grandchild was born in 1919—his long awaited grandson and namesake— his first remark to his wife, Adelaide, was "I want to know if he has a good head?" She replied, "Well come to think of it, his head is just like yours."

As grandfather, Henry Clay Frick played leapfrog with the children and, with great amounts of laughter, slid down the sliding board at Eagle Rock with them, landing, as his biographer Harvey noted, "with an awful bump." At the end of the day, he often sat on Eagle Rock's piazza and let the children climb into his lap. As they rested their heads against his chest in pretense of sleep, he would sit motionless until the children became restless and wiggled away.

Helen said that busy as her father was, whether in New York, Pittsburgh, or Eagle Rock, managing his business or personal affairs, he never missed a day when he did not either see his granddaughters or inquire for news of "the Babies." Since they and their parents lived in Philadelphia, he would telephone them several times a week. When the children were old enough to speak on the phone, Helen recalled, "It was always a great pleasure to him, just to hear [their] little voices say, 'Grandfather.'" In between times, he "loved to plot and plan how to get [his grandchildren] over to New York on a visit," often saying wistfully, "'How I wish we had the Babies with us.'" And when they came, he often let them play on the carpet with *his* toys, the smaller pieces in his newly acquired collection of bronzes from the Morgan estate.

When he returned from a late afternoon game of golf or bridge at Eagle Rock, Frick took the elevator to the second floor and Helen would know from the telltale bang of the door that her father was headed for the nursery. Although the children were in bed for their afternoon naps, they recognized his step, would call out, "Grandfather," and follow up his arrival with "the most wonderful amount of hugging and kissing, as well as a recital of the little songs they knew," songs he loved to hear. Frick enjoyed showing the love and tenderness he felt for the children and would watch with interest and indulgence as they developed physically and mentally during what Helen described as "the sweetest period in the lives of young children."

Frick cared so passionately for his grandchildren that, according to Helen, he suffered terribly when the children, sometimes otherwise occupied, did not notice him. Whether a sign of true love or true neediness on his part, of these occasions Helen explained, "If now and then you were a little unresponsive as children are apt to be at times, your Grandfather would leave the room feeling very sad—he was so brimful of love for you, that he sometimes forgot to reason that babies are little creatures with moods, and that there was nothing back of it."

Fig. 8-11. A few days before his death, Henry Clay Frick played
with his grandchildren in the Clayton, Long Island front hall.
Author's collection

In the grandchildren there was hope in the future. And yet, for Henry Clay Frick, there was no future. He was a very sick man. And a tormented one.

Luckily, when his car arrived at Clayton, he did not suspect that Helen had arranged to have the nurse accompany them. The children were playing outside and were so surprised to see their aunt and grandfather, their excitement quickly occupied Frick's attention and he did not notice the nurse's car.

He walked up the steps into the front hall (fig. 8-11) and sat down, looking very tired and pale. Ever interested in Frances's household arrangements, he made inquires about the new butler and settled in near the fire. The children then presented him with some pictures they had drawn. Delighted by their art work, he said of one granddaughter's drawing, "Who did this? It is very good indeed." Particularly pleased by the one his two-year-old granddaughter Martha had done, he added, "That picture has some snap to it."

Then the baby was brought down. As the girls gathered round their brother and started to play with him, Helen joined them on the floor. Always a favorite with the little girls, Helen found herself surrounded by them, as her father's voice, audible over the laughter, both teased and threatened, "They'd better be nice to their rich old Auntie."

After the excursion to Westbury, Frick and Helen returned to New York. Frick went to bed early. Unable to sleep, he lay on the couch in his private sitting room, surrounded by *The Purification of the Temple* (see fig. 4-21), *The Bullfight* (see fig. 4-22), *Motherhood* (see fig. 7-62), and *The Rehearsal* (see fig. 9-33). He played solitaire on and off through the night, and at 5:30 in the morning he went down to the library and slept on the sofa facing Hogarth's *Miss Mary Edwards* (see fig. 9-35) until nine o'clock. He signed some papers, dictated letters, and went over the designs for his namesake's first Christmas present—a set of dressing-table silver, every piece engraved with the likenesses of his three little sisters.

In the morning, however, Frick insisted he felt strong, had gained control of his illness and had the upper hand. After taking a half-hour drive around the reservoir, sleeping most of the time, he returned to spend time in the library and his office.

But Frick was in fact now dangerously near death. He walked with Helen into the gallery, carrying his blue silk comforter in his arms, past the Corots, Van Dycks, Rembrandts, and Veroneses. Occasionally, he would approach a special canvas and touch it as gently as one would a child, to see if the paint was in good condition.

When they entered the Enamel Room, Helen drew up some chairs and placed them in front of the windows overlooking Fifth Avenue so Frick could watch the people out for a stroll. He stayed for half an hour, musing about the way traffic came in bunches and commenting on the funny walks some people had. When he and Helen left the Enamel Room and walked back through the West Gallery, he turned to her thoughtfully, saying, "It's strange how when you get a fine collection, it becomes ordinary to you." That afternoon, he left for a bridge game at the Links Club, and Helen again became desperate. The doctors had not checked her father for four days. Dr. Evans seemed almost indifferent, and though her father insisted he was improving, he remained short of breath and miserable. Taking control from Helen, Frick called in a new doctor who sent him right to bed and put him on a liquid diet.

Helen tried to keep her father quiet and sent him his favorite roses. He admired them and told her, "It was very sweet of you to send me those roses, but you shouldn't spend your money on me." He then got out of bed and went downstairs for lunch. Against the new doctor's orders, he settled down to a chicken casserole, preceded by a hot scotch, and a cigar. Twice during lunch Helen was called away from the table, and twice her father grumbled, "It would be better if [you] didn't allow people to disturb [you] at mealtime." When lunch was over, Frick announced he wanted to play Russian

Bank. He and Helen moved to the library, and as they settled down, Oscar closed the door. Angered, Frick said, "Don't shut the door." But when Oscar explained, "I feel a draft, Mr. Frick," Frick quickly replied, "Certainly, shut the door."

At three, his car was ordered and Helen went with him for a drive. He dozed a little as he reminisced about the times he used to ride horses around the reservoir. He spoke about the house at Westbury, and as they approached 1 East Seventieth Street, he said, as if thinking himself back in the Overholt Homestead at West Overton, "Back to the old homestead—things look pretty familiar here."

He went immediately to the library, and when his friend and lawyer Mr. Grier arrived, they each had a drink and a cigar. When Grier protested about the drink, Frick beamed and said the doctor had ordered it for him. He then lost two games of Russian Bank and the "double or quits." When he sent Oscar upstairs for his wallet, Grier said not to bother as Frick "could not afford to lose $34 because he was not making any money these days." Frick's eyes twinkled as he replied, "That's the very reason why I can afford it, because I am not losing at the club. I'm saving money staying in."

That particular night, he seemed very bright and well. It was November 25 and Thanksgiving was only days away. He had, however, but eight days to live. He went to bed early and read his papers; but when Helen was talking on the phone, he suddenly uttered a sharp cry of pain. Helen called the doctor, but her father suffered for almost an hour before he arrived. The nurse gave him a hot foot bath with mustard and made him drink hot water with aromatic spirits of ammonia to relieve what his nurse believed was acute indigestion.

When the doctor arrived, he could not determine exactly what had caused the pain, but recognizing Frick's fear of having the pain return, the doctor gave him a hypodermic of morphine. Although Frick fell asleep, the doctor, anxious about his condition, spent the night with him.

In the morning, Frick announced that from now on he was going to be the boss. When family members interrupted him, a tactic they used to keep him from talking too much and thereby overtiring himself, he countered, "Now wait a minute." And when Helen expressed concern that her father scolded Oscar too harshly about little things, he held up his hand and warned, "That's steady enough," and Helen agreed that it was.

Frick played solitaire constantly, saying to Helen, "Watch me make it this time. If I don't make it this time, I'll eat my hat." And then, according to Helen, he suddenly announced he "would no longer take all those gargles and medicines," declaring, "There were no real doctors. They shake their heads and look very wise and say, 'Oh yes, I think you may do thus and so,' 'I think he may have a little—it won't do him any harm.'"

But Frick was far from being in control of the situation. His health was not improving and as Thanksgiving arrived, Frick had begun to ask for Dr. Garmany, whom until now Helen had succeeded in keeping away. To give him comfort, Helen finally acquiesced to her father's wish. When Dr. Garmany arrived, however, Helen took him aside and instructed him that because she was trying to keep from her father the severity of his illness, she did not want Garmany "to talk professionally" in front of him (fig. 8-12).

Fig. 8-12. Helen Frick instructs her father's doctors.
Frick Archives

Everyone was fearful of the outcome of the meeting with Garmany because Frick had insisted on seeing the doctor alone. After the consultation, a skeptical Frick immediately demanded the nurse retake his pulse and temperature. The nurse did as she was asked and reported his pulse rate at 58, his temperature as normal, knowing full well Garmany had told Frick differently.

Helen was afraid to enter her father's room, but when he sent for her, she knew she had no choice. He asked her, as she described, "in the gentlest way," if she had written to Garmany to discharge him when he first became ill. She replied Garmany had not been on the job, was not up to date, and all she wanted was for her father "to have the best."

Frick replied, "You did quite right. Garmany is a fool. He told me my pulse was 42 and the nurse took it and said it was 58. He also said I had a 99 degree temperature, and she said it was 90.9. I never want to see [Dr. Garmany] again—he's a bad number."

To Oscar, he said, "Garmany's a damn fool—throw all his medicines out of the window."

Relieved her father believed the nurse and herself, not Garmany, Helen said, "We felt our lucky star had been with us this time." Nevertheless, her father remained preoccupied by the conflicting diagnoses. He began to ask repeatedly for his pulse and temperature to be taken. Helen admitted, "It made us so anxious for fear he might learn the truth, become thereby discouraged and lose faith in us."

Helen came in and out of her father's bedroom throughout the night. She noticed he seemed to cough less, but the following morning, November 27, Thanksgiving Day, she was greeted with bad news. The doctor listened to her father's chest and heard a rushing sound. Although Frick's combination of symptoms would today have been recognized as heart failure, his doctor diagnosed a slight case of pleurisy, which pleased Frick because he thought pleurisy was what he had all along.

Helen, however, was distraught and particularly concerned about how to manage her father since the grandchildren were due to arrive at any minute for Thanksgiving lunch. Because he was so weak and tired, she was determined to keep him quiet.

Suddenly, at 12:30 P.M., Helen heard her father's voice calling from the upstairs hall, "Have the children arrived?" When Helen looked up the stairwell, there was Frick, dressed and getting into the elevator. He had ordered Oscar to bring his clothes and was up and out of his room before his nurse, or anyone else, had any idea what he was up to.

Helen flew around the house with the others, scattering in different directions, to light the fires in the rooms downstairs. With fire blazing beneath Hogarth's *Miss Mary Edwards*, Frick went to the library, settled himself into an armchair by the window, and waited for the children. When they arrived, Helen took three-year-old Frances in first. The child who most amused her grandfather, she had once forced him to relinquish his customary seat at the table by refusing to move. But on this visit, rather than feeling sure of herself, she felt frightened because her mother had lectured her about being quiet. So she behaved, sat on her grandfather's lap for a while, and then went upstairs to join the others.

Four-year-old Adelaide came down next. As the child chattered about the family's drive in from Westbury, her mother reminded Frick of his promise to give this granddaughter away when she married. Frances chided that he must take care of himself, "if he wanted to do [so]."

Frick smiled at his daughter-in-law and said, "That's right," and then began to discuss his pulse, saying "if his pulse was as he was told, a little exertion shouldn't be bad for him." He turned to Frances and said, "You don't suppose they are trying to deceive a man of my common sense?" He told her what Dr. Garmany had said about his pulse, and then dismissed Garmany's capabilities. Seeking comfort from his daughter-in-law, and respite from his confusion about the conflicting medical reports, he said, "You know, Frances, you and I are the only ones in the family that have common sense—they are all nice, but they are so fussy."

Then, in trying to lighten Frick's mood, Frances marveled at the paintings in the room saying, "Aren't you proud to have assembled all this?"

"No, I did not paint any of them," sighed the man who had declined all honorary degrees because he felt he had done nothing to "justify their acceptance." Shortly thereafter, at about two o'clock, Frick decided to go back upstairs. His pulse rate had increased from the exertion, and he seemed exhausted when he returned to his bed. Helen did not want the children to disturb him before they left for Westbury, but since their grandfather was calling for them, Helen allowed the children into his room. As he sat on the edge of his bed, little Frances sang him her "Pretty Little Frances Song," while young Martha (fig. 8-13) and Adelaide threw him good-bye kisses from the doorway.

Fig. 8-13. Martha and Frances Frick.
Author's collection

Helen stayed with her father that night, stroking his arm because he said it soothed him and he was afraid to cough. He dozed on and off and had a reasonable night. The following night, however, Frick was very nervous and only slept one hour. He perspired a great deal, threw off the bedclothes, and sat in his nightshirt at the foot of his bed. He called for Oscar at 4:00 A.M., had breakfast in his chair at 7:30 A.M., spoke to the doctor for about an hour and a half, and remained quiet all morning. Against doctor's instructions, he ordered for lunch: cream soup, sweetbreads, spinach (because he believed it was "the broom to the stomach"), au gratin potatoes, and a demitasse. His frustrated nurse quit, but Helen hired a replacement who arrived at dinnertime, just as her father was having a supper of milk toast.

Frick turned to the new nurse and said, in what Helen described as a "cunning way," "I hope you'll find me in a good humor in the morning." After she left, he said to

Helen, "I wonder if anyone ever died in this bed?" And she, ever quick, replied, "I don't imagine so, but I'm sure lots of people were born in it," at which her father smiled.

The weather turned dark and rainy and Frick's cough worsened. The doctors blamed the heavy congestion in his chest on the weather, and everyone tried to keep him quiet. The next morning, Frick sat in his armchair by the window and watched the passersby along Fifth Avenue. He used his far-sighted glasses, but after a time he became discouraged and turned to his nurse saying, "There are no beauties out this morning, so I'll go back to bed."

Helen brought him some chicken specially cooked by the ladies of an auxiliary guild called the Home Bureau. When she entered her father's room, he was sitting on the stool at the foot of his bed facing Romney's portrait of Lady Hamilton—Martha's teenage look-alike, had she lived. He said the chicken looked very nice, but wasn't cooked as his grandmother and sister Maria would have prepared it. He nevertheless served himself a large plateful and took a little of the rice and gravy, thoroughly enjoying it, as Helen described, "just like a boy." After lunch Helen played checkers with him and read aloud *The Council Assigned* by Mark Shipman Andrews. He listened intently to every word, never taking his eyes from Helen. Then, just as she came to the concluding line, he interrupted and recited it himself: "The man was the Judge."

Now, after almost four weeks of suffering, Frick brought something else to closure. When he fell ill, Frick asked James Howard Bridge to have the many art objects on approval from Joseph Duveen returned. The job had taken time to complete, but by November 29, all bills to Duveen were paid and $1,415,000 worth of items submitted for approval were removed.

Too weak to go downstairs and see how his collection looked without Duveen's articles, Frick asked Helen to go in his stead. When she returned, he asked if she had noticed much change. After assuring her father that his collection looked as fine as ever, Helen offered to play Russian Bank with him. As her father beat her soundly, her card piles growing larger the longer they played, he turned to her and said with a smile, "Am I playing too slowly for you?"

On December 1, Frick's pains returned, and his stomach became badly distended. Frances came to visit, as did Childs and Charles Carstairs. James Howard Bridge joined him for a few minutes as well, and was amused that as sick as his boss was, he was sitting up in bed with a half a dozen newspapers spread around him. He was equally amazed when Frick said, "Pull up a chair," and began questioning him, "Who will be the next President?"

But Bridge had a bad feeling about Frick's condition. He would later claim that after the ill-fated lobster luncheon attended by Boise Penrose, Frick had said to Bridge that he, Frick, "knew a great deal about some machines, but not the most important machine of all, his own body." Frick had also confided his "premonition of a tragic outcome of his indisposition."

That premonition was correct. The night of December 1, when Frick retired, he lay on his right side facing the only other painting in his bedroom—Lawrence's haunting portrait of Miss Louisa Murray, the love-child who resembled Martha as she looked in 1887 when she swallowed the pin. In trying to make her father comfortable, Helen offered him a heating pad instead of a hot water bag, but he turned her away saying in a very tired voice, "You'll have me so awake that I won't be able to go to sleep." And so, Helen leaned over to kiss him and wish him "a perfect night's sleep."

This was to be their last kiss. At eleven, the nurse tried to call the doctor for a sleeping potion, but he could not be located. Restless and in pain, Frick asked for a treatment of turpentine stoops, whereupon the nurse gave him six applications between eleven-thirty and twelve. At ten minutes after midnight, Frick complained to Oscar, "Oh, if I could only sleep." At five on the morning of December 2, he rang for Oscar, asked for a glass of water, and after taking hold of the glass and drinking, said to Oscar: "That will be all; now I think I'll go to sleep."

A few moments later, Helen entered her father's room and gave him something more to induce sleep. Not long afterward, the nurse tiptoed into the room. Hearing no sound, she came close beside the bed. Frick, described by the nurse as having a "pallid but wholly tranquil countenance," had died. Apparently Helen's remedy had precipitated more than sleep. For the rest of her life, Helen, who was accused of killing Frick by her brother and sister-in-law, would be tortured by that possibility.

Leon Wolff, in *Lockout,* said Frick had "died as he had lived: quietly, seemingly impassive, and alone." Frick, however, had died with Romney's *Lady Hamilton* (see fig. 3-18)—the teenager Martha might have resembled had she lived—above the mantelpiece. On the wall to the right of his bed was, of course, the haunting *Miss Louisa Murray* (see fig. 4-18) with her skirts filled with Martha's favorite flower, the pansy. Frick died as he had lived, longing for Martha.

❖

THE FOLLOWING DAY, at precisely five o'clock, the mortal remains of Henry Clay Frick returned from the undertaker to 1 East Seventieth Street for a brief service. His casket was carried up the marble staircase, beneath the organ screen with its *Singing Children* (see fig. 7-55), and past Renoir's *Mother and Children* (see fig. 3-10) at the entrance to the family quarters. It was placed in one of the rooms facing Fifth

Avenue, and while the house filled with flowers, the Fragonard Room, with its *Progress of Love* panels (fig. 8-14) and the Living Hall, with *St. Jerome* (see fig. 7-50), *Sir Thomas More* (see fig. 6-1), and *Thomas Cromwell* (see fig. 6-2), two Titians, and *St. Francis in the Desert* (see fig. 7-49), were chosen as seating areas for a short memorial service.

Only family, intimate friends, trustees of the Metropolitan Museum of Art, the directors of the U.S. Steel Corporation and the officers of the Links Club were invited. Because the actual funeral service was to be held a few days later at Clayton in Pittsburgh, with the burial service at the Homewood Cemetery, the New York ceremony was kept to fifteen minutes. No eulogy was given. Only the Sermon on the Mount was read, and after the service, those invited to do so went upstairs for a viewing.

Later that night, Frick's remains left 1 East Seventieth Street for the last time. The coffin, covered in roses, tulips, lily of the valley, and a small green wreath tied with white ribbon, was delivered to the Pennsylvania Railway Station for an 11:30 P.M. departure. The train, called the Iron City Express, had been ordered especially for Frick's

Fig. 8-14. Family and guests were seated in the Fragonard Room for the brief New York memorial service.
Author's collection

funeral cortege, comprising three cars, the Republic, the Claremont, and his own private car, the Westmoreland. One was reserved for flowers, one for the family, and the black-draped Westmoreland for Frick's remains.

Fifteen honorary pallbearers accompanied the casket from the house to the station. They included Judge Gary, George Harvey, Judge William H. Moore, of the failed Moore syndicate established to buy out Carnegie; and Charles Carstairs. As they followed the coffin down the station platform, the railroad men, as the prominent figures in the railroad industry were called, gathered on Track 15. With Adelaide and Helen heavily veiled, the men stood with hats off and heads bowed. Complications ensued, however, because the unusually wide coffin, with its custom-made square end, could not be taken through the Westmoreland's door. Finally, it was passed through one of the windows.

Once in place, the top of the coffin was lifted for friends and family to have a final viewing. Then the Iron City Express departed, making symbolic stops at all the stations familiar to Frick—Harrisburg, Altoona, Cresson Springs, and Johnstown. It made its final stop in Pittsburgh's East End at 9:30 A.M., December 4.

Upon arrival, the casket was taken to Clayton, placed in the parlor, and banked with flowers. Although plans were underway by Frick's executors for the public to come to Clayton and view the body, Childs stepped in and countermanded that arrangement. The city was outraged, and Frick's many friends upset, but Childs stood firm. Wanting to keep his father's funeral as private as possible, only one hundred people, close friends and family, were invited to the service the following day.

The morning of the funeral, Friday, December 5, Helen and Adelaide asked Andrew Mellon to come see them prior to the noon service. As he was executor of the will, he stayed with them for a long time, noting in his day-diary that they were "much broken up" (fig. 8-15).

At noon, the service commenced. The rector from Calvary Church stood on Clayton's stair landing with the stained-glass windows of *The Four Virgins* (see fig. 9-16) behind him. Christine Miller, a lifelong friend of Frick's, sang "Lead Kindly Light," "Peace Perfect Peace," and "Now the Day Is Over." The Twenty-third Psalm was read, as was Psalm 39, the prayer of a just man's peace and patience in a vain and troubled world. A reference, perhaps, to Frick's silence with respect to Pittsburgh's and Carnegie's betrayal in 1900, the psalm reads: "I will keep my mouth with a bridle, while the wicked is before me. . . . I was dumb with silence, I held my peace, even from good; and my sorrow was stirred." In the reading of Psalm 90, there was, perhaps, a hope that others would perceive the accomplishments of his life as God's work: "And let the beauty of the Lord our God be upon us: and establish thou the work of our hands upon us; yea, the work of our hands establish thou it."

Fig. 8-15. Helen and Adelaide in their mourning clothes at Eagle Rock, c. 1920.
Author's collection

More poignant than any passages read at the service was the reading from John 11, where Christ teaches the lesson of resurrection to Martha. Christ has challenged Martha for doubting he can raise Lazarus from the dead and tells her before working the miracle, "I am the resurrection, and the life: he that believeth in me, though he were dead, yet shall he live."

The honorary pallbearers, all Pittsburghers except J. P. Grier, included William Frew, Senator Philander C. Knox, Andrew W. Mellon, Richard B. Mellon, H. C. McEldowny, William Watson Smith, and Asa P. Childs, brother of Adelaide. They accompanied the casket from Clayton's music room to the waiting hearse, and then a procession of ten limousines wound its way from Clayton, up the short, steep hill to the gravesite in Homewood Cemetery. A chill wind blew, scattering snowflakes from the overcast sky. A tent sheltered the mourners from the bitter weather and protected the open grave. Martha's grave, and that of Frick's ill-fated infant son, still had no gravestones. They had been covered with boxwood for the ceremony. The site was identifiable only by the hand-chiseled inscription, "Frick," on the front of the large granite monument Frick ordered after his break with Andrew Carnegie in 1900.

Frick's flower-draped casket was placed over the copper-lined grave. At Adelaide's request, a wreath of American Beauty roses, her husband's favorite flower, was placed at the head of the casket.

As though referring to Frick's own anguish over Martha's life having been the ultimate sacrifice for his success, the minister read Revelation 14.10:

The same shall drink of the wine of the wrath of God, which is poured out without mixture into the cup of his indignation; and he shall be tormented with fire
and brimstone in the presence of the holy angels, and in the presence of the lamb.

After the burial service, the funeral party departed and the grave was sealed. In a
departure from normal procedure, 200 cubic feet of concrete was poured around and
on top of the casket's outer copper casing. Although the grave was five feet three inches wide and ten feet long, and covered with over a foot and a half of concrete, one further measure was taken to secure Frick's remains: a guard was stationed at the lot to
protect against grave robbers.

The headline in a Connellsville paper later that day read:

H. C. FRICK LAID TO REST BESIDE CHILDREN

Coincidentally, there were many other endings. The League of Nations, opposed by
Frick, was defeated. Walker D. Hines announced the railroads would be returned to
their owners on December 28 with a heavy rate increase, far exceeding Frick's recom-
mendation. Andrew Carnegie, whose mind had been failing for years, had died in
August. Carnegie had given over $350 million in his lifetime to social and educational
concerns, and now, the fortune Frick had made was also about to be redistributed in
charitable form.

By 1921, byproduct ovens had supplanted the beehive ovens in the coke-making
process. Frick's mines, though eventually depleted of coal, would continue to earn a
profit for U.S. Steel with their gas and other minerals. His filing and map system would
prove so efficient, even today it is used, rather than a computer.

The Overholt Distillery would stay open at Broad Ford for medicinal purposes,
while the original distillery at West Overton was closed because of prohibition.

Ironically, on December 2, the same day Frick had died, Pierre-Auguste Renoir,
who painted *Mother and Children,* also died. On December 3, the same day Frick's
remains returned to 1 East Seventieth Street for the brief memorial service, Alexander
Berkman was arrested in Chicago by the U.S. Department of Labor for deportation to
Russia because of his communist leanings, articles in radical newspapers, and advocacy of violence. The government considered him an "enem[y] of the United States of
America and of its peace and comfort."

Upon being taken into custody, when asked if he had heard Henry Clay Frick had
just died, Berkman cheered, "Deported by God," later adding bitterly, "It's too bad he

cannot take the millions amassed by exploiting labor with him." In further irony, at noon on December 5, as Frick's funeral service began, Berkman surrendered himself to authorities on Ellis Island, where he waited with hundreds of other immigrant radicals for his December 21 deportation. Of Frick he said philosophically, "Well, he left the country before I did." As his ship left New York Harbor the smoke from the stacks drifted back, obscuring the face and top portion of the Statue of Liberty, "the Mother of Exiles" as she was known by the deportees.

A curtain had dropped on the play's final act. And yet, with Frick's death, the drama of his life was not over. On June 25, 1927, Andrew Mellon wrote a poignant and prophetic letter to George Harvey, who was later commissioned by Helen to write a biography of her father. In the letter, Mellon recalled his lifelong friend and mentioned Frick's "strong character, good impulses, and broad as well as generous ideals." And he reflected: "It was with a strange feeling, after his sudden death . . . when I attended the funeral . . . in Pittsburgh on that wintry day, that I witnessed the performance of the last rites over his body. Was this the end of that eager, masterful character? It was hard to realize that he could even then be confined within those narrow bounds."

Andrew Mellon knew his friend well. This was indeed *not* the end of that eager, masterful character.

❖

AFTER THE HOMESTEAD STRIKE, a dead striker's mother said of Henry Clay Frick, "There is no more sensibility in that man than a toad." But Frick did not belong to a time when human rights issues were universally understood, much less contemplated. Typical of the capitalists of his day, Frick was a facts and figures man—a tough-minded accountant, not a social reformer. Hard on labor and perceived as generally insensitive to the suffering of the masses, he nevertheless was credited by newspapers in the Coke Region with "fair treatment of workmen," "genero[sity] in supplying the wants of the needy," a wage scale from 5 percent to 15 percent higher than at other works, as well as voluntary advances from 10 percent to 16 percent at Christmas. His company stores were praised as being "fairly conducted," and Adelaide Frick Ramsay, daughter of Frick's mine superintendent at Morewood, recorded in a family diary that the Frick mines were "operated on an intelligent and practical . . . basis. Every improvement that engineering talent and long-practical experience could devise had been introduced." A man who gave generously to charity (often anonymously) and particularly to those charities affecting children, Frick was remembered by his secretary at the time of the Homestead strike, Miss Sue Canfield, for "the spirit in which everything was given." Though no records exist of his donations, Frick's biographer, George Harvey, states that later, during the war, Frick and his family gave over $1 million for humanitarian causes such as the Belgian Relief Fund, the American Ambulance Hospital in France, the Maimed French Soldiers, the Families of Disabled French Artists, the Armored Motor Squadron, and the Allies' Bazaar.

The distribution in his will reflected this concern for the public good. He left only one-sixth of his fortune to his family. The remaining five-sixths were bequeathed to charitable institutions located in New York, Pittsburgh, and the West Overton–Connellsville Coke Region of his own, and his fortune's birth. The recipients primarily served the needs of the people and communities who had helped in the creation of his fortune. In 1918, three years after Frick's will was drawn, when his friend Philander Knox successfully included a clause in a Senate bill providing tax exemption for a gift such as Frick's to the public, the value of Frick's estate and, thereby, his bequests were greatly enhanced. He left $6 million to Princeton University for its unrestricted use and large sums to Harvard University and the Massachusetts Institute of Technology. In New York, his home for fourteen years, he gave a $1.5 million bequest to the City of New York Lying-In Hospital, and gave the public his home and art collection, together with a $15 million endowment. To Pittsburgh, home for almost forty years, he left a park encompassing 151 acres and endowed with a $2 million trust. Additionally, he gave $1.4 million to Pittsburgh's Mercy Hospital and made many large bequests to organizations and hospitals in Pittsburgh including the Educational Fund Commission, Children's Hospital, Allegheny General Hospital, the Home for the Friendless, the Kingsley House Association, the Pittsburgh Free Dispensary, the Pittsburgh Newsboys Home, the Western Pennsylvania Hospital, and the Central Young Women's Christian Association.

In the Coke Region, he made large bequests to hospitals in the towns central to his H. C. Frick Coke Company mining and coking operations: the Uniontown Hospital, the Cottage State Hospital in Connellsville, Westmoreland Hospital in Greensburg, and the Mt. Pleasant Memorial Hospital. And as far as the steel towns were concerned, he gave generous sums to the Braddock General Hospital and the Homestead Hospital.

Of this philanthropic gesture, the Knights Templar Tancred Commandery No. 48, stationed at Pittsburgh, Pennsylvania, noted of the Masonic knight they called "Sir Henry Clay Frick": "We know that the principles of Masonry were believed by him during his life; in his Last Will he gave the World evidence of these ideals in the disposition which he made of his vast wealth."

Nevertheless, many had suffered and died as Frick amassed his fortune. And now with his death, we shall see how his family, particularly Helen, had also been sacrificed.

Fig. 8-16. The Frick cenotaph.
Author's collection

My desire is to see you very happy and to see much of you — Love to all

Devotedly Your Papa

Tuesday

CHAPTER IX

Shrouded Legacy

I know you are anxious to please me, and will try to do what I desire.

—Henry Clay Frick to Helen Clay Frick, c. 1900

*I had another proposal for your hand today which I confined
to the wastebasket. You are becoming far too popular. . . .
this is only a line to assure you that you are always in my thoughts.*

—Henry Clay Frick to Helen Clay Frick, 1918

ON FRICK'S DEATH, THE BALANCE OF POWER within the family shifted. Adelaide, who had never played a leading role, remained a silent figure, though she could have taken legal action under the laws of Pennsylvania to get her widow's dower, which would have given her $68 million on an estate worth nearly $200 million. Whether or not Adelaide ever considered claiming the dower is unknown. She seems to have fallen into still greater ill health, passively accepting what she was bequeathed: $1 million outright, $5 million in trust, the contents of Eagle Rock and Clayton in Pittsburgh, as well as the right to live at 1 East Seventieth Street and Eagle Rock for the balance of her life.

Frick's son, Childs, then age thirty-six, inherited $2 million in trust and $1 million outright, while his wife, Frances Dixon Frick, received $2 million, to be held in trust.

After small bequests to relatives and friends, the remainder, unquestionably the lion's share, went to Frick's surviving, maiden daughter, Helen Clay Frick. Crowned "America's Richest Bachelor Girl" by the *New York Evening World* (fig. 9-1), even by a robber baron's standard the amount of her inheritance was vast, particularly for a woman of that time: $5 million outright, the $12 million Frick Building and Annex in Pittsburgh together with a $1 million endowment for its upkeep; the Iron Rail property in Wenham, Massachusetts; thirteen of the one hundred shares in her father's residual estate valued at approximately $6 million and bequeathed to her "in absolute and unqualified ownership"; any excess of the residual estate, after bequests to all institutions and legatees were satisfied; and the outright ownership of Eagle Rock upon her mother's death. As tribute to Helen, there was a secondary clause that provided for

Fig. 9-1. The day after Henry Clay Frick's death, the *New York Evening World* crowned Helen "America's Richest Bachelor Girl."
UPI/Corbis-Bettmann

her inheritance of the New York house and its entire contents, if on Frick's death plans for his gift to the public did not materialize.

In death, as in life, so it would seem, the firm and formidable hand of Henry Clay Frick reached across the grave to deliver a message to his survivors. Adelaide, though comfortably provided for, had long been lost to depression, a state into which she had withdrawn following the deaths of Martha and her infant son. An improbable candidate to fill Frick's shoes, she had remained a doting, clinging, kind, and sweet wife. During the course of their life together, she had been plagued by headaches, colds, and immobilizing accidents requiring, as her children were growing up, the constant care of doctors or the attention of her sister, Attie. While she enjoyed the trips to Europe and the gowns her husband bought her, she seemed to find in wine and trips to the casino the same solace her husband found in his pictures—and in his devoted daughter Helen. Referred to by her Childs relatives as a "sweet old thing" with "plenty of pluck," Adelaide had long suffered and was long suffering.

Childs had been comfortably provided for when he married in 1913. But he had largely been ignored by his father since childhood. Even though he produced the cherished grandson to carry on the Frick name, he had proved himself lacking in business capabilities. In fact, Childs was no better a candidate to be head of the family than Adelaide. Frick made Helen, therefore, the titular head, a decision that would not upset Adelaide, but would forever lock Helen into a love-hate relationship with her brother and, ironically, her deceased father.

As Otto Fenichel and other authorities on death and dying note, a conflicted relationship, such as Helen's to her father, creates a difficult mourning process. They maintain that if, as was the case with Helen, the relationship was marked by an abnormal emotional and financial dependency on the deceased, coupled with ambivalence about the situation and an anxious dependency on the relationship, the bereaved will try to both remain connected to the deceased and attempt to destroy him. There is a constant fear of the deceased returning to seek revenge. There is anger at the deceased. And there is guilt, a fear that their failed caretaking both caused the death and fulfilled the bereaved's latent wish that the person would die. The bereaved is haunted and, as Beverly Raphael describes the dynamic, there then arises the ironic need for the mourner to keep the deceased alive. By perpetuating the mourning, the bereaved can feel more in control, particularly if life is lived as it was when the deceased was alive, with all his possessions nearby, as if he will return. Tragically, the mourner's security now becomes dependent on maintaining a symbolic relationship with the deceased, creating a grief so entrenched it becomes a way of life. Since the deceased lives on in the grief, there is little motivation to relinquish either the grieving or the symbolic relationship. Completion of the mourning process would mean forgetting the deceased.

Helen became a classic illustration of this mourning process. Just as her father's unrelenting mourning was not understood in his day, her staggering childhood losses before age four—the death of two siblings, the loss of her mother to grief and depression, the loss of her father to protracted mourning, the loss of her teenage companion Annie, later to be followed by her move to New York, the loss of Clayton as home, and the loss of her beloved governess Mademoiselle Ogiz—predated modern grief therapy. Helen would, therefore, suffer in her own way from these losses, her own self-imposed guilt, and constant fears. As she began to devote her life to her father's memory and to establish him as a near saint, there would be no way for her to resolve her own distress, nor a way to break the link between her deceased father's possessions and the anger, sadness, guilt, and other emotions they embodied. For Helen, devastating childhood loss combined with her father's unbreakable spell promised that she would never unlock her own identity. Sibling death, parental grief, and most of all her father's voice and his paintings would forever retain their morbid control.

I N ORDER TO UNDERSTAND THE INTENSITY of Helen's losses and the unusual nature of the bond between Helen and her father—and its effect on Frick's art collection—we must go back to the past. This time we must look for Helen, the child whose life compass was forever set when she was just three; the pathological turn taken because of Martha's death; and in particular, the impact of Henry Clay Frick's unrelenting sorrow.

While death of a child was more expected in Henry Clay Frick's day, the tragedy, particularly by accident, was no less devastating. Death is death, and for the surviving parents and siblings the consequences were enormous. In *The Anatomy of Bereavement,* Beverly Raphael maintains that a bereaved's chronic grieving and emotions control the family dynamic. His or her pain can be transferred as anger onto a family member and results in excessive punishment of that person, while from others is elicited excessive care and sympathy. Raphael warns that surviving children—who react the same way as adults with their own searching, yearning, and guilt and who are impacted by their parents' grief reaction—may become "bound," "haunted," or "resurrected." A whole family system, and each person in the family unit, can therefore be described in terms of ongoing, pathological bereavement. Dr. Albert C. Cain and his colleagues offer a continuing and sobering thought: "A full preventive-therapeutic approach to the dead child's siblings, integrated with assistance to the grieving parents, remains to be carefully spelled out. But recognition of the need for such efforts represents a major step toward preventing . . . the senseless arithmetic of adding newly warped lives to the one already tragically ended."

In Frick's day, no one knew about chronic grieving, and even today research in the field of children's reaction to death has been neglected. John Bowlby holds that the significance of mourning in infancy and early childhood "has been and still is too little recognized." For one thing, it is hard to tell whether the child is reacting to the death of the sibling, the parents' grief, or the change in the parents' relationship with the surviving children. For the child's part, he or she may feel many losses—of a playmate, companion, buffer, or protector. If the mother withdraws into depression, as did Adelaide, there is the additional loss of a mother too bereaved to be physically or emotionally present to her children. With Adelaide not fully present, Henry Clay Frick became the driving force in his family, impacting the children with the full burden of his emotions, repressed or otherwise.

From the moment Frick left Cresson Springs in 1891 with Martha's body, accompanied by all the children's primary caretakers, their sense of security had been damaged. When he met them on the train platform after the funeral—ignoring Childs and kissing Helen—his surviving son's and daughter's fates were tragically sealed. Eight-year-old Childs seemed to go quietly about his business. One day he painted a picture of a distorted house with a pool of blood beneath a smashed picket fence. The land-

Fig. 9-2. Childs Frick (1883–1965), *House and Piers*, c. 1892.
Oil on canvas, 12 x 14 in. (30.5 x 35.6 cm).
Frick Art and Historical Center

scape also depicted dead trees, and half-closed black windows (fig. 9-2). In an unusual pastime for his day, he trapped animals in the woods behind Clayton and stuffed
the ones that died. As the eldest son and Martha's older brother and constant companion, these actions would seem to indicate that he too was traumatized, perhaps
also suffering from his own self-imposed guilt for failing to see Martha place the fatal
pin in her mouth. And, at some level, Frick may have also blamed him, either consciously or unconsciously.

Of the two children, Childs certainly seemed the one most obviously punished. Five
days before Alexander Berkman's 1892 attack, Frick hired Clyde Augustus Duniway to
be Childs's tutor. That fall, with the tutor accompanying the boy, Frick sent his son
away to school in Boston. Adelaide was very upset both because most nine-year-old
children remained home for their schooling and because Childs had never been far
away from his parents. Moreover, she had effectively lost her third child in two years.
Clearly worried that death by accident or disease might take the life of her only son, she
cautioned Duniway that if Childs were taken to the football games "the little fellow"

might become seriously ill. She insisted it was "a very, very bad season to have him exposed in the open air." She noted that the only son of their friends, the Dilworths, had been killed that week by an electric car when coming home from a football game in Allegheny and that two years before, Mrs. George Laughlin had "lost her life by taking cold at the football game."

Childs's father reacted differently. He reminded Duniway of his duty to be the boy's "teacher and friend—not his personal attendant" and insisted Duniway could best serve his son by "standing somewhat aloof from the course of his daily life." Clearly, Frick was anxious to make a man out of the boy and wanted to give him the education he, Frick, had been denied. He wrote Duniway, "Of course he will likely become homesick, and it may take the best part of a year for him to be reconciled to his present condition, but there must be no let up in this." And to his son he wrote, "I hope to have good reports at all times of you. I dreamed the other night that you had written me that you stood at the head of your class. I trust such will prove to be the fact."

Childs, however, proved a scholastic disappointment. His spelling was poor and his marks, within the first few weeks of school, were low. Frick admonished him:

> On my return home I got the news of your loss of class standing. This pains me very much for the reason that I am now sure if you had worked as you should, such result would have been avoided. If you want to please me, you must recover the lost ground quickly.
>
> I really thought when I learned it that I would write and say you could not return home Thanksgiving, and I have not decided that question yet, and your visit home will depend on how you get along between now and Thanksgiving.

As time went on, Frick's reprimands to Childs grew more and more severe. Childs was chastised for not dating his letters, and often Frick returned his son's letters with a red ring around all the incorrectly spelled words. He complained to his son about letters written in red ink, something Frick considered to be "in bad taste." He refused to pay for the stamps Childs wanted for his growing stamp collection, feeling he should buy them himself. He also scolded his son's efforts at bird shooting and wrote Childs: "You seem to be able to use that gun of yours to great advantage as to make it very uncomfortable for the little birds. As I understand it, you shot [at] four but only succeeded in getting one of them." (Childs, in 1916, hunted big game in Africa and donated many of his trophies to the New York Museum of Natural History and the Carnegie Institute in Pittsburgh. He gave over forty species and 370 trophies to the Carnegie alone and had them displayed in a simulation of their natural habitat, created from photos taken by Childs for that purpose. Later he became a paleontologist and the author of ground-breaking reference books on horned ruminants.)

When Childs began sending Adelaide samples of his verses, Frick immediately insisted he send "a specimen" of his poetry and not keep him "waiting very long." But even Childs's poetry did not meet Frick's standard. In a letter of May 2, 1894, he wrote, "I received [the enclosed] from a boy, who it seems is named for me, and who it seems is just about your age. It would be well for you to endeavor, as soon as possible, to compose as well as he does, and in fact I think he excels you both in spelling and writing." Although in adulthood Childs would publish his poetry, to Mr. Duniway an exasperated Frick said, "Suppose we will have to bear with him patiently, with the hope that he will some time wake up." So disappointed was Frick with his son he threatened "as soon as we get a report with all A's & B's, will pack up and start for Boston." And to Duniway he wrote: "We do not want him home unless he comes to tell us he will go back to Cambridge in the fall cheerfully."

Young Helen, however, proved an excellent student and, with Childs out of Frick's life as an object of active, affectionate concern, she apparently received an abundance of affection and praise. But always, Frick's interest in and love of Helen, genuine in part, was shaped and driven by the absence and loss of Martha.

In *The Hero's Daughter,* Maureen Murdock asserts that in the father-daughter syndrome, "destiny" is often the focus, particularly when the father's son has been a disappointment. Often, the father then "turns to his daughter to reflect his dreams and be his heir. He relates to her as a male, giving her certain responsibilities and privileges denied to other siblings. . . . Therefore, this father encourages his daughter's abilities and talents as long as they mirror his own. It appears that he supports her autonomy, but in fact he does not. Such a father sees his daughter solely as a reflection of himself."

As the Fricks' only surviving daughter, Helen was overprotected by her parents, particularly by her father, who perhaps was finding in Helen a way to assuage his guilt and seek solace. Indeed, death and dying research shows that the intense closeness a parent shows to a surviving child is often a way to be close to the dead child, not the surviving child. In this way Helen was immediately defined by the loss of her sister. To compound her distress, with Childs's departure for boarding school, Helen had now lost a third sibling within two years. This could only have felt like another death to her.

Helen's feeling of loss must have been further intensified by, first, her mother's slow, inexorable sinking into depression, and then by the elopement of the children's beloved teenage companion Annie following the 1892 Homestead strike. Thus, Helen was at once severed from the companionship of anyone who even whispered youth. And as an only child at home, she had no buffer between her father and his grief. Perhaps as a consequence, Helen became rebellious, refused to eat, and became very thin. A series of failed relationships with governesses ensued, and when a new Swiss governess named Mademoiselle Ogiz (fig. 9-3) (whom Helen would later come to adore for the

Fig. 9-3. Mademoiselle Ogiz.
Frick Archives

love and stability she provided) agreed to care for her, Helen hoped and prayed the ship bringing her from Europe to New York would sink.

Meanwhile, as Frick acquired art, he drew Helen closer to himself. Devoted and loving, he quizzed her governess about the progress of her lessons, most of which he graded himself. And soon he began to seek her out for companionship. But the special attention he gave her was also a form of abandoning her; he imprisoned her, demanding that her energies be spent in service to him, not in growing an independent self.

At meals, Helen normally sat beside her mother at the far end of the large mahogany dining-room table, but with Childs's departure to boarding school, she was moved to her father's end. In a letter that innocently identifies the shift in roles, George Megrew advised Childs, "Your sister Helen now occupies your place at the dinner table."

During dinner, Frick, who Helen later recalled rarely discussed his business affairs unless there was "something of particular interest to recount," would turn to Helen and go over her day's events. Helen later recorded in a memoir that her father and mother "often poked fun at each other during dinner." Helen enjoyed their jokes and laughter because her father was "always pleased when [her] mother got the best of him which often happened." But despite the occasional merriment, there were both subtle and silent reminders of Martha and the longing for her presence. As the orchestrion played the "Ave Maria" ("Pray, oh pray for us wretched sinners, Now and when the hour of our death o'er takes us") and "The Last Rose of Summer" from *Martha* ("I live in a dream / a dream that never dies"), Emile Friant's *Chagrin d'Enfant* (see fig. 3-6), evoking Annie as she looked when holding Martha in her lap to ease her pain, was just visible over Helen's shoulder in Clayton's front hall.

This silent communion continued after dinner as well. Apart from the fact that in a few years Dagnan-Bouveret's *Consolatrix Afflictorum* (see fig. 5-23) would grace the dining room and Helen, like her father, would soon gaze past her mother into the eyes of the Madonna, photographs of Martha covered tables, bureaus, and walls, throughout the house. Other paintings echoed her as well. When Frick, Adelaide, and Helen retired to the second-floor sitting room (fig. 9-4), Helen's parents pulled their big armchairs up to the gas-log fire and sat beneath *Pilgrims at Emmaus,* the copy of *Christ at Emmaus;* Chartran's portrait of Helen with Martha's locket portrait around her neck; and his portrait of her in the wreath of symbolic flowers—all this, while the orchestrion

Fig. 9-4. Upstairs sitting room, Clayton.
Author's collection

Figs. 9-5, 6. Clayton bedroom of Henry Clay Frick (east and south views), c. 1898.
Author's collection

played excerpts from Wagner's "Pilgrim's Chorus" and the sinners' prayer from *Tannhaüser* ("Oh, see my heart by guilt oppressed. I faint, I sink beneath my burden! Nor will I cease, nor will I rest, till heavenly mercy grants thy pardon").

When Helen as an adult wrote an account of her evenings at home, she never recognized how serious was the impact of her parents' distress on all their lives. She merely said of these Clayton evenings that after her father read the papers or played cards, he often got the "fidgets." Adept at gauging his moods, while others watched with apprehension, Helen would take her father's arm and walk with him, "first on one floor, then on another, steering [their] way around the furniture . . . [while] having fun doing it." Believing her relationship with her father was bound by love, not realizing it was pain, she wrote, these walks "seemed to relieve him and then he went early to bed."

With pictures and photographs of Martha everywhere, Frick's bedroom (figs. 9-5, 6), like the rest of the house, was a veritable shrine. Not atypical of other houses, then and now, where grief has taken an unreasonable hold on its occupants, Clayton was the kind of home described by Albert and Barbara Cain in their article "On Replacing a Child":

> The home . . . had an essentially funereal atmosphere. A tone of depression was pervasive with sorrow and yearning in the fore. But there was more than just a feeling "tone" or atmosphere involved: there were such matters as weekly—and in some cases daily visits to the grave; a house chosen because it was closer to the cemetery. . . . constant discussing of caretaking of the grave; nights filled with a mother's soft crying when a particularly poignant memory had been evoked; and discoveries of one's father staring for hours in a darkened room at the barely visible photograph of the dead child. The dead child lived on in a very concrete, day-to-day fashion. Photographs filled the household: in two cases the child's room was virtually turned into a shrine; each landmark in town elicited memories of what the child did there once; each recurrent event or holiday recalled how they had spent it together. The parents talked on and on about the dead child, even as much as ten or eleven years later.

And Helen, as the only daughter and a Victorian child, would, in fact, have been automatically cast in the role of family consoler. Children, particularly daughters, were seen then as angels who provided parents with happiness and comfort; their own emotional needs, if noticed at all, were considered secondary. Moreover, since the stability of the family unit was entirely dependent on the father—wife, children, and servants lived entirely for him because he was the wage earner—the dutiful daughter role was intensified.

To complicate the situation, with Adelaide's depression disqualifying her from assuming more of a place in her husband's life, Helen and her mother unconsciously

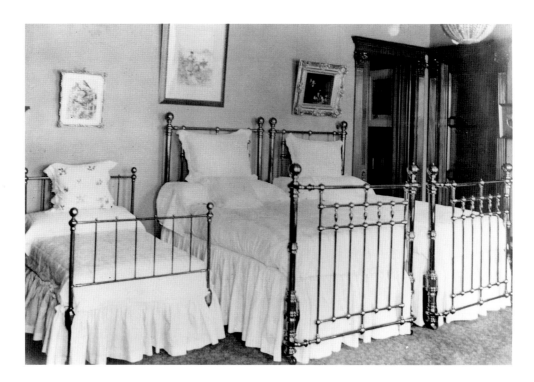

Fig. 9-7. Helen Clay Frick's bedroom with three beds.
Frick Archives

switched roles as Helen grew into womanhood. Adelaide became the child in need of care and protection and Helen became her mother's caretaker, as well as her father's confidante and surrogate spouse. Thus, her position evolved from a father's need to insure his needs would always be met. And Helen was trapped. Unlike her brother Childs, who as a man could earn a living in the outer world and was essentially tossed out of the nest by his father, Helen was entirely dependent upon him emotionally, financially, and spiritually. In later years, when Helen overdrew her checking account, she ignored this constraint. When her father made up the difference, she wrote in her diary: "it was just like her father" to send her two checks, calling them "an extra." But invariably, she was reminded of her subjugation. Her father explained that the extras "will not interfere with your regular."

Thus, Helen was locked into a psychologically conflicted role with her father. As the dutiful daughter who never married and was financially dependent on a grieving father in the Victorian age, she could know no independence. On one hand she was her father's flatterer and servant, on the other, a pawn in her mother's depression. In return for being her father's companion and confident, Helen lost her mother. But in exchange, she gained her father's ear, as well as excitement and a sense of power. Paradoxically, however, because she was also being disempowered, she was denied both her autonomy and the right to her own truth. She was satisfying her father's needs, not her own.

Helen wrote a story entitled, "Do All That You Can." It was about "a little star [that] said: I can not do much to make this world bright though as God had put me in the world, I must do something good. I can help to guide the boats along the waters at night." And as if describing the wreath of flowers in Martha's posthumous portrait that she wore in a locket around her neck, Helen wrote about "Four Little Sunbeams":

> Once there were four little sunbeams who were talking together. I will tell you what they said. "We must try to make some people happy," they said. The first one's name was Little Rose, the second Little Lily, the third, Forget-me-not, and the fourth, Little Margaret. . . . Little Rose went to a small cottage and played with a baby who had no toys at all, and her Mamma was away washing. . . . Little Lily went to see a poor old man who could not walk and brightened his little room up so that if he did not have pleasure out of doors he should have it in his home. Forget-me-not caressed a poor young girl who could not see and who was pale and thin and gave her a much rosier face than she had before. . . . Little Margaret went to a small garden where the flowers did not bloom but now made it smell good so when its owner came it was not the same sad little garden as before.

This ongoing mourning seemed to harbor hope, a secret hope that somehow Martha might return. Indeed, Helen's bedroom had three beds in it (fig. 9-7), and as she wrote: "One is Mademoiselle's the other is mine. No one sleeps in the other."

But there was another voice in Helen, a voice firm, startling, and rebellious (fig. 9-8). She had an innate practicality and an early understanding about money. In 1896, at age eight, she astonished her father by questioning the price he was paying for her chores, described by Helen as her "work." When she insisted he pay her in gold, Frick, not amused by his daughter, wrote Knoedler, "She said she understood that was what people generally demanded, and what I was in favor of, and she did not know why she should not be paid in gold, and would accept nothing else." Frick told Knoedler that as punishment, "I have discontinued purchasing her pictures for the present." With more money available for his own acquisitions, he chided, "Here is a great opportunity for you."

Fig. 9-8. Helen Clay Frick could put her foot down at an early age.
Frick Archives

Adelaide, who had become more interested in textiles and porcelains than paintings, often voiced her opinions, but it was Helen's conviction—strong, determined, and colored by the innocence of childhood—that most often influenced Frick. In 1897, Frick acknowledged his reliance on and confidence in her opinions and ideas, despite her tender age. He returned a picture by Chartran to Knoedler saying, "I want to exchange it for something better, by the gentleman, if I can. . . . It does not please me, nor do Mrs. Frick and my daughter seem to think it worthy of the artist." He also declined an offer for his Diaz (probably *Love Caresses*), writing Knoedler, "Helen would not consent to part with it." Yet another time, when Frick said he intended to exchange four paintings for a Charles-François Daubigny that was not considered as fine as the one he already owned, the seven-year-old Helen firmly announced that his "Detaille [title unknown] could go, as she did not care much for it, but the Chevalier [title unknown] and the Rico [*Fishermen's Houses in Venice* (1895)] could not be parted with, and, although she liked the Dupré [probably *The River*], yet she might be willing that it should go." Her father wrote Knoedler his reason for not purchasing the Daubigny: "You see the difficulties I would have had to encounter, even if I had decided to propose an exchange with you."

In 1898, Frick had a similar experience when taking his evening walk with Helen. He wrote to his then partner Andrew Carnegie that in pointing out the next-door Gillespie place, he said to Helen that he "regretted not having kept it when [he] owned it." Helen, however, was quick to reply: "Well, Papa, you got a great deal of money for it." In his letter, her father was quick to boast to Carnegie that he "had a daughter with a pretty good business head on her" and remarked that he "look[ed] forward to the time when Carnegie would receive as much pleasure from association with [his] little daughter as [he did]."

Shortly after, Helen showed her business acumen more forcefully. Her father had just acquired one of his first paintings by an old master, *Portrait of a Young Artist* (see fig. 6-7), then considered to be by Rembrandt. After the painting arrived, it was placed on an easel in the parlor. Adelaide chose red damask curtains to serve as background, and Frick requested that Knoedler find out as much as he could about the painting. In the meantime, Helen, then eleven, wrote Knoedler, who had sent her some photographs she had desired, that her canary, Mr. Mignon, and his family "send their chirping love to you . . . [and] As for the Rembrant [*sic*] I have not sold it yet, so you must come here and we will have a business talk about the subject."

And in 1900, when the Frick Building was completed in downtown Pittsburgh, Helen was asked, "Wasn't it lovely of your Papa to give you the finest, biggest building in the city for your very own?" She merely replied, "I'd rather he built me a hospital for sick dogs and cats."

Fig. 9-9. Helen Clay Frick, c. 1896.
Author's collection

Helen had become old beyond her years (fig. 9-9), something noted by Cecil Twyford, a London phrenologist who, on Frick's request, did character readings based on the size and shape of the bones in the skull. His 1896 report, "The Character of Miss Frick," noted that young Helen "is a strange mixture of a woman of thirty and a baby of three years old, and she must be treated quite suitably, according to which fit is on her. She must never be laughed at in either, for a more painfully sensitive disposition I never saw." In effect, he saw the little girl she was and the caretaker she was being made into—a role presaging the angry, often ridiculed woman circumstance would force her to become. Yet in his report, Twyford also anticipated Helen, the pioneer art historian and philanthropist. He felt Helen would always "try to get proper value for her money"

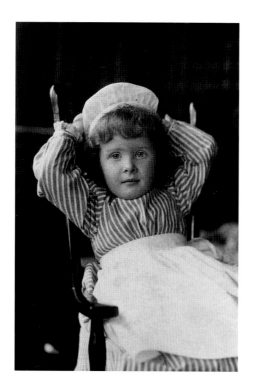

Fig. 9-10. Helen Clay Frick dressed as a nurse.
Frick Archives

and had "quite an idea of her own as to what that proper value either is or should be." In addition, he quite rightly identified her "magnificent organizing capabilities," her ability not only to "found a system" but also to "[get] it carried straight through," abilities that would allow her to found the Frick Art Reference Library in her father's memory and the Henry Clay Frick Fine Arts Department and Library at the University of Pittsburgh.

The startling thing was, however, the character reading reinforced the direction Helen's life had already taken. Twyford advised Frick, who was already a deep believer in this pseudo-science: "She has a nature that loves and requires change. It would never do for her to be shut up in a very strict disciplinary boarding school, away from those she most loved. In fact I should strongly advise her never being sent to a boarding school of any kind—it would warp her completely, change her natural character." Thus, he insisted Helen "be trained by some one who could give her more individual attention . . . than would be possible in any boarding school."

"She would," he said, "make a splendid matron of a hospital (fig. 9-10). Anyway, she should have a nurse's training "for she would later on become a heavenly visitor at a sick bedside, quite a patch of sunshine to light up weariness and suffering." She would also have a good memory for the doctor's orders, quick intuition as to a patient's wants, and great tact in managing the people in her care.

But Twyford warned Frick against Helen's ever marrying. He held that although one day Helen would "make a first class mother and wife if happily mated," she should "never be allowed to marry for money or position, or heartfelt affection." In his opinion, Helen would be best given "to an all around affection, and a very strict matrimonial rule would be intolerably irksome to her." He did add, however, that Helen was "just made up of love, and can really only be trained through her affections." He claimed, "were she loved, she would prove constant and true."

Guided by the report and persuaded by its findings, Frick drew his daughter closer to himself. One way Helen was shaped is manifest in her 1896 portrait by Chartran (see fig. 5-14). As we have seen, on the artist's first visit to Pittsburgh in 1895, he had painted a posthumous portrait of Martha, as well as a large oval portrait of the child dressed as Attie had been when Attie sat for her own childhood portrait. Additionally, he painted two miniatures of Martha: one fit nicely into a tortoiseshell frame on Adelaide's bureau, the other into a locket containing a piece of Martha's hair. This locket was made of turquoise—then considered a stone so negatively affected by the ill health of the wearer it becomes dull and can only regain its color when worn by a person in good health— and seed pearls, symbol of tears. It thus became both mourning jewelry and hex sign, designed on one hand to keep the memory of the deceased alive, and on the other, to constantly remind that death could strike young or old without warning. It was given to Helen to wear. When Chartran painted Helen, he portrayed her in plain, matter-of-fact terms with the turquoise locket around her neck.

Fig. 9-11. While Helen Clay Frick plays with her doll, she wears the locket containing Chartran's portrait of her deceased sister, Martha. Frick Archives

As consoler to her father's grief, apart from wearing her dead sister around her neck and being charged with caring for her memory, Helen would also be required to compete with her (fig. 9-11). As mentioned before, in 1895, on the tenth anniversary of Martha's birth, Frick had acquired his first picture from Knoedler, Bouguereau's *L'Espieglèrie (Mischievous Girl),* a portrait of a young child who looked like Martha. Regarded by René Gimpel as the start of Henry Clay Frick's collection, it was exhibited in Helen's bedroom over the fallen rosebud. A commemorative print of the painting, given to Helen by the artist, hung above the governess's desk in Helen's third-floor playroom (fig. 9-12).

With the idealization of Martha now the dominating psychic force in her family's life, and with her parent's calculated attempt to keep Helen identified with her dead sister, Helen's self-worth could only have been diminished. Her emotional development would naturally have been stifled by these constant reminders of Martha, reminders that forced Helen to live up to the ideal of her dead, perfect sister, reminders that since Martha died before she was old enough to rebel, defy, or disappoint, she, the *surviving* daughter, must become the "child" who might have been.

Moreover, as this treasured, surviving daughter, Helen was in demand as a companion, particularly by her father. Frick began taking her on evening walks around the neighborhood after work. They often went to Martha's grave and Gunn's Hill, a piece

Fig. 9-12. Clayton playroom with commemorative print of
Bouguereau's painting, c. 1895.
Frick Archives

of property where in the late 1890s Frick contemplated building a new home. A pioneer family had been massacred there by the Indians, and like many hillocks in the area, it had been fortified with gun embankments during the Civil War. The property, with a panoramic view of the steel mills along the Monongahela River, also provided a commanding view of Martha's grave. The neighbors watched father and daughter on these strolls. According to a family friend, Frick seemed delighted by the "antics of neighbors' children . . . [being] always quick to send a silver dollar spinning up in the air and into the outstretched palm as reward for a child's song or awkward dance." To these neighbors, it seemed that "strolling hand-in-hand through the trees and shadows of Homewood Cemetery, [was] their favorite spot for a walk every evening at twilight." As Frick wrote proudly to his then colleague and partner, Andrew Carnegie, "My experience is that little girls show their Mamas preference until they are about three years old and then the Papas seem to be appreciated."

At the age of seven, Helen also began practicing the role more and more bequeathed to her by her mother—hostess to Frick's friends. On Sunday mornings, after her father met in Clayton's second-floor library with Carnegie and Richard and Andrew Mellon, where they would talk about various art and business matters, the men would call on Helen in her third-floor playroom. Helen later wrote in her Clayton memoir that she "was always fully prepared to serve refreshments which they were kind enough to taste or else pretend to enjoy while they sat in chairs much too small to be comfortable [in] and at a table that was far from the proper size." Her Sunday ritual also came to include her father's visit to the next-door home of their artist friend Joseph R. Woodwell, where they would discuss painting and news of the art world.

As Helen gradually became immersed in Frick's world, his confidence, and his art collecting, her unmistakable impression must have been that she, not her mother, was the center of his world—that *she* was essential to her father's well-being, that she had extra power, that as her father's daughter she was to play a special role.

Helen also sensed, however, that with this position came a particular burden. She wrote in her later years that Clayton's walls "were rapidly being hung" and paintings "quite covered the walls." But her experience of her father's hobby, though she admired his ability to recall in exact detail the paintings he saw and appreciated the solace the paintings gave him, nevertheless burdened her. As if knowing she was bearing some inexplicable weight, when her father questioned her, "Now Helen, which would you prefer I should give you, this land or the pictures?" Helen had answered, "Papa, I would prefer the land as we can raise something on it."

Helen's burden *was* large. As Frick stood back to admire his ever changing collection, he encouraged Helen to express her opinion about the paintings. Although he did so partly from his enthusiasm and partly to prepare his daughter for society, he also did so as a father trains a son in a business he would one day inherit. Of these times, Helen later recalled, "It amused him to have me believe that my criticisms were of the utmost importance to him." But then, often when foreigners came to Pittsburgh, Clayton was one of the homes they wished to see. Because Frick was, as Helen later explained, "too busy to afford the luxury of returning home to meet these guests," she was "called upon to do the honors."

Once Frick tested his young daughter in a most profound way. Monsieur Coquelin, the famous actor from the Comédie Française and a close friend of several of the French artists whose works Frick collected, had come to Pittsburgh to play in *Cyrano de Bergerac* at the Alvin Theater, and he asked Frick if he could see Clayton. Because her father was busy and neither of her parents spoke French as well as she, Helen was asked to give the tour. Later, she recalled the horror she felt: "Never will I forget an order that was given [my nurse] Mlle. Ogiz: Have Helen recite in French to Monsieur Coquelin." Although Helen was taken to the theater to hear him and was, as she said, "thrilled of course," she later worried, "I wonder what his reaction must have been when he was obliged to listen . . . to a little American girl?"

But the little American girl represented herself well. Helen very clearly saw herself as the head of the household and assumed much of her identity from caretaking her parents. Often sent to her room by her governess for being rude, Helen was also very difficult to manage. In fact, Helen saw herself as parent to her parents, charging them to mind their health when they stayed in New York and cautioning them about exerting themselves too much. She referred to her mother as either "[my] preciously little baby Mama," "my sweet little 'baby,'" or "my dearest little baby" and though it was Helen who was inexplicably losing weight, Helen begged her mother to eat. During this period, when Helen signed her letters either "your bad child" or your "*horrid, horrid* Helen," she composed an essay about a young girl called Jane. She was a girl with a "careless but interesting" appearance who found entering womanhood "very trying"; a girl as awkward as a long-legged colt, whose gray eyes were "capable of being thoughtful, funny and fierce." As Helen wrote, "Kind, warm-hearted, bright and cheerful, Jane was the head of her family."

As Frick fell deeper into his melancholy, he increasingly turned to Helen and tied her to himself more forcefully than ever. Helen increasingly supported him, inexorably binding herself to a father who, though one of the toughest, wealthiest industrialists of his day, was, nevertheless, emotionally impoverished.

❖

Fig. 9-13. Jean-François Raffaëlli (1850-1924), *Woman in a White Dressing Gown*, c. 1898.
Acquired in 1898, Oil on canvas, 13¾ x 21¼ in. (34.9 x 53.9 cm).
Frick Art and Historical Center

WHILE HENRY CLAY FRICK TRAINED AND GUIDED HELEN, he insisted to her governess, Mademoiselle Ogiz, "Don't tell little girls fairy tales, teach them real things." He urged, "They need trained senses, keen observation, clear thinking, rapid reasoning, active, alert memories, trained imagination, expression in language, mental efficiency of every phase, so that the mind is as ready as the hand for every motion of which it is capable."

To this end, Frick regularly wrote Helen letters encouraging her to read. One dated July, 1903, went as follows:

> I hope you enjoyed this day? Am sure you did. Nothing will do you so much good as spending all the time you can in the air. Then you are in condition to read more intelligently, and how important it is to read and thoroughly understand things. Cultivate your mind and it will add so much to your happiness and to that of others who associate with you. Those who do not read are going back instead of progressing. I know you are anxious to please me, and will try to do what I desire.

Frick also used a combination of art and literature to teach Helen about "real things." In 1898, he purchased Jean-François Raffaëlli's *Woman in a White Dressing Gown,* now called *La Toilette* (fig. 9-13), depicting an adolescent girl in a white nightgown, a reinforcement perhaps of an earlier acquisition, *Little Red Riding Hood* (fig. 9-14), by the contemporary English painter George Frederic Watts. Apart from the fact that this latter painting was acquired by Frick at the onset of his long delayed grief reaction to Martha's death, a photograph of Frick and his family on a European trip with Andrew Carnegie in the early 1890s shows a timorous Helen similarly dressed in a hat and cape (fig. 9-15). She resembles the fairy-tale heroine who warns young girls about the lurking threat of seduction and, by extension, implies that a young girl can trust no man but her father. Not until 1906, when Helen was eighteen and had recently lost her Overholt grandmother, did Frick part with the painting, crediting it against a Maris and a Corot.

This painting—which Frick placed in the upstairs living room with Chartran's posthumous portrait of Martha and Dagnan-Bouveret's *Pilgrims at Emmaus*—together with its complicated connotations of morality and disturbing sexuality, perhaps more than any other foreshadowed the direction Frick was headed with Helen. By 1902, after his break with Carnegie and the formation of U.S. Steel, his symbolic warnings to his daughter about other men escalated. Although Frick at this time was beginning to actively consider a permanent move to New York, he invested over $100,000 on new furnishings and decorative art for Clayton, some of which encoded the psychology underpinning his messages to his fourteen-year-old daughter. Most prominent among

Above: Fig. 9-14. George Frederic Watts (1817–1904),
Little Red Riding Hood.
Acquired in 1895, Oil on canvas, 35.5 x 27 in. (88.9 x 67.3 cm).
Birmingham Museum and Art Gallery, Birmingham, England

Left: Fig. 9-15. Helen often wore clothes similar to those worn
by Little Red Riding Hood in the painting by George Watts.
Frick Archives

Fig. 9-16. Cottier and Company, *The Four Virgins (The Four Ladies of Literature)*.
Acquired c. 1902.
Frick Art and Historical Center

these are the stained-glass windows on Clayton's stair landing, *The Four Virgins* (fig. 9-16), now called *The Four Ladies of Literature*. From Cottier and Company in New York, they replaced windows called *Love in the Tower*. Each of the four new windows depicts the trial of an adolescent girl from the annals of literature, girls whose fates taught four valuable lessons about the perils of consorting with men: Miranda from Shakespeare's *The Tempest*, who after supporting her father in his time of struggle is finally allowed to marry a man who passes her father's every test; Marguerite from Goethe's *Faust*, whose sister has died. She has no mother to protect her, and in renouncing duty and virtue for sexual and material pleasure eventually goes insane and kills the baby she conceived with Faust, believing the infant to be contaminated by the devil; Isabella from Keats's "The Pot of Basil," who places the head of her murdered lover in a basil pot only to have her jealous brothers, his murderers, discover and break it, leaving Isabella to die of grief; and Madelaine from Keats's "St. Agnes Eve," who, unlike St. Agnes, ran off with her lover after he had secretly watched her undress, sleep, and awaken, the two then fleeing together into the night. Daily, as Helen passed up and down the stairs, she would be met by these figures, haunting in their luminosity, foreboding in their stories.

But there was something darker and even forbidden behind these pictures with their veiled warnings and silent implications. With her mother abdicating her position to her daughter, and Frick dependent on Helen's loyalty, trust, and companionship for his emotional needs, certain of Helen's personal boundaries were being broken. In a photograph taken around this time and discovered in a locked box in the Clayton library after Helen Clay Frick's death in 1984, it appears that Helen's father has blocked her passage to the bathhouse, that Helen is trying to get away, and that Frick is forcing an unwelcome kiss on her. The photograph seems to have been taken by someone hiding in the shadows of a bathhouse where Helen, who has just returned from a dancing class, intends to change her clothes. Dated 1903 in what appears to be Childs's handwriting, the picture may well have been taken by Childs, then a student at Princeton University and an enthusiastic amateur photographer with his own darkroom in the Clayton playhouse. In the envelope with the photograph was a letter to Helen from her father: "Sweetheart Mine. I hope to see much of you." Also in the envelope was the corner of a check engraved with the likeness of Martha (figs. 9-17-19).

While we cannot know the extent of this inappropriate behavior, there is evidence that Frick was fascinated by Helen. With the summer of 1904 coming to a close and Helen approaching her sixteenth birthday, Frick, who loved speed and enjoyed the thrill of an automobile at a time when there were few on the roads and no traffic laws, wrote her from Paris, describing what would have made his trip still more exhilarating: "Our Auto ride from Boulogne was the most delightful I have ever had—through the most beautiful country which at this season is especially charming as harvesting is in full swing—The roads are fine and with George [the chauffeur] in his 60 H. P. Mercedes and you beside me, I think it would be indescribable. We must try it some time."

And for this birthday, Frick personally designed a diamond necklace for Helen. No ordinary piece of jewelry, the necklace consists of 218 round cut diamonds in round platinum links with a marquise diamond clasp, the combined diamond weight being eighty karats; it measures four feet in length, long enough for a child's jumping rope or to wrap around one's neck at least four times. A few months later, in January 1905—months after his mother's death, just as the family was moving to the Vanderbilt house in New York, and just as Frick embarked on his collection of portraits of beautifully

Figs. 9-17–19. The 1903 photograph, with a fragment of a letter from Henry Clay
Frick to Helen and a corner of Helen's check with Martha's likeness.
Author's collection

dressed English ladies of the seventeenth and eighteenth centuries—he gave Helen a
large emerald ring and commissioned Chartran to do a life-size portrait of her as a Gibson Girl, the poised, intelligent, athletic woman whose good company and laughter
were idealized by high society (fig. 9-20).

Both ring and portrait, however, offended Helen deeply. Her anger over the ring,
which she regarded as a symbol of engagement, lasted her entire lifetime, as did her

Fig. 9-20. Théobald Chartran (1849–1907), *Portrait of Helen Clay Frick*, 1905.
Oil on canvas, 71½ x 39 in. (181.6 x 99.1 cm).
Private collection

objection to the portrait. On occasion she would vent her wrath about the ring to one of her grandnieces and would also huff angrily when the portrait was mentioned. Helen saw herself as a far different person from the feminine, sporty, sensual Gibson Girl ideal her father had projected upon her. A tomboy, Helen was ill at ease at parties, disliked dressing up, was awkward with boys, and throughout her life was uncomfortable with close physical contact, particularly kissing. Convinced she was a social misfit, Helen complained in a letter to her mother that "she danced like a real pig," and when writing in her journal about being taken to Mrs. Frew's dance, said "it was torture for me to go to it."

Helen was in a difficult position. Her father was smothering her with his attention and excessive demands; her mother was a depressive. By 1905, Helen was uprooted from her familiar Clayton surroundings and thrown into the New York social scene. Though far better educated than most girls her age, she was socially out of her depth. She lived in the Vanderbilts' famous mansion, universally known as the Vanderbilts' social "battering ram" because William K. Vanderbilt had constructed the house as a way to break into New York society. The house also symbolized the "Duchess for Dollars" craze, a craze begun in earnest when the Vanderbilt family became directly responsible for landing the "Duchess" title for four American heiresses. As the hallmark of the Vanderbilt empire and the social-climbing ostentation for which the Vanderbilts were known, the house not only intensified Helen's insecurity, but insulted and frightened her. Hers was the day when American heiresses—like Consuelo Vanderbilt, William H. Vanderbilt's granddaughter who in 1895 married the duke of Marlborough— often entered into loveless marriages to impoverished but titled Europeans, just so their newly rich parents could link their names to royalty. Although the heiresses became overnight celebrities, some found themselves drained both emotionally and financially by the cost of maintaining their husbands' palaces and grand life-styles.

Additionally, Helen was now separated from her closest friends in Pittsburgh. As a new face in Miss Spence's fashionable school, forced to mix with more cosmopolitan, socially aware girls than she, Helen was miserable. In a letter to Miss Duff, Clayton's housekeeper, Helen gave her "a large doze [sic] of my grumbling." Voicing her displeasure, she denounced the school as "a most bothersome and horrible place." She explained she started there "not knowing a soul . . . feeling as though I could chew everyone I saw. I did not know what to do! Everyone was pushing and screaming in that tiny, homely, house." Completely frustrated, Helen continued: "The rooms are not more than 10 feet square and there are about 8 girls and a teacher to a table and usually 8 tables to a room. There are so many rooms that it is very difficult for me to find my way around." An angry Helen despaired:

I *hate* the program. Miss Spence put French on it and Latin; she told everybody that there would be no changing before two weeks time but I certainly shall complain as I am "stuck" in with girls learning how to conjugate verbs in the former language! An awful come-down.

I had expected to take up German instead of Latin, this winter, and the villains are making me take Caesar—a most difficult task as nearly all the words are new. . . . Really this is a stupid school!

In fact, the phrenologist had been correct in his belief that Helen would suffer in a large educational scene. Her expectations and opinions had been shaped by the extraordinary tutoring she received from her beloved Mademoiselle Ogiz, whose lessons had put the young girl far ahead of her peers. Henry Clay Frick would say to Helen, "If it wasn't for that little Swiss woman, I don't know what would have become of you. You were so hard to manage." But the bond between Helen and her tutor went far deeper than Frick ever knew. Its full truth would later be evidenced in the strong resemblance between St. Anne (the Virgin's mother) in *The Education of the Virgin* (fig. 9-21)—now attributed to George de La Tour, an acquisition made in 1948 when the unmarried Helen was in her sixtieth year and head of the Acquisitions Committee for the Frick Collection—and Mademoiselle Ogiz (fig. 9-22). In 1905, Helen's letters increasingly confessed her longing to be home at Clayton: "I hope and expect to go home Friday to spend Saturday and Sunday there. Two days are not very much but a lot of talking for more did not seem to do any good so I have stopped; but I hope to spend many days home this Winter or else my health will certainly 'break down.' "

In a 1939 *New Yorker* profile, "Daughter of Her Father," John McCarten quotes the teachers as remembering Helen as "small and slender, with great nervous energy and little physical strength." She was referred to as "a docile student, with a tendency to swoon every now and then in an unobtrusive way . . . [sinking] to the floor sometimes when standing before the class." The Spence School also took note that "she faltered in recitation," and it seemed to them Helen had a certain "fastidiousness of taste. She would collapse in a heap when her history teachers mentioned some particularly brutal detail of war or a catastrophe."

Nevertheless, Helen dug in and proved an excellent student. She received top marks in everything from spelling to Chaucer, and from algebra to German. She was never late to class, completed every lesson, and had a perfect attendance record. Leather-bound volumes of her art history notebooks, recognized by her classmates as "the best of the group—one of a kind," because they were so beautifully written and illustrated, remain in the Frick Archives, proof of her obviously serious, scholarly, and loving approach to her studies.

Above: Fig. 9-21. Georges de La Tour (1593–1652),
The Education of the Virgin, c. 1650.
Acquired in 1948, Oil on canvas,
33 x 39½ in. (83.8 x 100.4 cm).
The Frick Collection

Right: Fig. 9-22. Mademoiselle Ogiz.
Frick Archives

In this respect, Helen benefited greatly from the grand tour of Europe she made annually with her father. It sparked her interest in and respect for archival material, something that would be evident when she later founded the Frick Art Reference library in the 1920s. In 1908 Helen visited the Record Office Museum in London and described it as "One of the most interesting places I have *ever seen*. There we saw a letter written to George III, just before the Declaration of Independence of the American Colonies, and signed by J. Hancock, S & J Adams, Patrick Henry, Benj. Franklin & others. Also a letter signed by Marie Antoinette." At the same time, she visited the Wallace Collection and revealed her own developing collector's eye when she visited the National Gallery: "I nearly went wild over so many pictures that I could have remained there forever. We visited first the English School. There we admired the marvelous Turners, Romneys, Reynolds, Gainsboroughs, and also the Lawrences . . . next the Italian, where I saw some dear old friends of mine, too numerous to recall. Then, the Dutch, and finally the Spanish. . . . We stayed until the bell sounded, and even then, were so slow to leave, that the guards had to hurry us away."

She also anticipated her father's eventual purchase of the great banker J. P. Morgan's Fragonard panels. Helen said of her visit to Morgan's "*wonderful house*": "[I] was too entranced by everything, for he has not alone wonderful pictures, but fine furniture; carvings; jeweled ornaments; 1000 superb miniatures of famous people, each framed by pearls & diamonds; [there is also a] large collection of memorandum cases etc. of his curiosities, [where] I was most interested by . . . [a] clock of Marie Antoinette, her hair . . . and of pictures . . . fine mural decorations by Fragonard."

Often in the company of renowned artists of the day, Helen traveled to Paris with Roland Knoedler's brother-in-law, Count Jan V. Chelminski. There she joined the Chartrans, who lived in Paris, and together they had wonderful times dining, attending the Opéra Comique, and admiring the artist's murals at the Sorbonne.

She visited Baroness Rothschild's house and the Musée des Archives in Paris, an "ancient residence" of which she wrote: "It contains hundreds of letters from celebrated people, but none interested me as much as the following: Last letter written by Marie Antoinette (to the Conciergerie & relating to her approaching death) last letter written to her father by Charlotte Corday, letters of Napoleon, Robespierre, of the many celebrated french writers, those of many Kings, Queens & others of the royal families."

Florence was also a favorite city. On a visit alone with her father, Helen wrote: "saw Santa Maria Novella! For the third time! How dearly I love it." She examined Ghiberti's bronze doors—the ones copied and gilded for 640 Fifth Avenue—and felt she was in "dream-land" as she flew through the Uffizi with Frick, also seeing the cathedral, baptistery, campanilo, the Pitti Gallery, the church of San Lorenzo, and the Brancacci

Chapel, all in one day. And she saw the church of Santa Croce, the Academy of Fine Arts, the Church of the Annunziato, the monastery of San Marco, and the Cathedral Museum, where she "admired for quite a while, the 4 exquisite singing-lofts by Donatello, but chiefly those of Luca della Robbia. His represent the Singing Children—those of Donatello, the Dancing Children."

Although Knoedler had made a small handbook of the pictures in the gallery at 640 Fifth Avenue a few years before, in 1908 twenty-year-old Helen decided to present her father with a Christmas gift, a catalogue of the portraits in his collection. Helen— who had now become an inveterate photographer, a diligent diary writer, and keeper of family scrapbooks—was not disappointed in Frick's reaction. The catalogue, as Helen recalled, "caused [her] father an enormous amount of pleasure"; so much so that the following year, she gave him a catalogue of the landscapes.

Her father, delighted with his daughter's interest, wrote a friend, Dr. Gorodiche, Helen "has been charming; occasionally gets a little obstreperous, but on the whole is everything we could wish her to be." And a good daughter she was. In addition to making catalogues, she chose the leather for the library and breakfast room at Clayton, as her mother should have done, and was now in fact truly the female head of the household.

❖

ON HELEN'S RETURN FROM EUROPE IN 1908, she was certainly old enough to take a serious interest in her father's collection. But she was also old enough to consider, like Consuelo Vanderbilt before her, "coming out"—becoming a debutante and being presented to society in a whirlwind of elegant luncheons, tea parties, and balls in hopes of finding a husband. With contract marriages still in vogue, and Consuelo Vanderbilt's 1906 separation from the duke causing a national and international scandal, Helen, ever intimidated by the press and the pleasure-seeking, title-seeking world, was fearful of the New York debutante circuit. Vulnerable and frightened by living in the famous Vanderbilt house, when Frick announced his intention to hold a debutante ball in her honor in the Vanderbilt picture gallery at 640 Fifth Avenue (fig. 9-23), Helen initiated her first outright rebellion against him.

Frick had always advised the press that Helen would "receive no notoriety as one of America's 'richest heiresses.' " In private, however, he enjoyed teasing Helen about her situation. In her later years, Helen wrote that when summering at Eagle Rock, after the organist played Handel's "Largo," her father never failed to request the "Ave Maria." He would then look at Helen "with a twinkle in his eye," and in a reference to

Fig. 9-23. The Vanderbilt picture gallery at the time of William Henry Vanderbilt, c. 1883.
Milton S. Eisenhower Library, Special Collections of the Johns Hopkins University

the fate of the pleasure-seeking queen Marie Antoinette, he would call the song the "Ave Marie."

And yet, in all of this, Helen needed to worry less about her being married off for a title or being perceived as an heiress, than she needed to worry about her father's increased need for her. Her initials, H.C.F., were his. His ring was on her finger. His diamond necklace was around her neck. He even named a flower—a new variety of purple chrysanthemum grown in Clayton's greenhouse—after her, dropping Helen's Christian name and calling the flower "Miss Clay Frick." Known as a "sport" and referred to as a "freak" in the newspapers, the flower was a spontaneous genetic mutation of the William Duckham cultivar, a beautiful and popular flower of its day. In dropping "Helen," and using only his nickname, "Clay," Helen's father had seen her only as an extension of himself, rather than a flower in her own right.

As the December date for her debutante party approached, Helen bolted. In a rare show of independence on her mother's part, as well, Adelaide waited for Frick to go downtown and then joined her daughter's rebellion, secretly boarding a train with her that was bound for Pittsburgh. Once at Clayton, Helen sent out invitations for a debut there, one designed to her specifications, not her father's. She chose December 16 as the date, as it was her mother's forty-ninth birthday, and invited family and close friends to a simple reception from three to six o'clock, followed by a supper and a ball.

Not surprisingly, Frick was outraged by the women's domestic revolt and refused to come to Pittsburgh for the party. But when Helen sent him an invitation with: "Papa mine, won't you come to my party?" inscribed on it, he relented.

The local newspapers remarked that although hundreds of bouquets sent by family and friends filled every room downstairs, mixing with the Christmas decorations, Helen carried a bouquet of lilies of the valley with a cluster of tiny pink rosebuds in the center. They noted that although she changed her bouquets throughout the afternoon, most of the time she carried the bouquet given to her by her father (fig. 9-24).

Helen also wore a necklace, a new gift from Frick consisting of a tiny, teardrop pendant with a minute single ruby, the martyr's stone, and a pearl, symbol of tears. But the success of her party and the reconciling gesture of the necklace had not satisfied Helen. She had always been promised by her father that on the day of her debut, he would grant her any wish. When Helen now asked him if his promise still held, and he said it did, Helen requested he give Pittsburgh a park, perhaps as an expression of her concern for the city's children, not so fortunate as she.

Fig. 9-24. Helen Clay Frick (seated far right) with her mother (center) at the Clayton debutante party, 1908.
(Meyer von Bremen's painting, *The Darlings*, in the background.)
Frick Archives

Fig. 9-25. The Iron Rail was established by Helen as a rest home for girls working in Boston's mills.
Frick Archives

Parks were few in Pittsburgh. The first one had been given in 1880 by Henry Phipps, and in 1905, when Frick left Pittsburgh for New York, he had given one block, complete with play areas, green grass, and a water fountain to Homestead. Helen must have hit a chord with her father, for he agreed to bequeath to Pittsburgh upon his death a 150-acre park composed of his informal golf course, the woods and ravines he and Helen had walked every evening at twilight, and the Gunn's Hill property abandoned as a home site when he moved to New York.

Obviously this land, so central to Helen's childhood, carried a special poignancy because it adjoined the cemetery where Martha was buried. Its forests and open fields, replete with squirrels, chipmunks, rabbits, opossums, raccoons, and deer, as well as every type of native bird, wildflower, and fern, was a world buffering the realm of the dead from the world of the living. In donating the park, Frick provided a $2 million endowment, thereby forever connecting Clayton and Helen's childhood to the quietude of the cemetery, in land to be forever a sanctuary.

And yet, generous as the bequest was, its timing as a gift to be transferred to the city after his death was another way Frick controlled his daughter. The underlying tension mounted between father and daughter and was soon manifest in a joke concerning two paintings—the ever loyal *Julia, Lady Peel* (see fig. 6-19) and El Greco's portrait of the misogynist *St. Jerome* (see fig. 7-50). As previously mentioned, Frick would favorably compare his daughter to Lady Peel, because the two often wore large black hats with feathers bursting from the crown: "A hundred years from now, people will point out this picture . . . and say, 'This is Miss Frick,' " he would tease, while Helen would turn "this little joke of ours" to daggers by pointedly replying, "And they will point to Greco's picture of the Cardinal and say, 'There's Mr. Frick.' "

Indeed, in just the few short years until 1910, when Helen entered her twenty-first year, the conflicted relationship between father and daughter intensified. Frick continued to seek Helen's advice, and together they considered potential acquisitions; they often playfully needled Knoedler by offering far less for a work than it was obviously worth. But a memoir Helen wrote in her later years inadvertently portrayed her as a person so hypervigilant she resembled a prisoner who, because her life is solely dependent on her jailer, notices her captor's every move. At Eagle Rock for the summer, for example, although Helen described herself as relaxed when cleaning her father's reading glasses or visiting him when he was having his daily massage, she watched him carefully, observing the rustling noise he made when reading his newspapers, the way he extended his arm almost straight when smoking and knocked the cigar ash with his fourth right finger, the sound of his footsteps when returning from golf, the "bang" of the elevator door as he went upstairs for his afternoon massage and the "bang" again as he got out on the third floor, even the scrape of his chair when he got up from his desk.

With Helen's entrée into the adult world, the dynamic of the father-daughter relationship increasingly became, as *The New Yorker* would later describe it, one of constant fights but loving scenes when they made up. In fact, observing the push-pull of their relationship, one could characterize their interaction as "she got if she gave; he gave if he received." As Helen drew her father into her humanitarian social causes, he drew Helen to himself. Just as Helen depended on her father financially for her causes, he relied on her for companionship.

If a tug of war had developed, in some respects Helen was winning. She had not only moved her debut to Clayton but had also received, as her debutante wish, the assurance of the park bequest, however eventual, and had by 1910 also established the Iron Rail (fig. 9-25), a summer home for girls working in Boston's mills and factories. To help Helen's humanitarian effort, her father bought large pieces of property around Wenham, Massachusetts, a town very near Eagle Rock. He paid all expenses for the project and within five years owned over three hundred acres of land, in the process becoming the town's largest landowner.

Even the *New York Times* complimented Helen for her work. It commended her for her "love for humanity in general, and for girls who toil in particular," explaining that her compassion "led her to found [this] private charity which ranks as the most unusual in the country."

The Iron Rail *was* indeed an unusual vacation home. The facility consisted of a white frame house with broad verandahs, hammocks, swing couches, sun parlor, gymnasium, tennis courts, and golf links. When visiting the Iron Rail, the girls stayed in cottages named Canary and Friendship. Rooms had special names—"Sunbeam Corner," "Four-leaf Clover," and "Wild Roseum." The girls were to have the day and evening to themselves, their only responsibility being to relax and rest. There were, however, rules. They were not allowed to wear "rats" or "puffs" in their hair, nor were they allowed to smoke, wear cosmetics, bob their hair, fib, flirt, gossip, or wear unnecessary frills. Male visitors were not allowed on the grounds, and when the girls returned to their work, they were instructed not only to "lower the eyes when strange men pass on the street, [but] to look at and only salute ministers." Helen prepared a "True Blue Hymnal," a selection of her favorites. "Health, Neatness and Sisterly Love" was the Iron Rail's motto.

⁙

As Helen began to put more and more of her energies into humanitarian causes, in addition to continuing to help shape, advise, and admire her father's art-collecting passion, so too she began to sense her destiny. An essay seventeen-year-old Helen had written at the Spence School, entitled "Myself at Eighty Years Old," perhaps foreshadowed her ultimate fate as a maiden lady:

> At eighty years old, I am a stooped, wrinkled, little old maid, very feeble-minded concerning questions of the present, but alive and active to those of the past. I always dress in gray, and wear a white kerchief fastened in the front with a pearl pin. The little hair I have left is parted down at the sides, and covered with a small lace cap. Although my face is very wrinkled by Father Time and my eyes are watery blue, my spirits are still very youthful, and I do not realize that I am no longer a girl. I love to *reminisce,* and whenever any of my girl-hood friends call on me—and there are but few alive—we talk of older times to our hearts' content.

In 1926, when Helen was thirty-six years old and well on her way to becoming this "old maid," she remembered her Clayton childhood. As chairman of the Acquisitions Committee for the Frick Collection, she steered the trustees toward the purchase of Jean-Baptiste-Siméon Chardin's *Lady with a Bird-Organ* (fig. 9-26). It was acquired on the fiftieth anniversary of Chartran's painting pictures of Helen's canaries on Clayton's

Fig. 9-26. Jean-Baptiste-Siméon Chardin (1699–1779), *Lady with a Bird-Organ*, 1751 (?).
Acquired in 1926, Oil on canvas, 20 x 17 in. (50.8 x 43.2 cm).
The Frick Collection

Fig. 9-27. The Clayton playroom where Helen spent her days and cared for her canaries, c. 1895.
Frick Archives

glass doors and recalls her beloved canary family and her Clayton playroom of the 1890s where the delicate birds lived (fig. 9-27). This painting expresses Helen's lifelong love of birds, her ability to identify their songs, and the joy their independent voices brought her. After her father's death she created a wildlife sanctuary on a section of her farm in Bedford Village, New York.

But the painting also expressed her captivity. A popular song of 1899 written by Arthur I. Comb and Harry von Tilzer describes Helen's situation:

> She's only a bird in a Gilded Cage,
> A beautiful sight to see.
> You may think she's happy and free from care.
> She's not tho' she seems to be.

And Helen perhaps described herself in the same way. A story she wrote in the 1920s about her canary, "Mr. Mignon," seems to capture something of herself:

> As I sit under the trees listening to the merry songs of the little birds on this hot June afternoon, suddenly time and surroundings are changed! I am a seven year old little girl again, holding in my hands a small square box-cage in which is imprisoned a canary. My mother has given it to me just a few minutes ago, and I watch the poor little creature with pity and wonder how people can be so cruel as to pent up an innocent bird in such a small place.

Helen's combined role as Frick's loyal daughter and emotional hostage to his guilt and longing, came together in a compelling way in 1910 with the purchase of Rembrandt's *The Polish Rider*. The painting, as mentioned previously, held many associations to Frick's early coking days—days when Frick mounted the gray horse named Billy and, like the Christian Knight in the picture, canvassed the coal bluffs after nightfall and before dawn, days when he sold his coke on the Mon Wharf with Mt. Washington towering above him.

But the painting appears to have had other associations for Frick. As Osbert Sitwell commented, Frick bought the painting "off his own bat." But the artistic importance of the painting, and its allusion to his early coking days, may have been only a small part of his motivation. Though not a portrait of Helen, it is at the very least a metaphor for her life. As one can see in the 1906 photograph of Helen mounted sidesaddle on Patricia (fig. 9-28)—her gray, pony-sized horse with a cropped tail—Helen is herself like Rembrandt's Christian Knight–Cossack (see fig. 1-38). The resemblance between them is noticeable, more so when a passport photograph taken of Helen in 1909 (fig. 9-29) is contrasted with the Polish Rider's face (fig. 9-30). Frick was often quoted as saying he would rather be a painter like Rembrandt than anything else, and with *The Polish Rider*, he shows why. It would seem Frick had added yet another look-alike family portrait to his collection.

In April 1910, Roger Fry, art advisor to the Metropolitan Museum, asked Frick if he wanted to buy the painting from Count Tarnowski. Frick, who traditionally took a long time deciding whether or not to make a purchase, made up his mind immediately. Excited by the prospect of owning the painting, he wrote Fry on May 12:

> I am much pleased with the way you have handled this matter; of course, I have been governed entirely by you as to its value, as I have great confidence in your judgment.
>
> As to your remuneration, I want to be quite fair with you. Would be glad to have from you an idea as to just what would be satisfactory. I have no doubt that in the future you will be able to secure many other important pictures for me.

He instructed Fry to "please deliver the painting to Knoedler [in Paris] . . . and show to no one except family or party having order from you or myself." Always considerate of his friend Roland Knoedler, who was in Paris with Helen and Adelaide, Frick apologized for using Fry as agent, saying: "Would have preferred to have purchased this Rembrandt through you, but I did not want to lose the opportunity of securing it; while I paid a high price, yet the picture is unique, being as I am told, one of two equestrian portraits by the artist."

Left: Fig. 9-28. Helen Clay Frick on Patricia, c. 1910.
Private collection

Top right: Fig. 9-29. Helen Clay Frick in 1909.
Frick Archives

Lower right: Fig. 9-30. Rembrandt Harmensz. van Rijn (1606–1669), Detail, *The Polish Rider,* c. 1655.
Oil on canvas, 46 x 53⅛ in. (116.8 x 134.9 cm).
The Frick Collection

Frick happily consented to lend Knoedler the painting for his upcoming exhibition and said in this same letter, quite cheerfully, "It gives me the keenest pleasure to see the interest Helen takes in art."

Helen's interest, in fact, as it related to *The Polish Rider,* soon turned to concern. At the end of the month, the painting went to London where a copy was made for the count by a thirty-two-year-old English portrait painter, Ambrose McEvoy. In the meantime, however, Fry's casual business methods had become worrisome. Frick wrote Knoedler: "If through any misunderstanding that picture should be sent to London before the 30th, please see that it is at once returned to Paris. I cabled Fry, but at this writing, have nothing from him; he, however, is not used to modern business methods, and may not have thought it necessary to reply to my cable, although I asked for one."

In June, Frick sent Fry his commission, asked for a receipt, and instructed him to ship the picture "as soon as it is copied." But by mid-December, *The Polish Rider* had not arrived, and Helen actively involved herself in the situation. She was unhappy about having the copy made, particularly since the descendants of European collectors were often guilty of selling a copy as if it were the original. She wrote Fry a number of letters, and by mid-December, when Fry did not reply, Frick wrote him a stern note: "No reply to my daughter's letter regarding what we should have regarding the Polish Rider." Anxious, he wrote again on December 29: "Please see that we receive from you such a letter regarding the Polish Rider as my daughter indicated we should have; in view of the fact that a copy of it was made, the question might arise in the future that we had the copy and not the original, and if we have a letter from you giving full particulars of the transaction, it will be most satisfactory."

Helen's fear *The Polish Rider* might one day become confused with the copy was, in an odd quirk of fate, later resolved. In 1927, seventeen years after her father's acquisition of the painting, and eight years after his death, the copy was destroyed when Count Tarnowski's castle burned to the ground. That same year the artist, Ambrose McEvoy, then only forty-nine years old, died suddenly. The opportunity to compare the Frick original to the Tarnowski copy was forever lost.

What was never lost, however, was Helen's emotionally charged relationship with her father. On the one hand, she showed her devotion by making a small pillow for him, embroidered with the word "Westmoreland," the county of his birth, and was rewarded with his delight that she had "worked with those dear little hands guided by that wonderful brain." He said to Helen, "you certainly [were] thinking of me as those letters were being formed and the evidence of your affection makes me very happy."

Meanwhile, Helen was also arguing bitterly with him. In 1910, perhaps as a reflection of her own status, she supported Teddy Roosevelt and the virtues of his trust-busting, while her father and his friends complained they had bought Roosevelt, "but he didn't stay bought." And yet Helen's rebellions were always short-lived. More a spouse than daughter, her increased subservience could easily be seen in a painting Frick commissioned from Edmund Tarbell in 1910, a painting now in the National Portrait Gallery, Washington, D.C., a painting Helen so disliked she returned it to the artist (fig. 9-31). The painting—done on or about Helen's twenty-first birthday—is a dual portrait of father and daughter as if seated in a carriage on their way to the opera. Frick dominates the painting's foreground, and Helen, pressed to the background, her face unhappy, her nose red as if from crying, is readily showing her discomfort. She disliked opera, and although she appears here more like her father's wife than his child, more

Fig. 9-31. Edmund C. Tarbell (1862–1938), *Henry Clay Frick and Daughter Helen,* c. 1910.
Helen's twenty-first birthday portrait.
Acquired c. 1910, Oil on canvas, 31 x 23¼ in. (78.8 x 59 cm).
The National Portrait Gallery, Smithsonian Institution

significant, she appears submissive. Her fragile white dress is starkly overshadowed by her father's black tuxedo, accentuating her vulnerability.

During the summer of 1912, after the family returned from their trip to Egypt, Helen did seem more wife than daughter to the father. When Henry Clay Frick decided to give a party at Eagle Rock in his daughter's honor, Helen, ever acting as her father's alter ego, and ever challenging, refused to have a party for just the social elite. She persuaded him to open Eagle Rock's gates in the afternoon to the local townspeople and merchants so that they could wander through the grounds, barns, and gardens. Sousa's band played on the lawn overlooking the Atlantic Ocean while that night, after the family went upstairs and changed into evening clothes, Frick, with Helen on his arm, received the socialites coming to their dinner dance.

But Martha's shadow always controlled their relationship. The following year, in December 1913, Helen gave Frick a 1914 Friendship Calendar for his sixty-fourth birthday. Each day of the year had its own page, and on each page Helen, or one of her father's friends, had written a poignant message or quotation. On one page, Helen pasted a photograph of the springhouse where her father was born and wrote: "I remember, I remember the place where I was born. The little window where the sun came streaming in at morn." On another she wrote, "I have you fast in my fortress and will not let you depart, but will put you down in the dungeon, in the round tower of my heart." But Helen had also carefully removed the page dated August 5, 1914, which was the twenty-ninth anniversary of Martha's birth.

Helen took other initiatives as well. She had been hard at work attaining from Knoedler's "the pedigree" of her father's recently acquired Van Dyck, *Paola Adorno, Marchesa di Brignole Sale;* the history of El Greco's *Purification of the Temple;* as well as the documented history of all her father's acquisitions dating from 1901. In constant communication with Knoedler's, she studied the articles on Holbein they sent to her, organized the shipment of paintings from their storage rooms to Eagle Rock, and reviewed the photographs of the paintings in her father's collection which she had requested Knoedler make.

The summer of 1914—the summer Frick suffered his near fatal attack of inflammatory rheumatism and was pressing his architects for completion of 1 East Seventieth Street—Helen showed more clearly than ever her devotion to him. She took charge of the paintings coming to Eagle Rock for the summer and after arranging them in the house, pleased with her efforts and the way Eagle Rock looked, she wrote Roland Knoedler, "The effect of the pictures up here is very attractive this year and shows what good taste you & I have!"

Fully capable of handling her father's collection, Helen was also fully adept at handling his emotions. Extremely concerned about his anxious emotional state, she tried,

Fig. 9-32. Childs Frick and Frances Dixon Frick with their
wedding party, 1913. Helen Clay Frick wears a black hat with
white plume and is standing behind Childs.
Author's Collection

in her own way, to humor him. She asked Knoedler's to forward Chartran's portrait of Martha, stored in their vault, to Eagle Rock. And to soothe her father's anger over the slow pace of the new house, in a gesture that almost mocked his egotism, Helen gave him the *Memoirs of Benvenuto Cellini,* a humorous exaggeration of Cellini's sense of importance and expertise. Frick seemed to enjoy the book, but clearly he missed the point. He continued to war with all parties involved in the building of his new home.

But even as Helen made gesture after gesture to show her love for her father, she was at odds with him. She had disliked living in New York from the moment she moved into the Vanderbilt house in 1905. When her family vacated the house in 1914, she said quite smugly, 640 Fifth Avenue "did not fill [her father's] fixed requirement of always the best." Although her father's new home was the best, Helen was as upset at having to live permanently in New York as she was by her father's behavior. In 1913, she had

Fig. 9-33. Edgar Degas (1834–1917), *The Rehearsal*, c. 1878–79.
Acquired in 1914, Oil on canvas, 18¾ x 24 in. (47.6 x 60.9 cm).
The Frick Collection

pasted a picture of Clayton on one of the Friendship Calendar's pages, writing "East to West, Clayton's best." To make her point, she taught her spaniel, Fido, "the cutest trick." As Helen explained to her Uncle Christian Overholt—a favorite uncle, who lived in Wooster with the rest of Frick's relatives—when she said, "Fido, what would you rather do than live in New York?" Fido was supposed to lie down and play dead. Unfortunately, according to Helen, "Fido didn't always do it." But when Helen mentioned a lot of other towns, as soon as she said "'Pittsburgh,' Fido jumped up."

There was reason for Helen to feel entrapped. On October 14, 1913, she had been a bridesmaid at the wedding of her brother Childs to Frances Dixon from Baltimore (fig. 9-32). Frick gave Childs a lifetime settlement of $12 million and immediately after the marriage ceremony quietly passed an envelope containing a check made out for $2 million to his new daughter-in-law, whose twenty-first birthday was also her wedding day.

On the other hand, Helen, five years older than Frances, was to have no such wedding, nor any such financial independence. As if demanding that Helen dance to his, not another's tune, in 1914 Frick acquired Degas's *The Rehearsal* (fig. 9-33). Widely regarded as an unusual purchase for Frick's day, particularly for Frick, who was then buying Old Masters, not modern French artists, the painting seems to follow Frick's pattern of acquiring art embedded with messages to family members. Apart from the fact that the graceless ballerinas recall Helen's childhood comment about having "danced like a real pig," the brooding figure of the violinist resembles Frick.

Degas had painted *The Rehearsal* in France in 1878 or 1879—a date perhaps significant to Frick because those were the years when he, as a bachelor in West Overton, was playing the violin at local dances. Frick would dance only five or six of the selections, so when a tune came up that he liked, he would give his violin to someone else, saying he was "going to dance this next one." After the dance, he would return to his violin, thank the person for holding it, and play the pieces having less appeal for him.

At the time Frick acquired *The Rehearsal* in 1914, Louisine Havemeyer, the widow of violin-playing Henry Osborne Havemeyer and a longtime collector of Degas's work, had become actively involved with the Women's Political Union which sought civil and political equality for women. Encouraged by Mary Cassatt, who had said to her, "Go home and work for the suffrage. If the world is to be saved, it will be the women who save it," Louisine later admitted, "It goes without saying that my art collection also had to take part in favor of the suffrage campaign."

One month after Frick bought *The Rehearsal*, Louisine decided to stage her second exhibition in as many years for the benefit of woman suffrage. She asked whether Frick would be willing to lend a painting to her show, which would feature a mixture of Old Masters, as well as works by Degas and Cassatt. Frick chose *The Rehearsal* for the new art and for an Old Master, he selected Van Dyck's portrait of Marchesa Giovanna

Fig. 9-34. Sir Anthony Van Dyck (1599-1641), *Marchesa Giovanna Cattaneo*, 1622-27.
Acquired in 1907, Oil on canvas, 40⅜ x 34 in. (102.6 x 86.4 cm).
The Frick Collection

Cattaneo (fig. 9-34). His choice of paintings may have revealed Frick's opinion of the suffragist movement. Certainly the ballerinas depict the "working class," as they grind out their routine with robot-like moves. In fact, their apathy and boredom seems a commentary on certain sinister aspects of the ballet, then a declining art form restricted to interludes held at the Paris Opéra. As was well known, the ballet profession had degenerated to the point where young ballerinas were routinely oppressed by their ballet masters, and the ballerinas themselves were often sold by their mothers to bourgeois men for financial favors.

By contrast, the marchesa, as a member of one of the original Italian families whose members included doges, cardinals, scholars, and statesmen, was a woman of high birth, breeding, and cultivation. She was also a woman bound by her family name;

she is pictured holding a heavy gold chain, known as a catena, thought to be a play on her family name, a pun also thought to be repeated in the C-shaped scrolls embroidered on her sleeves.

At the close of Louisine's exhibition, when the two paintings were returned to 1 East Seventieth Street, their placement in the house further revealed the very subtle, punishing dynamic from which Frick was working. The *Marchesa* was exhibited in the West Gallery with portraits of European aristocracy, while *The Rehearsal* was placed above Helen's desk in her father's private sitting room on the second floor, directly across from the doorway of her own upstairs library. More telling, the painting shared the company of El Greco's *Purification of the Temple* (see fig. 4-21) and Manet's *The Bull Fight* (see fig. 4-22)—paintings symbolic of Henry Clay Frick's crushing defeat of the rebellious working class at Homestead. *The Rehearsal,* like the El Greco and the Manet, was a subtle warning. Seen in the context of Helen's successful 1908 debutante rebellion, and her splendid 1912 party at Eagle Rock for both villagers and high society, *The Rehearsal* seemed to caution Helen to dance no steps of her own invention—unless they served Frick himself. In this way, *The Rehearsal* is like a sinister echo of this post-Homestead statement made by her father:

> Nobody could have more sympathy for the poor. Poverty has been my own lot, and knowing from experience the kind of life led by the poor, I felt, when I first entered the coke business, that by treating workmen properly I would never have any labor troubles. By the time the Homestead Strike came I had learned that the more a certain type of workmen get, the more arrogant and unreasonable they become. In the end, they wanted to run our business, to be dictators. Of course there could be only one boss.

At home as in the workplace Frick demanded there be "only one boss," as he wrote Carnegie of their Homestead employees. Helen, the bridesmaid, would never be bride.

The Rehearsal may have spoken to Helen with the voice described by the Jungian analyst, Maureen Murdock, when commenting on the "hero father," the controlling father. His words and actions say: "Challenge my authority and you'll lose my approval." "Compete with me and you'll lose my protection." "Expose my weakness and I'll leave you forever." The dark, brooding violin master, so like Frick, and the red-haired ballerina, so like Helen, indicated Frick would never allow her to be her own woman, the type of liberated female envisioned by the suffragists. Increasingly, Helen seemed less and less able to be a person in her own right, but more like one of her father's bronzes, a windup toy either silent or whirling, depending on his command.

A comment in Volume One of *The Frick Collection,* written under Helen's guidance, expresses the dark nature of this painting: "Our picture is one of [Degas's] best.

Fig. 9-35. William Hogarth (1697–1764), *Miss Mary Edwards*, 1742.
Acquired in 1914, Oil on canvas, 49¾ x 39⅞ in. (126.4 x 101.3 cm).
The Frick Collection

In it we find not only his characteristic drawing and composition but a clarity, a realism probing to the point of cruelty, an originality of statement and arrangement so daring that at first many were shocked by it."

But Frick's cautions and intimidation did not end with *The Rehearsal*. They extended to Hogarth's portrait of his good friend Mary Edwards (fig. 9-35), the richest woman in eighteenth-century England, another 1914 purchase. Not unlike a 1910 photograph of heiress Helen seated in a chair with Fido in her lap (fig. 9-36), Miss Mary Edwards sits with her own loyal spaniel looking up at her. Here Frick, like the artist-satirist, has trained his practiced eye on the dangers of heiresses entering into marriage. Miss Edwards had entered a hasty marriage and became the victim of her fortune-hunting husband. The marriage was short-lived: Miss Edwards declared herself a spinster and had the marriage annulled, although her son was thereby declared illegitimate. For the next few years, she managed the vast estates she had inherited from her parents, but she died prematurely at the age of thirty-eight, one year after Hogarth completed her portrait. By dictate of her will, she was buried with her father at Welham, where she had erected a monument in his memory.

Fig. 9-36. Helen Clay Frick and Fido, 1910.
Author's collection

Unknown to Helen or her father, however, Helen was only five years away from becoming, like Miss Mary Edwards, the richest woman in her country. In the meantime, as a special portrait, *Miss Mary Edwards* took the place of honor over the mantel in Frick's library. And ironically, apart from the fact that Frick would be buried on December 5, 1919—exactly five years to the day of his recorded purchase of *Miss Mary Edwards*—on his death, the *New York Evening World* would crown Helen Clay Frick, "America's Richest Bachelor Girl."

Intensifying the messages now literally hanging above her head, the portrait arrived at a time when there was a bitter marriage feud within the family. Helen's sister-in-law Frances, who had been Helen's closest friend until after her wedding, turned against Helen. Beautiful, cool, and calculating, in 1914 Frances told Helen she no longer had any use for her as she, Frances, now had what she wanted. As Helen's private secretary once explained, Helen often complained that Frances "was adorable until she hooked Childs."

Shortly after the wedding, the couple moved to Pittsburgh so Childs could take the reins of his father's business affairs. But when Childs, who to his credit had a brilliant scientific mind and later became an important paleontologist, proved a failure at business, he and his father had a falling-out. Childs left the financial world and with the subsequent estrangement from his father precipitated a bitter rivalry for Frick's affection. Cross with his son, afraid to lose Helen to another man, Frick changed his will in Helen's favor, leaving Childs jealous of the privileged position his unwed, younger sister held. Frances believed Helen was fueling the estrangement and undermining her marriage.

As the breach with Childs widened, Frick turned increasingly to Helen. Maureen Murdock contends that living out the father's destiny is the charge of the father-daughter syndrome, particularly when the son is a disappointment. To that end, Frick now certainly saw Helen as his "heir," and, as with Childs, was supportive of her only to the degree that she mirrored his talents and abilities, or, in other words, to the extent that she was a reflection of himself. In 1913, when the wedding of his son took place before Frick's eyes, the non-wedding of his twenty-five-year-old daughter had taken place in Frick's heart. The daughter, who was by the cultural norm prevented from marrying without her father's permission, the daughter who in her subordinate position to her father had neither money of her own, nor social, economic, or legal authority, was literally wedded to her father unless he gave her to another.

In *Addiction to Perfection: The Still Unravished Bride,* the Jungian analyst Marion Woodman examines the father-daughter syndrome as one where the daughter becomes a goddess, a heroine who has sacrificed herself so that she can be responsible for the father's well-being and creativity. When the father-daughter relationship is too intense, and is characterized by the bondage of the daughter to the father rather than by the

Fig. 9-37. Helen, at age twenty-six, had an artist paint a portrait
of herself as a six-year-old into a portrait miniature of Martha.
Private collection

father giving the daughter the tools to live a life independent of him, the syndrome typically results in the complete blocking of the daughter's own creative process. Instead, the father's-daughter strives "to create anything her father wants her to create, even to be anything her father wants her to be (whether it is natural to her or not) . . . to please Daddy."

And please her "Papsie," Helen did. In 1914, she had a miniaturist add her six-year-old likeness to a painting of Martha at that age (fig. 9-37). Additionally, during the years her father and brother were estranged, Helen's father bond tightened. Frick, to get a rise out of her, would compare himself to King Lear, the old, white-bearded king who used his wealth to buy love from his children. His message to Helen was clear and compelling. Although Lear goes insane when two of his daughters betray him, it is the third daughter, Cordelia, who initially refuses to love only him, who ultimately sacrifices her life by returning from France to redeem him. While Cordelia is hanged by the English as a traitor, her greater reward has been saving her father from family treachery and restoring him to sanity.

In this regard, we turn back to David's painting depicting Christ's descent from the Cross (see fig. 7-57; *The Deposition*), Henry Clay Frick's last religious acquisition. It describes one way he elicited sympathy and controlled Helen. As mentioned previously, it was acquired in 1915, the year Frick, who was still suffering from inflammatory rheumatism, executed his will. According to John Russell, it is a painting "where no-body got hurt." But someone did get hurt. When Frick drew up his will and acquired this painting, he had made Helen his virtual son and heir. At that time, apart from the fact that Frick began to charge her with the duties she was to perform in his name after his death, he began playing on Helen's fears. As she wrote in her diary, "to get a rise out of her" because she feared her father's death, he insisted on discussing his funeral plans. When Frick spoke of his "going," by her own admission Helen said "a terror used to seize . . . me." She believed her father enjoyed frightening her. In fact, Helen said that her distress "rather encouraged him to continue the subject." When eating dinner with Helen, Frick, perhaps alluding to their nine years in William K. Vanderbilt's house, would often recite Hiram Lord Spencer's laconic poem, "A Hundred Years to Come":

> We all within our grave will sleep,
> A hundred years to come:
> The living soul for us will weep,
> A hundred years to come
> But other men, our homes will fill
> And others then our lands will till
> And other birds will sing as gay
> And bright the sunshine as today,
> A hundred years to come.

When talking about his funeral arrangements, Helen so visibly showed her distress, he would say to Adelaide: "I wish Helen would let me talk about things sensibly—but she won't hear of it." For her part, however, Helen proudly maintained, "I never gave him the comfort of discussing the plans he wished to make for the future, because I could not bear to visualize what life would be without him." But her father had long instilled in Helen what her duty to him would be when he was gone. Having insisted on subservience during his life, he now expected his daughter to defend him aggressively in death.

Although Frick continued to compare himself to King Lear, he now began to compare himself to Job. He often told Helen he expected "to live to be ninety or a hundred" but was also "ready to go at any time," hoping that when his time came, he would "go to sleep and never wake up." But Frick could take such a philosophical approach because he had Helen to fight his emotional battles. Still bitterly preoccupied by Carnegie's betrayal, Frick would recite Psalm 55—the prayer of a just man persecuted by the wicked; the supplication of a man, like Christ, betrayed not by an enemy from without, but by a man who was "mine equal, my guide, and mine acquaintance"; a man who, like Carnegie, "took sweet counsel" with him and "walked unto the house of God in [his] company."

At dinner, Frick would recite the first part of the psalm, a lament:

> My heart is sore pained within me: and the terrors of death are
>   fallen upon me.
> Fearfulness and trembling are come upon me: and horror hath
>   overwhelmed me.
> And I said: Oh that I had wings like a dove! for then would I fly
>   away and be at rest.

But when he came to the lines dealing with the inequity, the wrongs still in the city, the usury and deceit still on its streets, the wicked men betraying the just, the psalm turned into a love duet. According to Helen, as he finished his lines, he "always smiled and put out his dear hand for me to squeeze," and then, as if Helen was consenting to deal with the fate of his enemies, after he was gone, she would complete the antiphony:

> Let death seize upon them, and let them go down quick into hell:
>   for wickedness is in their dwellings, and among them.
> As for me, I will call upon God; and the Lord shall save me.
> Evening, and morning, and at noon, will I pray, and cry aloud:
>   and he shall hear my voice.
> He hath delivered my soul in peace from the battle that was against me:
>   for there were many with me. . . .
> The words of his mouth were smoother than butter, but war was in
>   his heart: his words were softer than oil, yet were they drawn
>   swords. . . .
> Thou, O God, shalt bring them down into the pit of destruction:
>   bloody and deceitful men shall not live out half their days;
>   but I will trust in thee.

But then, Murdock posits that through the father's use of Scripture, the daughter becomes entrapped: "Because her father identifies so strongly with her, a father's

Fig. 9-38. Piero della Francesca (1410/20-1492), *The Apostle*, 1454-69.
Acquired in 1936, Tempera on poplar panel,
52¾ x 24½ in. (134 x 62.2 cm).
The Frick Collection

daughter is not allowed to experience or express emotions that he deems undesirable. Her father actually tries to control her feelings—such as anger, sadness, fear, and uncertainty—by extinguishing them with rational arguments." She also notes, "He may also be aware of, and perhaps appalled by, his feelings of attraction to her. He sublimates these feelings by . . . dominating her into submission by quoting chapter and verse from scripture."

Helen, therefore, was not unlike Lear who is betrayed and Job who is overburdened and crushed with pain. Although at some level she was angry with her father for his self-absorption and the burdens being thrown on her to deal with after his death, as Woodman explains, the father's-daughter "worships and at the same time hates because, on one level, she knows he is luring her away from her own life. Whether she worships him or hates him makes no difference, because in either case she is bound to him with no energy going into finding out who she herself is."

Helen's addition of Piero della Francesca's *The Apostle* (fig. 9-38) to her father's collection in 1936, the year after the Frick Collection opened to the public, demonstrates this dynamic. When *The Apostle* is juxtaposed with Frick's bookplate (fig. 9-39), the similarities—the white beard, large hands, broad forehead, and facial expression—can

Fig. 9-39. Henry Clay Frick's bookplate.
Author's collection

Above: Fig. 9-40. Jacopo Tintoretto (1518–1594), Circle of,
Portrait of a Venetian Procurator, prior to 1566.
Acquired in 1938, Oil on canvas,
44⅝ x 35 in. (113.3 x 88.9 cm).
The Frick Collection

Right: Fig. 9-41. Henry Clay Frick and Helen
at Eagle Rock.
Author's collection

hardly be denied. Moreover, one can appreciate that Helen may well have seen in the apostle her own father, who enjoyed reading primarily ethical books such as the disabled William George Jordan's *Self Control: Its Kingship and Majesty*, Marcus Aurelius' *Sayings*, and the *Jefferson Bible*. As we have seen, Frick also liked to quote Scripture to Helen, particularly the Sermon on the Mount, his favorite. Helen wrote of these moments: "Frequently, when I became rampant on some subject or other, he said to me, 'Read the Sermon on the Mount: Love your enemies' and then quoted whole passages, 'Blessed are the Peacemakers' . . . [for] Papsie was a peacemaker himself, and it always made him miserable to have one member of the family at outs with another." In other words, in Helen's eyes, although her father understandably continued to be preoccupied with hatred of Andrew Carnegie, he was, nevertheless, always just in his judgment of people and rarely critical of others.

In 1938, her fiftieth birthday year, Helen acquired *Portrait of a Venetian Procurator* (fig. 9-40), then attributed to Jacopo Tintoretto but now considered to be "from the Circle of." This painting brings the ambivalence of her father-daughter dynamic even closer to the surface. A 1919 photograph of Frick trying to kiss Helen (fig. 9-41), reverberates with the understanding of why, in later years, Helen grew to dislike the Tintoretto. No doubt a reaction to the way her father controlled her sexuality, her emotions, and her creativity, her objection to the portrait subject, with his immaculately trimmed white beard, indicates that she was transferring her anger at her father onto the portrait. According to Edgar Munhall, curator at the Frick Collection, Helen "loathed" the portrait subject's beard.

In later years, this same revulsion became evident in her dislike of the trustees' 1946 acquisition, Gainsborough's *Grace Dalrymple Elliott*, the tall, attractive daughter of an English barrister who divorced her husband after five years of marriage and subsequently took on many lovers. Undoubtedly acting from some self-imposed guilt, Helen grew to dislike the painting because of the subject's questionable morals. As far back as 1900, her distress at the inappropriate and deeply uncomfortable direction her relationship with her father had taken could be read in a prayer she wrote Mademoiselle Ogiz:

> Dear Mademoiselle.
> My voice shalt thou hear in the morning, O Lord. . . .
> Lord, behold, he whom Thou lovest is sick.
> Lord, if Thou wilt, Thou canst make me clean.

A painting today considered by the Frick Collection to be a 1918 acquisition by Henry Clay Frick, although records at Knoedler show it was purchased by Helen in 1916, provides a highly revealing look into Helen's mind. Entitled *Perseus and Andromeda*

Fig. 9-42. Giovanni Battista Tiepolo (1696–1770), *Perseus and Andromeda*, c. 1730.
Acquired in 1916 (1918), Oil on paper affixed to canvas, 20⅜ x 16 in. (51.8 x 40.6 cm).
The Frick Collection

Fig. 9-43. Helen placed *Perseus and Andromeda*
outside her bedroom door.
Author's collection

(fig. 9-42), the painting is by Giovanni Battista Tiepolo, the seventeenth-century decorator of palaces, villas, and churches who produced many religious, historical, and mythological paintings. The work is actually a small sketch in oil, done for a ceiling painting in the Palazzo Archinto, that illustrates the Greek myth of Andromeda, chained by her father, hand and foot, to a rock. Her mother, Queen Cassiopeia of Ethiopia, has made the mistake of boasting that she was as beautiful as the Nereids, the sea nymphs, and has thus incurred the wrath of Poseidon, who sent floods and a terrible sea monster to ravage the king's land. From an oracle, Andromeda's father, King Cepheus of Ethiopia, learns that to save his land, he must sacrifice his beautiful daughter to the sea monster. He therefore chains Andromeda to a rock, and awaits the death that will redeem him and bring his kingdom peace.

When Perseus flies over the country on his winged horse, Pegasus, he sees Andromeda and is so struck by her beauty he promises to rescue her if she will marry him. The painting depicts the exact moment of the rescue. Andromeda's shackles are broken. Both she and Perseus are carried by Pegasus, fleeing the monster as Hera and Zeus discuss their fate.

When the Tiepolo was acquired, Helen was being courted by Dr. Fordyce Barker St. John, a Princeton friend of her brother's who had been president of the student council and the Ivy Club. World War I had erupted in Europe and as America moved closer to war, Helen had involved herself in Red Cross work, outfitting St. John's entire front-line hospital unit with her money. Perhaps to convey a message of her own to her father, she had the $8,000 painting placed in the second-floor hall, immediately to the left of her bedroom door, a bedroom situated between her father's and her mother's rooms (fig. 9-43).

When America entered the European war in 1917, everyone expected Helen and St. John to announce their engagement, but the young man left for a casualty station on the Flanders front and no announcement was made. Shortly thereafter, a rebellious Helen, who as a Red Cross nurse hoped to go to the front herself, sailed for France to help repatriate Belgian refugees. The young heiress, in fact, spent the next six months in her Ford wagon, called Hunkatin (fig. 9-44), dashing among "her families" located in seventy-two French towns. She wrote to her father of her intention to establish a home for malnourished and orphaned refugee girls, explaining in a March 17 letter written from Knoedler's Paris apartment: "I refuse to go home without feeling that aside from a little personal service of my own, I haven't been able to really contribute *through you* to some really worthwhile cause, and I know it would disappoint you if I didn't when there is a big need to be filled."

Fig. 9-44. Hunkatin.
Frick Archives

For Helen, the seemingly never-ending war had now become "more like a hideous, hideous nightmare than a reality." Frightened by German bombings when in Paris, distraught by all she had seen and heard about the enemy's brutality, angered by the Germans' destruction of the beautiful cathedrals and monuments she had loved as a child, Helen complained, "How such atrocities can be committed and how these Huns can endure the way they have, makes one wonder where Justice comes in." And to Knoedler, in expressing her "feelings of appreciation . . . every time [she thought of his] wonderful kindness in letting the 'Old Maids' use [his] home as their 'headquarters,' " her own understanding of her fate had become clear.

Fig. 9-45. Helen (*top left*) and friends tour the battlefield at the Chemin des Dames.
Frick Archives

Fig. 9-46. Helen (*left center*) with the men in a cantonment on the Aisne.
These soldiers were killed three days later in a German offensive.
Frick Archives

On Thursday, May 16, 1918, however, she won the hoped-for opportunity to go to the front. Accompanied by Marshal Joffre of the French War Commission, who had stayed at 1 East Seventieth Street when in New York raising money for the war effort, Helen went to Soissons, sixty miles northwest of Paris on the Aisne River, almost at the Hindenburg Line, a system of German trenches behind the enemy's front lines. Helen had already seen the toll German atrocities, physical and otherwise, had taken on the Belgian refugees, but now she saw at first hand the cost both to cultural treasures and to human life. She saw the ruined cathedral of Soissons, and later, when making a scrapbook of her World War I adventure, she would juxtapose pictures of the ruined cathedral with ones showing how it had looked before the war. She toured the battlefield, entered a bunker with Joffre, and had her picture taken on the infamous Chemin des Dames (fig. 9-45), a dirt road running along a crest between the Aisne and Ailette rivers, in what Claudine Cowen, a contemporary French reporter, described as "the high place of horror in World War I," the violent theater of fighting that "bled France to death."

The Chemin des Dames would bleed Helen to death as well. Pictures of her in the World War I scrapbook show her in a cantonment on the Aisne surrounded by troops, men who were killed a few days later, on May 27, in the German offensive (fig. 9-46). By June, Helen had given all she had. She was fainting, craving sweets and carbohydrates, and vomiting regularly, a condition that had started a few years before her departure for France. Her tour of duty up after seven months, she returned to the

Fig. 9-47. Helen, far left, takes time out to enjoy the Bird Cage.
UPI/Corbis-Bettmann

Fig. 9-48. Pandora's Box, the Red Cross Shop's jewelry boutique.
Frick Archives

United States and joined her parents at Eagle Rock after a day or two in New York. Although ever afterward she had to walk around the perimeter of such open spaces as the main concourse of Grand Central Station for fear of fainting, she seemed oblivious to her own health problems.

Upon her return, she noticed immediately that her father did not look well. After dinner her first night, her father let Adelaide entertain their dinner guests so that he and Helen could talk alone together. Writing in her diary, Helen mused: "What wonderful hands he has—like Rembrandt's in his self portrait."

A few months later, on November 11, the war ended. In anticipation of the Christmas spending season and under the direction of the Goodwill Section of the Red Cross, Helen opened a four-story department store at 587 Fifth Avenue for the benefit of wounded soldiers recovering in American hospitals. The house, made available to her by Louis T. Haggin, was one of the first thrift shops of its kind. Knoedler donated paintings, society women tore through their attics and closets, men cleaned out their bureau drawers, cooks parted with equipment, antique dealers gave furniture, and famous jewelers donated fine pieces.

Helen created a tearoom, called the Bird Cage (fig. 9-47), that featured music, films of the war never before seen, and plays. It soon became a popular meeting spot,

NEW YORK HERALD, TUESDAY, MARCH 4, 1919.

Miss Frick's Red Cross Shop Spends Its Profits on Tours for Soldiers

CORPORAL GOTTLIEB BRUGGER

FIRST GROUP OF CONVALESCENT SOLDIERS SEEING NEW YORK

MRS. MORGAN JONES "BARKING" FOR THE SOLDIERS

Two Thousand Dollars a Week to Show Stranger Fighters Instructive Sights of the City.

Eighty convalescent soldiers who had never seen New York were taken on a sightseeing tour yesterday by the Red Cross Shop, of No. 587 Fifth avenue, of which Miss Helen Clay Frick is president. There were two large omnibuses filled with American fighters from Debarkation Hospital No. 5, in Grand Central Palace, and both were supplied with guides from among the women of society interested in the shop.

Among those who attended yesterday, under the direction of Mrs. Alfred C. Bossom were Mrs. Malcolm Goodridge, Miss Helen Clay Frick, Miss Anna Constable, Miss Georgiana H. Owen, Mrs. George Franklyn Lawrence, Mrs. George E. Brewer, Mrs. Arthur R. Gray, Miss Ellen S. Parks, Miss Sara Midlebrook, Mrs. Ramsay Hoguet, Mrs. James C. Auchincloss, Miss Margaret Crowninshield

and Mrs. Morgan Jones. Mrs. Jones acted as guide yesterday and through the megaphone told the soldier passengers about the interesting things they were seeing.

"Our shop has made a clear profit of $34,000 in three months," said Mrs. Bossom, "and we are going to spend $2,000 a week in this new system of educational sightseeing tours of the city for convalescent soldiers, sailors and marines in local hospitals.

"We shall take eighty of them every day, but they must be from out of town and never have seen this city before."

"Nearly all of them request to see the Brooklyn Bridge and Grant's Tomb. Today we shall take them to the bridge, to the Battery, to the Aquarium, Wall street, Grant's Tomb and Riverside Drive.

"Tea will be served to the soldiers at the Red Cross hut in Madison square, of which Mrs. T. M. Vinton is in charge."

Among the convalescent soldiers who enjoyed the tour yesterday was Corporal Gottlieb Brugor, of Ohio, who won the Belgian War Cross for having silenced three German machine guns and taken four prisoners single handed four or five hours before the armistice was signed.

Fig. 9-49. Bus tours for the wounded soldiers.
Frick Archives

as did one of the store's boutiques. Her mother, with the help of Duveen, decorated one room in the style of Louis XVI, named it Pandora's Box (fig. 9-48), and as the *New York Herald* describes, it sold "everything from a dollar trinket to a diamond."

The shop caused a small sensation when it received an anonymous gift of a showcase full of Cartier jewels. Unknown even to his own family, Frick had written the famous Fifth Avenue jewelry store to say that Adelaide and Helen were much interested in the opening of the Red Cross Shop in New York. Since Adelaide was to be in charge of the jewelry department, Frick sent Cartier a check for $10,000 to pay for jewelry which he requested be delivered to his wife at the shop in time for its opening. He requested, "each piece be plainly marked with the figure at which it should be sold for," and in his desire that the gift remain anonymous, he advised Cartier, "You could in delivering it say, it is from one who does not desire his name to be known, but it is a gift to the Red Cross."

On December 8, Helen took her father through the store. As the *New York Herald* noted, "Mr. Frick was delighted with the toy department because it was one hundred percent American. There was no trace of German made toys anywhere." He also described the jewel room as "perfect" and was said to have particularly admired "a flexible bracelet of diamond and onyx and a sixteenth century basket of crystal and gold." He found "the tea room superb" and in praise of the stock room, he said it was organized by "a system that leaves no room for improvement." His only criticism was of the posters that appeared in every room. "Pointing with his right forefinger Frick commented: 'Those posters with the inscription "Give, Give, Give" should be made to read "Buy, Buy, Buy."'"

Within the first three weeks, with Adelaide, Helen, and other ladies of the social elite as salesgirls, the store took in $16,000. Apparently people were as interested in buying as they were in seeing Miss Frick. According to *Town Topics,* this was "the first affair in New York at which she has come within range of the public eye." As they studied her, they noticed she was "short . . . [with] a fluff of golden hair fram[ing] her face." They also noted she was "slight and slim."

Frailty, however, was no deterrent to her determination. As sales mounted, and after visiting the soldiers in the U.S. General Hospital in Colonia, New Jersey, when she saw the necklaces and other things the men were making as part of their rehabilitation, Helen took their work, sold it in the store, and gave each man the entire profit of the sale. Soon, too, she started educational bus tours for the wounded soldiers, hoping to give them "a true appreciation of the wonders of New York and also . . . [to cultivate] the spirit of respect for and appreciation of American ideals" (fig. 9-49).

By May 1919, the shop project was drawing to a close. It had made a $34,000 profit in its first three months, and Helen, now determined to sell everything in the storeroom, issued an invitation. Designed to look like an official court summons, it called for the "Forthwith . . . appearance of [the invitee]," and "Waiv[ed] all excuses in the cause of humanity." By the time the door closed, the shop had made over $50,000. Then in June, Helen succeeded in getting Frick to construct a covered stand in his Fifth Avenue garden for 500 wounded soldiers, unable to march in a parade in their honor. In addition, the Fricks served the soldiers lunch and included not only the men, but their wives, mothers, sisters, and girlfriends.

Fig. 9-50. Helen Clay Frick.
Frick Archives

Whatever Helen's hopes for marriage may have been, at the close of World War I, they were shattered (fig. 9-50). As we know, unbeknownst to her, before St. John (fig. 9-51) left for the front, her sister-in-law Frances had warned him that Helen's father would never allow her to marry. Dr. St. John fell in love with a nurse from the front lines and married her after the war.

Whether or not Helen ever discovered what her sister-in-law had done is unknown. What is known, however, is that the breach between Frick and his son was now mending. In reconciliation, Frick had offered his daughter-in-law—now the mother of three daughters, one of whom was named after Martha—an expensive jewel. Frances declined, however, saying she would prefer a home in which to raise her children, a home she hoped would come to include the grandson and namesake for whom her father-in-law fervently wished. Frick, therefore, bought Frances the beautiful Georgian house in Westbury, Long Island, that he, as previously mentioned, enjoyed visiting prior to his final decline. The house, owned in the 1840s by the poet William Cullen Bryant, and later by Gen. Lloyd Bryce, was christened Clayton. Frick, who paid for all the renovations and interior decorating by Sir Charles Allom, warned Childs not to place more than one or two of his African trophies in his library as he did not want his grandchildren's home to be a "refuge of animal heads."

In the spring of 1919, Helen, whose own child-bearing years were slowly disappearing, made a poignant entry in her diary. She wrote that her father had said to her, "Weddings make me sad." On April 11, he sent her a letter revealing how impossible it would be for Helen to ever marry and have children like her sister-in-law, Frances: "I had another proposal for your hand today," her father wrote, "which I confined to the wastebasket. You are becoming far too popular . . . this is only a line to assure you that you are always in my thoughts."

Oddly, Helen referred to this note in her diary as "a sweet letter." An entry a week earlier showed how she could have interpreted such a devastating admission in that way. Helen had been visiting Pittsburgh, and upon learning her father had arrived in the city, she dashed from Clayton to his office. When told that her father was not there, but was with Andrew Mellon at the Mellon Bank, she left her father's office and hurried over. Helen, now thirty-one, wrote of her meeting with her father and unwittingly revealed both the severity of her arrested development and the physical familiarity between father and daughter. She said, "I sat on his lap and we talked a while, telling [him] all about [my] visit."

In the same entry, Helen also recalled that that afternoon, after she returned to Clayton, she found Frick in bed and apparently very tired. Dutifully, she offered to stay home, serve him tea, and keep him company. They were meant to dine at the Golf Club and, once Frick was refreshed, they decided to go early, by way of the cemetery. Her father picked a magnolia blossom from Clayton's garden and, as Helen wrote in her diary, "laid it tenderly on Martha's grave." Although she had friends staying with her at Clayton, she and her father "went to the lot alone."

It would seem that with the war's end and St. John's marriage, Helen had to resign herself to the reality that with her only important beau gone, the chances were she would never marry. On some sad level, her real bridegroom was her father, to whom she had "given" herself, subsuming her own goals, dreams, and desires for fear of his reprisals and as a way to compensate for his grief.

In a very real sense, when Henry Clay Frick died in 1919, Helen was left as his widow. To her he entrusted the greater part of the family's share of his fortune. To her he left his wish that she use this fortune in his memory—in the care and maintenance of his collection, as well as in the defense of his reputation. And, as we shall see, Helen would come to care for both with a kind of vengeance that underscored the depth of both his and her personal tragedies.

Fig. 9-51. Dr. Fordyce Barker St. John.
Frick Archives

CHAPTER X

Her Father's Voice

Certain of my wishes that are known to her.

—Will of Henry Clay Frick

WITH HENRY CLAY FRICK'S DEATH IN 1919, Helen officially took on the unfinished business of her father's life. In her book, *My Father Henry Clay Frick,* written in 1959 after a series of articles by that title ran in the *Pittsburgh Press,* Helen described her father by using a quote from Longfellow: "When a great man dies, the light behind him lies upon the paths of men." What Helen had not seen, however, was that although her father left a great light for the path of men, he also left a shadow for her, a shadow whose intensity stood in direct proportion to the light. Helen believed she walked in the path of her father's light and, in some respects, blessed by his love, she did. In other respects, cursed by his unresolved grief, she did not. Captivated by a highly seductive father, who made her feel she was more important to him than his wife, Helen was destined to expect that all men in her life would respond to her as had her father and to feel that no man was as good as he.

Many years after Frick's death, when Andrew Mellon recalled the snowy December day when Henry Clay Frick was buried, he remembered the difficulty he had had believing his forceful, masterful friend *was* confined to a grave. Indeed, Henry Clay Frick never was confined to the grave. He remained alive as a force deeply imbedded in Helen's psyche: this force, though tightly locked from her consciousness, was nonetheless the energy that continued to drive her life. Though silent to the ears of others, Henry Clay Frick's voice, not Helen's, was in control. And the dutiful father's-daughter, once dependent on the living father for approval, would continue to live out her father's destiny, not her own, as if still seeking his approbation. With her *own* checks now engraved with Martha's likeness, and as head of the Acquisitions Committee for the Frick Collection, Helen would be driven by grief—grief for Martha, grief for her father, grief for her failure to alleviate her father's grief, and grief for the loss of her own truth. Family, friends, and colleagues, unaware of the deeper sources of her behavior, came to regard Helen as bizarre, and even ridiculed her. Fanatic in her attempt to deify her father, she praised her father as faultless and glorified his devotion to her. In fact, when writing her memoir entitled "Grandfather" for Frick's grandchildren after his death, Helen noted the endearing names her father used for her: "Petty" and "Lovey-Dovey."

Fig. 10-1. Henry Clay Frick holding his granddaughter, Martha Howard Frick, under the grape arbor at Eagle Rock.
Frick Archives

As Helen entered the initial stages of mourning, however, she did so just as her father had for Martha, turning him into the sainted man, just as he made Martha the sainted child. She also began to link herself to him with objects carrying a sense of his presence. She started with seemingly little things that nevertheless carried enormous importance because they were among the last items Frick touched, or were the last concerns that occupied his thoughts. Just before the funeral service began in Clayton, for example, Frick's mantle was passed to his six-week-old grandson, the baby and namesake Frances had hoped to give him. The infant was brought to Clayton for the funeral and baptized Henry Clay Frick II. Twenty days later, on Christmas day, Helen gave the baby the silver dressing-table set with the likeness of his sister's faces, as engraved to his grandfather's specifications shortly before his death. In "Grandfather," Helen wrote: "This long-looked-for little grandson . . . can feel that this was the last present ever given to anyone by his dear grandfather." In other words, Helen now began creating the locus in which she could feel her father's continued presence.

Apart from the silver set, Helen next reorganized an album of what turned out to be her father's final summers at Eagle Rock, in 1918 and 1919. Although the album begins with the summer of 1918, the frontispiece is a 1919 picture of his granddaughter Martha (fig. 10-1), which Helen had torn from the back of the album. The photograph, showing Frick holding the child beneath a grape arbor, was taken either in July, the month his daughter Martha died, or in August, the month his Martha was born. More significantly, the photograph was taken in 1919 when his granddaughter was two years old, the same age his daughter Martha was when she swallowed the fatal pin.

As Helen continued to live her life within the context of loss and her father's grieving, she replaced her bed in 1 East Seventieth Street with the one he had occupied (figs. 10-2, 3). Before long, the concern she had felt for her father when he was alive was transferred to protecting his name from the outer world, reacting as if insults to her father were attacks on her, not him. In 1919, some felt the art collection gift was simply Frick's cynical way of using the charitable deduction provisions enacted into law in 1915 to reduce his estate taxes. Others, like the *Brooklyn New York Citizen,* criticized the gift by saying, just because "Mr. Frick intended to confer a great benefit upon the people of the city, [it] is no sufficient reason for accepting what may be called a 'white elephant' in the name of culture." But for Helen, her father's collection was sacred ground, a space so private and personal that to impinge in any way upon it would be an invasion of his and, by extension, her own privacy.

In a sense, her father's will both acknowledged the important role Helen had played in shaping the collection and suggested the part he wanted her to play after his death: "In the event that for any reason the devise and gifts in this Article [IV Section 8] made to the said corporation to be known as 'The Frick Collection' shall fail to take effect, then and in such event I give, devise and bequeath unto my daughter Helen C. Frick and her heirs forever all the property, real and personal, hereinbefore devised and bequeathed to or for the benefit of said corporation."

Paradoxically, however, although Helen received the largest share of the family wealth and was anointed titular head of the family, becoming Frick's "son," heir, and custodian of his "monument" to the world, and the art collection, in a real sense Frick abandoned Helen. He did not give her any formal or legal authority. But then, although Helen had always had her father's ear, Frick had not really "seen" her. He used her creativity and sympathies, but never visualized her as a person in her own right. Rather, in using Helen for his purposes, he objectified her. She was his echo, merely acting as her father wanted, making him happy by doing his bidding.

After his death, Helen was in an untenable position. *She* felt she had authority, even though her father had not created a context for it. Additionally, although the 1903 photograph of Frick kissing her could allow us to speculate that Helen's emotional and psychological wounding was extensive, her disempowered position was not unlike many women of her day. Women *were* voiceless; not until August 1920 were women granted the right to vote. During her father's last illness, he revealed just how powerless he felt women should be. In a situation obviously humiliating for Helen, when

Above: Fig. 10-2. Helen's bedroom at 1 East Seventieth Street.
Author's collection

Below: Fig. 10-3. After her father's death, Helen replaced her bed with her father's.
Author's collection

the subject of women's rights was gently alluded to by Adelaide, Frick replied that his daughter-in-law Frances, who was having his grandchildren, typified the woman who had "come to her own."

True, Helen was appointed an original trustee of her father's collection, but she and her mother were two women up against a board of high-powered businessmen such as John D. Rockefeller, Jr., and his friends Vanderbilt Webb and Frederick Osborne, a situation that intensified Helen's determination to act as she believed her father would have wanted. Though to others Helen's vast share of her father's estate marked her as financially independent, she was not. Frick had restricted her inheritance with a command stronger than the written, legal word—his wish. He said in his will that Helen's inheritance was hers outright, but he placed a caveat that bound her to forever serve his memory: his "wish" that she would "dispose of these amounts [so] that my general purpose in making these legacies should be accomplished." Additionally, Frick left her an extra $200,000 and stipulated: "While this bequest . . . is absolute and I impose upon her no trust or duty, expressed or implied, it will enable her to make effective certain of my wishes which are known to her."

While no one but Helen would ever know what her father's unstated wishes were, one thing was certain: America's richest bachelor girl was in fact penniless, wealthy only to the extent that she used her energies to serve her father and his unwritten demands. Helen would only be able to use her inheritance as she believed her father would have desired, in service to him. Survival still meant keeping "their secret," submitting to the facade of father-love for fear of being disgraced and rejected by her family and peers. Helen was as trapped by her father after his death as she had been trapped by him during his life. Her duty to the living father had been to satisfy his needs; her duty to the dead father was to sublimate her trauma by obsessively serving his memory and elevating to sainthood the man who had harmed her the most.

There was, however, a still greater tragic dimension to her entrapment than this self-protective canonization of her father. As Helen brandished his cross, she would soon be perceived by others as both spoiled and arrogant. Her sublimated father-rage, born of her captivity, her grief, the blurring of her personal boundaries, and her father's posthumous demands, would be transferred to those men who opposed her. Helen, therefore, started down a road of unending torment, her energies consumed by anger as she made war on anyone who wrongly blackened her "sainted" father's name.

❖

AT FIRST, HELEN WAS LOST without her father. Although his medical bills, doctors' fees, and funeral expenses had been paid, Helen, perhaps driven by the fear that she had killed her father, insisted on "personally settl[ing]" these bills by reimbursing his estate. As she began to mourn the father she may have unwittingly killed, Helen went abroad in the spring of 1920 and tried to connect herself to the paintings he had collected. Provided with letters of introduction from Roland Knoedler to important people in the art world, she sought out the sites of her father's British landscape paintings, places they had very likely visited together. She walked the Mall in St. James's Park and visited Salisbury Cathedral (fig. 10-4). Frustrated in her attempt to locate the site of Turner's *Mortlake Terrace: Early Summer Morning* (fig. 10-5) on the banks of the Thames, she asked the chauffeur to drive around in circles on London's west side until her well-trained eye caught Mortlake's distinctive roof line.

She visited the ancestral homes of her father's portrait subjects to glean information about their personal histories. She met with the Dowager Lady Ilchester who had owned Rembrandt's self-portrait and at Dulwich saw the Mazo copy of Velázquez's *Philip IV* (see fig. 7-2). She visited Warwick Castle, the former home of Van Dyck's portrait of Margareta Snyders and of Romney's *Henrietta, Countess of Warwick, and Her Children* (see fig. 7-3). Here the connections went deep. As mentioned before, Henrietta was both the daughter-in-law of Nattier's portrait subject, Elizabeth, countess of Warwick, and Henrietta was a niece by marriage to Lady Hamilton, painted by Romney. Additionally, Helen visited Castle Howard, once home to Van Dyck's portrait of Frans Snyders, husband of Margareta. The two Snyders were reunited by Frick in 1909, an act, that as previously mentioned, "gave [Frick] considerable sentimental satisfaction and on which, when in a holiday mood, he would comment in entertaining fashion."

Helen, however, was at a crossroads. Her restless search for information about her father's paintings was also a search for answers to her own conflict, a resolution of the long-fought tug-of-war between becoming her own person and remaining in service to her father. In *The Hero's Daughter,* Maureen Murdock describes the dilemma: "At some point in her life, a father's daughter is faced with a heart wrenching choice: either continue her hero worship of her father in order to preserve the intensity of their bond, or remove her father from his pedestal in order to live her own life." As Murdock explains, "To reclaim her own moral autonomy, her own destiny . . . the father as hero must die (metaphorically) in order for the father's daughter to live her own life with integrity." During Frick's life, for Helen to have claimed herself would have meant taking unthinkable risks. Apart from the fact that she might have been disinherited, she would have had to face the full-blown rage and revenge of the man who both broke the back of labor and defeated Andrew Carnegie. More unthinkable, in his death, she would have had to face her sexualized relationship with her father, an

Fig. 10-4. John Constable (1776-1837), *Salisbury Cathedral from the Bishop's Garden*, 1826.
Acquired in 1908, Oil on canvas, 35 x 44½ in. (88.9 x 112.4 cm).
The Frick Collection

Fig. 10-5. Joseph Mallord William Turner (1775-1851), *Mortlake Terrace: Early Summer Morning*, 1826.
Acquired in 1909, Oil on canvas, 36⅝ x 48½ in. (93 x 123.2 cm).
The Frick Collection

Fig. 10-6. T. C. Dugdale (1880-1952), *Sir Robert Witt in His Library.*
Courtesy the Witt Library, Courtauld Institute of Art, London

intimacy that in her day was neither understood and addressed by the medical field, nor eased by a sympathetic and forgiving public.

On May 20, 1920, the multiple layers of Helen's trauma and the solution she had been seeking to her conflict united in a single vision. Her letters of introduction from Knoedler and other friends had led her to the American consul in London, who in turn led her to Sir Hercules Read of the British Museum. He suggested she visit 30 Portman Square, the home of Sir Robert C. Witt, a trustee of London's National Gallery, who had a unique and extensive photo archive of European and American paintings in public and private collections dating from the twelfth century onward. Organized and catalogued into a ready-reference system, it would allow a scholar to study all the work of one artist in one place. The repository, created primarily to satisfy Witt's own interest, was to be bequeathed on his death to the National Gallery.

Upon seeing Witt's collection of images, books, pamphlets, and other material important to art research, all arranged alphabetically in boxed folios (fig. 10-6), Helen was so stunned she lost her breath. Excited by all that was before her, she at last had found a way to release her own creativity, while remaining in service to her father. She asked if she could copy his system. Witt agreed, offered to help her, and upon her return to the United States—after a tour of France and Belgium where she saw further evidence of German destruction of art—Helen petitioned the trustees of her father's collection to let her found a similar photo archive and art history reference library. Sensing that such a photographic repository would be an invaluable record should more great art be lost or damaged as it had been during the war, Helen underlined the fact that such a library would carry out her father's intention that his collection "encourage and develop the study of the fine arts . . . and promote the general knowledge of kindred subjects among the public at large."

Recognizing this would be the first such library in America, agreeing the library would be consistent with Henry Clay Frick's will, and realizing such a repository would be of great educational benefit and an exclusive and highly valuable asset for the Frick Collection itself, the trustees gave their approval. Rather than use the small library across from her father's second-floor sitting room, however, Helen took over the Bowling Alley (fig. 10-7). Within nine months her library spread to the outer hall and by 1924 was so extensive that the next-door building at 6 East Seventy-first Street, once set aside by her father for a sculpture gallery, was renovated to house the archive.

Helen dedicated the Frick Art Reference Library to her father's memory and named Sir Robert Witt its godfather. With a purpose of her own, something important to direct, and with the conditions of her father's will satisfied, Helen's state of mind improved and she seemed to be in a restful place. She was director of her library, had

Fig. 10-7. The Bowling Alley in 1 East Seventieth Street was the first home of the Frick Art Reference Library.
Frick Art Reference Library

Fig. 10-8. Anna Mary Robertson Moses, Grandma Moses (1860–1961), *Westmoreland Farm,* c. 1948.
Helen Clay Frick commissioned the artist to paint her farm with the author and her sisters playing in the snow.
Private collection

agreed to bequeath it to the Frick Collection on her death, and specified that it was to be "organized and operated exclusively for educational purposes," including the encouragement of art.

At the same time, with Frick gone, the generally poor relationship Helen had had with her mother seemed to be improving. She purchased a small farm in Bedford Village, New York—the first home of her own—and named it Westmoreland Farm (fig. 10-8) after the county of her father's birth. Her mother visited her there (fig. 10-9), maintaining her residences in New York and Prides Crossing. Helen also divided her time among the three places. Mother and daughter combed New England for American antiques suitable for Helen's country house, and although Adelaide often stayed behind in the hotel while Helen scoured Europe for her library, together they enjoyed Helen's escapades and adventures. Adelaide could only have delighted in the determination of this daughter, whose retort to her chauffer's lament when

Fig. 10-9. Adelaide Frick enjoyed her daughter's farm. She took walks, fished, and boated on the lake, but always wore her mourning clothes.
Author's collection

their car became mired in a mudhole, was "Go on!" and go on they did. More important, mother and daughter only met with the Frick Collection trustees once a year, so Adelaide, who had been granted a life tenancy, and Helen had the pleasure of managing 1 East Seventieth Street and the collection it housed.

In 1924, when her widowed mother was still living in 1 East Seventieth Street and before the house was open to the public, Helen and the trustees made their first posthumous addition to Henry Clay Frick's collection, a painting from Helen's favorite period, the Italian Renaissance, a period she loved because of the stories the paintings told. *The Annunciation* (fig. 10-10) by the fifteenth-century Florentine Fra Filippo Lippi, illustrates the moment when the Holy Ghost visits the Virgin Mary—a metaphor, certainly, for the godlike voice at work in Helen's psyche.

As tough as she was sentimental, in 1927, Helen coaxed the trustees to purchase *The Temptation of Christ on the Mountain* (fig. 10-11), one of the scenes from the reverse side of Duccio's celebrated *Maestà* altarpiece. So determined was she to have this painting in her father's collection, she offered to buy, on her own account, Barna da Siena's *Christ Bearing the Cross* (fig. 10-12) for $35,000 and give that painting to the collection if the trustees would buy the Duccio, a proposition they could not resist because Barna da Siena was the leading Sienese painter of the latter part of the fourteenth century.

Helen was, however, still listening to her father, doing as he had done, making associations between her past and her present when collecting art. This was the period when, as head of the Acquisitions Committee, she acquired Chardin's *Lady with a Bird-Organ* (see fig. 9-26) depicting a room similar to her Clayton playroom of 1895 where she kept her beloved canaries. In 1927, she acquired Jean-Auguste-Dominique Ingres's famous portrait of the melancholy, introspective Comtesse d'Haussonville (fig. 10-13), a woman who grieved the death of her own sister. Apart from being one of the finest examples of Ingres's work, the extraordinary portrait may have also appealed to Helen because the comtesse evokes the subject of Bouguereau's *L'Espieglèrie* (see fig. 5-15). This was the portrait her father acquired in 1895 because it so reminded him of Martha, the portrait he placed in Helen's Clayton bedroom, the portrait whose commemorative copy resided above the governess's desk in Helen's playroom.

In 1931, death revisited the Frick family. Adelaide Howard Childs Frick died of a stroke at the age of seventy-two. Until the time of her death, she had remained a recluse. She never exercised her right to vote and had seen only immediate family and a few of her more intimate friends. With her death, 1 East Seventieth Street officially became the Frick Collection and was now to be transformed into a public gallery.

Ever since Henry Clay Frick's death and the reading of his will, Childs and Helen, who had long been bitter rivals for their father's affection, had not spoken to each

Fig. 10-10. Fra Filippo Lippi (1406-1469), *The Annunciation*, c. 1440.
Acquired in 1924, Tempera on poplar panels;
left panel, 25⅛ x 9⅞ in. (63.8 x 25.1 cm), right panel, 25⅛ x 10 in. (63.8 x 25.4 cm).
The Frick Collection

Fig. 10-11. Duccio di Buoninsegna (c. 1255–1319), *The Temptation of Christ on the Mountain*, 1308–11.
Acquired in 1927, Tempera on poplar panel, 17 x 18⅛ in. (43.2 x 46 cm).
The Frick Collection

Fig. 10-12. Barna da Siena (active around 1350), *Christ Bearing the Cross*, c. 1350-60.
Acquired in 1927, Tempera on poplar panel, 12 x 8½ in. (30.5 x 21.6 cm).
The Frick Collection

Fig. 10-13. Jean-Auguste-Dominique Ingres (1780–1867), *Comtesse d'Haussonville*, 1845.
Acquired in 1927, Oil on canvas, 51⅞ x 36¼ in. (131.8 x 92 cm).
The Frick Collection

other. Although often in the same room when visiting their mother or at family gatherings, each would act as if the other was not there. Upon their mother's death and the impending task of remodeling their family home and opening it to the public, however, Helen wanted to resolve the animosity between herself and her brother. Although she retained Eagle Rock and Clayton, with their contents, and her mother's personal possessions at 1 East Seventieth Street, she immediately signed over her half-share in her mother's trust funds to Childs. She then began the arduous task of separating the family objects from the collection's. No easy assignment, the responsibility Helen faced was compounded by the fact that she was talking to her brother for the first time since their father's death and also dealing with John D. Rockefeller, Jr., an original trustee to the collection and chairman of the renovation process, who although a businessman and global philanthropist, was not interested in Frick family sentiment.

Rockefeller, therefore, became a particular problem for Helen. In an argument typical of Helen's future dealings with him, when the renovation plans called for the extension of the galleries eastward through Helen's small library building—requiring the removal of her papers, images, books, and assorted material—the two clashed. Helen felt the Frick Collection, not she, should purchase the next-door house at 10 East Seventy-first Street, an idea that Rockefeller adamantly opposed. He insisted that since her collection had to be moved, it should "be sent up to the Metropolitan Museum." Helen, ever determined, countered that she had been "both the creator and supporter of the Frick Art Reference Library and that it was dedicated to [her] father's memory and was to be part of the collection in the future." She said that she "felt certain [her father] would have approved of its being properly housed." Rockefeller replied, "It is unfortunate that Mr. F. is not here to speak for himself." Sarcastically he suggested Helen "should have obtained an affidavit from him," and balked, saying, "How we as Trustees can be true to the trust imposed upon us by Mr. Frick and spend a million and a quarter dollars for the site and construction of a new library over which we would have no ultimate control, I do not see."

Helen, however, won her new library building. In exchange for the purchase of the building by the Frick Collection and the continuation of her lifetime directorship, she again agreed to pay all the library's operating expenses and to endow it for the collection on her death. Grateful to her father's friend Andrew Mellon, who intervened on her behalf, Helen thanked him saying, "A little bird tells me that the successful outcome . . . is entirely due to your efforts. . . . I will always have to feel that it was because of you, who were Papa's closest friend, that the agreement was arrived at . . . permitting the Library to function as I had always hoped it might," that is without the trustees having any voice in its operation or management.

Though victorious over Rockefeller, Helen, who only employed women in her art reference library, was soon shadowed by ugly rumors that she was a lesbian. More likely, she was weary of the prevalent misogyny of her day and felt that a sisterhood would promise a safe, nonconfrontational environment for the development of her project. Certainly, if nothing else, her life experiences had taught her that a mixture of male and female employees, or a brotherhood, would threaten the stability she needed.

Additionally, she was shadowed by jealous former employees. A $250,000 lawsuit for libel was filed in the spring of 1932 by James Howard Bridge, Frick's former secretary, whom Helen had recently fired. She had never liked Bridge. In 1920, when she started her Frick Art Reference Library, Bridge, perhaps thinking Helen was going to be wildly extravagant and leave the hard work to others, had taunted her: "So, you are going to do this in a typical millionaire fashion?" Then in 1930, when he published *Portraits and Personalities in the Frick Galleries,* a fantasy in which the portrait subjects come alive and converse with each other, Helen considered having the book enjoined.

Fig. 10-14. Helen leaving the courthouse, c. 1935.
New York Times Pictures

Bridge had signed an agreement stipulating that he would not write about Henry Clay Frick's personal connection to the art, but in writing a fantasy, he had circumvented the agreement. Helen's lawyers advised her to leave the matter alone, that her suit would simply draw attention to the very thing she did not want to expose. She took the lawyers' advice, but when Bridge submitted a job resume to H. W. Warren of National Studios, saying he had been curator of Frick's collection, Helen wrote Warren that Bridge had not been curator and his work was "full of inaccuracies and adds nothing to art connoisseurship."

Bridge felt this letter damaged his reputation and filed suit. Thus Helen (fig. 10-14) was now burdened with preparing a legal defense, in addition to building her library and monitoring the renovation of her father's house and the other projects dedicated to her father's memory. Her Iron Rail was still in operation, and in 1922 she had formed the Westmoreland-Fayette Historical Society for the restoration and preservation of the old Homestead buildings in West Overton where Frick was born. She once considered remodeling the West Overton buildings as an orphanage in memory of her father, but in 1928, when she purchased Abraham Overholt's distillery building, she turned the house into a museum and used the distillery to display Native American mummies and local artifacts. She also donated to the University of Pittsburgh fourteen acres of undeveloped land worth $3.5 million. Located across from the Carnegie Institute and known as Frick Acres, the land would be used as the site for the university's Cathedral of Learning (fig. 10-15)—a vast tower inspired by Richard Wagner's "Magic Fire Music." Intended as a "temple of courage," the Cathedral was to be constructed "as high as steel can build." Then, in 1927, she founded the Henry Clay Frick Fine Arts Department, housed in this Cathedral of Learning, and started the Henry Clay Frick Fine Arts Library as well. Additionally, in response to the economic depression gripping the nation, she both organized the Forty Plus Club of Western Pennsylvania to help older men find employment and established a pension plan for the employees of her Frick Building, the first plan of its kind in Pittsburgh and a model later followed by other Pittsburgh office buildings.

When the suit came to trial in 1935, Bridge tried to defame the women for whom he had worked. A camera-shy Helen (fig. 10-16) wept when he accused her deceased mother of being an "arrogant woman." As rebuttal, Helen's lawyers then presented a proof sheet from Bridge's book *Millionaires and Grubb Street*. It showed if anyone was arrogant, he was. The proof sheet had been given to Adelaide to read shortly after her husband's death and noted "the conscious arrogance of the women of the ultra-rich [which] denoted a moral delinquency." It further argued that both the rich men and their wives were "in need of psychopathic treatment." Undoubtedly, as the lawyers explained how the sheet had shocked the grieving widow, it proved to the judge that Bridge had a long history of vindictiveness.

Helen, however, was less troubled by the accusations against herself and her mother than she was by Bridge's assertion that she was violating her father's will by failing to make public his $50 million art collection. When the court heard her argument that she was trying to keep her old library open during construction of both the new library building and the extension of the Frick Collection gallery, the judge ruled in her favor. And within the year, as her new building came to completion, she could boast of

Fig. 10-15. The Cathedral of Learning, 1937, was built on Frick Acres and housed both the Henry Clay Frick Fine Arts Department and the Henry Clay Frick Fine Arts Library for the University of Pittsburgh.
University Archives, University of Pittsburgh

other victories. Helen had protected the very private relationship her father had with his paintings, and she had met the responsibilities implicit in her father's will by using her inheritance to serve his name. In all this, her library office showed what gave her the energy and drive to handle so many things at the same time. A portrait of Martha hung behind her back over the mantelpiece (fig. 10-17) and pictures of her father were on her desk and wall (fig. 10-18). In her sitting room, fashioned in the Italian Renaissance style, she exhibited one of her first acquisitions for her own collection and perhaps the most telling of all: Apollonio di Giovanni's *Scenes from the Odyssey* (fig. 10-19), depicting the faithful Penelope awaiting her husband's return, as she staves off the three suitors standing outside her door by weaving and then unraveling a shroud.

Fig. 10-16. Helen was a very private person. She was camera-shy and upset by publicity.
UPI/Corbis-Bettmann

On December 12, 1935, a preview party for the Frick Collection was held. Fearing the anger of the working class and their resentment of Frick's name, all compounded by the Depression, a police bomb squad, together with a special detail composed of a precinct captain, a sergeant, and twelve patrolmen was dispatched to the premises. Guards in red uniforms and fifty other detectives watched the entrances, while thirty-five plainclothes detectives circulated in the galleries. Although Helen had succeeded in having Rockefeller strike her father's enemy and Carnegie loyalist, Charles Schwab, from the invitation list, seven hundred guests, including Andrew Carnegie's widow, whom the family had always liked, attended. The judge who had ruled against James Howard Bridge came as well. The guests followed a carefully arranged course through the art-filled rooms, around the family furniture that Helen insisted be left to maintain the collection's personal tone.

Then, on December 16, the collection was opened to the public. As the *New York World Telegram* noted, "One forgets all about Frick himself, his feud with Carnegie, the strikes, and everything else, and gives one self up to this heart-stirring experience."

And heart-stirring it was, particularly at levels beyond the public's awareness. In an act both symbolic and generous, Helen had left behind for her father's collection pieces of Sèvres porcelain for the Fragonard and Boucher rooms, tapestries for the new entrance hall, an important rug for the Boucher Room, a bust of her father by

Figs. 10-17, 18. Helen Clay Frick's penthouse office in the Frick Art Reference Library.
Frick Archives

Fig. 10-19. Apollonio di Giovanni (c. 1415-1465), *Scenes from the Odyssey: The Story of Penelope.*
Acquired by Helen Clay Frick for her own collection, c. 1920s.
Tempera on cassone panel, 7½ x 37⅜ in. (19 x 94.9 cm).
Frick Art Museum, Pittsburgh

Malvina Hoffman—all of which were rightly Helen's through her mother's estate, but were items she felt belonged more to her father's collection than to her.

Adelaide Frick's Boucher panels had been moved downstairs into a new gallery, now known as the Boucher Room. There Helen placed the Saly bust, so like Andreoni's bust of Martha at Clayton, beneath the panel entitled *Sculpture,* as it had been upstairs in her mother's room. Moreover, the collection opened on what would have been Adelaide's seventy-sixth birthday and in Martha's fiftieth birthday year. As if in recognition of this, the sole acquisition that year by the trustees was Lazzaro Bastiani's *Adoration of the Magi* (fig. 10-20) a painting of a gurgling Christ Child surrounded by adoring wise men and others dressed predominantly in rose-colored garments, a painting that represented the family's idealization of Martha and a collecting pattern that would repeat itself during Helen's near thirty-year tenure as head of the collection's Acquisitions Committee.

Helen lobbied hard to acquire such treasures as the Dreyfus bronzes (they eventually went to the National Gallery of Art in Washington, D.C.) and the famous Wilton Diptych (now in the National Gallery in London), and was bitterly disappointed when the trustees did not act on her advice. But in the posthumous additions that were made, Helen showed herself to be a collector consistent with her father's taste and enhanced by her scholarship. In 1926 the collection acquired *The Doge* by Gentile Bellini and later bought important works by Boucher, Goya, Constable, Monet, Rembrandt, Reynolds, and Gainsborough. Helen reintroduced Greuze to the collection, an artist her father had acquired for his Clayton collection, and she imprinted the Frick Collection with her preference for the Italian Renaissance.

Fig. 10-20. Lazzaro Bastiani (d. 1512), *Adoration of the Magi*, c. 1470s.
Acquired in 1935, Tempera on poplar panel, 20½ x 11 in. (52 x 28 cm).
The Frick Collection

Helen also was continuing Frick's habit of seeing paintings as links to people and events from the past. In 1936 and 1938 she acquired her father's look-alikes, the previously mentioned *Apostle* (see fig. 9-38) and *Venetian Procurator* (see fig. 9-40), and in 1939, what would have been Frick's ninetieth birthday year, she acquired a painting evoking Frick's experience of Martha's visitation—Andrea del Castagno's *The Resurrection* (fig. 10-21), an Italian, fifteenth-century work suggestive of the fused experiences of Christ's resurrection and ascension.

And yet, as Helen oversaw the renovation of her library and the transformation of her family home into a public building, and began to guide the acquisition policy for her father's collection, she continued to run up against the unyielding opposition of John D. Rockefeller, Jr., who objected to what he perceived as her sentimentality and her perpetration of a public institution as a personal memorial to its founder. Naturally, Rockefeller had no idea at what psychological level Helen was operating. The two, with their instinctive, philosophical, and practical differences, clashed immediately. She felt Rockefeller deliberately made things difficult for her—and in truth he did. As she said, "From the very start, there was friction between R. and the family. He was insincere and antagonistic and even rude to Mrs. F. and [me]. He was always opposed to any suggestions I made and this became more and more evident as time passed." In fact, as Helen later reflected, remembering the times when she called meetings to discuss the acquisition of a painting for the collection, these "were never pleasant affairs, and from the very start, Mr. Rockefeller seemed to take pleasure in being disagreeable." But Helen was not intimidated by Rockefeller, then or ever. While her father's close friend and trustee J. Horace Harding was alive, he, as Helen explained, "[Made] it plain [to Rockefeller] that my father and I had been very close and that I knew his wishes."

Within the first few years, however, Rockefeller's friends, and some of her brother Childs's, became board members. This situation made Helen's position increasingly awkward, particularly since Childs and Rockefeller had forged an alliance and were referring to her as a "stumbling block." They reminded Helen she was no longer officially in charge of her father's collection, and to distance her, Rockefeller refused to let her decide on the decoration of the new galleries or the placement of the artworks. Helen stated at a board meeting: "as a Trustee and as daughter of the Founder, [I] had a double responsibility and that [my] father had always wanted [me] to be interested in his greatest interest."

As a result, Rockefeller formed a three-man executive committee with himself as chairman, Childs as president, and a trustee other than Helen. Furious that Rockefeller and her brother—not she—were now in charge of Frick's collection, Helen warned she was "not going to keep out of her father's Collection" and fumed, "This has turned into

Fig. 10-21. Andrea del Castagno (before 1420–1457), attributed to, *The Resurrection.*
Acquired in 1939, Tempera on poplar panel,
11¼ x 13¼ in. (28.5 x 33.7 cm).
The Frick Collection

a Rockefeller Foundation." Rockefeller, on the other hand, replied that as she was head of the Acquisitions Committee, had been appointed director of the library for life over his protest, and was also secretary of the board of the collection, she had enough to do. According to Helen, he insisted it was unfortunate that her father could not speak for himself and declared that this was not to be a "Frick Institution."

All came home weary from the meetings, both brother and sister drained from the power struggle born of unresolved issues related to their father. But Helen was up against formidable adversaries. In 1936, after the transformation of 1 East Seventieth Street from private home to museum was complete, Rockefeller began to extend his authority into her domain: art acquisition for the collection. Helen admitted that Rockefeller had done a superb job in organizing the financial and practical aspects of the building transition, but acquisition of art for Henry Clay Frick's collection had been Helen's territory since the age of eight, or before. When Rockefeller began to press for a written acquisition policy, Helen countered there should be no such policy, written or otherwise, as she, better than they, knew what was appropriate for her father's collection.

Tension mounted. Rockefeller and the director of the Frick Collection, Mortimer Clapp (who helped Helen start the Fine Arts Library at the University of Pittsburgh and was hired by Helen), joined forces and developed an acquisition policy mandating the purchase of better examples of the artists Frick had collected to replace those on the walls. In conceiving of the collection "as it evolves, not as it existed in 1919," Clapp and Rockefeller insisted that the question of harmony with the existing collection "shall be regarded as of minor importance and not to be seriously considered." In words that could only have amazed Helen, Clapp described the collection as "free of historical or chronological obsessions [and] free of such obsessions as seek to perpetuate the accidents of personal taste." Furthermore, he recommended replacing what he considered less important pictures by ones more important and suggested a continual interchange between vaults and galleries. He, together with Rockefeller, also favored adding modern art—a medium Rockefeller did not like, although it was being avidly promoted by his wife Abigail Aldrich Rockefeller who was then turning their former New York residence into what became the Museum of Modern Art. Together, Rockefeller and Clapp claimed that when Henry Clay Frick acquired his first Corot in 1898, the painter was considered a modern artist. Moreover, as they tried to implement their art policy, they also tried to remove the family furniture in the Living Hall and Library (left in place by Helen to give a sense of her father's homelife) in favor of other pieces of greater artistic importance.

As Rockefeller and Clapp persisted, Helen met them with fierce resistance. Fearless in the face of a $50,000 extortion plot by a foreign nurse who was later arrested for her crime, she nevertheless came close to hysteria in her determination to preserve the one-man nature of her father's collection. Angry with Rockefeller, she personalized the dispute by insisting he was jealous of her father's accomplishment because he had never created anything of artistic merit. He, on the other hand, thought Helen was "lack[ing] balance and stability," a view enhanced by the fact that although Helen, like her father, was of German descent, she had developed a phobia for all things and people German. According to James Howard Bridge, then still in the Fricks' employ, when Helen was living with her widowed mother in the late 1920s, this phobia was already out of control. Bridge complained that Helen's reaction to the admittance of Dr. August L. Mayer, the famous director of the Munich Pinakothek, to the Frick residence was unforgivable. Apparently, had Mayer "been the anarchist who tried to assassinate Mr. Frick, he could not have produced a greater alarm," when Helen discovered he was German. Helen also refused entry to European guests of the Rockefellers because they had German-sounding names, and she censored all purchases of equipment for her Bedford farm, as well as Frick Art Reference Library materials, to be certain they were not made in Germany and, thereby, would not bolster the German economy. Moreover, she refused to permit people with Teutonic-sounding names in the Frick Art Reference Library—a restriction generally deplored and ridiculed even though Helen rightly feared her ready-reference library might assist the systematic theft of art by the Germans. Helen had seen the German pattern in World War I and feared a recurrence, particularly in 1936 when Germany reoccupied the Ruhr. Additionally, in the 1930s, a Wilhelm Frick was made Hitler's minister of culture. A rabid Nazi, who would later be convicted of war crimes and hanged, Wilhelm controlled the secret state police with Goering and was involved in post–World War I art thefts, an operation assisted by German spies who infiltrated archives and museums throughout Europe. Before long the world would in fact witness what Helen Frick feared and Wilhelm Frick promoted— massive German confiscation "in the public interest" of the great European collections in countries they occupied.

When the German blitz of London began in 1940, Helen tried to safeguard other European treasures, as well. She turned the stables at Eagle Rock into a dormitory for refugee British girls. Although she requested one hundred children, Helen was given only seven because she was a "maiden lady." After a ship transporting other children was torpedoed by the Germans, the evacuation was halted. While Helen's children adapted to life in America, she worried that a German incendiary bomb might hit her library or her father's collection. She photographed her now extensive library materials, placing the films in a New York bank vault for safekeeping.

To help the British war effort, she purchased, from the Red Cross, William Blake's original drawings for John Bunyan's *The Pilgrim's Progress* (fig. 10-22) for her father's

Fig. 10-22. William Blake (1757-1827), Illustration for *The Pilgrim's Progress*, "Christian in the Slough of Despond."
Acquired in 1943, Pencil, pen and watercolor.
5¼ x 7⅛ in. (13.3 x 18.1 cm).
The Frick Collection

print collection. The addition of the drawings may also be considered as another historical and psychological link in the father-daughter collecting pattern. We know, for example, that Blake was personally known to Constable, Romney, Hogarth, Hoppner, Turner, and Reynolds, all artists Frick collected. Sir Thomas Lawrence gave Blake money at the end of his life when he was dying in poverty. More important, Christian, with his bags of sins on his back, recalls the suffering man lying prostrate at the feet of the Madonna in Dagnan-Bouveret's *Consolatrix,* a man strongly resembling Henry Clay Frick. And although Blake was delusional and perhaps insane, he lived between the subjective and objective worlds. Preoccupied with other states of existence, obsessed with death, mortality, and resurrection, the poet's constant blending of reality and the supernatural may well, in this death-laden time, have reminded Helen of the energy at work in her father's psyche, the energy long at work in hers.

Four days after Helen sent her library films to the bank, the Japanese bombed Pearl Harbor, and America entered the war. Though few admitted it, Helen's German hysteria was at least partly justified. Further vindication came in 1942 when the U.S. Department of State established the American Commission for the Protection and Salvage of Artistic and Historic Monuments in Europe. Helen's library became a restricted area and was used by the War Department to make maps pinpointing the treasures of Europe in order to protect them when the Allies bombed German-occupied areas. And it was used by the War Department to track art stolen by the Germans.

As the horrific air war progressed, Helen, ever concerned about the welfare of her seven refugee English girls, moved them from Eagle Rock to a cottage on her farm. And while she foster-parented these young children, she became even more determined to keep her father prominent in the eyes of the Frick Collection trustees. In 1942, the trustees acquired Monet's *Vetheuil in Winter,* perhaps as a last look at a place about to be shattered by war. Then, in 1943, just as the Allies invaded German-occupied Europe, Helen had two portraits done of her father by the famous American portraitist John C. Johansen. She kept one (fig. 10-23) and presented the trustees with the other (see page 9). She insisted this portrait, with its dark, brooding background suggesting the smoke clouds of war, be exhibited in a place of importance commensurate with her father's—over the mantel in the Library where *Miss Mary Edwards* (see fig. 9-35) had always hung. Rockefeller, however, refused to accept any gift from Helen with strings attached. When Helen then said she would loan the painting, Rockefeller insisted it be shown where her father's *Salisbury Cathedral* had always resided, directly behind Frick's desk—a place Rockefeller maintained he was used to seeing Frick when he, Rockefeller, walked into the room. Helen replied she was used to seeing her father in every room of the house. She eventually had her way; she measured the panel above the mantel, had it adjusted to fit the portrait, and removed the famous heiress, *Miss Mary Edwards,* to the Dining Room.

Commenting on Helen's behavior, H. G. Dwight, assistant director of the collection, said to Rockefeller, "One wonders just how much Mr. Frick had in mind when he wrote in his will: 'I am conscious that . . . I am imposing upon these [trustees] a duty which may prove very burdensome.'"

In May 1945, Rockefeller and Dwight learned the full extent of Helen's "instability" and the "burden" they would soon carry. A collector friend of the Rockefellers' who greatly admired the collection asked Abby Rockefeller (who was then in ill health and a great supporter of German and left-wing modern artists) if gifts could be given to the collection. The Rockefellers, who still had some of their own collection to bequeath, immediately saw a repository for these items. Rockefeller felt that he, like Abby, did not have long to live and so asked Childs to investigate whether or not the trustees had the right to accept gifts. When Childs approached Helen and described the situation in broad terms, she knew immediately he was speaking of Rockefeller. She insisted that the trustees were only empowered to add to the collection with her father's $50 million endowment; more to the point, she was acting on her fear that Rockefeller's name would be plastered all over her father's collection, turning it into a Rockefeller, not a Frick institution.

Mortimer Clapp, now firmly aligned in Rockefeller's camp, was also fueling the philanthropist's desire to have the Rockefeller objects in the Frick Collection. According to Helen, when she accosted Clapp for refusing her phone calls and not answering her letters, the director went out the door of his office saying he would not have touched his job "with a red-hot iron, if [he] had known what the conditions were here."

That year, 1945, was also the sixtieth anniversary of Martha's birth, the year America dropped the atomic bomb on Hiroshima and Nagasaki, and the year the trustees acquired their second painting by Chardin, *Still Life with Plums* (fig. 10-24). It depicts fruit, a carafe, and a wineglass on a table and seems a metaphor for the stability for which the psyche must have longed at war's end. The painting, described in *The Frick Collection Handbook of Paintings* as "solidly designed," nevertheless leaves the viewer acutely aware of the fragile nature of the scene.

If Helen had hoped to freeze Rockefeller in his tracks as coldly as Chardin had painted the objects in *Still Life,* she was badly mistaken. In 1947, he resigned from the board, offered to return the $50,000 fee given him as an original trustee under Henry Clay Frick's will, and presented a written list of the art objects he intended to leave the collection, so the issue could be settled in court. The bequest of eleven paintings and two sculptures had been drawn up by Clapp, who was receiving $5,000 personal Christmas checks from Rockefeller. Helen, now age fifty-nine, went wild as Rockefeller

Fig. 10-23. John Christen Johansen (1876–1964), *Portrait of Henry Clay Frick*, 1943.
Oil on canvas.
Private collection

Fig. 10-24. Jean-Baptiste-Siméon Chardin (1699-1779), *Still Life with Plums,* c. 1730.
Acquired in 1945, Oil on canvas,
20 x 17 in. (50.8 x 43.2 cm).
The Frick Collection

and Clapp increased their pressure by arguing that Helen herself had already established the precedent of making gifts to the collection. The men insisted the Frick Art Reference Library was a gift because it was to pass to the collection upon Helen's death with a trust fund for its maintenance. Additionally, they cited as gifts the priceless articles from her mother's estate, the servants' furniture, personal items of Henry Clay Frick's, and other articles Helen had left behind after inheriting them from her mother.

H. G. Dwight told Rockefeller he was sorry for his resignation, but happy for him that he did not have "a certain pebble in [his] shoe." Helen roared, "I am mad as Hades." Over the past few years, she talked about their "high feather," and had drawn her battle lines, feeling elated when in the arguing she felt she had taken them off "their high horse." Now and again, however, rather than rage at her adversaries, Helen sat back waiting for their reactions, saying, "An' Brer Rabbit, he set tight."

In the meantime, Helen had placed a print of *Lady Hamilton* (see fig. 3-18), whom a teenage Martha would have resembled had she lived, over the fallen rosebud painted on the wall of her Clayton bedroom in 1892. She placed one of *Miss Mary Edwards*, the richest woman of her day who had her marriage annulled, in Attie's former Clayton bedroom. And she sold or gave friends and family many of the lesser paintings from her father's collections—George Bellows's *Dock in Winter* (1918), Bartolomé Esteban Murillo's *Self-Portrait* (1904), von Bremen's *The Darlings* (see fig. 2-10), Constant Troyon's *Wooded Lane* (1908), among others—and added two Gainsboroughs to the Frick Collection, portraits of Richard Paul Jodrell and Grace Dalrymple Elliott (1946). Later that same year—her sixtieth birthday year—she encouraged the trustees to add to the collection Georges de La Tour's *Education of the Virgin* (see fig. 9-21), the painting previously mentioned as honoring Helen's beloved governess, Mademoiselle Ogiz, who laid the foundations for Helen to become the scholar she was.

Helen, who did not regularly publish books or articles, also withdrew her manuscript on Jean-Antoine Houdon that had been accepted for publication. An important work of scholarship, Helen had written it from Houdon's letters, given to her by his family and translated by her. Her eyes, she claimed, were now too tired to do the necessary editing; and because she had been served with a complaint regarding the rights of the Frick Collection trustees—something the trustees referred to as friendly action—she had to devote all her energy to fighting Rockefeller.

Rockefeller wrote Helen to apologize for having opposed her so often. He said that he found the experience very painful and hoped that over time she would forget "the annoyance" he had caused her. Rockefeller insisted, however, that he would have been "untrue" had he not followed his best judgment carrying out what he believed were her father's wishes. And Helen, now suffering from migraine headaches as well as from failing eyes, replied that she did not know if the letter was drafted because of feelings of contrition on his part or for some other reason. She clamored: "the high purposes of my father in establishing The Frick Collection [were] surely as sacred to me as to anyone." She reminded him that her father relied on her knowledge of his "purposes and intentions" and had "confidence in her loyalty and devotion" to them. Were her father alive, she wrote, he would be "shocked and indignant" by Rockefeller's behavior and that as her father's daughter, she could "neither forget, nor condone" his actions.

Commenting on Rockefeller's reaction to Helen's reply, Rockefeller's lawyer, Thomas Debevoise, said "obsession is a polite and charitable word." Debevoise insisted that he had never heard of "a more disagreeable response to a gracious gesture" and added, "No court, I am sure, will ever be tempted to believe that the Trustees Mr. Frick chose were men he thought would follow the dictates of his daughter. It is possible that to some extent he had her in mind when he chose men who would follow only the dictates of their own judgment."

Once in court, Helen cited precedent for one-person collections, such as Isabella Stewart Gardner's museum in Boston, and testified to the personal nature of the collection by telling the judge her father referred to the paintings as either "my paintings" or "our paintings" and that gifts might impair its "personal character." But the judge ruled against Helen, writing in his decision that there was nothing in Henry Clay Frick's will to prevent the trustees' acceptance of gifts from the public. Undeterred and back in court on appeal, Helen called the Rockefellers cowbirds—the brown-headed, black-bodied, short-necked, conical-beaked vagabonds who lay their eggs in the nests of unsuspecting smaller birds. Opportunists and parasites, they leave the foster songbird mother to care for the cowbird fledgling, a fledgling who, because of its greater size, grabs more food and starves the baby songbirds, eventually driving the mating pair from the area.

Helen took Johansen's portrait of Henry Clay Frick on the stand with her, saying she hoped the likeness would help the judge "to know him," while also testifying: "It has been wrongly stated that my father was conceited and wanted self-glorification." She insisted he was a poor boy who "made, not inherited, his wealth" and that the Frick Collection was "the one great personal interest of his life [and] . . . was a very private concern."

But for all her efforts, on May 27, 1949, Helen lost the appeal. The judge, agreeing with the lower court's ruling, confirmed that nothing in her father's will precluded the trustees from accepting either money or gifts of artworks from donors outside the family. A crushing blow for Helen, particularly since this was her father's one-hundredth anniversary year, she, nevertheless, refused to admit defeat. Perhaps reminded of the well-known Overholt Whiskey label (fig. 10-25) depicting the Overholt boys hauling grain across Jacob's Creek, she encouraged the Frick Collection to acquire the Mennonite Jacob van Ruisdael's *Landscape with a Footbridge* (fig. 10-26). A poignant complement to Frick's Ruisdael and Hobbema collection, the painting, when juxtaposed with an Old Overholt Whiskey advertisement, attests to Helen's collecting eye and the long-ingrained collecting pattern of her father. The bridge was well known to Helen because she visited the area both as a child and after Frick's death, when she acquired the Overholt Homestead and turned it into a museum.

Additionally, in this one-hundredth anniversary year, Helen brought to publication a large illustrated folio of the Frick Collection that she had worked on since 1928. A memorial as well as the most sophisticated scholarship to date on the collection, it was a tribute to her father's "vision" and included an essay by Helen revisiting her position that Frick intended no gifts be made to his collection. She wrote: "the value of an endowed collection representing the taste of the founder and located in his dwelling is incontestable from an artistic point of view. It is comparable to an exquisite jewel within a setting specially designed to show off its beauty."

If Helen had not finished with Rockefeller and Clapp, they certainly were not finished with her either. They put together a second bequest comprised of over one hundred porcelains, a few paintings, and some large animal rugs. Rockefeller convinced his friends on the board of trustees that they could be exhibited in Helen's or her father's former bedrooms, or even in a wing on the east side of the building—a wing for which he had blueprints drawn. Helen protested these plans vigorously, and in the end the trustees turned down the second bequest, citing lack of space and their reluctance to add a new wing.

Fig. 10-25. Overholt Whiskey label showing the Overholt boys crossing Jacob's Creek.
West Overton Museums Archives

Fortune then began to change for Helen. Mortimer Clapp retired because of ill health, and the Rockefeller men on the board resigned. In 1950, the trustees acquired Piero della Francesca's *Monk and Nun* and a work of the Tuscan School, *The Flagellation of Christ*. In 1952, they acquired Césarine-Henriette-Flore Davin-Mirvault's portrait of the composer, musician, and conductor Antonio Bartolomeo Bruni. Also in that year, Helen settled for a written acquisition policy that charged the trustees to

Fig. 10-26. Jacob van Ruisdael (1628/29-1682), *Landscape with a Footbridge*, 1652.
Acquired in 1949, Oil on canvas,
38¾ x 62⅝ in. (98.4 x 159.1 cm).
The Frick Collection

"consider for acquisition only works of the highest quality and in excellent state of preservation, and then only if they 'belong' to The Frick Collection by harmonizing with existing exhibits."

In 1954, her mother's one-hundredth anniversary, she saw her father's collection acquire for $750,000 the prized *Virgin and Child with Saints and Donor* (fig. 10-27) then considered a Jan van Eyck, a painting Rockefeller himself had wanted. It had belonged to the Rothschilds and was exhibited only once in the last century; it was such a prize that a member of a competing art dealer's gallery, operating on his own, arranged to have Knoedler's telephone tapped so he could follow the bidding activity.

But this victorious period, capped by Rockefeller's withdrawal of his initial bequest in favor of his family and new wife, Martha Rockefeller, soon ended. On May 11, 1960, John D. Rockefeller, Jr., died. His widow, together with his children by his first marriage, exercised their right of first refusal, leaving in the bequest only three pieces that were more Abby Rockefeller's than her husband's. The trustees immediately voted to accept the artworks—Piero della Francesca's *Crucifixion* (fig. 10-28) and two marble busts of women, one by Andrea del Verrocchio and the other by Francesco Laurana—together with a $50,000 donation.

Although Helen had succeeded in staving off a flood of Rockefeller's art objects from entering the collection, rather than sigh in relief she continued to rage. She was now seventy-three years old, her mother's one-hundredth birthday had passed just five months earlier, and apart from having had her whole life consumed by her father, the last thirty years had been spent battling Rockefeller in her father's name. Helen stormed out of the trustees meeting saying, "I am leaving this organization forever." She raced down the stairs, tore through the west and east galleries, and after dashing through the secret door connecting the Frick Collection's east gallery to the Frick Art Reference Library, ordered the startled guard to "Lock this door and make certain it stays locked." According to Helen's nephew, Dr. Henry Clay Frick II, who had abstained from voting, Helen raged at him: "You are meant to run this Collection one day and you have shown yourself incapable." She removed her brother Childs as executor of her will and resigned from the board, appointing her niece, Martha Frick Symington, to take her place. On January 19, 1961, after forty-one years as trustee, she submitted a stinging letter of resignation to the press and washed her hands of the Collection. Citing her father's standard of highest quality and authenticity, Helen decried the damaged condition of the Rockefeller objects and their inferiority as artworks. Moreover, recalling how her father had formed his collection with love and understanding over a long period of years, she was outraged that no trustee had even been to see the objects being offered in the bequest before taking the final vote.

Fig. 10-27. Jan van Eyck (active 1422–1441), *Virgin and Child with Saints and Donor*, c. early 1440s.
Acquired in 1954, Oil on canvas,
18⅝ x 24⅛ in. (47.3 x 61.3 cm).
The Frick Collection

Fig. 10-28. Piero della Francesca (1410/20–1492), *The Crucifixion.*
Tempera on panel (irregular), 14¼ x 16³⁄₁₆ in. (37.5 x 41.1 cm).
The Frick Collection, bequest of John D. Rockefeller, Jr., 1961

Top left: Fig. 10-29. Francesco Laurana (c. 1430–c. 1502), *Bust of Beatrice of Aragon,* c. 1470s.
Marble, 14 x 15⅞ x 7⅞ in. (40.6 x 40.4 x 20 cm).
The Frick Collection, bequest of John D. Rockefeller, Jr., 1961

Lower left: Fig. 10-30. Abigail Aldrich Rockefeller at age six.
Rockefeller Archive Center

Top right: Fig. 10-31. Andrea del Verrocchio (1435–1488), *Bust of a Young Woman.*
Marble, 18⅞ x 19³⁄₁₆ x 9⅜ in. (48 x 48.7 x 23.8 cm).
The Frick Collection, bequest of John D. Rockefeller, Jr., 1961

Lower right: Fig. 10-32. Abigail Aldrich Rockefeller as a young woman.
Rockefeller Archive Center

Although she never said so publicly, Helen also undoubtedly resented the fact that the three pieces had a prior history of Frick-Rockefeller-Duveen intrigue. The busts had been acquired by Abby Rockefeller from the Dreyfus Collection through Duveen, who was on a $10,000-a-year retainer. At that time, the Frick Collection was considering purchasing the entire Dreyfus Collection of bronzes, so this acquisition presented a conflict of interest for Rockefeller. Worse, as the juxtaposition of the marble busts with photographs of Abby reveal, the subjects bear marked similarity to Abby. The Laurana bust (fig. 10-29) is recognized as having "delicate features [that] look almost childlike," something that, together with the swollen cheek, suggests Abby saw in it her own face as a young child (fig. 10-30). The Verocchio portrait subject (fig. 10-31), with her mass of tight curls, suggests Abby as a young woman (fig. 10-32). Significantly, Abby mentioned the resemblance between family members and the artworks she collected: she once compared her nose to the beak of a folk-art eagle she acquired for her early American art collection, and she often said of a portrait by Paolo Veneziano, part of Rockefeller's initial bequest but retained by the family, that the subject looked "weirdly like Laurance," her third son.

The small *Crucifixion* by Piero della Francesca had an equally troublesome legacy. It, like the marble busts, had previously been offered to the collection, but unlike the busts, the painting had been rejected. Duveen—whom Henry Clay Frick never liked, and of whom he was so suspicious he had a secretary present to record every word spoken in their meetings—was advised in 1915 by Bernard Berenson to sell the painting to Frick. He said, "Surely if Frick could be induced to buy the grimacing dead Christ falsely ascribed to Antonello da Messina [the *Pietà* (see fig. 6-26) Frick acquired in 1907, two years after his mother's death], it should not be hard to persuade him or his like to acquire such a gem as this by such a very great master." Frick did not buy *The Crucifixion* then, and when Duveen later recovered it from its eventual owner, he restored the painting, as Helen said, "most outrageously." She said, "It is now a ruined painting." Gimpel, Duveen's brother-in-law, agreed. He referred to it as being "rather tired." And although today the Frick Collection considers the painting "small, but monumental," Helen, who ever after referred to the Rockefellers as cowbirds, called the *Crucifixion* "That rag."

Helen, however, was not to be defeated by Rockefeller or the trustees. When she resigned in January 1961, she offered the trustees a quid pro quo—her small *Pietà* by the school of Konrad Witz (fig. 10-33), a twin to the painting her father had bought in 1907. In exchange, Helen asked the trustees to promise they would never exhibit Rockefeller's bequest in her father's collection. The trustees could ill afford to refuse the deal because the father-daughter paintings had often been exhibited together (fig. 10-34), and Helen's *Pietà* had been the subject in the late 1920s of an intense scholarly debate

Fig. 10-33. Konrad Witz (c. 1400-1447), follower of, *Pietà*, fifteenth century.
Acquired by Helen Frick for her collection, c. 1926. Tempera and oil on panel,
13⅛ x 17½ in. (33.3 x 44.4 cm).
The Frick Collection, gift of Helen Clay Frick, 1981

Fig. 10-34. "The Twins" on exhibition in the Enamel Room in 1 East Seventieth Street, 1927.
Author's collection

in which hers was declared the earlier, and finer, work. Thus, her "bribe" was accepted. For Helen, this was a particularly satisfying resolution. Duveen had insisted hers was the *later* version and backed his opinion with a bet against Gimpel, who held Helen's to be the earlier. Duveen was forced to admit his error, and in so doing, he offered Helen a $25,000 check to be given to one of hers, or her mother's, favorite charities. Helen had replied she did not take money from lost wagers and warned him: "Pride goeth before a fall."

In these last months as head of the Acquisitions Committee, when her grimacing Christ brought her revenge and stood guard in her stead over her father's legacy, Helen did more than insure the purity of her father's collection: she honored it by persuading the trustees to purchase Claude Lorrain's *The Sermon on the Mount* (fig. 10-35). This painting speaks to Frick's Mennonite heritage and the many times his grandmother read him this biblical passage when he was close to death from inflammatory rheumatism. It also recalls the time he asked Helen to bring him the Sermon on the Mount to read just before his own death. It is especially meaningful since only the Sermon on the Mount was read at Frick's New York memorial service, before his mortal remains were taken to Pittsburgh for burial.

Fig. 10-35. Claude Lorrain (1600-1682), *The Sermon on the Mount*, 1656.
Acquired in 1960, Oil on canvas, 67½ x 102¼ in. (171.4 x 259.7 cm).
The Frick Collection

Although Helen's *Pietà* stood guard over her father's collection and *The Sermon on the Mount* was a moving father's-daughter's blessing and good-bye kiss, Helen felt she had failed her father. Caught by the love-hate quality of her mourning process, Helen finally voiced her fear to her niece, Martha Frick Symington, that Childs and Frances had been right, that she *had* killed her father when she had given him something to help him sleep during the last night of his life. Now, in her anxiety, as she increasingly feared the reprisals of her dead father, she remained tormented by the fact that at one level she felt compelled to glorify Frick, while wondering if at another level she had acted out a need to destroy him.

Helen was searching for peace, and in the spring of 1965, she found her opportunity. Frances had died of pancreatic cancer in 1953, on August 5—Martha's birthday. But this death had done little to heal the brother-sister breach. Childs in 1965 had been quite ill with heart trouble and so Helen went to see him, hoping to reconcile their lifelong rivalry and recent differences. Childs and Helen still rarely spoke, so when Childs kept her waiting for over an hour, she left enraged.

Helen never saw her brother again. He dropped dead of a heart attack in his Long Island library a few months after her attempted visit. The following year, with Helen playing an instrumental role, the Frick Collection purchased two revealing artworks: François-Hubert Drouais's *The Comte and Chevalier de Choiseul as Savoyards* and Gentile da Fabriano's *Madonna and Child*. The former painting depicts two small, disheveled, but well-born children dressed in ill-fitting silk clothes. They are as the title promises—savoyards—disorderly and rude. Yet as wanderers, who earn money for their families back home by working at odd jobs, they are also, as *The Frick Collection Handbook of Paintings* notes, probably expressions of "filial devotion." The latter painting, an altarpiece, depicts St. Lawrence, who was burned alive by the prefect of Rome for distributing the wealth of the church to the poor, and St. Julian, who unwittingly murdered his parents and later, in search of forgiveness, built a hospital for the poor and a penitential cell for himself.

Helen's mind was obviously preoccupied with her failed reconciliation with Childs. Adding to her unease, she was again at war in her father's name, this time in Pittsburgh. In 1959, Helen had announced that if the University of Pittsburgh provided the land, she would give a small building, patterned after the Villa Giulia on the environs of sixteenth-century Rome, to house the Henry Clay Frick Fine Arts Department and Henry Clay Frick Fine Arts Library, as well as a teaching-art collection. In 1928, fearing the complete annihilation of Italy's art treasures in an inevitable air war against Germany, she had acquired two facsimiles of the finest examples of early Italian Renaissance painting. Now, in 1959 she acquired twenty-three additional facsimiles, all by Nicholas Lochoff, a Russian artist. These reproductions were commissioned in 1911 by the Czar of Russia,

Fig. 10-36. The Lochoff Cloister in the Henry Clay Frick Fine Arts Building.
Pittsburgh Post-Gazette

who wanted copies of the works not already belonging to, or unable to be transported to, the Hermitage in St. Petersburg. Since the revolution had precluded their delivery to the Czar, the copies, many of them frescoes, had remained in Italy until Bernard Berenson and the artist's son Boris sold them to her.

Helen had placed the Lochoffs—an extension of her photograph archives at the Frick Art Reference Library—in temporary storage, and in 1959, when she announced her intention to house the Fine Arts Department in a building dedicated to her father, she donated the facsimiles as well. When the Henry Clay Frick Fine Arts Building was completed in 1965, Helen had them installed on the cloister walls surrounding an open court designed by Umberto Innocenti (fig. 10-36), with the hope that the frescoes would inspire the scholars and laymen who used them for study. She also donated the Morgan bronzes and porcelains she inherited from her mother, as well as the organ from Eagle Rock, four mille-fleurs tapestries, and two white marble statues, bought by her in 1924 for her father's collection as works by Simone Martini. Four years later, however, the sculptures were discovered to be by the Italian master-forger Aleco Dossena.

In reaction, however, to a newly appointed director of fine arts who had a German ancestry, fiery temper, and little tact when dealing with Helen, Helen was now threatening to take back her building and art collection if the university hired German professors for the department or included modern art in its program. At a deeper level, however, her rage may have been rooted in the fact that the director wrote her a scathing letter on the Henry Clay Frick Fine Arts Department stationery, undoubtedly triggering all the bitterness she harbored against John D. Rockefeller, Jr., for infiltrating her father's collection, all her revulsion at the German destruction of cultural treasures and devastation of humanity in two world wars, and perhaps, at a deeply, deeply unconscious level, all her rage at the German father who invaded her personal space and stole her creativity, her freedom, and her life. Highly hysterical, she threatened to repossess the Henry Clay Frick Fine Arts Building. In a telling gesture, she acquired a painting by Carle Van Loo entitled *The Arts in Supplication* (fig. 10-37), showing Jove looking on as Atrapos, the goddess of death, readies herself to cut the cord connected to the arts and sciences. And to commemorate the Friends of Frick Fine Arts, she installed a bas-relief of an Indian elephant in the Lochoff cloister. The elephant who "does not fear gnats," though a moral allegory, is a metaphor of Helen. The elephant compensates for his short tail by enticing gnats into the crevices of his skin and crushing them when he contracts the wrinkles.

In January 1965, while she raged against the university, at age seventy-seven, Helen also filed a suit in equity against Sylvester K. Stevens, state historian of Pennsylvania from 1937 to 1956, for making "entirely false, scandalous, malicious, and defamatory" statements about her father in his *History of Western Pennsylvania*. She sought to enjoin Random House from distributing the book, claiming personal injury as a daughter who had "devoted her life to the promotion of projects of public welfare of the type encouraged and instituted by her father" and as a daughter who had "sought to honor the memory of her father." In her court papers, Helen claimed that "she had become associated with [Frick's memory] in the mind of the public, not merely because of the family relationship, but also because she [had] worked to carry on the tradition established by him of using her wealth for the public welfare." Thus, as she said, "any event tending to blacken [his memory had] a special significance to her and would tend to lower [her] in the esteem of the community."

Obsessed with defending her father's reputation, yet phobic about Germans, Helen's behavior was clearly a manifestation of her multilayered distress. Shortly after her brother's death, she went to the Carnegie Institute to see Dagnan-Bouveret's *Christ at Emmaus* (see fig. 4-17), the painting Frick had donated in honor of Martha. Upon entering the gallery where it was usually exhibited, however, Helen discovered that although he had given the painting on the condition it be kept on permanent display, the work had been put in storage. When she inquired why, the director, referring to her father's smaller copy of their *Christ at Emmaus* at Clayton, answered curtly that when

Fig. 10-37. Carle Van Loo (1705-1765), *The Arts in Supplication*, 1764.
Acquired by Helen Clay Frick for her own collection in 1966.
Oil on canvas, 30¼ x 26⅛ in. (76.8 x 66.3 cm).
Frick Art Museum, Pittsburgh

she hung her Dagnan-Bouveret in the Frick Collection, they would hang their Dagnan-Bouveret in the Carnegie.

Helen's copy never took its place in the Frick Collection, and her father's original was eventually returned to the exhibition halls of the Carnegie Institute, though without its memorial plaque. Henry Clay Frick's other Dagnan-Bouveret, *Consolatrix Afflictorum* (see fig. 5-23)—the "high-key" painting depicting the prostrate man, the Madonna, and Christ Child who looked respectively like Frick, Adelaide, and their deceased infant son, the painting he felt symbolized his collection—did continue to haunt her. In 1924, Helen had had the painting crated and sent to the University of Pittsburgh, where she later exhibited it in the lobby of the Henry Clay Frick Fine Arts Department in the Cathedral of Learning—built on the land she had inherited from her father. In 1934, two years after her mother's death, and for a period of thirty-six years thereafter, Helen relentlessly tried to divest herself of the moribund *Consolatrix*. She offered the painting to the Western Pennsylvania Hospital, the University of Pittsburgh, the Red Cross, and the Sisters of Mercy in Pittsburgh. But each refused the gift, claiming they had no exhibition space large enough. In 1942, Walter Read Hovey, the director of fine arts at the University of Pittsburgh, had suggested a way to make the painting more livable: cut the prostrate man at the Madonna's feet from the bottom of the canvas, just below her raised foot, thereby reducing the canvas to five feet in height, a size which might be "very effective on the end wall or [by] a fireplace in a room devoted to women's activities."

Helen decided against the alteration, but had she agreed, would such a superficial, surgical exercise have helped excise the unspoken, deeply ingrained layers of pathology beneath which Helen was trapped? By 1967, Helen Clay Frick, now age seventy-nine, was suffering the full circle and ultimate consequence of her wounding. In her anger, Helen Clay Frick the persecuted had become the persecutor; but even in this, she remained a helpless victim, clearly not in direction of her own life. Her actions as Henry Clay Frick's self-appointed surrogate brought her nothing but more pain and heartache. After almost ruining the University of Pittsburgh's Fine Arts Department and causing a national coalition of historians to protect their right to publish under the First and Fourteenth Amendments and the Civil Rights Act, Helen had her Henry Clay Frick Fine Arts Building seized from her by the university and lost her suit against Stevens.

As far as the building was concerned, Helen extricated her entire art, bronze, and porcelain collection, leaving behind only the Dossena fakes and the Lochoff frescoes. Then she immediately began construction of a new museum for her collection on the Clayton property.

In the lawsuit, the judge ruled that although Helen's feelings may have been hurt, she had suffered no injury; the author had been gentler to Henry Clay Frick than his actions probably warranted. The judge championed the public's right to know its history and insisted "an enlightened public opinion will take care of those who handle the truth carelessly or abandon it." In his opinion, however, the judge could not resist shaming the unsuccessful litigant. He wrote: "By analogy, Miss Frick might as well try to enjoin publication and distribution of the Holy Bible because, being a descendant of Eve, she does not believe that Eve gave Adam the forbidden fruit in the Garden of Eden, and that her senses are offended by such an ancestor of hers."

In 1973, just prior to the opening of her new museum, this demeaning voice seems to have evoked unpleasant memories of her Clayton childhood. Helen, who as a young girl loved to sing "Jesus Loves Me" and "Rock of Ages" at all hours of the day, but most particularly when in her bathtub early in the morning, was a serious piano student. Now, at age eighty-five, she acquired *The Music Lesson* (fig. 10-38) by Jan Steen, a brewer, tavern owner, satirist, and moralist inclined to excessive drinking and low life. The painting recalls her father's Vermeer, *Girl Interrupted at Her Music* (fig. 10-39), its allure perhaps a reminder of the moments when her own concentration was interrupted. One would think so, particularly given the fact that Helen was still an accomplished pianist, and Jan Steen, unlike Vermeer, became a household word. From the eighteenth century to the present, a home with rowdy children and marked by disarray is called a "Jan Steen household."

In this same year, Helen exhibited more distraught behavior. She generously agreed to lend her collection of Italian Renaissance paintings to the Frick Collection for an exhibition. Referring to them as "my darlings," and obviously suffering from her recent legal defeats, she insisted they be installed with an elaborate alarm system. A network of wires crisscrossed the Frick Collection basement, and twice a day Helen toured the galleries to be certain her paintings were safe. So high was her anxiety that she removed them two weeks after the exhibition opened, much to the exasperation of the curator in charge of the show.

When Helen's new museum opened, "her darlings" were beautifully and securely displayed in a magnificent re-creation of an Italian Renaissance room. The rest of her teaching-art collection was attractively displayed in other rooms and galleries, but *Consolatrix Afflictorum* remained in storage in the Frick Building in downtown Pittsburgh. It was discovered in 1985, a year after Helen's death. Its associations with childhood death and her father's mourning continued to work in Helen's psyche, particularly in her final years. She dedicated two maple trees in front of her new museum to her parents, trees for which the minister thanked God, as he also thanked Henry Clay Frick for the enrichment Pittsburgh gained because of his "careful teaching of Helen."

Fig. 10-38. Jan Steen (1626–1679), *The Music Lesson.*
Acquired by Helen Clay Frick for her own collection in 1973,
Oil on canvas, 12¼ x 10⅛ in. (31.1 x 25.7 cm)
Frick Art Museum, Pittsburgh

Fig. 10-39. Johannes Vermeer (1632–1675), *Girl Interrupted at Her Music*, c. 1660.
Acquired in 1901, Oil on canvas,
15½ x 17½ in. (39.3 x 44.4 cm).
The Frick Collection

There was, of course, much for Helen to be thankful for (fig. 10-40), but her anger and distress remained the darker, driving forces in her life. By 1980, Helen was ninety-two years old and very much alone with her past. She ordered graceful, plain tombs to replace the grass mounds of earth beneath which the remains of her parents and siblings rested. Still phobic about Germans, she continued to insist, "We are not German, we are Swiss." The temper flared again in telling how a German blew smoke in her face when, before World War I, she was traveling by train through Germany with her father. She constantly railed against her nurses. When they bathed her, she seethed, "You shall not conquer me." Yet she was surrounded by nurses who, though having no knowledge of the root of her trauma, nevertheless embraced her with their love, faith, and prayers. Living in Clayton with the windows shuttered and curtains drawn, Helen sat silently in her wheelchair, first in her mother's Clayton bedroom, then her father's. As the nurses wheeled her silently through the house, past Martha's bust, past *Chagrin d'Enfant* (see fig. 3-6), beneath *Pilgrims at Emmaus,* and Martha's portrait by Chartran, Helen went back in time. She wasn't senile, she just talked to her nurses about such things as the time Martha had prevented Childs from teasing her, making her cry, and then calling her ugly. Martha had scolded, "You shall not do that to my little sister."

Helen commented on how sad her parents were to have lost Martha, that had she benefited from modern medicine she might still be alive. She remembered how her father had given Martha his fingers to bite as the child was dying, because her pain was too much for her to bear. And Helen held a picture of her canaries and thanked them for the joy they brought into her life.

But when looking at a picture over her bedroom mantelpiece, a picture of herself between Martha and Childs, her wounds surfaced. She referred to herself as "the homely little girl in the middle." And when looking at reproductions in her father's bedroom of Chartran's portraits of herself and Martha, she teased her red-haired nurse Barbara, saying she, Helen, should get a red wig so they could be twins. She asked Barbara if she had a temper—"Redheads do, you know," she laughed. And she delighted that Barbara loved best the painting of red-haired St. Barbara (fig. 10-41)—patron saint of firearms and thunderstorms, who in spite of being locked in a tower by her pagan father to prevent her from marrying, had become a Christian, only to be beheaded by her father for her disobedience.

IN 1983, THE YEAR PRECEDING HER DEATH, Helen, age ninety-five, was dealt a mortal blow. She had become too infirm to remain active in her library, so for reasons of old age and deteriorating health, she was asked to resign the directorship and sign the library over to the Frick Collection. When presented with papers for her signature, a long, torturous meeting ensued. She asked Barbara to remain in the room, and although Helen showed no emotion, Barbara felt "the meeting was tearing her up; her heart was being ripped in two." Each time her nephew, her great-nephew, and her lawyer gave Helen a reason she must resign, Helen would "go quiet, very, very quiet, as the men paced the room." The meeting, Barbara thought "had to be killing her." But Helen was unrelenting in her determination: "She could vote by proxy," "She could fly to New York," "The trustees could meet at Clayton."

In the end, Helen reluctantly agreed. Her nurse said, however, that "although Helen had put the men through the ringer," she regretted the decision immediately, feeling the trustees had taken "her baby." A family member said Helen soon turned her face to the wall and said she wanted to die. In that time, while Helen sat in silent communion with Clayton's energies, she had also agreed to something else—to give outright as a gift to her father's collection her *Pietà*, the twin to her father's, the painting she had used to bar exhibition of the Rockefeller artworks.

In the last months of Helen's life, October and November 1984, she had numerous deathbed visitations from Martha and her mother. Although she spoke of the beauty and the peace of these visitations, and longed to die, Helen feared death. Not because she feared the state of death, but because she feared her father, and God. Maureen Murdock, in *The Hero's Daughter*, claims that "the fact that [the father] embodies the Father archetype greatly affects how his daughter will view God. If her father betrays her . . . her God will carry the threat of betrayal." In other words, the way she sees her father is the way she will relate to God.

Such was the case with Helen. Apart from believing she had killed her father when she seized control of his medical care and gave him his medication that fateful night, Helen was also afraid her deceased father would be angry with her for not properly defending him against the slanders of jealous people or the assault on the purity of his institutional efforts. She feared that because she had failed her deceased father, her

Father in Heaven would not accept her. She repeatedly asked her minister, "What will make me worthy to meet my mother and father? How can I be saved? Please find out how I can be forgiven."

Fortunately, Helen's minister was able to convince her that she did not need to do anything to win God's love or acceptance. And then, on November 9, 1984, when Helen's niece, Martha Frick Symington, telephoned to see how her aunt was doing, the peace came. Helen died. As her body was taken down Clayton's steps, past the *Four Virgins* on the stair landing, the Frick Art Reference Library in New York held a small ceremony and the Frick Collection's flag was lowered to half-mast. Although various Frick Collection catalogues would later give credit to Helen for the part she played in the formation of her father's collection, the minutes of the Frick Collection's board of trustees gave her no tribute. None had understood her. And none had guessed the price she had paid.

The year after Helen's death, with some family trustees opposing, some abstaining, and some voting for the reaccession, Rockefeller's *Crucifixion* and his two marble busts returned from Princeton University, where they had been displayed, and were silently put on exhibition in the Frick Collection. Perhaps Helen had anticipated the trustee's plan. Perhaps not. But in a section of her will drafted shortly after she lost her fight with Rockefeller on the one-hundredth anniversary of Frick's birth, Helen established no endowment for her Westmoreland Sanctuary, the Overholt Homestead, or the Frick Art Reference Library. She placed her entire fortune in the Helen Clay Frick Foundation, stipulating that these institutions only had the right to request money from the foundation. Additionally, her will instructed that her childhood Clayton home be preserved as a house-museum and restored to the 1890s. According to her wish, all personal photographs were to be divided among family members, except the large reproductions in her father's room—two of herself and one of Martha. Flowers were to be taken from the greenhouse and placed daily on the family graves at the Homewood Cemetery. And only the artworks original to Clayton could be exhibited there. Perhaps harboring a hope that one day the truth of her family's life would be understood, Helen made a revealing notation in her Clayton memoir: she wanted Clayton to become a house-museum so "others may know the kind of life that was lived within its walls."

Opposite: Fig. 10-40. Helen Clay Frick, c. 1982.
Private collection, courtesy Edgar Munhall

Fig. 10-41. Master of the Half Lengths, Hans Vereycke, early sixteenth century,
Madonna and Child with Angel; St. Catherine and St. Barbara, c. 1510.
Acquired by Helen Clay Frick for her own collection in 1970,
Triptych: oil on panels, 18⅛ x 22⁹⁄₁₆ in. (46.2 x 57.3 cm).
Frick Art Museum, Pittsburgh

Afterword

Today, as one tours Clayton and the Frick Collection, one can sense the presence of Henry Clay Frick. The paintings, like windows onto his psychic landscape, reveal the great industrialist's recognition that his self-enslavement to work and his insensitivity to others had cost him dearly, that the deaths of his cherished daughter and infant son were the price he paid. There seemed to be something devotional in his Martha-obsession, and something larger in his gift of his art collection and home than just the promise of enjoyment by the public. There was an element of neatness to his gesture, a tying-up, a reconciliation of debt and a payment. In giving five-sixths of his fortune and his art collection to the public, he seemed to be honoring his part in Martha's death and, at some deeper level, the deathblow he had dealt to others. Though forever anti-union and never repentant, through his highly selective philanthropy Henry Clay Frick seemed to be thanking those who helped him make his fortune while also acknowledging that a greater force had shaped all their destinies.

For all his wealth, power, success, and art, Henry Clay Frick was an unhappy man. Forced from childhood to carry an image dictated by culture and circumstance, his gentle side was devoured by a need to compete and control. Allowed only to be superhuman, he presented an ironclad facade to both the world and family. While his Midas touch turned much to gold, much that he touched became tarnished or was destroyed. In a sense, his mourning for Martha—intensified by the sudden removal of his four-year-old sister Maria from their home in 1852 and darkened by Carnegie's betrayal—was a self-mourning, a largely unconscious reaction to the loss of his own innocence, the hardening of his outer skin, and the resulting repression of his softer side.

Although Frick's wife and children had nothing but the best that material wealth could buy, they too were scarred by the family history of loss and Frick's poverty, particularly Helen. Just as lines of perspective recede from the dark silhouette of the officer in Vermeer's *Officer and a Laughing Girl* (see fig. i-1) and converge on the figure of the laughing girl, so too the events of Henry Clay Frick's life converged on Helen. If his unhealed sorrow over Martha's death was the visible turning point of his life, his vanishing point, and the vanishing point of his collection, so too his self-portrait became Helen's. Like her father, Helen's story became one of loss; a portrait of poverty and torment not wealth and peace. Although history may never forgive Henry Clay Frick for his stern business practices and his complicated relationship to Helen, or Helen for her now-comprehensible, but bizarre behavior, through their father-daughter art collection one can at least better recognize the nature of loss, the cost of wealth, and the consequences of protracted mourning.

The artistic personality pervading Henry Clay Frick's house-museums is so clearly felt, his memory can never fade or be destroyed. But in coming to know his emptiness through these combined collections, and by facing the consequences of his wounds, one learns more. One moves farther along in one's own journey by appreciating that because the harmony Frick sought stood in direct proportion to his ruinous shadow, his vanishing point gave history, and humanity, not only his two art collections, but also his daughter's unique New York and Pittsburgh art reference libraries, Pittsburgh's Clayton house-museum, the Henry Clay Frick Fine Arts Building, the Frick Art Museum, and the Henry Clay Frick Birthplace at the West Overton Museums—institutions that at once serve heart and mind.

Appendix

Combined Art Collections of Henry Clay Frick

This list includes *the majority of* the paintings in the New York and Pittsburgh collections of Henry Clay Frick, as well as certain sculpture and paintings he once owned or commissioned. An asterisk indicates that the painting mentioned in the text is no longer in either collection. The Frick Art and Historical Center (Clayton) owns the paintings credited to the Frick Art Museum, Pittsburgh. Although these paintings are mentioned in the text, they are not included in this list because they were acquired by Helen Clay Frick, not her father. Acquisitions by Helen Clay Frick are listed in Vincent Carl Fazio, "Helen Clay Frick: Architectural Patron and Art Collector," M.A. thesis, University of Pittsburgh, 1998, 3.

1879-1883: When Living in the Monongahela House

1881

George Hetzel	*Landscape with a River* (Frick Art and Historical Center, Clayton)
Luis Jiménez y Aranda	*A Revelation in the Louvre* (Frick Art and Historical Center, Clayton)
George Henry Boughton	*Priscilla*, engraving (Knoedler & Company)*
	Evangeline, engraving (Knoedler & Company)*

1882

George Henry Boughton	*Portrait of Henry Wadsworth Longfellow*, engraving (Frick Art and Historical Center, Clayton)
George Hetzel	*Fruit* (location unknown)*
A. Bryan Wall	*Fruit* (location unknown)*
A. Bryan Wall	*Wife and Sister* (Frick Art and Historical Center, Clayton)

1883–1905: When Living at Clayton (The Frick Art and Historical Center)

1884

James Archer	*Childs Frick* (Frick Art and Historical Center, Clayton)

1887

Tito Lessi	*Reading the Newspaper* (Frick Art and Historical Center, Clayton)
J. G. Meyer von Bremen	*The Darlings* (private collection)*

1889

Fr. Roseti	*Mrs. Henry Clay Frick and Children* (Frick Art and Historical Center, Clayton)

1890

Charles Courtney Curran	*Woman with a Horse* (Frick Art and Historical Center, Clayton)

1891

G. W. Waters	*Peaches* (Frick Art and Historical Center, Clayton)

1892

James Bonar	*Mine Mule* (Frick Art and Historical Center, Clayton)
Childs Frick (c.)	*House and Piers* (Frick Art and Historical Center, Clayton)

1898

P. A. J. Dagnan-Bouveret	Copy of *Christ and the Disciples at Emmaus* (Frick Art and Historical Center, Clayton)
	Childs Frick (Frick Art and Historical Center, Clayton)
	Consolatrix Afflictorum (placed on reserve)
Jean-Charles Cazin	*The Dipper* (Frick Art and Historical Center, Clayton)
Jean-Baptiste-Camille Corot	*Ville d'Avray* (The Frick Collection)
Jean-François Millet	*Shepherd Minding Sheep* (Frick Art and Historical Center, Clayton)
	The Knitting Lesson (Frick Art and Historical Center, Clayton)
Jean-François Raffaëlli	*Woman in a White Dressing Gown* (Frick Art and Historical Center, Clayton)
George Romney	*Miss Mary Finch-Hatton* (The Frick Collection)
John Macallan Swan	*Tigers Drinking by a Lotus Pool* (The Art Museum, Princeton University)*

1899

P. A. J. Dagnan-Bouveret	*Head of Christ* (Frick Art and Historical Center, Clayton)
Jean-Baptiste-Camille Corot	*The Pond* (The Frick Collection)
	Couronne de Fleurs (location unknown) *
Emile Friant	*Chagrin d'Enfant* (Frick Art and Historical Center, Clayton)
John Hoppner	*The Hon. Lucy Byng* (The Frick Collection)
Frank D. Millet	*How the Gossip Grew* (location unknown) *
Jean-François Millet	*The Sower* (Frick Art and Historical Center, Clayton)
	Le Puy de Dome (Frick Art and Historical Center, Clayton)
	The Cow-Herder (Frick Art and Historical Center, Clayton)
Jean-Marc Nattier	*Elizabeth, Countess of Warwick* (The Frick Collection)
Rembrandt Harmensz. van Rijn	*Portrait of a Young Artist* (The Frick Collection)
Constant Troyon	*A Pasture in Normandy* (The Frick Collection)

1900

William Henry Hunt	*Bird's Nest* (Frick Art and Historical Center, Clayton)
Antoine Vollon	*Still Life with Apples and Roses* (Frick Art and Historical Center, Clayton)

1901

P. A. J. Dagnan-Bouveret	*Consolatrix Afflictorum* (Frick Art and Historical Center, Clayton)
Virgile Narcisse Diaz de la Peña	*The Plain* (Frick Art and Historical Center, Clayton)
	The Bracelet (gift to D. H. Watson)
Jean Baptiste Camille Corot	*La Seine à Nantes* (location unknown)*
Claude Oscar Monet	*Bords de la Seine à Lavacour* (Frick Art and Historical Center, Clayton)
Jacob van Ruisdael	*A Waterfall with Rockey Hills and Trees* (private collection)
J. M. W. Turner	*Antwerp: Van Goyen Looking Out for a Subject* (The Frick Collection)
Johannes Vermeer	*Girl Interrupted at Her Music* (The Frick Collection)
Philips Wouwerman	*Cavalry Camp* (The Frick Collection)

1902

Théobald Chartran	*Signing the Peace Protocol Between Spain and the United States, August 12, 1898* (gift of Henry Clay Frick, The White House)*
Cottier and Company (c.)	*The Four Virgins* (Frick Art and Historical Center, Clayton)
Aelbert Cuyp	*Cows and Herdsman by a River* (The Frick Collection)
Meyndert Hobbema	*Village Among Trees* (The Frick Collection)
Sir Thomas Lawrence	*Marquise de Blaizel* (Frick Art and Historical Center, Clayton)
Sir Joshua Reynolds	*Lady Margaret Beaumont* (Frick Art and Historical Center, Clayton)
	Sir George Howland Beaumont (Frick Art and Historical Center, Clayton)

Pierre-Etienne-Théodore Rousseau   *The Village of Becquigny* (The Frick Collection)

1903

Gerard ter Borch   *Portrait of a Young Lady* (The Frick Collection)
Jean-Baptiste-Camille Corot   *The Boatman of Mortefontaine* (The Frick Collection)
George Romney   *Miss Frances Mary Harford* (The Frick Collection)
Joseph R. Woodwell   *Landscape with Cypresses* (Frick Art and Historical Center, Clayton)

1904

Charles-François Daubigny   *Dieppe* (The Frick Collection)
Sir Thomas Lawrence   *Julia, Lady Peel* (The Frick Collection)
Anton Mauve   *Shepherd with Sheep by a Snow Fence* (Frick Art and Historical Center, Clayton)
    The Shepherd (Frick Art and Historical Center, Clayton)
Jean-François Millet   *End of Day* (Frick Art and Historical Center, Clayton)
    The Gleaners (Frick Art and Historical Center, Clayton)
    Resting in the Shade (Frick Art and Historical Center, Clayton)
Bartolomé Estaban Murillio   *Self Portrait* (private collection)*
George Romney   *Lady Hamilton as 'Nature'* (The Frick Collection)
J. M. W. Turner   *Fishing Boats Entering Calais Harbor* (The Frick Collection)

Date Unknown

Jacobus Hendrikus Maris   *Man Plowing* (Frick Art and Historical Center, Clayton)

1905-1914: When Living at 640 Fifth Avenue

1905

Théobald Chartran   *Helen Clay Frick* (private collection)
Aelbert Cuyp   *Dordrecht: Sunrise* (The Frick Collection)
El Greco   *St. Jerome* (The Frick Collection)
Gabriel Metsu   *Lady at Her Toilet* (The Frick Collection)
Sir Henry Raeburn   *Mrs. James Cruikshank* (The Frick Collection)
Salomon van Ruysdael   *River Scene: Men Dragging a Net* (The Frick Collection)
Titian   *Pietro Aretino* (The Frick Collection)
Sir Anthony Van Dyck   *Ottaviano Canevari* (The Frick Collection)

1906

Jan van de Cappelle, follower of   *A View of the River Maas Before Rotterdam* (The Frick Collection)
Jean-Baptiste-Camille Corot   *The Lake* (The Frick Collection)
Frans Hals   *Portrait of a Painter* (The Frick Collection)
Jean-Francois Millet   *Woman Sewing by Lamplight* (The Frick Collection)
Rembrandt Harmensz. van Rijn   *Self-Portrait* (The Frick Collection)
Sir Joshua Reynolds   *Selina, Lady Skipwith* (The Frick Collection)

1907

Isack van Ostade   *Travelers Halting at an Inn* (The Frick Collection)
Sir Anthony Van Dyck   *Marchesa Giovanna Cattaneo* (The Frick Collection)
15th c. French   *Pietà* (The Frick Collection)

1908

John Constable   *Salisbury Cathedral from the Bishop's Garden* (The Frick Collection)
Childe Hassam   *The June Idyle* (Frick Art and Historical Center, Clayton)
Jean-François Millet   *La Sortie* (Frick Art and Historical Center, Clayton)
George Romney   *Henrietta, Countess of Warwick, and Her Children* (The Frick Collection)

| Joseph R. Woodwell | *Sand Dunes, Gloucester, Massachusetts* (Frick Art and Historical Center, Clayton) |

1909

Aelbert Cuyp	*River Scene* (The Frick Collection)
El Greco	*Purification of the Temple* (The Frick Collection)
J. M. W. Turner	*Mortlake Terrace: Early Summer Morning* (The Frick Collection)
Sir Anthony Van Dyck	*Frans Snyders* (The Frick Collection)
	Margareta Snyders (The Frick Collection)

1910

Frans Hals	*Portrait of an Elderly Man* (The Frick Collection)
Rembrandt Harmensz. van Rijn	*The Polish Rider* (The Frick Collection)
Sir Joshua Reynolds	*Elizabeth, Lady Taylor* (The Frick Collection)
Jacob van Ruisdael	*Quay at Amsterdam* (The Frick Collection)
Edmund C. Tarbell (c.)	*Henry Clay Frick and Daughter Helen* (The National Portrait Gallery, Washington, D.C.)*

1911

Thomas Gainsborough	*Frances Duncombe* (The Frick Collection)
Francisco Goya	*Julia Ascencio* (Frick Art and Historical Center, Clayton)
Meyndert Hobbema	*Village with Water Mill Among Trees* (The Frick Collection)
Sir Henry Raeburn	*James Cruikshank* (The Frick Collection)
George Romney	*Charlotte, Lady Milnes* (The Frick Collection)
Diego Velázquez	*King Philip IV of Spain* (The Frick Collection)
Johannes Vermeer	*Officer and Laughing Girl* (The Frick Collection)

1912

Henry Bacon	*On the Way to Karnak* (author's collection)
Hans Holbein the Younger	*Sir Thomas More* (The Frick Collection)
Paolo Veronese	*Allegory of Wisdom and Strength* (The Frick Collection)
	Allegory of Vice and Virtue (The Frick Collection)

1913

| El Greco | *Vincenzo Anastagi* (The Frick Collection) |
| Sir Anthony Van Dyck | *James, Seventh Earl of Derby, His Lady and Child* (The Frick Collection) |

1914

Edgar Degas	*The Rehearsal* (The Frick Collection)
Thomas Gainsborough	*Sarah, Lady Innes* (The Frick Collection)
Francisco de Goya y Lucientes	*An Officer* (The Frick Collection)
	Doña María Martínez de Puga (The Frick Collection)
	The Forge (The Frick Collection)
William Hogarth	*Miss Mary Edwards* (The Frick Collection)
Edouard Manet	*The Bullfight* (The Frick Collection)
Jacobus Hendrikus Maris	*The Bridge* (The Frick Collection)
Pierre-Auguste Renoir	*Mother and Children* (The Frick Collection)
After François-Jacques-Joseph Saly	*Bust of a Young Girl* (The Frick Collection)
J. M. W. Turner	*The Harbor of Dieppe* (The Frick Collection)
	Cologne: The Arrival of a Packet-Boat: Evening (The Frick Collection)
Sir Anthony Van Dyck	*Paola Adorno, Marchesa di Brignole Sale* (The Frick Collection)
James Abbott McNeill Whistler	*Robert, Comte de Montesquiou-Fezensac* (The Frick Collection)
	Miss Rosa Corder (The Frick Collection)
	The Ocean (The Frick Collection)

1915–1919: When Living at 1 East 70th Street (The Frick Collection)

1915

Giovanni Bellini	*St. Francis in the Desert* (The Frick Collection)
George Bellows	*Dock in Winter* (private collection)*
Agnolo Bronzino	*Lodovico Capponi* (The Frick Collection)
Francis Cotes	*Francis Vernon* (The Frick Collection)
Gerard David	*The Deposition* (The Frick Collection)
Jean-Honore Fragonard	*The Progress of Love: Reverie* (The Frick Collection)
Hans Holbein the Younger	*Thomas Cromwell* (The Frick Collection)
John Hoppner	*The Ladies Sarah and Catherine Bligh* (The Frick Collection)
Sir Peter Paul Rubens	*A Knight of the Order of the Golden Fleece* (The Frick Collection)
Titian	*Man in a Red Cap* (The Frick Collection)

1916

François Boucher	*The Arts and Sciences: Painting and Sculpture* (The Frick Collection)
	The Four Seasons (The Frick Collection)
	Drawing (The Frick Collection)
	Poetry (The Frick Collection)
	Girl with Roses (The Frick Collection)
Eugène Carrière	*Motherhood* (The Frick Collection)
Arthur Devis	*Sir Joshua Vanneck and His Family* (Frick Art and Historical Center, Clayton)
Thomas Gainsborough	*The Mall in St. James's Park* (The Frick Collection)
Sir Thomas Lawrence	*Miss Louisa Murray* (The Frick Collection)
Giovanni Battista Tiepolo	*Perseus and Andromeda* (The Frick Collection)
Carel van der Pluym	*Old Woman with a Book* (The Frick Collection)
James Abbott McNeill Whistler	*Mrs. Leyland* (The Frick Collection)

1917

Thomas Gainsborough	*Mrs. Peter Wiliam Baker* (The Frick Collection)
Frans Hals	*Portrait of a Man* (The Frick Collection)
Sir Anthony Van Dyck	*Anne, Countess of Clanbrassil* (The Frick Collection)

1918

Hendrik van der Burgh	*Drinkers Before the Fireplace (The Frick Collection)*
Thomas Gainsborough	*Richard Brinsley Sheridan* (Frick Art and Historical Center, Clayton)
Francesco Guardi	*View of the Grand Canal at San Geremia* (Frick Art and Historical Center, Clayton)
William Hogarth	*The Hon. John Hamilton* (Frick Art and Historical Center, Clayton)
John Hoppner	*Princess Sophia, Daughter of George III* (Frick Art and Historical Center, Clayton)
Jean-Baptiste Pater	*Italian Comedians* (The Frick Collection)
	The Village Orchestra (The Frick Collection)
Sir Joshua Reynolds	*Lady Cecil Rice* (The Frick Collection, after bequest in 1979)
Jacob van Ruisdael	*A Waterfall with a Castle and Cottage* (The Fogg Art Museum, Harvard University Art Museums)*
Gilbert Stuart	*George Washington* (The Frick Collection)
Sir Anthony Van Dyck	*Sir John Suckling* (The Frick Collection)
James Abbott McNeill Whistler	*Valerie, Lady Meux* (The Frick Collection)

1919

Johannes Vermeer	*Mistress and Maid* (The Frick Collection)

1919-1961: Posthumous Additions to the Frick Collection
(Helen Clay Frick, Chairman of the Acquisitions Committee)

1922

Malvina Hoffman	*Bust of Henry Clay Frick* (gift of Helen Clay Frick)

1924

French Burgundian	*Virgin and Child*
Fra Filippo Lippi	*The Annunciation*

1926

Gentile Bellini	*The Doge*
Jean-Baptiste-Siméon Chardin	*Lady with a Bird-Organ*

1927

Barna da Siena	*Christ Bearing the Cross*
Duccio di Buoninsegna	*The Temptation of Christ on the Mountain*
Jean-Auguste-Dominique Ingres	*Comtesse d'Haussonville*

1930

Paolo and Giovanni Veneziano	*Coronation of the Virgin*

1935

Lazzaro Bastiani	*Adoration of the Magi*

1936

Piero della Francesca	*The Apostle*

1937

François Boucher	*Madame Boucher*
Jacques-Louis David	*Comtesse Daru*

1938

Jacopo Tintoretto, circle of	*Portrait of a Venetian Procurator*

1939

Andrea del Castagno, attributed to	*The Resurrection*

1942

Claude Monet	*Vetheuil in Winter*

1943

John Constable	*The White Horse*
William Blake	Illustration for *The Pilgrim's Progress*: "Christian in the Slough of Despond"
Francisco de Goya y Lucientes	*Don Pedro, Duque de Osuna*
Jean-Baptiste Greuze	*The Wool Winder*
John Christen Johansen	*Henry Clay Frick* (gift of Helen Clay Frick)
Rembrandt Harmensz. van Rijn	*Nicholaes Ruts*
Sir Joshua Reynolds	*General Burgoyne*

1945

Jean-Baptiste-Siméon Chardin	*Still Life with Plums*

	1946
Thomas Gainsborough	*Richard Paul Jodrell*
	Grace Dalrymple Elliot
	1948
Georges de La Tour	*Education of the Virgin*
	1949
Jacob van Ruisdael	*Landscape with a Footbridge*
	1950
Piero della Francesca	*Monk and Nun*
Tuscan School	*Flagellation of Christ*
	1952
Césarine-Henriette-Flore Davin-Mirvault	*Antonio B. Bruni*
	1954
Jan van Eyck	*Virgin and Child with Saints and Donor*
	1959
Elizabeth Shoumatoff	Posthumous Portrait of *Adelaide Howard Frick* (gift of Helen Clay Frick)
	1960
Claude Lorraine	*The Sermon on the Mount*
	1961
Piero della Francesco	*The Crucifixion* (bequest of John D. Rockefeller, Jr.)
Andrea del Verrocchio	*Bust of a Young Woman* (bequest of John D. Rockefeller, Jr.)
Francesco Laurana	*Bust of Beatrice of Aragon* (bequest of John D. Rockefeller, Jr.)
Konrad Witz, follower of	*Pietà* (on permanent loan; in 1981, gift of Helen Clay Frick)

1961-1994: Trustee's Additions to the Frick Collection

1965

Pieter Bruegel the Elder — *The Three Soldiers*

1966

François-Hubert Drouais — *The Comte and Chevalier de Choiseul as Savoyards*
Gentile da Fabriano — *Madonna and Child, with St. Lawrence and St. Julian*

1968

Hans Memling — *Portrait of a Man*

1977

Anton Mauve — *Early Morning Plowing* (gift of I. Townsend Burden II)

1981

Conrad Witz, follower of — *Pietà* (gift of Helen Clay Frick)

1991

Jean-Antoine Watteau — *The Portal at Valenciennes*

1994

Jean-Baptiste-Camille Corot — *The Arch of Constantine and the Forum, Rome* (gift of Mr. and Mrs. Eugene Victor Thaw)

Abbreviations Used in the Notes

Individuals

James Howard Bridge	JHB
Andrew Carnegie	AC
Adelaide Howard Childs Frick	AHCF
Childs Frick	CF
Helen Clay Frick	HF
Henry Clay Frick	HCF
Martha Howard Frick	MHF
Roland F. Knoedler	RFK
Andrew W. Mellon	AWM
John D. Rockefeller, Jr.	JDR, Jr.

Institutions

Frick Archives, Pittsburgh, Pa.	FA
The Frick Collection, New York, N.Y.	FC
Knoedler Art Gallery Archives, New York, N.Y.	KA
Library of Congress, Washington, D.C.	LC
Office of Paul Mellon, Washington, D.C.	OPM
Rockefeller Archive Center, Sleepy Hollow, N. Y.	RAC
Rockefeller Family Archives, Sleepy Hollow, N. Y.	RFA
West Overton Museums Archives, West Overton, Pa.	WOMA
U.S. Steel Archives, Pittsburgh, Pa.	USX

Notes

Introduction

Page 14 Margaret Sanger and Alexander Berkman: This story was told to the author by her former brother-in-law, Alexander Sanger. For the intimacy of this relationship, see Alexander Berkman to Margaret Sanger December 1915, September 26, 1924, and December 28, 1924, Margaret Sanger Papers, New York University, (formerly in the Sophia Smith Collection, Margaret Sanger Papers, Smith College, Amherst, Massachusetts).

16 "As I controlled her life before": Ann K. Finkbeiner, *After the Death of a Child* (New York: The Free Press, 1996), 231.

16 "Time has brought me consolation": Thomas Mellon, *Thomas Mellon and His Times* (1885; rpt. Pittsburgh, Pa.: University of Pittsburgh Press, 1994), 234.

18 "He put [his collection] together": Charles Ryskamp and Bernice Davidson, *Art in the Frick Collection: Paintings, Sculpture, Decorative Arts* (New York: Harry N. Abrams in association with the Frick Collection, 1996), 15.

20 "a savior complex": Ron Chernow, *The House of Morgan* (New York: Simon & Schuster, 1990), 44.

21 "clearly dedicated": Hilliard T. Goldfarb, *The Isabella Stewart Gardner Museum* (New Haven, Conn.: Yale University Press, 1995), 37.

Chapter I: Birth of a Millionaire

Page 25 "a pretty tight sort": "Testimony of A. O. Tinstman," September 30, p. 21. Estate of Abraham Overholt, Orphans' Court of Westmoreland County, Pa. No. 7, August Term, 1908.

29 "make more ringers": J. M. Hantz to Karl Overholt, December 10, 1920, FA.

30 reciting "Twinkle Twinkle"; as Isaac's sister Ella wrote: Ella Sherrick to HF, March 1920, scrapbook on HCF, FA.

30-31 Clay's appearance and blushes: ibid.

31 "strong-willed": *New York Sun*, December 28, 1919.

31 "We children had to help": Glenn M. Sauder, "Hall of Distinction: Henry Clay Frick," *The Meadow Mart* 9, no. 2 (February 1977).

31 "most annoyed him"; "everyone was put": HF, "Grandfather," 15, FA.

32 "a very pretty pair": Ella Sherrick to HF, March 1920, scrapbook on HCF.

32 "Grandpap Overholt": George Harvey, *Henry Clay Frick: The Man* (New York: Scribner's, 1920), 9.

32 "to pay high for it": Karl Overholt, Diary, WOMA.

32 "If one got it": scrapbook on HCF.

32 "very angry": HF's diary of HCF's early life, 1849–1880, FA. Cited hereafter as HF's diary of HCF.

33 "the best likker": A. Overholt & Co., Inc., *A History of the Company and of the Overholt Family*, August 1940, Carnegie Library, Pittsburgh.

33 "hustler": Karl Overholt, Diary.

33 "Oh, I'll be worth $200,000"; "There is nothing to hinder me": scrapbook on HCF.

33-34 story of the boots; "[You] better go": Karl Overholt, Diary.

34 "Grandfather, won't you tell": ibid.

36 "Andy, please don't tell": Gertrude A. Mellon to Edgar Munhall, October 20, 1994, FC. The author is grateful to Edgar Munhall, curator of the Frick Collection, for generously sharing this letter.

37 Clay at the saw mill: Alfred Emerson to HF, February 19, 1923, FA.

44 Judge Mellon's comments on HCF: Andrew W. Mellon to George Harvey, June 25, 1927, FA.

44-45 Corey's report on HCF: *New York Times*, June 2, 1907.

47 HCF and Myers: Karl Overholt, Diary.

48 "without a peer": Edward Hungerford, *The Story of the Baltimore and Ohio Railroad, 1827–1927* (New York: G. P. Putnam's, 1928), 99.

49 "monument to Christian learning": Maria Stauffer Overholt, obituary, n.d., WOMA.

49 "sweet face": HF's diary of HCF.

49 "wasn't the brooding kind": Harvey, *Frick*, 58.

50 "They say Clay is": Abraham Overholt Tinstman, Diary, January 25, 1875, scrapbook on HCF.

50 "made up his mind": HF's diary of HCF.

51 "I regret very much": HCF to Mrs. Joseph Rice, May 13, 1891, FA.

51 "upon the understanding": Abstract Book 8007, p. 100, agreement dated October 11, 1895, USX.

51 "This is the best investment": Karl Overholt, Diary.

52 "John Frick": ibid.

53-54 HCF and James King: ibid.

56 HCF's thirtieth birthday: Harvey, *Frick*, 66; HF's diary of HCF.

65 "that if he could be given": HF, "Grandfather," 17–18; Sir Osbert Sitwell, introduction to *Catalogue of the Frick Collection* (New York: Frick Art Reference Library, 1949), 11.

73 "This was probably the first time": Richard Bissell, *The Monongahela* (New York: Rinehart, 1952), 78–79.

73 "unique as being one": HCF to Roger Fry, May 18, 1910, FC.

73-74 HCF Masonic records: Karl Overholt, Diary; Harvey, *Frick*, 370–71. Catherine Swanson, archivist at the Museum of Our National Heritage, in a letter to the author, December 22, 1997, states that although Frick "may well have been a high ranking Scottish Rite Mason, there is no record . . . to verify this fact." Their records indicate that the Fourteenth Degree was the highest one conferred on him.

75 Sitwell on the Polish Rider: Sitwell, introduction, 10.

Chapter II: Honeymoons and Horrors

Page 77 "an awful time": HF's diary of HCF.

79 "special reason": Harvey, *Frick*, 71.

79 HCF and Mellon conversation: Harvey, *Frick*, 66; see also William Larimer Mellon, *Judge Mellon's Sons* (Pittsburgh, Pa.: privately printed, 1949), 516.

79 "Your ancestors went": HF diary of HCF.

80 HCF on the Wallace Collection: Nicholas H. J. Hall, *Colnaghie in America* (New York: Colnaghie U.S.A. Ltd., 1992), 26; Helen Clay Frick with Mara O'Hara, *My Father: Henry Clay Frick* (Pittsburgh, Pa.: privately printed, 1959), 31; *Pittsburgh Press*, August 4, 1959; Elizabeth Shoumatoff, *F.D.R.'s Unfinished Portrait* (Pittsburgh, Pa.: University of Pittsburgh Press, 1990), 32.

80 "fair Emma": HCF to AWM, Dresden, August 6, 1887, AWM Papers, OPM.

80 "graciously facilitate[d]": Harvey, *Frick*, 72.

82-83 HCF and AWM conversation about Adelaide Childs: ibid., 73.

83 "a hard worker"; "go in but not stay": Karl Overholt, Diary.

83 Phrenology report: Professor O. S. Fowler, "The Phrenological Character of Henry Clay Frick," Boston, April 10, 1879, FA.

83 "[the] understanding . . . proved": Harvey, *Frick*, 72.

83 HCF's gifts to Adelaide: HF's diary of HCF.

85 "one of the most notable weddings": Karen Jones Hellerstedt, *Clayton, the Pittsburgh Home of Henry Clay Frick* (Pittsburgh, Pa.: Helen Clay Frick Foundation, 1988), 12.

87 "Will let you know": Kenneth Warren, *Triumphant Capitalism* (Pittsburgh, Pa.: University of Pittsburgh Press, 1996), 29.

87 "Surely, Andrew": HF's diary of HCF.

88 "leaving him alone": ibid.

88 "I would like your Mr. Hess": HCF to D. S. Hess and Company, January 1883, FA.

89 "I don't think his Papa": Frick Family Diary, 1882–1942, author's collection.

89 "providence has placed": Martha Howard Childs (mother) to AHCF, December 20, 1881, FA.

90 Martha's (Attie's) comments on Adelaide's marriage: Martha Howard Childs (sister) to AHCF, December 16, 1881, FA.

91 "I am free to say": Warren, *Triumphant Capitalism*, 34.

92 "sweetest little face": Annie Stephany, "Memoir of the Frick Family," FA.

92 "Did you ever study": *Catalogue of an Exhibition of the Work of Joseph R. Woodwell*, Henry Clay Frick Fine Arts Department, University of Pittsburgh, November 30, 1953–January 4, 1954.

93 Letters from Europe: HCF to AWM, Bremen, July 29, 1887; Hamburg, August 15, 1887; Dresden, August 6, 1887; Paris, August 25, 1887; London, September 15, 1887, AWM Papers.

95 Carnegie refuses to make HCF a shareholder: Warren, *Triumphant Capitalism*, 41, 42.

96 HCF offers to sell his coke company shares: Harvey, *Frick*, 86, 87.

96-97 "The loss to"; "Whilst a majority": Harvey, *Frick*, 86; Joseph Frazier Wall, *Andrew Carnegie* (1970; rpt. Pittsburgh, Pa.: University of Pittsburgh Press, 1989), 495; Warren, *Triumphant Capitalism*, 48.

97 "Frick and Company is almost his all": Warren, *Triumphant Capitalism*, 37.

97 Invitation and visit to AC; Rosie's illness: HCF to AWM, London, September 21, 1887, AWM Papers.

98 "You can't justly estimate": Harvey, *Frick*, 90.

98-100 Mrs. Frick and the new baby: Stephany, "Memoir."

103 Clay had constructed a dam: HF's diary of HCF.

103 John Fulton . . . had insisted: Nathan Daniel Shappee, "Spoilation and Encroachment in the Conemaugh Valley Before the Johnstown Flood of 1889," *Western Pennsylvania Historical Magazine* 23 (March 1940): 23, 39.

104 Others not only disliked: "Whose Fault Was the Johnstown Flood?" *Old News* (Marietta, Pa.), undated sample issue, 3.

104 "God have mercy": *Johnstown Democrat*, n.d.

107 "I saw it coming": *Illustrated Historical Combination Atlas of Cambria County, Pennsylvania* (Philadelphia: Atlas, 1890), 31.

112 George Swank, William Tice, Frank McDonald: quoted in David McCullough, *The Johnstown Flood* (New York: Simon & Schuster, 1968), 150, 172.

112 "I am going up there to fish": "Whose Fault was the Johnstown Flood?" 2.

112 James Reed: quoted in McCullough, *Flood*, 242. Philander Knox, secretary of the South Fork Fishing and Hunting Club, was ill at the time of the violent Memorial Day rain. When the club manager wired his concern over the rapidly rising lake waters, Knox tried to go to Johnstown. Legend says that his horse threw a shoe on the way to the station, causing him to miss the Day Express, the train that was engulfed by the Flood when standing in the East Conemaugh Yard. Ralph H. Demmler, *The First Century of an Institution: A Centennial History of Reed, Smith Shaw and McClay* (Pittsburgh, Pa., 1977), 18.

113 "words are inadequate": HCF to E. Y. Townsend, June 1, 1889, FA.

113 "This dreadful catastrophe: HCF to J. C. Morse, June 5, 1889, FA.

114 "Taking a view of": HCF to Reuben Miller, June 8, 1889, FA.

115 "a fair start": HCF to AC, June 13, 1889, FA.

115 "Dear Boys": AC to his partners, June 15, 1889, FA.

121-22 Frick informed Carnegie: Warren, *Triumphant Capitalism*, 54–55.

122 "We have been alarmed": AC to HCF, July 23, 1889, FA.123 "Not anything more": Warren, *Triumphant Capitalism*, 69.

124 "Please do not make": HCF to Frederick J. Osterling, March 28, 1891, FA.

130 "The iron trade": The Dispatch, March 13, 1891, scrapbook on the Coke Region, FA.

130 "storm center": undated news article, scrapbook on the Coke Region, FA.

130 "I don't know when": HCF to J. C. Morse, March 20, 1891, FA.

132 Thomas Lynch and his statements: *Greensburg Daily Tribune*, April 1, 1891, scrapbook on the Coke Region; *The Courier* (Connellsville, Pa.), vol. 12.

132 Thomas Lynch as manager: Thomas Lynch first managed one of Frick's company stores in a Westmoreland County mining patch. Lynch had never met Frick, but one day his employer arrived at the store and asked him, "How many potatoes are in that bin?" When Lynch replied, "Eight bushels, Mr. Frick," Frick asked him to empty the bin and count them. On seeing the pile was exactly eight bushels, Frick said, "Mr. Lynch, today is your last day on the job. You are no longer manager of this store. I would be grateful if, beginning tomorrow, you will supervise *all* of the company stores for the H. C. Frick Coke Company." Charles Altman to the author, November 24, 1998.

133 "It seems to me"; "much damage": HCF to Robert E. Pattison, April 2, 1891, FA.

133 "These ignorant people"; "not a single": HCF to AC, April 3, 1891, FA.

134 Frick warned Carnegie: HCF to AC, April 20, 21, 29, 1891, FA.

134 In an attempt to placate: HCF to J. C. Morse, April 29, 1891, FA.

141 "can you give me": HCF to W. R. Duham, Cresson Springs Hotel, 4:10 P.M., June 30, 1891, FA.

141 "Mrs. Frick does not": HCF to AC, June 30, 1891, FA.

142 "of unspeakable griefs": Nathan Daniel Shappee, "A History of Johnstown and the Great Flood of 1889," Ph.D. diss., University of Pittsburgh, 1940, 511.

143 "My sweetest Little Daughter": HCF to MHF, July 20, 1891, FA.

147 "no doubt everything": HCF to AHCF, telegram, 12:10 P.M., July 20, 1891, FA.

147 "Had a restless night": AHCF to HCF, telegram, 12:03 P.M., July 21, 1891, FA.

147 "My Dear Sweet Little Daughter": HCF to MHF, July 23, 1891, FA.

157 "unimportant shell": Charles O. Jackson, in *Death and Dying*, ed. Richard A. Kalish (Amityville, N.Y.: Baywood, 1972), 48.

164 "There never is a time": Warren, *Triumphant Capitalism*, 75.

Chapter III: As Martha Dies

Page 129 Annie had been coaxing Martha: Stephany, "Memoir." All material on Martha and her illness is from this memoir, unless otherwise indicated.

Chapter IV: Triumph Over Labor

Page 169 "We had reached the point": quoted in David E. Koskoff, *The Mellons* (New York: Thomas Y. Crowell, 1978), 74; Sauder, "Hall of Distinction," 6.

169 "unbearable panache": Leon Wolff, *Lockout* (New York: Harper & Row, 1965), 46.

170 Frick belittled the workers' fears: Sauder, "Hall of Distinction," 6.

170 "No better time": HCF to AC, April 21, 1892, FA.

170 Phipps "rejoiced": Koskoff, *The Mellons*, 74.

170 "it would be better": Harvey, *Frick*, 171.

170 "a very wise man": ibid.

171 "too anxious for a life of pleasure": *The New Milton Cross' Complete Stories of the Great Operas,* ed. Karl Kohrs (Garden City, N.Y.: Doubleday, 1955), 353.

172 "the halls to suit": George Megrew to A. J. Kimbal, Jr., March 11, 1892, FA.

174 "It required the greatest care": HF, "Clayton Memoir," FA.

175 "she does too much": George Megrew to HCF, March 9, 1892, quoted in Hellerstedt, *Clayton*, 15.

177 "After Tie's tutor": Stephany, "Memoir."

177 "Don't be alarmed at the bluster": AC to HCF, June 15, 1889, FA.

178 "I shall look forward"; "My hope is you will": AC to HCF, January 30, 1889, March 29, 1891, FA.

179 "only the bottom": Wolff, *Lockout,* 88.

180 HCF to Pinkerton: Harvey, *Frick,* 115.

180 Headline: *Commercial Gazette,* June 30, 1892.

180 "the stillness in a cemetery": *The Dispatch,* July 1, 1892, scrapbook on Homestead, FA.

180 "a genuine old fashioned drizzle": *The Dispatch,* July 4, 1892, quoted in David P. Demarest, Jr., and Fannia Weingartner, eds., *"The River Ran Red"* (Pittsburgh, Pa.: University of Pittsburgh Press, 1992), 58.

181 "as perfect a system": *Philadelphia Press,* July 4, 1892.

182-83 Fourth of July celebration: Stephany, "Memoir."

183 "only letting": HCF to AC, July 11, 1892, FA.

183 "of course, keep within the law": Warren, *Triumphant Capitalism,* 84.

183 "do no act of": Knox and Reed, general counsel to Carnegie Steel Company, Ltd., to HCF, July 2, 1892, copy given to Mr. Potter, general superintendent of the Homestead Steel Works, excerpt from U.S. Congress, House, Committee on the Judiciary, *Report 2447: Investigation of the Homestead Troubles* (Washington, D.C.: Government Printing Office, 1893).

184 "Don't let the blacksheep": Tim Ziaukas, "Lockout," *Pittsburgh,* June 1992, 26.

184 "In the name of God and humanity"; "We were sent here": Paul Krause, *The Battle for Homestead* (Pittsburgh, Pa.: University of Pittsburgh Press, 1992), 18.

185 white flag, pistols taken: Wolff, *Lockout,* 121, 125–26.

185 "Kill the murderers": *Pittsburgh Commercial Gazette,* July 7, 1892, scrapbook on Homestead, FA.

187 "All anxiety gone": AC to HCF, July 7, 1892, FA.

187 "While nobody could regret": Warren, *Triumphant Capitalism,* 85.

187 "There is no more sensibility": Ziaukas, "Lockout," 29.

187 "FRICK MAY BE INDICTED"; "If he was not in the right": *Pittsburgh Commercial Gazette,* July 9, 1892, scrapbook on Homestead.

188 "It is the sheerest nonsense": *Frank Leslie's Illustrated Weekly,* July 12, 1892.

188 "Governors action": AC to HCF, telegram, July 12, 1892, FA.

188 "Starting a few months sooner": AC to HCF, July 14, 1892, FA.

189 "Matters at home": Warren, *Triumphant Capitalism,* 93.

189 "not spoken written or cabled"; "Am with you to the end": AC to HCF, telegrams, July 14, 1892, FA.

189 "dynamite and death": undated news article, scrapbook on Homestead.

189 "sounded the awakening": Emma Goldman, *Living My Life* (New York: Da Capo Press, 1970), 84.

189 "The spirit of the heroic past": Alexander Berkman, *Prison Memoirs of an Anarchist* (New York: Mother Earth Publishing, 1912), 7.

189-90 "A blow aimed at Frick": Goldman, *Living My Life,* 87.

190 Berkman on Frick and Pittsburgh: Berkman, *Prison Memoirs,* 29, 31, 32.

190-94 This account of the assassination attempt is based on: scrapbooks on Homestead and the assassination, particularly clippings from *Pittsburgh Commercial Gazette, Pittsburgh Dispatch, Pittsburgh Leader, Pittsburgh Press, Philadelphia Press, The Sun,* FA; Berkman, *Prison Memoir;* Goldman, *Living My Life;* *Frank Leslie's Illustrated Weekly;* Harvey, *Frick;* Wall, *Andrew Carnegie;* Wolff, *Lockout;* Demarest and Weingartner, *"The River Ran Red";* and on James Howard Bridge, *Millionaires and Grubb Street* (New York: Brentano's, 1921).

194 "was the most magnificent": James Howard Bridge, *The Inside History of the Carnegie Steel Company* (1903; rpt. Pittsburgh, Pa.: University of Pittsburgh Press, 1991), 227.

194 HCF telegrams: Wall, *Carnegie,* 562.

194 "This incident will not change": ibid.

195 "Hello, I am glad to": *The Sun,* July 24, 1892.

195 "Lynch him": Bridge, *Inside History,* 226.

195 "I'll be back": *The Sun,* July 24, 1892, scrapbook on Homestead.

195 Attie returned to Clayton: except as noted, the following paragraphs are based on Stephany, "Memoir."

196 HCF's return to Clayton: Sr. M. Cornelius Meerwald states in her 1947 and 1959 histories of Mercy Hospital that during his convalescence HCF stayed incognito at Mercy Hospital. Family letters and diaries, however, support the author's account of HCF's Clayton convalescence. For the Mercy Hospital story see Kathleen M. Washy to the author, January 7, 1998; Sr. M. Cornelius Meerwald, "History of the Pittsburgh Mercy Hospital: 1843-1959," Mercy Hospital of Pittsburgh archives.

196 "Ada . . . , I will be": Louise Dilworth Childs to Mrs. George W. Dilworth, July 25, 1892, Mercy Hospital Archives; generously shared by Elizabeth Schoyer.

197 Headlines: *Pittsburgh Leader,* July 23, 1892, *The Sun,* July 24, 1892, scrapbook on Homestead.

197 "the unlawful act": Myron R. Stowell, *Fort Frick* (Pittsburgh, Pa.: Pittsburgh Printing Co., 1893), 216.

197 "Those who hate him most": *New York World* quoted in Stewart H. Holbrook, *The Age of the Moguls* (Garden City, N.Y.: Doubleday, 1953), 86.

197 "Too glad": AC to HCF, telegram, July 25, 1892, FA.

197 "the necessity of": Thomas Mellon to HCF, July 25, 1892, scrapbook on HCF.

197 "cause [his] fever to rise"; "It will not hurt me": *The Sun,* July 25, 1892.

198 "He was able to see me": John Elmer Milholland to the editor of *The Sun,* December 19, 1892, "Frick, The Man of Steel: His Resolute Character Shown in an Episode of the Homestead Strike," 3–4.

198 "fight the strike out": Harvey, *Frick,* 151.

198 "notably quick mind": ibid., 357.

199 "normal cool resolution": Warren, *Triumphant Capitalism,* 189.

199 "as clearly and as real": Sauder, "Hall of Distinction," 5.

201 "This week is the": Louise Dilworth Childs to Mrs. George W. Dilworth, July 25, 1892, Mercy Hospital Archives.

203 "A sensational chapter": clipping from Wheeling, Ohio, July 23, 1892, scrapbook on Homestead.

203-04 naming and death of Henry Clay Frick, Jr.: Stephany, "Memoir."

204 Arrest of Frick and Carnegie officials: *The Sun,* August 3, 1892.

204 "he was not ruffled": *Commercial Gazette,* August 4, 1892.

204 Did not read his mail; photographer called: Henry Clay Frick, Jr., death notice, undated news article, scrapbook on Homestead.

204-05 Description of funeral: Stephany, "Memoir."

206 "Born in the midst of": Bridge, *Inside History,* 235.

206 "had too much to do": *Pittsburgh Leader,* August 5, 1892.

206 "Hearty congratulations": AC to HCF, telegram, August 6, 1892, FA.

206 "If an honest American": Harvey, *Frick,* 142.

207 "young, fair and charming": quoted in Hellerstedt, *Clayton,* 12.

207 poisoning in the mill: *New York Sun,* December 12, 1892; Carnegie Papers, vol. 264, LC; Wolff, *Lockout,* 206–08.

208 "We will be amply repaid": HCF to AC, August 17, 1892, FA.

208 "The whole public is"; "I am glad you see"; "'the break' would come": AC to HCF, August 29, 1892, FA.

208 "sink [the] works": AC to HCF, August 27, 1892, FA.

208 "the firmness with which": HCF to AC, October 31, 1892, FA.

208 "The strike is a thing": Arthur G. Burgoyne, *The Homestead Strike of 1892* (1893; rpt. Pittsburgh, Pa.: University of Pittsburgh Press, 1979), 188.

208 "I with you": HCF to AC, September 10, 1892, FA.

209 "The pain I suffer": Warren, *Triumphant Capitalism,* 93.

209 "I think many times a day": AC to HCF, September 24, 1892, FA.

209 "We have had our trials": AC to HCF, September 30, 1892, FA.

209 "Victory-Early": quoted in Harvey, *Frick,* 172.

209 "Through the war"; "What a relief": AC to HCF, November 20, 1892, FA.

210 "Life is again worth living": AC to HCF, November 25, 1892, FA; Harvey, *Frick,* 172.

210 "Our victory is now": Harvey, *Frick,* 172.

210 "We had to teach our employees": quoted in Wolff, *Lockout,* 225; Warren, *Triumphant Capitalism,* 92.

210 "It is hard to estimate what blessings": HCF to AC, November 28, 1892, FA.

210 "Mr. Frick, who is a businessman": quoted in Warren, *Triumphant Capitalism,* 92.

212 "cast out all them": Matthew 21:12.

212 "church of true faith": AC to HCF, November 17, 1892, FA.

212 "muscular Christianity": Richard B. Woodward, "Everyone's Favorite Museum," *Art News* 85, no. 4 (April 1986): 126.

214 "battled contemporary opinion": Homer Saint-Gaudens, "Joseph R. Woodwell," *Carnegie Magazine,* May 6, 1932, 274.

215 "When the gray heron": William George Jordan, *The Majesty of Calmness* (New York: Fleming H. Revell, c. 1898), 10.

215 "Nothing I have ever had to meet": quoted in Wall, *Carnegie,* 570.

215 "lamentable matter"; "[I] am sure I never want to go": HCF to AC, July 11, 28, 1892, FA.

216 "I got one big 'religious' picture": AC to HCF, November 17, 1892, FA.

216 "It was mainly his cowardice": Berkman, *Prison Memoirs*, 66.

221 "internal prosecutors"; "assume a nightmarish": Theresa A. Rando, *Treatment of Complicated Mourning* (Champaign, Ill.: Research Press, 1993), 97.

Chapter V: Emotions, Apparitions, and Art

Page 225 "the public will vote": AC to HCF, April 23, 1898, Carnegie Papers, vol. 51, 9856, LC.

226 "little liked": John Ingham, introduction to Bridge, *Inside History*, xxix.

226 "It is better": Wall, *Carnegie*, 560.

227 "as an answer": Warren, *Triumphant Capitalism*, 40.

228 "no other guest": Cornelius Vanderbilt, Jr., *Farewell to Fifth Avenue* (New York: Simon & Schuster, 1935), 10–11.

228 "absolutely opposed": Warren, *Triumphant Capitalism*, 214.

228 "The U.S.A. is": Harvey, *Frick,* 369.

229 "[It is] too Frenchy": AC to HCF, September 24, 1892, FA.

229 "Oliver's ore bargain": AC to HCF, August 29, 1892, FA.

229 "When any of you": AC to HCF, stamped March 1894, FA.

231 "If the sheriff": *The Dispatch,* April 5, 1894, scrapbook on the Coke Region.

231 "It is not the intention": *Commercial Gazette,* April 9, 1894, scrapbook on the Coke Region.

231 "I am sorry": AC to HCF, April 21, 1894, FA.

231-32 "Regret very much": HCF to AWM, July 14, 1894, AWM Papers.

233 HCF advised Stone and warned Carnegie: Warren, *Triumphant Capitalism*, 214.

232 Rainey a "rascal" and "thief"; "leaving my feelings out": ibid., 215.

233 "had been trying ones"; "My mind from necessity": HCF to AC, December 18, 1894, Carnegie Papers, vol. 29, 5609-5611, LC.

232 HCF's decision to resign: ibid., HCF to AC, December 20, 1894, Carnegie Papers, vol. 29, 5624, 5625, LC.

233 AC refused to accept: AC to HCF, December 18, 1894 (first letter), Carnegie Papers, vol. 29, 5599, LC.

234 "your face appears to me": ibid.

234 "improper act": William Serrin, *Homestead* (New York: Random House, 1992), 109.

234 "I cannot consider your note": AC to HCF December 18, 1894 (second letter), Carnegie Papers, vol. 29, 5604, 5605, LC.

234 "calculated to produce": AC to HCF, August 29, 1892, FA.

234 "What will Rainey think"; "Be just my friend": Warren, *Triumphant Capitalism*, 216.

235 "My wish is": AC to HCF, December 23, 1894, FA.

235 "I do not wish to purchase"; "defer further action": HCF to AC, December 24, 1894, FA.

235-36 "And so Mr. Rainey": Warren, *Triumphant Capitalism*, 216.

236 HCF's New Year's letter: HCF to AC, January 1, 1895, FA; Carnegie Papers, vol. 30, 5707-5111, LC.

237 Carnegie replied: AC to HCF, January 3, 1895, FA.

237 "this Christmas"; "unless something was done"; "the wronged one": quoted in Peggie Phipps Boegner and Richard Gachot, *Halcyon Days* (New York: Harry N. Abrams, 1986), 17.

237 "In my opinion"; "You may be sure": Henry Phipps to AC, December 22, 1894, Carnegie Papers, vol. 29, 5639-40, LC.

238 "confining and exhaustive details": Warren, *Triumphant Capitalism*, 218.

238 "spare him[self] humiliation"; "dejected, haggard"; advantages of Frick's new position: ibid., 219.

238 "recovered his equilibrium": ibid., 220.

240 "strike as high a key"; "sweetness and light": Kenneth Neal, *A Wise Extravagance* (Pittsburgh, Pa.: University of Pittsburgh Press, 1996), 23, 4.

241 "Stopped at the Library": HCF to AC, October 26, 1895, FA.

241 "shake the hand": unpublished notice of Roland Knoedler's death, 1932, displayed in an exhibition at the Knoedler Galleries in New York, "The Rise of the Art World in America: Knoedler at 50."

242 knocked on the doors: interview with David C. Duniway, November 1991, in Salem, Oregon.

242 "More hurry": Clyde Augustus Duniway, Diary, 1893, David C. Duniway Archives. Generously shared with the author by David C. Duniway.

245 "strength and the spirit of conquest": J. Uzanne, *Figures Contemporaines, tirées de l'Album Mariani*, 11 vols. (Paris: H. Floury, 1896–1908). Translated for the author by Madame Von Meyer.

245 Chartran's antics: HF, "Clayton Memoir," 5.

245 "a sympathy which sometimes": Uzanne, *Figures.*

245 Bouguereau's prestige in Pittsburgh: Gabriel Weisberg, DeCourcy E. McIntosh, and Allison McQueen, *Collecting in the Gilded Age in Pittsburgh* (Pittsburgh, Pa.: Frick Art and Historical Center, 1997), 115, 168.

245 "alarmingly present": Fronia E. Wissman, *Bouguereau* (San Francisco: Pomegranate Artbooks, 1996), 60.

248 "spectacular light effects": Weisberg, *Gilded Age,* 231.

248 "a curious life-likeness": Ackerman, Gerald M., *Jean-Léon Gérôme (1824–1904),* exhibition catalogue, Dayton Art Institute, November 10–December 30, 1972, 94.

248 Beginning of Frick's collection: René Gimpel, *Diary of an Art Dealer,* trans. John Rosenberg, (New York: Farrar, Straus & Giroux, 1992), 232. Gimpel quotes Charles Knoedler.

248 Bouguereau portrait: *Mischievous Girl* remained in the Clayton collection until 1942—twenty-three years after Frick's death. HF gave the portrait to a family member. The gift coincided with the advent of HCF's great-grandchildren. The painting was later sold at auction.

253 "I am relying": HCF to RFK, September 16, 1895, FA.

253 "It seems to me better"; "I get more real pleasure": HCF to J. C. Morse, September 26, October 28, 1895, FA.

255 "It seems to improve": HCF to RFK, October 18, 1898, FA.

255 "All the paintings purchased by you": HCF to RFK, September 16, 1895, FA.

255 "[They] had better not": John of J. J. Gillespie & Co. to John W. Beatty, Carnegie Museum Papers, Carnegie Institute Collection, roll 1, file 00, letter 68, Archives of American Art, Smithsonian Institution, Washington, D.C.

255 "I furnished you with": HCF to John W. Beatty, October 15, 1895, FA.

258 "a man who comes to feel": William Anderson Coffin, "The Paintings of Dagnan-Bouveret," in John C. Van Dyke, ed., *Modern French Masters: A Series of Biographical and Critical Reviews by American Artists* (New York: Century Company, 1896), 245.

258 "radiated sympathy": Pascal-Adolphe-Jean Dagnan-Bouveret, *Catalogue des Oeuvres de M. Dagnan-Bouveret (Peintures)* (Paris: M. Rousseau, 1930), 4. Translated by Madame Von Meyer.

258 "curious blending": Gabriel Weisberg, "From the Real to the Unreal: Religious Painting and Photography at the Salons of the Third Republic," *Art Magazine* 60, no. 4 (December 1985): 61.

258 Headlines: *Chicago Tribune,* February 6, 1898.

258 "has surpassed himself": HCF to RFK, November 29, 1897, FA.

258 "Am quite anxious": HCF to Dagnan-Bouveret, October 21, 1897, FA.

260 "It is the best": *Pittsburgh Post,* February 8, 1898.

260 "Mr. Frick's employees": *Washington Post,* February 5, 1898.

260 "the modern world"; "the Catholic painters": *Pittsburgh Post,* February 8, 1898.

260 "cited before the holy"; "skeptic theologian": *Chicago Tribune,* February 6, 1898.

260 "His brow": *Boston Herald,* November 13, 1898.

261 "dazzled" by the sunburst: Edgar Munhall, "An Early Acquisition by Henry Clay Frick: Dagnan-Bouveret's *Christ and the Disciples at Emmaus,*" September 28, 1986, in *Reto Conzett, zum 15 Dezember 1986* (Zurich: privately printed, 1986), 4.

261 "often the parents' minds will": "Death in Childhood," *Canadian Medical Association Journal* 98 (May 18, 1968): 968.

261 "Guilt is one way": Finkbeiner, *After the Death of a Child,* 150.

262 "more painfully"; "to attend her more": Sauder, "Hall of Distinction," 5.

263 Dagnan's letter to his wife: Weisberg, *Gilded Age,* 391, n. 299. Translated for the author by Claudine Cowin.

265 "Please bear in mind": HCF to Edmund Simon, November 1, 1897, FA.

265 "Mrs. Frick and I"; "their little girl": HCF to William F. Frew, July 9, 1898, Carnegie Institute Collection, roll 3, letter 55, Division F, Archives of American Art, Smithsonian Institution, Washington, D.C.

266 "full particulars": Arthur Tooth and Sons to M. Knoedler & Co., June 17, 1903, FA.

266-67 In an additional note: Dagnan-Bouveret to Arthur Tooth and Sons for Knoedler, June 16, 1903, FA.

267 low forehead, low ears: Dr. Joseph Greenberg to the author, April 1992.

269 "Its [*sic*] too bad": AC to HCF, April 23, 1897, FA.

269 "You are crueler than": quoted in Marie-Louise von Franz, *The Way of the Dream* (Toronto: T. H. Best, 1987), 129.

Chapter VI: Pittsburgh Exodus

Page 273 "F is a marvel"; "Take supreme care": Wall, *Carnegie,* 499, 497.

273 "If his health be spared": Alexis Gregory, *Families of Fortune* (New York: Rizzoli, 1993), 66.

276 "We will see what the Judge": Serrin, *Homestead,* 110.

276 Drawer labeled "Gratitude": Wall, *Carnegie,* 522.

277 "too damp": Warren, *Triumphant Capitalism,* 224.

278 "quite savagely and went": ibid., 228.

278 "just a nice little present": Serrin, *Homestead,* 108.

279 "shift the focus": DeCourcey McIntosh, "Emile Friant," *Antiques Magazine,* April 1997, 588.

279 HCF told the managers: Warren, *Triumphant Capitalism,* 241, 243.

279 "I am yours to command": ibid., 244.

279 "No Sir, Frick": Serrin, *Homestead,* 109.

280 "Why was he not man": Warren, *Triumphant Capitalism,* 249.

280 "I shall receive": ibid.

280 George Lauder to AC: ibid., 250.

280 "Frick goes out": Serrin, *Homestead*, 109.

280 "a happy and united family"; "to tell Mr. Frick": Warren, *Triumphant Capitalism*, 251.

281 "ringing in his ears": ibid., 253.

281 "to prevent the evil": Bridge, *Inside History*, 365.

281 "be in the ridiculous position": Warren, *Triumphant Capitalism*, 254.

281 "You will find there are": Serrin, *Homestead*, 110.

281 "Raising his eyes": Harvey, *Frick*, 229.

282 "And if I don't": Serrin, *Homestead*, 110.

282 "with a net gain to": Harvey, *Frick*, 240.

282 "For years I have been": Wall, *Carnegie*, 753.

282 "the white whiskers": Andrew Tully, *Era of Elegance* (New York: Funk and Wagnalls Co., 1947),132.

282 "'John,' he remarked": Harvey, *Frick*, 230, 231.

283 "hastiness of one, and the touchiness of another": Henry Phipps to Andrew Carnegie, December 22, 1894, Carnegie Papers, vol. 29, 5639-40, LC.

283 "[Frick] gave his undivided attention": Harvey, *Frick*, 245.

283 Carnegie had "conceived": Bridge, *Inside History*, appendix, "The Equity Suit," 365–69.

283 "filed an abusive Bill": Harvey, *Frick*, 245.

283 "ungovernable temper"; "a man of imperious temper": Bridge, *Inside History*, 332–33.

283 "[we] will triumphantly defeat": Mr. Bilderback to AC, February 14, 1900, Carnegie Papers, vol. 73, 14039, LC.

284 "the Dr. Jekyll": Serrin, *Homestead*, 178.

284 "Settlement made": Harvey, *Frick*, 256.

285 rife with such claims as: Wall, *Carnegie*, 807.

285 "pity the poor millionaire": ibid., 796.

285 "I went over the matter": HCF to John W. Beatty, September 18, 1899, FA.

285 "You cannot trust many": Harvey, *Frick*, 257.

287 "give tone to"; "the exhibition was": HCF to RFK, October 27, 1896, FA.

288 "Frick poisoned himself": Warren, *Triumphant Capitalism*, 346.

290 "It seems to me": HCF to D. H. Burnham and Company, March 2, 1903, FA.

291 "very liberally"; "for the elimination of"; "Pray sleep soundly": Warren, *Triumphant Capitalism*, 298.

291 Carnegie's favorite lines; despairing memos: Wall, *Carnegie*, 857, 797.

296 Carnegie crowned: Donald Miller of the *Pittsburgh Post Gazette* believes the knight crowned by labor is the artist, not Andrew Carnegie.

297 "I am practicing golf": HCF to RFK, June 29, 1905, FA.

298-99 "leader of taste"; "greatest object seems to be": Hellerstedt, *Clayton*, 88, 90.

303 HCF particular about hats: HF, Diary, c.1930, FA.

303 "There's Miss Frick"; "And they will say": HF, "Grandfather," 19.

311 HCF on the Carnegie libraries: HCF to E. B. Gary, April 17, 1918, FA.

311 "Mr. Carnegie told me": Wolff, *Lockout*, 249. Bridge wrote to Horace Harding, February 3, 1912: "[Carnegie] says he does not bear a grudge against a soul, and his desire to die at peace with all his old associates is a very natural and pathetic one" (Bridge, *Millionaires*, 84–85).

311 "see Carnegie in Hell": Wall, *Carnegie*, 764. This story has been quoted in many works on Henry Clay Frick. Although no primary source exists, the anecdote was confirmed by HCF's grandson, Henry Clay Frick II, M.D.

Chapter VII: Bridging the Hereafter

Page 313 "look like a miner's shack": John McCarten, "Daughter of Her Father," *The New Yorker*, July 15, 1939, 24.

316 "Chartran maintained": Weisberg, *Gilded Age*, 217.

316 "a model in manners": Mellon, *Judge Mellon's Sons*, 117.

319 "holiday mood": Katherine McCook Knox, *The Story of the Frick Art Reference Library: The Early Years* (New York: The Frick Art Reference Library, 1979), 5.

320 Pittsburgh home on Gunn's Hill: HCF wrote D. H. Burnham : "It would be a great mistake for us to build anything like so large a house, and we may decide to have you take the matter up in a different shape, looking towards making a more moderate house, and relying on the art gallery for giving us such room as we might need when giving a large reception" (January 11, 1900, FA). See also, HCF to Burnham, January 8, 1912, FA: "I think if I ever build on the New York site, it will be a much smaller house, and arrange to leave a great deal of ground around it."

320 "a small house": *American Art News* 13, no. 22 , (March 1915).

320 "deeply interested": Charles Carstairs to RFK, April 2, 1912, KA.

320-21 "I go to see him": Bridge, *Millionaires*, 71.

321 HCF's preoccupation with the afterlife: Although family diaries contain no reference to Henry Clay Frick's canceled reservation on the *Titanic,* certain family members remember Helen Frick telling them this happened. The following magazine articles, generously shared by Marjorie Laing, document Frick's change of heart and lucky escape. If true, this narrow escape would very likely have augmented his conviction that the divine intervened in his life. See Webb Garrison, *A Treasury of Titanic Tales* (Nashville, Tenn.: Rutledge Hill Press, 1998), 145; Charles Hirshberg, "The Tragedy of the *Titanic,*" *Life Magazine*, June 1997, part 2, 63–71.

322 Someone had asked: Harvey, *Frick*, 372.

322 "As you had chosen": JHB to HCF, July 13, 1912, FA.

323 "Please see the ceilings": HCF to Sir Charles Allom, June 24, 1913, FC.

323 "We desire a comfortable": HCF to Sir Charles Allom, December 12, 1913, FC.

323 "I do hope we will not make any mistake": HCF to Sir Charles Allom, March 24, 1914, FC.

323 "fair and square": John Russell, "A Guide to the Discreet Changes at the Frick," *New York Times,* July 24, 1981.

323 Frick advised Miss de Wolfe: HCF to Elsie de Wolfe, May 27, December 12, 1914, FA.

325 "shall be done": D. B. Kinch to McElroy, 1919, FA.

325 "Went almost immediately": HCF to RFK, June 3, 1914, FA.

326 Atillio's hands: Josef Vincent Lombardo, *Atillio Piccirilli: Life of an American Sculptor* (New York: Pitman, 1944), xxii.

326 "coming on for a long time": Warren, *Triumphant Capitalism*, 348.

328 "[struck] down the only man": *New York Times,* June 29, 1914.

328 "My God! My God!"; "Sophie, remain": ibid., June 30, 1914.

328 "Helpless as a baby": Warren, *Triumphant Capitalism*, 348.

329 "proper setting for": Jerry E. Patterson, *The Vanderbilts* (New York: Harry N. Abrams, 1989), 80.

329 "Well it is too bad": HCF to S. L. Schoonmaker, August 13, 1914, FA.

329 "Conditions are such": HCF to Charles Carstairs, August 1, 1914, KA.

329 "move around with difficulty": HCF to Jasper Saligmann, September 26, 1914, FA.

329 "I am glad to say": HCF to White, Allom and Company, September 29, 1914, FA.

329 "locksmiths have been taken": Sir Charles Allom to HCF, October 30, 1914, FA.

329 "Simply outrageous": HCF to White, Allom and Company, October 29, 1914, FA.

330 "the family do[es] not": HCF to Knoedler & Company, September 29, 1917, FA.

331 "I really doubt": HCF to Charles Carstairs, December 4, 1914, KA.

332 "As requested": RFK to HCF, October 15, 1914, KA.

335 "arrivals and departures": John Russell, "Discreet Changes."

339 "It would take only thirty"; "So and so is just the age of Christ": HF, "Grandfather," 14.

339 "daring acquisition": Ryskamp and Davidson, *Art in the Frick Collection*, 23.

344 Helen and the mosaic path: the author is grateful to Everett Fahy for sharing this information.

345 "the Porchway Entrance": W. Kirk MacNulty, *Freemasonry* (New York: Thames and Hudson, 1991), 30–31.

350 The bowling alley as meeting room: the author is grateful to Everett Fahy for sharing this opinion.

350 "Slapping his hands": the author is grateful to Walter Cooley, now deceased, for sharing this story.

352 "an emblem of [Masonic] faith": Robert Macoy, *Masonic Burial Services with General Instructions* (Harwood Heights, Ill.: Ezra A. Cook, 1995), 26.

354 "infernal regions"; "resurrection": Henry C. Clausen, *Clausen's Commentaries on Morals and Dogma* (San Diego, Cal.: The Supreme Council, 33rd Degree, Ancient and Accepted Scottish Rite of Freemasonry, Southern Jurisdiction, U.S.A., 1974), 80.

357 "should inspire all": Albert G. Mackey, *An Encyclopedia of Freemasonry and Its Kindred Sciences* (New York: Masonic History Company, 1924), 2: 613.

357 animals as part of "the temple of creation": W. L. Wilmshurst, *The Meaning of Masonry* (New York: Bell, 1980), 77.

357 "Go now, and rebuild my church": Joseph Newton, *The Builders* (New York: McCoy Publishing and Masonic Supply, 1951), 162.

363 "the great trouble"; "it is difficult to": HCF to Locket Agnew, August 9, 1916, FA.

363 "I think by unremitting attention": HCF to Joseph Duveen, June 19, 1915, FC.

363 "I think [the house] is": HCF to Thomas Hastings, June 2, 1915, FA.

364 "a hallucinatory wishful psychosis": quoted in Rando, *Treatment of Complicated Mourning*, 83.

364 "the rooms would acquire": Helen Clay Frick, in "Henry Clay Frick and His Collection, in *"The Frick Collection An llustrated Catalogue of the Works of Art in the Collection of Henry Clay Frick,* vol. 1 (Pittsburgh, Pa.: University of Pittsburgh Press, 1949).

365 Frick sprang from his chair: Gimpel, *Diary*, 118.

365 "no real suffering": Russell, "Discreet Changes."

367 "[Frick] loved [his paintings]"; "Often late at night": Harvey, *Frick*, 335.

367 "find [Frick's] cigar ashes": Bridge, *Millionaires*, 103.

367 "He took so much joy": HF, "Grandfather," 17.

368 system of illumination: Bridge, *Millionaires*, 104, 86–87.

368 "How interesting it would be": HF, "Grandfather", 18.

368 To Bridge he mused: James Howard Bridge, *Portraits and Personalities in the Frick Galleries* (New York: Brentano's, [1935?]), vii.

368 "spoken of some event"; "the portraits had become": Bridge, *Millionaires*, 103–04.

368 "Come into the Gallery"; "Certainly they shall have"; "Come any day": HF, "Grandfather," 19.

369 "It seemed as though": ibid.

371 "twin gowns": HF, Diary, 1912, FA.

371 "It is so innocent": HCF to Polly Dixon, June 3, 1915, author's collection.

371 "I think [it] in every respect": HCF to Locket Agnew, August 9, 1916, FA.

371 "No great beauties": HF, Diary, 1919, author's collection.

375 "I have your letter": Samuel Mather to HCF, March 22, 1916. The author is indebted to Virginia Krumholz at the Cleveland Art Museum for sharing this letter.

375 "high in key": Mr. Whiting, director of the Cleveland Art Museum to HCF, May 24, 1916. The author is indebted to Virginia Krumholz at the Cleveland Art Museum for sharing this letter.

379 "a paragon of Freemasonry": John Sherer, The Masonic Ladder (Cincinnati, Ohio: R. W. Carroll, 1874), 70.

380 "one of the family": HCF to Philander Knox, September 2, 1918, FA.

380 "Frick comes in once or twice": Charles Knoedler to Charles Carstairs, October 16, 1918, KA.

380 "I want money only": Daily Courier (Connellsville, Pa.), December 11, 1919.

380 "I am very much richer"; "it hurt him to think": "What His Money Couldn't Bring," Forbes Magazine, cited in Neenah, Wisconsin News, April 1, 1920.

381 "The demands of modern life": Bridge, Inside History, viii.

Chapter VIII: Final Days

Unless otherwise noted, this chapter is based on a diary that Helen Clay Frick wrote c. 1920 as a way to document her father's fatal decline.

Page 383 "a more advanced stage of old age": The New Yorker, March 5, 1990, 77.

383 "You have done your country": HCF to Judge Gary, October 2, 1919, scrapbook on HCF.

384 "Why it seems to me": Warren, Triumphant Capitalism, 365.

384-385 Frick sent Hines a letter: Harvey, Frick, 283–84.

394 "a rather hard gaze": Gimpel, Diary, 41, entry for June 25, 1918.

394 "not a man to be permitted": Arthur T. Vanderbilt, Fortune's Children (New York: William Morrow, 1989), 314.

395 " 'Papsie!' what a host"; "Your welfare and happiness": HF, "Grandfather," 1, 4.

395 "That child smiled"; "Tiny as you were": ibid., 1.

395 "had brains": HF, "Grandfather," 13.

395-96 glowing accounts of grandchildren: ibid., 1.

396 "I want to know if": Harvey, Frick, 373.

396 "with an awful bump": ibid., 371.

396 "It was always a great pleasure"; "loved to plot and plan": HF, "Grandfather," 14, 2.

396 "the most wonderful amount"; "the sweetest period": ibid., 3.

396 "If now and then": ibid., 4.

401 "No, I did not paint": Martha Frick Symington to Emily duPont Frick, July 15, 1987, author's collection.

401 "justify their acceptance": Harvey, Frick, 370.

403-04 "knew a great deal about"; "premonition": Bridge, Millionaires, 69.

404 "That will be all"; "pallid but wholly tranquil": Harvey, Frick, 375.

404 "died as he had lived": Wolff, Lockout, 247.

404-06 The descriptions of the New York service, the train to Pittsburgh, the Clayton service, and the burial in Homewood Cemetery are compiled from various obituaries, FA.

406 "much broken up": AWM, Pocket Diaries, 1910–1921, entry for December 5, 1919, AWM Papers.

408 Description of the grave: Robert W. Wilson to the author, February 21, 1991.

408 Headline: undated news clipping (possibly from a Connellsville newspaper), scrapbook of Henry Clay Frick's obituaries, FA.

408 "enem[y] of the United States of America": Richard Drinnon, Rebel in Paradise (Boston: Beacon Press, 1970), 220.

408-09 "Deported by God"; "it's too bad he can't": New York City Tribune, December 3, 1919.

409 "Well, he left the country": New York Call, December 6, 1919.

409 Mellon's letter: AWM to Col. George Harvey, June 25, 1927, scrapbook on HCF.

409 Newspapers in the Coke Region: National Labor Tribune (Pittsburgh, Pa.), September 13, 1890; The Courier, June 19, 1891, October 13, 1893, January 19, 1894, March 22, October 4, and December 27, 1895; The Evening News (Uniontown, Pa.), July 14, 1893; The News Standard (Uniontown, Pa.), March 29, 1894.

409 "operated on an intelligent": Marjorie Ramsay Laing to the author, February 19, 1998.

410 "the spirit in which everything": Sue Canfield to HF, undated, FA.

410 donations during the war of $1 million: Harvey, Frick, 315–16.

410 "We know that the principles": citation given Adelaide Frick by the Knights Templar Tancred Commandery No. 48, Pittsburgh, 1919, FA.

Chapter IX: Shrouded Legacy

Page 413 Adelaide's widow's dower: The question was, in fact, considered. In a July 22, 1920, reply to AHCF's request that she be permitted to use money from Frick's estate to repair Eagle Rock, Philander Knox wrote:

"It seems incredible to me that, in view of the tremendous sacrifices you are making of your legal rights in order to carry out Mr. Frick's wishes for the benefit of the residuary legatees, that anyone would be so ungrateful as to object to the Executors carrying out his intentions respecting the necessary repairs to 'Eagle Rock,' law or no law.

"Moreover, I think you have a perfectly legitimate claim upon the estate to put 'Eagle Rock' in thoroughly good repair such as the character of the property demands and such as Mr. Frick contemplated was necessary to bring it up to the requirements of his taste, and to your usual standard of living.

"My reasons, in brief, for this opinion are these. Assuming Mr. Frick proposed to you that one of the items of his bequest to you, which he desired you to accept in lieu of your rights under the law, was a life interest in 'Eagle Rock' as a residence, such a proposition carried with it the implication that 'Eagle Rock' should be fit for that purpose at the time of his death in the sense heretofore indicated. That it was not so fit, his own declarations and preparations for repairs entirely establishes. Mr. Frick would have been the last person to have tolerated the thought that your willing acquiescence and cooperation in aiding him to carry out his great designs should be requited by turning over to you in deteriorated condition part of the comparatively little you were willing to accept in order that his benefactions might be increased.

"To me it seems your equities are so great, your surrenders so enormous and the obligations of the residuary legatees to you so direct and so vast that it is unthinkable that a question should be raised." Private collection.

413 Bequests to relatives: According to Kenneth L. Smith, a grandson of HCF's youngest brother, Jay Edgar Frick, HCF left $50,000 to each niece and nephew because he had been loaned this amount by his mother and grandmother when starting his coke business. Author's conversation with Kenneth L. Smith, January 10, 1999.

413 "America's Richest Bachelor Girl": *New York Evening World*, December 3, 1919.

414 "sweet old thing"; "plenty of pluck": poem written for a Childs family reunion at Clayton, October 11, 1912, FA.

415 the deceased lives on: Beverly Raphael, *The Anatomy of Bereavement* (New York: Basic Books, 1983), 132.

416 "bound"; "haunted" or "resurrected": ibid., 277.

416 "A full preventive": Albert C. Cain et al., "Children's Disturbed Reactions to the Death of a Sibling," *American Journal of Orthopsychiatry* 34 (July 1964): 751.

416 "has been and still is": John Bowlby, "Grief and Mourning in Infancy and Early Childhood," *Psychoanalytic Study of the Child* 15 (1965): 12.

417-18 Adelaide cautioned Duniway: AHCF to Clyde Augustus Duniway, November 10, 1891, David C. Duniway Archives.

418 HCF reminded Duniway: HCF to Clyde Augustus Duniway, July 18, 1892, October 18, 1893, David C. Duniway Archives.

418 "I hope to have good reports": HCF to Clyde Augustus Duniway, October 3, 1893, FA.

418 "On my return home": HCF to CF, November 2, 1893, FA.

418 "in bad taste": HCF to CF, December 1895, FA.

418-19 HCF letters on hunting and poetry: HCF to CF, May 31, May 2, 1894, FA.

419 "Suppose we will have to bear": HCF to Clyde Augustus Duniway, October 29, 1895, David C. Duniway Archives.

419 "as soon as we get": HCF to CF, undated letter, FA.

419 "We do not want him home": HCF to Clyde Augustus Duniway, June 17, 1894, FA.

419 Father-daughter syndrome: Maureen Murdock, *The Hero's Daughter* (New York: Ballentine Books, 1994), 85.

420 Helen hoped and prayed her ship would sink: the author is grateful to Julia Egan for sharing this story.

420 "Your sister Helen": George Megrew to CF, 1893, FA.

420-21 during dinner: Helen Clay Frick with Mara O'Hara, *My Father: Henry Clay Frick* (Privately printed, 1959), 27, 28.

421-23 An account of her evenings: HF, "Clayton Memoir," 3.

423 "The home . . . had": Albert C. Cain and Barbara S. Cain, "On Replacing a Child," *Journal of the American Academy of Child Psychiatry* 3 (1964): 446.

424 When her father made up the difference: HF, Diary 1915, entry for May 25, FA.

425 "Do All That You Can": HF, March 18, 1898, FA.

425 "Four Little Sunbeams": HF, essay, January 24, 1900, FA.

425 "One is Mademoiselle's": HF, "Description of My Bedroom," March 18, 1898, FA.

425 pay her in gold: HCF to RFK, September 22, 1896, FA.

426 "I want to exchange it": HCF to RFK, March 1897, FA.

426 "Helen would not consent": HCF to RFK, January 26, 1897, FA.

426 "Detaille could go"; "You see the difficulties": HCF to RFK, December 8, 1897, FA.

426 He wrote to his then partner: HCF to AC, March 19, 1898, FA.

426 Mr. Mignon and family: HF to RFK, November 5, 1899, FA.

426 Helen was asked: newspaper clipping, *Washington Post*, June 15, year unknown, FC.

427 "The Character of Miss Frick," Cecil Twyford, August 24, 1896, London, FA.

431 "antics of neighbors' children"; "strolling hand in hand": unnamed childhood friend and neighbor of HF quoted in the *Pittsburgh Press*, November 10, 1984.

431 "My experience is": HCF to AC, April 19, 1898, Carnegie Papers, vol. 51, 42, LC.

431 "was always fully prepared": HF, "Clayton Memoir," 9.

431 "were rapidly being hung": ibid., 5.

431 "quite covered the walls": HF, "Grandfather," 17.

431 "Now Helen, which"; "Papa, I would prefer": HCF to AC, March 19, 1898, FA; Carnegie Papers, vol. 50, LC.

432 "It amused him": HF, "Grandfather," 17.

432 "too busy to afford": HF, "Clayton Memoir," 5.

432 she recalled the horror: ibid.

432 she referred to her mother: these and other parental expressions can be found in the HF correspondence to AHCF, 1900–1904, FA.

432 Helen signed her letters: HF to AHCF, January 25, 1900, FA.

432 "A Young Girl Called Jane": HF, essay, 1903, FA.

434 "Don't tell little girls": Harvey, *Frick*, 369.

434 "I hope you enjoyed": HCF to HF, July 7, 1903, FA.

437 "Our Auto ride": HCF to HF, August 1904, FA.

440 "she danced like a real pig": HF to AHCF, November 11, 1903, FA.

440 "it was torture": HF, Diary 1904, FA.

440-41 a letter to Miss Duff: HF to Miss Duff, 1905, FA.

441 "If it wasn't for that little": HCF to HF, Diary, c. 1930, FA.

441 "I hope and expect": HF to Miss Duff, 1905, FA.

441 *New Yorker* profile: McCarten, "Daughter of Her Father," 23.

441 "the best of the group": Knox, *Story of the Frick Art Reference Library*, xiii.

443 Helen's European tour: HF, Diary, 1908–09, FA.

444 "caused [her] father": HF, Diary, c. 1910, FA.

444 "has been charming": HCF to Dr. Leon Gorodiche, November 10, 1909, FA.

444 "receive no notoriety": Sauder, "Hall of Distinction," 7.

444-45 "twinkle in his eye": HF, "Grandfather," 20.

446 "Papa mine": McCarten, "Daughter of Her Father," 24.

447-48 anecdote about *Julia, Lady Peel* and *St. Jerome*: HF, "Grandfather," 19.

448 The Iron Rail: When Helen was in Paris with her father, she refused his offer of a perfectly matched set of pearls for her twentieth birthday. She asked for the money instead because she wanted to "provide a place in the country where working girls from the mills of Lawrence, Lowell, Lynn, and Boston could spend a few weeks free vacation in the summer." In the spring of 1909 she wrote the South End Settlement House in Boston, the YWCA, and churches in Lawrence, Lowell, and Lynn requesting from each "ten promising, needy, Protestant working girls." Many girls also came from mills owned by her North Shore friends and neighbors such as William Wood of the American Woolen Company. She first housed them at the Stillman farm in Beverly and later at the Iron Rail, a thirty-seven acre farm in Wenham where her brother Childs kept his polo ponies and developed a practice polo field. The Iron Rail opened in 1910 with a social worker as director. The barn became a gymnasium. Rooms had fresh flowers daily. Fresh vegetables were grown and served. The girls sang hymns and learned etiquette. Their mothers were "welcome to come . . . for three-day getaways at no cost." Helen paid for many of the girls' higher education, established an emergency fund for them, and created club rooms in the mill towns where the girls could rest. These local clubs then reached out to children in need, following the motto of the True Blue girls. During World War I the girls bought two ambulances and sewed 55,000 dresses for the French war relief. In time the True Blue membership grew from sixty-two to over thirty-one hundred. The author is extremely grateful to Katherine Khalife, a former True Blue girl, for sharing this information. See Katherine Khalife, "Heyday! The Magazine That Remembers," *SeniorLifestyle* (Salem, N.H.), May, June 1993, 31–46.

448-49 "love of humanity": *New York Times*, July 14, 1912.

449 rules at the Iron Rail: *New York Times*, July 14, 1912; McCarten, "Daughter of Her Father," 21; *Pittsburgh Post Gazette*, November 10, 1984.

449 "Myself at Eighty Years Old": HF, essay, January 30, c. 1905, FA.

451 Mr. Mignon story: HF, "Mr. Mignon and Family," c. 1920, FA.

452 "off his own bat": "Mr. Frick's Royal Gift," *Literary Digest*, October 31, 1931.

452 "I am much pleased": HCF to Roger Fry, May 12, 1910, FC.

452 "please deliver": HCF to Roger Fry, undated letter, FC.

452 "Would have preferred": HCF to RFK, May 18, 1910, FA.

453 "If through any misunderstanding": HCF to RFK, May 19, 1910, FA.

454 Letters to Fry: HCF to Roger Fry, June 6, December 13, December 29, 1910, FA.

454 "worked with those dear"; "you certainly [were]": HCF to HF, December 19, 1910, FA.

454 "but he didn't stay bought": the author is grateful to Henry Clay Frick II, for sharing this story.

454 Edmund Tarbell portrait: According to Vincent Carl Fazio, "Helen Clay Frick: Architectural Patron and Art Collector," M. A. thesis, University of Pittsburgh, 1998, 3, the Tarbell portrait passed down through the Tarbell family. In 1981 Carolina Prints and Frames sold it to the National Portrait Gallery, Washington, D.C.

456 Friendship Calendar: given as a birthday present to HCF by HF, December 1913, FA.

456 "The effect of the pictures": HF to RFK, 1914, KA.

457 "did not fill": Harvey, *Frick*, 269.

459 Fido's trick: HF to to Howard Childs, September 17, 1906, FA.

459 "going to dance": HF's diary of HCF.

459 "Go home and work": Frances Weitzenhoffer, *The Havemeyers* (New York: Harry N. Abrams, 1986), 220.

459 "It goes without saying": ibid., 206.

461 catena as pun: The Frick Collection, *Handbook of Paintings* (New York: Frick Collection, 1978), 51.

461 "Nobody could have more sympathy": Sauder, "Hall of Distinction," 6.

461 His words and actions say: Murdock, *The Hero's Daughter*, 17.

461-63 "Our picture is one": The Frick Collection, *Illustrated Catalogue*, vol. 1, 178.

464 "was adorable": the author is grateful to Julia Egan, HF's secretary, for sharing this story.

465 "to create anything": Marion Woodman, *Addiction to Perfection* (Toronto: Inner City Books, 1982), 138.

466-67 "to get a rise out of her": the following paragraphs are based on HF, "Grandfather," 13–14.

467 "Where nobody got hurt": Russell, *"Discreet Changes."*

467-69 "Because her father identifies"; "He may also be aware": Murdock, *The Hero's Daughter*, 29, 53.

469 "worships and at the same time": Woodman, *Addiction*, 136.

471 "Frequently, when I": HF, "Grandfather," 13.

471 Helen "loathed" the portrait subject's beard: Edgar Munhall to the author, May 1, 1989.

471 "Dear Mademoiselle": HF to Mademoiselle Marika Ogiz, 1900, FA.

471 *Perseus and Andromeda*: The record of Helen Frick's purchase of Tiepolo's *Perseus and Andromeda* dated May 29, 1916 is located among Helen Frick's papers at Knoedler & Company.

474 "I refuse to go home without": HF to parents, March 17, 1918, FA.

474 HF on the never-ending war: HF to RFK, March 31, 1918, KA.

476 "the high place of horror": author's phone conversation with Claudine Cowen, January 1995.

477 "What wonderful hands": HF, Diary, 1918, entry for June 5, FA.

478 "everything from a dollar": newspaper clipping, December 9, 1918, scrapbook on the Red Cross Shop, FA.

479 Cartier jewelry: HCF to Cartier, December 6, 1918, FA.

479 "the first affair in": clipping from *Town Topics, The Journal of Society*, December 12, 1918, scrapbook on the Red Cross Shop.

479 "a true appreciation": undated newspaper clipping, *Evening Mail*, scrapbook on the Red Cross Shop.

479 invitation like a court summons: scrapbook on the Red Cross Shop.

480 Frances warned St. John: the author is grateful to her sisters and cousins for sharing this story.

480 "refuge of animal heads": HCF to Sir Charles Allom, January 24, 1919, FA.

480 "Weddings make me sad": HF, Diary, 1919, entry for March 29, FA.

480 "I had another proposal"; "sweet letter": HF, Diary, 1919, entry for April 11, FA.

480 "I sat on his lap": HF, Diary, 1919, entry for April 9, FA.

Chapter X: Her Father's Voice

Page 483 "When a great man": HF, *My Father,* 28.

485 "Mr. Frick intended to confer": *Brooklyn New York Citizen*, December 3, 1919.

485 "In the event that": Will of Henry Clay Frick, June 24, 1915.

487 "come to her own": HF, Diary, 1919, FA.

488 "personally settl[ing]": HF to Karl Overholt, February 6, 1920, FA.

488 The author is exceedingly grateful to Ashley J. Thomas, Educational Liaison at the Frick Collection, for clarifying the relationships among Elizabeth, countess of Warwick, Lady Hamilton, and Henrietta, countess of Warwick. AJT to the author, December 8, 1997.

488 "gave [Frick] considerable sentimental satisfaction": Knox, *Story of the Frick Art Reference Library*, 5.

488 "At some point in her life"; "To reclaim her own": Murdock, *The Hero's Daughter*, 92–93, 94.

492 "encourage and develop the study": Walker D. Hines to Lewis Cass Ledyard, August 27, 1920, FA.

493 "organized and operated exclusively": Agreement Between the Frick Collection and the Frick Art Reference Library, June 1933, FA.

494 "Go On!": Knox, *Story of the Frick Art Reference Library*, 41.

499 HF's clash with Rockefeller: HF to unnamed attorney, undated memo, FA; JDR, Jr., to Walker D. Hines, April 26, 1933, RFA, RG 2, series H, box 63, folder 472, RAC.

499 "A little bird tells me": HF to AWM, May 12, 1933, AWM Papers.

500 "So, you are going to": *New York World Telegram,* January 6, 1935.

500 "full of inaccuracies": *New York American,* January 16, 1935.

501 "temple of courage"; "as high as": John G. Bowman, *Unofficial Notes* (Pittsburgh, Pa.: Davis and Ward, privately printed, 1963), 44, 54.

501 "arrogant woman": *New York World Telegram,* January 6, 1935.

501 "the conscious arrogance"; "in need of psychopathic": *New York Times,* January 17, 1935.

502 "One forgets all about": *New York World Telegram,* December 14, 1935.

506 "From the very start": HF to unnamed attorney, undated letter, FA.

506 "were never pleasant affairs"; "[Made] it plain": HF, "Preparation of Facts," May 3, 1947, FA.

506 "stumbling block": conversation between HF and Mortimer Clapp, January 27, 1936, recorded by Miss Howland, undated transcript given to William S. Moorehead, FA.

506 "as a trustee and as a daughter": HF to an unnamed attorney, undated memo, FA.

506-08 "not going to keep out"; "This has turned into": conversation between HF and Mortimer Clapp, January 27, 1936.

508 "Frick Institution": HF to an unnamed attorney, undated memo, FA.

508 "as it evolves": "Policy of Acquisitions," February 14, 1939, RFA, RG 2, series H, box 64, folder 480, RAC.

508 "shall be regarded as": JDR, Jr., "Acquisition Memo," undated, ibid.

508 "free of historical": Mortimer Clapp, "Art Acquisition Policy," April 5, 1937, ibid.

509 "lack[ing] balance and stability: JDR, Jr., to Walker D. Hines, April 28, 1933, ibid., box 63, folder 472.

509 "been the anarchist": JHB to Mrs. Walker D. Hines, March 30, 1929, ibid.

512 "One wonders just how much": H. G. Dwight to JDR, Jr., June 19, 1936, ibid., box 64, folder 485.

512 "with a red hot iron": conversation between HF and Mortimer Clapp, January 27, 1936.

515 "a certain pebble": H. G. Dwight to JDR, Jr., June 2, 1947, RFA, RG 2, series H, box 64, folder 477, RAC.

515 HF's comments on Rockefeller and Clapp: HF to William S. Moorehead, February 4, 1949, January 30, 1947, May 8, 1947, FA.

515 "An' Brer Rabbit": HF to lawyer, January 10, 1946, FA.

515 Rockefeller wrote Helen: JDR, Jr., to HF, July 17, 1947, RFA, RG 2, series H, box 64, folder 477, RAC.

515-16 Helen replied: HF to JDR, Jr., July 24, 1947, ibid.

516 Commenting to JDR, Jr., on Helen's reply: Thomas Debevoise to JDR, Jr., July 30, 1947, ibid.

516 HF testimony, appeal: *New York Times,* January 30, May 1, July 11, 1948; May 27, 1949.

516 HF and "cowbirds": HF to William S. Moorehead (addressed to "Your Honors"), February 4, 8, 1949, FA. The author thanks the members of her family and others once closely associated with HF for adding insight to this story.

517 "the value of an endowed collection": HF, "Henry Clay Frick and His Collection."

519 "consider for acquisition only": Ryscamp and Davidson, *Art in the Frick Collection,* 31.

519 Knoedler's phone tapped: *New York Times,* January 14, March 19, August 26, 1956.

519 Helen stormed out: the author is grateful to her uncle, Henry Clay Frick II, for sharing this story.

523 having "delicate features": Ryskamp and Davidson, *Art in the Frick Collection,* 124.

523 "weirdly like Laurance": Bernice Kent, *Abby Aldrich Rockefeller* (New York: Random House, 1993), 223.

523 "Surely if Frick could be induced": Bernard Berenson to Joseph Duveen, May 3, 1915, FC.523 "most outrageously"; "It is now": HF, memo, April 23, 1947, FA.

523 "rather tired": Gimpel, *Diary,* 286.

523 "small, but monumental": Ryskamp and Davidson, *Art in the Frick Collection,* 25.

523 "That rag": the author is grateful to her sister, Helen Clay Chace, for sharing this story.

525 "Pride goeth before a fall": Gimpel, *Diary,* 220.

527 Helen's last visit to Childs Frick: the author is grateful to her uncle, Henry Clay Frick II, for sharing this story.

527 "filial devotion": *Handbook of Paintings* (New York: Frick Collection, 1978), 45.

529 Suit against Sylvester K. Stevens: Exhibit A to Complaint—Complaint in Pittsburgh Suit, Court of Common Pleas, Cumberland County, Pa., 16a, 17a, January Term, 1965.

531 "very effective on the end wall": Walter Read Hovey to John G. Bowman, February 4, 1942, FA.

532 the judge ruled: Final Adjudication Helen C. Frick vs. Sylvester K. Stevens, Court of Common Pleas, Cumberland County, Pa., January Term, 1965, In Equity, 33.

532 "her darlings": the author is grateful to Edgar Munhall for sharing this story.

535 "careful teaching of Helen": "Dedication Ceremony of Two Sugar Maple Trees in Memory of Mr. and Mrs.

Henry Clay Frick," May 22, 1980, Frick Art Museum, Pittsburgh, author's collection.

535 "We are not German": the author is grateful to her uncle, Henry Clay Frick II, and her cousin, I. T. Burden III, for sharing this story.

535 "You shall not conquer me": Ruth Mansfield to the author, undated letter, 1993.

535 "You shall not do that to my little sister": The author is grateful to Julia Egan for sharing this story.

535 "the homely little girl in the middle": except as noted, this account of HF's final years is based on the author's interview with Barbara Hunter, HF's nurse.

536 "the fact that [the father] embodies": Murdock, *The Hero's Daughter*, 149.

537 "What will make me worthy": the author is grateful to Reverend Tierny for sharing this experience.

537 "others may know": HF, "Clayton Memoir," FA.

Bibliography

Archival Collections

Allegheny County Courthouse. Pittsburgh, Pa.

B&O Railroad Museum Archives. Baltimore, Md.

The Burns Archives. New York, N.Y.

Calvary Church Archives. Pittsburgh, Pa.

Carnegie, Andrew. Papers. Library of Congress, Washington, D.C.

Carnegie Museum Papers. Carnegie Institute Collection, Archives of American Art, Washington, D.C.

Cleveland Museum of Art Archives. Cleveland, Ohio.

Duniway, David C. Archives. Salem, Ore.

Frick Archives. Helen Clay Frick Foundation, Pittsburgh, Pa.

Frick Art Reference Library Archives. New York, N.Y.

Hillman Library, Special Collections. University of Pittsburgh, Pittsburgh, Pa.

Homewood Cemetery. Pittsburgh, Pa.

Houghton Library Collection. Harvard University, Cambridge, Mass.

Johnstown Flood Museum Archives. Johnstown, Pa.

Knoedler & Company Archives. New York, N.Y.

Mellon, Andrew W. Papers. Office of Paul Mellon, Washington, D.C.

National Gallery of Art Archives. Washington, D.C.

New York Public Library Archives. New York, N.Y.

Princeton University Archives. Princeton, N.J.

Rockefeller Archive Center. Sleepy Hollow, N.Y.

Stanford, Leland, Jr., Stanford University Archives. Palo Alto, Cal.

State of Pennsylvania, Division of Archives and Manuscripts. Harrisburg, Pa.

The Metropolitan Museum of Art Archives. New York, N.Y.

U.S. Steel Corporation Archives. Pittsburgh, Pa.

U.S. Steel Resource Management. Uniontown, Pa.

Wallace Collection Archives. London.

West Overton Museums Archives. West Overton, Pa.

Wooster Cemetery. Wooster, Ohio.

Wooster Courthouse. Wooster, Ohio.

References

Art, Architecture, and Archaeology

Ackerman, Gerald M. *Jean-Léon Gérôme (1824–1907)*. Exhibition catalogue, Dayton Art Institute, November 10–December 30, 1972.

Arasse, Daniel. *Vermeer: Faith in Painting*. Trans. Terry Grabar. Princeton, N.J.: Princeton University Press, 1994.

Art in the Frick Collection: Paintings, Sculpture, Decorative Arts. New York: Harry N. Abrams, in association with The Frick Collection, 1996.

Bantens, Robert James. *Eugène Carrière: The Symbol of Creation*. New York: Kent Fine Art, 1990.

Bareau, Juliet Wilson. *The Hidden Face of Manet: An Investigation of the Artist's Working Process*. *The Burlington Magazine*. Rugby, England: Jolly & Barber, 1986.

———. *Manet, "The Execution of Maximillian": Painting, Politics, and Censorship*. London: National Gallery Publications, 1992.

Barr, Alfred H., Jr. *Painting and Sculpture in the Museum of Modern Art, 1929–1967*. New York: Museum of Modern Art, 1977.

Bonafoux, Pascal. *Rembrandt, Master of the Portrait*. Trans. Alexandra Campbell. New York: Harry N. Abrams, 1992.

Brenneman, Walter L., and Mary G. Brenneman. *Crossing the Circle at the Holy Wells of Ireland*. Charlottesville: University Press of Virginia, 1995.

Bridge, James Howard. *Portraits and Personalities in the Frick Galleries*. New York: Brentano's [1935?].

Brignano, Mary. *The Frick Art and Historical Center: The Art and Life of a Pittsburgh Family*. Pittsburgh, Pa.: Frick Art and Historical Center, 1993.

Burke, Doreen Bolger, et al. *In Pursuit of Beauty: Americans and the Aesthetic Movement*. New York: The Metropolitan Museum of Art; Rizzoli International Publications, 1986.

Chapman, H. Perry; Wouter Th. Kloek; and Arthur K. Wheelock, Jr. *Jan Steen: Painter and Storyteller*. Washington, D.C.: National Gallery of Art, 1996.

A Checklist of Painters c. 1200–1976 Represented in the Witt Library, Courtauld Institute of Art. Foreword by Sir John Witt. London: Mansell, 1978.

Chew, Paul, ed. *Southwestern Pennsylvania Painters, 1800–1945*. Greensburg, Pa: Westmoreland County Museum of Art, 1981.

———. *Southwestern Pennsylvania Painters: Collection of Westmoreland Museum of Art*. Greensburg, Pa.: Westmoreland Museum of Art, 1989.

Clark, Kenneth. *An Introduction to Rembrandt*. New York: Harper & Row, 1978.

———. *Rembrandt and the Italian Renaissance*. New York: New York University Press, 1966.

Clarke, Michael. *Corot and the Art of Landscape*. New York: Cross River Press, 1991.

Conway, Sir Martin. *The Sport of Collecting*. London: T. Fisher Unwin, 1914.

Cormack, Malcolm. *Constable*. Cambridge, England: Cambridge University Press, 1986.

Curran, Ann. "A Visit to Skibo." *Carnegie Mellon Magazine*, January 1997, 2, 18–23.

Davidson, Bernice. *Paintings in The Frick Collection*. Vol. 1, *American, British, Dutch, Flemish, and German*. Introduction by Harry D. M. Grier. New York: The Frick Collection; Princeton, N.J.: Princeton University Press, 1968.

Davidson, Bernice, assisted by Edgar Munhall. *Paintings in The Frick Collection*. Vol. 2, *French, Italian, Spanish*. New York: The Frick Collection, 1968.

Davidson, Bernice; Edgar Munhall; and Nadia Tscherny. *Paintings from The Frick Collection*. New York: The Frick Collection; Harry N. Abrams, 1990.

Davies, Randall. *Romney*. London: Adam and Charles Black, 1914.

Doob, Penelope Reed. *The Idea of the Labyrinth from Classical Antiquity through the Middle Ages*. Ithaca, N.Y.: Cornell University Press, 1990.

Dorsey, John. "The Artist of the Subtle and Serene." *Baltimore Sun*, December 10, 1995.

Dudar, Helen. "From Darkness Into Light: Rediscovering Georges de La Tour." *Smithsonian Magazine* (December 1996): 74–82.

——."Time Stands Still in the Harmonious World of Vermeer." *Smithsonian Magazine* 28, no. 8 (November 1995): 110–119.

Ferguson, George. *Signs and Symbols in Christian Art*. New York: Oxford University Press, 1955.

Fink, Lois Maria. *American Art at the Nineteenth-Century Paris Salons*. Cambridge, England: Cambridge University Press, 1990.

Frelinghuysen, Alice Cooney, et al. *Splendid Legacy: The Havemeyer Collection*. New York: The Metropolitan Museum of Art, 1993.

Frick Collection, The. "The Black Book" (paintings owned by Henry Clay Frick). Curatorial files, The Frick Collection.

——. *An Illustrated Catalogue of the Works of Art in the Collection of Henry Clay Frick*. Vol. 1, *Paintings Text*. Pittsburgh, Pa.: University of Pittsburgh Press, 1949.

——. *An Illustrated Catalogue of the Works of Art in the Collection of Henry Clay Frick*. Vol. 4, *Drawings and Prints*. New York: Frick Art Reference Library, 1951.

——. *An Illustrated Catalogue of the Works of Art in the Collection of Henry Clay Frick*. Vols. 5–6, *Sculpture*. New York: Frick Art Reference Library, 1954.

——. *An Illustrated Catalogue of the Works of Art in the Collection of Henry Clay Frick*. Vol. 9, *Paintings and Sculpture Acquired 1931–1955*. New York: Frick Art Reference Library, 1955.

——. *Guide to the Galleries*. New York: The Frick Collection. 1970.

——. *Handbook of Paintings*. New York: The Frick Collection, 1978.

——. *A Guide to Works of Art on Exhibition*. New York: The Frick Collection, 1989.

——. *"Mortlake Terrace": Turner's Companion Pieces Reunited*. New York: The Frick Collection, 1996.

——. "The Red Book" (paintings owned by Henry Clay Frick up to March 1914). Curatorial files, The Frick Collection.

Furst, Herbert E. A. *Chardin*. London: Methuen, 1911.

Garrett, Wendell. *Victorian America: Classical Romanticism to Gilded Opulence*. New York: Rizzoli International Publications, 1993.

Gassier, Pierre. *Goya: A Witness of His Times*. New York: Konecky & Konecky, 1983.

Goldfarb, Hilliard T. *The Isabella Stewart Gardner Museum: A Companion Guide and History*. New Haven, Conn.: Yale University Press, 1995.

Gregg, Robert C.; Karen Bartholomew; and Lesly Bone. *Stanford Memorial Church: Glory of Angels*. Palo Alto, Cal.: Stanford Alumni Association, 1995.

Haines, Gerald K. "Who Gives a Damn About Medieval Walls." *Prologue*, Summer 1976, 97–106.

Hall, James. *Illustrated Dictionary of Symbols in Eastern and Western Art*. New York: Harper Collins, 1994.

Hall, Nicholas H. J., ed. *Colnaghi in America: A Survey to Commemorate the First Decade of Colnaghi New York*. New York: Colnaghi U.S.A. Ltd., 1992.

Hellerstedt, Kahren Jones, et al. *Clayton, the Pittsburgh Home of Henry Clay Frick: Art and Furnishings*. Pittsburgh, Pa.: The Helen Clay Frick Foundation, 1988.

Henderson, Michael. "The Best That Money Can Buy." *London Times*, January 1997.

Hennessy, John Pope, and Terence W. I. Hodgkinson, assisted by Anthony F. Radcliffe. *Sculpture in The Frick Collection: An Illustrated Catalogue*. Vol. 4, *German, Netherlandish, French, and British*. New York: The Frick Collection; Princeton, N.J.:Princeton University Press, 1970.

Hooke, Samuel Henry, ed. *The Labyrinth: Further Studies in the Relation Between Myth and Ritual in the Ancient World*. New York: Macmillan, 1935.

Hovey, Walter Read. *Treasures of the Frick Art Museum*. Pittsburgh, Pa.: The Frick Art Museum / Helen Clay Frick Foundation, 1975.

Hughs, Peter. *The Founders of the Wallace Collection*. London: Trustees of the Wallace Collection, 1981.

Huttinger, Eduard. *Degas*. New York: Crown, 1977.

Ingamells, John. *The Wallace Collection*. London: Scala Books, 1990.

Jacobs, Michael. *The Good and Simple Life: Artist Colonies in Europe and America*. Oxford: Phaidon Press, 1985.

Janson, H. W. *History of Art*. New York: Harry N. Abrams, 1977.

Jones, Owen. *The Grammar of Ornament: The Victorian Masterpiece on Oriental, Primitive, Classical, Medieval, and Renaissance Design and Decorative Art*. New York: Portland House, 1986.

Knoedler & Company. "The Rise of the Art World in America. Knoedler at 150." New York: Knoedler & Company, 1996.

Leisser, Martin B. "Art in Pittsburgh." *Pittsburgh Gazette Times*, May 4, 1910.

Lewis, Arnold; James Turner; and Steven McQuinn. *The Opulent Interiors of the Golden Age*. New York: Dover, 1987.

Lombardo, Josef Vincent. *Atillio Piccirilli: Life of an American Sculptor*. New York: Pitman, 1944.

Lurker, Manfred. *The Gods and Symbols of Ancient Egypt: An Illustrated Dictionary*. Trans. Barbara Cummings. London: Thames and Hudson, 1980.

Lynes, Russell. *Good Old Modern: An Intimate Portrait of the Museum of Modern Art*. New York: Atheneum, 1973.

Masterpieces of English Painting: Hogarth, Constable and Turner. Chicago: Art Institute of Chicago, 1946.

Matthews, Boris. *The Herder Symbol Dictionary: Symbols from Art, Archaeology, Mythology, Literature, and Religion*. Trans. Boris Matthews. Wilmette, Ill.: Chiron, 1990.

Matthews, W. H. *Mazes and Labyrinths: Their History and Development*. New York: Dover, 1970.

Mauner, George. *Manet, Peintre-Philosophe: A Study of the Painter's Themes*. University Park: Pennsylvania State University Press, 1975.

Meiss, Millard. *Giovanni Bellini's "St. Francis" in The Frick Collection*. Princeton, N.J.: Princeton University Press, 1964.

Menzies, Lucy. *The Saints in Italy: A Book of Reference to the Saints in Italian Art and Dedication*. London: Medici Society, 1924.

Milner, John. *The Studios of Paris: The Capital of Art in the Late Nineteenth Century*. New Haven, Conn.: Yale University Press, 1988.

Mount, Charles Merrill. *John Singer Sargent*. New York: W. W. Norton, 1955.

Munhall, Edgar. "An Early Acquisition by Henry Clay Frick: Dagnan-Bouveret's *Christ and the Disciples at Emmaus*." In *Reto Conzett zum 15 Dezember 1986*. Zurich, 1986.

———. François-Hubert Drouais: *Portrait of the Comte and Chevalier de Choiseul as Savoyards*" Typescript, Curatorial Report, The Frick Collection, January 1966.

———. *Ingres and the "Comtesse d'Haussonville."* New York: The Frick Collection, 1985.

———. *Masterpieces of The Frick Collection*. New York: The Frick Collection, 1970.

———. *Little Notes Concerning Watteau's "Portal of Valenciennes."* New York: The Frick Collection, 1992.

———. *Whistler and Montesquiou: The Butterfly and the Bat*. New York: The Frick Collection; Paris: Flammarion, 1995.

Munz, Ludwig, and Bob Haak. *Rembrandt*. New York: Harry N. Abrams, 1984.

Neal, Kenneth. *A Wise Extravagance: The Founding of the Carnegie International Exhibitions*. Pittsburgh, Pa.: University of Pittsburgh Press, 1996.

Osborne, Carol M. *Museum Builders in the West: The Stanfords as Collectors and Patrons of Art*. Palo Alto, Cal.: Stanford University Department of Art, 1986.

Pach, Walter. *Renoir*. New York: Harry N. Abrams, 1983.

Paintings in the Collection of Henry Clay Frick, at One East Seventieth Street, New York. New York: privately printed, n.d.

Pickles, Sheila. *The Language of Flowers*. New York: Harmony Books, 1989.

Piper, David. *Painting in England, 1500–1870*. London: The Book Society, privately printed, n.d.

Randall, Lilian M. C. *Medieval and Renaissance Manuscripts in the Walters Art Gallery*. 3 vols. Baltimore: The Johns Hopkins University Press; Walters Art Gallery, 1989–1997.

Ratcliff, Carter. *John Singer Sargent*. New York: Artabras, 1982.

Reed, Henry Hope. *The New York Public Library: Its Architecture and Decoration.* New York: W. W. Norton, 1986.

Reeder, Ellen. *Pandora: Women in Classical Greece.* Baltimore: Trustees of the Walters Art Gallery; Princeton, N.J.: Princeton University Press, 1995.

Richardson, John. *Manet.* Oxford: Phaidon, 1982.

Robertson, Seonaid M. *Rosegarden and Labyrinth: A Study in Art Education.* Dallas, Tex.: Spring Publications, 1982.

Rosenberg, Jacob; Seymour Slive; and E. H. Terkuile. *Dutch Art and Architecture, 1600–1800.* London: Butler & Tanner, 1966.

Roth, Linda Horvitz, ed. *J. Pierpont Morgan, Collector: European Decorative Arts from the Wadsworth Atheneum.* Hartford, Conn.: Wadsworth Atheneum, 1987.

Rothstein, Edward. "Of Pinpoints and Cameras: The Science of Vermeer's Art." *New York Times,* January 14, 1996.

Russell, John. "A Guide to the Discreet Changes at the Frick." *New York Times,* July 24, 1981.

Ryskamp, Charles, and Bernice Davidson. *Art in The Frick Collection: Paintings, Sculpture, Decorative Arts.* New York: Harry N. Abrams, in association with The Frick Collection, 1996.

Saint-Gaudens, Homer. "Joseph R. Woodwell." *Carnegie Magazine,* May 6, 1932, 274.

Schneider, Norbert. *Vermeer, 1632–1675: Veiled Emotions.* Trans. Fiona Hulse. Cologne, Germany: Taschen, 1994.

Sill, Gertrude Grace. *A Handbook of Symbols in Christian Art.* New York: Macmillan, 1975.

Simpson, Colin. *Artful Partners: Bernard Berenson and Joseph Duveen.* New York: Macmillan, 1986.

———. *The Partnership: The Secret Association of Bernard Berenson and Joseph Duveen.* London: Bodley Head, 1987.

Sion, Georgia. *Degas' Ballet Dancers.* New York: Universe, 1992.

Sitwell, Osbert. Introduction to *Catalogue of The Frick Collection.* New York: Frick Art Reference Library, 1949.

Stein, Susan A., ed. *The Architecture of Richard Morris Hunt.* Chicago: University of Chicago Press, 1986.

Stern, Robert A. M.; Gregory Gilmartin; and John Massengale. *New York 1900: Metropolitan Architecture and Urbanism, 1890–1915.* New York: Rizzoli International Publications, 1983.

Strahan, Edward. *Mr. Vanderbilt's House and Collection.* New York: George Barrie, 1883–1884.

Sullivan, Lester. "The Leff Collection and the Collector." *Pitt Magazine,* Spring 1967.

Tabor, Margaret E. *The Saints in Art.* London: Methuen, 1913.

Thuillier, Jacques. *Fragonard.* New York: Rizzoli International Publications, 1987.

Tompkins, Calvin. *Merchants and Masterpieces: The Story of the The Metropolitan Museum of Art.* New York: Henry Holt, 1989.

Uzanne, J. *Figures Contemporaines, tirées de l'Album Mariani.* 11 vols. Paris: H. Floury, 1896–1908

Valenstein, Suzanne G. *A Handbook of Chinese Ceramics.* New York: The Metropolitan Museum of Art; Harry N. Abrams, 1989.

Van Dyke, John C., ed. *Modern French Masters: A Series of Biographical and Critical Previews by American Artists.* New York: Century Company, 1896.

———. *Rembrandt and His School: A Critical Study of the Master and His Pupils with a New Assignment of Their Pictures.* New York: Scribner's, 1923.

Walsh, Michael, ed. *Butler's Lives of the Saints.* San Francisco: Harper Collins, 1991.

Ward, Susan M., and Michael Smith, eds. *Biltmore Estate.* Asheville, N.C.: The Biltmore Company, 1989.

Watson, Peter. *Wisdom and Strength: The Biography of a Renaissance Masterpiece.* New York: Doubleday, 1989.

Weisberg, Gabriel. *Beyond Impressionism: The Naturalist Impulse.* New York: Harry N. Abrams, 1992.

———. "From the Real to the Unreal: Religious Painting and Photography at the Salons of the Third Republic." *Art Magazine* 60, no. 4 (December 1968).

Weisberg, Gabriel; DeCourcy E. McIntosh; and Alison McQueen. *Collecting in the Gilded Age: Art Patronage in Pittsburgh, 1890–1910.* Pittsburgh, Pa.: Frick Art and Historical Center, 1997.

Weitzenhoffer, Frances. *The Havemeyers: Impressionism Comes to America.* New York: Harry N. Abrams, 1986.

Wheelock, Arthur K., Jr., ed. *Johannes Vermeer.* Washington, D.C.: National Gallery of Art, 1995.

Wissman, Fronia E. *Bouguereau.* San Francisco: Pomegranate Artbooks, 1996.

Woodward, Richard B. "Everyone's Favorite Museum: The Frick at 50." *Art News* 85, no. 4 (April 1986): 123–27.

World of Manet, The. New York: Time-Life, 1968.

Zingman-Leith, Elan, and Susan Zingman-Leith. *The Secret Life of Victorian Houses.* Washington, D.C.: Elliott & Clark, 1993.

Autobiography, Biography, and Memoir

Ackroyd, Peter. *Blake: A Biography.* New York: Alfred A. Knopf, 1996.

Auchincloss, Louis. *J. P. Morgan: The Financier and Collector.* New York: Harry N. Abrams, 1990.

Baker, Jean H. *Mary Todd Lincoln: A Biography.* New York: W. W. Norton, 1987.

Balsan, Consuelo Vanderbilt. *The Glitter and the Gold.* New York: Harper & Brothers, 1952.

Behrman, S. N. *Duveen.* New York: Random House, 1951.

Berkman, Alexander. *Prison Memoirs of an Anarchist.* New York: Mother Earth Publishing, 1912.

Berner, Bertha. *Incidents in the Life of Mrs. Leland Stanford.* Ann Arbor, Mich.: Edwards Brothers, 1934.

Boegner, Peggie Phipps, and Richard Gachot. *Halcyon Days: An American Family Through Three Generations.* New York: Harry N. Abrams, 1986.

Bowman, John G. *Unofficial Notes.* Pittsburgh, Pa.: privately printed, 1963.

Brashear, John A. *The Autobiography of a Man Who Loved the Stars.* 1924. Reprint, Pittsburgh, Pa.: University of Pittsburgh Press, 1988.

Bridge, James Howard. *Millionaires and Grubb Street: Comrades and Contacts in the Last Half Century.* New York: Brentano's, 1921.

Campbell, Nina, and Caroline Seebohm. *Elsie de Wolfe: A Decorative Life.* New York: Clarkson N. Potter, 1992.

Chase, Mary Ellen. *Abby Aldrich Rockefeller.* New York: Macmillan, 1950.

Chernow, Ron. *The House of Morgan: An American Banking Dynasty and the Rise of Modern Finance.* New York: Simon & Schuster, 1990.

Clark, George T. *Leland Stanford: War Governor of California, Railroad Builder, and Founder of Stanford University.* Palo Alto, Cal.: Stanford University Press, 1931.

Collier, Peter, and David Horowitz. *Rockefellers: An American Dynasty.* New York: Holt, Rinehart & Winston, 1979.

———. *The Roosevelts: An American Saga.* New York: Simon & Schuster, 1994.

Donald, David Herbert. *Lincoln.* New York: Simon & Schuster, 1955.

Drinnon, Richard. *Rebel in Paradise: A Biography of Emma Goldman.* Boston: Beacon Press, 1970.

Fowler, Marion. *In a Gilded Cage: American Heiresses Who Married British Aristocrats.* New York: St. Martin's, 1993.

Frick, Helen Clay, with Mara O'Hara. *My Father: Henry Clay Frick.* Privately printed, 1958.

Gates, Frederick Taylor. *Chapters in My Life.* New York: Macmillan, 1977.

Gimpel, René. *Diary of an Art Dealer.* Trans. John Rosenberg. New York: Farrar, Straus & Giroux, 1992.

Goldman, Emma. *Living My Life.* New York: Da Capo Press, 1970.

Gregory, Alexis. *Families of Fortune: Life in the Gilded Age.* New York: Rizzoli International Publications, 1993.

Harr, John Ensor, and Peter J. Johnson. *The Rockefeller Conscience.* New York: Scribner's, 1991.

Harvey, George. *Henry Clay Frick: The Man.* New York: Scribner's, 1928.

Havemeyer, Louisine W. *Sixteen to Sixty: Memoirs of a Collector.* Ed. Susan Alyson Stein. New York: Ursus Press; The Metropolitan Museum of Art, 1961.

————. *Sixteen to Sixty: Memoirs of a Collector*. New York: privately printed, 1993.

Hessen, Robert. *Steel Titan: The Life of Charles M. Schwab*. 1975. Reprint, Pittsburgh, Pa.: University of Pittsburgh Press, 1991.

Horne, Alistair. *A Bundle from Britain*. New York: St. Martin's Press, 1993.

Hoyt, Austin, producer. *Andrew Carnegie: The Richest Man in the World*. PBS Video, 1997.

Ingamells, John. *The Third Marquess of Hertford (1777–1842) as a Collector*. London: Trustees of The Wallace Collection, 1983.

Jason, Sonya. *Icon of Spring*. Pittsburgh, Pa.: University of Pittsburgh Press, 1987.

Jensen, Oliver. "Filial Piety and the First Amendment." *American Heritage* 18, no. 6 (October 1967): 2–4.

Kent, Bernice. *Abby Aldrich Rockefeller: The Woman in the Family*. New York: Random House, 1993.

Koskoff, David E. *The Mellons: The Chronicle of America's Richest Family*. New York: Thomas Y. Crowell, 1978.

Kunhardt, Philip B., Jr. *Lincoln: An Illustrated Biography*. New York: Alfred A. Knopf, 1992.

Lewis, Oscar. *The Big Four: The Story of Huntington, Stanford, Hopkins, and Crocker and the Building of the Central Pacific*. New York: Alfred A. Knopf, 1938.

Lundberg, Ferdinand. *The Rockefeller Syndrome*. Secaucas, N.J.: Lyle Stuart, 1975.

McCarten, John. "Daughter of Her Father." *The New Yorker*, July 1939.

McCarthy, Kathleen D. *Women's Culture: American Philanthropy and Art, 1830–1930*. Chicago: University of Chicago Press, 1991.

Mellon, Paul, with John Baskett. *Reflections in a Silver Spoon: A Memoir*. New York: William Morrow, 1992.

Mellon, Thomas. *Thomas Mellon and His Times*. 1885. Reprint, Pittsburgh, Pa.: University of Pittsburgh Press, 1994.

Mellon, William Larimer. *Judge Mellon's Sons*. [Pittsburgh?]: privately printed, 1949.

Mohr, James C. *The Cormany Diaries: A Northern Family in the Civil War*. Pittsburgh, Pa.: University of Pittsburgh Press, 1982.

Nixon, Lily Lee. "Henry Clay Frick and Pittsburgh's Children." *Western Pennsylvania Historical Magazine* 29, nos. 1 and 2 (March–June 1946): 65–71.

Patterson, Jerry E. *The Vanderbilts*. New York: Harry N. Abrams, 1989.

Rockefeller, Abby Aldrich. *Abby Aldrich Rockefeller's Letters to Her Sister Lucy*. Ed. John D. Rockefeller, Jr. New York: privately printed, 1957.

Ruth, John L. *Maintaining the Right Fellowship: A Narrative Account of Life in the Oldest Mennonite Community in North America*. Scottdale, Pa.: Herald Press, 1984.

Sauder, Glenn M. "Hall of Distinction: Henry Clay Frick." *The Meadow Mart* (Shreve, Ohio) 9, no. 2 (February, 1977): 1–8.

Schreiner, Samuel A. *Henry Clay Frick: The Gospel of Greed*. New York: St. Martin's, 1995.

Shearman, Deirdre. *Queen Victoria*. New York: Chelsea House, 1986.

Shoumatoff, Elizabeth. *F.D.R.'s Unfinished Portrait: A Memoir*. Pittsburgh, Pa.: University of Pittsburgh Press, 1990.

Spencer, Ethel. *The Spencers of Amberson Avenue*. Pittsburgh, Pa.: University of Pittsburgh Press, 1983.

Stephany, Annie. "Memoir of the Frick Family." Pittsburgh, Pa.:Frick Archives.

Turner, Dorothy. *Queen Victoria*. New York: The Bookwright Press, 1989.

Tutorow, Norman E. *Leland Stanford: Man of Many Careers*. Menlo Park, Cal.: Pacific Coast Publishers, 1971.

Vanderbilt, Arthur T., II. *Fortune's Children: The Fall of the House of Vanderbilt*. New York: William Morrow, 1989.

Vanderbilt, Cornelius, Jr. *Farewell to Fifth Avenue*. New York: Simon & Schuster, 1935.

Vanderbilt, Gloria. *After the Death of a Child*. New York: Alfred A. Knopf, 1996.

Wall, Joseph Frazier. *Andrew Carnegie*. 1970. Reprint, Pittsburgh, Pa.: University of Pittsburgh Press, 1989.

Weintraub, Stanley. *Victoria: An Intimate Biography*. New York: E. P. Dutton, 1987.

Weitzenhoffer, Frances. *The Havemeyers: Impressionism Comes to America*. New York: Harry N. Abrams, 1986.

Death, Dying, Mourning, and the Afterlife

Altschul, Sol, ed. *Childhood Bereavement and Its Aftermath*. Madison, Conn.: International University Press, 1988.

Ariès, Philippe. *Western Attitudes Toward Death: From the Middle Ages to the Present*. Trans. Patricia M. Ranum. Baltimore: The Johns Hopkins University Press, 1974.

Baty, James Marvin, and Veronica B. Tisza. "The Impact of Illness on the Child and His Family." *Child Study* 34 (January 1956): 15–19.

Becker, Ernest. *The Denial of Death*. New York: Free Press, 1973.

Bowlby, John. "Grief and Mourning in Infancy and Early Childhood." *Psychoanalytic Study of the Child* 15 (1965): 9–52.

Brian, James Lewton. *The Last Taboo: Sex and the Fear of Death*. Garden City, N.Y.: Doubleday, 1979.

Brice, Charles W. "Paradoxes of Maternal Mourning." *Psychiatry* 54 (February 1991): 1–12.

Cain, Albert C., and Barbara S. Cain. "On Replacing a Child." *Journal of the American Academy of Child Psychiatry* 3 (1964): 443–56.

Cain, Albert C.; Irene Fast; and Mary E. Erickson. "Children's Disturbed Reactions to the Death of a Sibling." *American Journal of Orthopsychiatry* 34 (July 1964): 741–52.

Cobb, Beatrix. "Psychological Impact of Long Illness and Death of a Child in the Family Circle." *Journal of Pediatrics* 49, no. 6 (October–December 1956): 746–51.

Curl, James Stevens. *The Victorian Celebration of Death*. Detroit: Partridge Press, 1972.

Davis, J. A. "The Attitude of Parents to the Approaching Death of Their Child." *Developmental Medicine and Child Neurology* 6 (June 1964): 286–88.

"Death in Childhood." *Canadian Medical Association Journal* 98 (May 1968): 967–69.

Deutsch, Helen. "Absence of Grief." *The Psychoanalytic Quarterly* 6 (1937): 13–22.

Eadie, Betty J., with Curtis Taylor. *Embraced by the Light*. Placerville, Cal.: Gold Leaf Press, 1992.

Fanos, Joanna H., and Bruce G. Nickerson. "Long-Term Effects of Sibling Death During Adolescence." *Journal of Adolescent Research* 6, no. 1 (January 1991): 70–82.

Finkbeiner, Ann K. *After the Death of a Child: Living with Loss Through the Years*. New York: The Free Press, 1996.

Fisher, Joe. *The Case for Reincarnation*. Preface by the Dalai Lama. New York: Bantam Books, 1985.

Fitzgerald, Helen. *The Grieving Child: A Primer for Parents in Helping Their Children Through the Process of Grief*. Foreword by Elisabeth Kübler-Ross. New York: Simon & Schuster, 1992.

———. *The Mourning Handbook: A Complete Guide for the Bereaved*. New York: Simon & Schuster, 1994.

Foster, Genevieve W. *The World Was Flooded with Light: A Mystical Experience Remembered*. Pittsburgh, Pa.: University of Pittsburgh Press, 1985.

Friedman, Stanford B.; Paul Chodoff; John W. Mason; and David A. Hamburg. "Behavioral Observations on Parents Anticipating Death of a Child." *Pediatrics* 6 (October 1963): 610–24.

Furth, Gregg M. *The Secret World of Drawings: Healing Through Art*. Boston: Sigo Press, 1988.

Gershom, Rabbi Yonassan. *Beyond the Ashes: Cases of Reincarnation from the Holocaust*. Virginia Beach, Va.: A. R. E. Press, 1992.

Hagin, Rosa A., and Carol G. Corwin. "Bereaved Children." *Journal of Clinical Child Psychology* 3, no. 2 (Summer 1974): 39–40.

Harrison, Saul I.; Charles W. Davenport; and John F. McDermott, Jr. "Children's Reactions to Bereavement." *Archives of General Psychiatry* 17 (March 1967): 593–97.

Hilgard, Josephine; Martha F. Newman; and Fern Fiske. "Strength of Adult Ego Following Childhood Bereavement." *American Journal of Orthopsychiatry* 30 (October 1960): 788–98.

Jones, Barbara. *Design for Death*. New York: Bobbs-Merrill, 1967.

Kalish, Richard A., ed. *Death and Dying: Views from Many Cultures*. Amityville, N.Y.: Baywood, 1972.

Kalish, Richard A., and David K. Reynolds. "Phenomenological Reality and Post-Death Contact." *Journal for the Scientific Study of Religion* (1973): 209–21.

Kestenbergh, Judith S. "Psychoanalysis of Children of Survivors from the Holocaust: Case Presentations and Assessments." *Journal of the American Psychoanalytic Association* 28 (1980): 775–804.

Kübler-Ross, Elisabeth. *On Death and Dying*. New York: Macmillan, 1970.

Lindermann, Erich. "Symptomatology and Management of Acute Grief." *American Journal of Psychiatry* 101 (September 1944): 141–48.

Lubove, Roy. "Pittsburgh's Allegheny Cemetery and the Victorian Garden of the Dead." *Pittsburgh History*, Fall 1992, 148–56.

Moody, Raymond A., Jr. *Life After Life: The Investigation of a Phenomenon—Survival of Bodily Death*. Introduction by Elisabeth Kübler-Ross. New York: Bantam Books, 1976.

———. *Reunions: Visionary Encounters with Departed Loved Ones*. New York: Ivy Books, 1993.

Morse, Melvin, with Paul Perry. *Parting Visions: Uses and Meanings of Pre-Death, Psychic, and Spiritual Experiences*. Introduction by Betty J. Eadie. New York: Villard Books, 1994.

Nuland, Sherwin B. *How We Die: Reflections on Life's Final Chapter*. New York: Alfred A. Knopf, 1994.

Orback, Charles E. "Mulitple Meanings of the Loss of a Child." *American Journal of Psychotherapy* 13, no. 4 (October 1959): 906–15.

Poznanski, Orlow Elva. "The Replacement Child: A Saga of Unresolved Parental Grief." *Journal of Pediatrics* 81 (July–December 1972): 1190.

Randles, Jenny, and Peter Hough. *The Afterlife: An Investigation Into the Mysteries of Life After Death*. New York: Berkley Books, 1994.

Rando, Therese A. *Treatment of Complicated Mourning*. Champaign, Ill.: Research Press, 1993.

Raphael, Beverly. *The Anatomy of Bereavement*. New York: Basic Books, 1983.

Ruhling, Nancy, and John Crosby Freeman. *The Illustrated Encyclopedia of Victoriana: A Comprehensive Guide to the Designs, Customs, and Inventions of the Victorian Era*. Philadelphia: Running Press, 1994.

Schlereth, Thomas J. *Victorian America: Transformation in Everyday Life, 1876–1915*. New York: Harper Collins, 1991.

Taylor, L. *Mourning Dress: A Costume and Social History*. London: Allen & Unwin, 1983.

von Franz, Marie-Louise. *The Way of the Dream*. Toronto: T. H. Best, 1987.

Weiss, Brian L. *Many Lives, Many Masters*. New York: Simon & Schuster, 1988.

———. *Through Time Into Healing: Discovering the Power of Regression Therapy to Erase Trauma and Transform Mind, Body, and Relationships*. New York: Simon & Schuster, 1992.

Weston, Donald L., and Robert C. Irwin. "Preschool Child's Response to Death of Infant Sibling." *American Journal of Diseases of Children* 106, no. 6 (1963): 564–67.

Zeligs, Rose, ed. "Death Casts Its Shadow on a Child." *Mental Hygiene* 31, no. 1 (January 1967): 9–20.

Freemasonry

Baigent, Michael, and Richard Leigh. *The Temple and the Lodge*. New York: Arcade, 1989.

Beha, Ernest. *Dictionary of Freemasonry*. London: Arco, 1962.

Blakemore, L. B. *Masonic Lodge Methods*. Chicago: Masonic History Co., 1953.

Blanchard, J. *Scotch Rite Masonry Illustrated*. 2 vols. Harwood Heights, Ill.: Charles T. Powner Company, 1997.

Chesterton, G. K. *St. Francis of Assisi*. New York: Doubleday, 1957.

Clausen, Henry C. (Sovereign Grand Commander). *Clausen's Commentaries on Morals and Dogma*. San Diego, Cal.: The Supreme Council, 33rd Degree, Ancient and Accepted Scottish Rite of Freemasonry, Southern Jurisdiction, U.S.A., 1974.

Gies, Frances. *The Knight in History*. New York: Harper & Row, 1984.

Harris, Jack. *Freemasonry: Invisible Cult in Our Midst*. Collierville, Tenn.: Global Press, 1983.

Knight, Stephen. *The Brotherhood: The Secret World of Freemasonry*. London: Book Club Associates, 1984.

Lawler, Robert. *Sacred Geometry: Philosophy and Practice*. New York: Thames and Hudson, n. d.

Mackey, Albert G. *An Encyclopaedia of Freemasonry and Its Kindred Sciences*. New and rev. ed. Ed. William J. Hughan and Edward L. Hawkins. 2 vols. New York: Masonic History Company, 1917.

———. *An Encyclopaedia of Freemasonry and Its Kindred Sciences*. New and rev. ed. Ed. William J. Hughan and Edward L. Hawkins. 2 vols. New York: Masonic History Company, 1924.

MacNulty, W. Kirk. *Freemasonry: A Journey Through Ritual and Symbol*. New York: Thames and Hudson, 1991.

Macoy, Robert. *A Dictionary of Freemasonry: A Compendium of Masonic History, Symbolism, Rituals, Literature, and Myth*. New York: Bell, 1989.

———. *Masonic Burial Services with General Instructions*. Harwood Heights, Ill.: Ezra A. Cook, 1995.

Newton, Joseph. *The Builders: A Story and Study of Freemasonry*. New York: McCoy Publishing and Masonic Supply, 1951.

Partner, Peter. *The Knights Templar and Their Myth*. Rochester, Vt.: Destiny Books, 1990.

Percival, Harold Walden. *Masonry and Its Symbols: In the Light of "Thinking and Destiny," the Great Lessons of Masonry*. New York: World, 1952.

Pike, Albert. *Morals and Dogma of the Ancient and Accepted Scottish Rite of Freemasonry*. Richmond, Va.: L. H. Jenkins, 1927.

Robinson, John J. *Born in Blood*. New York: Evans, 1989.

Ronayne, Edmond. *Ronayne's Hand-Book of Freemasonry*. Harwood Heights, Ill.: Ezra A. Cook, 1994.

———. *Blue Lodge and Chapter Masonry*. Harwood Heights, Ill.: Ezra A. Cook, 1994.

Rooke, P. E., ed. *Theobolds Through the Centuries: The Changing Fortunes of a Hertfordshire House and Estate*. 1980. Reprint, London, October 1983.

Rutherford, Ward. *The Druids and Their Heritage*. London: Gordon & Cremonesi, 1978.

Sherer, John. *The Masonic Ladder, or The Nine Steps to Ancient Freemasonry*. Cincinnati, Ohio: R. W. Carroll, 1874.

Theobolds: A Historical Sketch. London: Meyers Brooks, n. d.

Waite, Arthur Edward. *A New Encyclopaedia of Freemasonry and of Cognate Instituted Mysteries: Their Rites, Literature, and History*. New York: University Books, 1970.

Williams, Jay. *Knights of the Crusades*. New York: American Heritage, 1962.

Wilmshurst, W. L. *The Meaning of Masonry*. 1927. Facsimile ed., New York: Bell, 1980.

History

Alberts, Robert C. *Pitt: The Story of the University of Pittsburgh, 1787–1987*. Pittsburgh, Pa.: University of Pittsburgh Press, 1986.

Alcamo, Frank P. *The South Fork Story*. Indiana, Pa.: A. G. Halldin, 1987.

Auchincloss, Louis. *The Vanderbilt Era: Profiles of a Gilded Age*. New York: Scribner's, 1989.

Barker, Nicolas. "The Frick Art Reference Library." Reprinted from *The Book Collector*, Summer 1992.

Bell, Thomas. *Out of This Furnace*. 1941. Reprint, Pittsburgh, Pa.: University of Pittsburgh Press, 1976.

Bissell, Richard. *The Monongahela*. New York: Rinehart, 1952.

Brestensky, Dennis F. *The Early Coke Worker*. Connellsville, Pa.: Connellsville Printing Co., 1994.

Bridge, James Howard. *The Inside History of the Carnegie Steel Company*. 1903. Reprint, Pittsburgh, Pa.: University of Pittsburgh Press, 1991.

Brown, Henry Collins. *Old New York*. New York: privately printed, 1913.

Brown, Mark M.; Lu Donnelly; and David G. Wilkins. *History of the Duquesne Club*. Pittsburgh, Pa.: Duquesne Club, 1979.

Burgoyne, Arthur G. *The Homestead Strike of 1892*. 1893. Reprint, Pittsburgh, Pa.: University of Pittsburgh Press, 1979.

Burns, Stanley B. *Sleeping Beauty: Memorial Photography in America*. Santa Fe, N.M.: Twelvetrees Press, 1990.

Butera, Ronald J. "A Settlement House and the Urban Challenge: Kingsley House in Pittsburgh, Pa., 1893–1920." *Western Pennsylvania History Magazine* 66, no. 1 (January 1983): 25–47.

Byington, Margaret F. *Homestead: The Households of a Mill Town.* 1910. Reprint, Pittsburgh, Pa.: University of Pittsburgh Press, 1974.

Claiter, Diana. *100 Years Ago.* New York: Moore & Moore, 1990.

Coal and Coke Resource Analysis: Western Pennsylvania and Northern West Virginia. America's Industrial Heritage Project. Washington, D.C: U.S. Department of the Interior, 1992.

Conti, Lt. Col. Philip M. (ret.). *The Pennsylvania State Police: A History of Service to the Commonwealth, 1905 to the Present.* Harrisburg, Pa.: Stackpole Books, 1977.

Coode, Thomas H. *Bug Dust and Blackdamp: Life and Work in the Old Coal Patch.* Rices Landing, Pa.: Comart Press, 1986.

Davies, Norman. *God's Playground: A History of Poland.* 2 vols. New York: Columbia University Press, 1982.

Demarest, David P., Jr., and Fannia Weingartner, eds. *"The River Ran Red": Homestead 1892.* Pittsburgh, Pa.: University of Pittsburgh Press, 1992.

Demmler, Ralph H. *The First Century of an Institution: Reed Smith Shaw & McClay.* Pittsburgh, Pa.: 1977.

Dolson, Hildegarde. *Disaster at Johnstown: The Great Flood.* New York: Random House, 1965.

Ellis, Franklin, ed. *History of Fayette County, Pennsylvania, with Biographical Sketches of Many of Its Pioneers and Prominent Men.* 1882. Reprint, Hickory Flat, Miss.: Whipoorwill Publications, 1988.

Elmore, Emily W. *A Practical Handbook of Games.* New York: Macmillan, 1930.

Faber, Doris. *The Amish.* New York: Doubleday, 1991.

Ferguson, Henry L. *Fishers Island, N.Y., 1614–1925.* 1925. Reprint, Harrison, N.Y.: Harbor Hill Books, 1974.

Foote, Timothy. "1846: The Way We Were—the Way We Went." *Smithsonian Magazine* (April 1996): 38–50.

Fretz, A. J. *A Genealogical Record of the Descendants of Martin Oberholtzer.* Milton, N.J.: The Evergreen News, 1903.

Garland, Joseph E. *Boston's Gold Coast: The North Shore, 1890–1929.* Boston: Little, Brown and Company, 1981.

Gates, John K. *The Beehive Coke Years: A Pictorial History of Those Times.* Uniontown, Pa.: John T. Gates, 1990.

Gitelman, Howard M. *The Legacy of the Ludlow Massacre: A Chapter in American Industrial Relations.* Philadelphia: University of Pennsylvania Press, 1988.

Goddard, Conrad Goodwin. *The Early History of Roslyn Harbor, Long Island.* N.p.: 1972.

Goodwin, Doris Kearns. *No Ordinary Time: Franklin and Eleanor Roosevelt.* New York: Simon & Schuster, 1994.

Gordon, Linda. *Cossack Rebellions: Social Turmoil in the Sixteenth-Century Ukraine.* Albany: State University of New York Press, 1983.

Gregory, Alexis. *The Golden Age of Travel, 1880–1939.* New York: Rizzoli International Publications, 1991.

Hatcher, Harlan. *A Century of Iron and Men.* New York: Bobbs-Merrill, 1950.

Heald, Sarah H., ed. *Fayette County, Pennsylvania: An Inventory of Historic Engineering and Industrial Sites.* America's Industrial Heritage Project. Washington, D.C.: U.S. Department of the Interior, 1990.

Hines, Walker D. (Director General of the Railroads, 1919–1920). *War History of American Railroads.* New Haven, Conn.: Yale University Press, 1928.

Hoerr, John P. *And the Wolf Finally Came: The Decline of the American Steel Industry.* Pittsburgh, Pa.: University of Pittsburgh Press, 1988.

Holbrook, Stewart H. *The Age of the Moguls.* Garden City, N.Y.: Doubleday, 1953.

Hungerford, Edward. *The Story of the Baltimore and Ohio Railroad, 1827–1927.* New York: G. P. Putnam's, 1928.

Illustrated Historical Combination Atlas of Cambria County, Pennsylvania. Philadelphia: Atlas, 1890.

Ingham, John N. *Making Iron and Steel: Independent Mills in Pittsburgh, 1820–1920*. Columbus, Ohio: Ohio State University Press, 1991.

Knox, Katherine McCook. *The Story of the Frick Art Reference Library: The Early Years*. New York: Frick Art Reference Library, 1979.

Korcheck, Robert A. *Nemacolin: The Mine—The Community, 1917–1950*. Nemacolin, Pa., 1980.

Krause, Paul. *The Battle for Homestead, 1880–1892: Culture, Politics, and Steel*. Pittsburgh, Pa.: University of Pittsburgh Press, 1992.

Lorant, Stephan. *Pittsburgh: The Story of an American City*. Garden City, N.Y.: Doubleday, 1964.

McClenathan, J. C., et al. *Centennial History of the Borough of Connellsville, Pennsylvania, 1806–1906*. Reprint, Salem, W. Va.: Walsworth Don Mills, 1982.

MacColl, Gail, and Carol McD. Wallace. *To Marry an English Lord, or How Anglomania Really Got Started*. New York: Workman, 1989.

McCullough, C. Hax, Jr. *One Hundred Years of Banking: The History of Mellon National Bank and Trust Company*. Pittsburgh, Pa.: Herbick & Held, 1969.

McCullough, C. Hax, Jr., with Mary Brignano. *Pillar of Pittsburgh: The History of Mercy Hospital and the City It Serves*. Pittsburgh, Pa.: Mercy Hospital, 1990.

McCullough, David. *The Johnstown Flood*. New York: Simon & Schuster, 1968.

Mauer, James H. *The American Cossack*. Reading, Pa.: Pennsylvania State Federation of Labor, 1915.

Maxwell, Marianne. "Pittsburgh's Frick Park: A Unique Addition to the City's Park System." *Western Pennsylvania Historical Magazine* 68, no. 3 (July 1985).

Mayo, Katherine. *Justice to All.: The Story of the Pennsylvania State Police*. Introduction by Theodore Roosevelt. New York: G. P. Putnam's, 1917.

———. *Mounted Justice*. New York: Houghton Mifflin, 1918.

———. *The Standard Bearers*. New York: Houghton Mifflin, 1930.

Mennonite Confessions of Faith. Scottdale, Pa.: Herald Press, 1963.

Mennonite Encyclopedia. Scottdale, Pa.: Mennonite Publishing House, 1956.

Miller, Levi. "The Growth and Decline of Mennonites Near Scottdale, Pennsylvania: 1790–1890." *Pennsylvania Mennonite Heritage* (October 1990): 2–15.

Mulrooney, Margaret M. *A Legacy of Coal: The Coal Company Towns of Southwestern Pennsylvania*. America's Industrial Heritage Project. Washington, D.C.: U.S. Department of the Interior, 1989.

Nicholas, Lynn H. *The Rape of Europa*. New York: Alfred A. Knopf, 1994.

Overholt, A., & Co., Inc. "A History of the Company and of the Overholt Family." August 1940.

Overholt, John L. "The Marcus Oberholtzer (1664–1725) Family." *Pennsylvania Mennonite Heritage* (October 1996): 26-40.

Palmer, Tim. *Youghiogheny: Appalachian River*. Pittsburgh, Pa.: University of Pittsburgh Press, 1984.

Paskoff, Paul F. *The Iron and Steel Industry in the Nineteenth Century*. Encyclopedia of American Business History and Biography. New York: Facts on File, 1988.

Peace, Faith, Nation: Mennonites and Amish in Nineteenth-Century America. Scottdale, Pa.: Herald Press, 1988.

Platt, Franklin. *Special Report on the Coke Manufacture of the Youghiogheny River Valley in Fayette and Westmoreland Counties*. Harrisburg, Pa.: Board of Commissioners for the Second Geological Survey, 1876.

Poliniak, Louis. *When Coal Was King: Mining Pennsylvania's Anthracite*. Lebanon, Pa.: Applied Arts, 1989.

Randall, Monica. *The Mansions of Long Island's Gold Coast*. New York: Hastings House, 1979.

Report of the American Commission for the Protection and Salvage of Artistic and Historic Monuments in War Areas. Washington, D.C.: Government Printing Office, 1946.

Ruth, John L. *Maintaining the Right Fellowship: A Narrative Account of Life in the Oldest Mennonite Community in North America*. Scottdale, Pa.: Herald Press, 1984.

Serrin, William. *Homestead: The Glory and Tragedy of an American Steel Town*. New York: Random House, 1992.

Sesquicentennial: Cambria County, 1804–1954. Ebensberg, Pa.: Cambria County Historical Association, 1954.

Shappe, Nathan Daniel. "A History of Johnstown and the Great Flood of 1889: A Study of Disaster and Rehabilitation." Ph.D. diss., University of Pittsburgh, 1940.

———. "Spoilation and Encroachment in the Conemaugh Valley Before the Johnstown Flood of 1889." *Western Pennsylvania Magazine* 23 (March 1940).

Sheppard, Muriel Early. *Cloud by Day: The Story of Coal and Coke and People.* 1974. Reprint, Pittsburgh, Pa.: University of Pittsburgh Press, 1991.

Shetler, Sanford G. *Two Centuries of Struggle and Growth, 1763–1963: A History of Allegheny Mennonite Conference.* Scottdale, Pa.: Herald Press, 1968.

Springer, H. J. *1910 Souvenir of Scottdale, Pa.* Scottdale: Westmoreland-Fayette Historical Society, 1996.

Stern, Robert A. M.; Gregory Gilmartin; and John Massengale. *New York 1900: Metropolitan Architecture and Urbanism, 1890–1915.* New York: Rizzoli International Publications, 1983.

Stevens, Sylvester K. *Pennsylvania, Birthplace of a Nation.* New York: Random House, 1964.

Stover, John F. *The History of the B&O Railroad.* West Lafayette, Ind.: Purdue University Press, 1987.

Stowell, Myron R. *Fort Frick, or the Siege of Homestead: A History of the Famous Struggle Between the Amalgamated Association of Iron and Steel Workers and the Carnegie Steel Company (Limited) of Pittsburgh, Pennsylvania.* Pittsburgh, Pa.: Pittsburgh Printing Co., 1893.

Tarbell, Ida M. *The Life of Elbert H. Gary: The Story of Steel.* New York: Appleton, 1925.

Taylor, Lou. *Mourning Dress: A Costume and Social History.* London: Allen & Urwin, 1983.

Tully, Andrew. *Era of Elegance.* New York: Funk and Wagnalls, 1947.

U.S. Congress. House. Committee on the Judiciary. *Report 2447: Investigation of the Homestead Troubles.* 52d Congress, 2d sess., 1892–1893. Washington D.C.: Government Printing Office, 1893.

Wall, James, and Joanne Wall. *Fishers Island: A Book of Memories.* Fisher's Island, N.Y.: Peninsula Press, 1982.

Warren, Kenneth. *Triumphant Capitalism: Henry Clay Frick and the Industrial Transformation of America.* Pittsburgh, Pa.: University of Pittsburgh Press, 1996.

"Water Baptism Not the New Birth." *Herald of Truth* (Elkhart, Ind.) 7, no. 3 (March 1870): 1, 47.

Wolff, Leon. *Lockout.* New York: Harper & Row, 1965.

Yoder, Edward. "The Mennonites of Westmoreland County." *Mennonite Quarterly Review* 15, no. 3 (July 1941): 155–69.

Ziaukas, Tim. "Lockout," *Pittsburgh,* June 1992, 20–45.

Homeopathy and Medicine

Brignano, Mary. *Inheritors of a Glorious Reality.* Pittsburgh, Pa.: Shadyside Hospital, 1991.

Clarke, Basil. *Psychological Medicine: Arthur Wigan and the Duality of the Mind.* Monograph Supplement. Cambridge: Cambridge University Press, 1987.

Copeland, Royal S. *The Scientific Basis of Homoeopathy.* Cleveland, 1960. Reprinted from *The Cleveland Medical and Surgical Reporter,* March 1906.

Dennis, Frederic S. *The History and Development of Surgery During the Past Century.* 1905. New York: privately reprinted, 1928.

———. *Selected Surgical Papers, 1876–1914.* 2 vols. New York: privately printed, 1934.

———. ed. *System of Surgery.* 4 vols. Philadelphia: Lea Brothers, 1895.

Diller, Theodore. *Pioneer Medicine in Western Pennsylvania.* Foreword by J. J. Buchanan, M.D. New York: Paul B. Hoeber, 1927.

Garmony, Jasper Jewett. *Operative Surgery on the Cadaver.* New York: Appleton, 1887.

Gauge, O. B., and R. W. McClelland. "Abdomen. Typhilitis & Perityphilitis. Obstetrics." Handwritten notebook, McClelland Papers, Historical Society of Western Pennsylvania, Pittsburgh, Pa.

Gerster, Arpad G., M.D. *The Rules of Aseptic and Antiseptic Surgery: A Practical Treatise for the Use of Students and the General Practitioner*. New York: Appleton, 1890.

Haeger, Knut. *Illustrated History of Surgery*. New York: Bell, 1988.

Hay, Louise L. *You Can Heal Your Life*. Santa Monica, Cal.: Hay House, 1987.

Hospital News (Pittsburgh Homeopathic Hospital) 1, no. 1 (April 1896).

Kaufman, Martin. *Homeopathy in America: The Rise and Fall of a Medical Heresy*. Baltimore: The Johns Hopkins University Press, 1971.

Kaufman, Martin; Stuart Galishoff; and Todd L. Savitt, eds. *Dictionary of American Medical Biography*. Vol. 1. Westport, Conn.: Greenwood Press, 1984.

Loria, Frank L. *Historical Aspects of Abdominal Injuries*. Springfield, Ill.: Charles C. Thomas, 1968.

McClelland, James H. Jubilee Address Delivered Before the American Institute of Homoeopathy 50th Anniversary. Denver, Colorado, June 14-20, 1894.

Paull, Barbara I. *A Century of Medical Excellence: The History of the University of Pittsburgh School of Medicine*. Pittsburgh, Pa.: University of Pittsburgh Medical Alumni Association, 1986.

Pioneers in Acute Abdominal Surgery. 1881. Reprint, London: Zachary Cope, 1939.

Richardson, Robert G. *The Story of Modern Surgery* (formerly *The Surgeon's Tale*). New York: Collier Books, 1958.

Rosenberg, Charles E. *The Care of Strangers: The Rise in America's Hospital System*. New York: Basic Books, 1987.

Shlotzhauer, Tammi L., and James L. McGuire. *Living with Rheumatoid Arthritis*. Baltimore, Md.: The Johns Hopkins University Press, 1993.

Stevens, Audry D. *America's Pioneers in Abdominal Surgery*. Melrose, Mass.: American Society of Abdominal Surgeons, 1968.

Stone, R. French, ed. *Biography of Eminent American Physicians and Surgeons*. Indianapolis: Carlon & Hollenbeck, 1894.

Van Baun, William Weed. "Immortality—Personality." Address in honor of James H. McClelland, M.D., delivered before the American Institute of Homoeopathy. Atlantic City, June 28, 1914.

Mythology

Alexander, Beatrice. *Famous Myths of the Golden Age*. New York: Random House, 1947.

Bulfinch, Thomas. *Bulfinch's Mythology*. New York: Avanel, 1978.

Campbell, Joseph. *The Hero with a Thousand Faces*. Bollingen Series. Princeton, N.J.: Princeton University Press, 1973.

————. *Myths to Live By: How We Re-create Ancient Legends in Our Daily Lives to Release Human Potential*. New York: Bantam Books, 1988.

Campbell, Joseph, with Bill Moyers. *The Power of Myth*. New York: Doubleday, 1988.

D'Aulaire, Edgar Parin, and Ingri D'Aulaire. *D'Aulaires' Book of Greek Myths*. New York: Doubleday, 1962.

Hamilton, Edith. *Mythology: Timeless Tales of Gods and Heroes*. New York: New American Library, 1969.

Phrenology

Benedikt, Moriz. *Anatomical Studies Upon Brains of Criminals*. Trans. E. P. Fowler, M.D. 1881. Reprint, New York: Wm. Wood & Co., 1981.

Combe, Andrew. *Mental Derangement*. 1834. Fascimile reprint of first American edition, New York: Delmar, 1972.

De Giustino, David. *Conquest of the Mind: Phrenology and Victorian Social Thought*. Totowa, N.J.: Rowan & Littlefield, 1975.

Leahey, Thomas Hardy, and Grace Evans Leahey. *Psychology's Occult Doubles: Psychology and the Problem of Pseudoscience*. Chicago: Nelson-Hall, 1983.

McCormick, L. Hamilton. *Characterology: An Exact Science*. New York: Rand McNally, 1920.

Morton, Samuel George. *Crania Americana*. Philadelphia: J. Dobson, 1839.

Sizer, Nelson. *Forty Years in Phrenology: Embracing Recollections of History, Anecdotes, and Experience*. New York: Fowler & Wells, 1882.

Spurzheim, Johann G. *Phrenology: The Study of Physiognomy*. Boston: Marsh, Capen, Lyon, 1883.

Psychiatry, Psychology, and Spirituality

Ariès, Philippe. *Centuries of Childhood: A Social History of Family Life*. Trans. Robert Baldick. New York: Alfred A. Knopf, 1962.

Armstrong, Louise. *Kiss Daddy Goodnight: Ten Years Later*. New York: Simon & Schuster, 1986.

Bass, Ellen, and Laura Davis. *The Courage to Heal: A Guide for Women Survivors of Child Sexual Abuse*. New York: Harper & Row, 1988.

Bradshaw, John. *Bradshaw On: The Family*. Pompano Beach, Fla.: Health Communications, 1988.

———. *Bradshaw On: Healing the Shame That Binds You*. Pompano Beach, Fla.: Health Communications, 1988.

Carmen, Elaine; Patricia Perri Rieker; and Trudy Mills. "Victims of Violence and Psychiatric Illness." *American Journal of Psychiatry* 141, no. 3 (March 1984): 378–83.

Clarke, Jean Illsley. *Self-Esteem: A Family Affair*. New York: Harper & Row, 1978.

Clawson, Mary Ann. "Early Modern Fraternalism and the Patriarchal Family." *Feminist Studies* 6, no. 2 (Summer 1980): 372–88.

Chernin, Kim. *The Hungry Self: Women, Eating, and Identity*. New York: Harper & Row, 1985.

De Salvo, Louise. *Virginia Woolfe: The Impact of Childhood Sexual Abuse on Her Life and Work*. New York: Ballantine Books, 1990.

Edelman, Hope. *Motherless Daughters*. New York: Dell, 1994.

Edinger, Edward F. *Goethe's Faust*. Toronto: Inner City Books, 1922.

Farrell, Warren. *The Myth of Male Power: Why Men Are the Disposable Sex*. New York: Berkley Books, 1994.

Forward, Susan, with Craig Buck. *Toxic Parents*. New York: Bantam Books, 1989.

Freedman, Alfred M., and Harold I. Kaplan, eds. *Comprehensive Textbook of Psychiatry*. Baltimore: Williams & Wilkins, 1967.

Gelinas, Cenise J. "The Persisting Negative Effects of Incest." *Psychiatry* 46 (November 1983): 312–32.

Gibson, Eric. "The Psychology of Hoarding." *New York Times*, 1 February 17, 1994.

Golomb, Elan. *Trapped in the Mirror: Adult Children of Narcissists in Their Struggle for Self*. New York: William Morrow, 1992.

Herman, Judith Lewis, with Lisa Hirscham. *Father Daughter Incest*. Cambridge, Mass.: Harvard University Press, 1981.

Hillman, James. *Kinds of Power: A Guide to Its Intelligent Uses*. New York: Doubleday, 1995.

Jordan, William George. *The Kingship of Self-Control*. New York: Fleming H. Revell, 1899.

———. *The Majesty of Calmness*. New York: Fleming H. Revell, c. 1898.

———. *The Power of Truth*. New York: Brentano's, 1902.

Jung, Carl G. *Answer to Job*. Vol. 2 of *The Collected Works of C. G. Jung*. Trans. R. F. C. Hull. Bollingen Series 20. Princeton, N.J.: Princeton University Press, 1969.

Kosof, Anna. *Incest: Families in Crisis*. New York: Franklin Watts, 1985.

Leonard, Linda. *The Wounded Woman: Healing the Father-Daughter Relationship*. Boston: Shambhala, 1983.

Lewis, C. S. *The Problem of Pain*. New York: Macmillan, 1976.

Mascetti, Manueta Dunn. *The Song of Eve*. New York: Simon & Schuster, 1990.

Mellody, Pia, with Andrea Wells Miller and J. Keith Miller. *Facing Codependence: What It Is, Where It Comes From, How It Sabatoges Our Lives*. San Francisco: Harper Collins, 1989.

Miller, Alice. *The Drama of the Gifted Child: The Search for the True Self*. Trans. Ruth Ward. New York: Meridian, 1986. Originally published as *Prisoners of Childhood*.

———. *For Your Own Good: Hidden Cruelty in Child-Rearing and the Roots of Violence*. Trans. Hildegard Hannum and Hunter Hannum. New York: Farrar, Straus & Giroux, 1983.

———. *Thou Shalt Not Be Aware: Society's Betrayal of the Child*. Trans. Hildegard Hannum and Hunter Hannum. New York: Farrar, Straus & Giroux, 1984.

Muensterberger, Werner. *Collecting: An Unruly Passion*. Princeton, N.J.: Princeton University Press, 1994.

Murdock, Maureen. *The Hero's Daughter: Through Myth, Story, and Jungian Psychology, an Exploration of the Shadow Side of Father Love*. New York: Ballantine Books, 1994.

Perera, Sylvia Brinton. *The Scapegoat Complex: Toward a Mythology of Shadow and Guilt*. Toronto: Inner City Books, 1986.

Russell, Diana E. H. *The Secret Trauma: Incest in the Lives of Girls and Women*. New York: Basic Books, 1986.

Van de Castle, Robert L. *Our Dreaming Mind*. New York: Ballantine Books, 1994.

Woodman, Marion. *Addiction to Perfection: The Still Unravished Bride*. Toronto: Inner City Books, 1982.

———. *The Pregnant Virgin: A Process of Psychological Transformation*. Toronto: Inner City Books, 1985.

———. *The Ravaged Bridegroom*. Toronto: Inner City Books, 1990.

Woodman, Marion, with Kate Danson, Mary Hamilton, and Rita Greer Allen. *Leaving My Father's House*. Boston: Shambhala, 1993.

Acknowledgments

Montaigne once wrote, "I have brought you a nosegay of flowers, but only the string that binds them is mine alone." I, however, claim no such string. Throughout the writing process, this book felt guided. Often it was helped by the miraculous appearance of hidden hands at a critical moment. I cannot help but feel that a force greater than I was at work. To those listed below, and all others not mentioned who know, as I do, how significantly they contributed to this work, I extend my deepest gratitude and return a bouquet bound with heartfelt thanks.

In particular, I would like to thank John E. Davis, Ph.D., founder and director of The Resource Group in Towson, Md. His support over the last ten years, as well as his gentle humor and great wisdom, sustained me as I wrote this book. If indeed there is a string that binds, I would suggest it came through him.

Frederick A. Hetzel, former director of the University of Pittsburgh Press, also supported me through those ten years. A native of the West Overton-Connellsville area, he introduced me to the Coke Region, scholars in my field, and professionals in the publishing world. He suggested that I fully research the Morewood riots of 1891 (as they had been largely overlooked by historians) and greatly assisted the development of the introduction and chapter 1.

The birth of this book I owe entirely to Judith Joseph, president of Joseph Publishing Services. Her friendship, her belief in the project, her wisdom, and her absolute determination to see this book published was inspirational. Her dedication to every facet of the process—from expanding the art program, to editing the text, and negotiating contracts—has been the driving force.

To Catherine Marshall, former editor-in-chief at the University of Pittsburgh Press, I owe my deepest gratitude. Her superb editing, excellent queries, demand for absolute accuracy, and sophisticated polish have given this book its accuracy and strength. Her patience with the many complexities of the manuscript and her perseverence while it underwent many revisions was heroic.

The beauty, elegance, and sophistication of this book I owe entirely to Alex Castro—designer, architect, and artist. To him I owe my introduction to Robert E. Abrams and Abbeville Press. I thank him for the privilege of being included in the design and printing processes; for making me aware of the parallels between Figures 2-14, 15, and Figures 5-26, 27; and for his wisdom, enthusiasm, sensitivity, and friendship. I also thank Alex for honoring this book with both his extraordinary chapter openings and his mysterious, compelling jacket—the latter kindly permitted by Alan Fern, director, The National Portrait Gallery, Washington, D.C., and Ellen G. Miles, curator of painting and sculpture. Alex's design, page layouts, and attention to the intricacies of the process have given this work a power far beyond my written word.

I would also like to thank Robert E. Abrams, collector in his own right and CEO of Abbeville Press, for publishing this book and making it a reality. Susan Costello, editorial director at Abbeville, Lou Bilka, production manager, and Owen Dugan, also deserve my thanks for their welcomed and appreciated expertise. Additionally, I extend my gratitude to Massimo Pizzi, Bruno Nicolis, Sandro Diani, Pamela Schechter, Elena Gaiardelli, Sergio Peresson, Germano Barban, Franco Ferrario, Claudio Scotti, Bruno Tintori, Fortunato Lessio, Walter Redaelli, Ezio Arosio, and Mariella Colombo of Amilcare Pizzi S.p.A. for the excellent print quality born of their care, committment, and absolute professionalism.

Additionally, this book could never have been written without the support, interest, and encouragement of my family. In particular, I am deeply grateful to my uncle Henry Clay Frick II, M.D., for giving me access to the Frick family archives and the opportunity to research the Frick family's personal and business papers. I am forever grateful for his permission to reproduce images from this extensive family collection.

My sisters Helen Clay Chace and Arabella Symington Dane greatly enriched this work. They shared insights about our great-aunt, Helen Clay Frick, and told me poignant stories about our family and the many Frick family homes. They made their own collections available to me, granted me permission to reproduce certain of the material in this book, and were ever enthusiastic about the project.

My brother-in-law Edward N. Dane gave me further understanding of my great-aunt and the Frick family summer home, Eagle Rock. My brother-in-law Minturn V. Chace also shared stories and insights about my great-aunt. Additionally, he combed microfilms of the *New York Times* for information on Henry Clay Frick and saved me much time by doing this valuable and painstaking research.

My aunt, Emily T. Frick, was always ready with encouragement and enthusiasm, as were my first cousins, the great-grandchildren of Henry Clay Frick—particularly Peter Blanchard, Jr., Childs Frick Burden, Frances Dixon Burden, I. Townsend Burden III, Frances Frick, Henry Clay Frick III, Elise Frick, and Adelaide Frick Trafton.

Our Overholt relatives—Sally Lott Burnhart, Jay Edgar Frick, Harold Overholt, and James Braddock Stevenson—gave me a much needed understanding of Henry Clay Frick's siblings and their life in Wooster, Ohio. My Childs relative, Elizabeth Schoyer, niece of Louise Dilworth Childs, shared a valuable family letter written at the time of the attempt on Henry Clay Frick's life. My Dixon relatives—Patricia Dixon, William Dixon, M.D., and Grace Hazzard—gave me important archival material and broadened my understanding of my grandmother, Frances Dixon Frick, and her relationship to both Henry Clay Frick and his daughter Helen.

Sheila Milikin, one of Helen Frick's World War II English girls, enriched my understanding of that period in my great-aunt's life. My father, J. Fife Symington, Jr., broadened my understanding of World War II. My cousin Sherri Symington gave me the first and most important articles on childhood bereavement.

Many members of other families connected to Frick history were equally generous: Barbara Janney Trimble, an artist and educator, and a great-granddaughter of Henry Phipps, read the manuscript an uncountable number of times and offered her sage advice and constant enthusiasm; Paul G. Pennoyer, Jr., trustee of The Frick Collection and the Frick Art Reference Library; Mr. and Mrs. Howard Phipps; Paul Mellon; Arthur Vanderbilt II; David C. Duniway, son of Childs Frick's tutor Clyde A. Duniway; Christopher Witt, grandson of Sir Robert Witt; William Herron Woodwell and John Woodwell, Jr., grandsons of Joseph R. Woodwell; Rosalind Havemeyer Roosevelt, great-granddaughter of Louisine and Henry O. Havemeyer; relatives of Andrew Carnegie—Linda Lawson Hills, Win Lauder, and Mrs. William Lawson; Mary Quinn, granddaughter of Thomas Lynch; Marjorie R. Laing, granddaughter of the superintendent of the Morewood coke works during the 1891 riots; Dr. James W. Ruff; Virginia Anthony Soule; Charles Guggenheim; and Alexander Sanger.

The following individuals shared poignant stories about Helen Clay Frick, Frances Dixon Frick, and Childs Frick: David Allen, former valet to Childs Frick; Helen Allen, housekeeper at Clayton, Long Island; James Mosaque, former chauffeur to Childs Frick; and members of Helen Clay Frick's household: Edward and Alice Boyle, housekeeper and cook; Walter Cooley, business manager; Julia Egan, secretary; and Barbara Hunter, R.N., and Ruth Mansfield, R.N., nurses.

Many individuals associated with Frick organizations also gave generously of their time and expertise. The staff of the Henry Clay Frick Birthplace at the West Overton Museums helped develop my understanding of the first thirty years of Henry Clay Frick's life through field trips and material in their valuable archives. Particular thanks go to former directors Susan Endersby and Kimberly Bringe; Rodney Sturtz, director; Robert Sandow; and Donald J. Snyder, Jr.

Many at the Frick Art and Historical Center spent valuable time and generously shared their expertise while providing me with material essential to this work. In particular, I would like to thank Decourcy McIntosh, executive director, for supporting the project in its early stages, Sheena Wagstaff, Nadine Grabania, Sarah Hall, Karren Barron, Robin Pflasterer, Terry Chapman, and Michele Griffin. Many who are no longer at the center provided valuable help and assistance: Ruth Ferguson, Joanne Moore, Steven J. Hussman, Robert L. Digby, and Lisa A. Hubeny. A particular thanks to the trustees, especially my sister Arabella Dane and my cousins Adelaide Trafton and Childs Burden.

My thanks to certain individuals at The Frick Collection, most particularly Samuel Sachs II, director; Charles Ryskamp, former director; Edgar Munhall, curator; Bernice Davidson, research curator; Susan Grace Galassi, associate curator; William Stout, assistant to the curator and registrar; Robert Goldsmith, deputy director for administration; as well as Amy Herman, Kate Gerlough, Martha Hackley, Richard di Liberto, and Ashley J. Thomas. My thanks also to Everett Fahy, former director of The Frick Collection.

The staff of the Frick Art Reference Library also lent essential support and expertise: Helen Sanger, former Andrew W. Mellon Librarian; Patricia Barnett, Andrew W. Mellon Librarian; as well as Lydia Dufour, Inge Reist, Don Swanson, David Schnabel, and Marie Keith.

Many individuals associated with the Henry Clay Frick Fine Arts Department at the University of Pittsburgh also gave generously of their time and shared their knowledge: Virginia Lewis, Ray Anne Lockhard, Matthew Roper, Marcia Rostek, Franklin K. Toker, and Davis G. Wilkins.

Other individuals in organizations closely connected to Frick family history were also of invaluable help. Richard Burkert, director of the Johnstown Flood Museum, Johnstown, Pa., located the Andrew Carnegie cottage where Martha Howard Frick died. Melissa De Madeiros, archivist at Knoedler & Company, showed me family letters and provided a list of paintings purchased by Henry Clay Frick and a list of those he returned. Darwin H. Stapleton, Erwin Levold, Harold W. Oakhill, and Thomas Rosenbaum of the Rockefeller Archive Center made available valuable material on the Frick-Rockefeller relationship. Ellen M. Rosenthal at the Historical Society of Western Pennsylvania, Carolyn S. Schumacher, and William J. Gaughan were of invaluable assistance in securing images for reproduction. Ellen Reeder, at the Walters Art Gallery, Baltimore, was teacher, friend, and guiding light throughout the writing process; thanks to her I was given introductions to others at the Walters Art Gallery who were helpful: Gary Vikan, William R. Johnston, Lillian Randall, Elise Thall Calvi, Murial Toppan, and Susan Tobin. Kathleen Henshaw Baldwin at the Biltmore Estate, Ashville, N.C., provided me with material related to George Vanderbilt and Henry Clay Frick's rental of 640 Fifth Avenue. At Stanford University, Margaret Kimball, Diana Strazdes, and Darrell Carey provided an understanding of the relationship between art and the Stanford family's bereavement. Stanley B. Burns, M.D., at the Burns Archives provided daguerreotypes of the dead.

Certain Freemasons and Masonic organizations helped me research Freemasonry in general and Henry Clay Frick's Masonic career in particular: William H. Thornley, Jr., Homer Errett, Julian Perry, J. M. Hamill, Grand Lodge of F. A. & A. Masons of Scotland, Masonic Library and Museum of the Supreme Council, 33rd Degree, Washington, D.C.; John Hamilton, Glenys A. Waldman, Rexford F. Cox, and Martin L. Miller.

In my quest, many individuals in the religious life became invaluable friends, advisors, and spiritual guides. I would like to thank the Carmelite Sisters of Baltimore, particularly Sister Veronica Emmick, Sister Robin Stratton, and Sister Patricia Josephine McEvoy. Thanks also to Sister Anna Mary Gibson, Sister Cornelius Merrwald, Sister Camille Marie, Louise Wells, Reverend Philip Tierney, and Sally Robinson.

Many in the medical field broadened my understanding of medical practices in the nineteenth century; homeopathy; the psychology of death, dying, and bereavement; and the father-daughter syndrome. In addition to John E. Davis, I would like to thank Barbara M. Sourkes for reading the manuscript, widening its lens, and giving me the epigraph for this book. I would also like to thank Elisabeth Kübler-Ross, Thomas Benedek of the American Association of the History of Medicine, Charles W. Brice, Mary Brignano, Wendy Lomicka, E. B. Buchanan, Melissa Cantekin-Jones, J. Greenberg, Sally Hardon, Earl P. Galleher, Jr., Peter Hinderberger, Peter Hornefer, Jonathan Erlin, Hunter Wilson, and Gregg Furth.

To all other individuals and organizations, I am equally and eternally grateful: Julia Allen, Carnegie Library, Connellsville; Charles Aston, Hillman Library, University of Pittsburgh; David Bain, Middlebury College; William Balsley, historian, Connellsville, Pa.; Dorothy Beatty, Carnegie Library at Homestead; Charles A. Becker, Pittsburgh WW II air war veteran based in Italy for German bombing runs; Birmingham Art Museum; Caroline Beisswanger, Thames and Hudson; George and Jo de Bolt, Mon Valley Initiative and Homestead Preservation, Homestead, Pa.; Karen Bowdin, Historical Society of Western Pennsylvania; Ann Brooks; Catherine Brown, curator, Medieval Art, The Metropolitan Museum of Art; Thomas Buchanan, Esq.; Caron Capizzano, archive assistant NYU Medical Center; Barry Chad, Maria Ziti, and Marilyn Holt of the Pennsylvania Room, Carnegie Library, Pittsburgh; Ann Colhoun, Librarian, B&O Railroad Museum, Baltimore; Jay Costa, Jr., Register of Wills and clerk of Orphan's Court Division of the Court of Common Pleas, County of Allegheny, Pa.; Paul Chew, Ph.D., Westmoreland Museum of Art, Greensburgh, Pa.; Linda Ciatto, descendent of John Fulton of Johnstown, Pa.; Dennis Ciccone of White Oak Publishing; John Clarke, Art Department, University of Texas; Jerry Conlon, WW II Pittsburgh air war veteran, based in Italy for German bombing runs; Philip M. Conti, Lt. Colonel, Philadelphia State Police (Ret.); Walter Costlow, president of the 1889 South Fork Fishing and Hunting Club Historical Preservation Society; Claudine La Haye Cowen; Elissa Curcio, Clark Museum; William Defibaugh, Sr., historian, Bedford Springs; David Demarest, Jr., historian; Daniel J. Duda, Sr., IFS Intercoal Fuel Supplies; Charles Ferguson, Fishers Island, New York; Thomas R. Ferrall, director-public affairs, U.S. Steel Group, Pittsburgh, Pa.; Robert Gangwere, Carnegie Museum of Art; Brent D. Glass, *Pennsylvania Heritage Magazine;* Anthony J. Graziani, Director, U.S. Steel Resource Management, Uniontown, Pa.; Robert M. Gibson, vice president Raymond C. Yard Inc. Jewelers, N.Y.C.; Lizabeth S. Gray, *Pittsburgh Post-Gazette;* Joseph Guinta, research consultant United States Steel Technical Center, Monroeville, Pa.; Hahneman University; Herbert A. Harwood, author and authority on B&O Railroad, Baltimore; Randolph Harris, Mon Valley Initiative and Homestead Preservation, Homestead, Pa.; Herbert H. Harwood, Jr., railroad historian, former railroad worker; Bill P. Hayden, Child Abuse and Sex Offense Unit State's Attorney's Office, Towson, Md.; John Herbst, former director of the Historical Society of Western Pennsylvania; Amy Herman; Nancy Heywood, Essex Institute, Salem, Mass.; Gregory Hines, photographer; Edwin and Katherine Horning, curators, The Henry L. Ferguson Museum, Fishers Island, New York; Angela Horton, assistant to the curator, The White House, Washington, D.C.; Austin Hoyt, WGBH Boston; Ann P. Hurt, Carnegie Library at Homestead; Audry Iacone, Historical Society of Western Pennsylvania; John N. Ingham, Professor of History University of Toronto, Canada; Dan Ingram, curator, The Johnstown Flood Museum, Johnstown, Pa.; Patricia Ivinski, Clark Museum; Margaret Johnson, Brownsville Public Library, Brownsville, Pa.; Jon F. Kaloski, general manager, Mon Valley Works, Dravosburg, Pa.; Janet P. Kettering, The Homewood Cemetery; Walter Kidney, Pittsburgh History and Landmarks Foundation, Pittsburgh, Pa.; John King, Belpre, Ohio, and Connellsville, Pa., railroad authority; Bonnie Knox, librarian, Wayne County Public Library, genealogy; Robert A. Korcheck, historian; Virginia M. Krumholz, The Cleveland Museum of Art; Jay C. Leff, Jay C. Leff Collection, Pittsburgh, Pa.; Arthur Lindo of the Andrew Carnegie house, New York, now the Cooper Hewitt; Eric N. Lindquist; George Lockhart, former patient of the Doctors McClelland, Pittsburgh, Pa.; Laura Lingle, assistant curator, Metropolitan Museum of Art; Louise Lippincott, curator of fine arts, Carnegie Museum of Art; Mrs. Frank McCowen, granddaughter of E. M. Ferguson, Fishers Island, New York; David H. Lohr, general manager, USX Mon Valley Works; Hax McCullough, Jr., historian; Frederique Thomas-Maurin, Conservateur au Musée des Beaux-Arts & d'Archeologie, Besançon, France; Maureen McCormick, registrar, The Art Museum, Princeton University; Sharon Maurow,

Historical Society of Western Pennsylvania; David G. Malosky, recorder of deeds of Fayette County; Maureen Melton, archivist, Museum of Fine Arts Boston; Charles Miller, President, Cresson Area Historical Association, Inc., Cresson, Pa.; Rita Molio, Frick Park; Jennifer Morgan; Edward T. Morman, Ph.D., librarian, The Johns Hopkins University School of Medicine, Institute of the History of Medicine; Seely G. Mudd, Princeton University Archives; Edward K. Muller, History Department, University of Pittsburgh, Pa.; Kenneth Murray, former owner of the Andrew Carnegie house, Cresson Springs, Pa.; Leroy Newby, WW II air war veteran; Maxwell Nobel, owner, Shoaf Coke Works, Uniontown, Pa.; Marion Osborn, Fishers Island, New York; Monica and Ethan Penner; Mark Piel, librarian, the New York Society Library; Ann Poulet, curator, Museum of Fine Arts, Boston; Mary Pursglove, Brownsville Historical Society; Max Reidman, railroad authority, mine tipple operator at Davidson works, Connellsville, Pa.; Karen Richter, The Art Museum, Princeton University; Mrs. John T. Roberts, Horticulture Society, Chevy Chase, Md.; David K. Roger, Heritage Development, Uniontown, Pa.; Anne Roquebert, Musée d'Orsay, Paris; Robin Rummel, archival assistant, Johnstown Area Heritage Association; David Ruppersberger, University of Pittsburgh Archives, Special Collections; Cynthia and Nathan Saint-Amand; Rosalinde Saville, director, The Wallace Collection, London; Barbara Schweikert, Carnegie Institute; David Searsman, special collections, Hillman Library, University of Pittsburgh; Corey Sheehan, Historical Society of Western Pennsylvania; Hilliard T. Goldfarb, chief curator, The Isabella Stewart Gardner Museum, Boston, Mass., together with Susan Sinclair and Lowell W. Bassett; Mary Singer, historian, Mountain House at Cresson Springs; Robert Sink, archivist and records manager, The New York Public Library; Patrick Smithwick; Mary Sommerville, daughter of Annie Stephany, Pittsburgh, Pa.; Jonathan R. Stayer; Richard Stoner, photographer; Sotheby's Inc., New York; Butch Suages, Mountain House at Cressons historian, Cresson Springs, Pa.; John Sunderland, Witt Librarian, Courtauld Institute, London; Charlotte Tancin, librarian, Hunt Botanical Library, Hunt Institute for Botanical Documentation, Carnegie Mellon University; Judith Throm, Archives of American Art; Larry Trombellow, Allegheny Portage Railroad NHS, National Park Service, Portage, Pa.; Richard B. Tucker; Suzanne Valenstein, Research Curator, Metropolitan Museum of Art, N.Y.C.; Madame Von Meyer; Susan Ward, curator, Phipps Conservatory, Pittsburgh, Pa.; Professor Joseph Wall, Andrew Carnegie's biographer; Kenneth Warren, business historian and author of *Triumphant Capitalism,* who read this manuscript, offered the greatest encouragement, sage advice, and gave many statistical and historical corrections concerning the Coke Region and U.S. Steel; Edward Watkins, photographer; George T. Weber, Jr., General Manager Coking Operations, U.S. Steel Clairton Works, Dravosberg, Pa.; Al Weher, APEX Manager, Edgar Thomson Plant, United States Steel; Gabriel and Yvonne Weisberg, art historians; Jack Wilkins, former archivist Homewood Cemetery, Point Breeze historian, Pittsburgh; Helen Wilson, Historical Society of Western Pennsylvania; Robert W. Wilson, Homewood Cemetery; Jack Wilson, USX; Susan Yonkers; Nanci Young, Princeton University Archives; Greg Ziberoski, National Park Service, South Fork, Pa.; and Arthur P. Ziegler, Jr., president, Pittsburgh History and Landmarks Foundation.

I am indebted to Josephine Trueschler, essayist, teacher of writing and literature, College of Notre Dame, Baltimore, Md., for her editing advice in the early stages of the manuscript; to Elsa Van Bergen for pulling this book out of my first manuscript; to Susan Leon for the structural changes and editing of that new manuscript; to Nancy Wolff for the index; and to Philip Reynolds for the proofreading.

A final thank you to the home team: James Astrachan and Douglas Worrall for their legal advice; Mark Weigman, Len Richards, and Richard Gasperini for their financial assistance; Huntington Williams for reading the manuscript and offering advice; Anetta and Philip Goelet for their friendship and enthusiasm; Isabel Spaulding Roberts and Laurence Page Roberts for the stimulating and comforting conversations over lunch and tea, as well as for their numerous readings of the manuscript, their advice, and their "cheering me on." Kurt Rosenthal for his friendship, his keen eye, and his patience as he redecorated my house when I was in the last stages of publishing the book, as well as for ten years of listening to the book's ups and downs. To Robert Talbert for watching over me and my mastiffs, keeping my ice box full, and beautifully maintaining the house and grounds; Sandy Storck, Libby Smith, and Flo Thate for their constant encouragement, for keeping the house running, and me smiling; most of all, to my three daughters, Annie Darrow, Laura Roe, and Michele Sanger, who for ten years have never failed to ask, "How's the book coming?" And to my two sons-in-law, Rob Darrow and David Roe, and to Natalie Brengle, who joined in this refrain. To them all I can now cheerfully say, "The book's finished."

In addition to the many institutions that made photographs available for this book, I wish to acknowledge the following photographers: Neena Ewing, author's photograph in the genealogy; Gregory Hines, figs. 2-10, 9-37, 10-23; Richard Stoner, frontispiece, figs. 1-22, 1-23, 1-24, 1-26, 1-27, 1-33, 1-34, 2-2, 2-3, 2-4, 2-9, 2-11, 3-6, 4-2, 4-3, 4-4, 4-16, 4-24, 5-11, 5-13, 5-14, 5-18, 5-19, 5-20, 5-22, 5-23, 5-30, 6-5, 6-18, 7-46, 7-68, 8-16, 9-2, 9-13, 9-16; and Ed Watkins, figs. 3-5, 4-6, 4-7, 4-8, 4-9, 4-10, 4-11, 4-13, 4-15, 5-14, 7-11, 7-13, 7-15, 7-47, 9-16.

ELECTRONICALLY MANIPULATED IMAGES

The following are the components of the illustrations facing each chapter opening:

Jacket: Edmund C. Tarbell, *Henry Clay Frick and Daughter Helen*, National Portrait Gallery, Washington, D.C.; The front gates at 1 East Seventieth Street, 1927, author's collection.

Introduction: Martha Howard Frick, author's collection; Childs Frick, *House and Piers*, Frick Art and Historical Center.

Chapter I: Frick dollar bill, Frick Archives; Henry Clay Frick, c. 1875, Frick Archives; "Among the Coke Furnaces," *Harper's Weekly*, January 30, 1886, Historical Society of Western Pennsylvania.

Chapter II: Clayton, c. 1900, Frick Archives; Fr. Roseti, *Mrs. Henry Clay Frick and Children*, on loan from Henry Clay Frick II to the Frick Art and Historical Center.

Chapter III: Henry Clay Frick, c. 1895, Carnegie Library, Pittsburgh; Martha Howard Frick with eyebrows and hair penciled in, Frick Archives; mine cave-in, private collection; Helen Clay Frick's dolls, author's collection.

Chapter IV: The Dining Room at Clayton, Frick Art and Historical Center; Henry Clay Frick, Jr., Frick Archives; the assassination attempt, *Harper's Weekly*, August 6, 1892, New York Society Library; searchlight on the Monongahela River, *Frank Leslie's Illustrated Weekly*, July 14, 1892, New York Society Library.

Chapter V: Théobald Chartran, *Henry Clay Frick*, private collection; Adolphe-William Bouguereau, *L'Espieglèrie (Mischievous Girl)*, private collection; Pascal-Adolphe-Jean Dagnan-Bouveret, *Consolatrix Afflictorum*, Frick Art and Historical Center.

Chapter VI: Helen Clay Frick, private collection; 640 Fifth Avenue, *Frank Leslie's Illustrated Weekly*, May 30, 1891, New York Society Library; Henry Clay Frick's cenotaph, Carnegie Library, Pittsburgh.

Chapter VII: The mosaic path, author's collection; Currier and Ives, *George Washington as a Mason*, Masonic Library and Museum of Pennsylvania; men drawing coke, *Harper's Weekly*, July 7, 1888, Historical Society of Western Pennsylvania.

Chapter VIII: The Living Hall at 1 East Seventieth Street, 1927, author's collection; Walter Gay, *One East Seventieth Street Living Hall*, Frick Art Museum, Pittsburgh.

Chapter IX: Théobald Chartran, *Helen Clay Frick*, 1905, private collection; Henry Clay Frick and Helen, author's collection.

Chapter X: Master of the Half Lengths, Hans Vereycke, *Madonna and Child with Angel; St. Catherine and St. Barbara*, Frick Art Museum, Pittsburgh; Henry Clay Frick, author's collection; Helen Clay Frick, author's collection; Cathedral of Learning, University of Pittsburgh.

Index

Note: Page numbers in *italics* refer to illustrations.

THIS BOOK WAS DESIGNED AND COMPOSED BY

ALEX CASTRO

IN ADOBE KEPLER FONTS

AND WAS PRINTED BY

AMILCARE PIZZI, MILAN